ADVERTISING MANAGEMENT

GRID SERIES IN ADVERTISING AND JOURNALISM

Consulting Editors
ARNOLD M. BARBAN, University of Illinois
DONALD W. JUGENHEIMER, University of Kansas

OTHER BOOKS IN THE GRID SERIES IN ADVERTISING AND JOURNALISM

ADVERTISING MANAGEMENT:
Criteria, Analysis, and Decision Making

John D. Leckenby
University of Illinois at Urbana-Champaign

Nugent Wedding
University of Illinois at Urbana-Champaign, Emeritus

Grid Publishing, Inc., Columbus, Ohio

©COPYRIGHT 1982, GRID PUBLISHING, INC.
2950 North High Street
P. O. Box 14466
Columbus, Ohio 43214

Printed in the United States.

1 2 3 4 ⊠ 5 4 3 2

Library of Congress Cataloging in Publication Data

Leckenby, John D.
  Advertising management.

  (Grid series in advertising and journalism)
  Includes index.
  1. Advertising management. 2. Advertising management—Case studies. I. Wedding, C. Nugent, 1912-   . II. Title. III. Series.
HF5823.L43   659.1'11   81-6912
ISBN 0-88244-244-9   AACR2

CONTENTS

PART 2
ASSESSING OPPORTUNITY AND SETTING OBJECTIVES

PART 3
DETERMINING ADVERTISING DECISIONS

PREFACE

Advertising is one of the most exciting areas of human endeavor because, unlike some other areas of life, it is not possible to stereotypically describe any part of it at all satisfactorily. On the one hand, an individual viewing television commercials might think almost anyone on earth could create such artifacts; on the other hand, a person working in advertising for a living soon finds such commercials more difficult to construct than a movie extravaganza. As a social influence, advertising is said to be a mirror which holds up the reality of our society to us; it is also said to be a prime shaper of our social values. It is art yet is is science. It is said to be a prime component in business enterprise as part of the marketing system; it is also characterized as a mass communication system with a life apart from general business practice. Some emphasize advertising's role in generating a profit for business while others emphasize its role as a consumer information source. On the one side advertising is viewed as a creative system properly belonging in the realm of Hollywood, while on the other side it is positioned next to Wall Street and analyzed in a highly quantitative manner. In sum, advertising could be characterized as an enigmatic institution. It is precisely this characteristic which attracts individuals to its study and practice. It is this same characteristic which also makes it challenging to teach and learn; it cannot be neatly categorized into "learning blocks" very easily.

There is no one generally accepted method, therefore, of the manner in which students should approach the learning of advertising management. Some instructors favor the study of advertising management from an *inductive* point of view; this stems from the traditional Harvard Business School case study method. The approach suggests that the student should be able to induce a theoretical framework after studying many different instances which illustrate a general idea; from many specific instances, the general idea is obtained. Others, in keeping with more recent developments in consumer behavior and quantitative methods, would emphasize the *deductive* approach to advertising management. In this instance, it is assumed that enough is known about advertising phenomena to state the general principle or theory first; the student then applies this general theory to individual instances which are called applications or problems. The strength of the inductive approach has traditionally been given as that of providing the student with "real-life" knowledge and first-hand experience; it is recognized, however, that ultimately "real life" is not contained in a textbook but must finally be experienced first hand. The strength of the deductive approach has generally been viewed as that of providing the student with a general means of learning to think about problems; the drawback has very often been, however, that the learning frameworks provided have been too grand and ambitious to be of much value in actual "real-life" advertising situations. This book attempts to employ the strengths of the two approaches and minimize their respective weaknesses.

The authors have used the text and case chapters in their classes in advertising management at the undergraduate level before putting the book in the form presented here. These senior students found the melding of the two approaches discussed above to be helpful. If advertising is a subject matter for which boredom in the classroom is possible (and we doubt this), then the case analyses seemed to provide a balance. Some of the cases are rather lengthy (The Anheuser-Busch Company) while others are quite brief (Personna Blade). This has been purposely planned by the authors so that the instructor can select a few of each or all of one length to use in the course. The longer cases are similar to the traditional case analyses while the shorter cases are more like exercises or problems which can be used to illustrate some of the text material. We find the numerous examples are helpful in explaining some of the more difficult concepts in a practical way.

This book is organized around a central, core organizational scheme of decision making in advertising management. It emphasizes the selection of *criteria* or goals upon which *analyses* will be conducted during the *decision making* process. The book is divided into five overall parts:

Part 1   Perspectives on Advertising Strategy
Part 2   Assessing Opportunity and Setting Objectives
Part 3   Determining Advertising Decisions
Part 4   Coordinating Promotion Management
Part 5   Considering the Regulatory Environment.

Within each of these overall categories of the subject matter, the organizational scheme is set up. This scheme is graphically reiterated at the beginning of each text chapter so that the student understands the point in the overall process of advertising management decision making which is currently being examined. The decision making scheme consists of *Planning Areas* or steps in the decision making process. The authors view this planning process according to the following scheme (each of which is considered in one or more text and case chapters):

Planning Area I	Inputs to Advertising Planning
Planning Area II	Advertising Opportunity Analysis
Planning Area III	Advertising Objectives
Planning Area IV	Market Segmentation
Planning Area V	Management of the Advertising Budget
Planning Area VI	Advertising Creative Strategy
Planning Area VII	Advertising Media Strategy
Planning Area VIII	The Promotion Program
Planning Area IX	Advertising Regulation.

This book, of course, includes a concept originally developed by one of the authors for use in advertising management: *Advertising Opportunity Analysis*. This concept is set forth and broadened in Chapter 3 and forms the foundation upon which it is assumed the advertising program will be built. Considerable emphasis on this simple yet critical idea in advertising management is given in this chapter. If the advertising opportunity analysis shows that the prospects for advertising in the marketing mix are indeed poor, perhaps the best advertising decision would be that of conducting *no* advertising program at all! This concept will enable students to determine when such situations exist; if advertising is called for in the marketing program, advertising opportunity analysis will point to the particular areas which require considerable care and attention in the development of the advertising program. Chapter 1 makes it clear that the authors strongly view advertising in the context of the marketing program *in toto*. It is not possible to develop an acceptable advertising program apart from the other marketing factors: product, distribution, and price.

This book provides a substantial departure from more traditional texts on advertising management in the areas of budgeting, creative, and media decision making. An entire chapter is devoted to the concept of *response function* as the foundation for current concepts in budgeting decision making models. An entire chapter is also given over to in-depth discussion of *copytesting methods* on a theoretical as well as a practical level. In this one chapter, the student can find material gathered together on the highly important topic of copytesting which cannot be found elsewhere. Furthermore, the "practical" methods of copytesting are related to the overall theoretical scheme relating criteria to decision making in the creative strategy area. Finally, an entire chapter is also devoted to a highly important yet often neglected topic, *media exposure distribution models*. The advertising decision maker must be aware of the problems and possible solutions involved in the most fundamental form of advertising analysis: the determination of how many people or households are reached by the advertising message. This is a highly complex yet deceptively simple area of advertising analysis and decision making. To the authors' knowledge, this material is also not gathered together elsewhere in a concise format.

It is the fundamental hope of the authors that students will, through the use of this book in small part, find the field of advertising to be *challenging* to their thought processes. And, given the very nature of the field of advertising, it is well for the student as well as teacher to keep in mind the phrase of Hobbes: "No discourse whatsoever can end in absolute knowledge of fact." To this, Santayana has added:

> Absolute knowledge of fact is immediate, it is experiential. . . . Intellectual knowledge, on the other hand, where it relates to hidden existence, is faith only, a faith which in these matters means trust.

ACKNOWLEDGEMENTS

A great many individuals must be thanked for such admirable qualities as might exist in parts of this book. Professor Arnold Barban, Head of the Department of Advertising at the University of Illinois at Urbana-Champaign, has been extremely giving of his time and advice on the organizational scheme as well as reading every word of the text. His comments and suggestions have very often been implemented in the book. His encouragement is greatfully appreciated. He first suggested a need for such a book to us.

Thanks go also for suggestions by Professor Donald Jugenheimer of the University of Kansas, Professor Jesse Teel of the University of South Carolina, and Professor J. Stephen Kelly of DePaul University. Professor Richard Beltramini and Professor Nancy Stephens of Arizona State University, for use of the Morton Salt revision of Nugent Wedding's original case, are also thanked. Thanks to Professor John C. Murphy of the University of Texas-Austin and Professor Charles Patti of Arizona State University for use of the Gulf Oil case. A special thanks goes to Professor Spencer F. Tinkham of the University of Georgia for his suggestions on consumer behavior and analysis which appear in Chapter 3.

The authors also wish to thank doctoral student Shizue Kishi and master's candidate Sirish Mani for their help on the case material. The tremendous help of the staff of the Department of Advertising office at the University of Illinois at Urbana-Champaign in the persons of Mary Lowrey and Susan Turner is greatly admired and appreciated.

Finally, a big thanks goes to all our students who have used the material in our classes and provided us with insights on the interpretation of our ideas.

TO OUR STUDENTS: Past, Present and Future

PART 1:
PERSPECTIVES ON ADVERTISING STRATEGY

- Advertising Decision Making and Marketing
- Inputs to Advertising Planning

ADVERTISING DECISION MAKING AND MARKETING

- Advertising and the Marketing Concept
- Market Segmentation and Marketing Integration
- Perspectives on Advertising and Promotion
- Case Analysis and Advertising Management
- Models and Advertising Management
- Decision Making Organization of This Text
- Criteria, Analysis and Decision Making

ADVERTISING DECISION MAKING AND MARKETING

"Advertising performs the function of interpreting the want-satisfying qualities of services, products, or ideas in terms of the needs and desires of consumers."

—C.H. Sandage
Advertising Educator

This book develops the ideas and methods by which the manager of an advertising program can plan, implement and control advertising for the purpose of making it as effective and efficient as possible. In contemporary practice, advertising management begins with a thorough analysis of the needs and wants of consumers with respect to possibilities of particular products in meeting these needs. This consumer orientation has come to be called the "marketing concept." This view of advertising must be placed in the context of the role of advertising in generating profits for the firm. There sometimes may be a tension between these two roles of advertising. The manager of an advertising program must serve to mesh and balance these two primary functions of advertising. This task is the subject matter of advertising management and is illustrated in Figure 1-1.

ADVERTISING AND THE MARKETING CONCEPT

The initial separation of marketing from other facets of business operations was a natural outgrowth of the Industrial Revolution and its specializations in the United States and the allied development of markets at increasing distances from the basic sources of supply.

The needs of business specialization fostered extensive departmental development, with specialists who tended to operate exclusively within their own particular area. The production personnel thought only of making a product in the most efficient manner, sales managers thought only of the movement of a volume of merchandise, controllers considered only the profit picture. As the complexities of the distribu-

Figure 1-1   Balancing the Two Roles of Advertising

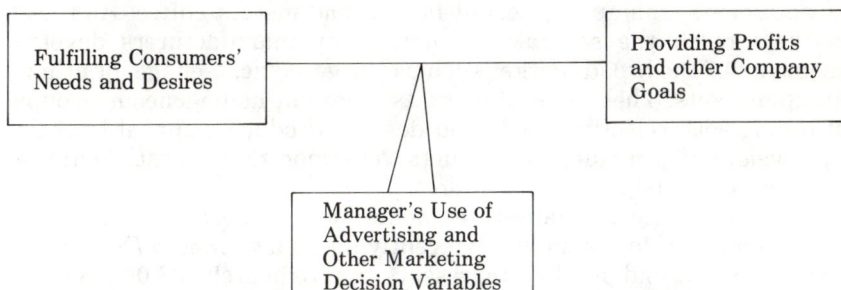

Fulfilling Consumers' Needs and Desires		Providing Profits and other Company Goals

Manager's Use of Advertising and Other Marketing Decision Variables

tion process increased, marketing sub-functions grew into specialties such as advertising, merchandising, market research, sales management, and forecasting. Similar trends in specialization were taking place in the production function.

The overall importance of the field of marketing and the critical relationships within marketing's own specialized functions began to be recognized after World War II as business prepared to take advantage of the tremendous opportunities of the product-hungry American market. Just as production had been the dominant business function during the early stages of the Industrial Revolution, and financial operations had taken the center of the business stage at the turn of the century and through the era of the 1920's, the dominance of distribution, incubated in the depression of the 1930's, reached out for leadership in the mid-1940's. There was a growth of recognition for the necessity of a working partnership between production and marketing, the idea that a mass production system without mass marketing is an illusion.

MARKET SEGMENTATION AND MARKETING INTEGRATION

The importance of production-marketing integration was further accentuated by the development of completely new products or important product modifications which have become part of profitable selling. In the keen competition of advertised brands, it has become more difficult for a corporation to retain its position within a given industry. If such a corporation hopes to improve its competitive position, it is almost a necessity for it to produce relatively diversified merchandise designed to fulfill the needs of specific segments of consumers within the overall market. As products with a generally universal appeal, purchased by a large number of consumers, move into the market place and competition among them increases, the number of product brands offered by the various manufacturers has invariably increased.

This has been apparent in many industries marketing such products as detergents, shampoos, peanut butter, and instant coffee. As these markets reach the saturation point, many manufacturers develop segments of the broad market such as the geriatric, teenage, or ethnic group markets. These special markets represent homogeneous groups of people with selective needs and desires. Producers appeal to them by developing or modifying products to harmonize more satisfactorily with these special needs and desires.

The importance of market segmentation can be observed in the teenage market, for example, as recently profiled by *Media Decisions*.[1] The 12-19-year-old market represents approximately 33,000,000 individuals who spend over $25 billion annually. But although teenagers compose only 13 percent of the female population of the United States, teen girls account for over 20 percent of the beauty products purchased each year. Clearly, managers of advertising for beauty products would be interested in paying particular attention to the teenage market segment when developing their advertising programs.

The combination of increased brand competition, the pressures of more complex market segmentation as discussed above, increasingly involved channels of distribution, along with such increasing risk as those connected with new-product introductions, necessitated a re-evaluation of marketing philosophy. This re-examination resulted in the unification of marketing functions with control under a single executive, often called the brand manager.

This counterbalance to specialization is designed to integrate all marketing forces and also to link together other facets of the manufacturer's organization such as production and finance. Decisions in one area influence those to be made in other areas. The type of product and price influence both the type of advertising effort and the results which are possible from such promotion. Manufacturing costs influence expenditures for advertising and other promotion. The costs involved in the expansion of the personal sales force cannot be divorced from the monetary resources allocated to the advertising budget when the controller makes profit projections.

This awareness of the interdependence of business functions was one critical factor leading to the development of the "marketing concept." The stress on the interdependence of marketing functions of the firm, combined with the second critical factor, the conviction and knowledge that successful marketing should be consumer-oriented, form the marketing concept. Both of these ideas, interdependence of business functions and consumer orientation, underlie the approach to advertising management to be examined in this text.

PERSPECTIVES ON ADVERTISING AND PROMOTION

There are several different approaches which have been taken in the study of advertising management. These can generally be divided into: (a) the case study approach and (b) the model-building approach.

Probably the first book written on advertising from the managerial perspective was that by Neil Borden and Martin Marshall, *Advertising Management: Text and Cases*. This book was first published in 1950 and revised in 1959.[2] This book differed from earlier treatments of advertising since it confronted students with an actual advertising management situation. The student was required to analyze the advertising problem, perhaps develop an advertising budget, prepare a media plan, and select advertising copy. Such an approach is decision-oriented whereas earlier texts provided a description of various advertising institutions and techniques. This approach has the strength of illustrating actual advertising decision-making problems. Based upon the study of many case situations, it is the task of the student to inductively arrive at applicable analytical frameworks which may help solve particular case problems. A specific analytical approach suitable for a variety of case situations is not ordinarily provided.

The second approach to advertising management, model-building, is relatively newer than the first. Models dealing with the selection of advertising media vehicles were the first advertising application of the approach; this began in the early 1950's with the media selection work conducted at the advertising agency, Batten, Barton, Durstine and Osborne.[3] The first advertising management text written which utilized this approach was *Advertising Management* by David Aaker and John G. Myers in 1975.[4] The systematic compilation of model-building approaches to advertising management is, thus, relatively new. This approach has the strength of providing specific analytical frameworks which might be applied to specific advertising management problems. Such approaches, however, tend to be somewhat complicated by nature. It has been difficult to explain such approaches in a straight forward and understandable manner, let alone illustrate specific means by which the methods can be applied to solve advertising problems.

Both of the above approaches have their value in advertising management situations. This book will, therefore, attempt to combine the strengths of each approach. Case analyses involving the application of alternative thinking will be used extensively throughout the book. These serve to encourage creative thinking in terms of possible solutions to advertising problems. Where appropriate and capable of implementation in actual advertising management situations, models will be discussed and developed. The emphasis will be on the manner in which such models can be applied to help in the solution of difficult advertising management problems.

CASE ANALYSIS AND ADVERTISING MANAGEMENT

The cases presented in this text are designed to illustrate specific instances of broad categories of problems which arise in the management of advertising programs. It is not possible for one case to encompass all aspects of advertising problems, and, consequently, the cases focus on a particular advertising decision area. For example, The Oron Paper Company case in Chapter 9 is designed to illustrate one particular aspect of the advertising budgeting decision for a consumer goods company. The Sears Roebuck case in Chapter 12 focuses on the creative strategy decisions which needed to be made in the context of the entire advertising program for that company. Clearly, however, since advertising decision variables are interdependent, it is not possible to discuss and consider only one decision area at a time. The decision about advertising budgeting will be affected by the nature of the creative strategy decision for the particular company. This is so in the practice of advertising management, but is difficult to implement in the case study approach. To include every aspect of the advertising problem in a single case would be, in most instances, impracticable, if not undesirable. It is unlikely that one company would illustrate sufficiently the broad range of problems which arise in the spectrum of advertising management. The approach in this text has, therefore, been to highlight a particular decision problem in each case as much as this has been possible to do so. Cases are included which highlight the following problems: market demand stimulation, advertising budgeting and control, creative strategy, media planning, promotion management, and the regulation of advertising.

CASE ANALYSIS METHOD

It is desirable to apply a general analytical method in the analysis of case material. The "five-step method" of case analysis includes the following elements:
  (1) Definition of the Case Problem
  (2) Statement of Alternative Courses of Action
  (3) Evaluation of Alternatives
  (4) Recommendation of Course of Action
  (5) Justification of the Recommendation.

Definition of Problem. The first of the five steps in the above method of case analysis is perhaps the most important. Skill and practice are required to develop the ability to clearly and concisely sort out and define the most important, central problem or issue in a given problem circumstance. For example, focusing on the problem of how much to spend for a given brand on its advertising program when deeper, more broadly significant issues or problems lie with the brand itself could result in some serious errors in decision making.

Statement of Alternatives. One of the more important values of case analysis exercises is that of stimulating alternative thinking in the decision making process. There is often the temptation to go with the first "common sense" idea in the solution of a problem; this can create problems from two standpoints. First, though the idea may be a good one, others may be more desirable; if a conscious effort is not made to propose alternative courses of action, these other ideas would not ever be considered. Second, the proposed course of action for the solution of a problem ordinarily will need to be justified to management; one of the most effective means of justifying a course of action is to compare it to alternative actions which might be taken in its place.

Evaluation of Alternatives. Any course of action will have strengths and weaknesses, pros and cons. Every effort should be made to explicitly consider the pros and cons for each alternative being considered as a possible solution to a particular problem. Very often these strengths and weaknesses will be relative to other alternative courses of action.

Recommendation. After a review of the above evaluation, it should be possible to make a statement or recommendation about what ought to be done to solve the problem at hand. Clearly, the recommended course of action should be the most desirable of the considered alternatives from the standpoint of strengths and weaknesses. The recommended alternative might have more advantages and fewer disadvantages than any of the other alternatives which were considered as possible solutions to the problem. It might also be the case that the recommended course of action, while not having more pros and fewer cons than other alternatives, has strengths which carry more "weight" than those of other alternatives. One critical advantage for an alternative might outweigh seven or eight disadvantages.

Justification. A simple, short, and concise statement needs to be made of why the recommended alternative is the most desirable of those examined. This statement should capture the essence of the strengths and weaknesses of the alternative relative to the others proposed in the case analysis.

The above method of case analysis is illustrated in Appendix A to this chapter.

MODELS AND ADVERTISING MANAGEMENT

The concept of model building in advertising can be traced back only as far as the early 1950's, and the literature dealing with this approach since about 1967 is more than twice that which appeared prior to that time. A brief chronological history of the development of this approach illustrates the problems that have been faced and the approaches that have been used in addressing the issues.[5]

EMULATION OF OPERATIONS RESEARCH: 1950-1964

Operations Research as a field developed during World War II primarily for the purpose of solving war-related problems of a strategic nature. The approach was characterized by the drawing together of individuals who specialized in very different fields of knowledge. For example, an operations research group might consist of a sociologist, a mathematician, a psychologist, and an engineer. The theory set forth under the OR approach was that any problem consists of many very different dimensions of human and machine interaction and that no one individual could be an expert in dealing with all of these dimensions. In practice, and over some period of time, the operations research approach came to be identified with the application of quantitative methods, particularly statistics, to problems.

This period of development of models in advertising management was characterized by the wholesale application of mathematical techniques to advertising problems. The emphasis was on quantitative method sophistication rather than on the advertising problem per se. The advertising problem was contorted so as to fit the requirements of the technical methods employed. An outstanding example of work in this period of development was the application of linear programming to the media selection problem.[6]

BIGGER AND BETTER: 1964-1970

A major problem during the early time period was the naive manner in which the response to advertising was specified. For example, in the case of linear programming, the response function was, of course, of a linear or straight-line nature. The reaction to such simplicity and incompleteness was to build gigantic and theoretically elegant advertising models. In the media selection and planning area, an example of one such model was COMPASS, developed by several advertising agencies. This model was fairly complex and incorporated most of the important issues confronting the media planner. There were, however, at least two problems which developed in relation to this model. First, since it was extremely technical and complex, it was difficult to explain to non-technically inclined media managers in any detail. Second, the model required heavy input of data from the marketplace. This expensive and time-consuming data collection process discouraged usage of the model. Considerably scaled-down versions of the model are in use today by at least one major advertising agency. In retrospect, the original model seems an exercise in overkill.

SIMPLICITY, SUBJECTIVITY, AND USABILITY:
1970 TO PRESENT

A major change in the directions of model building in advertising took place with the development of the concept of "Decision Calculus" by John D.C. Little. He used the term to describe models that would process judgments *and* data in a manner which would assist the manager in decision making. Such models, he suggested, should have the following properties:[7]

(1) They should be simple and understandable from the manager's standpoint.

(2) Such models should be robust, that is, the structure should constrain answers from the model to a reasonable and plausible range of values.

(3) They should be easy to control. The manager should be able to set input levels in order to obtain nearly any outputs. Management judgment should be a major component of the model.

(4) The models should be adaptive, that is, they should be easy to change when new information or viewpoints are developed.

(5) The models should be complete on the most important issues or variables involved in the problem. The factors that the management considers important in the problem should be capable of representation in the model by one of two ways: (a) explicitly in the model structure or (b) as conditioning factors for specific parameters.

(6) Finally, it should be easy for managers to communicate with the model. This usually means use of computer terminals in an interactive mode.

In summary, models to be discussed in this text will focus on *decision relevance* and *implemenation* rather than on theoretical elegance and complexity.

Along with the advent of models that are more readily understandable and more easily used than earlier counterparts, has come increased acceptance on the part of advertising managers. For example, agencies working with one large automobile manufacturing division have computer terminals in their offices linked to the client's computer. In addition to the client's data, these terminals provide access to various models which the client has developed. MEDIAC, a media planning and selection model, and ADBUDG, an appropriation model, have been employed in recent years by managers of advertising.[8] Faculty members of the Stanford Graduate School of Business have developed models which have proved useful in a variety of advertising management applications.[9] The N.W. Ayer advertising agency developed a new-product planning model that has been utilized extensively.[10] Other examples might be enumerated, but the implication is that the acceptance and usage of models to assist in advertising planning and decision making has become an increasingly important part of the tools available to the advertising manager.

However, it is still a well-accepted proposition that advertising management and decision making will not be reduced to completely systematic relations in *any* model. It is, interestingly, probably true that part of advertising which escapes specific definition is also that part which, in many instances, provides intrigue and amazement to both students and practitioners in the field of advertising.

Clearly, models should be viewed as but one more aid to those who must make decisions about extremely complex matters. In fact, one of the useful functions of model-building is that of revealing the nature of the complexity of advertising decision-making. These difficult decisions will not be made by even the best computerized model but rather by a combination of available data and experience-based judgment. A reasonable model may, however, assist the manager in organizing the elements of a problem in such a way that they may easily be used in the decision making process.

THE MEANING OF MODEL BUILDING

A model is an explicit representation of some larger reality. For example, a child's model airplane is a more or less accurate representation of a full-scale airplane. From it one can get some idea of the general appearance of large airplanes. The extent to which the model plane gives an accurate picture of the large plane depends upon the detail and accuracy of the elements of the child's plane. A faithful, detailed, and quite small model airplane might be useful, for example, in testing the behavior of the larger plane in a wind tunnel. It would be preferable to know prior to the real plane's first flight just how well it behaves in certain wind conditions. It is certainly less expensive, in human life and dollars, to test new ideas about wing construction on the model than on the real thing.

Similar reasoning can be applied to model-building in advertising management. If a model of the advertising process accurately reflects the larger reality of the marketplace, then the manager can test new assumptions and strategies using the model more quickly and less expensively than could be done in the actual marketplace. For example, an advertising model might include a specification of the response of sales to advertising expenditures. If this model is a fairly accurate representation of the realities of the marketplace, then the advertising manager can use the model to find the sales results which accompany various levels of advertising spending.

Models may be *implicit* or *explicit* in nature. Advertising decision makers, including those who avoid the use of explicit models, actually use implicit models. Underlying a decision to spend a certain amount on advertising will be an implicit notion as to the relation between advertising and sales, for example. The advertising manager may feel that one particular commerical is preferable to another; behind this feeling is an implicit theory of consumer reaction to commercials. The problem with implicit models is that their underlying assumptions are not stated. Explicit models, on the other hand, require a direct statement of assumptions about how advertising works in the marketplace. Explicit models are preferred to implicit models because, once the assumptions are directly stated, the projected results from the model can be explained logically to others. The explicit model makes clear the theory upon which the advertising manager is operating, and that theory can then be debated if necessary. The development of explicit models is basically a four-step process:

(1) Determination of the manager's "implicit model" of how the advertising process works for the particular product.
(2) Translation of the implicit model into a "formal" structure.
(3) Development of procedures for "parameterizing" the model.
(4) "Numerical evaluation" using the completed model.

Each of the above four steps in the model-building and using process is illustrated through an example in Appendix B to this chapter.

DECISION MAKING ORGANIZATION OF THIS TEXT

This text first considers the backdrop upon which the advertising decision making process rests: *corporate and marketing objectives and planning.* Given this background, the first important decision making task considered in Chapter 3 concerns the decision as to whether or not advertising should play an important role in the overall marketing plan and strategy; this decision involves the *assessment of advertising opportunity.* The decision maker is then in a position to set *advertising objectives* based upon an understanding of *advertising criteria*; these issues are addressed in Chapter 5. The four primary decision making variables *(Market, Money, Media and Message)* are then considered in detail in Part 3: Determining Advertising Decisions. This is followed in Part 4 with a consideration of the relation of advertising planning and tactics to other forms of promotion (personal selling and sales promotion, including publicity); this involves the development of a *promotion coordination* strategy and policy. Finally, in Part 5, the role of one particular constraint on advertising planning, *advertising regulation*, is examined at a general level.

As noted above, there are four *primary factors* in advertising which require decisions to be made by the manager: (1) Market, (2) Money, (3) Media, and (4) Message. If the marketing plan has not already determined the emphasis to be placed on different consumer markets, then the advertising manager must first define or target the *market segments* which will be emphasized in the advertising program. These market segments are defined rather precisely in terms of such demographic variables as income, occupation, geographic region as well as others. In recent years there has been some movement, although not dramatic, to the use of psychographic variables, such as might be defined by various psychological profiles or on an ad hoc basis, in the definition of target markets. Since this information is not

14

generally available about the audiences of media, the psychographic or lifestyle approach to segmentation has not been widely utilized.

The amount of *money* to be spent on the advertising for some period of time, frequently for one quarter of business operations, must be determined. The determination of the total size of the advertising budget for a particular brand is one of the most difficult problems facing the advertising manager. The budget should be determined based upon the projected response of sales to the amount of money spent on advertising; this is a very difficult task since so many factors other than the amount of money spent on advertising determine the response of consumer sales.

The *media* plan to be employed in delivering the messages in the various media must be decided upon. Should television be used for a particular product? Should the television schedule consist of network buys or spot buys or both? Should magazines be used in the schedules? The answers to such questions depend upon such factors as the product type, the amount of money available, the type of consumers reached by the various media vehicles, the advertising message to be used, and the price of the product, among many other factors.

Which television commercial should be used to convey the selling message? Development of the advertising *message* requires a thorough understanding of the entire marketing backdrop of the product in question. One type of message will be appropriate for a high-priced product while another completely different message will be required for a low-price product. One media vehicle will demand one kind of message while another will require a completely different message. One market segment, for example, low-income consumers, will respond more favorably to one type of message while a high-income group will require a different approach.

It is worthwhile to note at this point that some would include a fifth "M" of advertising in the above list of decision variables; measurement is sometimes considered as a separate area for decision making. While it is clear that a decision must be made regarding the undertaking of research and the specific type of research procedures to be employed, the purpose of that measurement or research decision is to provide information to support decision making on the four primary decision variables: Market, Money, Media, and Message. Decisions might be made about these factors, after all, without the benefit of any formal research input. It will become clear that the present authors view information as a necessary and preliminary part of decision making in each of the four advertising areas. It is not their view that research or measurement should be considered as distinct or separate from the four basic management areas in advertising, but rather as an integrative element in the entire advertising management process. Accordingly, there is no separate section in this text dealing with research methodology.

It should also be noted that the first and most fundamental decision which the advertising manager must make is whether or not advertising should be conducted at all for a particular company, product, brand, service, or idea. In Chapter 3 the appraisal of advertising opportunities will be discussed as the basis for making such a decision. Though this decision is not, strictly speaking, of the same nature as the 4M's of advertising management, it is just as important as the four substantive advertising management decision areas.

Figure 1-2 shows the context in which decisions must be made with respect to the 4M's of advertising (Market Segmentation, Money, Media, and Message). The Marketing Plan represents the backdrop against which advertising decisions must be made. The type of *product,* the *place* in which it is sold (the distribution system), the *price* to be charged, and other types of *promotion* (personal selling and sales promotion tools such as free calendars) all will affect the type of decision which should be made on the four advertising decision variables. The decisions made by the marketing personnel, often the brand manager, on these four general categories of marketing factors result in the "Marketing Mix." One type of marketing mix will require a different type of advertising decision making than another for maximum effectiveness of the advertising program.

Figure 1-2 also shows the link of the four advertising decision variables to consumer response criteria. It is critical to note that it is impossible to effectively make decisions about the four advertising factors without reference to one criterion or to a set of criteria. The criteria determine the basis upon which the effectiveness of the advertising decision making process will be judged. These criteria must be selected and agreed upon prior to the advertising decision making process. Will sales be the sole basis upon which the advertising results will be judged? Or will sales as well as brand awareness and brand attitude be used to assess effectiveness? Advertisement Exposure, Awareness (whether awareness of consumers of the brand name or recall of the advertisements), Attitude (toward commercials or toward brands), and Intentions-to-Buy the brand are referred to as *intermediate* criteria of effectiveness. While sales, market share, and profits are observable factors, criteria such as awareness are unobservable directly. Advertising decision makers (particularly those at advertising agencies) tend to prefer advertising evaluation in terms of intermediate criteria while client personnel often lean toward sales, share, or profit criteria. Though it would be desirable to evaluate advertising in terms of what it is ultimately designed to do, make money for the company using it, this is not an easy task in many situations. Ease of measurement of consumer response on criteria declines on the travel from Exposure to Profits while desirability for management purposes goes in the opposite direction. This conflict between ease of accurate assessment on a criterion and that criterion's desirability for management purposes is not easy to resolve; approaches to this problem will be discussed in great detail later in the text. The primary difficulties in the accurate assessment of effectiveness of advertising decisions, regardless of which criterion is employed, have to do with *intervening* factors. The best-conceived advertising program can be sidetracked by actions of competitors. The

Figure 1-2 Decision Making Organization of This Text

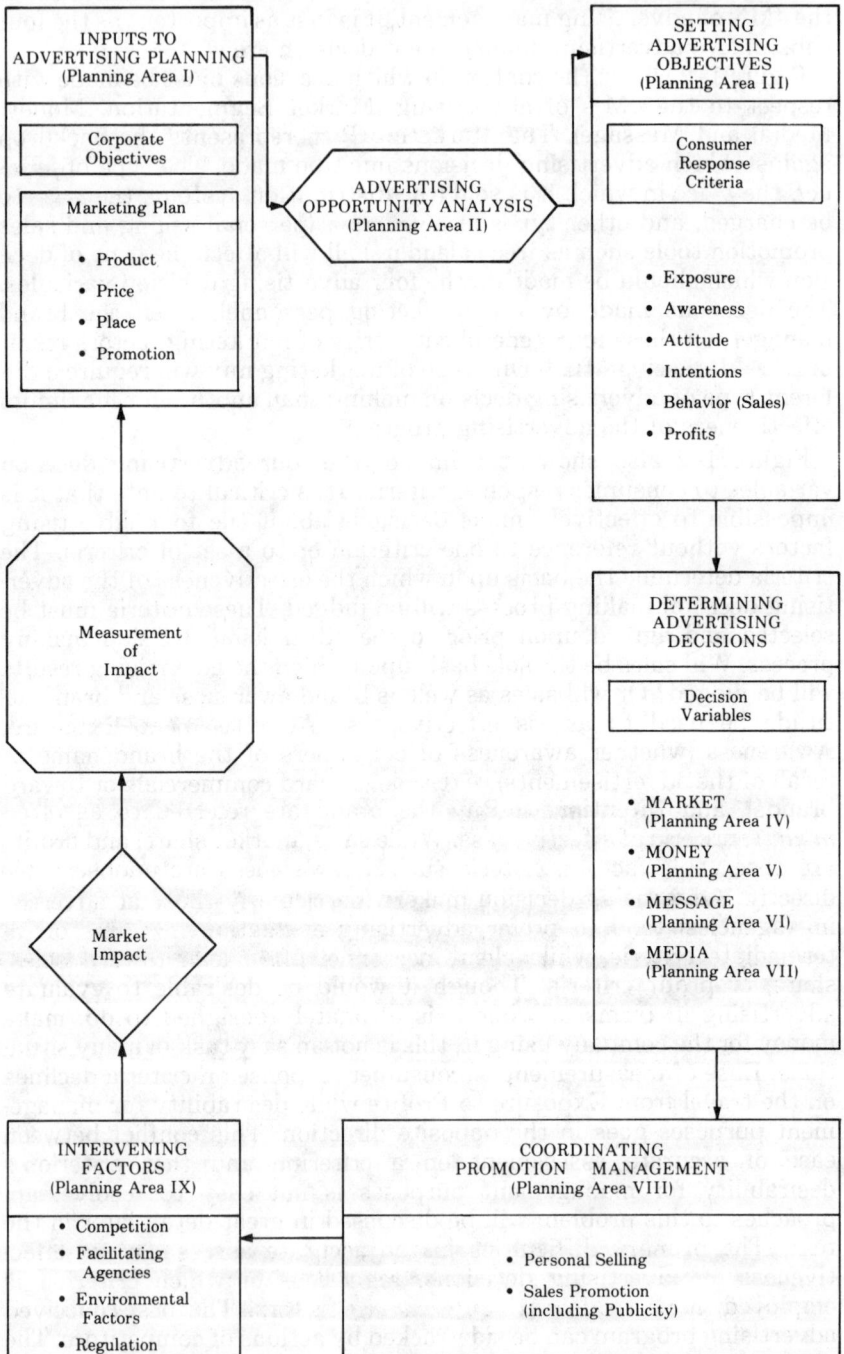

```
┌─────────────────────────┐                              ┌─────────────────────────┐
│   INPUTS TO             │                              │      SETTING            │
│ ADVERTISING PLANNING    │                              │    ADVERTISING          │
│   (Planning Area I)     │                              │    OBJECTIVES           │
│                         │                              │  (Planning Area III)    │
│ ┌─────────────────────┐ │                              │ ┌─────────────────────┐ │
│ │    Corporate        │ │        ADVERTISING           │ │     Consumer        │ │
│ │    Objectives       │ │      OPPORTUNITY ANALYSIS     │ │     Response        │ │
│ ├─────────────────────┤ │      (Planning Area II)      │ │     Criteria        │ │
│ │   Marketing Plan    │ │                              │ └─────────────────────┘ │
│ │                     │ │                              │                         │
│ │  • Product          │ │                              │   • Exposure            │
│ │  • Price            │ │                              │   • Awareness           │
│ │  • Place            │ │                              │   • Attitude            │
│ │  • Promotion        │ │                              │   • Intentions          │
│ │                     │ │                              │   • Behavior (Sales)    │
│ └─────────────────────┘ │                              │   • Profits             │
└─────────────────────────┘                              └─────────────────────────┘

      ┌──────────────┐                                   ┌─────────────────────────┐
      │ Measurement  │                                   │   DETERMINING           │
      │     of       │                                   │   ADVERTISING           │
      │   Impact     │                                   │   DECISIONS             │
      │              │                                   │ ┌─────────────────────┐ │
      └──────────────┘                                   │ │     Decision        │ │
                                                         │ │     Variables       │ │
       ╱────────────╲                                    │ └─────────────────────┘ │
      ╱              ╲                                    │                         │
     ╱    Market      ╲                                   │   • MARKET              │
     ╲    Impact      ╱                                   │     (Planning Area IV)  │
      ╲              ╱                                    │   • MONEY               │
       ╲────────────╱                                    │     (Planning Area V)   │
                                                         │   • MESSAGE             │
                                                         │     (Planning Area VI)  │
                                                         │   • MEDIA               │
                                                         │     (Planning Area VII) │
                                                         └─────────────────────────┘

┌─────────────────────────┐                              ┌─────────────────────────┐
│   INTERVENING           │                              │   COORDINATING          │
│   FACTORS               │                              │   PROMOTION MANAGEMENT   │
│   (Planning Area IX)    │                              │   (Planning Area VIII)  │
│                         │                              │                         │
│  • Competition          │                              │                         │
│  • Facilitating         │                              │   • Personal Selling    │
│    Agencies             │                              │   • Sales Promotion     │
│  • Environmental        │                              │     (including          │
│    Factors              │                              │      Publicity)         │
│  • Regulation           │                              │                         │
└─────────────────────────┘                              └─────────────────────────┘
```

general economic climate has a great deal to do with the overall result obtained from the advertising program. Such intervening factors are largely not under the control of the advertising decision maker. One intervening factor which is under the control of the advertiser is that of the facilitating agencies. Research organizations are often hired by the advertiser or agency to provide consumer information, as well as other categories of information, for the purpose of helping to establish the link between the decisions made on the four advertising decision variables and the criteria used to assess the decisions. Measurement of consumer recall of commercials is an example of the way in which facilitating research firms are used to provide this linkage.

Figure 1-2 also shows the planning element of coordinating the overall promotion program. As will be seen in Chapter 16, the effectiveness of the advertising decision making process very much depends upon its coordination with other methods of promotion—personal selling and sales promotion (including public relations). The advertising manager or brand manager must pay particular attention to the coordination both within (internal coordination) the company among these overall promotion elements and without (external coordination) the company. Wholesalers, distributors, and retailers must be informed and involved in the manufacturer's promotion program if it is to reach maximum effectiveness.

Figure 1-2 shows the organizational plan of this book. The book is basically divided into nine *planning areas* of major importance in the decision making sequence in advertising management. Each of these planning areas is associated with one or more text chapters. The relation between planning areas in the decision making sequence and text chapters is indicated in the Table of Contents. The planning areas are listed below:

Planning Area I   *Corporate and Marketing Objectives*
Planning Area II: *Advertising Opportunity Analysis*
Planning Area III: *Advertising Objectives and Criteria*
Planning Area IV: *Market Segmentation*
Planning Area V: *Money (The Advertising Budget)*
Planning Area VI: *Message (Creative Strategy)*
Planning Area VII: *Media (The Budget Allocation)*
Planning Area VIII: *Promotion Coordination*
Planning Area IX: *Advertising Regulation*

Each of these planning areas is discussed in this text in the above sequence.

CRITERIA, ANALYSIS AND DECISION MAKING

The title of this text is *Advertising Management: Criteria, Analysis and Decision Making*. The subtitle of the text is intended to emphasize the basic and elemental connections in the decision making process in advertising. That is, the advertising decision making process, conceived at its broadest level of meaning, consists of "connecting" *adver-*

tising criteria, on the one hand, with *advertising decision variables* on the other hand. The extent to which this *connection process* is successful in the ultimate development of advertising programs depends on the quality of the *analysis* utilized in the connection process itself. The emphasis in this text will be aimed at developing an understanding of criteria issues and the analytical methods which need to be employed to make successful linkages or connections between the decision variables and the criteria.

The *criteria* to be considered in this text, as shown in Figure 1-2, consist of the following: Exposure, Awareness, Attitude, Intention, Behavior, and Profits. The issues to be considered in the discussion of criteria include the question as to which criterion should serve as the indicator of effective advertising, whether one criterion or several criteria should serve as the indicator, and the relationships among the criteria listed above. These issues are discussed extensively in Chapter 5.

The *decision making* variables to be considered in this text are: Market Segmentation, Money (the budget or appropriation), Media, and Message (the advertisements). Each of these areas is discussed separately in isolation from the others in separate chapters in the text. However, the various models and cases considered in this text often require the simultaneous consideration of each of these four decision variables. This means that some appreciation of the *interaction* of one with the other must be developed. How will the selection of a particular message strategy or theme for the advertising campaign affect the media strategy and scheduling decision process? How will the amount of money to be appropriated for the advertising campaign affect the media decision making process? How will the target market definition relate to the media decision making process? How will the market segmentation decision impact on the message decision? Clearly, the integration of the advertising decision variables requires an understanding of the relationships between each of them. Much of this text will, therefore, concentrate on developing an understanding of the interaction of the four primary decision variables of market, money, media, and message.

The methods of *analysis* to be examined in this text cover a wide variety of approaches. As indicated previously, cases analyses will be used both in separate chapters as well as more briefly in examples within the text chapters proper. Model building methods will be emphasized, particularly in the budgeting chapters and the media chapters. Some of the tools of analysis require the application of statistics while others require arithmetic, algebra and, in one case, calculus. *Judgment*, of course, is the most basic tool of all and is indispensable.

This text, then, attempts to provide an understanding of advertising criteria in relation to advertising decision making variables. This understanding rests upon the intelligent application of various analytical methods and judgment. The basic point to understand, however, is that there can be effective decision making in advertising only when such decision making is conducted in the context of, and with reference to, advertising criteria. Without the explicit consideration of criteria, advertising decision making cannot be considered in any systematic manner.

APPENDIX A TO CHAPTER 1

AN EXAMPLE OF ALTERNATIVE THINKING

The general steps to pursue in the use of alternative thinking are described in the "five-step" method listed below:
  (1) Define the problem
  (2) State alternative courses of action
  (3) Evaluate the alternatives
  (4) Recommend the course of action
  (5) Justify the recommendation
Given below is an example which applies the above five-step method of analysis:
Problem: What should be the relative emphasis to be placed on Brand X Aerosol versus Stick deodorant?

Alternative #1: Advertise Only the Aerosol

Basic Advantages	Basic Disadvantages
a. A large, undiluted budget	a. Stick has no advertising support
b. Promotional emphasis on the only truly different product the company has	b. Stick market appears to be a growing market
c. Copy has a greater potential exposure	c. A male stick as a counterpart to present stick may be planned for introduction

Alternative #2: Advertise Only the Stick

Basic Advantages	Basic Disadvantages
a. Aerosol has already achieved a maximum market penetration and product loyalty is fairly good	a. The major present source of revenue is from aerosol, which is the more profitable of the two
b. Possibility that the stick may not dig sharply into aerosol sales	b. The future growth potential of the stick as a type of product is not guaranteed (at the present time, sticks have less than 40 percent of the market)
c. Possibility that the stick may actually have the greatest future potential, particularly in light of the tremendous amount of support other advertisers will put behind stick deodorants	

Alternative #3: Advertise the Aerosol and Stick
Nationally Together but Emphasize the
Aerosol in All Advertising

Basic Advantages	Basic Disadvantages
a. Produces dual support with emphasis on the leading revenue producer	a. May lead to consumer confusion
	b. Not readily adaptable to television; it lacks media flexibility
b. Produces greater flexibility in adapting advertising to specific market pictures (in other words, emphasis on either of the two products can be varied depending on which way the wind is blowing in the various markets)	c. May actually encourage internal market brand shifting so that the present aerosol user shifts to the stick, which does not build business additionally for the company

Alternative #4: Change the Name of Stick and Advertise
the Stick and Aerosol as Two Different Products

Basic Advantages	Basic Disadvantages
a. Permits concentration of funds to maximize budget efficiency (in areas where there is spending on each product, projected national advertising expenditure will be quite high)	a. Tacitly undercuts the concept of the national franchise for either one of the products
	b. Might result in substantial decline in aerosol business in the secondary areas because of lack of support
b. Permits concentration of funds so that the successful type of product—the one that has the momentum gets the benefit of the promotion	

Alternative #5: Advertise the Aerosol and Stick Regularly and
Separately on a Non-Overlapping Basis

Basic Advantages	Basic Disadvantages
a. Cuts brand confusion and reduces the internal competitive situation	a. Requires stick advertising expenditure on an investment rate basis
b. Puts the stick on its own feet as a product	b. Does not have any advantage of the existing brand name carry-over

Alternative #6: Advertise Aerosol and Stick Separately on Basis
of Different Strategy for Each

Basic Advantages	Basic Disadvantages
a. Permits maintenance of brand-name national franchise	a. Requires that stick support be confined to larger markets
b. Does not "give up" in poorer aerosol areas	
c. Stick will be separately supported	

Alternative #1 was discarded because it was completely unrealistic not to give the current distribution support, even in weak-selling areas.

Alternative #2 was discarded because, although the stick market seems to be rapidly expanding, the aerosol forms the core of the company's business.

Alternative #3 was discarded because it was not considered possible to effectively marry these two products in copy without diluting the effectiveness of major aerosol appeal.

Alternative #4 was discarded because the company had gone too far in the production of the stick to make a fundamental change in nomenclature.

Alternative #5 was discarded because of the feeling that the present national franchise should not be cut back.

The recommended advertising policy on the relationship of the aerosol to the stick is Alternative #6:

(1) Advertise the aerosol nationally and separately.

(2) Advertise the stick as a separate brand in selected key areas.

Furthermore, now and in the foreseeable future, the prime basis of income is the aerosol business. It is believed that one of the keys to opening the profit door in this business has been the exclusivity of the product coupled with an effective copy story, dramatically told on television. The company felt very strongly that they could not in any way afford to jeopardize this franchise.

APPENDIX B TO CHAPTER 1

AN EXAMPLE OF MODEL BUILDING AND USAGE

A simplified example of model-building will illustrate the procedure. Later in the text, it will be determined why the following illustration would probably be a fairly unrealistic representation of the advertising process. But for the purposes of a beginning understanding of the model-building process this example should be instructive.

(1) Suppose the advertising manager believes that the single most important marketing factor responsible for the sales of the company's product is advertising. Furthermore, suppose it is also believed that it is the weight or dollars spent on advertising which is most important, not the creative materials or the media schedules. Based upon some years of experience with the product the manager believes that, in general, for every one dollar spent on advertising, three dollars in sales result. The assumption here is that the response of sales to advertising is straight-line in nature; this is called a linear advertising response function and is shown in Figure 1-3.

(2) Given the implicit model in (1) above, a formal or explicit model can be developed: Sales are a function of three times advertising expenditures or $S = 3(A)$. The parameter in this response function is assigned the number three. A parameter in any model is a factor which takes on a given number in a specific situation. At the heart of the model-building process is the estimation of the parameters of the model. To the extent that the parameters of a model are estimated accurately *and* the extent to which the relations in the model are specified correctly, the model will produce accurate projections of the "real" situation it is intended to represent.

(3) For example, $S = 3(A)$ above represents the manager's judgment of the relation between advertising and sales. Suppose the manager is considering the results which might occur next year if 2 million dollars are spent on advertising. Using the model, $3(2) = 6$ million dollars in sales would be

projected by the model. If the manager then spends 2 million dollars next year and the sales resulting from the expenditure are 5 million dollars, the parameter "3" in the response function has been inaccurately estimated and/or the model relations have been inaccurately specified. In this case, the parameter can be estimated using more information and using other methods than judgment, for example, regression analysis of several quarters of

Figure 1-3   A Linear Advertising
Response Function

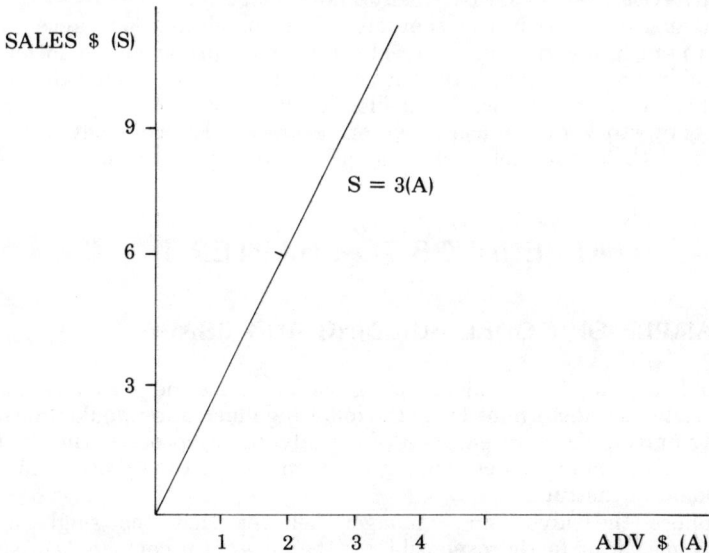

SALES $ (S)

$S = 3(A)$

ADV $ (A)

advertising and sales data. If the accuracy of the model does not improve after re-estimation of the parameter value, then the relation must be re-specified; the relation between advertising and sales for the company's product may not be linear. Rather than $S = b(A)$ the correct specification of the relation may be $S = b(A)^{1/2}$ where b is the parameter to be estimated and "½" indicates the square root of advertising, that is, a non-linear response function.

(4) Assuming that $S = 3(A)$ is an accurate response function, this information can then be used to extend the model. Suppose for this company, net profits (NP) are equal to revenue (sales in dollars) less fixed costs (FC) and advertising expenditures: $NP = S - FC - A$. Then, by substitution of the response function into the profit function, $NP = 3(A) - FC - A$.

(5) Suppose that fixed costs are estimated for the advertising manager's company next quarter to be one million dollars. Then $NP = 3(A) - 1,000,000 - A$ is the actual net profit model for the company in relation to advertising expenditures. The advertising manager now wishes to examine possible profits which might result from an expenditure of 2 million dollars next quarter compared to an alternative expenditure of 2.5 million dollars next quarter.

Alternative (a): $\underline{A = \$2,000,000}$
$$NP = 3(2,000,000) - \$1,000,000 - \$2,000,000$$
$$NP = \$3,000,000$$

Alternative (b): $\underline{A = \$2,500,000}$
$$NP = 3(2,500,000) - \$1,000,000 - \$2,500,000$$
$$NP = \$4,000,000$$

Given the accuracy of this model as a representation of reality (in this highly simplified case this is very questionable), alternative (b) would represent the preferable spending level on advertising.

In the following chapters, many models will be presented in different advertising applications. A knowledge of the approaches and structure of these models will serve to discipline and direct analyses of the various cases which are presented separately in various chapters throughout the text. The case study approach and the model-building approach should be viewed as complementary to each other; theory and application go hand in hand.

QUESTIONS AND PROBLEMS

1. Discuss the way in which the role of advertising will differ when an industrial product is involved rather than consumer packaged goods. What part of the overall marketing program will advertising play in each case?
2. What role does marketing integration play in the development of advertising as it is today? How does the acceptance and development of the marketing concept relate to the development of advertising?
3. It has been said that it is the role of advertising to help meet the needs and wants of consumers by informing them of the availability of products which might meet such needs. How does this role of advertising, if you believe this is the role of advertising, relate to the use of advertising by business people for the purpose of making a profit?
4. In this chapter, one particular method was suggested for the analysis of advertising case material, the "five-point" method. Can you suggest some alternative ways of analyzing case material? How does the suggested method in this chapter relate to methods of problem-solving which have been discussed by such individuals as Von Neuman and Morgenstern (see such a discussion in R. Alderson and P. Green, *Planning and Problem Solving in Marketing* (Homewood, Il.: Richard D. Irwin, 1964)?
5. Why is model building in advertising today not so closely allied with the field of operations research as it was in the early 1950s? What contribution to advertising modeling did operations research provide?
6. Why were advertising agencies the first to explore, develop and apply mathematical models to advertising decision making processes?
7. In the quest to learn more about how advertising works, in what ways might the case study approach and the model-building approach be considered complementary? Why have these approaches been considered in such different lights historically? What is the relationship of inductive and deductive learning to case studies and model-building analyses?
8. In what ways do models in the "decision calculus" model differ from the operations research approach to model building?
9. What are the strengths and weaknesses of "implicit" and "explicit" models?

10. Review the material in Appendix B to this chapter. Following this four-step procedure for model building and usage, develop a somewhat more acceptable example of a budgeting model than is shown in that appendix (from the standpoint of the assumptions made about the response function utilized in that example).

ENDNOTES

1. "The Teens," A Three-part Series in *Media Decisions,* August, October and November, 1976.
2. Neil H. Borden and Martin V. Marshall, *Advertising Management: Text and Cases,* rev.ed. (Homewood, Il.: Richard D. Irwin, 1959).
3. Harry Deane Wolfe, James K. Brown, G. Clark Thompson, and Stephen H. Greenberg, *Evaluating Media* (New York: National Industrial Conference Board, 1966), p. 115.
4. David A. Aaker and John G. Myers, *Advertising Management* (Englewood Cliffs, New Jersey: Prentice-Hall, Inc., 1975).
5. This discussion draws from David B. Montgomery and Charles Weinberg, "Modeling Marketing Phenomena: A Managerial Perspective," *Journal of Contemporary Business* (Autumn 1973), pp. 42-51.
6. H.D. Wolfe, *et.al., op.cit.*
7. John D.C. Little, "Models and Managers: The Concept of A Decision Calculus," *Management Science* 16 (April 1970), pp. B466-B485.
8. John D.C. Little and Leonard M. Lodish, "A Media Selection Model and it Optimization by Dynamic Programming," *Industrial Management Review* (Fall 1966), pp. 15-23.
9. George S. Day, Gerald J. Eskin, David B. Montgomery, and Charles B. Weinberg, *Cases in Computer and Model-Assisted Marketing: Planning* (Cupertino, California: Hewlett Packard Company, 1977).
10. H.J. Claycamp and L.E. Liddy, "Prediction of New Product Performance: An Analytical Approach," *Journal of Marketing Research* (November 1969), pp. 414-420.

INPUTS TO ADVERTISING PLANNING

- Organization and Advertising Decision Making
- The Meaning of Strategy
- Elements of Marketing Planning
- Outline of the Marketing Plan

Decision Making Organization of This Text

```
┌─────────────────────────────┐                              ┌─────────────────────────────┐
│   INPUTS TO                 │                              │        SETTING              │
│ ADVERTISING PLANNING        │──────────┐        ┌─────────▶│      ADVERTISING            │
│   (Planning Area I)         │          │        │          │       OBJECTIVES            │
├─────────────────────────────┤          │        │          │    (Planning Area III)      │
│     Corporate               │          ▼        │          ├─────────────────────────────┤
│     Objectives              │      ╱─────────────╲          │      Consumer               │
├─────────────────────────────┤     ╱  ADVERTISING  ╲        │      Response               │
│   Marketing Plan            │    ⟨ OPPORTUNITY ANALYSIS⟩    │      Criteria               │
├─────────────────────────────┤     ╲ (Planning Area II)╱    │                             │
│   • Product                 │      ╲─────────────╱          │    • Exposure               │
│   • Price                   │                              │    • Awareness              │
│   • Place                   │                              │    • Attitude               │
│   • Promotion               │                              │    • Intentions             │
└─────────────────────────────┘                              │    • Behavior (Sales)       │
            ▲                                                 │    • Profits                │
            │                                                 └─────────────────────────────┘
```

INPUTS TO ADVERTISING PLANNING (Planning Area I)

- Corporate Objectives
- Marketing Plan
  - Product
  - Price
  - Place
  - Promotion

ADVERTISING OPPORTUNITY ANALYSIS (Planning Area II)

SETTING ADVERTISING OBJECTIVES (Planning Area III)

Consumer Response Criteria

- Exposure
- Awareness
- Attitude
- Intentions
- Behavior (Sales)
- Profits

Measurement of Impact

DETERMINING ADVERTISING DECISIONS

Decision Variables

- MARKET (Planning Area IV)
- MONEY (Planning Area V)
- MESSAGE (Planning Area VI)
- MEDIA (Planning Area VII)

Market Impact

INTERVENING FACTORS (Planning Area IX)

- Competition
- Facilitating Agencies
- Environmental Factors
- Regulation

COORDINATING PROMOTION MANAGEMENT (Planning Area VIII)

- Personal Selling
- Sales Promotion (including Publicity)

INPUTS TO ADVERTISING PLANNING

"Advertising people, like everybody else, ought to figure out the *right* thing to do and then do it!"

—Carl Ally
Advertising Practitioner

More than 34 billion dollars were spent on advertising in 1980 in the United States. This exceeds by a considerable amount the funds invested in all of higher education in that year.[1] As the reader is undoubtedly aware, the advertising industry is very large and complex indeed. The institutional arrangements which have been developed to facilitate advertising confront the advertising management personnel with a bewildering array of entanglements. The advertising manager must come to some understanding of these institutional settings in order to determine the correct procedures to follow in the development of an advertising program and insure its effective implementation.

Beyond an institutional understanding of advertising, the manager must develop a systematic comprehension of the way in which an advertising program can be produced within the corporate setting. This requires an understanding of the elements of marketing planning and its relation to the advertising plan. This involves an appreciation of the relation of advertising decision variables (market, money, media and message) to the marketing mix as a whole.

ORGANIZATION AND ADVERTISING DECISION MAKING

There are three principal institutions which are involved in the national advertising setting: (1) the advertiser, (2) the advertising agen-

28

cy, and (3) the media. A brief overview of each of these three elements of the advertising system is given below.

THE ADVERTISER

Advertising expenditures in the United States by advertisers (both national and retail) have increased tremendously since the founding of this country. Table 2-1 shows the steady increase in advertising expenditures since that time; these expenditures have doubled in the past decade or so alone. As shown in Figure 2-1, advertising and related expenditures by advertisers have been rising faster than the

Table 2-1   Advertising Expenditures in the U.S.—
1776 to 1979
(in Millions of Dollars)

Year	Amount	Year	Amount	Year	Amount
1776	0.2	1925	2,600	1951	6,420
1780	0.21	1926	2,700	1952	7,140
1790	0.4	1927	2,720	1953	7,740
1800	1.0	1928	2,760	1954	8,150
1810	1.6	1929	2,850	1955	9,150
1820	3	1930	2,450	1956	9,910
1830	5	1931	2,100	1957	10,270
1840	7	1932	1,620	1958	10,310
1850	12	1933	1,325	1959	11,270
1860	22	1934	1,650	1960	11,960
1867	40	1935	1,720	1961	11,860
1876	150	1936	1,930	1962	12,430
1880	175	1937	2,100	1963	13,100
1890	300	1938	1,930	1964	14,150
1900	450	1939	2,010	1965	15,250
1904	750	1940	2,110	1966	16,630
1909	1,000	1941	2,250	1967	16,870
1914	1,100	1942	2,160	1968	18,090
1915	1,100	1943	2,490	1969	19,420
1916	1,240	1944	2,700	1970	19,550
1917	1,380	1945	2,840	1971	20,740
1918	1,240	1946	3,340	1972	23,300
1919	1,930	1947	4,260	1973	25,120
1920	2,480	1948	4,870	1974	26,820
1921	1,930	1949	5,210	1975	28,160
1922	2,200	1950	5,700	1976	33,690
1923	2,400			1977	37,920
1924	2,480			1978	43,840
				1979	49,690

* preliminary
** forecast

SOURCE: Adapted from ADVERTISING AGE (July 5, 1979), p. 41.

Table 2-2   100 Leading National Advertisers

(Total Ad Dollars in Millions: 1979)

1 Procter & Gamble Co.	$614.9	52 DuPont	89.4
2 General Foods Corp.	393.0	53 Eastman Kodak Co.	87.8
3 Sears, Roebuck & Co.	379.3	54 Quaker Oats Co.	86.6
4 General Motors Corp.	323.4	55 Nestle Enterprises	86.0
5 Philip Morris Inc.	291.2	56 American Brands	83.5
6 K mart Corp.	287.1	57 Toyota Motor Sales U.S.A.	80.3
7 R. J. Reynolds Industries	258.1	58 Schering-Plough Corp.	78.0
8 Warner-Lambert Co.	220.2	59 Miles Laboratories	77.8
9 American Telephone &		60 Clorox Co.	72.6
Telegraph Co.	219.8	61 CPC International Inc.	72.0
10 Ford Motor Co.	215.0	62 Jos. Schlitz Brewing Co.	71.6
11 PepsiCo Inc.	212.0	63 H. J. Heinz Co.	71.5
12 Bristol-Myers Co.	210.6	64 Mars Inc.	69.5
13 American Home Products	206.0	65 Nissan Motor Corp.	66.1
14 McDonald's Corp.	202.8	66 MCA Inc.	66.0
15 Gulf + Western Industries	191.5	67 Mattel Inc.	66.0
16 General Mills	190.7	68 Trans World Corp.	62.0
17 Esmark Inc.	170.5	69 Campbell Soup Co.	60.5
18 Coca-Cola Co.	169.3	70 Squibb Corp.	60.0
19 Seagram Co.	168.0	71 Liggett Group	59.0
20 Mobil Corp.	165.8	72 Warner Communications	57.6
21 Norton Simon Inc.	163.2	73 American Express Co.	55.4
22 Anheuser-Busch	160.5	74 Union Carbide Corp.	55.1
23 Unilever U.S. Inc.	160.0	75 Volkswagen of America	55.0
24 RCA Corp.	158.6	76 Greyhound Corp.	53.8
25 Johnson & Johnson	157.7	77 UAL Inc.	52.5
26 Heublein Inc.	155.0	78 Polaroid Corp.	50.5
27 Beatrice Foods Co.	150.0	79 Brown-Forman	
28 CBS Inc.	146.1	Distillers Corp.	50.0
28 U.S. Government	146.1	80 MortonNorwich	49.2
30 Loews Corp.	144.5	81 Wm. Wrigley Jr. Co.	48.5
31 General Electric Co.	139.4	82 Beecham Group Ltd.	46.7
32 International Telephone &		83 American Motors Corp.	44.6
Telegraph Corp.	132.4	84 North American	
33 Pillsbury Co.	131.5	Philips Corp.	44.2
34 American Cyanamid Co.	127.0	85 American Honda Motor Co.	44.0
35 Gillette Co.	126.9	86 Pfizer Inc.	43.7
36 Richardson-Merrell	123.8	87 ABC Inc.	42.0
37 Colgate-Palmolive Co.	122.5	88 Eastern Air Lines	40.4
38 J. C. Penney Co.	122.0	89 Noxell Corp.	40.2
39 Kraft Inc.	119.7	90 S. C. Johnson & Son	40.2
40 Chrysler Corp.	118.0	91 Borden Inc.	39.0
41 B.A.T. Industries Ltd.	116.4	92 Levi Strauss & Co.	38.6
42 Ralston Purina Co.	108.0	93 A. H. Robins Co.	37.0
43 SmithKline Corp.	107.7	94 Scott Paper Co.	36.8
44 Chesebrough-Pond's	107.3	95 Standard Brands	36.4
45 Consolidated Foods Corp.	105.0	96 American Airlines	35.0
46 Time Inc.	102.4	97 Delta Air Lines	33.5
47 Revlon Inc.	101.0	98 Milton Bradley Co.	31.3
48 Transamerica Corp.	95.0	99 International Business	
49 Sterling Drug Co.	$92.0	Machines	31.1
50 Kellogg Co.	91.6	100 Mazda Motors of America	28.4
51 Nabisco Inc.	91.3		

SOURCE: ADVERTISING AGE (September 11, 1980), cover

Figure 2-1

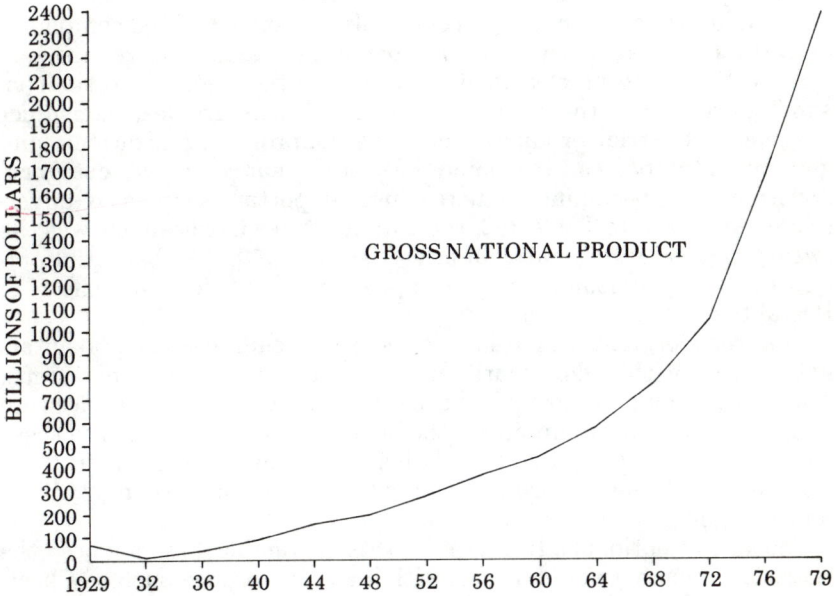

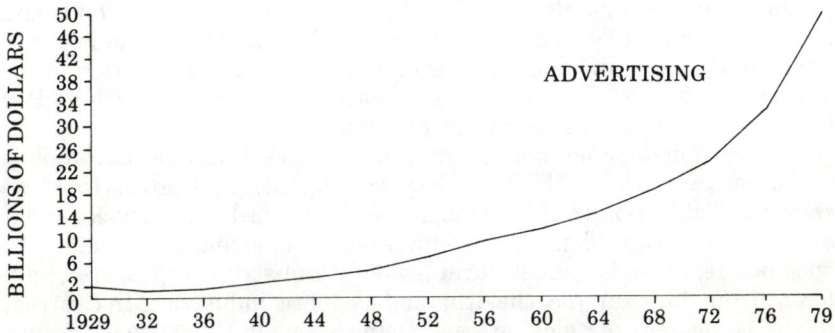

gross national product, national income, carloadings, or almost any measure of business activity. As shown in Table 2-2, the advertising appropriation for the leading national advertiser, Procter & Gamble Company, now exceeds the total amount spent by all advertisers at the beginning of this century.

There is a great deal of variation in the amount of money spent by companies manufacturing products in different industries. A convenient way to compare amounts of money spent on advertising in different industries is through advertising dollars expressed as a percentage of sales dollars. The highest percentage of sales spent on advertising is in the proprietary drug industry; some proprietary drug companies spend in excess of 50 percent of sales on advertising on some of their brands of over-the-counter drugs. On the other hand, the average percent of sales spent on advertising in 1978 in the frozen foods industry was about 2 percent. Only 10 percent of the companies in that industry spent more than 5 percent of sales on advertising.

Advertisers can be classified according to the segment of the consuming economy they serve: consumer non-durables, consumer durables, industrial products, retailers, nonprofit organizations, and governmental bodies. It should be noted that this last category, government, is becoming an increasingly important segment of advertising. As shown in Table 2–2, the United States Government was the twenty-eighth largest national advertiser in 1979. A substantial portion of its expenditures come from the armed services and the U.S. Postal Service.

Nonprofit organizations such as schools, churches and hospitals have many of the same marketing problems faced by corporations. They need to pinpoint groups of consumers for whom their services are targeted and then communicate the benefits of their offerings to these consumers. This job is increasingly being done by advertising; in 1973, it is estimated that nonprofit organizations spent more than $2 billion on advertising.[2]

The largest national advertiser, Procter & Gamble, has long been the leader in consumer non-durables with mainstay brands such as Cheer, Tide, Oxydol, and Ivory. P & G also manufactures non-soap consumer products such as Pringle's Potato Chips and other brands of foods and coffees. About sixty of Procter & Gamble's brands are handled and advertised by ten different advertising agencies. A large portion of the advertising budget for companies operating in industries such as P & G tends to be spent in television advertising.

In the non-durable consumer goods market, three automobile manufacturers are in the top forty leading national advertisers, as shown in Table 2–2. In 1979, General Motors, Ford and Chrysler spent $726,000,000. But when this is expressed as a percentage of sales, the automobile, as well as most durable goods industries, appear quite different from, for example, the drug and cosmetic industries. In contrast to the 16 percent of sales on advertising spent in the cosmetic industry, the advertising to sales ratio for the automobile industry is less than 2 percent. General Motors Corporation, the nation's second largest advertiser, is organized into ten divisions; each division has considerable autonomy with respect to its advertising. Each division's advertising is handled by a major advertising agency.

Industrial advertisers differ considerably from those companies advertising to the consumer market. Industrial advertising, which entails all non-consumer advertising, tends to use considerably different advertising media than that employed in consumer advertising. Most expenditures go in business papers which reach buyers in specific corporate areas, for example, plant maintenance equipment. The advertising conducted by industrial advertisers tends to be considerably more detailed and technical than that by consumer advertisers, since the industrial audience consists of professionals knowledgeable in their particular areas.

In recent years there has been a marked trend toward organization of consumer advertising according to the brand management concept. This type of organization for advertising activity is depicted in Figure 2-2. The brand manager is responsible for all marketing facets for a particular brand, including its advertising. There generally will be an advertising manager who coordinates all advertising activity for the entire company, whether this advertising is planned and executed by a brand manager or the product group manager. Both the brand managers and the advertising manager have contact with the personnel at the advertising agency in charge of handling the company's advertising.

THE ADVERTISING AGENCY

The advertising agency system originated in the work of freelance individuals, such as George P. Rowell, who sold space in different media vehicles to advertisers. The media for whom these people sold advertising space compensated them by providing a commission on all space sold. Eventually, in order to attract more advertisers, these space salesmen began offering creative services. The creation of the advertisement was offered to advertisers at no additional charge beyond that of the space in which the advertisement was run. Later, additional services such as media planning and research were provided by these salesmen who by this time came to be known as advertising agents. The commission paid to advertising agencies has for many decades been customarily set at 15 percent.

Many agencies operate under a non-commission called the "fee system." Under this approach to compensation, a general fee is assessed the advertiser for all services rendered; this is similar to the manner in which a lawyer charges the client for professional advice and counsel. In most cases, the commissions are counted as part of the fee charged. For example, if the advertiser and the agency have agreed to a fee of $200,000 for some given time period and for certain work, and the commissions from advertising placed in the media during this time amounted to $110,000, the advertiser would pay the agency $90,000.

There are three primary reasons why most large national advertisers, in contrast to retail advertisers, generally employ advertising agencies to prepare and place their advertising. First, and perhaps most importantly, the advertiser would usually pay media the same amount of money for space and time even if the agency were not used; in essence, the agency's services are free. Second, advertising agencies employ practitioners skilled in each of the various functions of advertising: creative, media, planning, and research. These people have spent their careers learning about and practicing advertising. Finally, the advertising agency may be able, under certain circumstances, to provide a more objective assessment of the advertising and marketing problems of the advertiser than could the advertiser's own employees.

Figure 2-2   Organization Chart for Corporation Using
Brand Management Concept

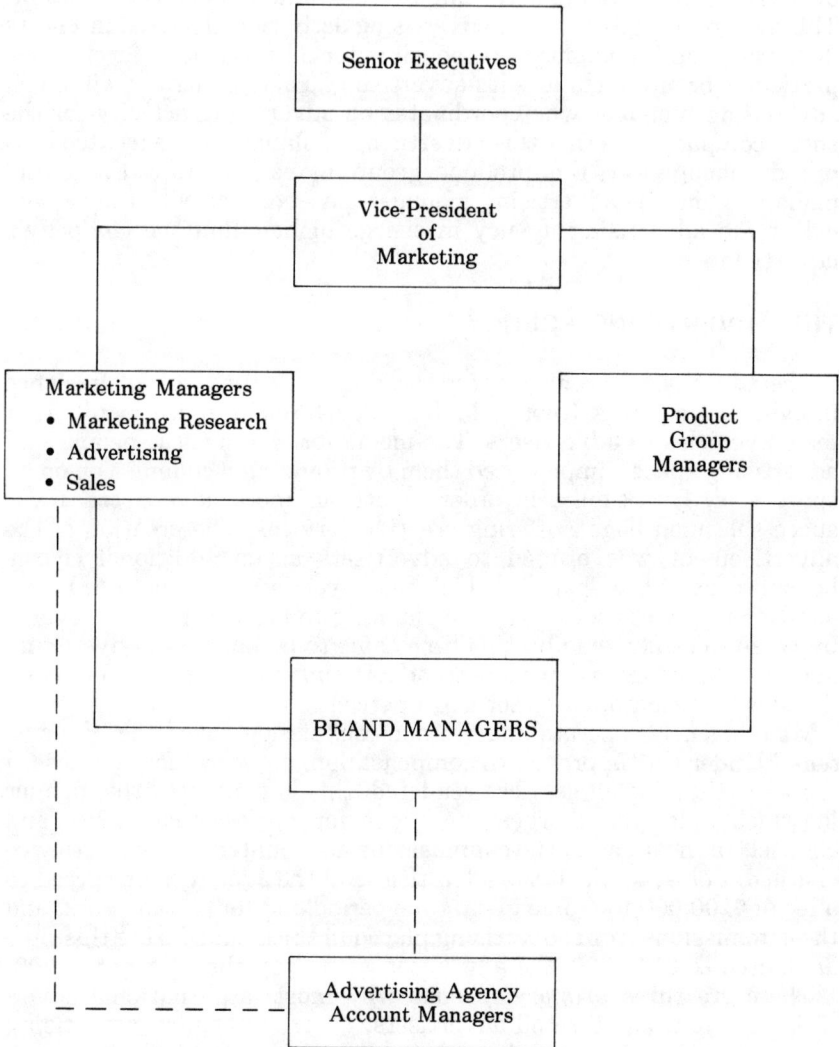

Figure 2–3 shows the organization of the typical advertising agency by functions. The account services section consists of account supervisors and account managers or executives whose job it is to coordinate and plan the advertising program in conjunction with the client. Account managers are the primary contact with the advertiser. Advertising and marketing research functions are usually grouped under the

Figure 2-3

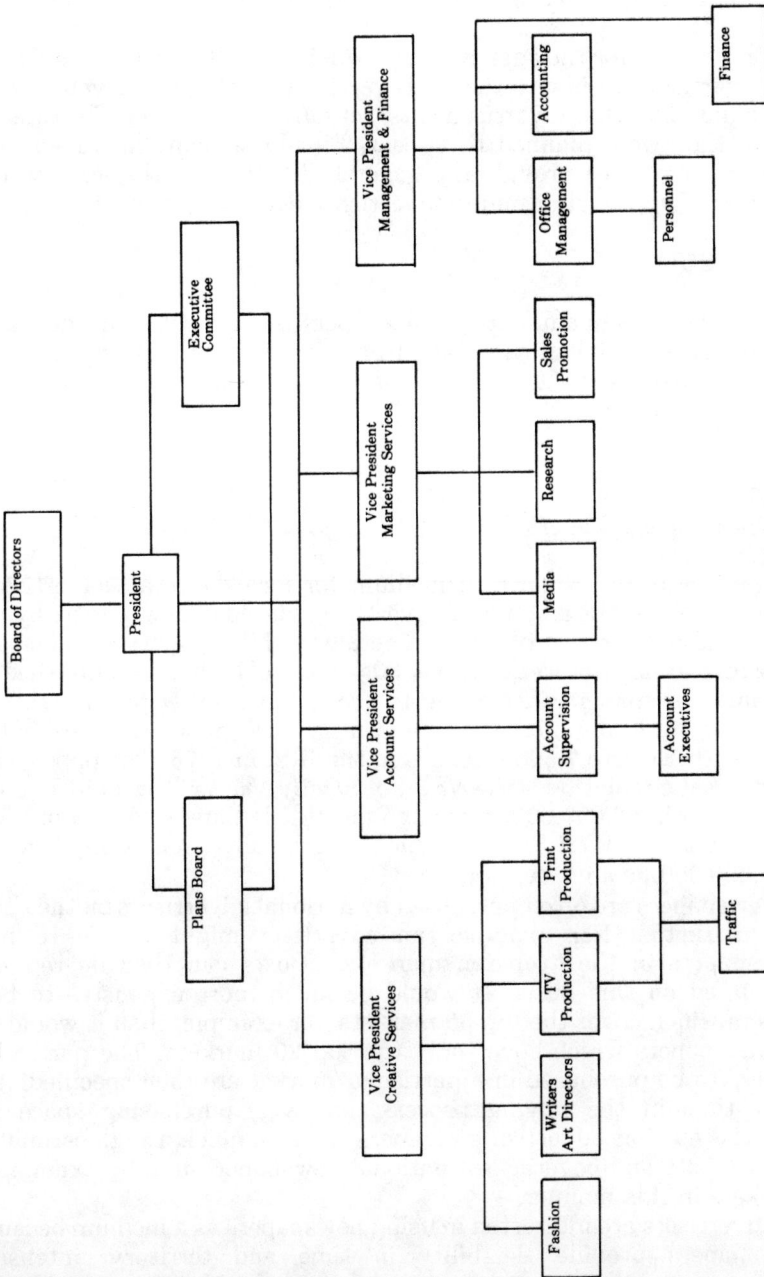

Board of Directors — **President**

Executive Committee

Plans Board

Vice President Creative Services
- Fashion
- Writers / Art Directors
- TV Production
- Print Production
  - Traffic

Vice President Account Services
- Account Supervision
  - Account Executives

Vice President Marketing Services
- Media
- Research
- Sales Promotion

Vice President Management & Finance
- Office Management
  - Personnel
- Accounting
  - Finance

SOURCE: American Association of Advertising Agencies.

marketing services umbrella along with sales promotion. Under the creative services department will be art directors, copy writers, producers and other creative specialists who prepare the advertisements. The internal financial operations of the agency are grouped under a finance director. Often a "new business" unit will be formed to search for new clients for the agency. There will be a traffic unit which tracks all advertising to insure that it is received by the media vehicles on time and that the advertisements actually appeared at the time in which they were planned to appear. Finally, a plans board and executive committee provide the general direction for the agency and make final approval of major advertising decisions for clients.

THE MEDIA

In terms of total amount of money spent by advertisers in the major media types, they can be ranked from most to least important as:
(1) Newspapers
(2) Television
(3) Direct Mail
(4) Radio
(5) Magazines
(6) Business Papers
(7) Outdoor

Newspapers are primarily a medium for local or retail advertisers; about six times the amount of advertising placed in newspapers by national advertisers is placed by retailers. Newspapers are usually classified as daily or weekly. Over 80 percent of dailies are published as evening newspapers. According to the National Newspaper Association, the trade organization representing newspapers in the United States, there were 7,500 weeklies in the U.S. in 1976. The paper with the largest circulation is the *New York Daily News* with a daily circulation exceeding 2,000,000. Although most daily papers serve a particular locality, the *Wall Street Journal*, with a daily circulation in excess of 1,400,000, is an exception.

Newspapers are often purchased by national advertisers on the basis of "markets." For example, an advertiser might decide to buy newspapers in the "top ten markets." Costs can then be roughly estimated on this basis. It would be much more expensive to buy papers which cover the top 50 markets, for example, than it would be to buy papers which cover only the top 20 markets. The particular papers to be purchased in a particular market are then specified at a later time in the buying process; however, purchasing space by markets enables advertising planners to make quick, rough estimates of the costs and coverage of national newspaper buys by examining markets in this manner.

Advertisers are interested in using newspapers as a medium because newspapers provide flexibility in time and territory, intensive coverage of a market, and the community prestige offered by the individual newspaper in association with the advertiser's product. The newspaper also has disadvantages as an advertising medium, however. The newspaper has a short life, is read hastily, and generally provides poor reproduction quality.

Newspapers, as well as other advertising media, are usually represented to advertisers by agents called "media reps." These firms handle non-competing media and attempt to sell the advantages of these particular media to advertising agencies. In fact, media rep firms are the contemporary counterpart of agencies; advertising agencies began as space salesmen for the newspaper industry.

Although magazines rank fifth among the media in terms of total amount of money spent in them by advertisers, more advertisers use magazines than use any other mass medium. Magazines are generally classified as consumer magazines, farm magazines, or business publications. Consumer magazines are designed for people who buy products for their own use; farm magazines circulate to farmers and their families; and business publications are trade papers (designed for retailers and wholesalers), industrial magazines (addressed to businesspeople involved in all aspects of manufacturing), and professional magazines (directed to lawyers, professors and other professional groups).

Magazines are attractive vehicles for advertisers because they provide selectivity in terms of the types of people who read particular magazines; they have good-quality reproduction and a relatively long life. Some magazines, such as *The New Yorker*, can lend a prestige image to the advertiser. But magazines also have some drawbacks for national advertisers. They are not so flexible with respect to deadlines or with respect to territory covered as are newspapers. This territory limitation is overcome somewhat by the 100 or so consumer magazines which offered regional editions in 1977. *Time* magazine is the most flexible in this regard; it can be purchased in over 100 city markets.

Although direct mail is not actually a mass medium, it is a very important one. In 1980, it ranked third among all media types in terms of the expenditures by advertisers. Direct mail advertising has increased its efficiency tremendously in recent years. Mailing lists have become more precise by focusing on very specific groups of consumers; for example, those consumers interested in bass fishing can be reached by direct mail through purchase of their names from companies specializing in the compilation of mailing lists. These companies have been aided a great deal by the development of computerized mailing lists. The direct mailing pieces have now become more personal in nature due to the advances in computerized writing of them.

Direct mail is used by advertisers because it provides the ultimate degree of selectivity of audiences. Whether the advertiser is looking for a small audience or one numbering in the millions, whether the advertiser wants high or low income groups, it is possible to work out an acceptable coverage plan. Direct mail also provides the advertiser with speed in the delivery of the message to the right prospects, flexibility in the mailing piece format, personal tone, and the capability to develop intensive coverage through repeated mailings to the prospects. The limitations of direct mail to advertisers lie in the high costs per reader, the difficulties of maintaining and updating costly mailing lists, and customer resistance to so-called "junk" mail.

Outdoor advertising has come under increasing demand by advertisers in recent years while the availability of posters has declined, due largely to environmental standards by governmental bodies. Two-thirds of the $388,000,000 spent on outdoor advertising in 1980 was spent by national advertisers. Outdoor advertising is usually classified into three categories: (1) posters (such posters are often referred to as billboards) which are usually "24- or 30-sheets", though they no longer consist of that many printed sections; (2) painted bulletins, which are often specially designed outdoor advertising to meet the needs of individual advertisers; and (3) spectaculars, which are illuminated, and sometimes also animated, signs which are often located in high-traffic locations such as in-city expressways. The value of outdoor advertising to the advertiser lies largely in its ability to provide message repetition and a reminder of the product message close to the point of sale. The limitation which is probably most evident is the possible irritation of consumers who object to outdoor advertising's intrusiveness on the landscape.

When television arrived on the scene in a large way in the early fifties, many in the advertising industry believed it would replace newspapers as the primary advertising medium. This has not occurred. But in terms of dollar volume, it has become the second most important advertising medium. Although television is a relatively new medium, there has developed a surprising amount of information on the medium available to advertisers. There is more research information on the effect of television advertising than of any other type. This further enhances its attractiveness to the advertiser. Television advertising is thought of as network, spot or local. Network advertising is placed with the major television networks such as CBS and appears simultaneously all over the United States where the network has affiliate stations. Spot television is advertising purchased by a national advertiser, but, as opposed to network advertising, is purchased directly from local television stations or their media representatives. It is usually purchased on the basis of markets, for example, the purchase of spot television in the "top ten markets." Local television advertising is purchased at local stations by retail advertisers in their own communities.

Television advertising offers many advantages to the advertiser. More than any other medium, it provides impact for the message which no other medium can deliver because of the use of action, sight and sound. It offers a mass coverage to audiences, the possibilities of message repetition, flexibility of message format (and in the case of local advertising, time flexibility), and the possibilities of prestige deriving from such quality programming as the "Hall of Fame" series. Budweiser has gained prestige with their distributors, for example, through their association with the Johnny Carson Show and Ed McMahon. The disadvantages of television advertising can be found in the cost (though low for the number of viewers reached, the total cost is prohibitive to many advertisers), the temporary nature of commercials compared to magazine ads, for example, and the lack of audience selectivity.

Radio can be considered the number one medium in terms of the size of the potential audience which it offers. Nearly 99 percent of all homes own at least one radio. The number of AM stations available to advertisers has tripled between 1945 and 1960; in 1980 there were more than 4,500 AM and 3,200 FM stations on the air. As in the case of television, radio advertising is classified as network, spot and local. Advertisers use radio for its immediacy (which derives primarily from frequent airing of short news programs), its low cost (both in terms of cost per listener and total absolute cost), its flexibility in format possibilities for the advertising, its rather high degree of audience selectivity for particular types of programming (rock station audiences, for example, will undoubtedly be quite different than easy listening audiences), and its mobility (car radios and portable radios). Its limitations as an advertising medium are to be found in its transient quality (the message is gone after 30 seconds), the fragmentation of the audience (in large cities ten or more stations must compete for the audience), and the general lack of research data on radio effectiveness relative to that provided by television.

THE MEANING OF STRATEGY

Strategy in marketing and advertising involves the plans and objectives of the company. It considers the longer-run implications of the alternative actions confronting the decision maker. These are broad decisions which influence other decisions and are formulated so as to provide the best action in the event of any one of several possible happenings. Flexibility should be considered as one of the characteristics involved. Tactics are concerned with the implementation of and day-to-day requirements in the execution of company strategy, taking place within the broader strategic plan.

In the simplest terms, *strategy* is "What you are trying to accomplish" and tactics are "How you are going to do it." The critical importance of this distinction goes far beyond subtle differences in terminology and can have far-reaching effects on a firm.

THE CRITICAL IMPORTANCE OF STRATEGIC DECISIONS

In advertising as well as in other areas of business, immediate tactical operations bury strategic needs. The day-to-day requirements of a business may well dominate the decisionmaker's time. Valuable time is spent in correcting yesterday's mistakes when the real emphasis should be on planning for tomorrow's eventualities.

As an illustration, suppose a firm produces a proprietary drug item that acts both to relieve headaches as well as the after-effects of the dining table or a night of over-enjoyment and over-indulgence. Without adequate information, the firm's leader decided that more people have headaches and that the firm's strategy will be to attempt to secure the major share of that dominant market.

That strategic decision goes beyond the development of appropriate advertising copy. That decision thrusts the dual-purpose remedy in direct competition with straight headache remedy producers, all of whom are exceptionally heavy advertisers. Logically, the advertising budget will have to be increased so there can be effective competition in an already message-saturated market. With that decision came the acceptance of the seasonal nature of the advertising budget, which might differ from the seasonal pattern characteristic of the "over-indulgence" market.

Prospective consumer grouping (sex, age or socio-economic, for example) differences were accepted, as the over-indulgence appeal curve will probably be skewed in the direction of males of the middle and upper income brackets living in larger cities. Competitive pricing will be determined by the selectivity of the market, as the "new look" approach will place the drug in direct competition with established single-purpose, quick-turnover items already occupying the pharmacy and supermarket shelves. Package redesign is virtually a must, all because of the new emphasis dictated by the selection of a new operating strategy.

A strategic decision must consider the myriad of prospective effects and implications. It should not be made without intelligent investigation, evaluation, discussion of alternatives, and a complete inspection of the potential consequences. The formulation of a sound strategic plan is a relatively inexpensive procedure compared to the cost of field operations. If basic planning is wrong, the best sales personnel, the best creative advertising and media will not match competitors having superior selling programs.

Not recognizing the total significance of a decision mirrors a lack of appreciation of the leverage of strategy. A tactical decision can be more easily corrected, since its influence is limited. A strategic decision, however, digs deep with consequences, and its leverage is tremendous. Buying a television program that is not up to par in its delivery power and efficiency, or designing a promotion piece that has poor color combination each represents tactical mistakes. In most cases, these mistakes can be costly, but they can be corrected relatively swiftly, without having a compounding effect on a whole series of fundamental decisions.

ELEMENTS OF MARKETING PLANNING

In defining a marketing plan or an advertising plan, it is useful to outline its objectives and the function it is to perform. In marketing and advertising, a plan can be said to have the following critical characteristics.

INTEGRATION OF DECISION VARIABLES

It reflects the integration of all the relevant marketing and advertising decision factors related to the specific problems under consideration. All areas directly or indirectly related to the decision-making aspects of the plan are covered as intensively as necessary. If the characteristics of a given product (compared with a competitor's product) have influenced both pricing and creative advertising decisions, the physical structure of the product, together with its assets and liabilities, versus competitive items should be discussed. In more mature and sophisticated corporations, there may be no such formal document as an advertising plan. There may be, rather, an overall marketing plan within which the advertising recommendations are outlined and discussed.

FACTS

It contains the complete organization of available and relevant facts. In one sense an important part of planning involves the creative interpretation of organized facts. Unfortunately, many plans are formulated without sufficient factual data to narrow the area of management decision making. Regardless of the scope of the facts available, however, they all should be covered in the plan.

ALTERNATIVE ACTIONS

The plan should consider, outline, and discuss alternative actions. The very nature of planning requires a recognition and consideration of diverse approaches to the solution of marketing and advertising problems. There may be no one and only solution to a stated problem; rather, there is usually a preferred solution at which management arrives after studying its objectives, the available facts, the longer-term implications of the decision, the marketing ingredients involved in the total mix, and as complete a listing as possible of all other feasible actions.

OBJECTIVES

For the architect, the blueprint is a physical translation of the building objectives to be achieved. In marketing, unfortunately, the objectives cannot be depicted visually, or laid out in a physical model form. They should, however, be established as precisely as possible; without a clean and clear statement of objectives, it is impossible to understand and evaluate a recommended action. An objective frequently may be stated in too broad or general terms as: To increase company sales. A more helpful, practical approach would suggest something similar to the following: To increase company sales 10 percent during the next fiscal period by—

(1) Promoting new uses of the product.

(2) Expanding product distribution by opening 600 retail outlets in new sales territories.

LONG AND SHORT TERM ACTION

A plan, by definition, should not consider only short-term aspects of recommended action. Since "long" term varies from company to company, the relative phrase "longer term" is used here. For example, to suggest that a brand conduct a price promotion without considering the effects on trade and consumer attitudes towards the brand, as well as competitive counter-action, reflects a short-term point of view and does not give adequate consideration to the longer-term implications of such action.

In normal managerial situations, conflicting objectives are almost certain to exist; before the conflict can be resolved, its elements must be listed and analyzed. Suppose, for example, a price increase is being considered in order to turn up more dollars per unit to promote the given brand. The procurement of additional promotion money is in itself an obviously desirable objective in a competitive market. If, however, competition should not match the price increase, the reaction of consumers may be critical. Immediately, there are conflicting objectives; on one side to turn up more money for advertising; on the other side, avoiding the possibility that such a step might have a negative effect upon the brand's standing in the market. The best decision obviously cannot be made without a thorough inspection and analysis of all feasible alternatives including a forecasting of competitive counter-action as well as consumer reaction.

COURSE OF ACTION

Finally, a plan should indicate or suggest, in general, a course of action for accomplishing objectives.

OUTLINE OF THE MARKETING PLAN

To be applicable to the myriad of situations and problems which may be encountered in the marketing context, any suggested approach to planning must be characterized by flexibility and adaptability. Companies with differing marketing objectives require different plans; products with different problems, different histories, varying degrees of advertising involvement have differing marketing environments and require quite different plans. Some products may require longer, more involved and detailed marketing plans; others may be quite brief. The discussion which follows delineates and briefly discusses the key areas which should be covered in an integrated advertising program.

THE PRODUCT

An examination should be conducted of the product in production's relation to marketing rather than of marketing alone. This examination should serve as a reminder about the constituent elements of the product and of the processes used to manufacture it, including production superiorities, in-plant research and testing, and the manufacturer's evaluation of the product.

In some instances, product research information will not be available. In such cases, product research might be recommended. An example might be a local beverage account where blind testing of ginger ale was recommended in order to get some insight into whether a declining sales curve was influenced by the product's taste differences.

Product information is usually very familiar to important executives of the company. However, the organization of such data acts as a catalyst for thinking in the area and, very importantly, provides organized information to departments working on the accounts who cannot have top management's intimate product familiarity. Such information might subtly remind the production personnel, via a factual framework, of certain basic facts of life about the product. For example, it might remind a pharmaceutical company that a depilatory has only limited effectiveness, something production people may know, but do not like to think about. Placed in the environment of a marketing plan it can be quietly communicated.

THE PACKAGE

Packaging, outside of its relation to merchandising policy and pricing policy, has two vital functions: (1) physical, and (2) psychological.

If the physical appearance and "reachability" of the package need revision, the assets and liabilities of the package should be examined. For example, the fact that the name of the brand was printed only on one side of a dog food package was a distinct liability on the grocery shelf and needed to be modified.

The psychological aspects of the package may well be important for a particular product. For example, in the case of Streamline Beverages, a local soft drink, it was felt that the label design did not communicate the slimness that should be associated with the brand, but was rather gross in its appearance. Once a product is purchased, the package remains in the home, and its psychological influence is sometimes subtle but strong in the long run.

The relative selling power of different sizes of a product should be analyzed. The relationship between size and price, for example, was of considerable importance with respect to the introduction of a new toiletry brand. In this instance, measured in ounces of product, the appearance (if not the fact) of larger size and the price, represented the variables to which the consumer reacted in terms of the total value being received. The final value combination was a vital ingredient in determining overall strategy, and importantly influenced the prospective advertising investment pattern.

THE PRICE

This nearly always represents an area of policy importance within the structure of a marketing plan.

In the brand's pricing area, any recent changes of price at plant, price at retail, discount structure and terms of sale should be examined. If available, the financial structure of the brand's operation, most particularly its profit margins, should be considered. In addition, the extent of price sensitivity in the market should be analyzed. The past history of consumer reactions to pricing policy changes needs to be examined. For example, in connection with the introduction of a new proprietary foot-care product, the ability to turn up significant advertising dollars in a field with limited product turnover (infrequent purchase) was importantly dependent on the feasibility of pricing the product at a premium. Such a decision, intimately related to advertising policy, cannot, of course, be made without extensive investigation into the pricing area.

If retailers, for example, loaded with an inventory of television sets, tend to use a given brand as a "price football," an advertising message strategy featuring the concept of superior quality may be antithetical to the selling environment on the retail floor.

THE MARKET

The size of the market for the particular product needs to be estimated. What is the volume? How does this volume break down as far as consumer groups are concerned, i.e., to what extent is the product used? For example, the volume of flashcubes is concentrated among relatively few consumers. On the other hand, in the soft drink business, while different segments of the market have different consumption patterns, there is little new market territory to be developed.

The characteristics of the market such as sales with respect to the geographical concentration and distribution of dollars needs to be assessed. The market characteristics with respect to people as well as sales needs to be examined; people with respect to age, sex, income, geographical location, occupation, and other usable profile indicators.

THE DISTRIBUTION

The distribution factor's influence on the total market forces should be examined. It is of particular importance, for example, in the beer industry that supermarket purchasing of packaged beer has displaced the tavern's draft beer as the primary seller. With some manufacturers in the cosmetic industry, the drug wholesaler represents an important method of distribution, while others use only direct retail selling. Obviously, this difference in distribution policy has an effect on overall promotion policy. In the hard goods business, whether a steel kitchen equipment manufacturer has factory branches or uses independent distributors is almost certain to have an important effect on cooperative advertising policy.

THE ADVERTISING PLAN

In the above context, the elements of the advertising plan, as indicated in the plan of this book in Chapter 1 and illustrated in Figure 1-2, are as follows:
  I. *Corporate and Marketing Objectives*
     A. Product
     B. Price
     C. Place
     D. Promotion (General Overview)
 II. *The Advertising Strategy*
     A. Advertising Opportunity Analysis
     B. Advertising Objectives and Criteria
     C. Market Segmentation Strategy
     D. Money (Budget Plan)
     E. Media Strategy and Tactics
     F. Message (Creative) Strategy and Tactics
III. *Overall Promotional Coordination*
     A. Personal Selling Strategy and Tactics
     B. Other Sales Promotion Planning and Tactics
 IV. *Intervening Factors and Constraints*
     A. Competitive Analysis
     B. Facilitating Agencies
     C. Environmental Influences
     D. Regulation
  V. *Summary of Recommendation*
 VI. *Statement of Long-Term Strategy.*
This represents the general structure of planning and its relationship to advertising decision making.

Now, with an understanding of the total marketing orientation of this book's treatment of advertising, the functional differences between different types of advertising as well as promotion, a review of the importance of basic strategy together with its relationship to integrated planning, and a sketch of the core of basic planning, ground-work is laid for the first critical management decision: the decision to use advertising as an important marketing tool.

QUESTIONS AND PROBLEMS

1. Why, in the United States, have advertising expenditures increased at a rate faster than most other indicators of business activity as shown in Figure 2-1? What factors would account for this growth?

2. Why has brand management become such a popular method of organizing marketing activity for brands? How does advertising fit into the brand management concept? How different would advertising organization appear in one company embodying the brand management concept versus another company using a less integrated approach to marketing organization?

3. Evaluate the 15 percent commission system under which most national advertising is developed.

4. How do you evaluate the role of so-called "house agencies" which some large corporations have developed to take the place of third-party, independent, traditional advertising agencies? How does this all relate to the commission system?

5. What similarities and differences do you see in the development of advertising campaigns for the U.S. Postal Service and Pontiac Motor Division of General Motors?

6. The advertising decision maker lives in a world of uncertainty; this uncertainty is, in some respects, greater than other aspects of business because of the very nature of advertising. What are the major ways in which the advertising decision maker can reduce this uncertainty?

7. What is the difference between an advertising program and a marketing program?

8. Do you see any ways in which magazines might be made a more attractive medium for advertisers? Why have large circulation magazines such as the old *Life, Look,* and *Post* disappeared? What has taken their place? Why?

9. Why has television not replaced the newspaper as the most popular advertising medium as judged by the total expenditures in each of these media types in the United States in any given year?

10. In what ways is measurement in advertising (research) not a distinct decision variable comparable to market segmentation, money, media, and message? How does this measurement relate to these other decision variables?

11. Provide some examples of the manner in which advertising interacts with other marketing decision variables to produce the final mix.

12. What is an advertising decision? Give your own version of how advertising decisions are made (thinking in the context of a product such as Pringle's Newfangled Potato Chips).

ENDNOTES

1. Total expenditures by institutions of higher education (in billions of 1975-76 dollars):

1975-76	$39.7	
1976-77	41.5	projected
1977-78	43.7	projected
1978-79	45.8	projected
1979-80	47.8	projected
1980-81	49.6	projected

Source: *Projection of Education Statistics to 1985-86,* Department of Health, Education, and Welfare, Education Division, National Center for Education Statistics, 1977. P. 77 for 1975-76 figure and 1976-77. P. 78 for 1977-78.

2. Philip Kotler, "Advertising in the Nonprofit Sector," Working Paper, Northwestern University, Evanston, Il, 1973.

PART 2: ASSESSING OPPORTUNITY AND SETTING OBJECTIVES

- Advertising Opportunity Analysis
- Cases in Opportunity Analysis
- Advertising Objectives

ADVERTISING OPPORTUNITY ANALYSIS AND CONSUMER BEHAVIOR

- Characteristics of Market Demand
- The Appraisal of Advertising Opportunity
- Factors Influencing Advertising Opportunity
- Product Analysis
- Marketing/Financial Analysis
- Consumer Analysis
- Sales Forecasting

Decision Making Organization of This Text

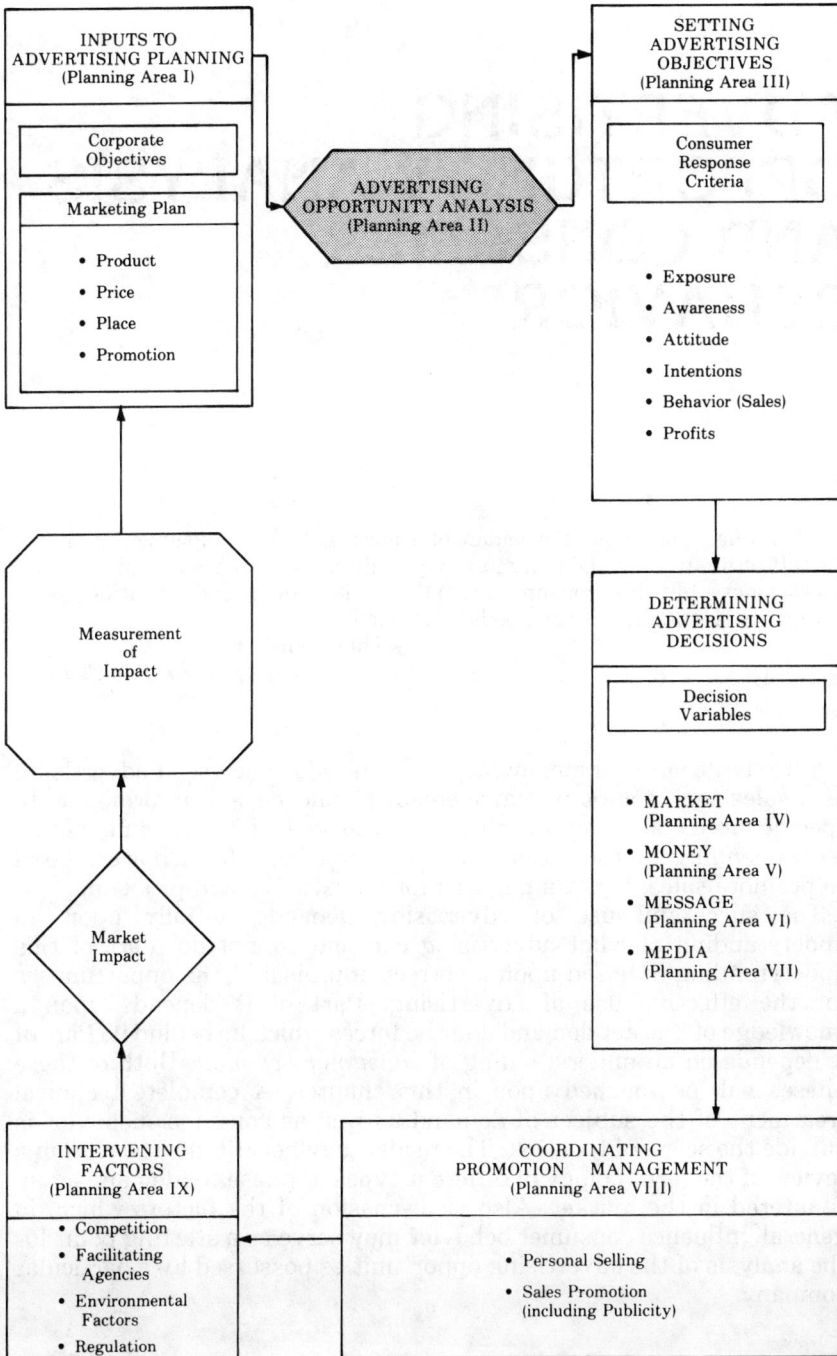

INPUTS TO ADVERTISING PLANNING
(Planning Area I)

Corporate Objectives

Marketing Plan

- Product
- Price
- Place
- Promotion

ADVERTISING OPPORTUNITY ANALYSIS
(Planning Area II)

SETTING ADVERTISING OBJECTIVES
(Planning Area III)

Consumer Response Criteria

- Exposure
- Awareness
- Attitude
- Intentions
- Behavior (Sales)
- Profits

Measurement of Impact

DETERMINING ADVERTISING DECISIONS

Decision Variables

- MARKET
  (Planning Area IV)
- MONEY
  (Planning Area V)
- MESSAGE
  (Planning Area VI)
- MEDIA
  (Planning Area VII)

Market Impact

INTERVENING FACTORS
(Planning Area IX)

- Competition
- Facilitating Agencies
- Environmental Factors
- Regulation

COORDINATING PROMOTION MANAGEMENT
(Planning Area VIII)

- Personal Selling
- Sales Promotion
  (including Publicity)

ADVERTISING OPPORTUNITY ANALYSIS AND CONSUMER BEHAVIOR

"The quasi-peaceable gentleman of leisure not only consumes of the staff of life beyond the minimum required for subsistence and physical efficiency, but his consumption also undergoes a specialization as regards the quality of the goods consumed."

—Thorstein Veblen
The Theory of the Leisure Class

Since large sums of money may be required in the use of advertising as a sales tool, company management should be well informed as to specific needs and opportunities for the use of advertising before recommending appropriations for it. Advertising, while a powerful tool to promote sales, is not a panacea for all sales ills and problems.

The successful use of advertising depends initially upon an understanding of what advertising can and cannot do. Part of this understanding is based upon a correct appraisal of the opportunities for the effective use of advertising. Part of it depends upon a knowledge of market demand and the forces which lie behind it. Part of it depends on an understanding of *consumer behavior*. Both of these phases will be touched upon in this chapter. A complete technical treatment of the subject of demand as well as consumer behavior is outside the scope of this text. The reader may benefit, however, from a review of the terminology of different types or phases of demand as encountered in the market. Also, a discussion of the factors which, in general, influence consumer behavior may serve as a starting point for the analysis of the advertising opportunities possessed by a particular company.

CHARACTERISTICS OF MARKET DEMAND

Market demand for a product may be considered as a special case of the broader, more general problem of mass behavior. The task of determining or anticipating the demand for a product is concerned with predicting what consumers may or may not do under the everyday conditions of the market.

Consumers' purchasing decisions depend upon and stem from the complex economic and sociological conditions under which people work and live. Consumers' wants and needs tend to be based upon the utility of commodities, that is, upon their ability to satisfy human wants. These desires arise out of the way people live; out of their occupations, environments, cultural levels, and religions; and out of the habits and preferences developed by all of the economic and social forces which go to make up a complex society. Buying decisions are conditioned by such factors as income, education, environment, occupation, climate and religion, as well as age, sex distribution and family status. Differences in demand stimulation problems are to be found in different market situations.

The general factors suggested above which influence consumer demand may be summarized under four sets of factors:

(1) The character of consumers' wants and needs as influenced by the factors suggested above;
(2) The qualities and prices of goods capable of satisfying these wants;
(3) Consumer purchasing power;
(4) Attempts to influence buyers' actions through advertising and selling efforts.

GENERIC AND BRAND DEMAND

In their efforts to clarify the problem of demand, economists have described and classified a number of different types or variations of demand. The following are probably of greatest interest to the advertiser. *Generic* or primary demand is the demand for a class of product, for the output of an industry. The demand for meat, air conditioners, or automobiles is a generic one.

Brand or selective demand is a segment of generic demand. It is the demand for the branded product of an individual member of an industry competing for a share of total industry demand. The demand for Armour's Star meat, Fedders air conditioners, and Thunderbird automobiles are examples of brand or selective demand. Whether the demand problem is generic or selective will have a great bearing on the methods used to stimulate demand.

DEMAND ELASTICITY (PRICE ELASTICITY)

Market demand may be described either as elastic or inelastic. Elasticity of demand is a term used to describe the degree of sensitivity of market demand to changes in price of the product. Specifically, demand is considered to be *elastic* if an increase or decrease in the price of a product brings about a more than proportionate change in the number of units sold. If price is reduced, and demand is elastic, net revenue will be increased. Conversely, an increase in price would have the effect of lowering net revenue. Demand elasticity is relative and may be operative within certain limits or ranges. For example, to lower a price from $2.25 per unit to $1.99 may produce enough additional sales to increase total revenue. A further decrease in price to $1.75 may not produce the same effect.

The degree of demand elasticity for a product depends upon the degree of sensitivity of demand to price or income changes. A relatively small price increase or decrease in the number of units purchased in response to a price adjustment is not sufficient to have an elastic demand. The product faces an *inelastic* demand if changes in price or purchasing power result in less-than-proportionate changes in market demand.

Elasticity can be defined in the following manner:

$$e = \frac{\text{Percentage Change in Sales}}{\text{Percentage Change in Price.}}$$

In symbolic terms, e (price elasticity) is calculated as:

$$e = \frac{(S_t - S_{t-1})/S_{t-1}}{(P_t - P_{t-1})/P_{t-1}}$$

where: S_t = sales in current period "t"
S_{t-1} = sales in the preceding period "t−1"
P_t = price in current period "t"
P_{t-1} = price in the preceding period "t−1"
e = price elasticity coefficient.

Example 3-1. For the purpose of calculating a price elasticity, suppose the following information on price and sales is given for a particular product:

Time Period	Price	Sales
Winter 1980 (t−1)	$2.25	1.2 million units
Spring 1981 (t)	$1.99	1.7 million units

$$\text{Then: } e = \frac{(1.7 - 1.2)/1.2}{(1.99 - 2.25)/2.25}$$

$$e = -3.60.$$

In this instance, for every one percent *decrease* in price, sales are expected to *increase* by 3.6 percent. If in the Summer of 1981, price is decreased for this product by two percent, sales would be expected to increase by 7.2 percent ($-2\% \times -3.6 = 7.2\%$). The price decrease from $1.99 down two percent to $1.95 would be expected to produce sales of 1.82 million units ($.072 \times 1.7 = .12 + 1.7 = 1.82$). This type of demand analysis assumes, of course, that the only factor changing in the Summer 1981 quarter from the preceding quarters would be the price of the product. To the extent that this assumption does not hold, the predictions of demand from the price elasticity coefficient will be in error.

FACTORS INFLUENCING DEMAND ELASTICITY

Demand elasticity, while the result of a complex group of factors, is influenced by the following factors among others, some of which are under the control of management and some are not:
(1) The qualities of the product involved
(2) The number of and prices of adequate substitutes for the product
(3) The attitudes and opinions of consumers toward the product
(4) The number and importance of competitors in the industry
(5) The type of demand involved.

In evaluating the first factor, qualities of the product, the element of first-rate importance is the degree to which the product, and the product alone, can satisfy the wants and needs of a particular segment of the market. The amount and type of product differentiation and the number and variety of uses for the product directly influence the reaction of consumers to changes in prices.

If there are a large number of readily available substitutes, a very slight increase in price of a product may switch a large segment of the market away from the product to these substitutes. If there are many possible uses for the product, a slight decrease in price may bring about a great increase in demand. Even the sale of a staple necessity can feel the effect of a price drop, as, for example, one that brings the cost of salt down to the point where it can be used more widely in eliminating ice and snow hazards.

Durable and non-durable products face a different customer reaction to price change. A durable product with an indefinite life may be continued in use if customers feel that a price advance is un-warranted. The compulsion for immediate replacement found in some products is not present in the same degree here.

The demand for so-called essentials is generally relatively inelastic. Food may serve as an example of this demand. If food prices all increase by 10 percent, the decline in the total volume of sales might be small. People would tend to sacrifice consumption of other items in order to maintain an adequate food intake. While this tends to be true for food as a general class of products, it would not necessarily hold true for individual items of food. If this price increase were related to one item such as chickens, the sales of this commodity would almost certainly decline more sharply than food in general. That people need food is true, but there are many substitutes which they could purchase in place of chickens.

The number and importance of the members of an industry also have a bearing on demand elasticity. This is especially true when this factor is coupled with product differentiation. In an industry such as farming there may be a million growers of corn all producing and selling a similar—almost identical—product. In other industries there may be only one or a very few producers. In the early forties, for example, Bausch and Lomb Optical Company was the only producer of scientific precision glass in the United States. Until World War II, ALCOA was the sole producer of aluminum in this country. It is obvious that a single seller has greater freedom in pricing than a firm with a million competitors, and the chances for an elastic demand are also greater.

The attitudes and opinions of consumers toward a product are important factors in determining elasticity of demand. To a great extent, these attitudes are the result of product qualities and differentiations and of efforts to influence consumer attitudes and opinions through advertising and sales promotion efforts. These factors lie closer to the area of management control than others mentioned above. Through product development and modification, product utilities may be deliberately cultivated and the variety of uses broadened.

These differentiated features, when adequately interpreted to the public by advertising and sales promotion, may enhance the value of the product in the eyes of consumers to such a degree that demand elasticity is modified. The actions of the Morton Salt Company illustrate this device. This company differentiated its product from that of competitors by making it less susceptible to caking and hardening. This was done by modifying the shape of the salt crystals. This modified feature removed Morton from the close price competition which had been typical of the industry when "salt was salt" and allowed Morton to increase their prices above others on the market. Their product advantage was successfully advertised in campaigns based on their slogan "When It Rains It Pours."

At a later period, when competing companies imitated their process of reducing caking and hardening, Morton further differentiated their salt by adding iodine and advertising an "Iodized" salt. Product modification and promotion permitted Morton to maintain their price differential. This combination of product differentiation coupled with advertising and promotion is vitally important. It is not only what qualities a product has which are important; it is what people think of the product which really counts when the decision must be made either to pay more for a preferred product or to seek a substitute. This marketing approach can currently be seen again by the Morton Salt Company in the marketing of Lite Salt, a low-sodium product.

Price adjustments may cause a relatively small change in sales of an article that is used in conjunction with another more expensive product. In the joint demand for golf clubs and golf balls, the demand for balls would tend to be relatively inelastic. It would take a sizable increase in the price of golf balls to cause any change in sales. If balls increase 10 percent in price, avid golfers with a relatively large investment in golf clubs are not going to give up the game. They may reduce somewhat the purchase of new balls by using a ball a little longer or by hunting more persistently for lost balls. This decline in demand, if less than proportionate to the amount of increase in price, is not an example of an elasticity of demand. It merely illustrates the functioning of the general law of demand.

EXPANSIBLE DEMAND (ADVERTISING RESPONSE COEFFICIENT)

A variation of market demand has been termed an expansible demand. Through a combination of product differentiation and aggressive advertising and selling efforts, not accompanied by changes in price or income, it is frequently possible to increase the number of units of a product which a market will absorb. This result is referred to as an expansion of demand, in order to distinguish it from elasticity of demand resulting primarily from price changes.

The measure of demand expansions has been termed the *advertising response coefficient*. It can be defined in the following manner:

$$a = \frac{\text{Percentage Change in Sales}}{\text{Percentage Change in Advertising.}}$$

In symbolic terms, a (advertising response coefficient) is calculated as:

$$a = \frac{(S_t - S_{t-1})/S_{t-1}}{(A_t - A_{t-1})/A_{t-1}}$$

where: S_t = sales in current period "t"

S_{t-1} = sales in the preceding period "t−1"

A_t = advertising dollars in current period "t"

A_{t-1} = advertising dollars in the preceding period "t−1"

a   = advertising response coefficient.

Example 3-2. For the purpose of calculating an advertising response coefficient, suppose the following information was available for a particular product:

Bimonthly Time Period		Adv (million $)	Sales (million $)
November-December 1981	(t−1)	1.30	22.30
January-February 1982	(t)	1.45	26.80
March-April 1982	(t+1)	?	?

$$\text{Then:} \quad a = \frac{(26.8 - 22.3)/22.3}{(1.45 - 1.3)/1.3}$$

$$a = 1.75.$$

The calculated advertising response coefficient can be interpreted as follows: For every one percent *increase* in the amount of money spent on advertising for this product, sales dollars are expected to *increase* by 1.75 percent. Suppose advertising expenditures were to be increased in March-April 1982 to a level 15 percent above that spent in January-February 1982 to $1.67 million (.15 × 1.45 = .22; .22 + 1.45 = 1.67). This 15 percent rise in advertising spending would indicate a 26.25 percent increase in sales according to the advertising response coefficient calculated above (1.75 × 15 = 26.25). The expected sales in dollars in the March-April 1982 time period would be $33.84 million. This can be seen from the following relations:

$$\%\Delta\ \text{Sales}_{t+1}\ =\ a(\%\Delta\ \text{Adv}_{t+1}) \qquad \text{where } \Delta\ =\ \text{"change"}$$
$$\text{Sales}_{t+1}\ =\ \text{Sales}_t\ +\ \text{Sales}_t(a)(\%\Delta\ \text{Adv}_{t+1})$$
$$33.84\ =\ 26.80\ +\ 26.80(1.75)(.15).$$

FACTORS INFLUENCING DEMAND EXPANSIBILITY

An expansion in demand may be brought about in several ways. New customers and users of the product may be cultivated. Those customers already using a certain number of units may be induced to increase their rate of consumption either for the original purpose or for new and different product uses. In many cases something more than a mere increase in volume of advertising will be necessary to bring about an expansion of demand if no price decrease is involved. New uses for the product may be suggested or discovered. Arm & Hammer Baking Soda is an excellent example of the utilization of this approach; over the years not only the volume of its advertising has increased but also the creative strategy involved the suggestion of new and varied uses of the product. Not only is the product excellent for baking purposes (the original product purpose) but it is also excellent for use in deodorizing refrigerators, maintaining fresh swimming pool conditions, keeping cat litter odors at minimum and so forth. The basic product did not need to be modified to suggest these new applications. In many instances new values or utilities may be uncovered or deliberately added; for example, the addition of vitamins to margarine might increase its utility to certain market segments.

The student of advertising should realize that an expansion in demand may stem from causes other than advertising and paid promotional efforts. Advances in education and increases in income and leisure time have been contributing causes for many variations in demand. The increase in consumption of leafy green vegetables during the past 40 or 50 years may be attributed largely to increased knowledge of their value in the diet. Increases in income and leisure time are to a great extent responsible for the tremendous expansion in sales of sporting goods and recreational equipment of all kinds. The most effective use of advertising may come when it is coupled to the promotion of something which people are already doing or have indicated they have an interest in doing.

THE APPRAISAL OF ADVERTISING OPPORTUNITY

One of the most important advertising management decisions is that regarding the use of advertising as a sales tool. This involves the consideration of the part, *if any*, which advertising should play in the promotion program. This decision, which is one of the fundamental questions of the management of advertising, is ultimately a matter of executive judgment. However, this judgment should be based upon a thorough appraisal of the opportunities to use advertising effectively and economically. This is usually taken to mean whether or not the use of advertising can succeed in bringing about an increase in sales revenue large enough to cover costs, including costs of advertising, and still make a contribution toward net profit. A simple, but effective, tool which might be used by advertising management in this regard is that of break-even analysis.

BREAK-EVEN ANALYSIS

The "break-even point" in the type of analysis to be described here is defined as the amount in dollars of sales revenue required to support increased (over the preceding time period) advertising expenditures to the point where profits will equal the preceding time period profits. Break-even analysis is used, then, to determine the sales levels required to provide profits which "break-even" with last time period's profits for a given advertising expenditure. Here it will be assumed that non-advertising costs of doing business (except those involved in producing the product) will remain constant from one time period to the next. The following example will illustrate the break-even analysis procedure.

Example 3-3. Suppose the following abbreviated financial statement is operative for a particular advertised brand for period "t" (this might be one year or one quarter):

	Year t Statement
Net Sales	$20,000,000
Cost of goods sold	14,000,000
Gross Margin	6,000,000
Other Expenses:	
Administrative &	
Marketing	4,000,000
Advertising	1,000,000
Net Profit	$ 1,000,000

Some explanation of the above financial terms might be helpful before going further with this example. Net sales refers to sales revenues after all returns (damaged goods, etc.) have been deducted. If the particular company is a manufacturer, then the revenue is with respect to wholesale prices so that price times quantity (number of units) sold equals gross revenue less returns equals net revenue or net sales. Cost of goods sold (abbreviated c.g.s) refers to the total costs of producing the product; this would include such factors as labor, manufacturing equipment, and raw materials. Administrative & marketing expenses refer to all salaries for administrative personnel (both marketing and non-marketing personnel) and other marketing expenses (all marketing costs except those dealing with advertising). Advertising costs are excluded from the marketing costs so that the advertising manager can keep track of them explicitly. Net profit is the amount of money the company makes prior to such matters as taxes, dividends and other such items. The following basic accounting relationship defines how the abbreviated statement above is derived:

$$GM = S - c.g.s.$$
$$NP = GM - \text{Admin/Mktg} - A$$

where: GM = Gross Margin
S = Sales
c.g.s. = cost of goods sold
NP = Net Profit
Admin/Mktg = Administrative & Marketing Expenses
A = Advertising Expenditure.

Suppose the manager for this company's advertising program is considering spending $2,000,000 on advertising in the next time period "t+1". What revenue would be required to break-even with last period's profits of $1,000,000 if the manager doubles the advertising expenditure to $2,000,000? To answer this question, an abbreviated statement is projected for year t+1 as described below:

Year t+1 Statement

Net Sales	$23,333,333
c.g.s	16,333,333
GM	7,000,000
Other Expenses:	
Admin/Mktg	4,000,000
Adv	2,000,000
Net Profit	$ 1,000,000

This statement was derived in the following manner:
(1) The "new" or t+1 advertising expenditure was put in place of the old $1,000,000 expenditure on the Year t Statement.
(2) The "Break-Even" profit level of the "old" or Year t statement is used ($1,000,000).
(3) It is assumed in the analysis that non-advertising other expenses will remain the same in year t+1 as in the preceding year t, that is, $4,000,000. This assumption should be made since the concern here is with the increased sales needed to support the increased advertising expenditure as opposed to other types of expenditures.

(4) Since Gross Margin must equal net profits plus advertising plus administrative/marketing these are summed to provide the "new" year $t+1$ Gross Margin: $7,000,000 = (1,000,000 + 2,000,000 + 4,000,000)$.

(5) In this analysis, it is assumed that cost of goods sold will increase in proportion to net sales (a linear increase) so that the following ratio may be used to find "new" year $t+1$ net sales:

$$\frac{\text{"old" GM (year t)}}{\text{"old" Sales (year t)}} = \frac{\text{"new" GM (year t+1)}}{\text{"new" Sales (year t+1)}}.$$

The above reads "old gross margin is to old sales as new gross margin is to new sales." After plugging in the known values, the fourth is solved for by cross-multiplication:

$$\frac{6,000,000}{20,000,000} = \frac{7,000,000}{X}$$

$$
\begin{aligned}
6,000,000 \ (X) &= 7,000,000 \ (20,000,000) \\
X &= 7,000,000 \ (20,000,000)/6,000,000 \\
X &= 23,333,333.
\end{aligned}
$$

(6) The "new" $t+1$ c.g.s. is found by subtracting the "new" GM of 7,000,000 from the "new" sales of \$23,333,333 found in step #5 above $(23,333,333 - 7,000,000 = 16,333,333)$.

The final step in such analysis is for the manager to determine whether or not the 16.67 percent increase in sales required in $t+1$ to support the \$2,000,000 advertising expenditure can be achieved $(16.67 = (23,333,333 - 20,000,000)/20,000,000)$. If the average sales increases for the company in question have been only 8 percent for the last several time periods (and the next time period is not expected to appear radically different than these previous time periods), then it would not be advisable for the advertising manager to undertake such a recommendation. In fact, if the advertising manager recommends the \$2,000,000 in this example and the 16.67 percent increase in sales is not achieved, it is possible that the additional \$1,000,000 allocated to advertising for year $t+1$ may have to be paid for by the \$1,000,000 profits of the preceding period (year t).

ADVERTISING OPPORTUNITY ANALYSIS

The above example illustrates the important point that it is the basic, fundamental responsibility of advertising management to generate at least enough revenue to pay for the advertising and still make a contribution toward profits. In appraising each advertising opportunity it is recognized that advertising may not produce equally good results for all products in all business situations. In addition, it is recognized that other factors are involved in a profitable use of advertising: a skillful, creative copy approach, a proper volume of advertising in the right media, etc. These factors tend to be more directly under the control of the advertiser than is the basic opportunity. Hence, the first step in decision-making is an appraisal of the opportunity.

It may be possible to take an advertising opportunity rated as fair or even poor and by virtue of intensive and usually creative advertising effort make a reasonable success from it. If, however, the same degree of advertising skill and effort were to be applied to a situation with a better advertising opportunity, sales and profit returns would be even more successful.

The analysis of the basic advertising opportunity is not dissimilar to that of analyzing the fertility of soil in a farmer's field, or of comparing the relative fertility of soil in one field with that of another. When a

Figure 3-1   Analysis of Advertising Opportunity and
Advertising Decision Making

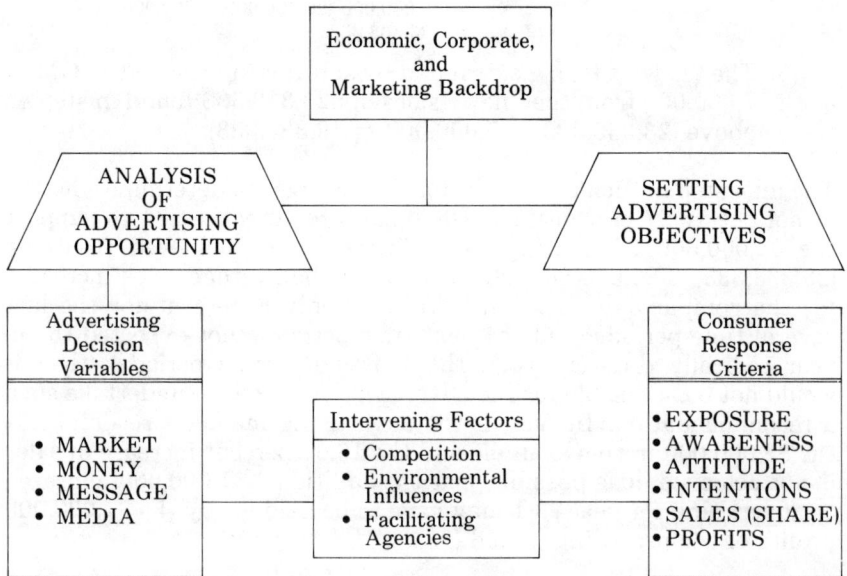

given amount of seed, fertilizer, and cultivation effort are applied to two fields of different fertility, with the same climatic conditions for both, the field with the higher relative fertility will produce a greater yield. Similarly in the case of advertising, a comparable amount and quality of advertising effort put on products facing different advertising opportunities will also produce different sales and profit results.

Figure 3-1 shows the relationship of appraisal of advertising opportunity to the management decision making scheme discussed in Chapter 2 and illustrated in that chapter in Figure 2-4. In the overall decision making scheme, the first step should be that of appraising the advertising opportunity. As will be seen shortly, this involves some estimate of consumer response on various dimensions (perhaps attitude change, perhaps net profits) as well as the overall economic and marketing conditions. The advertising objectives (to be considered in detail in Chapter 4) can then be set in the context of the *Advertising Opportunity Analysis* previously conducted. After advertising objectives are set, decisions can then be made on each of the four advertising management decision variables: Market, Money, Message, and Media. Both the advertising objectives and the decision variables are viewed in light of consumer response criteria: Exposure, Awareness, Attitude, Intentions, Sales, and Profits.

FACTORS INFLUENCING ADVERTISING OPPORTUNITY

PURPOSES OF BRANDING

The essential objective of branding and identification is the opportunity it provides for advertising and promoting brand sales and control over the market. It is common practice to refer to four different degrees of brand control, depending upon what the advertiser has been able to accomplish with consumers in the market or market segment. Beginning with the weakest of these and showing the ladder of success, the degrees are:

I. Brand Recognition
II. Brand Acceptance
III. Brand Preference
IV. Brand Insistence.

The advertiser who succeeds in converting any part of the market to insistence upon the company's brand, that is, the acceptance of no substitutes, has a type of monopoly control over this segment of the market. The risks as well as the stakes may be high. As in the case of generic demand analysis, management should appraise the risks and possible opportunities for a successful use of advertising prior to spending any company funds for this purpose.

The adoption and promotion of a brand carries no assurance that the effort will result in a financial success. The decision to use a brand does not mean that it can be advertised successfully; it may not mean that it should be advertised at all.

With this indication of the uncertainty which faces a prospective advertiser, it is appropriate to suggest that the decision to use or not to use advertising should be a careful and deliberate decision. It should be based upon an evaluation of the factors in the situation which indicate the possibilities of a successful use of advertising weighed

**Figure 3-2   Appraising the Opportunity for the Effective
Use of Advertising**

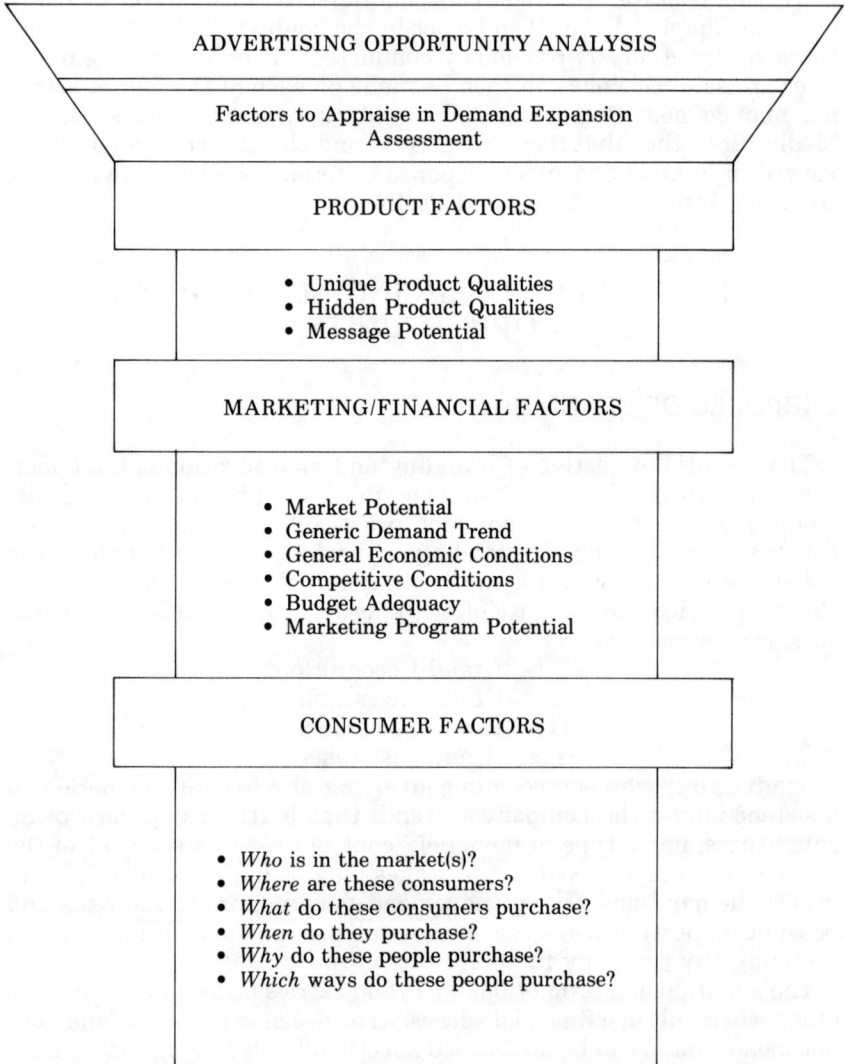

ADVERTISING OPPORTUNITY ANALYSIS

Factors to Appraise in Demand Expansion
Assessment

PRODUCT FACTORS

- Unique Product Qualities
- Hidden Product Qualities
- Message Potential

MARKETING/FINANCIAL FACTORS

- Market Potential
- Generic Demand Trend
- General Economic Conditions
- Competitive Conditions
- Budget Adequacy
- Marketing Program Potential

CONSUMER FACTORS

- *Who* is in the market(s)?
- *Where* are these consumers?
- *What* do these consumers purchase?
- *When* do they purchase?
- *Why* do these people purchase?
- *Which* ways do these people purchase?

against those which would tend to act against success.[1] The analysis may be based upon *Product, Marketing/Financial,* and *Consumer* factors which are depicted graphically in Figure 3-2.[2]

PRODUCT ANALYSIS

The analysis should start with a study of the product and its utilities. Management should attempt to determine whether or not the product warrants advertising. The important question involved is how much difficulty may be encountered in persuading people to want the product. Three points may be stressed in this phase of the analysis.

UNIQUE PRODUCT QUALITIES

This is a key factor in advertising and expansion of brand demand. Since the aim is to build brand sales and share, the most favorable opportunity for this exists when the product has qualities which set it apart from, and make it more desirable than, competing products. The advertiser then has an opportunity to swing sales to the product by playing up these product advantages in the advertising messages.

HIDDEN PRODUCT QUALITIES

If there are product qualities which are hidden and which are not apparent upon examination, or even use of the product, the opportunities for using advertising effectively are enhanced. Advertising chances may be considered better because of the opportunity in advertising copy to explain and interpret these hidden, want-satisfying qualities.

MESSAGE POTENTIAL

Are there strong motivating factors which favor the use of the product? The opportunities for effective advertising are better if the product lends itself well to strong advertising appeals. Management should seek to determine how well strong product appeals can be aligned with self-interest of consumers. Such appeals as sex, parental affection, fear, beauty, health, and security are examples of appeals which usually are capable of stimulating people to desired action with a minimum of time and effort.

MARKETING/FINANCIAL ANALYSIS

In addition to the factors relating directly to the product and its qualities, there are important factors stemming from the market which management should include in this appraisal.

MARKET POTENTIAL

Management must determine whether or not the total sales of the industry are sufficient to justify the expenditure of funds necessary for brand development. The stakes must be sufficiently large to justify the risks and costs. An industry such as the household table cutlery industry which has had total sales in the vicinity of $9 to $10 million per year would obviously not be adequate to justify the million-dollar-plus budget which might be necessary for a national advertising campaign for one brand of cutlery.

GENERIC DEMAND TREND

Management should be concerned with future industry sales prospects as well as present sales. If the prospective advertiser's firm is a member of an industry which is experiencing an expanding sales trend, the prospects of an effective use of advertising to build brand sales are better than if the industry trend is a steady or declining one. In an expanding market, where sales are growing each year, every member of the industry stands to gain in dollar sales without any change in the relative market share or market position. This usually makes the sales problem of individual industry members relatively easier than if the market is contracting and sales are diminishing. If the product is facing an adverse trend of consumer acceptance as a result of changes in social, cultural, or occupational habits, efforts to change these desires through advertising may either be impossible or prohibitively expensive.

GENERAL ECONOMIC CONDITIONS

Employment and consumer purchasing power are important factors to consider here. The ability of consumers to buy has an influence on the quality of the market or the advertising climate. It should not be assumed, however, that sales opportunities are always greater for all products in periods of high business activity than in periods of recession. Sales of some products tend to follow a trend inverse to that of consumer income.

COMPETITIVE CONDITIONS

In an analysis of any market, a look at the competitive situation is desirable. Both the number of competitors and the quality of competition should be considered since both influence market position and share of market. Quality of competition is based on the relative qualities of competing products and the type of marketing and promotional efforts put behind these products.

It may be difficult to obtain objective information on these points. Some effort at appraisal is worthwhile, however, since these factors may have an important bearing on the responsiveness of the market to brand advertising.

BUDGET ADEQUACY

There must be adequate funds available before any advertising effort has a fair chance of succeeding. In every market a certain minimum intensity of advertising effort is necessary to make an adequate impression on consumers. The amount of pressure necessary will, of course, vary with the market, the product, the amount and quality of competition, and the various other factors involved. The amount of funds available must be large enough to make an adequate impact upon the market. The program must be sustained over a period of time necessary to build sales to profitable proportions. Success frequently should not be expected during those first years of advertising. Even for products whose differentiated features make them desirable, a period of several years may be necessary to build the necessary consumer following for the brand.

During the introductory period for a new product, the amount of money needed for advertising and promotion may equal, or for a time even exceed, total sales revenue. To be justified, advertising must in the long run build enough additional sales revenue to cover costs of advertising and make some contribution to net profit. Management should determine a break-even point. Considering gross margin available for advertising, what volume must be sold in order to cover advertising and promotional costs? This type of analysis has been illustrated earlier in this chapter in Example 3-3. More is involved in the question of adequacy of funds than whether or not there are dollars available which might be devoted to advertising. Sales volume and margin possibilities are the important questions if advertising ultimately is to stand on its own feet and pay its own way in the company.

MARKETING PROGRAM POTENTIAL

Clearly, the successful marketing of a product involves the complex interaction of many marketing factors in addition to advertising. If it is not possible to achieve successful distribution for the product for whatever reasons, then the opportunities for advertising are limited by the low potential for the marketing program as a whole. The higher the probability of successfully implementing decisions on each of the major marketing variables other than advertising, the greater is the opportunity for advertising to contribute to the overall health of the brand.

CONSUMER ANALYSIS

In addition to a successful analysis of the product as well as the marketing/financial background, a major required ingredient in *Adver-*

tising Opportunity Analysis is Consumer Analysis. The following six questions encompass the most important of the consumer factors and, if answered adequately, will insure that an understanding of consumer behavior in the context of the particular brand or corporate advertising problem has been achieved:

The Six W's of Consumer Analysis

I. *Who* is in the market(s)?
II. *Where* are these individuals and groups?
III. *What* do these people purchase?
IV. *When* do they purchase?
V. *Why* do these people purchase?
VI. *Which* ways do these people purchase?

Each of these six issues of consumer analysis will be considered as a means of illustrating the various aspects of consumer behavior which are crucial to the assessment of advertising opportunity. These issues will be addressed below in the order in which they are listed above (see Figure 3-3).

Figure 3-3 The Six W's of Consumer Analysis

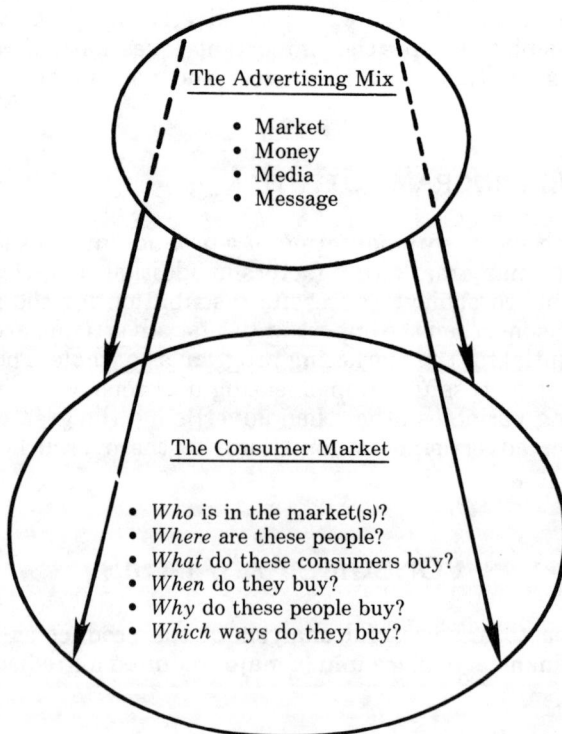

The Advertising Mix

- Market
- Money
- Media
- Message

The Consumer Market

- *Who* is in the market(s)?
- *Where* are these people?
- *What* do these consumers buy?
- *When* do they buy?
- *Why* do these people buy?
- *Which* ways do they buy?

I. WHO IS IN THE MARKET(S)?

The first step in consumer analysis is to determine who the prospects for the product, service or idea might be and then to define these in terms which will be of use in the planning of the advertising program. In general, prospects consist of any individuals or groups for whom the product will fulfill a need or want. In some instances, particularly when utilitarian needs might be satisfied by the product, it may be possible to define the prospects in terms of these needs as well as to describe these prospects based upon demographic, life style or personality variables. In most instances, however, it will be desirable to identify prospects based upon one or both of the following: (1) those people who currently use the product in question; and (2) those people who can be identified as using a product which is in some manner related to the product in question.

Current Users. This approach is most appropriate for a product which has been on the market for some time or for a new product in an existing product category. Information for the usage of this approach is readily available (from Simmons Market Research Bureau, for example) and, if more detail is required, can easily be obtained through fairly straightforward consumer research. For example, Table 6-3 in Chapter 6 shows a sample SMRB report for regular cola drinks. That table shows that of the 155,794,000 adults in the United States, it is estimated from sample data that 104,574,000 drink regular cola drinks (carbonated, not diet).

This approach is simple, but it probably provides useful information for products which are mature and well-established. The number of people using products in a mature product category remains fairly stable. On the other hand, for new product categories, the initial count of users may be quite misleading regarding the potential number of prospects for the product. The current number of users of videotape recorders may not be a reliable indicator of the number of prospects available for the purchase of new laser disc television playback equipment. For a product such as regular, carbonated cola drinks, this approach will be quite useful.

Prospects with Related Characteristics. A practical method for locating prospects is that of finding those people who have some characteristic which is related to the product in question. For example, people who own videotape recorders will most certainly be prospects for videotape. Prospects for renter's insurance will be renting their homes rather than owning them. Subscribers to a stereo magazine may be prospects for high quality stereo equipment. In such instances, the prospects can be identified by examining a related characteristic which is observable. If the number and description of current purchasers of videotape equipment is not available, for example, it may be possible to obtain a count of those people subscribing to cable television. This related characteristic is less direct than the preceding examples; the theory would be that these people are most concerned about television in general, and, therefore, may represent better prospects than all people owning television sets.

Prospect Description. Once the prospects have been defined, for practical implementation of advertising programs it is necessary to describe or define these prospects in terms of demographic profiles or in terms of life style and/or personality variables. This will most often occur in terms of demographic variables alone though "psychographic" descriptions are available on a limited basis from such syndicated services as SMRB.

A list of suggested demographic subcategories that are useful in media planning during the development of the advertising program is given in Chapter 6 in Table 6-1. Breakdowns based upon the following factors are given in that table:

(1) Age
(2) Sex
(3) Income
(4) Occupation
(5) Education
(6) Life Cycle
(7) Family Size
(8) Social Class
(9) Race
(10) Religion
(11) Geographic Region
(12) County Size
(13) City Size
(14) Population Density.

For example, the "heavy users", as shown in Table 6-3, of regular cola drinks can be described in terms of education and county size in the following manner:

Education	Number of Adults
Graduated College	2,645,000
Attended College	4,495,000
Graduated High School	13,146,000
Did Not Graduate High School	10,272,000
Total	30,558,000

County Size[3]	Number of Adults
County Size A	10,563,000
County Size B	9,916,000
County Size C	5,703,000
County Size D	4,376,000
Total	30,558,000.

Breakdowns on the other demographic variables for heavy as well as medium and light users are shown in Table 6-3 for regular cola. Such descriptive information exists for most product categories in the consumer goods area.

Detailed information on the selection and description of target markets as well as on the concepts of life style and psychological or "psychographic" segmentation is provided in Chapter 6 on the topic of market segmentation. But it should be understood that the development of a prospect profile must precede the selection and development of the target market segments as described in Chapter 6. The target market, or as in many cases, the target markets must be selected from the consumer prospect profile. Though the prospect list may be a large one, it will generally be desirable to zero in on particular segments of the profile list from the standpoint of efficiency in using advertising resources.

It should be noted that Chapter 6 provides a more detailed account of the sources to which the advertising planner may go for the purpose of developing information to construct the prospect profile.

II. WHERE ARE THESE CONSUMERS?

The question "where are these consumers?" really involves addressing two separate issues. In the first case, it is important to know, physically speaking, how many of the prospects reside in particular *geographic regions*, cities, and counties throughout the country so that advertising outlays can be allocated geographically according to potential. This information, as indicated in the previous section, can be obtained from syndicated research services since geographic area as well as county size and others are standard demographics which are regularly reported by these services. Table 6-3 illustrates this for regular cola drinks:

Region	Number of Adults
Northeast	22,082,000
North Central	26,955,000
South	36,160,000
West	19,377,000
Total	104,574,000.

Such information reveals, for example, that 72.8 percent of those adults residing in the South consume regular cola compared with only 62.6 percent in the Northeast. This fact has obvious implications for the advertising program for any cola drink.

Beyond the issue of where the consumer prospects for a product might reside is the question of *where these consumers purchase the product.* The retailing, wholesaling, and other channel characteristics of the distribution system must be known in relation to the behavior of consumers for the product category. If the product is one which is not ordinarily purchased in a retail outlet, for example, the advertising for this product will vary markedly from a product which has a quite different purchasing environment.

Marketing Channels and Consumer Analysis. Table 3-1 shows the variety of marketing intermediaries which can be used to get the product from the producer to the institutions who finally sell the product to the ultimate consumer. The point to be made is that the behavior of consumers in the market place can often become a function, in part, of the particular method used to move the merchandise to them. One type of middleman operation may increase the price over another by the time the product reaches the consumer; this will have an impact on the behavior of price-conscious consumers. In some instances, on the other hand, it is not clear which came first: the intermediary institution or the desire of consumers to utilize such institutions. For example, in retailing totally new institutions have emerged many different times over the past one hundred years.

Table 3-1   Definitions of Various Marketing Intermediaries

Agent. A business unit which negotiates purchases or sales or both but does not take title to the goods in which it deals. The agent usually performs fewer marketing functions than does the merchant. He commonly receives his remuneration in the form of a commission or fee. Examples are: broker, commission merchant, manufacturer's agent, selling agent, and resident buyer.

Broker. An agent who does not have direct physical control of the goods in which he deals but represents either buyer or seller in negotiating purchases or sales for his principal. The broker's powers as to prices and terms of sale are usually limited by his principal.

Commission house (sometimes called *Commission merchant*). An agent who usually exercises physical control over and negotiates the sale of the goods he handles. The commission house usually enjoys broader powers as to prices, methods, and terms of sale than does the broker, although it must obey instructions issued by the principal. It generally arranges delivery, extends necessary credit, collects, deducts its fees, and remits the balance to the principal.

Dealer. A firm that buys and resells merchandise at either retail or wholesale.

Distributor. In its general usage this term is synonymous with "wholesaler."

Facilitating agencies in marketing. Those agencies which perform or assist in the performance of one or a number of the marketing functions, but which neither take title to goods nor negotiate purchases or sales. Common types are banks, railroads, storage warehouses, commodity exchanges, stock yards, insurance companies, graders and inspectors, advertising agencies, firms engaged in marketing research, cattle loan companies, furniture marts, and packers and shippers.

Jobber. This term is widely used as a synonym of "wholesaler" or "distributor." The term is sometimes used in certain trades and localities to designate special types of wholesalers.

Manufacturer's agent. An agent who generally operates on an extended contractual basis; often sells within an exclusive territory; handles noncompeting but related lines of goods; and possesses limited authority with regard to prices and terms of sale. He may be authorized to sell a definite portion of his principal's output.

Merchant. A business unit that buys, takes title to, and resells merchandise. The distinctive feature of this middleman lies in the fact that he takes title to the goods he handles. Wholesalers and retailers are the chief types of merchants.

Middleman. A business concern that specializes in performing operations or rendering services directly involved in the purchase and/or sale of goods in the process of their flow from producer to consumer. Middlemen are of two types, *merchants* and *agents*.

Retailer. A merchant, or occasionally an agent, whose main business is selling directly to the ultimate consumer.

Selling agent. An agent who operates on an extended contractual basis, sells all of a specified line of merchandise or the entire output of his principal, and usually has full authority with regard to prices, terms, and other conditions of sale. This functionary is often called a "sales agent."

Wholesaler. A business unit which buys and resells merchandise to retailers and other merchants and/or to industrial, institutional, and commercial users, but which does not sell in significant amounts to ultimate consumers. Those who render all the services normally expected in the wholesale trade are known as *service wholesalers:* those who render only a few of the wholesale services are known as *limited-function wholesalers.* The latter group is composed mainly of *cash-and-carry wholesalers,* who do not render the credit or delivery service; *drop-shipment wholesalers,* who sell for delivery by the producer direct to the buyer; *truck wholesalers,* who combine selling, delivery, and collection in one operation; and *mail-order wholesalers,* who perform the selling service entirely by mail.

SOURCE: *Marketing Definitions: A Glossary of Marketing Terms,* compiled by the Committee on Definitions of the American Marketing Association, Ralph S. Alexander, Chairman (Chicago: American Marketing Association, 1960).

Department stores first came into the American buying scene in the 1860's; soon after this development, mail-order companies such as Sears Roebuck (1886) were founded. The now ubiquitous chain-store operations were largely begun in the 1910's and 1920's. The 1930's saw the development of a radical retailing institutional form, the supermarket; in the late 1940's came the regional, planned shopping centers. Discount houses, such as K-Mart, were developed in the 1950's and expanded in the 1960's. Vending machines appeared on a large scale in the 1950's to introduce the advent of completely automatic retailing. The 1960's were marked by the wide-spread introduction of fast-food stores, convenience stores, such as 7-eleven stores, and superstores including supermarkets, discount houses, and drug stores all under one roof and name. In the 1970's, boutiques, home improvement centers, furniture warehouse showrooms and warehouse grocery stores were introduced. Each of these revolutions in retailing has produced a shift in consumer behavior; where people do their purchasing has largely been influenced by such developments.

With particular respect to advertising management, a recent retailing growth area has been that of *direct marketing systems.* A growing number of manufacturers and other producers have turned to direct marketing to bypass or supplement the activities of other middlemen traditionally employed by them. Direct marketing systems take on four forms: (1) mail-order selling; (2) mass-media selling; (3) telephone selling; and (4) on-premise selling. Mass-media selling has been particularly evident on television; the often-observed example is that of direct selling of records through television which cannot otherwise be purchased in retail outlets. On-premise selling refers to the age-old practice, such as that used by Electrolux vacuum cleaners, of bringing the merchandise to the prospects' homes and selling to consumers on their own premises. Tupperware has been the often-cited pioneer success story in this field of merchandising.

III. WHAT DO THESE PEOPLE PURCHASE?

This question of consumer analysis needs to be understood from two points of view: (1) the advertiser should be aware of where the product stands in relation to standard categorization of all products; and (2) the advertiser can benefit by understanding that types of products are purchased by consumer prospects *in addition to* the product in question. Each of these will be considered in turn.

Two standard categorizations are often used to describe the goods people buy: (1) Durable goods, nondurable goods and services; and (2) convenience goods, shopping goods, and specialty goods. *Durable* goods are tangibles which survive many uses such as refrigerators, clothing and automobiles. *Nondurable* goods include such items as meats, soap and other products which are normally fully consumed in one or two uses. *Services*, on the other hand, are distinguished from durable and nondurable goods since they are intangible in nature; they are also generally perishable, variable and personal.

Convenience goods are those which the consumer usually purchases often and uses a minimum of effort in comparison and buying. Such goods as soap, canned goods, toothpaste, and beer are convenience goods. *Shopping* goods, on the other hand, are those which are generally high-ticket items and the consumer "shops around" and expends considerable effort in comparison shopping before making a purchase. Furniture, used automobiles, and major appliances are examples of shopping goods. *Specialty* goods are those which have unique characteristics or brand identification for which a large group of consumers will habitually make a special purchasing effort to acquire. Such items as stereo equipment, photography equipment, designer jeans, and fancy canned goods are examples of specialty goods.

Each of the above types of goods is characterized by a different accompanying form of consumer behavior. If the product for which the advertising program is to be developed is a convenience good, the advertising program will be totally different, ordinarily, than one for a shopping good. Examine the manner in which television is utilized in an advertising campaign for laundry detergent in comparison to that for automobiles. Even the copy research system utilized to help in the development of such television commercials will usually be quite different, let alone the content of the commercial as well as the media scheduling for the commercial.

Product Clusters and Consumer Analysis. From the second standpoint, an analysis of consumer prospects will benefit through an understanding of the whole *cluster* of product types and brands which given groups of consumers purchase. It is very likely that a person is more likely to be a prime candidate for a brand of beer if this person has a bowling ball in his home rather than a violin; this is stereotyping of people, but often such stereotyping has some minimal basis in fact. It is often possible to make valid inferences about the nature of a consumer based upon an entire cluster of products which this person purchases.

Very often, consumer researchers have been successful in finding a relationship between personality and clusters of product usage by consumers. For example, Life Style research is characterized by a search for those demographic characteristics, media preferences, activities, interests, and opinions as well as *product clusters* which distinguish heavy, medium, light and nonusers of a product from each other. This approach to Life Style segmentation as utilized by Wells at Needham, Harper & Steers Advertising agency, among others, is illustrated in

Table 3-2 for heavy users of eye makeup and vegetable shortening.[4] That particular study showed that heavy users of eye makeup were also *heavy* users of liquid face makeup, lipstick, hair spray, perfume, cigarettes, and gasoline. Heavy users of shortening were also *heavy* users of flour, sugar, canned lunch meat, cooked pudding, and catsup. Life Style research as the basis for segmentation is examined in greater detail in Chapter 6.

Table 3-2   Life Styles of the Heavy User of Eye Makeup and the Heavy User of Shortening

Heavy User of Eye Makeup	*Heavy User of Shortening*
Demographic Characteristics	
Young, well-educated, lives in metropolitan areas	Middle-aged, medium to large family, lives outside metropolitan areas
Product Use	
Also a heavy user of liquid face makeup, lipstick, hair spray, perfume, cigarettes, gasoline	Also a heavy user of flour, sugar, canned lunch meat, cooked pudding, catsup
Media Preferences	
Fashion magazines, *Life, Look,* Tonight Show, adventure program	*Readers Digest,* daytime TV serials, family situation TV comedies
Activities, Interests, and Opinions	
Agrees more than average with	
I often try the latest hairdo styles when they change	I love to bake and frequently do
I usually have one or more outfits that are of the very latest style	I save recipes from newspapers and magazines
An important part of my life and activities is dressing smartly	The kitchen is my favorite room
I enjoy looking through fashion magazines	I love to eat
I like to feel attractive to all men	I enjoy most forms of housework
I want to look a little different from others	Usually I have regular days for washing, cleaning, etc., around the house
Looking attractive is important in keeping your husband	I am uncomfortable when my house is not completely clean
I like what I see when I look in the mirror	I often make my own or my children's clothes
I comb my hair and put on my lipstick first thing in the morning	I like to sew and frequently do
I take good care of my skin	I try to arrange my home for my children's convenience
Sloppy people feel terrible	Our family is a close-knit group
I would like to take a trip around the world	There is a lot of love in our family
I would like to spend a year in London or Paris	I spend a lot of time with my children talking about their activities, friends, and problems
I like ballet	Everyone should take walks, bicycle, garden, or otherwise exercise several times a week
I like parties where there is lots of music and talk	Clothes should be dried in the fresh air and out-of-doors
I like things that are bright, gay, and exciting	It is very important for people to wash their hands before eating every meal

Table 3-2 continued

Heavy User of Eye Makeup	*Heavy User of Shortening*
Agrees more than average with	

I do more things socially than do most of my friends	You should have a medical checkup at least once a year
I would like to have a maid to do the housework	I would rather spend a quiet evening at home than go out to a party
I like to serve unusual dinners	I would rather go to a sporting event than a dance
I am interested in spices and seasonings	
If I had to choose, I would rather have a color television set than a new refrigerator	
I like bright, splashy colors	
I really do believe that blondes have more fun	

Disagrees more than average with	
I am a homebody	I would like to have a maid to do the housework
I like grocery shopping	My idea of housekeeping is "once over lightly"
I enjoy most forms of housework	Classical music is more interesting than popular music
I furnish my home for comfort, not for style	I like ballet
I try to arrange my home for my children's convenience	I'd like to spend a year in London or Paris
It is more important to have good appliances in the home than good furniture	
Women should not smoke in public	
There is too much emphasis on sex today	
Spiritual values are more important than material things	
If it was good enough for my mother, it's good enough for me	

A study by Laumann and House on living room styles and social attributes also illustrates the point of understanding clustering behavior of consumers with respect to product purchases.[5] Laumann and House observed the products and other home furnishing items exhibited in over one-thousand consumers' living rooms in Detroit and conducted a cluster analysis to find the common occurrence of products with each other in such living rooms. For example, they found the following objects tend to appear in the same living room:

Cluster VII:
(1) Wall mirror
(2) Still life paintings
(3) Artificial flowers
(4) Clock
(5) Religious objects.

In still another cluster, they found groups of consumers whose living rooms were typified by the following groups of items:

Cluster XVIII:
(1) Abstract paintings
(2) Sculpture
(3) Modern furniture.

Clearly, the consumers represented by Cluster VII would appear to be different prospects for an offering, for example, of a reproduction of some art object in the $100 price range by the Museum of Modern Art in New York City than would those consumers typified by Cluster XVIII. There may also be a higher probability that those consumers in Cluster XVIII would represent better prospects for designer jeans, for example, than would those in cluster VII.

IV. WHEN DO CONSUMERS PURCHASE THE PRODUCT?

One dimension of the issue of "when" consumers buy products concerns the frequency of usage of the product category. Frequency of purchase depends upon consumers' rate of consumption of the product; this in turn will be influenced by many factors. For example, homes with children will consume hot dogs more frequently than will homes with only one adult; this will influence the time when consumers will purchase hot dogs. This thinking underlies the common segmentation practice of dividing consumers into groups based upon consumption rate: High, Medium, Light and Non-users are frequently utilized categories for this purpose.

The seasonal pattern of purchasing products should also be examined in any consumer analysis. Ice cream, for example, has a higher consumption rate in the summer than winter months; this may call for counter-cyclical advertising programs where more effort is expended on influencing purchase in the winter or "off seasons" than at the season of highest consumption. Seasonal and weather conditions influence the demand for such items as snowmobiles, snow and water ski equipment, vacations, and heating equipment for the home.

Consumers also vary by daypart and weekpart in which purchasing of certain types of products is conducted. Many grocery stores remain open 24 hours each day in order to accommodate the purchasing time needs of consumers; women often do shopping in grocery stores in the evening since their widespread, full-time employment in the labor force has become the rule rather than the exception. Weekend purchasing is also characteristic for some product categories for certain groups of consumers.

It should also be noted that "when" a purchase is made may also depend, for certain groups of consumers, on the general economic climate of the moment. For shopping goods, this is particularly true when the economic climate influences the cost and availability of credit. Consumers may postpone the purchase of a large-ticket, shopping good, such as a new automobile or air conditioner, until the general economic condition improves.

V. WHY DO CONSUMERS PURCHASE?

The reasons why consumers purchase a particular brand or product are, quite naturally, as varied and as many as there are individual consumers. But a general picture must be drawn of the typical reasons "why" large groups of consumers purchase in the way they do. The answer to "why consumers purchase" is perhaps the most important answer which can be obtained from any consumer analysis. It is the most important of the six W's of consumer analysis. An understanding of why consumers purchase will enable the advertising planner to develop a promotion program which will attempt to provide the consumer with information and/or motivation which provides a "why" or reason which corresponds closely with the "why" which the consumer has in mind. For analytical purposes, these "whys" are depicted in Figure 3-4.

**Figure 3-4   Consumer Factors Influencing
Purchasing Behavior**

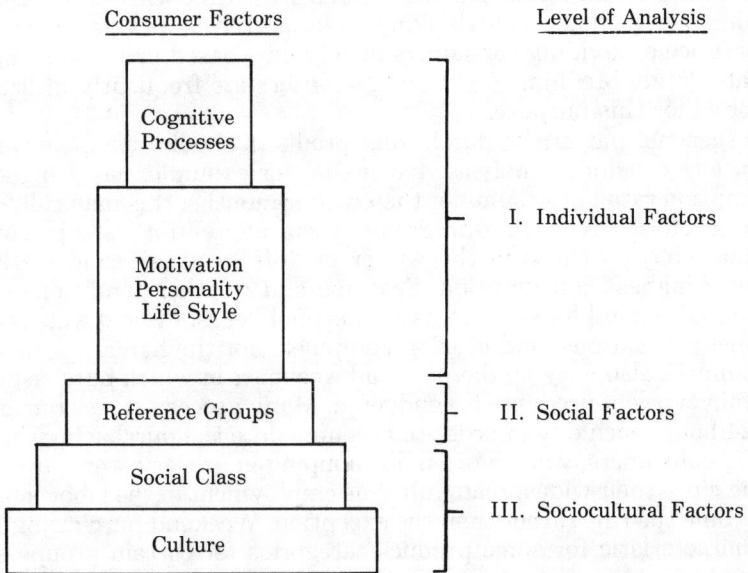

Consumer Factors   Level of Analysis

Cognitive Processes	
Motivation Personality Life Style	I. Individual Factors
Reference Groups	II. Social Factors
Social Class	III. Sociocultural Factors
Culture	

It is clear that characteristics in addition to those depicted in Figure 3-4 are influential in consumers' purchasing decision making. The factors illustrated there concern only those inherent in the consumers' cultural, social and individual psychological factors which operate in these individuals' lives. In general, a full answer to the "why" question involves an investigation of the following elements:

(1) Consumer Factors
(2) Producer Characteristics
(3) Product Characteristics
(4) Situational Characteristics.

In addition to the cultural, social and psychological "set" of a given consumer, the nature of the *producer* or seller in terms of the overall "image" conveyed to the consumer will influence the consumer's purchasing decision. The nature of the *product* will provide "cues" which will ordinarily be taken into account when the consumer makes a buying decision. Finally, various *situational* factors, such as the amount of time the consumer has in which to make a purchasing decision, will influence purchasing behavior.

Nonetheless, in this section dealing with the overall issue of Advertising Opportunity analysis, the concern is specifically with *consumer* factors; the other three main ingredients in the "why" of buying behavior have been considered earlier in this chapter in the sections concerning product and financial/marketing analysis. This section will examine briefly some fundamental issues of the influence of culture, social class, reference group, goals, motivation, and personality. Of the two remaining consumer factors shown in Figure 3-4, Life Style has been discussed earlier in this chapter and will be discussed in greater detail in Chapter 6 on Market Segmentation. Cognitive processes, the remaining factor in Figure 3-4, will be considered in detail in the following section dealing with the last of the 6 W's: In *which* ways do consumers purchase? In this section, culture, social class, reference group behavior, personality, motivation, and goals will be examined in turn.

Cultural Factors. Culture is depicted at the bottom of Figure 3-4 because it is the fundamental foundation upon which all social and individual factors rest. Culture serves as a filter through which a newborn child will learn values and behaviors appropriate to the society in which this child will live.

Linton has defined culture as " . . . the configuration of learned behavior and results of behavior whose component elements are shared and transmitted by the members of a particular society."[6] This configuration is developed over long periods of time for the purpose of helping the society solve recurring problems of its constituents; it is shaped by biological and geographical influences. "The culture of a people consists of their distinctive modal patterns of behavior and the underlying regulatory beliefs, norms, and premises," according to Krech, Crutchfield, and Ballachy.[7]

Within a complex overall culture such as the United States, a number of subcultures exist. These are based upon distinguishable features such as language, religion, skin color and other characteristics which lead to unique ways of behaving. Such subcultures have great implications for advertisers. Separate media plans and creative strategies may be required for particular subcultural groups. Such advertising must "talk the language" and utilize the cultural mores of the subculture and must appear in media vehicles which will reach the subculture in order to be effective in reaching the advertiser's goals.

International advertising programs require an understanding on the part of the advertiser of the cross-cultural differences between one country and another. It is rarely possible to successfully transplant a campaign wholesale from one country to another. A campaign must take into account the indigenous culture of the country in which the advertising program is to be conducted. Many illustrations of this often "hard-to-learn" lesson of cultural differences and their influence on marketing and advertising effectiveness are provided by Dunn and Lorimor.[8]

Social Class. All societies exhibit a certain degree of social stratification; this may take on the form of a caste system where children are raised in an extremely rigid manner to a station in life from which there is no escape as an adult. More frequently, however, a less rigid stratification system exists and is usually referred to as "class." Social class can be defined as "relatively permanent and homogeneous divisions in a society into which individuals or families sharing similar values, life styles, interests and behavior can be categorized."[9] Such social classes have, generally, the following characteristics: (1) All of the members of a given social class *tend* to behave alike; (2) members of a given social class tend to compare themselves to superior or inferior positions; (3) social class is usually thought of along a single dimension but is usually measured along several dimensions; and (4) though in theory social classes are discrete divisions in society, in practice this is rarely observed and classes are treated on a continuum. Individuals in a mobile society are constantly moving to higher classes or dropping to lower ones, and the divisions of the classes themselves are constantly in a state of flux in such a mobile society as the United States.

Table 3–3 shows the most often-utilized operational definitions of social classes in the United States as developed by W. Lloyd Warner.[10] Warner's classification scheme consists of four indicators: occupation, source of income, residential area, and type of dwelling. Using this scheme, he divided American society into the six classes shown in Table 3–3.

Table 3-3   Social Class Behavior in America

Upper upper

Upper uppers are the social elite of society. Inherited wealth from socially prominent families is the key to admission. Children attend private preparatory schools and graduate from the best colleges.

Consumers in the upper upper class spend money as if it were unimportant, not niggardly but not with display either, for that would imply that money is important. For some products a "trickle-down" influence may exist between social classes. The social position of these individuals is so secure that they can deviate from class norms if they choose to without losing status.

Lower upper

Lower uppers include the very-high-income professional people who have "earned" their position rather than inherited it. They are the *nouveaux riches,* active people with many material symbols of their status. They buy the largest homes in the best suburbs, the most expensive automobiles, swimming pools and other symbols of conspicuous consumption, making them innovators and good markets for luxury marketing offerings.

Upper middle

The key word for upper middles is "career". Careers are based on successful professional or graduate degrees for a specific profession or the skill of business administration. Members of this class are demanding of their children in educational attainment.

The *quality* market for many products is the upper middle class and gracious living in a conspicuous but careful manner characterizes the family's life style. The home is of high importance and an important symbol of the family's success and competence.

Lower middle

Lower middle class families are "typical" Americans, exemplifying the core of respectability, conscientious work habits and adherence to culturally defined norms and standards. They believe in attending church and obeying the law and are upset when their children are arrested for law violations. They are not innovators.

The *home* is very important to the lower middle family and they want it to be neat, well-painted, and in a respected neighborhood They may have little confidence in their own tastes and adopt "standardized" home furnishings—perhaps from Levitz or Wickes. This is in contrast to the upper middle housewife who feels freer to experiment with new styles and new arrangements and with the upper lower housewife who is not very concerned about the overall plan for furnishing the home. The lower middle housewife reads and follows the advice of the medium-level shelter and service magazines in her attempt to make her house "pretty".

The lower middle class housewife "works" more at her shopping than other women and considers purchase decisions demanding and tedious. She may have a high degree of price sensitivity.

Upper lower

Upper lower social classes—the largest segment of society—exhibit a routine life, characterized by a day-to-day existence of unchanging activities. They live in dull areas of the city, in small houses or apartments. The "hard hats" are included in this class, with many members working at uncreative jobs requiring manual activity or only moderate skills and education. Because of unions and security, many may earn incomes that give them considerable discretionary income.

The purchase decisions of the working-class wife are often impulsive but at the same time she may have high brand loyalty to national brands. Buying them is one way to "prove" her knowledge as a buyer, a role in which she feels (probably correctly) that she has little skill. She has little social contact outside the home and does not like to attend civic organizations or church activities. Social interaction is limited to close neighbors and relatives. If she takes a vacation, it will probably be a visit to relatives in another city. Upper lowers are concerned that they not be confused with the lower lowers.

Lower lower

The lower lower social class contains the so-called disreputable people of the society who may try to rise above their class on some occasions but usually fail to do so and become reconciled to their position in society. An individual in the lower lower class often rejects middle class morality and "gets his kicks" wherever he can—and this includes buying impulsively. This lack of planning causes purchases that cost too much and may result in inferior goods. This person pays too much for products, buys on credit at a high interest rate and has difficulty evaluating the quality or value of a product.

SOURCE: Engel et al., Consumer Behavior, 1972.

From the advertising management point of view, the coincidence of socio-politico-economic interests shown by the divisions in Table 3–3 is of great concern. This grouping allows a market to be segmented into meaningful units for the purpose of using differential message appeals and media vehicles which are in line with the specific characteristics, value systems, and habits of each class.

Reference Groups. Reference groups include all those social groups who influence the beliefs, values, and opinions of an individual. Some of these are *primary* groups such as family, close friends, fellow employees and similar groups. *Secondary* groups include professional organizations, fraternal organizations and those with similar goals and objectives; these generally produce less influence on the individual's behavior than do primary groups. People may not be members of a particular group but wish they could be; such groups can be referred to as *aspirational* groups. Individuals modify their behavior to comply with the written or unwritten rules of groups to which they either are current members or aspire to be members. Reference groups also include both *formal* and *informal* groups. Formal groups have a defined structure and usually specified membership rules and regulations; informal groups occur on the basis of proximity, interests or other bases which are less specific than in the case of formal groups.

Reference groups fulfill several functions in society: (1) Adult and childhood socialization; (2) providing a basis for attitude formation; (3) providing for compliant behavior; and (4) providing for self-concept evaluation.

In terms of socialization functions of reference groups, it has been noted that such groups insure such socialization functions as teaching:[11]
  (a) The basic *goals* of the organization.
  (b) The preferred *means* by which those goals should be attained.
  (c) The basic responsibilities of the member in the role which is being granted to him by the organization.
  (d) The *behavior patterns* which are required for effective performance in the role.
  (e) A set of rules or principles which pertain to the *maintenance* of the identity and integrity of the organization.

At one time it was thought that socialization was a phenomenon which was important only in the development of the child. In recent years it has become accepted that adults continue to undergo socialization processes which can be almost as important as those under which they labored as a child. The acceptance of a product by an adult may be influenced in much the same way as changes brought about in some adults during the 1960's and 1970's with respect to drug use; their reference groups persuaded them to engage in behaviors which they previously might have regarded as abhorrent. The influence of the reference group is also thought to be a major influence on the drug-related behaviors of teenagers.

The socialization function of reference groups is an important basis for understanding the formation of attitudes and beliefs. Newcomb conducted a classic study illustrating the role of reference groups in the formation of attitudes. His study was concerned with attitude change of college females as they began attending college and became influenced by their fellow students. Newcomb found, "Attitudes are not acquired in a social vacuum. Their acquisition is a function of relating oneself to some group or groups, either positively or negatively."[12]

The functions of reference groups are often referred to as "normative" in nature since they cause people to behave in similar ways; they are also "evaluative" since they provide a reference point by which an individual can view his or her own behavior. Reference groups provide the *norms* by which behavior is guided and with which it must more or less comply. Norms are defined as quantitative statements or beliefs by the majority of group members which define what the activities of the group members should be in the ideal. Group pressure causes group members to conform to or comply with such group norms.

A reference group also provides a basis for individuals to evaluate their self concepts. A person's self-concept causes the individual to see himself or herself through the eyes of other persons; in doing this, the individual takes into account the behavior of these other group members as well as their beliefs, attitudes, and approval and disapproval. An individual's self concept is strongly related to the way in which other people are seen to approve or disapprove of that individual. The importance of self-concept from the advertising point of view lies in the idea that the symbols that people manage as a function of their "selves" include the products they purchase and the way in which these products are used. Purchasing a Honda automobile, for example, may improve the individual's self concept because the consumer sees himself or herself to be an individual of quality; this conception may, in part, stem from the product qualities and, in part, from the advertising which emphasizes the quality characteristics of Honda automobiles. The importance of a self-concept which includes "quality" would originally, in part, have stemmed from the way in which the individual wishes to be seen by particular reference group members.

Personality. The term personality is used by psychologists to mean a consistent pattern of responses to the world that impinges upon the individual internally and externally. In general, individuals react in a consistent, usually stable fashion to a variety of environmental situations. It is not this consistency which is remarkable; it is the fact that so infrequently do people behave inconsistently which is quite remarkable. It is this consistency of behavior which is examined under the rubric of personality.

It should be noted that personality as an important marketing and advertising decision making factor has waned in recent years. This may be traced to the abuse with which early utilizers of the concept in marketing and advertising applied it. Engel, Kollat and Blackwell have noted, "To date, most research attempts have ended in failure in that personality variables have not differentiated adequately between relevant groups. It seems that the evidence to date falls short . . ., and personality has not been demonstrated convincingly as a useful means of market segmentation."[13] It has been further pointed out, however, that personality, used properly and cautiously in the development of consumer analysis, can be helpful when the following four approaches are considered:[14] (1) market segmentation through tailor-made personality inventories; (2) market segmentation through attitude, interest, and opinion inventories (AIO's as indicated in Table 3-2); (3) use of personality as a moderator variable (personality may be more predictive in one particular situation than another); and (4) the use of personality as an intervening variable (where, for example, heavy, light, and nonusers of a product are compared on personality profiles rather than segmented directly on the differences of personality profiles).

Theories of personality which can be of use, when properly applied as noted above, include *Psychoanalytic Theory, Social-Psychological Theory*, and *Trait-Factor Theory*.[15] Psychoanalytic theory stems, of course, from Freud and his disciples. Freud organized motivation into three main systems of psychological forces: the *id*, the *ego*, and the *superego*. In his own view, behavior was a function of the interaction of these three systems; the dominant personality characteristics of an individual were dependent upon that person's fixation at one of the four developmental phases through which every child passes: oral, anal, phallic, and genital. In his system, Freud defined the id to consist of the aggressive, destructive, and infantile impulses which are present in every child at the time of birth. The superego is constituted of moralistic inhibiting factors. The ego is the reality principle; it is the arbiter between the id and the superego. It provides for integrated and rational behavior on the part of the individual. The differences in personalities of different individuals, therefore, stem from the differences in the balances struck in these individuals between the id and the superego.

Social-psychological theories of personality stem from such individuals as Adler, Horney, Fromm, and Sullivan. These theories differ from psychoanalytic theories in two respects. First, social variables are considered to be more important than biological variables in the production of personality characteristics. And second, motivation of human behavior is seen to be conscious as opposed to Freudian subconsciousness. It is supposed that individuals know what they want and need and direct their behavior to obtain fulfillment of such wants and needs. The classical application of Horney's social-psychological personality theory in marketing and advertising was conducted by Cohen.[16] His CAD scale measured consumers' compliance, aggressiveness, and detachment using a paper and pencil test. He found significant differences in brand preference for convenience goods based upon the mix of compliant, aggressive, and detached characteristics in a given individual.

Trait-factor theories of personality represent a quantitative approach to the study of the concept. This theory generally posits that personality is composed of definite predispositions which are called *traits*. A trait is defined as "any distinguishable, relatively enduring way in which one individual differs from another."[17] The attempt is made to "type" people using such traits. Analytical techniques such as factor analysis are often applied to massive paper and pencil inventories provided by respondents, in an effort to isolate distinct "factors" or traits along which different personalities lie. The work of Cattell is typical of those working in this area of personality research.[18]

A beer company wishes to use personality in its advertising by showing people who possess certain personality traits or characteristics in conjunction with its brand of beer; these people are selected for usage in the commercial because they possess the characteristics most similar to those consumers in the target market for the brand or most similar to individuals the target groups of consumers considers as desirable people. The beer is thus provided with an "image" or personality of its own in the process. Countless other examples from media strategy, segmentation strategy, and creative strategy might be suggested in the application of the personality concept in advertising programs.

Motivation. A *motive* drive is a stimulated need that is sufficiently pressing that a person becomes directed toward the goal of satisfying that need. When such a need is satisfied, the individual's tension is discharged, and the person is returned to a state of equilibrium. One of the most prominent theories of motivation which has been developed is that of Maslow and his "Hierarchy of Needs." Maslow's theory is based upon the following premises:[19]

(1) An individual will have many different needs.
(2) These needs will vary in importance and, therefore, can be rank-ordered in a hierarchy of needs.
(3) The individual will seek to satisfy the first-ranked needs first.
(4) When the person succeeds in satisfying this first-ranked or most important need, this need will cease to be a motivating factor for the person.
(5) The person will turn next to fulfilling the needs rank-ordered in the second most important position.

This general concept is depicted in Figure 3-5. As shown in that figure, Maslow considered needs to be organized in the following order: *physiological needs, safety needs, social needs, esteem needs,* and *self-actualization needs.* Physiological needs concern the fundamentals of survival, including hunger and thirst. Safety needs are those concerning physical survival using prudence which might be overlooked when striving to satisfy hunger or thirst. Belongingness and love needs concern the striving to be accepted by intimate members of one's family and to be an important person to them; this striving also includes others to whom the individual feels close. The need for esteem shows in a striving to achieve high standing relative to others in professional or other endeavors. Maslow claims that the highest goal for human beings is that of self-actualization. Even if a person's needs (physical and social) are satisfied, it may still be expected that the individual will grow restless. The individual wishes to become the person he or she thinks himself or herself to be and wishes to reach the goal of using the full potential available. It is the desire for self-fulfillment.

Even a casual observation of American advertising will show that most of the ads are not directed toward fulfilling the physical needs of consumers. Rarely does an ad say "ABC saltines will fill your stomach fuller than any other brand." Instead, social needs are more often prevalent themes in such advertising. "Use ABC brand saltines with fine wines and cheeses." The idea is to show quality in the choice of saltines and impress friends.

Figure 3-5   Maslow's Hierarchy of Needs

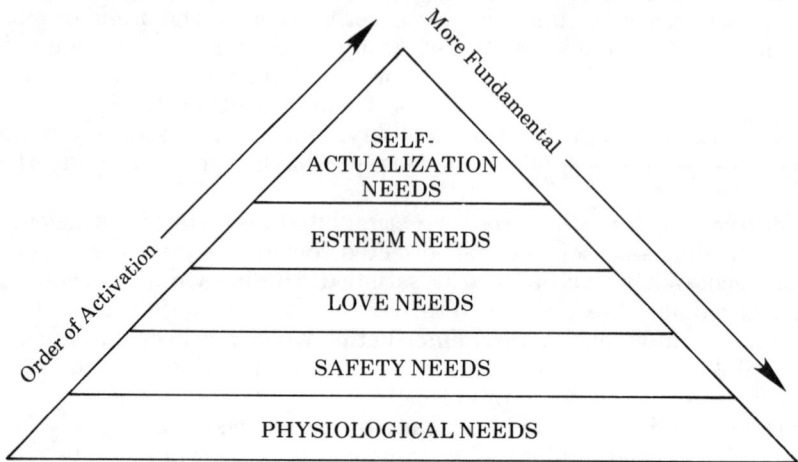

VI. IN WHICH WAYS DO CONSUMERS PURCHASE?

An answer to the issue of *which* ways people purchase involves an examination of *processes* of consumer decision making. Processes will be examined in this section in four different ways: (1) the individual psychological processes of perception, selective exposure, inference, selective retention, learning, and attitude formation; (2) the complexity of decision making processes by levels; (3) different decision making rules or models used by individuals; and (4) overall, comprehensive consumer decision making models.

Psychological Processes. As will be seen at the end of this section, individual psychological processes combine in different ways in different individuals and, as a unit, define an overall process of decision making. At this point, such psychological processes will be examined in isolation from the overall scheme of decision making of which each is a part.

Perception is the process by which an individual selects, organizes, and interprets information inputs to create a meaningful picture of the world.[20] Two people can be exposed to the very same set of informative circumstances yet act quite differently in response to this situation because each "sees" the situation differently; this is due to differences in perceptual processes between these two people. Perception is different in different individuals because it depends not only on the nature of stimuli incoming as information but also on the relation of these stimuli to the surrounding environment and on a general "set" within the individual.

Three processes may be used to explain, in part, why people have different perceptions of the same thing: (1) selective exposure; (2) inferential processes; and (3) selective retention. *Selective Exposure* refers to the processes by which a person is more likely to be exposed to some stimulus objects than to others; most stimuli will be screened out altogether. The following three propositions, together known as Weber's Law, explain selective exposure:

(a) People are more likely to notice stimuli which relate to a current need.
(b) Individuals are more likely to notice stimuli which they anticipate receiving.
(c) People are more likely to notice stimuli which are quite different from the normal stimuli encountered by the person.[21]

Of the tremendous number of advertisements to which people are exposed each day, they selectively attend to only a small number of these. The task of the advertiser is to break through the "clutter" of commercial messages so that consumer groups important to the advertiser will selectively attend to the message.

Inferential Processes are those which people utilize to shape and form incoming information to fit their own preconceptions and needs. People are not passive processors of information which comes from advertisers and marketers; rather they are active interpreters of all such information. One consumer may infer the producer of a given product is a charlatan while another consumer may infer the seller is honest when both have been exposed to the same information. Both of these consumers may be able to "playback" the message from the advertiser with complete "objective" accuracy yet draw completely different conclusions from the information which can be accurately recalled and is essentially the same for both consumers. Clearly, the inference process is largely not under advertiser control so that undesirable "messages" may be generated through this process even though the message sent by the advertiser says desirable things about the product, service or idea. The assessment of inferential generative capabilities of a particular message is increasingly being recognized in copy research as an important area of assessment of message effectiveness.

Selective Retention refers to selective forgetting or "sifting out" of all the information material available for storage in long- or short-term memory. People tend to retain information that supports their attitudes and beliefs. Material which is inconsistent with pre-existing beliefs is forgotten more readily than that which is consistent or supportive. Claims in a competitive ad for tires which "knock" a consumer's own brand of tire will not be remembered by that consumer as well as the content of ads for the consumer's own brand of tire, providing this consumer is satisfied with the particular tire brand purchased.

Learning refers to changes in behavior resulting from experience. Most behavior can be said to be learned; exceptions are behaviors which stem from instinctive responses, growth, and such physiological conditions as hunger and fatigue. Learning theory generally posits that learning is produced through the interaction of drives, stimuli, cues, responses and reinforcement.

A *drive* is some internal stimulus which impels that individual to action. An overweight person might have an internal drive to reduce weight. This drive becomes a *motive* and directs the person to a particular drive-reducing *stimulus* object, for example, a self-help exercise book. The person's *response* of purchasing the book is a result of conditioning cues, in part; *cues* are minor stimuli which determine the specific manner in which a person responds. A print ad in a general magazine may serve as a cue which may affect purchase of the book. The experience of purchasing and reading the book may be positively rewarding so that the purchase is *reinforced;* the particular response may be *generalized* and additional self-help exercise books might be purchased. A countertendency to generalization is *discrimination;* this refers to a person's ability to discriminate between similar cue configurations. The person discussed above may find some self-help books to be, in fact, quite helpful while "learning" that certain "cues" define a less desirable self-help manual.

   Attitude Formation takes place through the learning process. People acquire their beliefs and attitudes. *Beliefs* are subjective probability statements connecting two objects. A belief might be that "Boz detergent is effective in cleaning dirt." This belief statement connects Boz detergent with the concept of effective cleaning. Based upon "salient" sets of beliefs, an attitude may be formed. *Attitude* concerns a positive or negative feeling toward some object.[22] A person might hold the attitude "Boz detergent is a good detergent." This could be based upon the attribute linked through a belief that Boz is an effective cleaner; this assumes that "effective cleaning" is a salient attribute and that a particular "rule" of information processing is at work as will be seen in the subsequent discussion of decision making rules. The task of the advertiser, of course, is to provide material which will provide for the formation of salient beliefs upon which a favorable attitude toward the brand might be developed.

   Complexity of Decision Making Processes. The level of complexity of the decision making process in operation within an individual at a given time depends largely upon the "familiarity" of the consumer with the particular consuming problem at hand. Howard and Sheth divide the decision making process into four stages of complexity: (1) Extensive Problem Solving (EPS); (2) Limited Problem Solving (LPS); (3) Routinized Response Behavior (RRB); and (4) Boredom or Exploratory Problem Solving (BPS).[23] In *Extensive Problem Solving* the individual is unfamiliar with the product class. No well-defined criteria upon which to make a decision exist for this person and, as a result, the individual experiences a high degree of brand ambiguity. There are many brands in the "evoked set" to which the consumer holds no strong feeling for or against.

   In *Limited Problem Solving* the consumer has gained enough information so that choice criteria are well defined. There are fewer brands in the evoked set than under EPS. The consumer's predisposition toward these brands is quite high. There is still, however, some brand ambiguity and the individual is not certain which brand is best to buy.

In *Routinized Response Behavior* the individual has well defined choice criteria, is familiar with the product class and the brands in that class, and feels no ambiguity. There are very few brands in the evoked set, and the individual's predisposition toward *one* of these brands is very high. The selection of the brand under RRB is, in fact, automatic or habitual behavior.

For consumers who habitually purchase the same brand over and over, the RRB may, at times, produce a boredom with the situation in that product class. For such consumers things have become too simple and routine. These people feel a need to complicate the buying situation in order to restore a minimal level of interest in it. In *Boredom Problem Solving* the consumer increases the search for different brands and other stimuli where this exploration behavior is aimed at finding stimulation from any source that is sufficiently interesting. A person may go to the refrigerator, for example, and find that it contains no milk. Automatically, this person goes to the grocery store and automatically selects the usual brand of milk. This is Routinized Response Behavior. On the other hand, this same person may run out of paper towels and go to the grocery store to get a new supply. The person may think "boring" upon confrontation with the usual brands of paper towels in the usual aisle of the supermarket; this thought may prompt the person to go to the "generic aisle" just to try something different; this is to engage in a sort of gambling operation just to relieve the boredom of purchasing such a mundane product. This behavior would be referred to as Exploratory or Boredom Problem Solving.

Decision Making Rules. Decision rules are basically of two general types: (A) Noncompensatory; and (B) Compensatory. *Noncompensatory* rules or models are those in which the brands under consideration for purchase are compared on an attribute by attribute basis. For example, toothpaste brands might be compared on the attributes of taste, color, and consistency. A brand's weakness on one attribute cannot be compensated for by its strength on another attribute, and thus the name noncompensatory. Three noncompensatory models will be briefly discussed: (1) the Conjunctive model; (2) the Disjunctive model; and (3) the Lexicographic model.

In the *conjunctive* model a minimum acceptable level for each product attribute is set forth. A given brand is considered to be acceptable only if each of its attributes equals or exceeds the minimum level set forth for that attribute. If the brand falls below the minimum acceptable level on any one attribute, the brand is rejected.

In the *disjunctive* model one or more attributes are identified as being very important to the purchase decision. For a brand to be acceptable, it must exceed a predetermined level on one or more of these attributes. Suppose that a consumer decides that the only thing that matters in toothpaste is its taste; the brand which provides the desired taste will be selected regardless of whether or not it contains fluoride or is of a particular consistency, if the disjunctive model is in operation.

In *Lexicographic* models the decision maker first ranks the product qualities according to their importance. The brand in this product category which is evaluated as "best" on the attribute ranked most important is the brand which is selected under this decision rule. If two or more brands tie for the highest ranking on this attribute, the second attribute is examined. The third attribute is examined if the tie cannot be broken on the second attribute; this process is continued until the ties are broken.

Compensatory models are those in which a weakness of a brand on one particular attribute can be "compensated" for by a strength on another attribute. Two types of compensatory models will be examined briefly: (1) the weighted linear compensatory model; and (2) the unweighted linear compensatory model. *Weighted Linear Compensatory* models can be expressed in the following way:

$$E_j = \sum_{i=1}^{n} W_i X_{ij}$$

where: E_j = the individual's evaluation of brand j

X_{ij} = a rating for the ith attribute for brand j

W_i = subjective importance of attribute i.

The *Unweighted Linear Compensatory* model can be stated as:

$$E_j = \sum_{i=1}^{n} X_{ij}.$$

The weighted linear compensatory model is one in which the individual constructs a weighting function which indicates the degree of attribute salience. The magnitude of compensation in this situation depends upon the weighting function constructed by the person. In the unweighted linear compensatory model, on the other hand, the magnitude of compensation does not depend upon the weighting function cognitively constructed by the consumer; this is determined by the summation of the stimulus ratings. The basic difference between the two models is that all attributes are assumed to have the same weight of importance in the unweighted model. It might be noted that the conjunctive and disjunctive models are not appropriate for the purpose of ranking alternative brands in terms of preferences or affect. The two models are only appropriate as the basis for dividing alternative brands into two sets, one of which is acceptable and the other of which is unacceptable.

Comprehensive Decision Making Models. Figure 3–6 shows one particular overall or comprehensive scheme to represent the total consumer decision making process. The heart of such a model is illustrated in Figure 3–6 in the column labeled "Decision Process Stages." The

Figure 3-6 A Comprehensive Decision Process Model

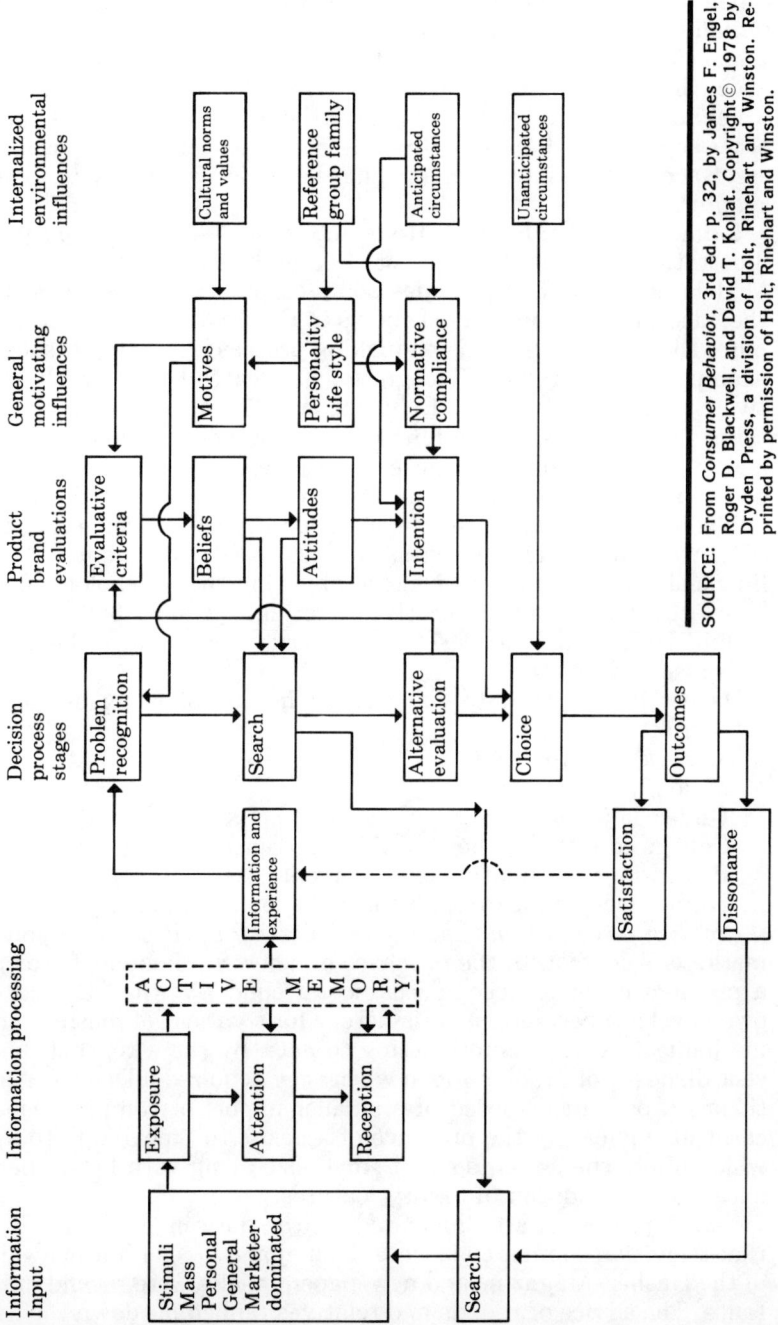

SOURCE: From *Consumer Behavior*, 3rd ed., p. 32, by James F. Engel, Roger D. Blackwell, and David T. Kollat. Copyright© 1978 by Dryden Press, a division of Holt, Rinehart and Winston. Reprinted by permission of Holt, Rinehart and Winston.

consumer must first recognize that a purchasing problem exists; this is called *problem recognition,* Next, a *search* for information, either externally or internally, takes place. This search provides a basis for the *evaluation of alternative* ways of solving the problem; a *choice* about which brand to purchase is made. This choice results in *outcomes* which are varied in terms of being satisfactory or unsatisfactory. All other elements of Figure 3-6 represent inputs into this decision process. Each of these input elements has been discussed previously in this chapter.

Using a Decision Process Model (Example 3-4). For the purposes of illustrating the application of Comprehensive Decision Making Models, Example 3-4 provides some consumer analysis based upon the "decision making" model shown in Figure 3-6 for Dasher automobiles. Elements of the decision making process illustrated through this example are: (1) Problem Recognition; (2) Search Behavior; (3) Alternative Evaluation; (4) Choice Behavior; and (5) Outcomes.

For most people, the purchase of a new and previously unknown make of automobile requires extended problem-solving (EPS) behavior. Experience with the Dasher, introduced to the American public in January 1974 (see the introductory advertisement in Figure 3-7), was limited to awareness of the Volkswagen name. Also, the financial commitment was considerable, and the psychological stakes in selecting the right alternative were high. Almost 300 people who bought Dashers in April 1974 were interviewed. Some of the key finds are presented below.

Dasher buyers tend to concentrate in the following demographic categories:

Married (74.8 percent)
Male (77.1 percent)
Under 35 (42.3 percent)
College educated or beyond (77.2 percent)
Professional occupation (40.1 percent)
Higher income (nearly two thirds beyond $15,000)

Problem recognition usually results from factors beyond the marketer's control. In the purchase of a new automobile, for example, a problem becomes recognized most frequently when the currently owned vehicle becomes unsatisfactory for a variety of reasons, such as mechanical wear. It is interesting to note, by the way, that 34.8 percent disposed of a Volkswagen when they acquired a Dasher. An additional 20 percent disposed of a smaller import or compact American car, thus indicating the presence of a desire to "move up" to a make which offers the advantages of small size along with better performance and the addition of luxury features.

Search processes are illustrated by the data in Table 3-4 indicate that television commercials were the major source of initial awareness of the Dasher. Magazine and newspaper articles were second in importance. The advice of friends and relatives ranked far down the list, undoubtedly because of the newness of this make. Results often are quite different with a more established make.

Figure 3-7　Example of Introductory Print Advertisement

SOURCE: Reprinted by permission of Volkswagen of America. Note, however, that this ad has been superseded, and the information in it is no longer valid.

Table 3-4   Sources of Initial Awareness of the Dasher

TV commercial	36.7%
Articles (magazines/newspapers)	16.4
At dealership (showroom/salesmen)	15.7
Advice of friends/relatives	6.8
Through Fox/Passat	5.3
Newspaper ads	4.7
Advertising (general)	4.6
Magazine ads	4.2
Other	5.6
Total	100.0%

SOURCE: From *Contemporary Cases in Consumer Behavior*, p. 370, by Roger D. Blackwell, James F. Engel, and W. Wayne Talarzyk. Copyright©1977 by Dryden Press, a division of Holt, Rinehart and Winston. Reprinted by permission of Holt, Rinehart and Winston.

The *evaluative criteria* utilized by Dasher buyers are itemized in Table 3-5. Of these ten, gas mileage proved to be the dominant consideration. Manufacturer's reputation was next in order as might be expected from the large number who traded in a Volkswagen Beetle. Apparently, previous experience with this company had been satisfactory. Quality of workmanship and warranty coverage were the only additional criteria receiving frequent mention. It is highly revealing to compare the customer's specifications with the sales points mentioned in the dealer's showroom. These appear in Table 3-6. There should be a close match between them, but that apparently did not prove to be the case. Gas mileage did receive the most frequent mention, but there was a large discrepancy from that point on. For example, quality of workmanship rarely was stressed. Little attempt was made to capitalize upon reputation of manufacturer and previous positive experience with Volkswagens. The salesperson tended either to do little or no real selling or to stress performance characteristics that were of less importance to the buyer. It should come as no surprise that initial sales results of the Dasher were far below expectations. The problem may lie at the level of the dealership. The Dasher carried a higher price

Table 3-5   Evaluative Criteria Mentioned at Least Once
as Reasons for Purchase of the Dasher

Gas mileage	79.7%
Manufacturer's reputation	28.9
Quality of workmanship	22.8
Previous experience with make	21.3
Warranty coverage	18.2
Resale value	18.0
Handling ease	13.4
Interior room	13.0
Value for money	6.6
Exterior styling	6.5

SOURCE: From *Contemporary Cases in Consumer Behavior*, p. 373, by Roger D. Blackwell, James F. Engel, and W. Wayne Talarzyk. Copyright©1977 by Dryden Press, a division of Holt, Rinehart and Winston. Reprinted by permission of Holt, Rinehart and Winston.

tag than the traditional Beetle. Only 15.9 percent of the people interviewed said that the price was about what was expected. Nearly half said that it was a little more than expected, and more than a third said it was a lot more than expected. The justifications given by salespersons for the price are in Table 3-7. Quality of workmanship was stressed most frequently along with general inflation. Quality as an explanation should have been well received given the importance of this factor in the purchase decision.

Table 3-6   Sales Points Mentioned at Time of Purchase

Gas mileage/economy	28.8%
Roominess	17.0
Front-wheel drive	16.2
None (poor salesmanship)	14.8
Handling/ease of driving	14.4
Economy of operation	12.9
Owner's security blanket/computer analysis	8.5
No sales points necessary (presold, knew more than salesman)	8.1
Engine, water-cooled/front-mounted	8.1
Performance	5.9
Design/style	5.5
Features (standard on Dasher but options/accessories on other makes)	5.5
Service	5.5
Quality of workmanship/construction	4.4
Safety	4.4
Engineering	4.4
Other	45.1

SOURCE: From *Contemporary Cases in Consumer Behavior*, p. 370, by Roger D. Blackwell, James F. Engel, and W. Wayne Talarzyk. Copyright©1977 by Dryden Press, a division of Holt, Rinehart and Winston. Reprinted by permission of Holt, Rinehart and Winston.

Table 3-7   Salesman's Justification for Greater-than-Expected Price of the Dasher

Quality workmanship	17.7%
General inflation	17.1
Didn't (salesman did not attempt to justify)	12.5
Dollar devaluation	11.8
Features (standard on Dasher, extra on other makes)	9.2
No reductions from list price	7.8
Unique car (superior/new)	6.5
Couldn't (salesman tried to justify but, according to customer, failed)	6.5
Increased value of trade-in	5.9
Low operating cost	5.2
Value for the money	3.9
Owner's security blanket	3.9
Performance	3.9
Increased production costs	3.9
Gas mileage	3.2

SOURCE: From *Contemporary Cases in Consumer Behavior*, p. 371, by Roger D. Blackwell, James F. Engel, and W. Wayne Talarzyk. Copyright©1977 by Dryden Press, a division of Holt, Rinehart and Winston. Reprinted by permission of Holt, Rinehart and Winston.

Part of the *choice process* is selection of the dealer. The data in Table
3-8 indicate that physical proximity was the dominant consideration,
with previous experience a distant second. Other factors were of less
importance.

Table 3-8   Primary Reason for Dealership Selection

Closeness to dealer	40.9%
Previous experience	10.6
Service	8.2
Dealership personnel	7.8
Dealer reputation	7.2
Only one	6.2
Trade-in	5.8
Advice of friends	4.0
Other	9.3
Total	100.0%

SOURCE: From *Contemporary Cases in Consumer Behavior*, p. 370, by Roger D.
Blackwell, James F. Engel, and W. Wayne Talarzyk. Copyright©1977 by
Dryden Press, a division of Holt, Rinehart and Winston. Reprinted by per-
mission of Holt, Rinehart and Winston.

Outcomes can be described as follows. Ownership satisfaction is of
critical importance in continued loyalty to a given company. In the
case of the Dasher, satisfaction was related to reaction to price. If the
price was about as expected, the buyer tended to be quite satisfied,
whereas satisfaction was much lower when the price was more than expected. (See Table 3-9.)

Table 3-9   Satisfaction vs. Initial Reaction to Price

	Dasher Price Was	
	about what expected	a little/lot more than expected
Completely/very satisfied	70.7%	50.7%
Fairly well satisfied	19.5	26.9
Somewhat dissatisfied	4.9	19.2
Very dissatisfied	4.9	3.2
	100.0%	100.0%

SOURCE: From *Contemporary Cases in Consumer Behavior*, p. 371, by Roger D.
Blackwell, James F. Engel, and W. Wayne Talarzyk. Copyright©1977 by
Dryden Press, a division of Holt, Rinehart and Winston. Reprinted by per-
mission of Holt, Rinehart and Winston.

Sales of the Dasher fell below expectations. Price appeared to be a
major factor, and the relationship of reaction to price and buyer
satisfaction is a real danger sign. The dissatisfied owner rarely keeps
quiet about these reactions and, thus, is bound to affect future sales.
Furthermore, the quality of salesmanship at the dealer level reflected a

poor grasp of buyer expectations. A reversal of the negative trend will depend in large part on remedial action taken in the marketing program.

SALES FORECASTING

In Example 3-3 in this chapter an illustration of Break-even Analysis was shown in which the determination was made that 16.67 percent increase in next time period's sales was required in order to support a two million dollar advertising expenditure in that time period. It should be noted that this analysis does not assume a "causal" connection between the advertising figure used in the analysis (two million dollars in this case) and the sales figure generated by the analysis ($23,333,333 in the example). From an accounting point of view, all the analysis indicates is that $23,333,333 in sales is required to "pay for" the two million dollars in advertising. The final question in break-even analysis is always: "Will sales increase next time period by at least 16.67 percent over the current period sales?" Just as the break-even analysis does not take explicit account of the relationship of advertising and sales, so generally the answer to the question regarding the expected level of next time period sales also does not. The answer to the above question will generally be arrived at independently of the level of advertising effort befing considered for the time period by means of *sales forecasting methods*.

Sales forecasting methods ordinarily consist of extrapolation of the underlying pattern in a series of sales observations over time. This pattern will not ordinarily be simple in appearance so that some rather detailed methods are employed to analyze the time series so that this pattern might be revealed and used as the basis for a projection of next time period sales. In advertising decision making, then, sales forecasting methods go hand-in-hand with the application of break-even analyses.

COMPONENTS OF A TIME SERIES

The recording of sales for a particular brand or company as a function of time results in a set of numbers called a *time series*. A time series might consist of sales for Kellerman Ketchup as shown in Table 3-10 organized from 1978 through 1982. The variations in these sales figures over the five-year period ordinarily would be assumed to result from four different components: (1) Trend—TR; (2) Seasonal variation—SE; (3) Cyclical variation—CY; and (4) Irregular variation—IR.

Trend. Trend is defined as the long-term movement in a time series. For example, it may be known that sales of Kellerman Ketchup have increased 32 percent over the past 18 years.

Seasonal Variation. This component of the sales movement pattern refers to fluctuations in sales which repeat themselves within a fixed time period, usually of less than one year. Suppose it is known that sales of Kellerman Ketchup are greatest during the summer quarter of each year; this quarterly increase in sales for each year would be referred to as a seasonal increase in sales.

Table 3-10   Sales of Kellerman Ketchup for 1978-1982
(in thousands of dollars)

Year	t	S	t^2	$t \times S$
1978	−2	$ 6	4	−12
1979	−1	8	1	− 8
1980	0	12	0	0
1981	1	13	1	13
1982	2	18	4	36
Sum	0	57	10	29

Cyclical Variation. The cyclical variation in sales patterns refers to those repetitions over time periods of differing length, ordinarily longer in duration than one year. It may be determined, for example, that part of the sales "ups and downs" for Kellerman Ketchup is due to recessionary elements in the economy as a whole. Recessions are not always of the same length but are invariably followed by recovery and

Figure 3-8   The Four Components of a Time Series

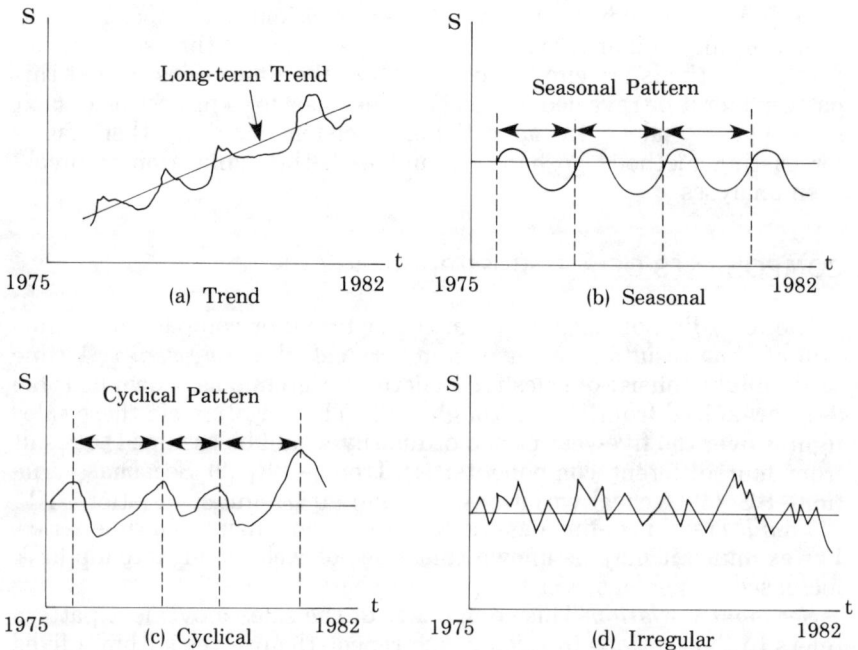

(a) Trend

(b) Seasonal

(c) Cyclical

(d) Irregular

prosperity cycles. This business cycle will be present in the sales patterns of most products, though some categories may be immune or insulated from such cyclical fluctuations.

These four components of time-series fluctuations are illustrated in Figure 3-8. It should be noted that not all time series must have all four types of fluctuation. In general, however, sales forecasting is an attempt to find and isolate or remove certain of these components, if they exist, in the series so that the underlying trend can be observed. This underlying trend may then serve as the basis for forecasting.

The General Time-Series Model. The general model, then, in sales forecasting will consist of the four components described above. Though the model may take on various forms, often the model will be either of an *additive* nature or a *multiplicative* nature. In the additive case, the assumption is made that the four components of the series are independent of each other; changes in one component are assumed not to affect the other components. On the other hand, the multiplicative model assumes dependence among the four components; in this case, a change in any one factor will create changes in the other components:

Additive Model: $S = TR + SE + CY + IR$
Multiplicative Model: $S = TR \times SE \times CY \times IR$.

For purposes of model fitting (by means of regression analysis usually), the multiplicative model can be transformed to linear format as required by regression models by taking the logs (either natural or to the base ten) of both sides of the equation:

Transformed Multiplicative Model:
$$LN\,(S) = LN(TR) + LN(SE) + LN(CY) + LN(IR)$$

where: LN = log to the base e (natural logarithms).

For estimation purposes, SE, CY and IR are often treated as deviations from trend. Therefore, trend is estimated first using simple regression analysis; then the variation in the sales series which can be attributed to trend is removed from the series. The remaining variation after trend in the sales must then be attributable to either seasonal, cyclical, or irregular factors. These elements can then, in turn, be isolated in the series. Some elementary methods for accomplishing this will now be illustrated through the use of the Kellerman Ketchup example.

USING REGRESSION TO FIND THE TREND LINE (EXAMPLE 3-5)

Table 3-10 presents sales data for Kellerman Ketchup from 1978 through 1982. In addition to the sales figures (in thousands of dollars), Table 3-10 also assigns a number from -2 through $+2$ for each of the years involved in the time series; this variable is called "t" for trend or time. For convenience in the regression calculations, t has been squared as well as multiplied times S for each time period in the series. As can be seen in Table 3-10, it is often convenient to assign the number zero to the year falling in the middle of the series; negative numbers are then sequentially assigned to years below the middle year while positive numbers are assigned sequentially to years falling above the middle year.

The regression equation to be estimated follows the algebraic representation of a straight line: $y = a + b(x)$ where "a" and "b" are called parameters of the function and represent, respectively, the point at which the line intersects the y axis (called the intercept) and the tilt or slope of the line. In this example, the letter y will be replaced by the dependent variable S (sales) and the independent variable x will be replaced by time (t) so that the function becomes:

$$S = a + b(t).$$

Regression analysis will allow the calculation of a specific intercept and slope for the Kellerman data shown in Table 3-10. Once a and b are found for the data, it becomes possible to "plug in" a value for the next time period (+3 in this case would represent 1983) and multiply through the function to find a predicted S or sales for Kellerman Ketchup for 1983 based upon the trend in the data series. The following two "reduced form" equations may be used in this case to calculate a and b for the data in Table 3-10:

$$a = \frac{\sum_{i=1}^{n} S_i}{n}$$

$$b = \frac{\sum_{i=1}^{n} t_i S_i}{\sum_{i=1}^{n} t^2_i}$$

where: n = number of time periods in the series.

Using the above reduced form formulas, $a = 57/5 = 11.4$; $b = 29/10 = 2.9$. Therefore, The trend equation can be stated as: $S = 11.4 + 2.9(t)$. And the estimate of sales of Kellerman Ketchup for 1983 (represented by +3 in the function) would be calculated as:

$$\hat{S} = 11.4 + 2.9(3)$$

$$\hat{S} = 20.1.$$

The trend line is plotted in Figure 3-9.

Figure 3-9   Trend Line for Kellerman Ketchup

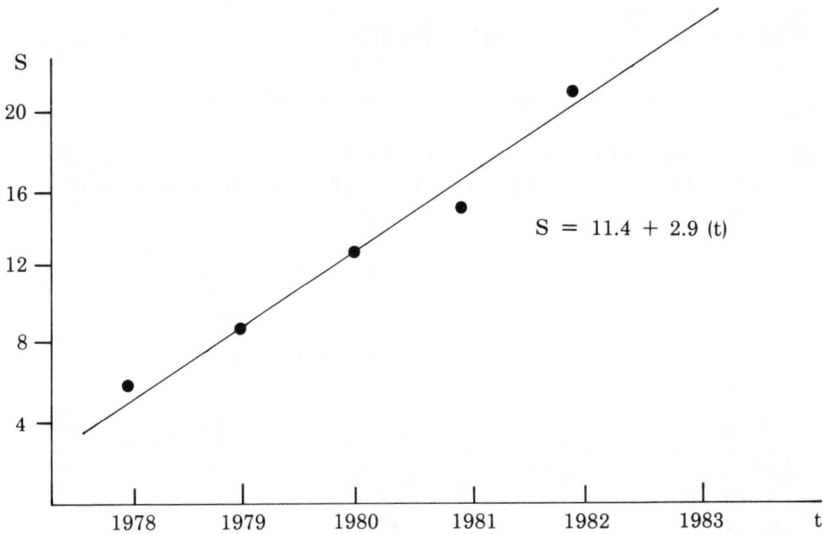

$$S = 11.4 + 2.9 \,(t)$$

NONLINEAR TREND

In the preceding example, it was assumed that the trend component in the Kellerman data was linearly related to sales. This assumption results, of course, in a straight-line trend as shown in Figure 3-10. It may be the case, however, that the trend in the data exhibits a nonlinear relationship to sales; if this is the case, then a linear trend computation will not represent the relationship in the series as well as a nonlinear function. Some forecasting accuracy will be lost in this instance. Several nonlinear forms should be examined if nonlinearities are suspected to determine if the "fit" of the trend line improves over the linear fit. Fit can be measured by the sum of the squared deviations of the actual sales figures in each year from that "predicted" by the regression equation for that year. If this figure is divided by the number of observations and the square root then taken, the resulting statistic is referred to as the "standard error of the estimate" in regression analysis.

Though several nonlinear functions may be examined in each case, the example below shows the use of an exponential function applied to the Kellerman data. Some other functions which might be examined in forecasting are:

Modified Exponential: $S = \overline{S} + ab^t$

Logistic Function: $S = 1/(\overline{S} + ab^t)$

Gompertz Function: $S = \overline{S}a^{b^t}$

where: $\overline{S}$ = upper asymptote on sales (the largest amount sales can reasonably expect to reach in the forecasting period).

Example 3–6. The exponential function is generally given as:

Exponential Function: $S = ab^t$.

This can be transformed into linear format for purposes of fitting via regression analysis by taking the natural log of both sides of the function:

$$LN(S) = LN(a) + LN(b)t.$$

Figure 3-10 Exponential Trend Line for Kellerman Ketchup

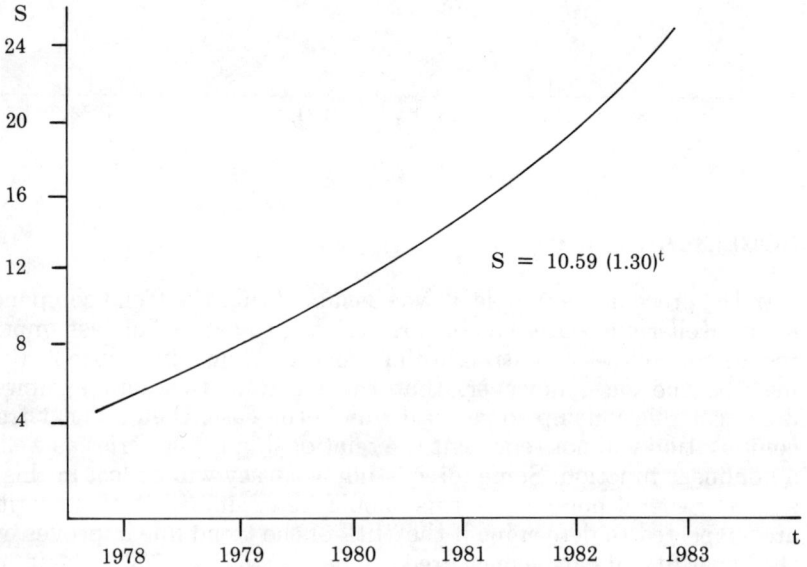

$S = 10.59 \ (1.30)^t$

Table 3-11 Transformed Sales for Kellerman Ketchup for 1978-1982 (in thousands of dollars)

Year	t	S	LN(S)	t^2	$t \times LN(S)$
1978	−2	$ 6	$1.79	4	−3.58
1979	−1	8	2.08	1	−2.08
1980	0	12	2.48	0	0.00
1981	1	13	2.56	1	2.56
1982	2	18	2.89	4	5.78
Sum	0	57	11.80	10	2.68

Table 3-11 provides the transformed sales data and transformed sales times "t" so that the equations in Example 3-5 (reduced form regression equations) can be used to calculate LN(a) and LN(b) for the exponential function simply by using LN(S) rather than S as was the case in Example 3-5. Following this thinking, a = 11.8/5 = 2.36 and b = 2.68/10 = .268. The function then becomes:

$$LN(S) = 2.36 + .268(t).$$

The antilog (e^x) of 2.36 is 10.59 and of .268 is 1.30 so that, in terms of the original exponential function, the trend curve can be stated as:

$$S = 10.59(1.30)^t.$$

This is the case since 2.36 equals LN(a) and .268 equals LN(b) when the calculations in the regression equation use LN(S) rather than S as in Example 3-5. Using this exponential function to predict or forecast for 1983 yields:

$$\hat{S} = 10.59(1.30)^3$$

$$\hat{S} = 23.26.$$

The plot of this exponential function for Kellerman Ketchup is shown in Figure 3-10 and is slightly concave-upward in shape. It might be noted that a prediction in this example of 23.4 is considerably different (remember the units are in thousands) than that provided by the linear function in Example 3-5 (which was 20.1). Which of the two predictions or forecasts might be more reliable? This is a difficult question; however, one way to examine this issue is to look at the squared deviations of actual versus predicted values for each of the two functions for all five observed years, 1978-1982. The lower the sum of the squared deviations (called Residual Sum of Squares), the better the "fit" of the function. All other things aside, the function with the smaller residual sum of squares should be used for the forecast. The RSS (residual sum of squares) for the linear function is calculated to be 2.82 while the RSS for the exponential function is 2.71. Based upon this measure of goodness of fit, the exponential function, and, therefore, its forecast, would be preferred to the linear function.

MOVING AVERAGES TO SMOOTH A SERIES

In the above examples it was assumed that a trend line could be calculated without first removing or minimizing the effect of seasonal, cyclical, and irregular fluctuations from the series. It may be more convenient, at times, to estimate the trend using the foregoing methods by applying them not to the original data series but rather to one in which the seasonal, cyclical, and random fluctuations have been removed. One way of doing this is to use techniques called "smoothing." One such method, called Moving Averages, will be illustrated with Kellerman Ketchup data in the following example.

Example 3-7. The data for Kellerman for Examples 3-5 and 3-6 have been expanded by adding on ten prior years of sales data; these expanded data are shown in Table 3-6. The original, unsmooth 15-year series is shown in the first column of Table 3-12. An inspection of these fifteen years of data will reveal a cyclical pattern which repeats itself every five years. Roughly speaking, 1969 sales are 33 percent greater than 1968 sales. Sales for 1970 are 50 percent greater than 1969, 1971 8 percent greater than 1970, and 1972 38 percent greater than 1971. Proportionately, this pattern of 33, 50, 8, and 38 percentage points increase from year to year is almost exactly repeated in the years 1973 through 1977 and also again in the five-year period from 1978 through 1982. This provides the basis for constructing a five-year moving average to "smooth out" the cyclical variations in the series.

Table 3-12   Fifteen-Year Time Series and Smoothed Series
for Kellerman Ketchup
(Sales in thousands of dollars)

Year	Original Sales	Smoothed Sales
1968	.4	—
1969	.6	—
1970	.9	.9
1971	1.0	1.1
1972	1.4	1.4
1973	1.6	1.9
1974	2.2	2.4
1975	3.3	3.1
1976	3.6	4.0
1977	5.0	5.2
1978	6.0	6.9
1979	8.0	8.8
1980	12.0	11.4
1981	13.0	—
1982	18.0	—

The five-year moving average is constructed by first taking the average of the first five years in the fifteen-year series; this is calculated as $\frac{1}{5} \times (.4 + .6 + .9 + 1.0 + 1.4) = .9$. The average of the first five years, .9, is then placed at the midpoint of the first five years from which it was calculated. This is shown in the second column of Table 3-12. Then a second average is calculated by summing the next five years stepping one year down from the top of the series; beginning with 1969, then, the second moving average is found to be $1.1 = \frac{1}{5} \times (.6 + .9 + 1.0 + 1.4 + 1.6)$. It is placed directly underneath the first five-year average in the second column of Table 3-12. In a similar manner, a total of eleven five-year averages can be constructed for the fifteen-year times series in Table 3-12. These eleven mean scores can then serve as substitute sales figures for the original fifteen sales figures and are called "smoothed sales figures." Of course, the greater the seasonal, cyclical, or irregular fluctuations present in the series originally, the greater will be the effect of replacing the original series with the smoothed series. In this instance for Kellerman Ketchup, though the effect is not dramatic, a smoothing effect is clearly evident when the original and smooth data are plotted as shown in Figure 3-11. A drawback of smoothing consists in the loss of observations; the greater is the length of the cyclical pattern, the greater will be the loss of data. It can be surmised from Figure 3-11 that it will be easier to find a curve which adequately fits the smoothed curve than the somewhat more "jagged" original curve. And this is the primary purpose of smoothing; it should generally be easier to fit a trend line to a series after the removal of cyclical, seasonal, or random fluctuations in this manner.

It should be noted that many specialized procedures exist for removing the various components of a time series. Seasonal indices are often

Figure 3-11   Kellerman Ketchup Time Series Smoothed
with Five-Year Moving Average
(for fifteen-year series shown in Table 3-3)

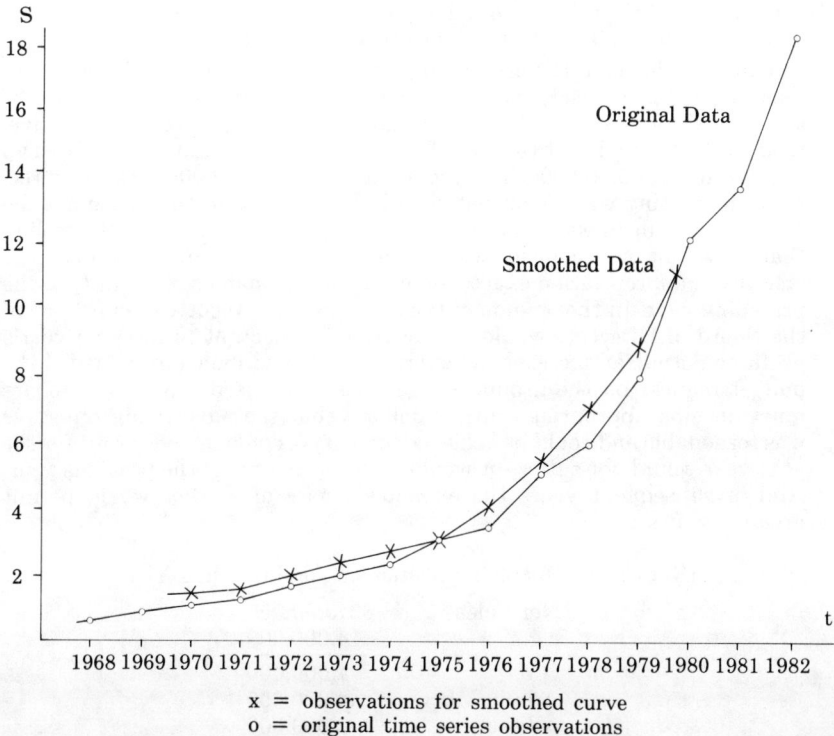

x = observations for smoothed curve
o = original time series observations

constructed for the purpose of isolating seasonal variations in the series. Another method to do this is called the Ratio-to-Trend method. All methods, however, attempt to first remove either seasonal, cyclical, or random fluctuations before fitting a linear or nonlinear trend line in the manner suggested in the above examples.

With this outline of the elements of Advertising Opportunity Analysis in mind, it is assumed that the decision can be made as to whether or not advertising should play a role in the overall marketing program of the brand. Once this decision is made, the question of advertising objectives arises. The following chapter is devoted to a consideration of objective setting in advertising and its relationship to advertising management.

QUESTIONS AND PROBLEMS

1. Discuss the different nature of an advertising program when the objective is that of stimulating generic demand as opposed to brand or selective demand.

2. Why is elasticity usually negative? If elasticity is positive, what factors might account for this? What differences would you expect to see in the advertising program for a product which had a positive elasticity versus one which had a negative elasticity?

3. Discuss the similarities between demand elasticity and demand expansibility. Can the coefficient of advertising response be viewed in a similar manner to the demand elasticity coefficient? Why or why not?

4. In planning the advertising campaign for the next fiscal period, the advertising manager for the Kenwright Company set an increase in sales of 10% as the goal for the advertising program. The manager used the objective-task method to arrive at the size of the appropriation and recommended an expenditure of $3,000,000. The budget last year was $2,000,000. The director of marketing was somewhat skeptical of the size of this recommendation and was inclined to reject it. This was based, in part, on the feeling that it was not mere coincidence that the increase in the budget figure over last year's appropriation exactly equalled the company's net profit for the preceding year. In the opinion of the director, the Executive Committee of the Board of Directors would be exceedingly reluctant to forego a year's profit to permit an increase in advertising. The ad manager defended the budget request on the ground that it was recognized that input dollars must develop appropriate output dollars; that the advertising objective was reasonable and could be achieved; and, if so, company net profit for the next year would not suffer—it would be equal to that of the previous year. And in subsequent years the expanded share of market would permit greater profits.

(Kenwright Operating Statement for Preceding Year)

Net Sales	$21,000,000
c.g.s.	14,000,000
GM	7,000,000
Admin/Mktg	4,000,000
Adv	2,000,000
Net Profit	$ 1,000,000

Evaluate the ad manager's defense of the budget request.

5. The Rabman Company manufactures a line of aerosol floor cleaners. The recent data on sales, advertising, and profits for Rabman are given below:

Year	ADV (millions $)	SALES (millions $)	Net Profits ($)
1979	4.5	9.0	1,100,000
1980	4.0	9.2	1,200,000
1981	3.8	9.4	1,300,500
1982	3.7	9.7	1,250,000
1983	?	?	?

The advertising manager for Rabman conducted an analysis of advertising expenditures and determined, through use of the objective-task approach, that the expenditure for 1983 should amount to 3.4 million dollars. The manager forwarded this recommendation to management for their approval. It was estimated by company management that administrative/other marketing costs for 1983 would amount to about $2.0 million. They expected to charge a price of $2.55/unit wholesale; production costs/unit were estimated for 1983 as $1.00.

Evaluate the advertising manager's recommended spending level for 1983 using the concept of advertising response coefficients.

6. What is the relationship between advertising opportunity analysis and the setting of advertising objectives? Why is it important, as the very first step in advertising decision making, to conduct an advertising opportunity analysis?

ENDNOTES

1. This analysis is more appropriate for consumer goods than for industrial goods.
2. A major portion of the points presented in this discussion were suggested originally by Neil H. Borden in *Economic Effects of Advertising* (Homewood, IL: Richard D. Irwin, Inc., 1942), p. 424. This discussion also appeared in somewhat different form in Nugent Wedding and Richard S. Lessler, *Advertising Management* (New York: The Ronald Press Company, 1962).
3. Counties are ordinarily classified as:
   County Size A: All counties belonging to the 26 largest metropolitan areas.
   County Size B: Counties over 120,000 population that are not in Class A plus counties that are part of the metropolitan area of cities in such B counties.
   County Size C: Counties not included in Classes A or B having over 32,000 population plus counties that are a part of the metropolitan area of cities in such C counties.
   County Size D: All counties not included in Classes A, B, or C.
4. See a full discussion of Life Style analysis based upon personality theories in William D. Wells and Arthur D. Beard, "Personality and Consumer Behavior," in Scott Ward and Thomas S. Robertson, eds., *Consumer Behavior: Theoretical Sources* (Englewood Cliffs, N.J.: Prentice-Hall, Inc. 1973), pp. 141-199.
5. Edward O. Laumann and James S. House, "Living Room Styles and Social Attributes: The Patterning of Material Artifacts in a Modern Urban Community," in Harold Kassarjian and Thomas S. Robertson, *Perspectives in Consumer Behavior* (Glenview, IL: Scott, Foresman and Company, 1973), pp. 43-440.

110

6. Ralph Linton, *The Study of Man* (New York: Appleton-Century-Crofts, 1936).
7. D. Krech, R. S. Crutchfield, and E. L. Ballachy, *Individual in Society* (New York: McGraw-Hill, Inc., 1962).
8. S. Watson Dunn and Ann Lorimor, *International Advertising and Marketing* (Columbus, Ohio: Grid Publishing, Inc., 1981).
9. James F. Engel, David T. Kollat and Roger D. Blackwell, *Consumer Behavior*, Second Edition, (New York: Holt, Rinehart and Winston, Inc., 1973), p. 112.
10. W. Lloyd Warner, Marchia Meeker, and Kenneth Eck, *Social Class in America: A Manual of Procedure for the Measurement of Social Status* (Chicago: Science Research Associates, 1949).
11. Edgar H. Schein, "Organization Socialization and the Profession of Management," in David A. Kolb, Irwin M. Rubin, and James M. McIntyre (eds.), *Organizational Psychology* (Englewood Cliffs, N.J.: Prentice-Hall, Inc., 1971), pp. 1-14.
12. Theodore M. Newcomb, "Attitude Development as a Function of Reference Groups: The Bennington Study," in Eleanor E. Maccoby, Theodore M. Newcomb, and Eugene L. Hartley (eds.), *Readings in Social Psychology*, 3rd edition, (New York: Holt, Rinehart and Winston, 1958), pp. 265-275.
13. Engel, Kollat and Blackwell, *op.cit.*, p. 296.
14. *Ibid.*, p. 297.
15. This categorization is adapted from Kassarjian and Robertson, *op.cit.*, pp. 196-200.
16. Joel B. Cohen, "An Interpersonal Orientation to the Study of Consumer Behavior," *Journal of Marketing Research*, vol. 4 (August 1967), pp. 270-278.
17. J. P. Guilford, *Personality* (New York: McGraw-Hill, Inc., 1959), p. 6.
18. Raymond B. Cattell, *The Scientific Analysis of Personality* (Baltimore: Penguin Books, 1965).
19. Abraham H. Maslow, *Motivation and Personality* (New York: Harper & Row, Inc., 1954).
20. Bernard Berelson and Gary A. Steiner, *Human Behavior: An Inventory of Scientific Findings* (New York: Harcourt Brace Jovanovich, 1964), p. 88.
21. See, for example, the discussion of Weber's Law in Steuart Henderson Britt, *Psychological Principles of Marketing and Consumer Behavior* (Lexington, Mass: Lexington Books, 1978), p. 133.
22. Martin Fishbein and Icek Ajzen, *Belief, Attitude, Intention, and Behavior: An Introduction to Theory and Research* (Reading, MA: Addison-Wesley, 1975).
23. John A. Howard and Jagdish N. Sheth, *The Theory of Buyer Behavior* (New York: John Wiley & Sons, Inc., 1969).

4

CASES IN OPPORTUNITY ANALYSIS

- Sunkist Growers, Inc. (A)
- Gordon Textile Company
- Coastal Fisheries, Inc. (A)
- The Johnson Baking Company
- The Atlas Tool Company
- The Morton Salt Company
- The Miramar Grocery Company
- Supersweet Sugar Refining Company
- Timken Roller Bearing
- Personna Blades

CASES IN OPPORTUNITY ANALYSIS

Case 4-1—Sunkist Growers, Inc. (A)

In 1893 chaotic marketing conditions in the citrus fruit industry led to the organization of a non-profit marketing cooperative known as the Southern California Fruit Exchange. The marketing situation was such that a majority of the members of the citrus industry were unable to obtain market prices for their fruit sufficient to meet costs of production. Haphazard marketing efforts by individual growers resulted in low prices, glutted markets in some areas, and inadequate coverage of other markets, all acting to hinder the growth of the industry.

It was anticipated that the evils in this situation could be corrected through joint efforts of all growers. This action resulted in organization of the Southern California Fruit Growers Exchange. In 1905, the organization was renamed the California Fruit Growers Exchange. In 1952, the name was further changed to Sunkist Growers, Inc., to incorporate into its corporate name the organization's leading brand name which had been used since 1908. Through the years, the organization has made a substantial contribution to members' welfare by stimulating market demand for fresh citrus and processed citrus products; extensive use of research on nutritional, by-product, and merchandising fields; and through developing dependable sources of production and packinghouse supplies.

BACKGROUND INFORMATION ON ORGANIZATION AND OPERATION

Sunkist Growers, Inc. is a non-stock, nonprofit cooperative association which markets on a worldwide basis, in fresh and processed form, citrus fruit produced by its some 6,000 grower members in California and Arizona. The members of Sunkist in addition to the growers are about 43 local cooperative associations known as "Local Associations" and some 13 regional cooperative associations known as "District Exchanges". All growers are members of either a Local Association or a District Exchange, as well as Sunkist. All Local Associations are also members of a District Exchange.

All growers have their fruit packed in facilities provided either by one or more member Local Associations or by one or more of about 29 nonmember Licensed Packers authorized to perform that service by Sunkist and a District Exchange. Fruit not suitable for sale in fresh form is delivered by those packing facilities to Sunkist for processing into citrus products.

Individual growers sign a membership agreement to market through Sunkist the citrus fruit grown on acreage specified in the agreement. Membership agreements may be terminated at the end of any season.

The packing units are responsible for preparing the fruit of their affiliated growers for market and for loading cars for shipment. They employ picking crews which move from orchard to orchard, deliver the fruit to the packing house, wash, grade, size, and pack the fruit from the growers. During the packing season, each packing unit is inspected daily by a member of the Sunkist field service department to determine whether fruit being packed there meets the Sunkist quality standards. A packing unit cannot add the name Sunkist to its product unless the fruit is of a grade or quality equal to Sunkist standards.

The control of the system is democratic. At the final stage of authority, the district exchanges, based upon the volume of fruit handled, elect one or more members to the Sunkist Board of Directors. This Board meets in open session at regular intervals through each month. These meetings are open to all members and other interested parties.

Operating expenses of the organization are met by a schedule of assessments per carton of fruit handled. The schedule is based upon expected fruit yields and on anticipated expenses and is determined in advance of November 1, which is the beginning of the new fiscal year. The headquarters of the organization is in Los Angeles.

SUNKIST MARKETING OPERATIONS

The primary marketing objective of Sunkist is the profitable sale of their members' citrus fruit. Sunkist maintains sales offices in every major market in the United States and Canada for maximum distribution. There are 37 district sales offices, staffed by salaried employees, to help maintain daily contact between producer and distributor.

While the sale of fresh fruit is the most profitable to the grower, all fruit harvested is utilized insofar as that is possible. The portion of the crop not absorbed by the "fresh" market, including fruit which is below Sunkist standards for fresh fruits, is processed by Sunkist. Sunkist's major volume of revenue comes from the sale of oranges, lemons, grapefruits and tangerines, plus the sale of processed citrus juice and peel products.

The principal methods utilized by the co-op over the years to accomplish their marketing goals were improved efficiencies in marketing operations and an expansion of consumer demand for citrus fruit by advertising and sales promotion. In 1981, Sunkist celebrated 73 years of Sunkist advertising. In the early years of their operations, the principal markets for citrus fruits were in the Midwest and East. Fruit was pooled and shipped on regular schedules throughout the year. The organization took full advantage of all developments in rail transportation. The crop was iced for shipment, and later refrigerated cars were used. Lower freight rates, faster transit, and better delivered condition of fruit have resulted from their efforts. In later years, population shifts to the West have modified this situation somewhat, although Eastern and Midwestern markets have continued to occupy an important part of the attention of Sunkist management. The size of these markets plus the keen competition from Florida and Texas fruit tend to make certain of this.

In their operations, the principles of orderly marketing have constituted an important part of their operations. The central office acts as a clearing house for the district offices. The representatives who are placed in important markets all over the country supply information constantly regarding market conditions and prices. The objective has been to see that every carlot market in the country shall be supplied with that quantity of citrus fruit which it can consume from day to day or week to week and also that the entire crop shall be distributed over the shipping season in such a manner as to satisfy consumer demand, avoiding an oversupply at one period and shortages at other times. The total supply is fixed by natural conditions and cannot be increased or decreased within the season. Distribution is through wholesalers and jobbers, and direct buying retailers. Export sales are made to markets throughout the world. The five most active markets in 1978-79 were Japan, Hong Kong, Benelux, Poland and France.

SUNKIST RESEARCH

The Sunkist Growers maintain an unremitting quest through the research department for new facts of health and consumer usefulness of citrus products and invests substantial sums each year in scientific research. Continuing Sunkist research has uncovered hidden nutritional elements in fresh citrus, such as vitamin C, protopectins, bioflavinoids, and others.

Scientific studies dealing with the therapeutic value of citrus fruits are also sponsored at medical schools throughout the country. Cooperative relations are maintained with the medical, dental, and dietetic professions.

Sunkist produces over four hundred consumer, industrial, and pharmaceutical products from citrus fruit. Sunkist products include pectin, citric acid, soft drink concentrates, oils, meal and other items used by bakers, confectioners, canners, and beverage manufacturers. These are regarded chiefly as a means of minimizing losses when crops exceed demand. Sometimes an abundant crop will permit the production of more than a full year's supply of these by-products. Under these circumstances, the surplus is carried in inventory until a more advantageous marketing opportunity appears.

ADVERTISING AND SALES PROMOTION

The advertising program of the California Fruit Growers' Exchange was started in 1907 with an initial budget of $10,000. In 1908 the Sunkist trademark was adopted as the symbol for the quality fruit which the organization marketed and as a basis for demand stimulation. This advertising effort has been continued and greatly expanded over the years with a multimillion dollar budget.

The initial objective of the association advertising was the expansion of generic demand for citrus fruits. The Exchange was one of the pioneers in this type of advertising effort. In recent years, the advertising approach has been to place principal emphasis upon the Sunkist brand and to stimulate demand for specific fruit sizes and grades.

Advertising plans and budgets each year for the association are developed jointly by the advertising committee and the advertising department. These plans are set up in detail and recommended to the board of directors. After the board has approved the recommendations, or their modifications, the plans are returned to the advertising department, which, in cooperation with the advertising agencies, is responsible for execution of the plans. The advertising committee has authority to approve recommendations of the advertising manager for deviations from the plans unless these involve major changes in policy or strategy. In this manner, needed flexibility is introduced into the program.

For the year 1978-79, a sharp drop in funds available for fresh fruit advertising cancelled all major national campaigns. The lack of funds was due in part to the great freeze during that growing season. The absence of national advertising exposure was compensated for by the company's consumer services division and home economist. Releases were made throughout the year including recipes, magazine articles, radio and TV talk and feature shows, to help maintain public awareness of the brands and their availability.

The company sets its budgets as of November 1, which is the beginning of its fiscal year. If the crop is larger than expected, budgets may be increased in midyear.

At present, separate budgets and campaigns are developed for each variety of product. Lemon advertising, for example, has its own budget and is administered as a separate program. The association believes that different supply and demand conditions and different advertising problems and costs require this separation. (see Case 12-3).

The company follows a conservative policy in the nutrition and

116

medical claims made in their advertising. Before making any claim, the advertising department makes certain that research has been soundly done and is well substantiated and that the findings are well known to and accepted by the medical profession. They believe that this policy has resulted in a high degree of credibility and acceptance of Sunkist advertising by the public. Exhibit 4-1 shows traceable advertising expenditures for Sunkist products 1974-79.

Exhibit 4-1   Estimated Traceable Expenditures Sunkist Products 1974-79

1974	Consumer Mags (000)	Supplements (000)	Net TV (000)	Newspapers (000)	Spot TV (000)	TOTALS (000)
Sunkist fresh lemons	1,785.1					1,785.1
Sunkist frozen concentrate orange juice blend	16.8					16.8
Sunkist fresh oranges			2,929.7	472.5		3,402.2
TOTALS	1,801.9		2,929.7	472.5		5,204.1
1975						
Sunkist fresh lemons	1,509.0				396.8	1,905.8
Sunkist fresh oranges			3,114.2	337.1		3,451.3
Sunkist frozen lemon juice		15.3		24.8		40.1
TOTALS	1,509.0	15.3	3,114.2	361.9	396.8	5,397.2
1976						
Sunkist fresh lemons	1,248.2			128.5		1,376.7
Sunkist fresh oranges	74.8		3,000.8		304.8	3,380.4
Sunkist growers gen. promo.	6.2					6.2
Sunkist fresh grapefruits				6.7		6.7
Sunkist frozen orange juice				16.0		16.0
TOTALS	1,329.2		3,000.8	151.2	304.8	4,786.0

Exhibit 4-1 continued

1977	Consumer Mags (000)	Supplements (000)	Net TV (000)	Newspapers (000)	Spot TV (000)	TOTALS (000)
Sunkist fresh lemons	1,399.4					1,399.4
Sunkist sweepstakes	98.9					98.9
Sunkist citrus fruit				41.1		41.1
Sunkist grapefruit				5.9		5.9
Sunkist fresh oranges				379.2	3,297.3	3,676.5
Sunkist frozen orange juice				32.2		32.2
TOTALS	1,498.3			458.4	3,297.3	5,254.0
1978						
Sunkist fresh lemons	1,170.0			216.4		1,386.4
Sunkist mail order promo.	187.0					187.0
Sunkist citrus fruit			905.5			905.5
Sunkist fresh oranges	110.6			614.1	2,742.1	3,466.8
Sunkist frozen orange juice				27.5		27.5
TOTALS	1,467.6		905.5	858.0	2,742.1	5,973.2
1979						
Sunkist fresh lemons				340.3		340.3
Sunkist gen. promo.	12.6					12.6
Sunkist fresh oranges	222.4			151.8		374.2
TOTALS[1]	235.0			492.1		727.1

[1]Figures for 1979 based on partial reports

RESULTS OF THE PROGRAM

The sales results of the operation of the cooperative from 1959 are shown in Exhibit 4-2.

Exhibit 4-2   Value of Sunkist Fresh Sales of Oranges,
Lemons & Grapefruit

Year	Sales Values[1]
1959	192,000,000
1960	176,000,000
1961	169,000,000
1962	151,000,000
1963	177,000,000
1964	186,000,000
1965	193,000,000
1966	228,000,000
1967	234,000,000
1968	200,000,000
1969	245,000,000
1970	252,000,000
1971	274,000,000
1972	270,000,000
1973	301,500,000
1974	335,300,000
1975	406,700,000
1976	356,100,000
1977	397,300,000
1978	462,100,000
1979	486,700,000

---

[1]Figures from 1960-61 down reflect non-FOB prices.

Exhibit 4-3 presents statistics on per capita consumption of fresh fruit, both citrus and deciduous. These figures permit comparisons in consumption of various types of fruit over a 46 year period.

QUESTIONS FOR DISCUSSION

1. Have results of the advertising and sales promotion program of Sunkist Growers justified the expenditures of the Association?
2. Evaluate the opportunities that existed in 1907 for the Association to make use of advertising to expand the generic demand for citrus fruits.
3. What opportunities for the role of advertising do you see for Sunkist Growers as of 1979?

Exhibit 4-3   Per Capita Consumption (pounds)

Crop Year	Fresh Citrus Fruit					Apples	Bananas	Fresh Deciduous Fruits					All Deciduous	All fresh fruits[3]
	Tang. & oranges	Lemons	Grapefruit	Limes	Total[2] citrus			Grapes	Peaches	Pears	Strawberries	Eight other fruits		
1955	27.5	3.5	10.7	.2	41.9	20.0	19.5	5.0	6.1	3.4	1.2	4.8	60.0	101.9
1956	24.5	3.1	10.5	.2	38.3	38.3	18.9	4.7	9.0	3.8	1.5	4.1	80.3	99.5
1957														
1958														
1959														
1960	20.5	2.9	10.0	.12	33.7	18.3	20.5	3.9	9.5	2.6	1.3	3.6	59.7	93.4
1961	17.9	2.8	9.8	.12	30.8	16.4	20.0	3.5	9.7	2.6	1.6	3.9	57.7	88.6
1962	17.2	2.8	9.0	.11	29.5	17.4	16.4	4.0	8.1	2.6	1.6	3.8	53.9	83.4
1963	13.8	2.5	6.4	.13	22.1	16.7	16.7	4.0	7.6	2.0	1.6	3.8	52.4	74.5
1964	15.7	2.6	7.5	.12	26.2	17.9	16.9	3.6	6.0	2.4	1.7	4.1	52.6	78.8
1965	17.9	2.4	8.3	.14	29.1	16.3	17.9	3.9	6.8	1.8	1.8	4.0	52.0	81.1
1966	17.8	2.3	8.4	.12	29.1	16.1	18.3	3.8	6.2	2.4	1.4	4.1	52.3	81.5
1967	19.6	2.3	9.0	.10	31.6	16.2	18.3	3.1	4.9	1.8	1.5	3.7	49.5	81.0
1968	15.3	2.2	8.0	.14	26.2	15.7	18.5	3.4	6.6	2.0	1.8	4.0	52.0	78.2
1969	17.6	2.1	7.8	.15	28.2	14.9	17.9	3.1	6.8	2.3	1.7	3.6	50.3	78.7
1970	17.5	2.1	8.2	.17	28.6	18.3	17.6	2.5	5.7	2.1	1.8	4.7	52.7	81.7
1971	17.5	2.2	8.6	.16	29.2	16.2	18.2	2.1	5.7	2.3	1.9	4.3	50.7	72.1
1972	15.9	1.8	8.6	.19	27.2	17.4	18.1	1.8	4.1	2.4	1.7	4.3	49.8	77.0
1973	16.0	1.9	8.6	.19	27.3	14.5	18.4	2.1	4.4	2.5	1.6	4.9	48.4	75.6
1974	16.1	2.0	8.3	.19	27.3	15.9	18.7	2.3	4.3	2.3	1.8	5.7	51.0	78.4
1975	18.1	2.0	8.5	.24	29.8	17.9	19.8	3.3	5.1	2.8	1.8	5.2	55.9	85.7
1976[1]	16.8	1.8	9.3	.25	29.2	17.0	21.6	3.2	5.2	2.7	1.7	5.7	57.1	86.3

[1] 1976 preliminary figures
[2] Total citrus includes tangelos
[3] All fresh fruit includes nectarines, apricots, avocados, cherries, cranberries, figs, pineapples, plums & papayas

Case 4-2—Gordon Textile Company

ADVERTISING POLICY FOR CHEESECLOTH

The executives of the Gordon Textile Company were engaged in a review of their advertising and sales promotion program. The Gordon

Company produces and distributes cheesecloth and similar textiles. One of their principle goals was to expand sales of cheesecloth in packaged form which they were selling under the Gordon brand. This was a somewhat unusual step since other companies in the industry sold cheesecloth by the yard, unbranded. Cheesecloth is a highly competitive commodity, carrying a relatively low gross margin.

In the meeting the executives were not able to agree on whether the company should direct the sales promotion activities to consumers or to the trade-wholesalers, retailers, and chain organizations.

The Gordon Company employs 14 salesmen who solicit orders for its products from both wholesalers and retailers. It also employs seven missionary salesmen to cooperate with the wholesalers' salesmen in introducing packaged cheesecloth in localities where the potential volume of sales is considered sufficient to warrant such an expenditure.

In addition to these forms of sales promotion, the Gordon Company has been spending from $20,000 to $30,000 each year in direct mail and business publications advertising to the trade.

The Gordon Company had, with one exception, done no consumer brand advertising. This exception was a type of test effort in cooperation with a department store. The Cobden Department Store, in a Midwestern city, had been persuaded to put in a special display for one week of Gordon Branch cheesecloth in handy-sized packages. Gordon ran a half-page advertisement in a local paper on Sunday; the department store displayed Gordon cheesecloth on two counters during the following week. This promotion was considered an outstanding success. The Cobden store sold over 20,000 yards of cheesecloth, which was 50% of its previous year's sales of this product.

The Gordon Co. management could not agree on the proper interpretation of these results. They were not sure, for example, how much of the success of this promotion could be attributed to the advertising and how much should be credited to the effectiveness of the store displays.

The sales promotion manager came out strongly in favor of an expanded use of brand advertising. He said he believed that building customer preference for the Gordon brand by advertising would be the best and quickest way of increasing company sales and profits. He proposed a broader and more expensive test of the power of advertising. In his plan the s. p. manager recommended keeping a budget of $30,000 for direct mail and business publication advertising to the trade and appropriating an additional $100,000 for what he called a "thorough" test of consumer brand advertising.

He proposed to develop brand sales by suggesting to housewives new uses for it. By educating consumers to regard cheesecloth as a household necessity, he hoped to induce druggists and hardware dealers to carry packaged cheesecloth. The convenience of the handy-sized packages could be expected to remove most of their objections to carrying it in bulk. The sales promotion manager planned to conduct this campaign for nine months, commencing with intensive advertising in the spring, decreasing it during the summer months, and finishing the campaign with increasing amounts in the fall.

The sales manager was convinced that company funds might be used to better advantage in soliciting orders directly from retailers by means of additional missionary salesmen or by means of additional direct-mail advertising. The Gordon Company already had 300 retail and 100 wholesale accounts; the sales manager advocated undertaking to increase sales to those accounts by educating the retailers to the new uses for cheesecloth and to the value of advantageous display, and by furnishing dealer helps to retailers and wholesalers.

The general consensus of the meeting was not to appropriate funds for the campaign of consumer advertising and for the present, to concentrate on advertising in trade papers, on missionary sales work, and on dealer helps, with the aim of improving relations with dry goods wholesalers and retailers.

The company also introduced a package containing three "handicloths," each a yard in length. It was expected that hardware stores, drug stores, and automotive equipment stores would be more willing to carry packages of this size than those of the larger sizes.

The following is a condensed statement of last year's operations:

Net sales	100%	$2,400,000
Cost of goods sold	80	1,920,000
Gross margin	20	480,000
Adm. & marketing Exp.		50,000
Per. selling Exp.		320,000
Adv.		30,000
Net profit	4%	$ 80,000

QUESTIONS FOR DISCUSSION

1. Assess the opportunity for advertising in the promotional program of The Gordon Company.
2. Do you think branding of the packaged product by Gordon requires a consumer advertising program?
3. What relative value would you place on direct mail and business publication advertising versus consumer advertising for the new packaged cheesecloth?

Case 4-3—Coastal Fisheries, Inc. (A)

Coastal Fisheries, located in the state of Washington, is one of the nation's leading producers of tuna fish for human consumption. Annual sales for the tuna industry are in the vicinity of 850 million dollars. Coastal Fisheries has 10 percent of the market. Sales are made to food chains, food cooperatives, and grocery wholesalers through a national organization of ninety-three food brokers.

In an effort to expand sales and utilize more fully available production and marketing resources, the company decided to enter the cat-food business. Most cat foods have some type of fish base, and tuna cat food had been placed on the market in the late 1950's. Since a tuna cat food could be made with that part of the fish which was not desirable for a quality tuna packed for human consumption, the company could make a profitable use of tuna which, heretofore, had been discarded at low prices. Since cat food is sold primarily through grocery outlets, the company's present marketing and distribution facilities could be used for the introduction and sale of the new product without undue expansion. The apparent ideal nature of the circumstances indicated strongly the opportunities for success in the proposed venture, and company management authorized the vice-president in charge of marketing to study the cat-food industry completely. The scope of his investigation included a study of the type of product which Coastal Fisheries should develop, a brand name, package, and recommendations for an advertising and promotion plan to gain distribution and consumer acceptance.

THE MARKET FOR CANNED CAT FOOD

During the 1970's, the market for canned cat food demonstrated a strong and consistent growth trend. As noted in Exhibit 4-4, from 1976 through 1979 sales of canned cat food increased by approximately 9 percent annually. The 1979 market at retail was estimated at $560.0 million. A conservative projection would place the 1980 retail market at $610 million.

This growing market evolves from the fact that approximately one out of eight of the nation's families owns a cat. As some 14 million families own over 23 million cats, the average cat-owning family possesses "1.6" cats.

Exhibit 4-4   Sales for Selected Pet Products

Year	Canned Dog Food Retail Sales (millions)	Percent Change	Index	Canned Cat Food Retail Sales (millions)	Percent Change	Index
1972	$520	—	100	$330	—	100
1973	$594	+14.2	114	$377	+14.2	114
1974	$637	+07.2	123	$437	+15.9	132
1975	$642	+00.8	123	$466	+06.6	141
1976	$546	−15.0	105	$463	−06.4	140
1977	$703	+28.6	135	$505	+09.1	153
1978	$685	−02.6	132	$509	+07.9	154
1979	$725	+05.8	139	$560	+10.0	170

SOURCE: *Advertising Age*, 1972-79, John C. Maxwell, Jr.

CAT FOOD PRODUCTS

During the course of his investigations, the vice-president of marketing learned that prepared cat foods are available in a variety of forms. Moist cat foods, which constitute the smallest segment of the market, generally consist of meal- or cereal-based products. They are frequently sold in kibbled or small biscuit form. The major part of the market consists of the wet or canned cat foods. In this segment of the market, the leading products are those which consist of formulated products with an all-nutrient composition. These are composed either of a fish or meat base in combination with ground corn, soybean oil meal, wheat, barley, salt, and a vitamin-E supplement. The fish-base products are used more frequently than those with a meat base. Some products combine both the fish and meat base with the cereal supplements in their formulation.

During the late 1950's, a number of producers introduced all-tuna-fish cat food supplemented with vitamin E. This high-protein food is more expensive than the formulated mixtures but is highly preferred by the cats. The common variety of tuna-fish cat food, unfortunately does not offer a well-rounded and adequate diet for the cat. Because of this, as well as the high cost of the tuna product compared to formulated cat foods, tuna is not used in an important manner as part of the cat's sustaining diet. Many cat owners feed tuna to their pets as a supplement to their normal diet or as a treat. Veterinarians are of the opinion that an all-tuna diet, even when fortified with vitamin E, will not provide adequate nutrition and can lead to illness.

As noted below, there is a substantial difference between the cost per ounce of the popular fish or meat, meal-base products, and that of the all-tuna foods. Based upon this information, it is apparent that the cost of tuna cat food is at least double that of the larger-selling fish-and-base products for the same quantity of food. Puss'n Boots, for example, costs the consumer 2.4 cents per ounce compared to 6.2 cents per ounce for Nine Lives tuna cat food. (Exhibit 4-5).

Exhibit 4-5   Market Share and Price, 1979

Brand Name	Market Share Canned Food	Can Size (ounce)	Retail Price (cents)	Cost Per Ounce
Puss 'N Boots	.04	15	36	2.4
9 Lives	.28	6	37	6.2
Friskies	.21	6½	38	5.8
Tabby	.02	6½	37	5.7
Bright Eyes	.03	13	50	3.8
Purina	.07	6	37	6.2
Kal Kan	.13	6½	31	4.8
Bonnie	.02	6	33	5.5

SURVEY OF PET OWNERS

During the late 1970's several studies were done concerning pets and their owners. Although the data could not be projected rationally, they did present some interesting points.

The survey included questions on various characteristics of the households in order to determine patterns of cat and dog ownership. The following characteristics pertained to the interviewees:[1]

1) Most (62.9%) owned their own homes and 37.1% lived in rented homes.

2) The occupation of the head of each household was ascertained as follows: not employed, 33.5%; professional-technical, 17.7%; managerial, 8%; clerical-sales, 9.4%; skilled worker, 13.5%; semiskilled worker, 5.1%; unskilled worker, 2.7%; service 3.5%; and farmer, 6.6%.

3) There were 32.9% males and 67.1% females.

4) The ages of heads of households, grouped by decades and expressed as percentages, were: 18 to 29 years, 27.9%; 30 to 39 years, 19.0%; 40 to 49 years, 17.8%; 50 to 59 years, 14.5%; 60 to 69 years, 10.1%; and 70 to 93 years, 10.6%. The mean age was 43.4 years, and the median was 40.7 (standard error, 0.735; standard deviation, 17.599).

5) Total family income, grouped in $5,000 increments and expressed by percentage of households, was as follows: < $5,000, 33.5%; $5,000 to $9,999, 24.3%; $10,000 to $14,999, 20.4%; $15,000 to $19,999, 11.5%; $20,000 to $24,999, 4.7%; and ≥ $25,000, 5.8%. The mean income was about $10,000, the median was slightly less.

6) Number of children < 18 years of age in household, by percentage of households, was: none, 56.5%; one, 12.1%; two, 17.6%; three, 10.1%; four, 2.3%; five, 0.8%; and six, 0.5%. The mean number of children < 18 years old per household was 0.94, and the median was 0.38 (standard error, 0.052; standard deviation, 1.270).

7) Number of children < 12 years of age in household, by percentage of households, was: none, 67.1%; one, 13.8%; two, 13.3%; three, 5.3%; four, 0.3%; and five, 0.2%. The mean number of children < 12 years old per household was 0.58, and the median was 0.24 (standard error, 0.039; standard deviation, 0.950).

ADVERTISING AND PROMOTION OF CAT FOOD

At the time of the planned introduction of Coastal's new product, a multitude of new brands of cat food were being introduced to the market. Numerous fish canners found that with little effort they could use waste products for the production of a cat food. Very few of these producers, however, had the facilities or ability to advertise and promote their products adequately. Although there were virtually hundreds of brands on the market, only two received any significant degree of advertising support.

With respect to brand share of market, surveys conducted by John C. Maxwell, Lehman Brothers, and Kuhn Loeb Research show that 9-Lives, a tuna and meat formula product by Heinz, was undoubtedly the leader in the field with a market share in the vicinity of 30 percent. Friskies, held second place with an approximate market share of 21 percent. Kal Kan produced by Mars Inc. had a market share in the vicinity of 13 percent. The predominant quantity of cat food purchased undoubtedly was of the canned variety, with two brands enjoying the major share of the market.

THE DEVELOPMENT OF COASTAL'S PRODUCT

The information reviewed here was presented to the company's board of directors by the vice-president in charge of marketing, accompanied with a firm recommendation that Coastal enter the cat food business. The company accepted his recommendation and decided to develop a cat food that was adequately supplied with vitamins and other nutritional supplements so that it could serve as a complete cat diet and not merely as a supplementary treat. Company management believed that this type of product would not only give Coastal a competitive advantage over other manufacturers of tuna cat food, but it would also expand the product's potential sales since it was designed for use as the sole source of nourishment for the cat and not merely as a supplementary "dessert."

Company chemists developed a product made of red tuna and adequately supplemented with thiamine, riboflavin, pantothenic acid, and vitamins A and E. The new product was named Hep Cat. In order to cut down on the offensive fishy smell of this new type of product and increase palatability, a smokey flavor was added. The product is bite size and chunky, not pasty, and is uniform in appearance and quality from can to can. Hep Cat was priced to sell at retail for 5.6 cents per ounce.

QUESTIONS FOR DISCUSSION

1. Appraise the marketing opportunity for a new cat food and the advertising opportunity for the Hep Cat product.
2. Is Coastal Fisheries in a position to support an effective advertising program for Hep Cat in light of the competitive situation?
3. Is there a sufficient market for Hep Cat food?

ENDNOTES

1. *Journal of American Veterinary Medicine Association*, September 1977, p. 1334.

Case 4-4—The Johnson Baking Company

The Johnson Baking Company is one of the top five bakers of cakes and breads in the country. The distribution for the company covers the area east of the Rockies. In this area Johnson plays a dominating marketing role. The company has combined high-quality products and an extensive use of advertising to build and maintain its position in the industry.

INTRODUCTION OF FROZEN DONUTS

Executives of the Johnson company had long been of the opinion that a satisfactory market existed for a frozen donut of superior quality. Towards the end of 1979 Johnson introduced Homaid, a quick-frozen donut, in the Allentown, Pennsylvania, market for testing purposes. Homaid was an exclusive product, since there was no other like it on the market. The donuts were frozen and packed in foil heating bags so that they could be served hot after a brief warming period. For a flavorful extra treat, the purchaser could add sugar and optional spices to the foil heating bag and shake it up. This operation afforded the purchasers the opportunity of adding their own creative touches to the product. Homaid donuts could be served with milk, coffee, or hot chocolate, as well as with sundry dessert sauces and foods.

The introduction of Homaid to Allentown was planned as a test market operation to obtain data which would serve as a guide for the expansion of the distribution of the product to other areas. The product was backed by a heavy schedule of radio and newspaper advertising and received excellent distribution in a very short period of time.

At the time of Homaid's introduction, Johnson's management learned that their leading competitor was prepared to introduce a similar product nationally without the benefit of test marketing. Johnson's executives were convinced that it was desirable to be first in the market with this product because of the publicity value involved. They believed that the second brand to enter the market would have to spend more on advertising and would not get the same recognition and sales results as the first brand. Accordingly, they were anxious to get their product on the market before their competitor did.

MARKET RESEARCH PROGRAM

It was decided that market research should be used to measure the level of consumer awareness and acceptance of and attitudes towards Homaid. Of particular concern to company management was some measure of the effectiveness of the advertising campaign in inducing trial and repeat purchase of the product. The research was conducted after 4 weeks of advertising. This period of time was deemed adequate for a perishable convenience good with a short repeat-purchase cycle. A survey was used in which respondents were selected at random from the Allentown telephone book. The belief was that a sample drawn from the telephone directory would be reasonably representative of the market. Any sample bias introduced because there are some households that do not subscribe to telephone service would be unimportant, because Homaid was a premium-priced product which would probably not appeal to low-income households without telephones. Since the food "purchasing agent" for the household is the housewife, only female heads of household were accepted as qualified respondents in the survey.

RESEARCH RESULTS

At the end of the first 4 weeks after Homaid donuts were introduced, the situation in Allentown was as follows:

1. Of all housewives 48 percent had heard of Homaid. The level of awareness was somewhat high in larger households—those with more children—than it was in the smaller households.
2. Of all housewives 15 percent had purchased Homaid. About one-third as many housewives had purchased Homaid in the past month as had purchased any type of donut. The level of trial was somewhat higher in larger households.
3. Over *one-third* of all purchasers (38 percent) had *repurchased* Homaid. These repurchasers averaged 3.25 purchases each. In households where the initial Homaid purchase was made 3 weeks before the time of the interview, 45 percent had repurchased, and this average repurchaser purchased Homaid 3.4 times.
4. Very few non-purchasers could give a reason for not purchasing. Only 6 percent of the non-purchasers mentioned Homaid itself as a reason for not purchasing: 4 percent said "too expensive" and 2 percent said "too much bother."
5. Slightly over half of all non-repeat purchasers (56 percent) could give a reason for not repurchasing Homaid. The physical qualities of Homaid were most frequently mentioned as the reason for not repurchasing.
6. Housewives are not particularly aware of the Homaid price—only 34 percent could recall the correct price. Four of every 17 who recalled the correct price felt that the Homaid price was "too high."
7. Among all purchasers favorable comments about Homaid outweighed unfavorable comments by a ratio of two to one. "Tastes like home made," "flavor-taste is good," and "crisp outside-soft inside" were the most frequently mentioned favorable comments. "Too expensive" and "get hard after heating" were the most frequently mentioned negatives.
8. There are no serious product negatives connected with Homaid. While all features—taste, texture, appearance and size—are favorably received by consumers, it seems that taste is the most favorable and appearance is the least favorable.

QUESTIONS FOR DISCUSSION

1. Would you recommend that Johnson Baking Company introduce Homaid Donuts throughout their entire market?
2. State the conclusions which you believe should be drawn from the market research conducted by Johnson Baking.
3. How do you view Johnson Baking's theory about the relationship between the first brand and second brand on the market with respect to the advertising for those brands?

Case 4-5—The Atlas Tool Company

The Atlas Company of Newark, New Jersey manufactured a large and varied line of pneumatic tools and air appliances such as air drills and hammers for rock drilling and clay digging. The principal markets for its products were among operators of ore and coal mines.

The advantages which the company claimed for its products over competing products were higher cutting speed, greater ease in holding, less vibration (therefore greater productivity and less fatigue to the operator) and lower repair expenses because of the rugged construction of the machines even though they were of light weight.

Advertising played a relatively small part in the company's selling program. The sales manager believed that the function of the company's advertising should be similar to that of general publicity, namely, to keep the name of the company and its products before mine-operating officials such as superintendents, foremen, purchasing agents. The actual selling was accomplished by company salesmen in competitive demonstrations. No middlemen were used.

The Atlas Company management decided to expand its product line. In addition to its line of mining tools, it started to manufacture demolition tools such as paving and concrete breakers, clay diggers, and rock drills for excavating work. From a production point of view, this was not different, since, with a few changes in design, tools of this type could be adapted from the original line of mining tools. The markets for these products, however, were entirely different from the original line of products. The new tools which the company believed would be most successful were a type of rock drill especially suited to rock-quarry work and excavating work for new construction, and a pneumatic paving breaker for use in tearing up old pavements. These would be sold to operators of rock quarries, construction companies, road builders and municipalities which did some or all of their own street and sidewalk maintenance and repair work.

After successful trials with the tools of the new line among road builders and construction contractors, the company started to develop a national market for these tools. The company chose selected contractors' supply firms and dealers in contractors' tools and machinery as channels of distribution.

The company encountered certain advertising problems with its new line. In entering the new field, the company had to develop its distribution system. This was a problem since it was now competing with companies which were well-established in making and distributing tools of this type. In competitive tests, however, the company had demonstrated to its own satisfaction that its tools could accomplish more work in a given time, with less fatigue to operators and with less repair costs, than could any competing tool. The price was approximately the same as competitors' prices for tools of similar standard.

In their marketing and promotion program, company management decided to put a considerably heavier reliance upon advertising in the sale of the new product than in its other products. A budget was allocated which represented an expenditure more than double the size of that which the company had ever used for the products sold to the mining market. There was a strong opposition to this decision from several members of the management group who believed that this increased expenditure was not justified. Their opposition could be summed up as follows: "We have never found it necessary to throw money like this into advertising. Why should we begin now?"

QUESTIONS FOR DISCUSSION

1. How would you answer the question raised by the Atlas Tool executive who remarked, "We have never found it necessary to throw money like this into advertising. Why should we begin now?"
2. What is the relative role for advertising versus other marketing functions in the marketing program for a product such as that developed by Atlas?
3. Compare the markets in terms of size and other characteristics in the traditional Atlas marketing program with that suggested in the new program.

Case 4-6—Morton Salt[1]

George Tate strolled down Michigan Avenue on a warm spring afternoon in Chicago. He had spent the entire morning with Morton Salt's advertising agency, reviewing the company's past promotions and discussing possible plans for the upcoming fiscal year, which would begin on July 1st. As he walked, he pondered the problems facing the company, particularly with regard to table salt, traditionally Morton Salt's major product.

WHEN IT RAINS, IT POURS

In the early part of the 20th Century, consumers bought salt in brown paper bags, which had been put up by a grocer from bulk salt he had purchased in barrels. The salt business was keenly competitive, and no firm had been able to gain significant consumer demand or a price advantage. Morton's product was exactly like that of its competition.

If Morton Salt could be differentiated in some way, however, they could improve consumer demand, and thus improve profit margins. By 1920, they developed an innovative way to keep salt from caking or hardening from moisture, and introduced a moisture-proof, two pound cylindrical package with an aluminum spout for easier pouring. With these improvements, Morton embarked upon a modest advertising program, utilizing primarily women's magazines. "When It Rains, It Pours" was adopted as a slogan for the advertisement, and was also printed on the package (see Figure 4-1).

The idea of branding and advertising was a new one in the salt market, but it seemed to work as Morton's sales and market share grew. With this increased degree of control over consumer demand, Morton began to gradually increase prices until their packaged salt sold for double that of any competitor (10¢ per package, compared to 5¢ for unbranded bags).

NO SALT SALTS LIKE MORTON SALT SALTS

Since Morton's product and package improvements were unprotected by patents, competitors were quick to imitate. As a result, some consumer resistance to the price differential began to affect Morton Salt sales. At this point, therefore, Morton needed another innovation.

Because of its leadership in the salt industry, Morton was approached by health authorities and medical organizations who had discovered that an insufficient amount of iodine in the body was a cause of goiter (an enlargement of the thyroid gland, often visible as a swelling in the lower part of the front of the neck). Since salt was a universally used food product, these authorities suggested that Morton take the lead in adding iodine to their sale, in a ratio of 1 part iodine to 5,000 parts salt, for goiter prevention.

Iodized salt was introduced in the early 1920s with advertising support, and by 1926 Morton's iodized salt was outselling plain salt. It was able to continue its market leadership and brand preference for many years, maintaining a premium price.

However, in the early 1960s Morton saw its sales and market share slipping again as competitors had matched product innovations, and had engaged in price-cutting tactics. In addition, consumer lifestyles had changed to produce a declining demand for salt. More people were eating away from home, and more prepared, presalted foods were being consumed at home.

Morton expanded its advertising to focus on the 30 to 40 age group (then found to consume 75 percent of all salt sold), and reemphasize the company's early innovations in the salt market. Magazines, television, and radio carried the message "No Salt Salts Like Morton Salt Salts" to this target audience. In 1968 Morton was able to enjoy the largest market share of any year in the decade.

THE NEXT BEST THING TO THE REAL THING

By the late 1960s, Morton had also expanded its product offerings beyond table salt. Company divisions had been established to produce prepared foods, chemicals, and agricultural goods, partially as a result of their 1969 merger with Norwich Pharmacal Company.

Future growth depended upon properly defining the firm's business position. As consumers had changed, Morton was no longer just in the "salt business," it was in the "seasonings business."

In 1970 after extensive product and market research, Morton introduced a new consumer product, Salt Substitute. Morton Salt Substitute was initially available in two varieties, regular and seasoned. It was composed of potassium chloride, and had already been in limited use by people on medically supervised, low sodium diets.

The introduction of Salt Substitute as a consumer product was supported by a $242,000 advertising campaign which emphasized taste rather than the product's medical uses. "The Next Best Thing to the Real Thing" was chosen as the slogan, and appeared in magazine and newspaper advertisements. Further, a 10¢-off coupon was featured to stimulate trial purchase of the innovative product. By the end of the decade, Morton's sales achieved higher levels than all other salt brands combined.

MORTON, THE SALT YOU'VE BEEN PASSING FOR GENERATIONS

The decade of the 1970's brought increasing attention and concern among Americans about the potential relationship between the use of salt and certain diseases. Medical researchers observed that when certain patients suffering from hypertension or high blood pressure were fed a diet severely restricted in sodium, their blood pressure decreased. Few researchers were willing to state categorically that sodium *caused* hypertension, but some troubling questions were posed.

Several years later, the U.S. Senate Select Committee on Nutrition and Human Needs responded to concerns about salt usage by including it in a set of Dietary Goals for the United States. One of the stated goals was that salt consumption be reduced to approximately five grams per day from the average of ten or twelve grams normally ingested. Such a goal might be achieved, some suggested, by eliminating most highly salted processed foods and condiments, and by eliminating salt added at the table.

Health concerns about salt intake did not escape Morton management, and in 1973 (well ahead of the U.S. Senate Committee recommendations) Morton Lite Salt was introduced to consumers. Lite Salt was the first iodized salt mixture with the taste of regular salt, but with only half the sodium. Unlike Salt Substitute which was not positioned directly against regular salt, Lite Salt was expected to cannibalize Morton's regular salt to some extent. This was not a major concern to Morton management, however, since Lite was seen as "the salt of the future."[2] A $1 million advertising campaign, largely in television, accompanied the roll-out of Lite Salt.

During the 1970's Morton tested several other new seasoning products including Butter Buds, Sugar Cure, Tender Quick, and Nature's

Seasons. Some of these products were reasonably successful and remained on the market, while others were withdrawn due to insufficient sales.

To supplement Morton's fluctuating advertising budgets during this period (see Tables 4-1, 4-2, and 4-3), several sales promotion programs were employed. The first attempt was a set of four porcelain mugs offered for $2 plus a spout seal from a 26 oz. table salt package. Each mug featured a different Morton girl from the four periods of the company's history (see Figure 4-2).

In 1975, another sales promotion program was developed to provide additional uses for salt. Morton introduced salt sculpture (a mixture of flour, water, and salt) for holiday decorations (see Figure 4-3). Film strips were offered to elementary schools, and a ten minute film was sent to television stations, explaining salt sculpture. Print advertising in women's magazines offered Morton's "Dough It Yourself" Handbook for $1.

The promotions for salt sculpture ran during the Christmas season, and were continued during Easter and July 4th for two years. By 1977, company executives estimated that 700,000 "Dough It Yourself" Handbooks had been sold, and distribution was expanded to craft stores as well.

Despite a series of successful consumer and trade promotions, 26 oz. table salt could not sustain the company. "It's a strong cash producer," commented Morton's president in 1977, "but not a growth market."[3] At the same time, management recognized that table salt could not be abandoned completely for although it represented only five percent of tonnage sales, it produced at least thirty-five percent of dollar sales.

Therefore, it was decided in 1977 to continue the sales promotion for Morton 26 oz. table salt. To capitalize on Americans' increased interest in genealogy, Morton sponsored a "Visit the Land of Your Ancestors" Sweepstakes. Also featured were mailed kits which contained recipes from the homelands of Americans of current and past generations. The sweepstakes was tied in with the advertising theme, "Morton, the salt you've been passing for generations" (see Figure 4-4). Morton table salt maintained its number one position among table salts in 1977 with an all time high market share.

A third promotion (in addition to the salt sculpture and sweepstakes promotions) was begun in 1978. Special salt packages with labels from four past container designs (1914, 1921, 1933, and 1941) were featured in retail stores. Consumers were urged through media advertising to collect the entire "Keepsake Collection" (see Figure 4-5). These innovations in sales promotion were another solution to the perennial problem of maintaining brand preference for a parity product.

SUMMARY

As George Tate opened his office door, marked Director of Communications, he realized that some important decisions now faced

Table 4-1   Morton Salt

BLUE PACKAGE
MEDIA HISTORY

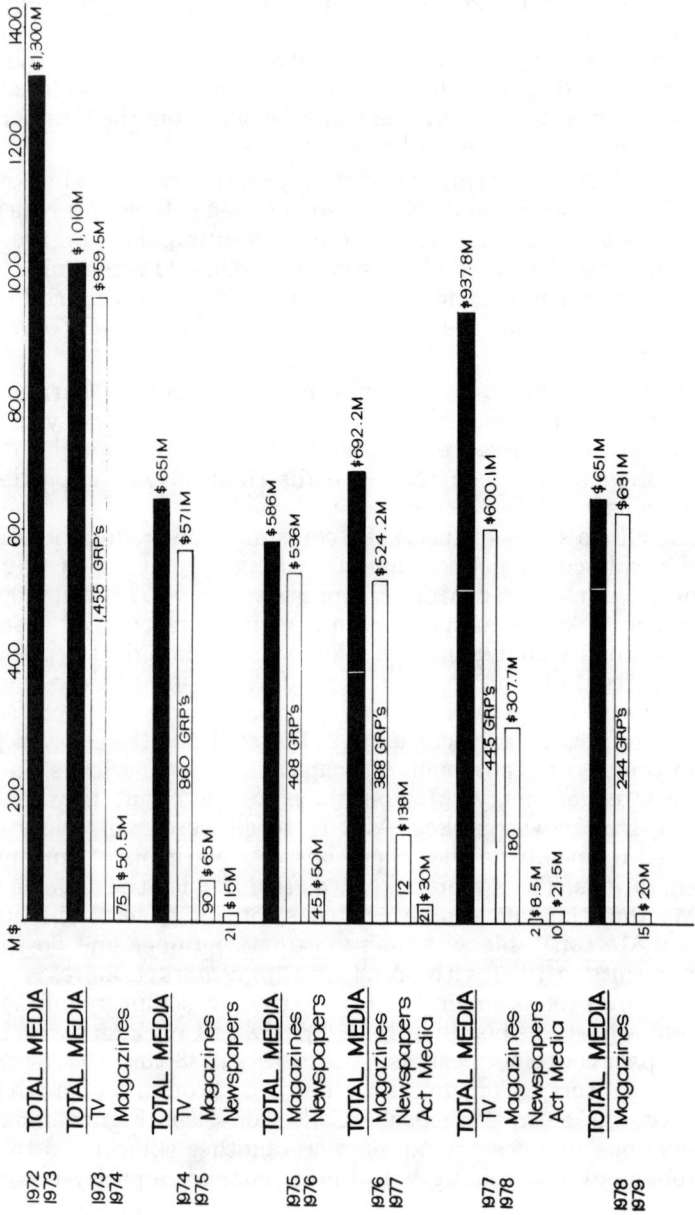

Year	Category	Value
1972 / 1973	TOTAL MEDIA	$1,300M
1973 / 1974	TOTAL MEDIA	$1,010M
	TV	1,455 GRP's — $959.5M
	Magazines	75 — $50.5M
1974 / 1975	TOTAL MEDIA	$651M
	TV	860 GRP's — $571M
	Magazines	90 — $65M
	Newspapers	21 — $15M
1975 / 1976	TOTAL MEDIA	$586M
	Magazines	408 GRP's — $536M
	Newspapers	45 — $50M
1976 / 1977	TOTAL MEDIA	$692.2M
	Magazines	388 GRP's — $524.2M
	Newspapers	12 — $138M
	Act Media	21 — $30M
1977 / 1978	TOTAL MEDIA	$937.8M
	TV	445 GRP's — $600.1M
	Magazines	180 — $307.7M
	Newspapers	2 — $8.5M
	Act Media	10 — $21.5M
1978 / 1979	TOTAL MEDIA	$651M
	Magazines	244 GRP's — $631M
		15 — $20M

M$ 200   400   600   800   1000   1200   1400

Table 4-2   Morton Salt

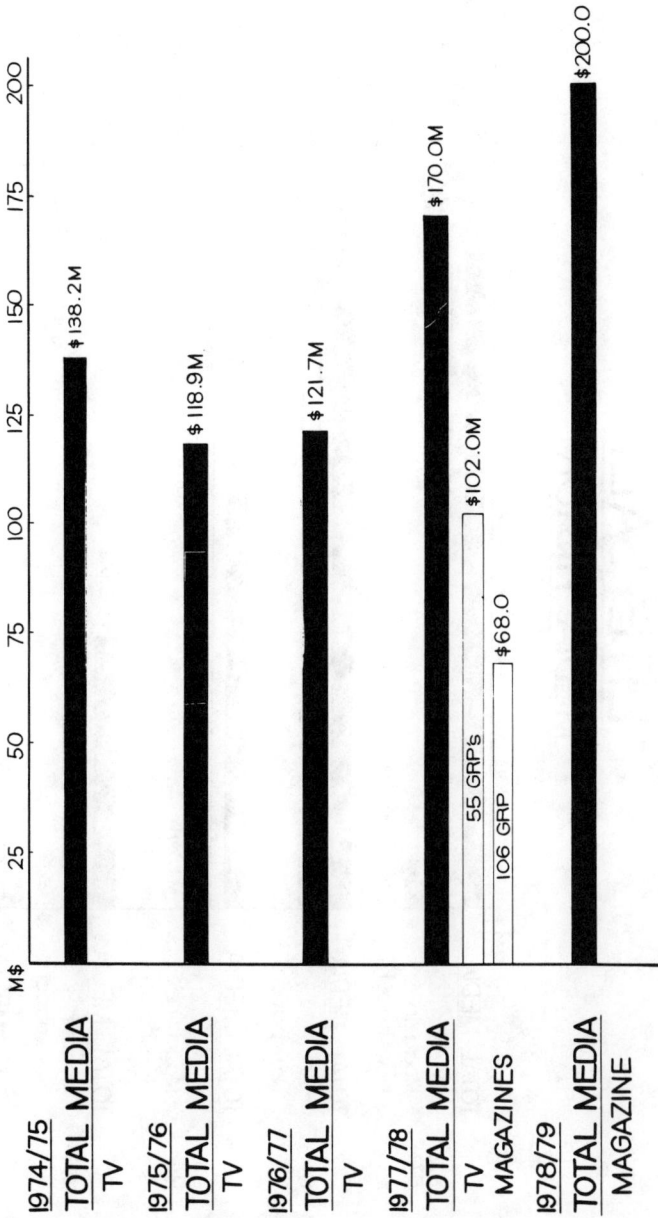

SALT SUBSTITUTE
MEDIA HISTORY

M$

1974/75
TOTAL MEDIA
TV — $138.2M

1975/76
TOTAL MEDIA
TV — $118.9M

1976/77
TOTAL MEDIA
TV — $121.7M

1977/78
TOTAL MEDIA
TV — $170.0M
55 GRP's — $102.0M
106 GRP — $68.0

1978/79
TOTAL MEDIA
MAGAZINE — $200.0

Table 4-3   Morton Salt

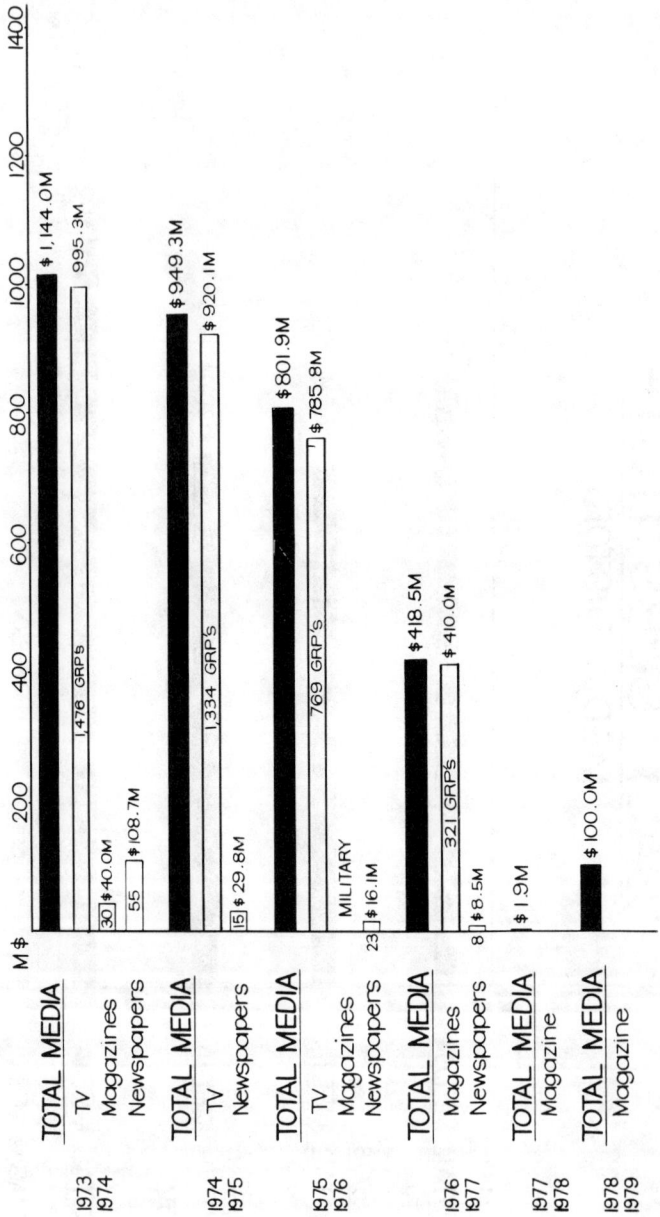

LITE SALT
MEDIA HISTORY

1973	TOTAL MEDIA	$ 1,144.0M
1974	TV	995.3M
		1,478 GRP's
	Magazines	30 $40.0M
	Newspapers	55 $108.7M
1974	TOTAL MEDIA	$ 949.3M
1975	TV	$ 920.1M
		1,334 GRP's
	Newspapers	15 $ 29.8M
1975	TOTAL MEDIA	$ 801.9M
1976	TV	$ 785.8M
		769 GRP's
	Magazines	MILITARY
	Newspapers	23 $16.1M
1976	TOTAL MEDIA	$ 418.5M
1977	Magazines	$ 410.0M
		321 GRP's
	Newspapers	8 $ 8.5M
1977	TOTAL MEDIA	$ 1.9M
1978	Magazine	
1978	TOTAL MEDIA	$ 100.0M
1979	Magazine	

M$ 200   400   600   800   1000   1200   1400

Figure 4-2   Morton Salt

A SLIGHTLY SENTIMENTAL OFFER

The Morton Girls: 1914, 1921, 1956, 1968.

They're all yours for two dollars and a spout seal.

Figure 4-3   Morton Salt

Make Yourself A Merrier Christmas.

There's nothing more priceless at Christmas than homemade gifts and ornaments. And they've never been so easy to make.

Just start by blending... 1 cup of Morton® Salt, 2 cups of flour (tap to level measure) in a bowl, adding 1 cup of water as you go. After kneading for 7-10 minutes, roll the dough ¼" thick. Then using either cookie cutters or your imagination, you're ready to create dozens of items just like the ones pictured above.

Attach any separate pieces of dough by first moistening them with water. Then bake at 325 degrees for 30 minutes or until hard. When cool, varnish to protect from moisture. (Naturally, your masterpiece should not be eaten.)

If you'd like to get fancy, send for our "Dough-It-Yourself"® Handbook. A step-by-step guide with instructions for over 60 great ideas that are not only fun for the whole family, but perfect for almost every occasion—especially Christmas.

Morton Salt Company, Division of Morton-Norwich Products, Inc., Chicago, Illinois 60606

"Dough-It-Yourself"® Handbook
P.O. Box 9067
Kankakee, Illinois 60901

I have enclosed $_____ check or money order (not responsible for cash). Please send me _____ "Dough-It-Yourself"® Handbooks at $1.00 each.

(Allow up to six weeks for delivery)

Name_____

Address_____

City_____

State_____ Zip_____

Void where taxed, restricted or prohibited.   M-N8

Figure 4-4 Morton Salt

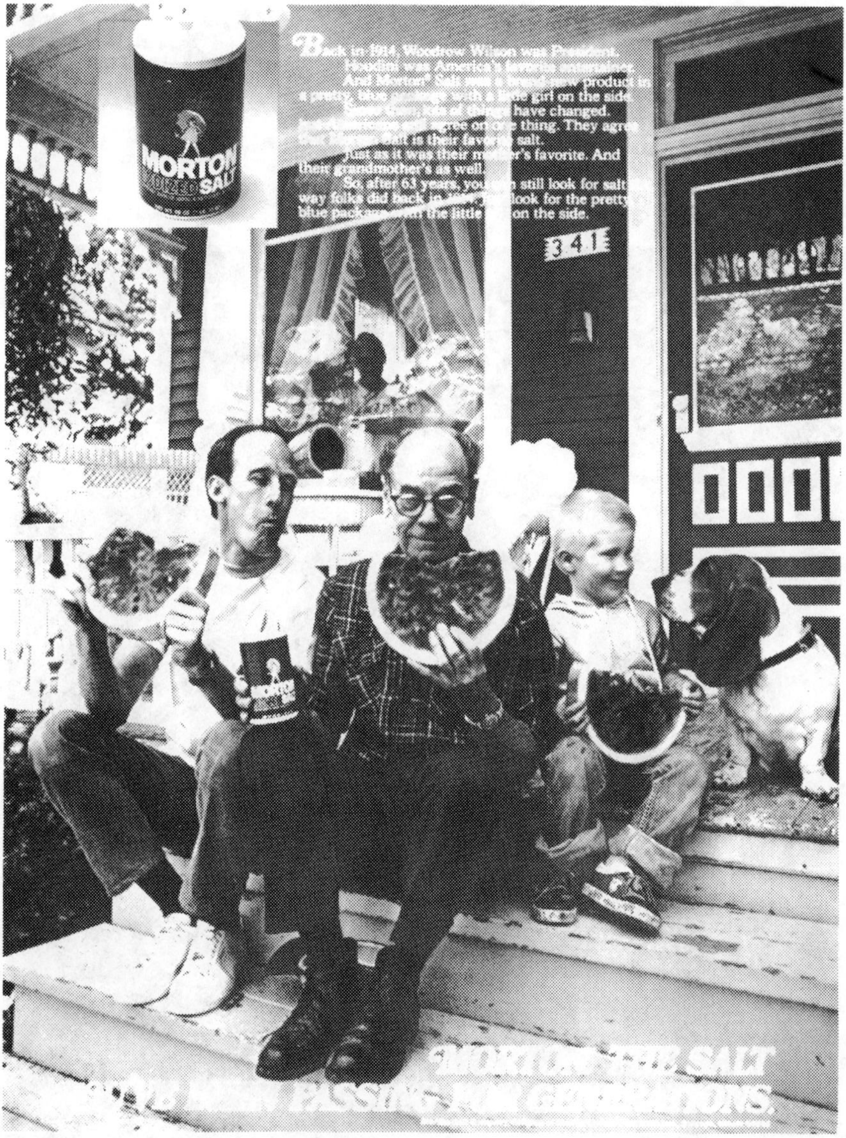

Figure 4-5   Morton Salt

1914 Woodrow Wilson had moved into the White House, and our little girl had moved into the kitchen.

1921 The twenties were roaring and Morton's little girl was pouring.

1933 Jazz was king. And as it reigned, our little girl poured.

1941 While our boys were starting off to war, our little girl was serving at home

Our little girls of yesterday are yours today.

In 1979 this Keepsake Collection of four Morton packages is available at your grocer. So now, for a limited time, you can pick up our little girls of old. And pass the salt from generations past.

MORTON. The salt you've been passing for generations.

MORTON SALT, DIVISION OF MORTON-NORWICH PRODUCTS, INC., CHICAGO, ILLINOIS 60606

Morton Salt. Salt Substitute and Lite Salt were leading the market in their respective product categories, and Nature's Seasons was growing in sales as well. Regular table salt seemed to be doing well as a result of the sales promotions, although the medical concerns of the 1970's were not expected to fade.

It seemed to Tate that innovations in product development, in packaging, and in sales promotion had always solved past problems. However, he was now concerned with an advertising innovation as a remedy.

QUESTIONS FOR DISCUSSION

1. What was the future of Morton's regular table salt—the product upon which the company was founded, and to which it owed much of its success?
2. Could consumer sales be sustained through advertising, and if so, how much should be budgeted in which media?
3. Was it wise to continue special offers, sweepstakes, and similar sales promotions?

ENDNOTES

1. This case was made possible by the cooperation of the Morton Salt Company and the author of the original Morton Salt case, Dr. Nugent Wedding. It was prepared by Nancy Stephens and Richard F. Beltramini, Assistant Professors of Marketing at Arizona State University, as a basis for class discussion rather than to illustrate either effective or ineffective handling of an administrative situation. Comments, views or conclusions stated herein are not to be construed as those of the Morton Salt Company, and the case authors are solely responsible for content.
   Morton, the Umbrella Girl design, When it rains it pours, Morton Lite Salt, Sugar Cure, Tender Quick, Nature's Seasons and Dough-It-Yourself are registered trademarks of Morton-Norwich Products, Inc.
   Copyright © 1980 by Nancy Stephens and Richard F. Beltramini.
   Distributed by the Intercollegiate Case Clearing House, Soldiers Field, Boston, Mass. 02163. All rights reserved to the contributors. Printed in the U.S.A.
2. "Morton Lite ties into 'RD' special insert," *Advertising Age*, October 29, 1973.
3. "Morton pours more ad dollars into image-building bid," *Advertising Age*, August 8, 1977.

Case 4-7—The Miramar Grocery Company[1] (Problems of Brand Management)

INTRODUCTION OF A NEW LINE OF PRODUCTS

The Miramar Company, a food processor with sales in the vicinity of $500,000,000 yearly, has developed a new line of products. These are flavored ketchups which sell under the company blanket brand. They include such flavors as Pizza, Hickory, Steak House, Onion, and Barbecue. The flavored ketchup, management believes, may be a profitable supplement to the regular tomato ketchup selling under the Miramar brand.

The problems of brand management, especially in the introduction of new brands, constitute a major business risk. Since the question of introducing a new brand or product variation is such an important decision, the Miramar Company has used a test market as a means of helping to predict the ultimate sales performance of the new products and to reduce the overall risk inherent in this innovative stage of marketing.

PREVALENCE OF BRANDS

In our present-day food stores, there are large numbers of brands competing for shelf space and consumer dollars. In a study by the A.C. Nielsen Company, 35,035 different packaged grocery items were identified as being offered for sale in a representative cross section of 100 supermarkets in the U.S.[2] Each individual supermarket, however, usually has shelf space for only about 6,000 items. These figures indicate the extremely keen competition for this scarce shelf space.

BRAND FAILURE RATES

The failure rate, or turnover, of brands in this area of business is very high and adds considerably to the costs of marketing. The failure of a brand may cost a company from $75,000 to $100,000 in a test market to ten or fifteen milllion for a national marketing failure. Several surveys over the past 20 years have set the rate of failure of new brands above 90%.

In a 1968 study, it was found that 9,450 new brands were introduced into U.S. supermarkets during the year, less than 20% of which met sales goals.[3] This rate of failure, while still excessively high and costly, indicates some decrease in the turnover rate. In another Nielson Company study of brand introduction and discontinuance, researchers found that during one year period 5543 items in the grocery field were entirely removed from the market and 7,303 new brands were added to grocers' shelves.[4]

The following serve as examples of new brands in both food and drug fields that failed to meet desired sales goals:

Food:

Campbell's Red Kettle Soups
Corn Crackos Cereal
Dynamo Liquid Laundry Detergent
Easy-Off Household Cleaner
Gablinger's Beer
Heinz Happy Soups
Knorr's Dry Soup Mix
Post Cereals with Freeze-Dried Fruit

Drug:

Code 10 Hair Dressing	Mighty White Toothpaste
Cope Sedative	Noxzema Medicated Cold Cream
Cue Toothpaste	007 Men's Toiletries Line
Duractin Analgesic	Revlon's Super Natural Hairspray
Fact Toothpaste	Reed Mouth Wash
Hidden Magic Hairspray	Resolve
Measurin Analgesic	Subdue Anti-Dandruff Shampoo
Manicurist Nail Polish	Vote Toothpaste

When coupled with the rather considerable costs of distribution and promotion of brands, this high mortality rate makes brand introduction a very significant business risk.

CAUSES OF BRAND FAILURES

Many factors may contribute to the success or failure of a brand in the market. In general these stem from what are considered the elements of marketing management: the qualities and characteristics of the product itself—the significance of product differentiation of superiority; the packaging; the price of the brand; the adequacy of distribution; and the advertising and promotion efforts put behind it, are among the important aspects to be considered in brand success or failure. The activities of competitors in all of these phases should be included. Many otherwise excellent plans have been scuttled by activities of aggressive competitors when management did not properly anticipate or recognize their actions in the market.

In addition, management should consider the adequacy of the potential market to which the brand appeals. In a market typified by market segmentation with a large number of brands competing for market share, continued efforts to differentiate products may result in the development of a brand the qualities of which appeal to a market segment too small to support a profitable marketing operation.

Most of these studies indicate that the single most important cause of failure of new brands is lack of significant product differentiation—significant, that is, from the consumer point of view. Marketing management, in general, is well aware of the important part which unique, distinctive product qualities play in any effort to build brand control in the market. The problems are several. In many cases the unique feature of the brand does not interest a sufficient number of consumers to permit building adequate sales volume. In other situations the advertiser is unable to communicate the unique and different qualities of the brand in an effective, convincing manner. It should also be recognized that the problem may be that the product does not measure up to advertising claims; after trying the brand, consumers are disappointed and do not repurchase it.

Menly & James introduced Duractin in late 1962. The unique feature of this product was a sustained release analgesic which, presumably, gave relief from pain for a period of eight hours. The product failed to reach sales goals because of one or more of the reasons given above. The cost of failure for the Western region only was estimated at $1,500,000.

In 1968 American Home Products Company introduced a new household cleaner called Easy-Off. The distinctive feature of this brand was an aerosol foam formulation. Consumers seemed to see little advantage to this product. American Home lost about $850,000 trying to communicate the unique and superior qualities of an aerosol foam product to a market which is dominated by liquid cleaners.

Copy strategy problems for these unsuccessful brands seem to fall into one of three areas—insignificant; confused; or mismatched. "Insignificant" means that the consumer is not interested. This, of course, is a direct reflection of insignificant product differentiation. "Confused" means the consumer doesn't understand, or is not convinced of product values. An example of confused creative strategy is the Revlon brand of hairspray called Super Natural. This brand, introduced in early 1960's lost several million dollars for Revlon. In the industry, *Super* means "more holding power;" *Natural* means "less holding power." Consumers evidently were never quite sure just what the product represented.[5]

"Mismatched" strategy means product performance doesn't match the appeal or the claims made for the product. It is likely that much of the failure of the Duractin "Eight-hour relief" story may be attributed to the inability of the product to measure up to copy promises.

MARKET TESTS

A test market may be a valuable method of gauging and minimizing potential risks in the introduction of new brands. If such a test is properly conducted using markets which are representative, with adequate controls, and is run for a sufficient length of time, it is frequently possible to predict and project future market performance with considerable accuracy. In addition, marketing management may determine the reasons behind the performance—either good or bad—of a new brand and suggest measures which may further improve and enhance market acceptance. It should be recognized that such tests are often slow, costly, and the results are not always completely reliable, particularly in the case of determining repeat sales performance. In many cases a test will not reveal all of the product problems because the unique aspects of the product are artifically highlighted in the test or the test period is too short to permit consumers to detect product shortcomings which will affect repurchase.

Part of the problem may be the inability or unwillingness of management to interpret test results properly or to accept results which may not agree with predetermined personal preferences. General Foods lost $5,000,000 several years ago in an attempt to introduce a line of Post cereals with freeze-dried fruit. The company used not one but three separate market tests of this product innovation, none of which seemed adequately to reveal product shortcomings. These cereals had a high rate of initial purchase but insufficient repeat purchases. This seemed to be principally because the dried fruit did not reconstitute fast enough and the cereal became soggy.

DECISION TO USE TEST MARKET

After an appraisal of the risk involved in attempting to introduce the new product line, Miramar Company management engaged the services and facilities of the Market Research Corporation of America for an integrated test-marketing program. This included the use of MRCA's nation-wide, consumer panel, retail sales audits, and consumer surveys covering brand awareness and attitudes.

TEST RESULTS

After running for six months, the results of the test were analyzed and certain aspects found not particularly encouraging to management. Purchase results obtained from members of the national consumer panel revealed that the "trial" rate—i.e., families buying the product for the first time—was significantly below the objective which management had established as acceptable for the brand. Store audits showed no weakness in distribution, display or shelf facings. This rate of initial purchase was viewed by some members of the management team as sufficiently discouraging to warrant dropping the test and discontinuing any further efforts to market the product. Figure 4-6 below shows a visual comparison of the rate of actual trial with company goals:

Figure 4-6   Rate of Trial

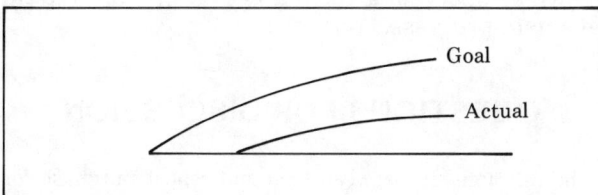

Management had also established a repeat purchase goal. Careful study of repeat sales from the panel shows a somewhat more encouraging picture than that obtained from initial purchase results. When compared to initial purchases, the percentage of families which bought the new products two or more times was approximately equal to the expectations and goals originally established by management. (See Figure 4-7 for this comparison.)

Figure 4-7 Repeat Purchases

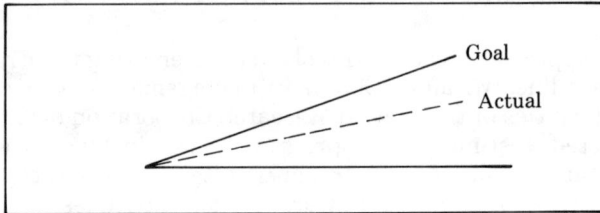

The results of consumer surveys furnished additional information on the test results, particularly in connection with factors influencing the rate of trial. These surveys showed that consumer brand awareness or brand recognition equalled company goals. There were also indications that consumer interest in flavored ketchups was relatively low. Some of the large users of ketchup are teen-agers who had relatively low interest in flavored ketchups, in general, and an active dislike, in particular, for the onion flavor.

Although the purchase price was only slightly higher than regular ketchups, consumer attitude studies suggested that some respondents considered the purchase of the product to be high and that the relatively high price may have discouraged some potential consumers from trying it.

COMPANY EVALUATION

With this information available the project director called a meeting of the committee supervising the market test to analyze the research data and evaluate progress.

QUESTIONS FOR DISCUSSION

1. What is the relationship between trial and repeat purchase for a product such as that being developed by Miramar?
2. Do you believe there is a substantial market for such a product? How do you determine this?
3. Does the current information available to Miramar executives warrant going ahead with the new product?
4. Give an overall appraisal of the opportunity for advertising for this new product.

ENDNOTES

1. Company name has been disguised.
2. From a speech by A.C. Nielsen Jr., President—to American Association of Advertising Agencies, Pittsburgh, Pa., Nov. 17, 1967.
3. See Angelus, T.L., "Why Most New Products Fail," *Marketing Insights*, May 12, 1969, p. 14.
4. From a speech by Franklin Graf, of A.C. Nielsen Co. to Grocery Manufacturer's Association, June 20, 1967.
5. Examples from Angeles, T.L. "Why Most New Products Fail," cited above.

Case 4-8—The Super Sweet Sugar Refining Company: A Marketing Program for Sugar

The executives of the Super-Sweet Sugar Refining Company were engaged in a review of their over-all marketing program.

SUPER-SWEET COMPANY LOCATION AND OPERATIONS

The Super-Sweet Company is a relatively small refining and distributing company located in Pittsburgh, Penna., a location selected in part because of the cheap transportation offered by the Ohio River. The bulk of company sales come from a 5-state area—Pennsylvania, Ohio, West Virginia, Indiana, and Kentucky.

The company produces a full line of bulk and packaged sugar for industrial and home use. About 30-35% of company output is sold to wholesalers, chain organizations, and retail grocers for use in the home. About 65-70% of company sales go to food processors, bakers, and manufacturers of such products as candy, ice cream and soft drinks.

COMPANY AND INDUSTRY PROBLEMS

The Super-Sweet Company and the entire industry are bothered by a number of problems: excess refining capacity; keen competition; inability to develop brand preferences; no control over prices; and a decline in the per capita consumption of sugar throughout the United States.

The sugar industry is over-expanded and demand is able to consume only about half of the total productive capacity of the industry in any one year. Because of the standardized, undifferentiated nature of the product, it is virtually impossible for one company to gain any degree of control over price. Any reduction in price by one refinery is met almost immediately by other companies, so that the price cut usually results in a narrower operating margin for all competitors.

The relatively low utilization of plant capacity and low prices resulted in high production costs, low efficiency and low gross margins. The cost of production for companies in the industry usually averaged well above 80% of net sales.

SUPER SWEET COMPANY PROBLEMS

The influence of these industry problems on Super Sweet is apparent by examining a typical company operating statement:

Net sales	$15,000,000	100%
Cost of gds sold	13,125,000	87.5%
Gross Margin	1,875,000	12.5%
Adm. & Mktg. Expense	1,800,000	
Net Profit	$ 75,000	.5%

A cost of production figure of 87.5%, resulting in a 12.5% gross margin leaves very little opportunity for an active, aggressive marketing program. With a narrow net profit of ½ of 1%, small declines in sales or prices may very quickly result in losses.

In another area of the marketing spectrum—Distribution—Super Sweet also faced a troublesome problem. Adequate distribution at the retail level is an essential ingredient in a successful marketing program for sugar. Super Sweet has had trouble getting and maintaining what management considered an adequate distribution system.

Keen competition at the retail level results in low prices and profit margins. Wholesale, retail, and chain grocers are usually not able to secure a mark-up sufficient to cover all costs of handling sugar. The result is that sugar is handled as a loss leader. Because of the low margins, many retail store managers would not stock sugar at all if they had a choice. Since sugar is a household staple, however, they have no option. As a result of this low interest, retailers rarely stock more than one or two brands of sugar. This situation makes it difficult for Super Sweet to compete for shelf space with the larger, better-known companies such as American, National, and C and H.

ADVERTISING AND SALES PROMOTION EFFORTS

Advertising, increased personal selling, point-of-purchase materials, and innovations in packaging were among the promotion possibilities brought up for discussion in the meeting. All of these seemed to offer some opportunity for increasing sales and retail distribution. All of them, however, had the disadvantage of involving expense.

Each additional salesman hired by the company will cost about $25,000 a year considering both salary and expenses. No estimates were given for point-of-purchase costs, but this was not considered a highly promising area. The low interest of retailers in handling sugar did not encourage its use. Expenses included design and production of suitable material and distribution and setting up all materials by company representatives. In addition, many of the larger chains are now making a charge for such promotion space in the store.

New packaging ideas were met with some skepticism by committee members. Super Sweet had, in the past, experimented in the design of special packages or cartons, but these seemed to have been most successful in marketing such low volume specialty items as powdered sugar. The experience of Super Sweet and other companies in the industry offered rather strong evidence that consumers were unwilling to pay an additional amount per pound for granulated sugar sufficient to cover the added costs of packaging.

Several of the executives present expressed interest in the possibilities which advertising offered, both in promotion of the Super Sweet brand and as a means of counteracting the decline in sugar consumption. This favorable attitude existed in spite of the fact that advertising had not played a major part in the marketing programs of suger refiners. American and National, the two largest companies in the industry, had spent relatively modest sums principally in newspaper advertising for a number of years. Their budgets had averaged between $200,000 and $400,000 per year, which was considerably less than 1% of sales. The results had not seemed to be overly impressive. It was the general opinion throughout the industry that this advertising had not succeeded in building a degree of brand preference for either company sufficiently strong to permit a control over price. It did seem, however, that brand recognition and acceptance by consumers had been helpful in gaining interest and support of wholesalers and retailers in the food field.

The sugar industry, through the Sugar Institute, had attempted to expand total consumption of sugar by an industry-wide advertising program. This effort took place during the depression years of 1930 and 1931 when the Institute spent about $400,000 each year in magazine advertising. No noticeable change in generic demand had resulted.

Near the close of the meeting one of the members of the group raised an intriguing question. He was concerned with trying to determine what might be considered the minimum requirements in a marketing program for the successful production and marketing of sugar.

The question raised a lively discussion among the members present. Unfortunately the meeting adjourned without reaching a consensus.

QUESTIONS FOR DISCUSSION

1. Analyze the problems of the sugar refining industry and Super-Sweet in particular with respect to opportunities for effective advertising programs.
2. Can Super Sweet financially support an effective advertising program?

3. What role should packaging, personal selling, point-of-purchase, and advertising play in the overall marketing program for Super Sweet?

Case 4-9—The Timken Company: (Advertising Branded Parts)

The Timken Company is one of the country's largest producers of bearings for all types of mechanical equipment. Net sales for The Timken Company in 1980 were $1,338,499,000, and sales in 1946 were $80,483,521.

This marked increase in sales volume was largely the result of a program of diversification of market during this period. In addition to tapered roller bearings, the original product of the Company, The Timken Company now produces steel products in the form of seamless tubing, bars and forgings. In addition, The Timken Company manufactures rock bits for use in mining and drilling. All of this complex output of components and materials may be classed as industrial goods; no finished products are sold to the ultimate consumer market.

PROMOTION OF COMPANY PRODUCTS

Throughout its history The Timken Company has carried on a very thorough and aggressive marketing program for its products. This includes adequate use of Company salesmen selling to Timken Company customers; an advertising program in trade and business papers to Timken's very wide potential markets; use of direct mail whenever this medium is appropriate. They also made use of exhibits, displays and demonstrations at trade shows and conventions and utilized publicity in trade journals whenever that was possible.

ADVERTISING TO ULTIMATE CONSUMERS

In spite of the concentration of Company output for the industrial goods market, and a substantial advertising and sales promotion effort for these products, The Timken Company has for many years carried on a program of advertising to the ultimate consumer market. The consumer-oriented ads, carried in such general magazines as the *Saturday Evening Post*, utilized such themes as "Keeping America on the Go—With Timken Tapered Roller Bearings."

One such full-page 4-color advertisement in the *Post*, featured a wheat field near Four Lakes, Washington. Headline: "How 2½ million fewer farmers feed 30 million more people." The copy developed the theme that mechanization has made this possible and Timken bearings have played a part by making trouble-free operation of machinery possible through reducing friction.

Another such *Saturday Evening Post* advertisement, also in four-color showed an illustration of a Southern Railroad freight car, with a trainman in the foreground holding a set of Timken roller bearings in each hand: Headline: "Now it's the Southern that's going 'Roller Freight'—with 260 new freight cars on Timken bearings." Copy messages developed the theme that ". . . freight cars rolling on Timken bearings will bring a new high in on-time deliveries for Southern's customers. 'Roller Freight' can take high speeds over long distances without danger of a hot box holding up the whole train."

Timken Company's advertising has also appeared in *The Wall Street Journal.* One such advertisement, (April 28, 1967, p. 24) tied Timken Company advertising in with the Canadian Exposition in Montreal.

The illustration featured a shoe—with a headline reading: "Probably the only transportation system at Expo '67 that doesn't have a single Timken bearing!" The copy read as follows: "At Expo '67 you can escalate on Timken bearings and elevate on them. You can amusement-ride on them. Expo Express on them. And Metro on them.

"Fact is, walking's one of the few ways you'll move without the aid of Timken bearings. (We can't remember ever having installed one in a shoe.)

"Timken bearings are sold in 116 countries. They're manufactured in Australia, Brazil, Canada, England, France, South Africa and the U.S.A.

"So it's really no surprise to find them where more than 70 countries get together."

QUESTIONS FOR DISCUSSION

1. How does the advertising opportunity for branded parts differ generally from that for finished goods?
2. Is there a sufficient opportunity for the advertising of branded parts to warrant Timken advertising them?
3. Should Timken conduct advertising aimed at consumer markets generally?

Case 4-10—The Personna Blade Company

The Personna Blade Company manufactured a line of high-grade table cutlery in addition to Pal and Personna razor blades. Marketing and promotion plans for the razor blade division were pretty well set for the coming year, with advertising appropriations amounting to $3½ million already approved. You are a member of a committee assigned the task of formulating marketing plans for the cutlery division. Their marketing objectives, although not stated in precise terms were directed generally toward maximizing sales and profits.

Personna table cutlery was made in 13 styles. The packages ranged from a single carving knife to a four-piece carving set. The four-piece set consisted of a ham slicer, steak slicer, utility knife, and parer. The usual combination was a three-piece set, consisting of knife, fork, and steel. The sets were fair-traded at retail prices of $15.95 to $44.95. The prices for Personna cutlery were somewhat higher than those for similar sets of other companies. Personna officials believed that this differential was in keeping with the fine quality of their cutlery.

The trade reported a considerable seasonal fluctuation in household cutlery sales. The chief selling season was in the months from September through December. Sales volume was less in months after Christmas, although considerable sales for the wedding-gift market occurred in June. Summer sales were relatively low.

Household cutlery sets were often purchased as gifts. Consequently, they were among items featured for Christmas, Father's Day, Mother's Day, June weddings, housewarmings, and anniversaries.

Personna cutlery was sold from coast to coast by a force of 15 salesmen. Ten were regional salesmen, who concentrated on the several thousand wholesalers in the hardware and jewelry businesses. The remaining five men served as missionary salesmen and called on retail stores.

Total sales of the household cutlery industry at this time were estimated at $3 million. Personna had a 15% share of market, with a gross margin of 40% and a net profit for the cutlery division of 5%. Ekco Products Company and the Robeson Cutlery Company were the two leading competitors of Personna.

During the discussion, one member of the sales department pointed out that both Ekco and Robeson advertise nationally and since Personna had national distribution, we also should back our product with national advertising. He recommended a minimum budget for this of $400,000.

QUESTIONS FOR DISCUSSION

1. Conduct a break-even analysis of the recommended budget of $400,000 suggested by Personna's sales department.
2. Can Personna conduct its advertising program competitively?
3. What do you believe the opportunity for advertising is in this case relative to the opportunity for personal selling activities?

5

ADVERTISING OBJECTIVES

- The Role of Advertising Objectives
- Hierarchy of Effects and Objective Setting
- Intermediate Criteria
- Behavioral Criteria

Decision Making Organization of This Text

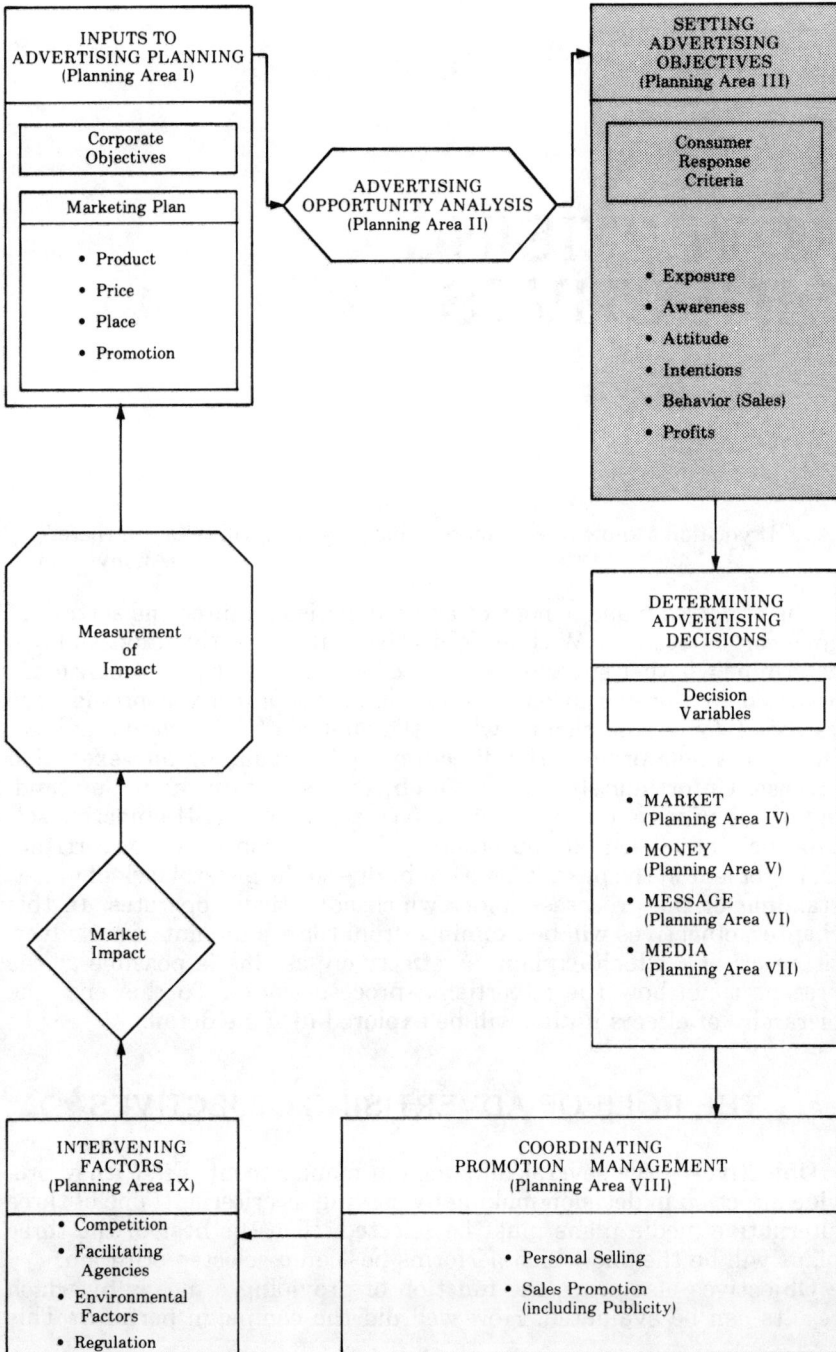

INPUTS TO ADVERTISING PLANNING
(Planning Area I)

Corporate Objectives

Marketing Plan

- Product
- Price
- Place
- Promotion

ADVERTISING OPPORTUNITY ANALYSIS
(Planning Area II)

SETTING ADVERTISING OBJECTIVES
(Planning Area III)

Consumer Response Criteria

- Exposure
- Awareness
- Attitude
- Intentions
- Behavior (Sales)
- Profits

Measurement of Impact

DETERMINING ADVERTISING DECISIONS

Decision Variables

- MARKET
  (Planning Area IV)
- MONEY
  (Planning Area V)
- MESSAGE
  (Planning Area VI)
- MEDIA
  (Planning Area VII)

Market Impact

INTERVENING FACTORS
(Planning Area IX)

- Competition
- Facilitating Agencies
- Environmental Factors
- Regulation

COORDINATING PROMOTION MANAGEMENT
(Planning Area VIII)

- Personal Selling
- Sales Promotion
  (including Publicity)

5

ADVERTISING OBJECTIVES

"If you don't know where you're going, any road will take you there."
—Anonymous

The effective management of any enterprise requires the setting of goals or objectives. Without objectives, it is nearly impossible to determine whether superior, adequate, or inadequate performance has occurred in the execution of some activity. Objectives provide the yardstick (or yardsticks) by which the quality of work can be judged. Objectives also provide the direction for the planning and execution process. Unfortunately, the use of objectives requires an understanding of the process for which objectives are to be set. If objective setting has not been an outstandingly vivid aspect of advertising management in the past, it is no doubt due to the general lack of understanding of the processes under which advertising operates. In this chapter, objectives will be examined from the standpoint of the advertising criteria which explain, as effectively as this is possible at the present time, how the advertising process works. To this end, the hierarchy of effects notion will be explored in some detail.

THE ROLE OF ADVERTISING OBJECTIVES

Objectives serve several functions in management. First, they provide direction in decision making by serving as criteria. If one of three alternative media plans must be selected, then the best of the three plans will be the one which performs best on a selected criterion.

Objectives also serve the function of providing a means by which results can be evaluated. How well did the campaign perform? This question can only be answered with respect to some pre-determined objective and the accompanying criterion variable or variables. What is meant by "well"? Did the campaign do *well* in generating profits for the company? Or did the campaign do *well* in terms of the number of units sold in the last quarter of the fiscal year? Or did the campaign do *well* with respect to increasing the number of individuals in the target market who were aware of the brand? An explicit management agreement on the objectives for such a campaign could help in resolving the above dilemma.

Another function of objectives is to enhance communication within the organization. Ideas can be communicated along chains of command since if objectives have been determined all those involved have an opportunity to understand the precise nature of the task facing them.

And, very importantly, objective-setting processes force those involved to strive for a deeper understanding of the processes underlying their particular problems. Advertising objectives cannot be set without some fairly sophisticated understanding of the manner in which the advertising process works, at least in the case of particular products or companies, if not in general.

THE NATURE OF OBJECTIVE SETTING

The process of objective setting is best illustrated by example. Figure 5-1 shows response profiles for two different brands. The current state of each brand has been measured among its target market segment (the market segment upon which most marketing and advertising effort will be placed because of the potential it provides relative to other segments) on three criteria: Awareness, Trial, and Satisfaction. Awareness refers to the percentage of the market which is aware of the particular brand. Trial refers to the proportion of the target market which has tried the product at least once. And Satisfaction concerns the percentage of the segment which, having tried the product, was satisfied with it.[1] A more detailed discussion of measurement issues involved in the preparation of such brand profiles will be provided later in this chapter.

Clearly, Brand A is in a better position than Brand B on two of the three criteria. For Brand A, 90 percent of the total market segment is aware of the brand, 70 percent of the aware 90 percent have tried the brand, and of these individuals, 25 percent were satisfied with the brand. The distribution is quite different for Brand B. Only 40 percent of the total market is aware of the brand, only 20 percent have tried the brand, but fully 90 percent of those who have tried Brand B were satisfied with it. Without question, these two profiles have very different implications for the setting of advertising objectives for the brand.

In the case of Brand A, the advertising in the past has succeeded in getting high awareness levels and a large proportion of the market try-

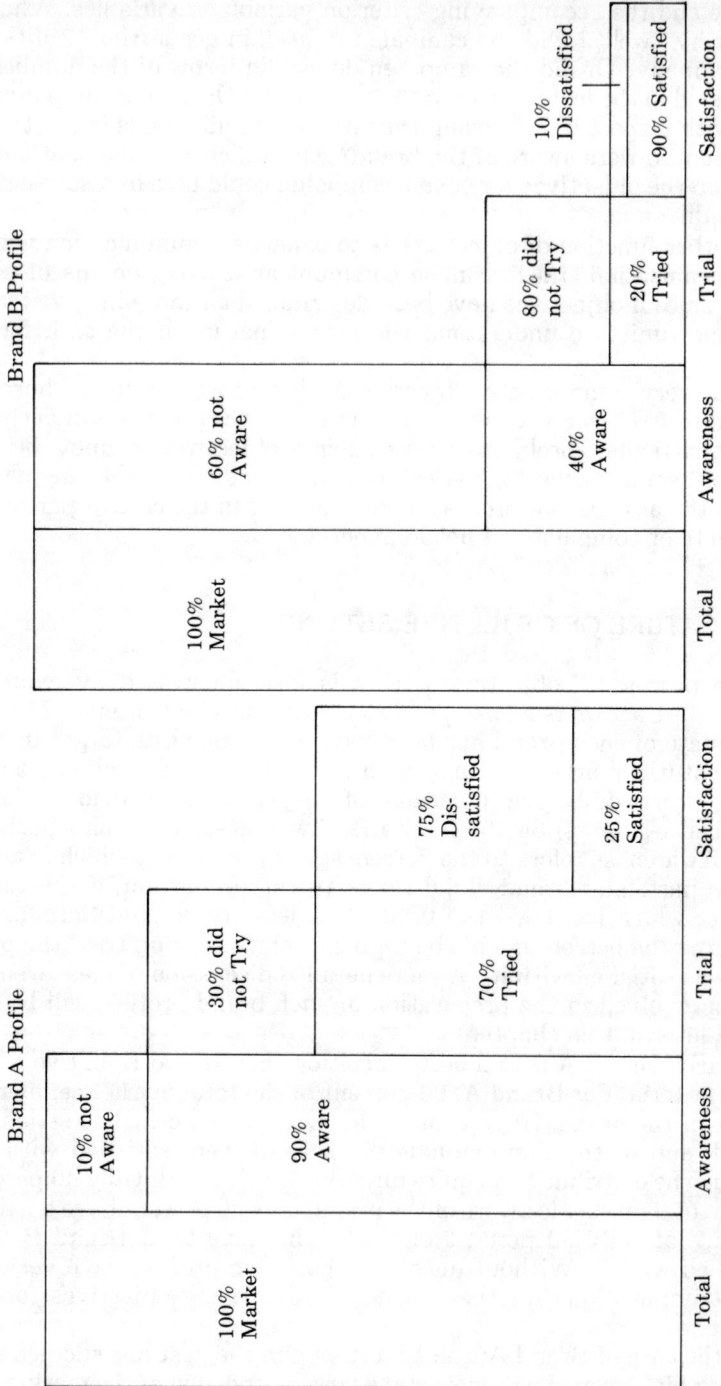

Figure 5-1   Consumer Response Profiles for Two Brands

ing the brand. However, there must be a product-related problem with Brand A since only one-fourth of those trying are satisfied with the brand's performance. The problem with Brand B is just the opposite. The creative and media work in the advertising program are not generating high levels of brand awareness or trial. When the product is tried by consumers, their satisfaction with Brand B appears high. Clearly, the objectives for Brand B must involve the criterion variables of Awareness and Trial or perhaps, at minimum, Awareness alone. Some combination of creative, media, and budgeting strategy must be found to raise Awareness levels. Though these same criteria would continue to be of interest to Brand A's management, their focus might shift to the satisfaction criterion somewhat while attempting to maintain, through the advertising program, the current levels of Awareness and Initial Trial.

In this example, the distinction should be noticed between objectives and criteria. Advertising *criteria*, to be discussed in the following sections, are the elements or building blocks of statements of objectives. For example, in the case of Brand B above, an objective might be stated as, "To raise Awareness from 40% to 60% by the end of the second quarter of 1982 for Brand B." Notice that an *objective* is a specific statement involving numerical values on a criterion variable, in this case, Awareness. Clearly, there is no point in stating objectives if the criteria involved in the statements are not fully understood or cannot be measured. Operational objectives are to be desired; in order for an objective to be operational, the criterion variable involved in the objective statement must be susceptible to measurement and generally agreed-upon interpretations. The Leo Burnett Company, a large advertising agency, developed an interesting procedure for operationalizing the above example of objective setting called CAPP.

CONTINUOUS ADVERTISING PLANNING PROGRAM

The Continuous Advertising Planning Program (CAPP) was developed by the Leo Burnett Company for use with some of its clients and as a means of operationalizing objective setting. The particular criterion variables in this system are shown in Figure 5-2. The criteria in this consumer demand profile are Brand Awareness, Brand Acceptance, Brand Bought Last, and Brand Satisfaction. The acceptance level indicates that the brand is acceptable to an individual in the target market, that is, that the brand meets the individual's minimum requirements for a brand in the product category. Brand Preference was assessed on a four-point scale and indicates the percentage of the product class users who rate the brand higher than any other brands in the category. Brand Satisfaction indicates the proportion who are satisfied with the performance of the product after purchase and repeat buying of the brand.

Each of these criteria were measured monthly during a campaign for a particular brand (or collection of brands from different product

Figure 5-2   Consumer Demand Profile

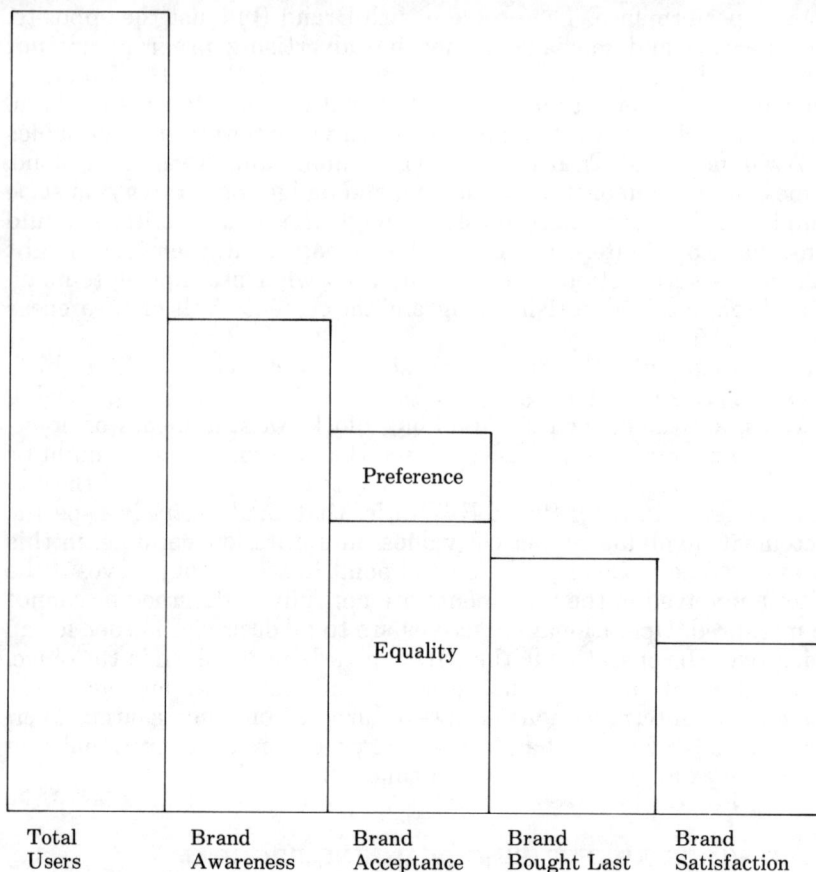

| Total Users | Brand Awareness | Brand Acceptance | Brand Bought Last | Brand Satisfaction |

SOURCE: John C. Maloney, "Attitude Measurement and Formation," paper presented at the Test Market Design and Measurement Workshop, American Marketing Association, Chicago, Il., April 21, 1966.

categories). A cross-sectional sample of 1000 households was interviewed on a continuing basis; in addition to the CAPP measurements, data were collected regarding the media exposure habits of the households. The important aspect of the CAPP system was this continuing measurement system. It provides the possibility for tuning the campaign as it progresses to the criterion area most needing improvement at a particular time. This is in contrast to static pre/post measurement (one measurement before and one measurement after a campaign) which is often observed. The CAPP system was a dynamic objective-setting system providing timely information which could be acted upon.

One of the developers of this system, John Maloney, has suggested a decision rule for the use of CAPP in setting objectives.[2] He proposed that the ratio of the size of adjacent levels or criteria be used to decide which criterion to emphasize in objective setting. For example, the number of households having Brand Awareness would be divided by the number of households having Brand Acceptance. If this ratio is high, then the criterion to concentrate on would be the one in the denominator of this ratio, in this case, Brand Acceptance. This decision rule follows the general idea that it is desirable to concentrate marketing and advertising efforts on larger rather than smaller market segments. This ratio helps identify the segment which contains the greatest number of people. What is meant by "high" in terms of this ratio would need to be determined through normative data based upon experience with many different brands over time.

HIERARCHY OF EFFECTS AND OBJECTIVE SETTING

The CAPP System outlined above is an attempt to apply the principles and ideas set forth by Russell Colley in his classic work, *Defining Advertising Goals for Measured Advertising Results.*[3] His suggested approach is usually noted by the acronym, DAGMAR, and has the major objective of differentiating sales or behavioral objectives from *intermediate* objectives such as those illustrated by the CAPP procedure. The DAGMAR approach has been influential in stimulating many different approaches to objective setting. Most of these approaches, however, have one aspect in common; they generally follow one variation or another of the basic "hierarchy of effects" scheme. Before examining the hierarchy of effects schemes, it is worthwhile to note that an additional idea set forth in DAGMAR was the *specificity* of objective setting. Colley emphasized the thinking that, in advertising as in other business areas, the more specific the objective, the more desirable is that objective. For example, an objective might be stated as, "To increase the awareness of Brand X." It would be preferable to replace this statement with a more specific one such as, "To raise awareness from the current 57% to 80% in the next quarter of operations."

The term "hierarchy" in the hierarchy of effects concept refers to the idea that the criteria in the hierarchy follow logically from each other. For example, in the CAPP system, it is assumed that Brand Awareness must first occur before Brand Acceptance can be developed among the target market population. There have been several variations of the hierarchy notion which have been suggested over the years. The first to suggest the idea was E.K. Strong in his *Psychology of Selling* in 1925.[4] Strong believed that the consumer must be moved by the advertising through four basic steps if the advertising was to be considered successful: Attention, Interest, Desire, and Action. This model is often referred to as the AIDA model of communication effects.

The hierarchy of effects concept was popularized in a practical manner by the copywriting sage, Clyde Bedell.[5] He believed that each advertisement must move the consumer sequentially through the following stages: Attention, Interest, Desire, Conviction, and Action. Bedell atempted to define the mechanisms by which an ad could move the consumer through the criteria in this hierarchy. Not until 1961 were these stages linked to contemporary notions of social psychology and given the label "hierarchy of effects."[6] Lavidge and Steiner used different labeling than Strong and Bedell (Awareness, Knowledge, Liking, Preference, Conviction, and Purchase) and categorized each of the "steps in the hierarchy ladder" as belonging to the cognitive, affective, or conative dimensions of attitude as conceived by the so-called "three-dimensional" attitude theorists.[7]

In the "Diffusion of Innovations" literature, the adoption process is viewed as a hierarchy of effects with still other labels for the steps or criteria: Awareness, Interest, Evaluation, Trial, and Adoption.[8] The most recent formulation of the hierarchy is termed "Information Processing" and has been given the following steps by McGuire: (1) Presentation of the message; (2) Attention to the message; (3) Comprehension of the conclusion in the message; (4) Yielding to the conclusion; (5) Retention of the belief formed as a result of exposure to the message; and (6) Behaving on the basis of the new belief.[9] These different conceptions of the hierarchy of effects, and, thus, different conceptions about how advertising works, are summarized and categorized by the three dimensions of effectiveness (Cognitive, Affective, and Conative) in Figure 5-3.

PERSPECTIVES ON HIERARCHY OF EFFECTIVENESS

Robertson notes that each of the hierarchy models share the same shortcomings: (1) the consumer may make decisions in a "nonrational" manner. That is, he or she may not secure, process, or carefully evaluate all the available information; (2) there is not a specified sequence of stages which must occur. Any such model must make allowances for consumers to "skip" stages; and (3) must also provide feedback loops since such a process will not necessarily be linear and uni-dimensional.[10] It is the recognition of these shortcomings which has motivated the major research dealing with the hierarchy issue.

Lavidge and Steiner, in their original conception of the three-dimensional nature of the hierarchy, did not provide any evidence that such a process actually operates in consumer behavior situations. Subsequently, Palda analyzed secondary data reported in studies which utilized variables related to those discussed by Lavidge and Steiner; he concluded there was little or no evidence in the studies he surveyed that such a hierarchy process operated at all.[11] A brief review of additional studies on this matter will help clarify the present situation with respect to the hierarchy viewpoint.

Brand Awareness and Attitude. A large-scale review was conducted by Haskins of the studies which included both awareness and at-

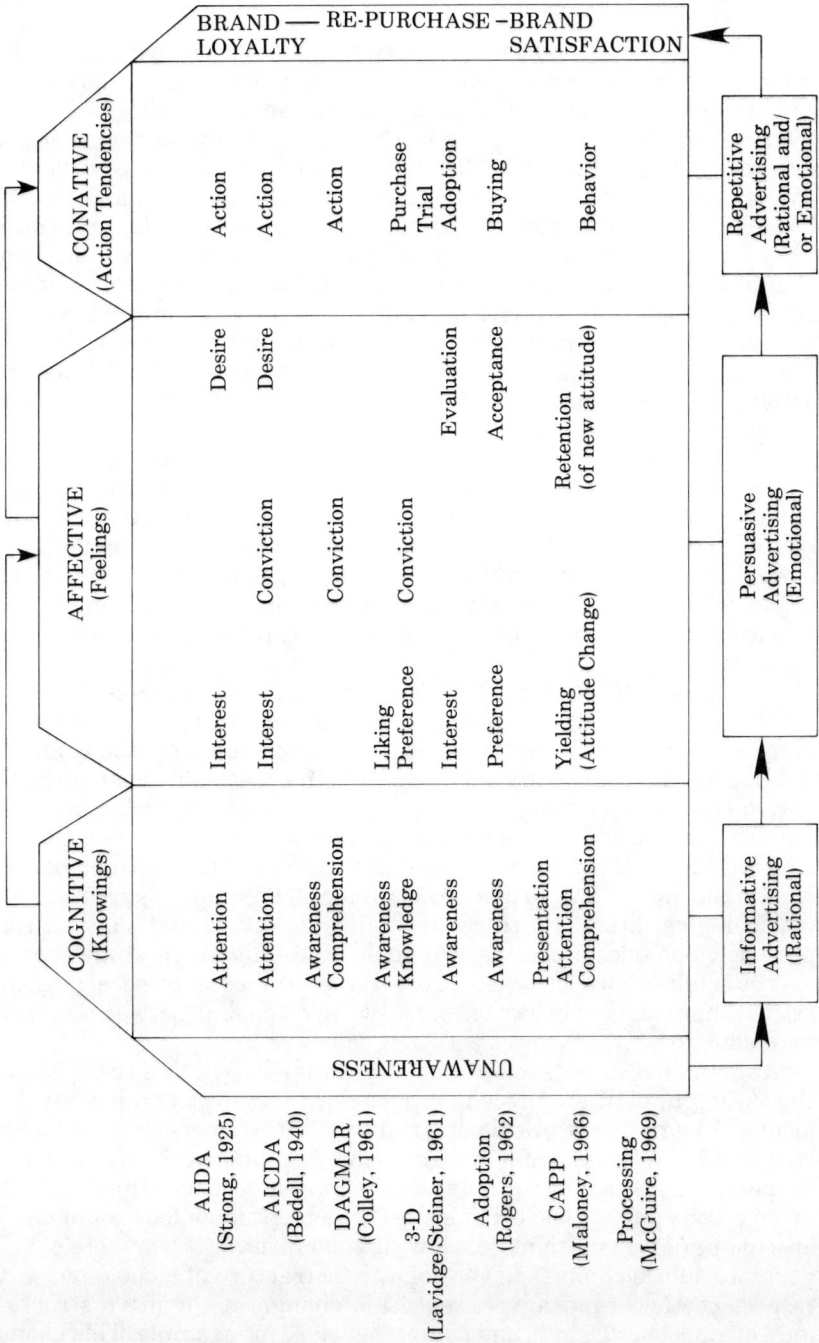

Figure 5-3   Conceptions of Hierarchy of Effects

BRAND LOYALTY — RE-PURCHASE — BRAND SATISFACTION

Model	COGNITIVE (Knowings)	AFFECTIVE (Feelings)	CONATIVE (Action Tendencies)
AIDA (Strong, 1925)	Attention	Interest / Desire	Action
AICDA (Bedell, 1940)	Attention	Interest / Conviction / Desire	Action
DAGMAR (Colley, 1961)	Awareness / Comprehension	Conviction	Action
3-D (Lavidge/Steiner, 1961)	Awareness / Knowledge	Liking / Preference / Conviction	Purchase
Adoption (Rogers, 1962)	Awareness	Interest / Evaluation	Trial / Adoption
CAPP (Maloney, 1966)	Awareness	Preference / Acceptance	Buying
Processing (McGuire, 1969)	Presentation / Attention / Comprehension	Yielding (Attitude Change) / Retention (of new attitude)	Behavior

UNAWARENESS

Advertising stages:
- Informative Advertising (Rational)
- Persuasive Advertising (Emotional)
- Repetitive Advertising (Rational and/or Emotional)

titude.[12] The results of his survey, which covered studies conducted over a ten-year period, showed that there was little relationship between high brand awareness and favorable attitude or vice versa. Out of twenty-one studies in communications research, two of them showed a positive relationship between changes in awareness and changes in attitude or behavior, two showed a negative relationship, and the remainder showed little or no relationship at all.

One of the most recent tests of the hierarchy notion was that conducted by Aaker and Day.[13] They conducted 19 telephone surveys at two-month intervals to a national probability sample of 1,200 households who were users of the product to be studied, instant coffee. They measured four variables in the study: brand awareness, brand attitude, advertising recall, and purchase behavior. The results of this study showed that advertising influenced both awareness and attitude, while awareness and attitude influenced behavior. The influence of advertising went directly from awareness to behavior, not through attitude. Thus, the hierarchy model of communication effects was found to be only partially correct.

There is little evidence to show that brand awareness must necessarily precede the development of a favorable attitude towards the brand or, indeed, that awareness and attitude are necessarily related to each other. It may be reasonable to consider "impulse" purchases as an example of this; the buyer is essentially unaware of the brand when making the purchase in the impulse situation. In this situation, the action or purchase step would precede all others in the hierarchy.

Attitude and Behavior. The hierarchy of effects suggests that after attitude is "caused" by awareness, attitude, in turn, "causes" or precedes behavior. This notion has been challenged by the cognitive dissonance hypothesis by Festinger which essentially puts forth the notion that engaging in behavior causes attitude to develop.[14] For example, if an individual purchases an automobile (a behavior), the person will "adjust" his or her attitude to "fall in line" with or become consonant with the behavioral impact. Festinger surveyed the psychological literature to see if studies demonstrated that attitude preceded behavioral change. He could find only three studies which even included both criteria. These three studies showed a negative rather than the hypothesized positive relationship between attitude and behavior.[15]

Krugman has also developed an alternative hypothesis to the hierarchy notion of attitude preceding behavior in his work on low involvement.[16] Krugman's work dealt primarily with television advertising. He considered television a low-involving medium; watching television is quite unlike reading a magazine where conscious effort must be made on the part of the consumer. The perceptual defenses are low or absent under conditions of low involvement. A commercial will generate subtle changes in the cognitive structure of a consumer with respect to the brand advertised. This change in cognitive structure may mean a change in brand comprehension, for example. This change is sufficient to cause a change in behavior even though it is too weak to affect attitude. This alteration in comprehension can then lead to an un-deliberate purchase of the brand. As in the cognitive dissonance framework, this behavioral response then has a feedback effect on attitude. In essence, the suggestion is that, under conditions of low involvement, the effect is directly from awareness to behavior without the intervention of attitude (see Figure 5-4).

Figure 5-4   Learning Under Low Involvement

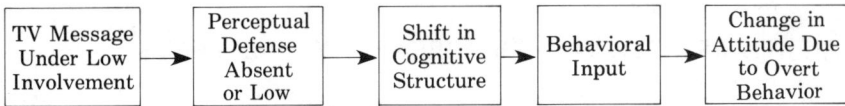

TV Message Under Low Involvement	→	Perceptual Defense Absent or Low	→	Shift in Cognitive Structure	→	Behavioral Input	→	Change in Attitude Due to Overt Behavior

SOURCE: David A. Aaker and John G. Myers, *Advertising Management* (Englewood Cliffs, N.J.: Prentice-Hall, Inc., 1975).

William D. Wells of the Needham, Harper & Steers advertising agency has recently suggested an interesting hypothesis regarding attitude and behavior, or, as he puts it, liking and sales effectiveness.[17] Wells asserts that there will be a high or low relationship between attitude towards the commercial and brand purchase depending upon the type of product and the type of commercial or advertisement developed for that product. He places products along an "Avoidance-Approach" continuum. *Approach* products are those which are intrinsically enjoyable. They include most foods, most beverages, nice clothes, vacations, new cars, pets, jewelry, new furniture, and almost anything associated with enjoyment. Traditionally, advertising has been used to highlight the enjoyable aspects of such products and tends to be entertaining, aesthetically appealing, or gratifying in some manner.

Avoidance products are those which would not be bought if they did not help the consumer do something (these can be thought of as products which are purchased for negative rather than positive reasons). These products include proprietary medicines, most cleaning products, insurance, denture adhesives, and products which help control unpleasant odors. The primary problem in the advertising of such products is that the vivid portrayal of the unpleasant situation which the product will remedy through its use is almost certain to remind consumers of negative life situations. Products such as paper towels do not fit nicely in either category, and so Wells refers to them as *utilitarian* products.

Wells' hypothesis can be summarized in the following way. For an approach-type product, there will be a positive relationship between attitude and sales. For avoidance-type products, there will be a negative or inverse relationship between liking the advertising and sales, that is, the greater the sales effect of the advertising, the less the advertising is liked. For utilitarian-type products, the relationship between liking and sales could be in either direction, depending upon the objective of the advertising. In general, however, for such products the most effective advertising is the type which is neither strongly liked or strongly disliked. This hypothesis is summarized in Figure 5-5. Though Wells's hypothesis is a plausible and interesting one, it is presented here primarily as speculation regarding the sometimes observed lack of relationship between attitude and behavior in advertising situations.

AN INTEGRATIVE VIEW OF HIERARCHY OF EFFECTS

Ray and his colleagues have conducted more research of the hierarchy than have others.[18] As a result of his extensive investigations, he has suggested that there is not one hierarchy of effects but rather three: (1) Learning Hierarchy; (2) Dissonance-Attribution Hierarchy; and (3) Low-Involvement Hierarchy. These hierarchies are conceived in terms of the ordering of the cognitive-affective-conative dimensions as these may develop under different circumstances. He defines the orders as follows (and as shown in Figure 5-6): (1) The Learning Hierarchy: Cognitive-Affective-Conative; (2) The Dissonance-Attribution Hierarchy: Conative-Affective-Cognitive; and (3) The Low-Involvement Hierarchy: Cognitive-Conative-Affective.

The particular hierarchy for a given situation is governed by primarily four factors: (1) The extent of the involvement of the individual with the object of the message; (2) the extent to which there is a clear differentiation among alternatives to that proposed in the message; (3) whether the source of the message is the mass media or interpersonal communication; and (4) the so-called "compensation principle." The Aaker and Day study mentioned above could probably be viewed in the Three-Hierarchies conception as an example of the operation of the Low-Involvement Hierarchy with the cognitive-conative-affective form since a slight relationship of purchase preceding attitude development was also found in their study.

Ray and his associates have been able to produce empirically the appearance of the Low Involvement Hierarchy and the Learning Hierarchy by manipulating the three explanatory variables indicated above of source, level of involvement and differentiation of alternatives. The studies have typically been conducted in advertising laboratories with multiple exposures to the same advertisements. For example, Sawyer conducted a study in the laboratory involving two test advertisements and a competitive ad from each of five product classes.[19] The test ads were exposed to the same subjects six times while the competitive ad was given two exposures. "Top recall" indicated the percentage of respondents recalling the test ad before the competitive (cognitive dimension measure), "Top attitude" was the proportion rating the test

Figure 5-5 Approach-Avoidance Hypothesis for Attitude/Sales Relationship

	APPROACH Product	UTILITARIAN Product	AVOIDANCE Product
FAVORABLE ATTITUDE toward Advertising	High Sales	High Sales*	Low Sales
NEUTRAL ATTITUDE toward Advertising	—	High Sales	—
NEGATIVE ATTITUDE toward Advertising	Low Sales	Low Sales*	High Sales

*If product is "converted" to an Approach product by adding psychological values through advertising.

Figure 5-6 Three-Hierarchies Approach

LEARNING HIERARCHY	DISSONANCE HIERARCHY	LOW INVOLVEMENT HIERARCHY
• High Involvement • High Differentiation • Mass Communication Source	• High Involvement • Low Differentiation • Interpersonal Source	• Low Involvement • Low Differentiation • Mass Communication Source
COGNITIVE → AFFECTIVE → CONATIVE	CONATIVE → AFFECTIVE → COGNITIVE	COGNITIVE → CONATIVE → AFFECTIVE

brand higher than competitive ads, and "Top purchase intention" was the proportion saying they were more likely to purchase the test brand than the competitive one (conative dimension measure). Over the six repetitions of the message, it was found that the cognitive measure was not affected, followed by the conative measure, followed by the affective measure. Ray has been able to show this effect in low involvement situations in several other studies.[20] In addition, Silk and Vavra found in their survey of the literature on the effects of pleasant and unpleasant advertising formats that significant findings less often result with evaluation (affective) measures than with recall or action measures; this would seem to indicate an earlier effect of communications on the cognitive and conative dimensions as opposed to the affective.[21]

It was noted above that a factor which explains, in part, which of the three hierarchies is operative in a given situation is the "compensation principle." This principle was first stated by McGuire as a result of his extensive studies in communication effectiveness.[22] He believes that a message which has high positive effect on any two of the three dimensions will tend to have a depressing effect on the remaining dimension. For example, Heeler showed recall (cognitive) and purchase intentions (conative) increased with the number of exposures to advertisements for low involvement products while preference (affective) decreased.[23]

The Three-Hierarchies approach developed by Ray is an integrative approach. It is clear from the various formulations of the hierarchy of effects shown in Figure 5–3 that no one conceptualization fits all situations. It is clear that the order of the criteria in the hierarchy changes depending upon several factors in a given situation. In general, Ray has found that for convenience goods which are low involving for consumers, which use mass communication (advertising) to communicate with consumers, and which are relatively undifferentiated from competitive products, the Low Involvement Hierarchy would likely be the most appropriate conception of the advertising process. That is, the process for such a brand would be conceptualized as Learning, Behavior Change, and then Attitude Change (cognitive, conative, and affective, in that order). Soaps, soups and mouthwashes might fall into the Low Involvement category. For shopping goods such as portable televisions, washing machines, and foundation garments for which consumers tend to depend more on personal sources of communication (sales personnel) and which are more differentiated across brands than are convenience goods, in general, the Learning Hierarchy is likely to be operative. That is, the process for brands of such goods would likely be Learning, Attitude Change, and then Behavior Change (cognitive, affective, and then conative) or basically as originally conceptualized by Strong in the original hierarchy of effects.

It makes a good deal of sense to conceive of Three Hierarchies rather than of one, not only because of the empirical support such a conception has received, but also because each hierarchy corresponds to a theoretical tradition of some standing. The Learning Hierarchy (Learning-Attitude Change-Behavior Change) corresponds to learning theory in psychology; the Dissonance-Attribution Hierarchy (Behavior Change-Attitude Change-Learning) stems from Festinger's cognitive dissonance tradition; and the Low Involvement Hierarchy (Learning-Behavior Change-Attitude Change) relates to the emerging theory of low involvement of Krugman. Further, as a practical matter, the observer of the advertising process can easily understand each of the processes operating in different contexts, that is, the Three Hierarchies "makes common sense" to advertising people. The Three-Hierarchies approach is summarized in Figure 5–6.

With this conception in mind, it is worthwhile for the reader to consider the problems involved in operationalizing and measuring the criteria in hierarchies of effect. Accordingly, intermediate criteria (exposure, awareness, attitude and intentions) will first be discussed. Subsequently, behavioral criteria (sales and other observable criteria) will be examined.

INTERMEDIATE CRITERIA

The various intermediate criteria will be considered with respect to the Three-Hierarchies categories of cognitive, affective, and conative dimensions of effectiveness.

COGNITIVE CRITERIA

The following cognitive criteria will briefly be examined: Vehicle Exposure, Advertising Exposure, Brand Awareness, Advertising Awareness, and Advertising Recall.

Vehicle Exposure. There are two levels of exposure with which the advertising manager must be concerned. The first of these concerns the number or percentage of target market individuals or households who can be expected to see and/or hear the vehicle in which the message will appear. The second level, to be discussed subsequently, deals with actual exposure of the message to target market individuals or households. It is not clear, for example, that if *Time* magazine reaches 23 percent of the defined target market for a product that the same proportion of the target market will also see the advertising message which might be placed in *Time* magazine. Nonetheless, vehicle exposure often serves as the criterion in one form or another for the comparison of alternative media vehicles and alternative media schedules. This is so because of the difficulty, particularly in broadcast media, of obtaining reliable estimates of Advertising Exposure levels.

Various syndicated services provide information which can be purchased on a routine basis regarding the audience sizes of various print and broadcast vehicles. The most widely accepted measure of magazine audiences is the *Study of Selective Markets and the Media Reaching Them,* which is produced by Simmons Market Research Bureau (SMRB), on an annual basis. The service measures audiences of many leading magazines and a few large newspapers. In the 1979 study, the audiences of 140 publications were measured. The measurements deal with total audiences, demographic breakdowns on a variety of bases, data for two-issue accumulative audience, and frequency. In addition, information is developed on ownership, purchase, and use of specific products and services. In addition, some limited information about television viewing and radio listening is provided.

The Nielsen Television Index provides the measurement of national audiences for network television programs. This service reports home audience data based on the measurement of home viewing developed from electronic meters. The Index measures the number of homes in which television sets are in use, the channels to which these sets are tuned, and reports these measurements in terms of total homes and percentage ratings and shares. These data are broken down by selected demographics which include geographic area, county size, household size, household income, presence of non-adults, and so on. The Index is based upon measurements of four-week cumulative program audiences. A companion Nielsen service called the Nielsen Audience Composition Service provides additional information to supplement the channel tuning data derived from metering in the Television Index Service. The Audience Composition Service information is derived from diaries which are kept by a representative national panel of viewers. The essential difference between this service and the Television Index Service is that the Audience Composition reports on the basis of individual viewing rather than sets in use since individuals record their viewing in their own diary as opposed to having the viewing recorded electronically by meter attached to the sets.

Local television audiences are measured by the Arbitron Company as well as the Nielsen Media Research division of the A.C. Nielsen Company. These services are competitive with each other and provide very similar types of data on local stations. Arbitron, for example, measures the number of homes in which television sets are in use, the channels to which these sets are tuned, and these are reported in terms of total homes, percentage ratings and shares. Data are reported for the metro area or central market area and the area of dominant influence (ADI's). These measures are broken down by sex and age demographics. ARB uses the diary method for collection of viewing data. These diaries are filled in by the viewers themselves without the help of interviewers.

Most prominent among those measuring radio audiences is the Pulse, Inc. This firm uses the roster recall method of measurement in which personal interviewers ring doorbells and ask the person who answers what programs he or she heard for the preceding week prior to the interview. Each interviewer carries a roster of programs broadcast the week before and lets the householder look at the roster while answering. Demographics are also collected and reported by The Pulse.

These measurements allow for the examination of the audiences of individual vehicles. When vehicles are combined into media schedules, the problem of estimating the number of persons exposed to the schedule as a whole becomes very complex. This estimate, called schedule reach, must take into account the overlapping coverage of the vehicles in the media schedule. For this purpose, various methods have been developed to estimate "unduplicated" reach of a schedule. These methods all require the basic vehicle exposure data outlined above. The nature of these methods will be considered in some detail in Chapter 14.

Advertising Exposure. The problem of measuring the number of people exposed to a television commercial which is run on a commercial network is a complex one; there is no service which routinely measures the national audiences of the commercial itself. This is clearly logistically and economically out of the question. For magazines, since the total number of them involved is not as great as the number of television programs, and also the frequency of issue is often monthly with a few weeklies, the problem of measuring exposure to specific ads in these vehicles is more manageable. The prominent measure of exposure to magazine advertisements is the recognition method developed in the 1920's by Daniel Starch and routinely measured by Starch Readership Studies, Inc.

Starch Readership Studies make three basic measurements among persons who claim readership of specific magazines and can prove they have read some part of the issue by playing back that part accurately to the interviewer:

(1) The Noting Score: This is a measure of the percentage of readers who noted specific advertisements when they first looked at the issues of the magazine (prior to the personal interview);

(2) The Seen Associated Score: This measures the percentage of readers who associated the product advertised with the advertiser;

(3) Read Most Score: The percentage of the readers who claimed to have read 50 percent or more of the copy in the advertisement.

In the interviewing procedure, the interviewer pages through the magazine issue, once the reader has been qualified as a true reader of the particular issue, pausing at each advertisement one-quarter page or larger, asking if the respondent recognizes it, associates the product with the advertiser, and has read most of the copy. It should be noted that the validity of the recognition method is questionable since the respondent may say he or she saw the ad the first time reading the issue regardless of whether or not this is so; there is no objective method of determining whether or not the interviewee's answer is a factual one. The reliability of this method is apparently fairly acceptable.[24] Nonetheless, care must be used when viewing recognition scores in an absolute sense; since these measurements have been made for 50 years, it is probably desirable to view them relative to the norms established over this long period of time for the various product categories.

A more objective method than recognition has occasionally been used to assess the advertising exposure for magazines. This method is called the "glue seal method." In this procedure, an imperceptible amount of glue is attached by the magazine's publisher at the time of printing to the page facing the advertisement page. After the magazine is delivered to subscribers, interviewers call to examine the magazine issue. If the seal has been broken on the page containing the advertisement, it is assumed the subscriber was exposed to the advertising page. Various other laboratory methods have been developed which attempt to measure advertisement exposure, but these must necessarily deal with a very small sample of individuals and are of more interest as criteria in copy development than in media evaluation. The tachistoscopic approach is prominent among these laboratory methods.[25] The tachistoscope is a projector that can project objects on a screen at rates faster than normal operation or perceptual processes. The frame speed is altered to the point that subliminal messages pass through the perceptual threshold, and the point at which respondents indicate an understanding of the message is recorded. The theory suggests that the more "catchy" creative elements, headline and so forth, will be noticed more rapidly than those messages which are less interesting to the audience.

Brand Awareness. Though there are many different ways of measuring brand awareness, all methods have in common the attempt to determine if the marketing effort of a given brand has made an impact on consumer consciousness. One popular method of measuring brand awareness is called "share of mind." Consumers are asked to mention the first brand or brands they think of when a given product class is mentioned. It is assumed that if the brand in question is not in the consumer's "top of mind," he or she is less likely to purchase the brand.

Share of mind awareness utilizes unaided recall. It is also possible to measure brand awareness using the recognition idea discussed above. Consumers are given a list of brand names and asked to indicate which ones they have heard of before being shown the list. Sometimes fictitious or "bogus" brand names are added to the list to control for the yea-saying and nay-saying tendencies of some respondents, over which the recognition method has no check.

An interesting experiment by the Oscar Mayer & Company has been reported by Twedt which used brand awareness as the major criterion variable.[26] The objective of this study was to determine the effect of repeated advertising exposure on brand awareness and purchase. In this study, the radio broadcasts of the Milwaukee baseball team were sponsored for the entire season. After the season, some 1200 completed interviews were conducted. Each respondent was asked how many baseball games they had heard, who the sponsor was, and amount and brands of hotdogs purchased within the last month. As indicated in Figure 5–7, sponsor identification (brand awareness) increased directly by number of exposures. Notice that brand purchase remains about constant until the 15th broadcast. Twedt concluded that a minimum of 15 exposures was necessary before brand awareness was increased to a sufficient degree to have an impact on purchase behavior.

Figure 5-7   Relation of Brand Awareness to Purchase

Oscar Mayer Brand Purchase

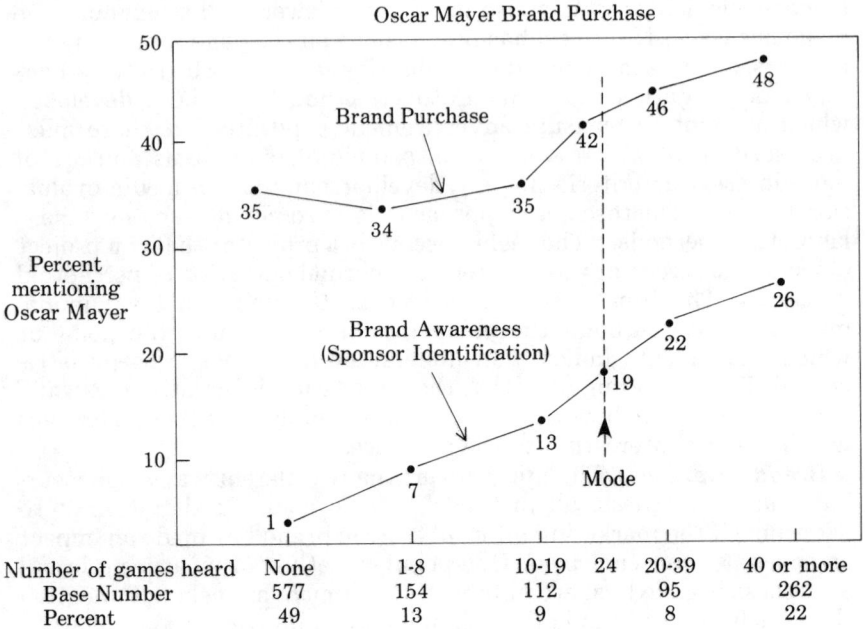

Number of games heard	None	1-8	10-19	24	20-39	40 or more
Base Number	577	154	112		95	262
Percent	49	13	9		8	22

SOURCE: Dik W. Twedt, "How Can the Advertising Dollar Work Harder?"
Journal of Marketing (April 1965), p. 61.

Advertising Awareness. Awareness of the advertising (as opposed to the brand name) can be measured in absolute or relative terms. This measure usually serves as a criterion in media planning to help determine whether the combination of reach and frequency in the schedule is sufficient to attract consumer attention. Consumers are asked to indicate the brands for which they have heard or seen advertising within some given period of time. Both aided and unaided approaches are utilized in advertising awareness assessment.

Relative advertising awareness can be measured by having consumers indicate which brands have had the most advertising in a given time period. Consumer belief about advertising weight for a particular brand can be compared with the actual expenditures for the brand relative to those perceived weights and expenditures for the competitive brands. Clearly, a brand is in an excellent position, relative to the competition, with respect to advertising awareness if less money is spent on its advertising than for competitive brands but consumer awareness of its advertising is greater than that for these competitive brands.

Faison reports a study relating advertising awareness to sales.[27] This study was conducted in six cities over a period of 18 weeks during the time that a new heavy-duty detergent was being introduced to the market. Advertising awareness was assessed by asking the question, "Have you seen or heard any advertising for _____ ?" This was an aided recall question. Sales were assessed by asking respondents what brands of detergents had been purchased during the last six months. Every two weeks, 200 telephone interviews were conducted in each of the six test cities. An introductory advertising schedule was run that consisted of heavy television for an 18-week period. There were also newspaper ads containing coupons for the first four weeks which were run. The total media schedule was highest in expenditures for the first four weeks and then gradually reduced for the remainder of the 18 weeks. Figure 5–8 shows that advertising awareness and purchase follow similar patterns. However, it should be noticed that the pattern of advertising awareness in Figure 5–8 closely follows the expenditure pattern in the media schedule.

Figure 5-8   The Relation of Advertising Awareness to Purchase Over Time

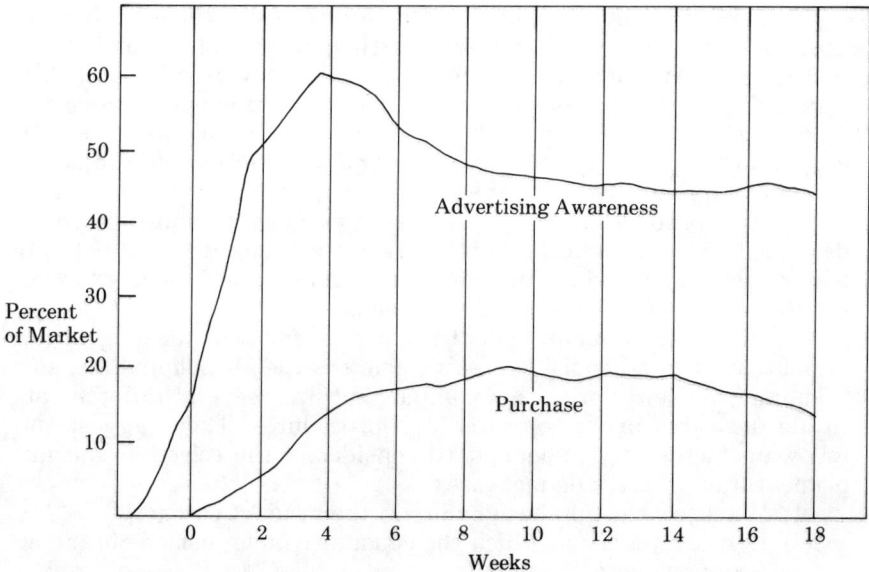

SOURCE: Edmund W. J. Faison, *Advertising: A Behavioral Approach for Managers* (New York: John Wiley & Sons, 1980), p. 716.

Advertising Recall. Advertising recall differs from advertising awareness inasmuch as the object in recall is to determine whether or not specific aspects of the copy approach have been communicated in such a way that consumers can remember these aspects. Day-after

Recall, as developed by the Burke Marketing Research Company, is the most prominent among the research organizations which measure advertising recall. The DAR system of Burke has become the industry standard for the assessment of this cognitive criterion.

DAR tests will be discussed in some detail in Chapter 11 since they have become one of the most important methods of evaluating advertising creative strategies. At this point, however, a brief overview of the nature of this cognitive criterion variable will be provided.

Day-after recall tests measure the percentage of consumers who prove they can recall specific elements of test commercials that they have seen the day before, in their own homes, during regular television viewing. Several types of scores are developed from such tests, but the top-line score is usually the Related Recall Score. In addition, the verbatim responses of the viewers as recorded by the telephone interviewers are provided for the 200 or so respondents who usually qualify for inclusion in the commercial audience base (those who have had the opportunity to actually see the commercial).

AFFECTIVE CRITERIA

There are probably as many methods for assessing the affective (attitudinal) dimension of effectivenes as there are people investigating such issues. Attitude can be measured based upon the use of "attributes" of a brand or advertisement; such measurement employs one type of attitude model or another. Models are desirable to use if it is important to know *why* consumers like or dislike the attitude object; if it is only required that the manager know *how much* consumers like or dislike the product, then *global* measures such as most of those described below (the exception is the Likert scale used in Figure 5-11) may be used. The student interested in attitude models might examine the Fishbein model and related approaches.[28]

Attitude Measurement. One of the prominent firms dealing in the measurement of advertising creative work is the McCollum/Spielman Company of New York. This company utilizes several different attitude measures in its copy research procedures. They suggest the following factors are important to consider in the selection and implementation of attitude measures:[29]

(1) What are the purchase habits in the product category?
(2) Is it a category in which the consumer buys just one brand or many brands?
(3) How frequently is the product-type purchased?
(4) Does the consumer habitually purchase one or several packages of this product?
(5) How many brands are in the product category?
(6) What is the nature of brand share, brand loyalty and competition in the product category?
(7) What are the objectives of the advertiser?
(a) To convert competitive brand users?

(b) To retain current users?

(c) To increase consumption among current users?

(d) To change the way people view the product?

The simplest of the measurements used by this firm is the *single choice pre/post brand attitude shift*. It is often used for frequently purchased packaged goods such as cosmetics, drug products and foods. These are the categories where the consumer habitually uses a single brand. In this system of measurement, the consumer is awarded a brand in a prize market basket both pre- and post-exposure to the test commercials. The brand list includes enough brands to account for at least 70 percent of all market shares. To avoid bias from order position, the test brand appears in a constant fourth position on the list so that normative comparisons are similar with respect to this characteristic. This procedure is shown in Figure 5-9.

Figure 5-9   Single Choice Pre/Post Brand Attitude Shift

PRE: Which one brand of hair coloring do you use most often? (circle only one.)

POST: Which one brand of hair coloring do you want in your $10 Market Basket? (circle only one.)

BRAND LIST

Balsam Color	Happiness
Preference	Excellence
Clairesse	Miss Clairol
Nice n' Easy	For Brunettes Only
Color Silk	Loving Care

Some other brand
Do not use hair coloring

The previous measure is not suitable for product categories where the consumer usually buys more than one brand in the product category. Such product categories include snack foods, soft drinks, cereals, and many others. In these product categories it would not be appropriate to force the respondent to make a single brand selection. An alternative procedure (variations of which are very common in advertising copy research) is the *constant sum measure*, illustrated in Figure 5-10. The points in the constant sum system are allocated by respondents in one of two different ways. If there are no major price disparities between the brands utilized in the procedure, respondents are asked to allocate a fixed number of packages among the brands. Where price differentials do exist, the respondents are requested to allocate a fixed dollar amount among the brands. As shown in Figure 5-10, for example, this procedure allows the person who normally buys lemon-lime, root beer, and cola soft drinks to select all three.

Figure 5-10   Constant Sum Allocation Pre & Post

Indicate how you would distribute $10 among the brands on this list. The more you prefer a brand, the more dollars you should give it. You may assign as many or as few dollars—even no dollars—to each brand, but the total number of dollars must equal 10.

		Dollar Distribution
COLA:	A. Coca-Cola	_____
	B. Pepsi-Cola	_____
	C. RC Cola	_____
	D. Dr. Pepper	_____
	E. Diet Pepsi	_____
	F. Tab	_____
	G. Some other cola brand	_____
ROOT BEER:	H. Dads	_____
	I. A & W	_____
	J. Hires	_____
	K. Barrelhead	_____
	L. Shasta	_____
	M. Some other root beer brand	_____
LEMON & LIME:	N. Sprite	_____
	O. 7-Up	_____
	P. Fresca	_____
	Q. Some other lemon/ lime brand	_____
OTHER:	R. Some other brand and flavor	_____
	TOTAL	$10

This firm also uses attitude scaling measures as described in the preceding section when it believes these are appropriate. They term this the *test vs. control image/attribute battery,* shown in Figure 5-11. These are utilized where the objective is not to sell a specific product but rather to bring about some change in the way people think about a corporation, institution, service, commodity, or public issue. In other words, the attitude scaling system is used in the most complex communication contexts. In this particular design, the same items are administered to two matched samples, one which has seen no advertising (control group) and another which has been exposed to the test message (test group). An examination of Figure 5-11 will show that this system utilizes the Likert scale procedure. McCollum/Spielman has found that attitudinal image batteries have also been found to be appropriate and useful supplemental measures for clients engaged in selling specific products. For example, they use this system for clients selling beer, soft drinks, chewing gum, fragrances, and pipe tobacco; these products are often sold on the basis of the image generated rather than on actual product attributes of a physical nature.

**Figure 5-11   Control vs. Post Exposure
Image/Attribute Battery**

How strongly do you agree or disagree with each of these statements about the _____ Oil Company?

   I. Is a leader in the oil industry

  II. Sincerely committed to meeting the energy needs of the country now and in the future

 III. Is a company worthy of the public's trust

 IV. Company's efforts will benefit American consumers.

                          SCALE: 1. Agree strongly
                                          2. Agree somewhat
                                          3. Disagree somewhat
                                          4. Disagree strongly

CONATIVE CRITERIA

Behavioral intentions, behavioral predispositions and consideration are all measures of the conative dimension of effectiveness. Such measures will be more or less predictive of actual behavior (to be discussed in the next section) based upon three primary factors: (1) the complexity of the behavior in question; (2) the specificity with which the intention, predisposition or consideration measure is taken; and (3) the time interval between the assessment of intentions, predispositions or considerations and the expected performance of the behavior.[30] In general, the relationship between assessed intentions and behavior will be greater the less complex is the behavior at issue, the more specifically the intention question is asked of the respondent, and the less the time lapse between the intention assessment and the observation of the behavior. For example, suppose it is desired to predict whether or not an individual will attend a given showing of a movie at a particular theater. It would be expected that intentions to go or not to go to this showing would be more predictive of behavior if the question is asked at a time as close as possible to the date of showing (clearly, assessing the intention to purchase a particular brand of automobile is a risky business).

However, even if an individual indicates he or she will attend the particular theater later on the same day the question is asked, other events could occur during that time interval; perhaps a friend important to this person will not go along to the theater that evening and thus change the individual's mind about going to the showing. In the advertising context, one would expect intentions to purchase a particular brand would be more predictive of actual purchase in a simulated shopping environment system (such as the theater copy research conducted by ASI Market Research, Inc.) where purchase takes place almost immediately after questioning than in a system where purchase would be observed in a natural environment with its inherent time lapse.

Buying Predisposition. One of the most popular conative criteria is buying predisposition. This measure is obtained from a scale, such as that shown in Figure 5-12. Using such a scale, Wells has shown a fairly strong relation between buying predisposition and actual purchase for two types of products.[31] In the cases of a toilet goods item and a grocery item (both packaged, convenience goods), Wells showed, for the 900 housewives studied, strong relations for the aggregate measures of predisposition and purchase; predisposition was defined as the percent of respondents saying that they will buy right away or might buy soon; purchase was defined as the percent of respondents buying within four weeks of the time the predisposition-to-buy was assessed.

Figure 5-12 Buying Predisposition Scale

	Buying Continuum	Intention Scale
1.	Firm and immediate intent to buy a specific brand.	"I am going to buy some right away." "I am going to buy some soon."
2.	Positive intention without definite buying plans.	"I am certain I will buy some sometime." "I probably will buy some sometime."
3.	Neutrality: might buy, might not.	"I may buy some sometime." "I might buy some sometime but I doubt it."
4.	Inclined to buy the brand, but not definite about.	"I don't think I am interested in buying any." "I probably will never buy any."
5.	Firm intention not to buy brand.	"I'm not interested in buying any." "If somebody gave me some, I'd give it away."
6.	Never considered buying.	"I have never heard of the brand."

SOURCE: William D. Wells, "Measuring Readiness to Buy," *Harvard Business Review*, (July-August 1961), p. 82.

Consideration. The McCollum/Spielman Company utilizes a consideration measure they call the "4 × 4 Matrix."[32] They utilize this measure in the copy research conducted on high ticket items such as appliances and automobiles or for certain types of services such as insurance and travel. In these product or service categories, purchase is not necessarily immediate and the buying process is very complex. Therefore, the objective of advertising in such product categories is usually to bring about some change in the consumer's mind which renders that brand or service more desirable or more likely to be considered when purchase time arrives.

The 4 × 4 Matrix procedure is illustrated in Figure 5-13. Respondents are presented with a list of brands and are asked to indicate: (1) their favorite or first choice: (2) alternatives which they might consider if the first choice were not available; and (3) those brands which they would not consider at all. This measuring process yields a brand profile in four groups; three of these groups are listed above, and the fourth is the default, "test brand not mentioned."

INTERMEDIATE CRITERIA AND PURCHASE PREDICTION

Though it is difficult to generalize about the relation of intermediate criteria to behavioral observations such as purchase, it is worthwhile to note a classic study which was conducted by Axelrod in 1968.[33]

Axelrod studied ten different intermediate criteria in a large-scale examination of convenience goods. Of the ten intermediate criteria included in his study, first brand awareness (defined by the question, "If you were to go out shopping right now for 'product class', what brand do you think you would buy?") and a constant sum scale measure of buying intentions performed best on reliability and sensitivity criteria. Sensitivity is a characteristic of measures which indicates the extent to which the measure shows differences, for example, between two commercials, when such differences actually exist. These two measures, first brand awareness and constant-sum buying intention, produced the best combination of short-term sales prediction as well as diagnostic information which was sensitive and stable.

BEHAVIORAL CRITERIA

The first distinction which must be made in any consideration of behavioral criteria has to do with the level of criterion analysis. Behavioral measures fall into two general categories: Aggregate and Individual Difference criteria.

AGGREGATION VS. INDIVIDUAL DIFFERENCES

An aggregate measure is one which lumps many individual responses together in such a way that the manner in which any given

Figure 5-13 The 4 × 4 Matrix Consideration Method

PRE AND POST:

1. If you were going to buy a new color TV tomorrow, which of these brands would be your *first choice?*

2. If your first choice were not available, what *other* brands would you consider?

3. Which brands would you *definitely not consider?*

BRAND LIST (shown three times)

—Philco
—General Electric
—Magnavox
—RCA
—Quasar
—Admiral
—Sears
—Sylvania
—Zenith
—Sony
—Some other brand

Resulting Matrix for Advertised Brand

POST

PRE	First Choice	Second Choice	Not Mentioned	Not Considered
First Choice	C	−	−	−
Second Choice	+	C	−	−
Not Mentioned	+	+	C	−
Would Not Consider	+	+	+	C

Score = Positive Movement (+) less Negative Movement (−)
where C = Constant Pre and Post.

individual behaved is not possible to determine from the measure. For example, the criterion "percent of individuals who indicate they definitely will buy brand X" is an aggregate measure. Total dollar sales for brand X in a given time period is also an aggregate measure. Which particular individuals in the target market purchased brand X cannot be detected from such a measure.

On the other hand, individual difference measures, as the name implies, retain specific information by individuals so that information on one measure for an individual, for example, purchase predisposition, can be compared with another measure, for example, purchase of brand, for that particular individual. As will be seen in later chapters, aggregate data are very often utilized as criteria in advertising appropriation models and procedures while individual difference measures are more likely utilized in copy research situations.

Individual Difference Behaviors. It should be noted that the manner in which the behavioral criterion itself is defined will likely have an impact on the closeness of such criteria as attitude and intentions to actual behavior on an individual-by-individual basis. An individual difference behavior might be defined as a single act and measured dichotomously. This is often the case in advertising studies where only purchase or non-purchase is measured on a single occasion of measurement. A single act could also be measured on a continuum; here, for example, the number of cartons of Pringle's Newfangled Potato Chips from "0" on up would be recorded in the behavioral measurement with the assumption being that two cartons indicates greater positive evaluation on the part of the purchaser than only one carton.

A single act behavior could also be observed on more than one occasion. For example, in a theater testing situation (such as ASI's system mentioned earlier), respondents may be requested to go through the simulated shopping environment on several occasions during the screening which might involve more than one exposure to the same commercial. This single act, repeated-observation behavioral criterion could be observed under homogeneous conditions (where no changes are made in price of product, shelf position, etc.) or under heterogeneous conditions (where non-advertising or advertising variables are manipulated from one observation period to the next).

Behavior might be defined as a multiple act. For example, observation might be made on the same individual for two or more different behaviors with respect to Pringle's Potato Chips. It might be noted whether or not the respondent makes a purchase of the chips during a visit to a grocery store and also whether or not the respondent makes a taste test at a special promotion booth set up in the grocery store at the same time; it might also be noted whether or not the same respondent sends in a coupon for free chips which was picked up at the taste booth.

There are at least three behaviors defined in the above hypothetical situation; many others could no doubt be considered. These behaviors may differ with respect to the amount of positive or negative evaluation about the object which they indicate. When a multiple act criterion is utilized in behavioral measurement, it could be considered in the context of an attitude scale development procedure.[34]

Aggregate Behaviors. Aggregate behaviors refer to such criteria as sales in dollars, sales in units, market share, net profits and the like. In many instances it would be inappropriate for an aggregate behavioral measure to serve as the criterion of advertising effectiveness. However, if at least two conditions are met, sales and related criteria might usefully serve as advertising decision making criteria. First, advertising will clearly be the major cause of sales; that is, other marketing variables such as distribution, price, and other promotions will not be as important as is advertising in the ultimate sale of the product. Second, there will be little or no carry-over effect; that is, current time period sales will be caused by current time period advertising. Past advertising will have little effect on the current time period sales measurements.

There are only two advertising situations which come really close to meeting these two criteria: direct mail advertising and advertising by retailers, that is, local advertising. In direct mail advertising, non-advertising marketing factors such as shelf position, store location, and sales personnel are not involved. Also, there is no carry-over effect since, assuming no further purchases, the advertising has done its job when the customer sends in the order in response to the advertisement. In the case of retail advertising, there is probably little carry-over effect of advertising of a store-wide sale, especially when the ads cover the product line with which the store is already associated. Also, although shopping trips are influenced by many different variables, there are situations in which advertising can have an important and immediate effect on store traffic.

Even though most national advertising for packaged goods and other types of products does not usually meet the two criteria defined above (advertising as major cause of sales and no carry-over effects), it is clear that the purpose of using advertising is to generate sales beyond those which would occur without its use for the purpose of making a profit. It should also be noted that, in the process, it is desirable that the needs and wants of consumers are adequately met while striving to make such a profit. The resolution of this dilemma usually takes on the format described by Simon:[35]

> Ever since Warren's Shoe Blacking became the first nationally advertised brand in England at the beginning of the nineteenth century, advertisers have studied their quarterly and yearly sales and advertising figures just as they studied other parts of the balance sheet, trying to determine how much sales volume their advertising created. Very quickly they learned the frustrating truth that it is impossible to relate a yearly advertising expenditure to the total amount of sales in that year, because the sales created by advertising are spread over a period of time longer than a quarter or a year.
>
> This teaches us that the measurement of advertising is composed of two tasks. The first task is determining how much sales volume a given advertising expenditure will cause *within an initial period* of, say, a year

or a quarter. The second task is determining how much sales volume will occur in *subsequent periods relative to the initial period.* . . .

The problem of carryover effects in relation to budget setting will be discussed fully in Chapter 8. The point to be made, however, is that if carry-over effects of advertising are explicitly taken into account, then it may still be possible and appropriate to utilize an aggregate behavioral criterion such as dollar sales per unit of time to plan the advertising program.

SALES GENERATED BY ADVERTISING

There are many ways in which it is clear that the sales have been "caused" by advertising in nationally-advertised brand situations. Anderson and Barry note the following examples of this fact:[36]
(1) Increase the use of a product
(2) Increase the frequency of use
(3) Increase the variety of uses
(4) Increase the frequency of replacement
(5) Increase the length of the buying season
(6) Present a promotional campaign (such as two-for-one sales)
(7) Bring a family of products together
(8) Turn a disadvantage into an advantage.
The "Avis Tries Harder" campaign as well as Listerine's campaign which turned "bad" taste into a desirable feature of the product are examples of advertising's power to generate sales under the last method listed above. Many other instances could no doubt be supplied for each of the above items. Under such circumstances, where it is clear that advertising has a major opportunity to "cause" sales to increase, an aggregate behavioral criterion might best serve in the decision making process to relate advertising input to advertising output.

QUESTIONS AND PROBLEMS

1. Considering the three dimensions of effectiveness (cognitive, affective, and conative), Ray hypothesizes three different orderings in his Three-Hierarchies model. The number of permutations of three things is six; that is, there are clearly six different orderings or permutations of the three effectiveness dimensions. What interpretations might be placed on the three orderings which Ray has left out of his hypothesis?

2. Consider the Leo Burnett CAPP model discussed in this chapter. What diagnosis of the brand's problems would you make if brand acceptance was 40 percent but brand preference was only 8 percent? Would your diagnosis differ depending upon whether the product involved was an underarm deodorant or an automobile?

3. Considering the various Hierarchy of Effect models summarized in Figure 5-3, why do you suppose different individuals have developed so many different conceptions of the elements (brand awareness, comprehension, etc.) which go to make up the cognitive, affective, and conative stages?

4. Describe a specific instance or example of how Krugman's low involvement theory of communication effects might work in advertising.
5. Can you develop any evidence to support the hypothesis developed by Wells regarding the "Approach-Avoidance" categorization of products relative to attitude/behavior relationships? Is this a reasonable hypothesis? Why or why not?
6. Which of the Three-Hierarchies suggested by Ray do you think most often characterizes national advertising situations? Why?
7. Design a study which would reliably and accurately measure *advertising exposure* levels for a television media schedule.
8. In what ways could the Starch Recognition Method be improved?
9. Categorize the criteria discussed in this chapter with respect to their primary usefulness in decision making for a particular advertising decision variable, that is, market segmentation, money, message, or media.
10. What factors explain the existence of a carry-over effect of advertising for certain products? How could advertising have an effect many years after it first appeared? Why is this of concern to advertising management?

ENDNOTES

1. This discussion draws from Philip Kotler, *Marketing Decision Making* (New York: Holt, Rinehart, and Winston, 1971), pp. 436-438.
2. John D. Maloney, "Attitude Measurement and Formation," paper presented at American Marketing Association, Test Market Design and Measurement Workshop, Chicago, Illinois, April 21, 1966.
3. Russell H. Colley, *Defining Advertising Goals for Measured Advertising Results* (New York: Association of National Advertisers, 1961).
4. E.K. Strong, *Psychology of Selling* (New York: McGraw-Hill Book Co., 1925).
5. Clyde Bedell, *How to Write Advertising that Sells* (New York: McGraw-Hill Book Co., 1940).
6. R.J. Lavidge and G.A. Steiner, "A Model for Predictive Measurements of Advertising Effectiveness," *Journal of Marketing* (October 1961), pp. 59-62.
7. For example, see this viewpoint in D. Krech, R.S. Crutchfield, and E.L. Ballachey, *Individual in Society* (New York: McGraw-Hill Book Co., 1962).
8. E. Rogers, *Diffusion of Innovations* (Glencoe, Illinois: The Free Press, 1962).
9. W.J. McGuire, "An Information Processing Approach to Advertising Effectiveness," in H. Davis and A.J. Silk (eds.), *The Behavioral and Management Sciences in Marketing* (New York: Ronald Press, 1974).
10. T.S. Robertson, *Innovation and The Consumer* (New York: Holt, Rinehart and Winston, Inc., 1971).
11. Kristian S. Palda, "The Hypothesis of a Hierarchy of Effects: A Partial Evaluation," *Journal of Marketing Research* (February 1966), pp. 13-24.
12. Jack B. Haskins, "Factual Recall as a Measure of Advertising Effectiveness," *Journal of Advertising Research* (March 1964), pp. 2-8.
13. David A. Aker and George S. Day, "A Dynamic Model of Relationships Among Advertising, Consumer Awareness, Attitudes, and Behavior," *Journal of Applied Psychology* 59 (1974), pp. 281-286.
14. Leon Festinger, *A Theory of Cognitive Dissonance* (New York: Harper & Row, 1957).
15. Leon Festinger, "Behavioral Support for Opinion Change," in *Dimensions of Communication*, Lee Richardson (ed.), (New York: Appleton-Century-Crofts, Inc., 1969).
16. Herbert E. Krugman, "The Impact of Television Advertising: Learning without Involvement," *Public Opinion Quarterly* (Fall 1965) pp. 349-356.

17. William D. Wells, "Liking and Sales Effectiveness: A Hypothesis," *Topline* (A publication of McCollum/Spielman, Inc., New York), February 1980.
18. Michael L. Ray, "Marketing Communications and the Hierarchy of Effects," in Peter Clarke (ed.), *New Models for Mass Communication Research*, Vol. II, *Sage Annual Review of Communication Research* (Beverly Hills: Sage Publications, Inc., 1973).
19. Alan G. Sawyer, "A Laboratory Experimental Investigation of the Effects of Repetition of Advertising," unpublished doctoral dissertation, Stanford University, 1971.
20. Ray, *op.cit.*
21. A.J. Silk and R. Vavra, "The Influence of Advertising's Affective Qualities on Consumer Response," paper presented at the Association for Consumer Research, American Marketing Association Workshop on Consumer Information Processing, Chicago, Illinois, 1972.
22. W.J. McGuire, "Personality and Attitude Change: An Information Processing Theory," in A.G. Greenwald, T.C. Brock, and T.M. Ostrom (eds.), *Psychological Foundations of Attitudes* (New York: Academic Press, 1968), pp. 171-196.
23. R.M. Heeler, "The Effects of Mixed Media, Multiple Copy, Repetition and Competition in Advertising: A Laboratory Investigation," unpublished doctoral dissertation, Stanford University, 1972.
24. Daniel Starch, *Measuring Advertising Readership and Results* (New York: McGraw-Hill, 1966).
25. For a more detailed discussion of laboratory methods in the evaluation of advertising creative processes, see D.B. Lucas and S.H. Britt, *Measuring Advertising Effectiveness* (New York: McGraw-Hill, 1963).
26. Dik W. Twedt, "How Can the Advertising Dollar Work Harder?" *Journal of Marketing* (April 1965), pp. 60-62.
27. E.W.J. Faison, *Advertising: A Behavioral Approach for Managers* (New York: John Wiley & Sons, 1980), p. 716.
28. Martin Fishbein, "Attitude and the Prediction of Behavior," in Martin Fishbein, *Readings in Attitude Theory and Measurement* (New York: John Wiley & Sons, Inc., 1967), p. 477.
29. "Choosing the Right Attitude Measure," *Topline,* a publication of the McCollum/Spielman Company, Great Neck, New York (April 1980).
30. Fishbein, *op.cit.,* pp. 288-334.
31. W.D. Wells, "Measuring Readiness to Buy," *Harvard Business Review* (July-August 1961), pp. 81-87.
32. "Choosing the Right Attitude Measure," *Topline, op.cit.*
33. Joel N. Axelrod, "Attitude Measures that Predict Purchase," *Journal of Advertising Research* (March 1968), pp. 3-17.
34. For a more detailed discussion of these and related issues, see John D. Leckenby, "Conceptual Foundations for Copytesting Research," working paper no. 2, February 1976, Department of Advertising, University of Illinois at Urbana-Champaign.
35. Julian Simon, *The Management of Advertising* (Englewood Cliffs, New Jersey: Prentice-Hall, Inc., 1971), pp. 13-14.
36. R.L. Anderson and T.E. Barry, *Advertising Management: Text and Cases* (Columbus, Ohio: Charles E. Merrill Publishing Co., 1979), pp. 165-166.

PART 3:
DETERMINING
ADVERTISING DECISIONS

- Market Segmentation
- Management of the Advertising Budget
- Response Functions and Budgeting
- Cases in Advertising Budgeting
  and Control
- Advertising Creative Strategy
- Creative Strategy and Copy Research
- Cases in Creative Strategy Decisions
- Advertising Media Strategy
- Media Strategy and Exposure
  Estimation
- Cases in Media Strategy Decisions

MARKET SEGMENTATION

- The Meaning of Market Segmentation
- Market Segmentation Strategies
- Bases for Market Segmentation
- Market Segmentation Data

MARKET SEGMENTATION

- The Method of Market Segmentation
- Market Segmentation Strategies
- Steps in Market Segmentation
- Market Segmentation Data

Decision Making Organization of This Text

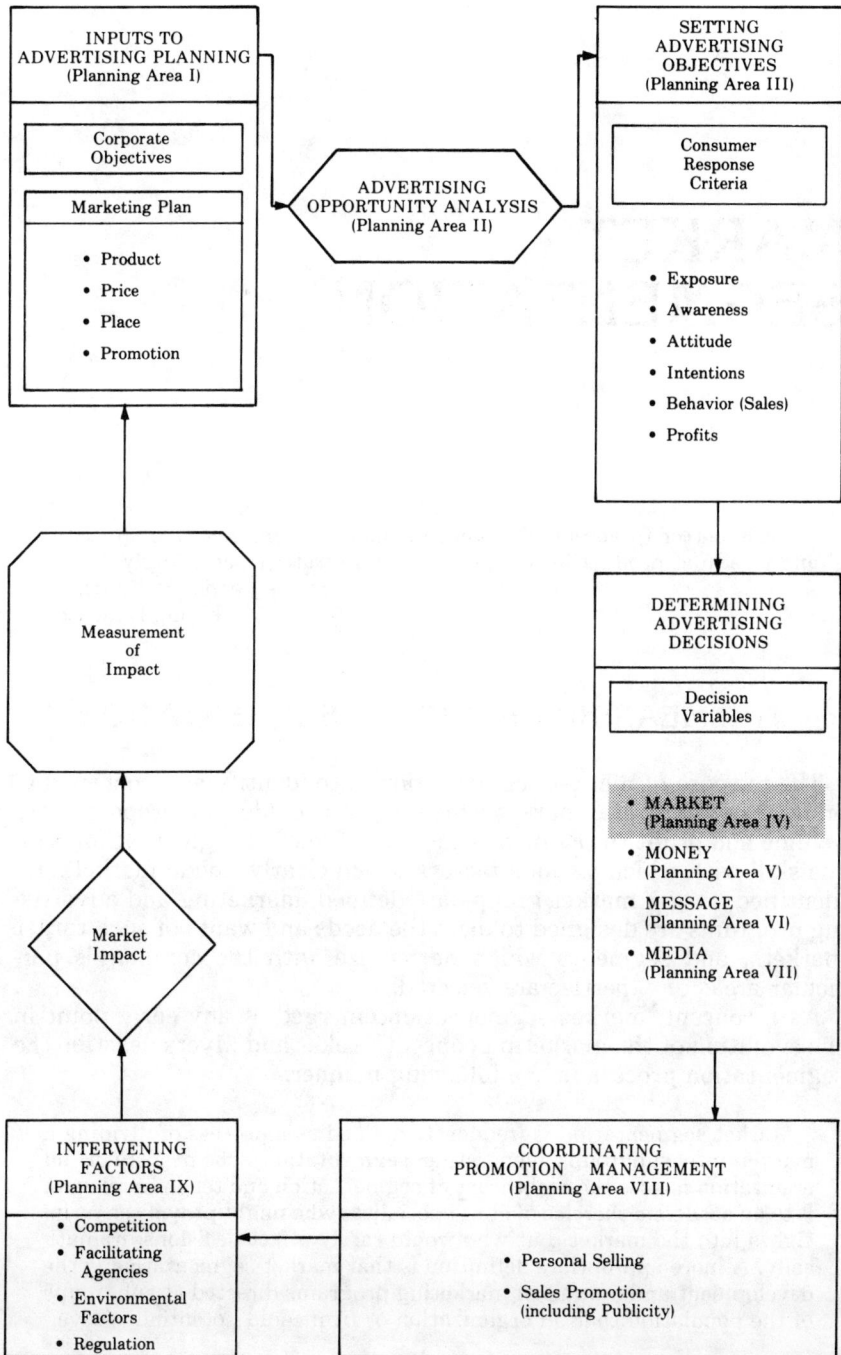

```
┌─────────────────────────────┐              ┌─────────────────────────────┐
│       INPUTS TO             │              │        SETTING              │
│ ADVERTISING PLANNING        │              │     ADVERTISING             │
│   (Planning Area I)         │              │      OBJECTIVES             │
│                             │              │  (Planning Area III)        │
│  ┌───────────────────────┐  │              │                             │
│  │    Corporate          │  │              │  ┌───────────────────────┐  │
│  │    Objectives         │  │              │  │     Consumer          │  │
│  ├───────────────────────┤  │  ADVERTISING │  │     Response          │  │
│  │   Marketing Plan      │  │  OPPORTUNITY │  │     Criteria          │  │
│  │                       │  │   ANALYSIS   │  └───────────────────────┘  │
│  │   • Product           │  │ (Planning    │                             │
│  │   • Price             │  │   Area II)   │   • Exposure                │
│  │   • Place             │  │              │   • Awareness               │
│  │   • Promotion         │  │              │   • Attitude                │
│  │                       │  │              │   • Intentions              │
│  └───────────────────────┘  │              │   • Behavior (Sales)        │
└─────────────────────────────┘              │   • Profits                 │
                                             └─────────────────────────────┘
```

INPUTS TO ADVERTISING PLANNING (Planning Area I)

Corporate Objectives

Marketing Plan

- Product
- Price
- Place
- Promotion

ADVERTISING OPPORTUNITY ANALYSIS (Planning Area II)

SETTING ADVERTISING OBJECTIVES (Planning Area III)

Consumer Response Criteria

- Exposure
- Awareness
- Attitude
- Intentions
- Behavior (Sales)
- Profits

Measurement of Impact

DETERMINING ADVERTISING DECISIONS

Decision Variables

- MARKET (Planning Area IV)
- MONEY (Planning Area V)
- MESSAGE (Planning Area VI)
- MEDIA (Planning Area VII)

Market Impact

INTERVENING FACTORS (Planning Area IX)

- Competition
- Facilitating Agencies
- Environmental Factors
- Regulation

COORDINATING PROMOTION MANAGEMENT (Planning Area VIII)

- Personal Selling
- Sales Promotion (including Publicity)

MARKET SEGMENTATION

"It is better to accept divergent demand as a market characteristic and to adjust product lines and marketing strategy accordingly."
—Wendell R. Smith
Marketing Educator

THE MEANING OF MARKET SEGMENTATION

The purpose of market segmentation is to identify and concentrate on fractions of a total market which might provide a disproportionate volume and profit to the firm. The focus of market segmentation is on the skill with which various factors which clearly divide markets are identified, target market groups are defined, marketing and advertising programs are designed to meet the needs and wants of such target markets, and segments which harmonize with the company's particular areas of expertise are selected.

As a concept, market segmentation emerged at any early point in the evolution of the marketing concept. Aaker and Myers describe the segmentation process in the following manner:

> Market segmentation is frequently defined as a process of dividing a market into subgroups (generating segmentation schemes). Such an orientation misses the real thrust of segmentation and tends to relegate it to an academic exercise of staff specialists who might provide some insights into the market, but who would rarely affect decisions dramatically. A more appropriate definition is that market segmentation is the development and pursuit of marketing programs directed at subgroups of the population that an organization or firm could potentially serve.[1]

BENEFITS OF SEGMENTATION

There are several distinct benefits which have been attributed to the role of market segmentation in marketing planning and execution:[2]

(1) A segmentation perspective leads to a more precise definition of the market in terms of consumer needs. Segmentation thus improves management's understanding of the customer and, more importantly, *why* he or she buys.

(2) Management, once it understands consumer needs, is in a much better position to direct marketing programs that will satisfy these needs and hence will parallel the demands of the market.

(3) A continuous program of market segmentation strengthens management capabilities in meeting changing market demands.

(4) Management is better able to assess competitive strengths and weaknesses.

(5) It is possible to assess a firm's strengths and weaknesses through identification of market segments.

(6) Segmentation leads to a more efficient allocation of marketing resources.

(7) Segmentation leads to a more precise setting of market objectives. Targets are defined operationally, and performance can later be evaluated against these standards.

Specific benefits can be suggested for the application of market segmentation to advertising decision making. With respect to the advertising budget, setting market segmentation objectives allows the spending of money, say on a geographic basis for example, where the potential sales volume is greatest at a particular time. In the message decision making area, knowledge of the characteristics of a particular market segment, say the "young married without children" segment, helps in the development of the creative strategy since it can be prepared with particular people in mind rather than everyone in the United States. In the advertising management area of marketing, perhaps one of the most useful areas in which segmentation concepts are applied is in media planning. As indicated by Barban and others, the principle underlying the efficient use of advertising time and space is matching markets and media—that is, the media planner tries to invest advertising dollars in those media vehicles which have audiences that closely parallel the description of the target market. The better the match, the less money wasted on delivering messages to consumers for whom the product was not intended in the first place.[3]

Assumptions of Segmentation. The whole idea of market segmentation rests basically upon three major assumptions.[4] These can be stated as follows:

(1) The concept of segmentation is based on the proposition that *consumers are different.*

(2) A second assumption of segmentation is that *differences in consumers are related to differences in market demand.*

(3) That *segments of consumers can be isolated within the overall market* is the third assumption.

It might be thought that a product such as toothpaste, which, after all, almost every individual uses, would be thought of in similar ways by consumers regardless of their differences. Following this thinking, the advertiser of toothpaste would use advertising media which have extremely broad coverage to the entire United States in an attempt to sell the particular brand to everyone who will listen. Yet there is evidence to show that the three assumptions of segmentation are often correct, even in the case of a mass consumption product such as toothpaste. *Different* consumers demand *different* kinds of toothpaste; it is possible to reach these different kinds of consumers through *different* media vehicles in advertising. Aim toothpaste has apparently been a successful product because the managers of that brand were able to identify a market segment whose needs and wants were not satisfied by the already available brands. Crest provided fluoride protection while Close-up provided a "gel" consistency rather than a paste consistency. Aim combines both these attributes in one product and thereby captures those individuals who liked the gel of Close-up but wanted the protection of fluoride.

Usage of Segmentation. The alternative to the following of a market segmentation strategy is usually termed "product differentiation" strategy. Product differentiation strategies are dependent upon the promotion of product differences, whether these are real or imagined. A product differentiation policy is highly dependent on some unusual aspect of the seller's product, the advertising media utilized to communicate this aspect, selling messages, package designs and so forth. The distinction between the differentiation strategy and the segmentation strategy has been described by Kotrba as follows:[5]

> The marketer employing the strategy of product differentiation tries to build sales by offering a product that can be easily distinguished from similar products, and usually directs marketing efforts at the typical consumer in the group of potential buyers for the product.
> The marketer who segments the market of potential buyers for the product directs marketing effort at exclusive consumer groups or submarkets. This person believes that each group will probably buy that product which best satisfies their particular needs.
> This means that the "product differentiators" are more sensitive to product characteristics, and the "market segmenters" more sensitive to consumer characteristics.

Clearly, neither strategy, differentiation or segmentation, is likely to be employed exclusively in most situations. Some mix of each will likely be exhibited in practice. Nonetheless, the advertising manager must make a conscious decision as to which of these "leanings" is most appropriate under the circumstances prevailing for a particular product. The decision to go with one strategy more than with the other will depend, on at least the six factors indicated in Figure 6-1. These factors are: (1) Size of the market; (2) Consumer sensitivity; (3) Product life-cycle; (4) Type of product; (5) Number of competitors; and (6) Typical competitor strategies.

Figure 6-1   Differentiation vs. Segmentation Strategy Selection Chart

	Use Product Differentiation	Strategy Selection Factors	Use Market Segmentation
	Promote Product Differences		Emphasize Market Differences
Market Factors	Narrow	SIZE OF MARKET	Broad
		O X	
		1 2 3 4 5 6 7 8 9 10	
	High	CONSUMER SENSITIVITY TO PRODUCT DIFFERENCES	Low
		O X	
		1 2 3 4 5 6 7 8 9 10	
Product Factors	Introduction Stage	PRODUCT LIFE CYCLE	Saturation Stage
		O X	
		1 2 3 4 5 6 7 8 9 10	
	Commodity	TYPE OF PRODUCT	Distinct Item
		O X	
		1 2 3 4 5 6 7 8 9 10	
Competitive Factors	Few	NUMBER OF COMPETITORS	Many
		O X	
		1 2 3 4 5 6 7 8 9 10	
	Differentiation Policy	TYPICAL COMPETITOR STRATEGY	Segmentation Policy
		O X	
		1 2 3 4 5 6 7 8 9 10	

SOURCE: Adapted from R. W. Kotrba, "The Strategy Selection Chart," *Journal of Marketing* (July 1966), pp. 22–25.

When a market is already small, further cutting up of this market on geographic, demographic or other bases will probably be undesirable. For example, the market for hearing aids is small to begin with and probably not segmented further from an economic point of view. If consumers' sensitivity to product differences in a particular product category is low, say as in the case of lawn rakes, then a differentiation strategy will probably be unsuccessful. On the other hand, detergents apparently represent a category of products where "newness" is something people are invariably interested in. Once primary demand for a product has been developed, for example, as in the case of home video-tape recorders, it becomes practical for a firm to produce the additional product versions required by a strategy of market segmentation. For a product category where most brands are new and have just come on the market, it may be preferable to follow a product differentiation strategy to initially help promote primary or generic demand. If the product is similar to a commodity (sugar, wheat, etc.), then it will be difficult to find ways to modify it and product differentiation strategies will be inappropriate. As the number of competitors increases in a product category, it becomes increasingly difficult for any single firm to differentiate its product from the competitors' product; in such cases a segmentation strategy might be preferable. Finally, if the majority of the competitors are applying a segmentation strategy, it may be difficult for a firm to compete with a policy of differentiation.

In Figure 6-1, the "0" might refer to a product such as gasoline while the "X" might represent a product category such as television sets. These products are evaluated on the six factors mentioned above to illustrate the manner in which a decision might be made about segmentation. In the example, gasoline products would no doubt tend more towards a product differentiation strategy while television would tend more towards segmentation.

MARKET SEGMENTATION STRATEGIES

Product differentiation policies and segmentation policies, as suggested above, can be viewed as blends on a continuum where the endpoints of that continuum are "customer self-selection" and "controlled coverage of marketing effort" as defined by the manner in which the marketing tools are utilized. An examination of segmentation strategies from this vantage point will provide a broader perspective on the possibilities in utilizing segmentation.

ELEMENTS OF SEGMENTATION STRATEGY

Figure 6-2 shows four different types of segmentation strategies corresponding to the four cells (which are numbered 1 through 4) in the illustration.[6]

The situation represented in cell 1 is best described by typical product positioning activities. The product is designed and often made available to the general market; however, the characteristics of the product will often be differentially attractive to potential customers. The company relies on *customer self-selection* to deliver the product appeal to the target market segments. For example, in the past it might have been suggested that Coke concentrated on selling its product to everyone in the United States as well as abroad. In recent years, however, Coca-Cola has pursued a policy of differentiating its product

Figure 6-2   Elements of A Market
Segmentation Strategy

Method of Targeting the Marketing Effort	Marketing Decision Variables	
	Product Characteristics and Appeals	Advertising, Price and Distribution
Customer Self-Selection	(1)	(2)
Controlled Coverage of Marketing Effort	(3)	(4)

SOURCE: Adapted from R.E. Frank, W.F. Massy and Y. Wind, *Market Segmentation* (Englewood Cliffs, N.J.: Prentice-Hall, Inc., 1972), p. 7.

line in terms of container sizes and types as well as the introduction of diet drinks. This product differentiation will naturally lead to customer self-selection of the product. Customers interested in weight control will tend to become self-selected purchasers of the diet version of Coke. Customers in the low income market segment might tend to purchase larger sizes of the product due to the volume price decrease. Higher income consumers might be willing to pay for the convenience of "throw-away" containers. Customer self-selection strategies such as this are at the "low" end of the segmentation continuum and are really product differentiation policies at base.

When the type of strategy represented in cell 1 above is supplemented by marketing efforts more directly under the control of the manager, the situation in cell 3 results. Here, in addition to designing the product with particular segments in mind, the product might be sold only in stores frequented by members of a particular target market, free samples of the brand could be sent to households with the appropriate target market profile, and so on. For example, suppose a company sold a premium line of baseball gloves. This product would be differentiated in the sense that it was made of superior materials and designed with professional baseball features. It could be sold or made available to consumers only through specific sporting goods stores outlets; it would not be offered through regular department stores or through discount department stores. This strategy of retail placement of the gloves would tend to insure that only those interested in high quality, professionally constructed gloves would constitute the market for them.

The most important application of the *controlled coverage* strategy is in advertising, specifically. The objective is to make the message available through specific media vehicles to the target market and, at its most effective level of implementation, to no one else. This element is represented in Figure 6–2 by cell 4. The steps involved in the application of controlled coverage segmentation strategies are:

(1) Determining how use opportunities for the product and probable responses to advertising vary within the population.

(2) Determining how well the relevant media vehicles can be targeted to various groups of potential customers.

(3) Defining operational market segments and assessing their worth. A segment is operational if (a) it is sufficiently different from other segments to make disproportionate allocation of money worthwhile and (b) it can be reached efficiently through the available media vehicles.

(4) Finding the optimal distribution of effort among the various segments for each of the media vehicles.

For example, suppose the Bantin Camera Company manufactures and markets a line of cameras for which they have developed a new lense adaption feature which improves the ease of using different lenses. Suppose that this camera is complex to operate. It has many features, in addition to the new one, of a professional camera. It is to be used by semi-professionals who desire high quality, and it is moderately priced relative to the competition. The Bantin management might define their target market segment as those individuals who have moderate to high income in order to afford purchase of the camera, who have considerable knowledge of the technical aspects of camera work, and who are highly motivated to improve the quality of their photographic work. Suppose *Photography* magazine possessed the following characteristic: 43 percent of the subscribers have moderate or high income. It might be assumed that people who purchase such a magazine are, by and large, interested in improving their photographic skills and learning more about photography. Suppose Bantin management estimates that if just 3 percent of those consumers who subscribe to *Photography* magazine and who also have high or moderate incomes purchase one Bantin camera in the period of one business quarter, this camera line could operate at a profit for the company. Clearly, Bantin would seem well-advised to place advertising in this magazine and follow a controlled coverage segmentation strategy.

It should be noted that, though it is often assumed, it is not clear that Bantin Camera Company should automatically pursue the controlled coverage strategy outlined above. There are two general inefficiencies to be recognized in the use of such a segmentation strategy. First, such an approach leads to primary usage of non-mass coverage media vehicles rather than mass coverage vehicles such as *Reader's Digest*, for example. Such mass coverage vehicles are more efficient than *Photography* magazine in the sense that a huge audience is reached, thus lowering the cost of advertising per selling contact. Second, the controlled coverage approach forces the manager to forego marketing and advertising application to segments other than the prime or target segment; it is possible that even some low-income individuals who are extremely interested in photography might forego some other purchases in order to buy a good-quality camera. Using the ultimate controlled coverage strategy in which only moderate to high income individuals are reached by the selling messages would eliminate the potential purchasers from the advertising effort who reside outside the strictly defined market segment of prime interest. Advertising in a mass vehicle, such as *Reader's Digest,* on the other hand, would offer the opportunity to reach many of these people. Clearly, the advantages and disadvantages of the controlled coverage segmentation strategy must be weighed against each other in a particular instance; the important thing is that the manager should not automatically assume that the strategy represented in cell 4 in Figure 6-2 is always the superior one.

Cell 2 in Figure 6-2 illustrates the final major category of segmentation strategy. This cell illustrates the situation where customer self-selection is used in the development of a segmented advertising strategy. The manager may select media which reach a broad section of the market but tailor the message to one particular segment or a group of segments. Alternatively, the planner might use broad, general message appeals but rely on the format of the commercial to provide the desired market segment self-selection. For example, a commercial for Irish Spring toilet soap might stress deodorant protection (a general appeal) but be directed at either men or women by altering the format or context in which the appeal is presented. The format, in order to appeal primarily to men, might deal with a logging operation where several men get the suggestion from a woman that they should use Irish Spring to "cure" the current problem; this commercial might appear on a television program which has about equal numbers of male and female viewers. It, accordingly, would rely on customer self-selection strategies to provide the desired male market for Irish Spring.

In the context of the above primary dimensions of segmentation strategy, there is one, overriding matter which must be kept in mind. This element of segmentation strategy is so easily over-looked or else actively engaged in that it has been given the name, "The Majority Fallacy." This issue is discussed below.

THE MAJORITY FALLACY

There is a pitfall which is easy to be taken in by in the development of market segmentation strategy; this pitfall is common enough in occurrence to have been given a name: "The Majority Fallacy." One approach often followed in the development of a segmentation strategy is to first determine who the large users of the product are and then use this information as the basis of identification of the target market segment. The problem with this procedure is that, very often, competitors will also be following the same process in the identification of their target markets. They have also identified the segment with the "large" potential and are directing their marketing and advertising efforts at it. This large, attractive segment then has several different brands of the same product competing fiercely for its business. This undoubtedly will leave a smaller segment of this market with no brand, or very few brands, attempting to serve it. This segment could possibly provide greater profits than the larger, more attractive segment since the largest market segment is not necessarily the most profitable. It may be the case that it is more profitable to attempt to gain the business of a small segment which has been ignored in the past than to fight eight or nine competitors for a share of a segment which represents 70 percent of the sales in the product category even though that small segment might only represent 6 or 7 percent of the category sales. It is costly to wage a promotional battle with several other companies in a large market segment. This error in segmentation strategy is called the majority fallacy, and it is no doubt a common phenomenon.

BASES FOR MARKET SEGMENTATION

CRITERIA FOR MARKET SEGMENTS

In general, for a market segment to be of any use to the advertising planner, it should possess the following characteristics: (1) it should be large enough in size and potential to warrant the expenditure of money on it (while at the same time keeping in mind the "majority fallacy"); (2) the segment should be able to be reached by the available media; and (3) it should demonstrate variation in market behavior relative to other segments of the market; that is, the advertising directed at, say the young adult market segment, should not produce the same result in teenage, middle-age and older adult markets as in the young adult market if this segmentation scheme is to be useful.

Whether or not a specific market segmentation variable, for example, age, is a useful basis for segmentation for a particular product is more specifically defined by Frank, Massy and Wind using the following criteria:[8]

(1) The variables should divide a market into homogeneous segments that tend to respond differently to the firm's promotional activities. More specifically, this requires the establishment of the following relations:

   (a) Between the segmentation variable(s) and the criterion variable in the segmentation problem (for example, total consumption, consumption of a given brand, and brand loyalty).

    (b) Between the variable(s) and the performance characteristics
        of the various marketing inputs (such as media usage and so
        forth).
(2) The variable(s) should be measurable.
(3) The variable(s) should be accessible to the firm's promotional
    activities.
(4) The variable(s) should lead to increased profits from
    segmentation.

In practice, the selection of the segmentation variables is one of the
most difficult aspects of the entire segmentation process. One problem
which must be avoided is the usage of too many segmentation variables in the definition of the target market. Each time another
demographic variable is added to the definition, the effect is to narrow
the size of the market segment. As Barban, *et al.* note, "The desirable
balance between defining targets too broadly or too narrowly is just
this: the target should be defined specifically enough so that the media
planner will know what type of audience to look for in making media
comparisons, but should not be defined so narrowly that a significant
number of real prospects are excluded from the target."[9] Figure 6-3
shows what can happen to the size of the target market when too many
segmentation bases are used in the target market definition. When
only one variable is used, that is, sex, the market size is 66,087,000
men; when education, home ownership, marital status, geographic,
and income variables are added on to the definition, the segment size
becomes 4,668,000. This is a reduction from the initial segment size
(defined only on the basis of sex) of 93 percent.

A CLASSIFICATION SCHEME

Figure 6-4 shows the classification of major bases for segmentation
of markets. In cell 1 are demographic variables; these are *general*
characteristics of consumers in the sense that they are not dependent
upon particular buying and consumption decisions. Demographic
characteristics are also *objective* bases for segmentation in the sense
that they are directly observable.

In cell 2 are personality traits and life style bases for segmentation.
These variables must be *inferred* and, in this sense, are not directly and
objectively observable (measurable). These segmentation variables,
like demographics, are also general with respect to customer
characteristics.

In cell 3 are product consumption patterns; these are objectively
observable and depend upon the specific purchase of particular products in particular circumstances, that is, they are *situation-specific*.

Finally, in cell 4 of Figure 6-4 are the situation-specific variables of
attitude, perceptions and preferences regarding particular product
purchases.[10] These measures are inferred rather than objectively observable. The most commonly utilized of all these segmentation variables
are the demographic variables and consumption patterns (light,

Figure 6-3   The Effect of Additional Segmentation
Variables on Segment Size

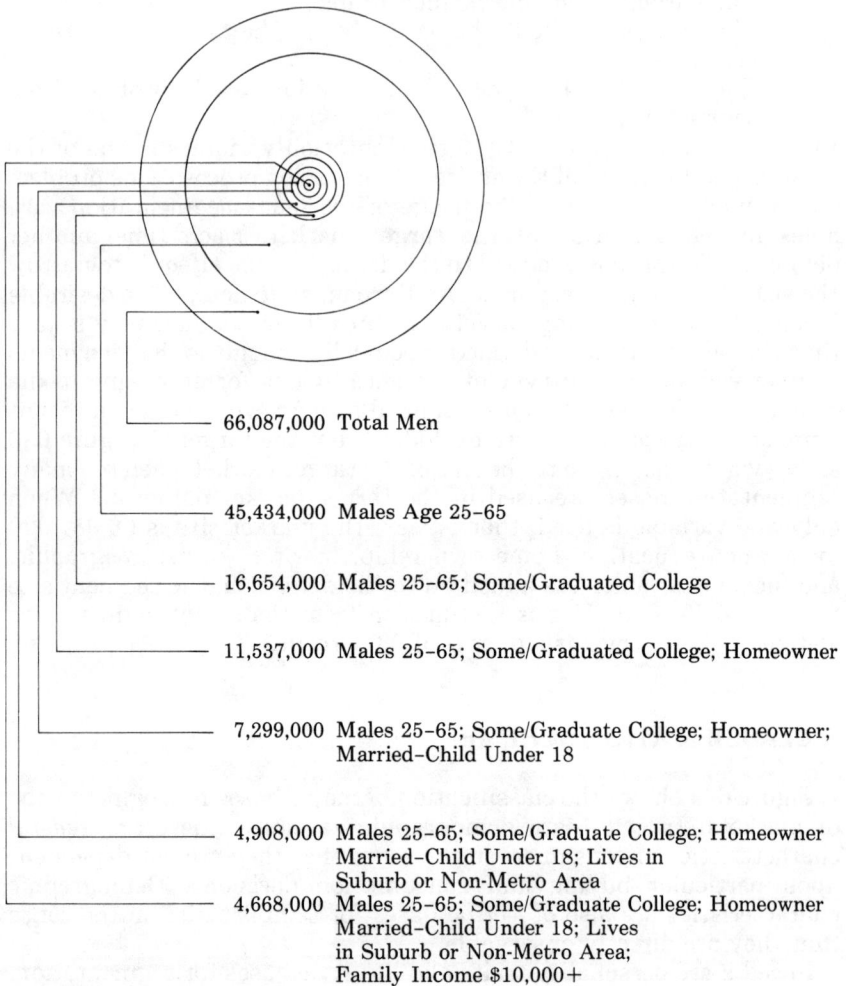

66,087,000 Total Men

45,434,000 Males Age 25-65

16,654,000 Males 25-65; Some/Graduated College

11,537,000 Males 25-65; Some/Graduated College; Homeowner

7,299,000 Males 25-65; Some/Graduate College; Homeowner;
Married–Child Under 18

4,908,000 Males 25-65; Some/Graduate College; Homeowner
Married–Child Under 18; Lives in
Suburb or Non-Metro Area

4,668,000 Males 25-65; Some/Graduate College; Homeowner
Married–Child Under 18; Lives
in Suburb or Non-Metro Area;
Family Income $10,000+

SOURCE: A.M. Barban, S.M. Cristol and F.J. Kopec, *Essentials of Media
Planning: A Marketing Viewpoint*, p. 32.

medium and heavy usage). Of the ten segmentation bases classified in
Figure 6-4, three general categories are discussed in some detail
below: (1) demographic variables; (2) socio-psychological variables; and
product usage variables (consumption patterns).

Demographic Segmentation Bases. Standard demographic variables
include age, sex, income, occupation, education, family life cycle

Figure 6-4   A Classification Scheme of Alternative
Bases for Market Segmentation

| | | Customer Characteristics | |
		General	Situation-Specific
M e a s u r e s	Objective	(1) Demographic Factors (Age, Stage in Life Cycle, Sex, Place of Living, Etc.) Socioeconomic Factors	(2) Consumption Patterns (Heavy, Medium, Light) Brand Loyalty Patterns Buying Situations
	Inferred	(3) Personality Traits Life Style	(4) Attitudes Perceptions and Preferences

SOURCE: R.E. Frank, W.F. Massy and Y. Wind, *Market Segmentation* (Englewood Cliffs, N.J.: Prentice-Hall, Inc., 1972), p. 27.

(marital status and age of children), family size, social class, race, religion, geographic region, county size, city size and population density. The suggested breakdowns within each of these variables, that is, the subcategories such as "under 6 years of age," are shown in Table 6-1.[11] It should be reiterated that it is not necessary for the target market to be defined on each and every one of these demographic categories. It may be sufficient for a given product to define the target market based only on one variable, for example, age; the target market might be defined simply as "all adults over 34 years of age." In addition, it is clear that several of the demographic variables will be highly correlated with each other, and, therefore, provide redundant information to the advertising decision maker. For example, high income will be related to particular professions and excluded from other professions. Those in certain professions will have higher educational levels than those in other job categories. Social class is, in large part, a function of income, education, and occupation. In many instances, therefore, it is unnecessary to define the segment on each of these variables. As indicated in the previous section, those variables should be chosen which most nearly, in a given product situation, meet the basic criteria for the usefulness of segmentation variables indicated in that section.

Sociopsychological Segmentation Bases. Description of consumers based upon their objectively observable characteristics, for example, demographics, tells a great deal about them but not nearly as much

Table 6-1   Suggested Demographic Subcategories

Variable	Breakdowns
Age	Under 6; 6-11; 12-17; 18-34; 35-49 50-64; 65+
Sex	Male; Female
Income	Under $5,000; $5,000-$7,999; $8,000-$9,999; $10,000-$14,999; $15,000+
Occupation	Professional and technical; Managers, Officials, and Proprietors; Clerical, Sales; Craftsmen, Foreman; Laborers; Farmers; Retired; Students; Housewives; Unemployed
Education	Grade School or Less; Some High School; Graduated High School; Some College; Graduated College
Family Life Cycle	Young, Single; Young, Married, No children; Young, Married, Youngest child under 6; Young, Married, Youngest child 6 or older; Older, Married, with Children; Older, Married, No Children under 18; Older, Single; Other
Family Size	1-2; 3-4; 5+
Social Class	Lower-Lower; Upper-Lower; Lower-Middle; Upper-Middle; Lower-Upper; Upper-Upper
Race	Caucasian; Negro; Oriental
Religion	Protestant; Catholic; Jewish; Other
Geographic Region	Pacific; Mountain; West North Central; West South Central; East North Central; East South Central; South Atlantic; New England
County Size	A; B; C; D (A.C. Nielsen Company)
City Size	Under 5,000; 5,000-19,999; 20,000-49,999; 50,000-99,999; 100,000-249,999; 250,000-499,999; 500,000-999,999; 1,000,000-3,999,999; 4,000,000+
Population Density	Urban; Suburban; Rural

SOURCE: A.M. Barban, S.M. Cristol, and F.J. Kopec, *Essentials of Media Planning: A Marketing Viewpoint* (Chicago: Crain Books, 1976), pp. 29-30.

about them as would be desirable from the point of view of the person constructing the advertising messages. This is so since two people who are exactly the same age, have the same occupation, have the same annual income, are of the same sex and so forth will still think, believe, and behave in different ways. This is due to the differences between these two people which are "unobservable" or which reside in their mental states. Sociopsychological bases of segmentation attempt to take up where demographics leave off in terms of description of consumers.

Early attempts to develop this approach often dealt with the concept of personality. Studies which were conducted in an attempt to relate personality to such factors as brand preference, brand loyalty, store preference, and other types of consumer purchasing behavior were disappointing, with very few exceptions.[12] In light of these findings, personality as a segmentation basis has been largely abandoned in favor of the concepts of "psychographics" and "life styles." The psychographic classifications utilized by one syndicated research firm are illustrated in Figure 6–5.

Plummer has suggested the following benefits of utilizing life styles as a basis for segmentation:[13]

(1) Life style segmentation provides a richer redefinition of the target audience . . .

(2) It provides an overview of the market in a multidimensional sense . . .

(3) Life style information can be employed to position a product based on the inferences drawn from the portrait of the consumer both in terms of his or her basic needs and how the product fits into his or her life . . .

(4) For the creative person in advertising it provides a richer, more life-like picture of the consumer; it helps him or her set the "tone of voice" for the advertising; it is helpful in developing advertising that "rewards" people in their activities and interests and portrays people in advertising in roles the target consumer sees himself or herself . . .

(5) Life styles help develop sounder overall marketing and media strategies.

A method of developing life styles is that of using AIO scales which attempt to measure the activities, interests and opinions of consumers. Table 6–2 lists the elements of such AIO measures.[14]

It should be noted, however, that the entire area of psychographic and life style segmentation is subject to some debate regarding its definition and usefulness. As Ziff has suggested, for example:

> . . . the very definition of "psychographics" remains a controversial one. Some have used the term to refer to basic personality characteristics . . . some have applied it to life style variables . . . others have preferred definitions involving attitudes, values and beliefs. . . . Finally, still others have given primary emphasis to the specific benefits individuals specify in a particular product.[15]

At least one study warns on overstressing the value of psychographics in practice.[16] The Newspaper Advertising Bureau suggests that: (1) psychographics are least useful for products which enjoy almost universal use; and (2) psychographic analysis is of minimal use in selecting media unless the product or the media are highly specialized.

Product Usage Segmentation. One of the most useful, at least in the initial stages of analysis, means of segmenting markets is based upon levels of product usage. These are ordinarily defined as: (1) Non-usage; (2) Light usage; (3) Moderate usage; and (4) Heavy usage. Product usage segmentation is especially useful when used in conjunction with

Figure 6-5 Psychographic Classifications: Definitions

Self-Concept

Classifications of Self-Concept are based on self-ratings with respect
to groups of adjectives on a five-point scale:

1. Agree a lot
2. Agree a little
3. Neither agree or disagree
4. Disagree a little
5. Disagree a lot

The adjectives, and the scale-points which define the classifications
in each case are:

AFFECTIONATE, passionate, loving, romantic	1
AMICABLE, amiable, affable, benevolent	1
AWKWARD, absent-minded, forgetful, careless	1,2
BRAVE, courageous, daring, adventuresome	1,2
BROADMINDED, open-minded, liberal, tolerant	1
CREATIVE, inventive, imaginative, artistic	1
DOMINATING, authoritarian, demanding, aggressive	1,2
EFFICIENT, organized, diligent, thorough	1
EGOCENTRIC, vain, self-centered, narcissistic	1,2,3
FRANK, straightforward, outspoken, candid	1
FUNNY, humorous, amusing, witty	1
INTELLIGENT, smart, bright, well-informed	1
KIND, good-hearted, warm-hearted, sincere	1
REFINED, gracious, sophisticated, dignified	1,2
RESERVED, conservative, quiet, conventional	1
SELF-ASSURED, confident, self-sufficient, secure	1
SOCIABLE, friendly, cheerful, likeable	1
STUBBORN, hardheaded, headstrong, obstinate	1,2
TENSE, nervous, high-strung, excitable	1,2
TRUSTWORTHY, competent, reliable, responsible	1

Buying-Style

Classifications of Buying-Style are based on agreement or disagreement with the following statements on the same five-point scale used
for Self-Concept:

BRAND LOYAL   1
   I always look for the name of the manufacturer on the
   package.
CAUTIOUS   1
   I do not buy unknown brands merely to save money.
CONFORMISTS   1,2,3
   I prefer to buy things that my friends or neighbors
   would approve of.
ECOLOGISTS   1
   All products that pollute the environment should be
   banned.
ECONOMY-MINDED   1
   I shop around a lot to take advantage of specials or
   bargains.
EXPERIMENTERS   1,2,3
   I like to change brands often for the sake of variety and
   novelty.

IMPULSIVE   1
  When in the store, I often buy an item on the spur of
  the moment.
PERSUASABLE   1,2
  In general advertising presents a true picture of the
  products of well-known companies.
PLANNERS   1
  I generally plan far ahead to buy expensive items such
  as automobiles.
STYLE-CONSCIOUS   1
  I try to keep abreast of changes in styles & fashions.

Table 6-2   Major Dimensions of Activities, Interests and Opinions

Price Conscious
  I shop a lot for "specials."
  I find myself checking the prices in the grocery store even for small items.
  I usually watch the advertisements for announcements of sales.
  A person can save a lot of money by shopping around for bargains.
Fashion Conscious
  I usually have one or more outfits that are of the very latest style.
  When I must choose between the two I usually dress for fashion, not for comfort.
  An important part of my life and activities is dressing smartly.
  I often try the latest hairdo styles when they change.
Child Oriented
  When my children are ill in bed I drop most everything else in order to see to their
  comfort.
  My children are the most important thing in my life.
  I try to arrange my home for my children's convenience.
  I take a lot of time and effort to teach my children good habits.
Compulsive Housekeeper
  I don't like to see children's toys lying about.
  I usually keep my house very neat and clean.
  I am uncomfortable when my house is not completely clean.
  Our days seem to follow a definite routine such as eating meals at a regular time, etc.
Dislikes Housekeeping
  I must admit I really don't like household chores.
  I find cleaning my house an unpleasant task.
  I enjoy most forms of housework. (Reverse scored)
  My idea of housekeeping is "once over lightly."
Sewer
  I like to sew and frequently do.
  I often make my own or my children's clothes.
  You can save a lot of money by making your own clothes.
  I would like to know how to sew like an expert.
Homebody
  I would rather spend a quiet evening at home than go out to a party.
  I like parties where there is lots of music and talk. (Reverse scored)
  I would rather go to a sporting event than a dance.
  I am a homebody.
Community Minded
  I am an active member of more than one service organization.
  I do volunteer work for a hospital or service organization on a fairly regular basis.
  I like to work on community projects.
  I have personally worked in a political campaign or for a candidate or an issue.

Credit User
I buy many things with a credit card or a charge card.
I like to pay cash for everything I buy. (Reverse scored)
It is good to have charge accounts.
To buy anything, other than a house or a car, on credit is unwise. (Reverse scored)
Sports Spectator
I like to watch or listen to baseball or football games.
I usually read the sports page in the daily paper.
I thoroughly enjoy conversations about sports.
I would rather go to a sporting event than a dance.
Cook
I love to cook.
I am a good cook.
I love to bake and frequently do.
I am interested in spices and seasonings.
Self-Confident
I think I have more self-confidence than most people.
I am more independent than most people.
I think I have a lot of personal ability.
I like to be considered a leader.
Self-Designated Opinion Leader
My friends or neighbors often come to me for advice.
I sometimes influence what my friends buy.
People come to me more often than I go to them for information about brands.
Information Seeker
I often seek out the advice of my friends regarding which brand to buy.
I spend a lot of time talking with my friends about products and brands.
My neighbors or friends usually give me good advice on what brands to buy in the grocery store.
New Brand Tryer
When I see a new brand on the shelf I often buy it just to see what it's like.
I often try new brands before my friends and neighbors do.
I like to try new and different things.
Satisfied with Finances
Our family income is high enough to satisfy nearly all our important desires.
No matter how fast our income goes up we never seem to get ahead. (Reverse scored)
I wish we had a lot of money. (Reverse scored)
Canned Food User
I depend on canned food for at least one meal a day.
I couldn't get along without canned foods.
Things just don't taste right if they come out of a can. (Reverse scored)
Dieter
During the warm weather I drink low calorie soft drinks several times a week.
I buy more low calorie foods than the average housewife.
I have used Metrecal or other diet foods at least one meal a day.
Financial Optimist
I will probably have more money to spend next year than I have now.
Five years from now the family income will probably be a lot higher than it is now.
Wrapper
Food should never be left in the refrigerator uncovered.
Leftovers should be wrapped before being put into the refrigerator.
Wide Horizons
I'd like to spend a year in London or Paris.
I would like to take a trip around the world.
Arts Enthusiast
I enjoy going through an art gallery.
I enjoy going to concerts.
I like ballet.

SOURCE: William D. Wells and Douglas J. Tigert, "Activities, Interests, and Opinions," *Journal of Advertising Research* 11 No. 4 (August 1971): 35.

demographics and/or sociopsychological bases for segmentation. This is illustrated in Figure 6–6 for the Flavorfest Company (company name is fictitious).[17]

Figure 6-6   Segmentation Findings for Flavorfest

I. *Heavy Users* (39 percent of the market)
  a. Demographic attributes—housewives aged 20–45; well-educated, higher-income categories, small families with most children under 5, concentration in Northeast and Midwest and in suburban and farm areas.
  b. Motivational attributes
   1. Strong motivation not to be old-fashioned, and a desire to express individuality through creative action and use of exciting new things.
   2. The traditional role as a housewife viewed with displeasure, and experimentation with new foods done to express individuality—not to please the family.
   3. Exciting and exotic taste suggested by the image of Flavorfest. Favorable reaction in terms of taste, appearance, and food value. Highly prized in experimental cooking. Hence, substantial compatibility between values of the user and product image.

II. *Light to Moderate Users* (20 percent of the market)
  a. Demographic attributes—housewives aged 35–54; large families with children under 12, middle-income groups, location mostly in Southeast, Pacific states, and Southwest.
  b. Motivational attributes
   1. A strong desire to express individuality through creative cookery, but constrained somewhat by a conflicting desire to maintain tradition and subordinate herself to the family's desires.
   2. The desire to experiment with new foods constrained by a lack of confidence in the results of experimental cooking.
   3. Favorable image of Flavorfest. The product liked in all respects, but confined largely to use with one type of food. Viewed as unacceptable for other uses. Hence, vision limited regarding new uses for Flavorfest.

III. *Nonusers* (41 percent of the market)
  a. Demographic attributes—older housewives; large families, lower-income brackets, location mostly in the eastern states and some parts of the South.
  b. Motivational attributes
   1. A strong motive to maintain tradition and emotional ties with the past; identification with her mother and her role in the home.
   2. A conservative nonventuresome personality.
   3. Experimental cookery discouraged by self-concept of role as a mother and housewife. Flavorfest thus regarded unfavorably. Exotic flavors and a degree of modernity, which is unacceptable, connoted by the image of Flavorfest.
   4. No interest expressed in new uses and experimentation with Flavorfest, for the product not representative of the values embraced by these housewives.

SOURCE: James F. Engel, Hugh G. Wales, and Martin R. Warshaw, *Promotional Strategy*, rev. ed., (Homewood, II.: Richard D. Irwin, Inc., 1971), Ch. 9.

The Flavorfest Company bottles and distributes a well-known condiment product. The company has long dominated the market with a share of about 85 percent. The company management undertook a segmentation study so that they could better understand the market for their product (which included spices and seasoning items in addition to the bottled condiment). The segmentation study disclosed three distinct segments, as shown in Figure 6–6.

It is clear from this study, that Flavorfest would have a difficult time entering and making progress with the nonuser segment of the market. These consumers do not engage in experimental cookery where the Flavorfest product may be most appropriate. The image of Flavorfest connotes to these consumers a degree of modernity which does not "jibe" with their own self-concepts.

The heavy user segment is the largest market segment, and Flavorfest is relatively well-regarded by this group. Because of the product's use in experimental cookery and its role in demonstrating individuality in cooking, the potential exists for stimulating greater demand in this large segment.

The greatest opportunity for increased sales for Flavorfest perhaps resides with the light to moderate user segments. The product is liked in nearly all respects by these segments, but the desire for creative cookery is constrained by the desire to maintain tradition and a lack of confidence by those in these segments in the results of experimental cooking. The company could attack these constraining forces with recipes which emphasize "fail-safe" cooking and stressing the favorable family reaction to the new cooking by family members in any advertising which might be conducted. Clearly, it would be a mistake for this company to attempt to appeal to one mass market, that is, deciding not to follow a segmentation strategy, with one message in its advertising program.

MARKET SEGMENTATION DATA

To make it possible to implement segmentation strategies, it is, of course, necessary to have certain types of information about markets. There is a great deal of information available from syndicated services (services which supply the same information to many companies, thus reducing its cost to any particular company); other types of specialized information must be developed on a primary basis by individual companies. The general types of data which are required are: (1) Information about total industry sales for the product category; (2) Information about the firm's sales; (3) Information about the principal competitors' sales; and (4) Information to aid in the forecast of market potential for the product.

Information about industry sales, company sales, and competitors' sales can be obtained from such syndicated services as Simmons Market Research Bureau (SMRB). Table 6–3 shows sample information of the type provided by Simmons for the cola soft-drink market;

Table 6-3   SMRB Product Usage Data

REGULAR COLA DRINKS (CARBONATED, NOT DIET): USAGE
(ADULTS)

	TOTAL U.S. '000	ALL USERS A '000	B % DOWN	C % ACROSS	D INDX	HEAVY USERS A '000	B % DOWN	C % ACROSS	D INDX	MEDIUM USERS A '000	B % DOWN	C % ACROSS	D INDX	LIGHT USERS A '000	B % DOWN	C % ACROSS	D INDX
TOTAL ADULTS	155794	104574	100.0	67.1	100	30559	100.0	19.6	100	33203	100.0	21.3	100	40812	100.0	26.2	100
MALES	74722	52725	50.4	70.6	105	17240	56.4	23.1	118	16407	49.4	22.0	103	19079	46.7	25.5	97
FEMALES	81073	51849	49.6	64.0	95	13320	43.6	16.4	84	16796	50.6	20.7	97	21734	53.3	26.8	102
18 - 24	28385	22364	21.4	78.8	117	9018	29.5	31.8	162	7187	21.6	25.3	119	6160	15.1	21.7	83
25 - 34	34725	27249	26.1	78.5	117	8536	27.9	24.6	125	8672	26.1	25.0	117	10041	24.6	26.9	110
35 - 44	24972	18615	17.8	74.5	111	5348	17.5	21.4	109	6179	18.6	24.7	116	7089	17.4	28.4	108
45 - 54	23611	14373	13.7	60.9	91	3312	10.8	14.0	72	4343	13.1	18.4	86	6719	16.5	28.5	109
55 - 64	21139	11608	11.1	54.9	82	2334	7.6	11.0	56	3334	10.0	15.8	74	5940	14.6	28.1	107
65 OR OLDER	22962	10365	9.9	45.1	67	2012	6.6	8.8	45	3488	10.5	15.2	71	4865	11.9	21.2	81
18 - 34	63109	49613	47.4	78.6	117	17554	57.4	27.8	142	15859	47.8	25.1	118	16200	39.7	25.7	98
18 - 49	99601	75547	72.2	75.8	113	24653	80.7	24.8	126	24322	73.3	24.4	115	26572	65.1	26.7	102
35 - 49	36492	25934	24.8	71.1	106	7100	23.2	19.5	99	8463	25.5	23.2	109	10372	25.4	28.4	108
GRADUATED COLLEGE	22011	13622	13.0	61.9	92	2646	8.7	12.0	61	3817	11.5	17.3	81	7160	17.5	32.5	124
ATTENDED COLLEGE	25047	17222	16.5	68.8	102	4495	14.7	17.9	91	5184	15.6	20.7	97	7543	18.5	30.1	115
GRADUATED HIGH SCHOOL	59229	41600	39.8	70.2	105	13146	43.0	22.2	113	13195	39.7	22.3	105	15259	37.4	25.8	98
DID NOT GRADUATE HIGH SCHOOL	49508	32130	30.7	64.9	97	10272	33.6	20.7	106	11007	33.2	22.2	104	10851	26.6	21.9	84
EMPLOYED	95157	67864	64.9	71.3	106	21036	68.8	22.1	113	21186	63.8	22.3	104	25642	62.8	26.9	103
EMPLOYED FULL-TIME	82534	59503	56.9	72.1	107	18948	62.0	23.0	117	18611	56.1	22.5	106	21944	53.8	26.6	101
EMPLOYED PART-TIME	12622	8361	8.0	66.2	99	2088	6.8	16.5	84	2575	7.8	20.4	96	3698	9.1	29.3	112
NOT EMPLOYED	60638	36711	35.1	60.5	90	9523	31.2	15.7	80	12017	36.2	19.8	93	15170	37.2	25.0	96
PROFESSIONAL/MANAGER	27167	18611	17.8	68.5	102	4161	13.6	15.3	78	5534	16.7	20.4	96	8915	21.8	32.8	125
CLERICAL/SALES	22793	15501	14.8	68.0	101	4634	15.2	20.3	104	4628	13.9	20.3	95	6240	15.3	27.4	105
CRAFTSMEN/FOREMEN	13261	10065	9.6	75.9	113	3730	12.2	28.1	143	3427	10.3	25.8	121	2908	7.1	21.9	84
OTHER EMPLOYED	31936	23687	22.7	74.2	110	8512	27.9	26.7	136	7596	22.9	23.8	112	7579	18.6	23.7	91
SINGLE	29964	21571	20.6	72.0	107	7294	23.9	24.3	124	6794	20.5	22.7	106	7484	18.3	25.0	95
MARRIED	100516	67803	64.8	67.5	100	19004	62.2	18.9	96	21682	65.3	21.6	101	27117	66.4	27.0	103
DIVORCED/SEPARATED/WIDOWED	25315	15200	14.5	60.0	89	4261	13.9	16.8	86	4727	14.2	18.7	88	6211	15.2	24.5	94
PARENTS	59271	46416	44.4	78.3	117	14789	48.4	25.0	127	15102	45.5	25.5	120	16525	40.5	27.9	106
WHITE	136138	89794	85.9	66.0	98	25879	84.7	19.0	97	28325	85.3	20.8	98	35590	87.2	26.1	100
BLACK	17013	12773	12.2	75.1	112	4061	13.3	23.9	122	4182	12.6	24.6	115	4529	11.1	26.6	102
OTHER	2643	2008	1.9	76.0	113	619	2.0	23.4	119	696	2.1	26.3	124	693	1.7	26.2	100
NORTHEAST-CENSUS	35289	22002	21.1	62.6	93	5771	18.9	16.4	83	6925	20.9	19.6	92	9386	23.0	26.6	102
NORTH CENTRAL	38851	26955	25.8	69.4	103	7586	24.8	19.5	100	8159	24.6	21.0	99	11211	27.5	26.9	110
SOUTH	49702	36160	34.6	72.8	108	12640	41.4	25.4	130	12309	37.1	24.8	116	11211	27.5	22.6	86
WEST	31953	19377	18.5	60.6	90	4562	14.9	14.3	73	5811	17.5	18.2	85	9004	22.1	28.2	108
NORTHEAST-MKTG.	37818	23561	22.5	62.3	93	6181	20.2	16.3	83	7268	21.9	19.2	90	10112	24.8	26.7	102
EAST CENTRAL	23186	16683	16.0	72.0	107	5212	17.1	22.5	115	5093	15.3	22.0	103	6377	15.6	27.5	105
WEST CENTRAL	27057	18558	17.7	68.6	102	4513	14.8	16.7	85	5790	17.4	21.4	100	8255	20.2	30.5	116
SOUTH	42053	30790	29.4	73.2	109	11095	36.3	26.4	135	10535	31.7	25.1	118	9160	22.4	21.8	83
PACIFIC	25681	14982	14.3	58.3	87	3558	11.6	13.9	71	4517	13.6	17.6	83	6908	16.9	26.9	103
COUNTY SIZE A	61378	39287	37.6	64.0	95	10563	34.6	17.2	88	12338	37.2	20.1	94	16387	40.2	26.7	102
COUNTY SIZE B	44543	31329	30.0	70.3	105	9916	32.4	22.3	113	10071	30.3	22.6	106	11343	27.8	25.5	97
COUNTY SIZE C	27986	19036	18.2	68.0	101	5703	18.7	20.4	104	5808	17.5	20.8	97	7526	18.4	26.9	103
COUNTY SIZE D	21887	14922	14.3	68.2	101	4376	14.3	20.0	102	4987	15.0	22.8	107	5557	13.6	25.4	97
METRO CENTRAL CITY	47722	31942	30.5	66.9	100	9889	32.4	20.7	106	9932	29.9	20.8	98	12121	29.7	25.4	97
METRO SUBURBAN	67114	44779	42.8	66.7	99	12216	40.0	18.2	93	14333	43.2	21.4	100	18230	44.7	27.2	104
NON METRO	40959	27853	26.6	68.0	101	8454	27.7	20.6	105	8938	26.9	21.8	102	10461	25.6	25.5	97
HSHLD INC $35,000 OR MORE	17217	11037	10.6	64.1	96	2394	7.8	13.9	71	3140	9.5	18.2	86	5502	13.5	32.0	122
$25,000 OR MORE	41274	27482	26.3	66.6	99	6854	22.4	16.6	85	8040	24.2	19.5	91	12588	30.8	30.5	116
$20,000 - $24,999	20306	13923	13.3	68.6	102	4409	14.4	21.7	111	4369	13.2	21.5	101	5145	12.6	25.3	97
$15,000 - $19,999	23109	16817	16.1	72.8	108	5061	16.6	21.9	112	6060	18.3	26.2	123	5696	14.0	24.6	94
$10,000 - $14,999	33677	22745	21.8	67.5	101	7447	24.4	22.1	113	6507	19.6	19.3	91	8791	21.5	26.1	100
$ 5,000 - $ 9,999	22314	14389	13.8	64.5	96	4057	13.3	18.2	93	5051	15.2	22.6	106	5281	12.9	23.7	90
UNDER $5,000	15115	9219	8.8	61.0	91	2732	8.9	18.1	92	3175	9.6	21.0	99	3311	8.1	21.9	84
HSHLD OF 1 OR 2 PEOPLE	68122	39278	37.6	57.7	86	9868	32.3	14.5	74	12192	36.7	17.9	84	17218	42.2	25.3	96
3 OR 4 PEOPLE	59043	43863	41.9	73.3	109	13625	44.6	22.8	116	14432	43.5	24.1	113	15806	38.7	26.4	101
5 OR MORE PEOPLE	27029	21434	20.5	77.0	115	7067	23.1	25.4	129	6579	19.8	23.6	111	7788	19.1	28.0	107
NO CHILD IN HSHLD	86593	50523	48.3	58.3	87	13053	42.7	15.1	77	15593	47.0	18.0	84	21877	53.6	25.3	96
CHILD(REN) UNDER 2 YRS	11451	9483	9.1	82.8	123	3093	10.1	27.0	138	3467	10.4	30.3	142	2923	7.2	25.5	97
2 - 5 YEARS	21779	18043	17.3	82.8	123	6613	21.6	30.4	155	5527	16.6	25.4	119	5903	14.5	27.1	103
6 - 11 YEARS	31760	25758	24.6	81.1	121	8348	27.3	26.3	134	8660	26.1	27.3	128	8751	21.4	27.6	105
12 - 17 YEARS	35811	26660	25.5	74.4	111	8039	26.3	22.4	114	8408	25.3	23.5	110	10212	25.0	28.5	109
RESIDENCE OWNED	105243	69729	66.7	66.3	99	18074	59.1	17.2	88	22734	68.5	21.6	101	28921	70.9	27.5	105
VALUE: $40,000 OR MORE	53331	34157	32.7	64.0	95	7771	25.4	14.6	74	10486	31.6	19.7	92	15900	39.0	29.8	114
VALUE: UNDER $40,000	51912	35572	34.0	68.5	102	10303	33.7	19.8	101	12248	36.9	23.6	111	13020	31.9	25.1	96

Table 6-4 SMRB Brand Usage Data

REGULAR COLA DRINKS (CARBONATED, NOT DIET): BRANDS
(ADULTS)

	TOTAL U.S. '000	COCA COLA A '000	B % DOWN	C % ACROSS	D INDX	PEPSI COLA A '000	B % DOWN	C % ACROSS	D INDX	ROYAL CROWN COLA (R.C.) A '000	B % DOWN	C % ACROSS	D INDX	SHASTA COLA A '000	B % DOWN	C % ACROSS	D INDX
TOTAL ADULTS	155794	67605	100.0	43.4	100	64835	100.0	41.6	100	18755	100.0	12.0	100	8238	100.0	5.3	100
MALES	74722	34997	51.8	46.8	108	33346	51.4	44.6	107	9809	52.3	13.1	109	4370	53.0	5.8	111
FEMALES	81073	32609	48.2	40.2	93	31489	48.6	38.8	93	8946	47.7	11.0	92	3868	47.0	4.8	90
18 - 24	28385	15093	22.3	53.2	123	14949	23.1	52.7	127	4449	23.7	15.7	130	2203	26.7	7.8	147
25 - 34	34725	16890	25.0	48.6	112	17937	27.7	51.7	124	4854	25.9	14.0	116	1988	24.1	5.7	108
35 - 44	24972	11478	17.0	46.0	106	12403	19.1	49.7	119	4127	22.0	16.5	137	1557	18.9	6.2	118
45 - 54	23611	9209	13.6	39.0	90	8242	12.7	34.9	84	2423	12.9	10.3	85	966	11.7	4.1	77
55 - 64	21139	7786	11.5	36.8	85	6146	9.5	29.1	70	1494	8.0	7.1	59	•778	9.4	3.7	70
65 OR OLDER	22962	7149	10.6	31.1	72	5158	8.0	22.5	54	1408	7.5	6.1	51	746	9.1	3.2	61
18 - 34	63109	31983	47.3	50.7	117	32886	50.7	52.1	125	9303	49.6	14.7	122	4191	50.9	6.6	126
18 - 49	99601	47981	71.0	48.2	111	49620	76.5	49.8	120	14870	79.3	14.9	124	6312	76.6	6.3	120
35 - 49	36492	15998	23.7	43.8	101	16734	25.8	45.9	110	5567	29.7	15.3	127	2121	25.7	5.8	110
GRADUATED COLLEGE	22011	9954	14.7	45.2	104	8248	12.7	37.5	90	2273	12.1	10.3	86	1000	12.1	4.5	86
ATTENDED COLLEGE	25047	11912	17.6	47.6	110	10465	16.1	41.8	100	2728	14.5	10.9	90	1632	19.8	6.5	123
GRADUATED HIGH SCHOOL	59229	25521	37.8	43.1	99	27294	42.1	46.1	111	8016	42.7	13.5	112	3373	40.9	5.7	108
DID NOT GRADUATE HIGH SCHOOL	49508	20219	29.9	40.8	94	18829	29.0	38.0	91	5738	30.6	11.6	96	2233	27.1	4.5	85
EMPLOYED	95157	43916	65.0	46.2	106	42698	65.9	44.9	108	11900	63.4	12.5	104	5460	66.4	5.7	109
EMPLOYED FULL-TIME	82534	38420	55.8	46.6	107	37702	58.2	45.7	110	10511	56.0	12.7	106	4868	59.1	5.9	112
EMPLOYED PART-TIME	12622	5496	8.1	43.5	100	4996	7.7	39.6	95	1388	7.4	11.0	91	•600	7.3	4.8	90
NOT EMPLOYED	60638	23689	35.0	39.1	90	22137	34.1	36.5	88	6855	36.6	11.3	94	2770	33.6	4.6	86
PROFESSIONAL/MANAGER	27157	13202	19.5	48.6	112	10919	16.8	40.2	97	2479	13.2	9.1	76	1202	14.6	4.4	84
CLERICAL/SALES	22793	9761	14.4	42.8	99	9660	14.9	42.4	102	2956	15.8	13.0	108	1238	15.0	5.4	103
CRAFTSMEN/FOREMEN	13261	5966	8.8	45.0	104	6819	10.5	51.4	124	2060	11.0	15.5	129	•912	11.1	6.9	130
OTHER EMPLOYED	31936	14987	22.2	46.9	108	15301	23.6	47.9	115	4404	23.5	13.8	115	2118	25.7	6.5	125
SINGLE	29964	15129	22.4	50.5	116	14228	21.9	47.5	114	4350	23.2	14.5	121	2387	29.0	8.0	151
MARRIED	100516	42223	62.5	42.0	97	41955	64.7	41.7	100	11921	63.6	11.9	99	4556	55.3	4.5	86
DIVORCED/SEPARATED/WIDOWED	25315	10253	15.2	40.5	93	8652	13.3	34.2	82	2484	13.2	9.8	82	1296	15.7	5.1	97
PARENTS	59271	28493	42.1	48.1	111	30923	47.7	52.2	125	8966	47.8	15.1	126	3590	43.6	6.1	115
WHITE	136138	67463	85.0	42.2	97	56098	86.5	41.2	99	15614	83.3	11.5	95	6521	79.2	4.8	91
BLACK	17013	8886	13.1	52.2	120	7493	11.6	44.0	106	2852	15.2	16.8	139	1612	19.6	9.5	179
OTHER	2643	1257	1.9	47.6	110	1244	1.9	47.1	113	•289	1.5	10.9	91	••105	1.3	4.0	75
NORTHEAST-CENSUS	35289	14328	21.2	40.6	94	13430	20.7	38.1	91	3333	17.8	9.4	78	947	11.5	2.7	51
NORTH CENTRAL	38851	15483	22.9	39.9	92	19740	30.4	50.8	122	6416	34.2	16.5	137	2164	26.3	5.6	105
SOUTH	49702	27161	40.2	54.6	126	18533	20.6	37.3	90	6326	33.7	12.7	106	2565	31.1	5.2	98
WEST	31953	10634	15.7	33.3	77	13132	20.3	41.1	99	2600	14.3	8.4	70	2562	31.1	8.0	152
NORTHEAST-MKTG.	37818	15598	23.1	41.2	95	13909	21.5	36.8	88	3754	20.0	9.8	82	1004	12.2	2.7	50
EAST CENTRAL	23186	10046	14.9	43.3	100	11849	18.3	51.1	123	4010	21.4	17.3	144	•882	10.7	3.8	72
WEST CENTRAL	27057	10121	15.0	37.4	86	13587	21.0	50.2	121	4078	21.7	15.1	125	1917	23.3	7.1	134
SOUTH	42053	23413	34.6	55.7	128	15386	23.7	36.6	88	4794	25.6	11.4	95	2312	28.1	5.5	104
PACIFIC	25681	8427	12.5	32.8	76	10103	15.6	39.3	95	2119	11.3	8.3	69	2124	25.8	8.3	156
COUNTY SIZE A	61378	25185	37.3	41.0	95	24778	38.2	40.4	97	7096	37.8	11.6	96	3115	37.8	5.1	96
COUNTY SIZE B	44543	20504	30.3	46.0	106	19864	30.6	44.6	107	5758	30.7	12.9	107	2537	30.8	5.7	108
COUNTY SIZE C	27986	11954	17.7	42.7	98	11785	18.2	42.1	101	3281	17.5	11.7	97	1476	17.9	5.3	100
COUNTY SIZE D	21887	9963	14.7	45.5	105	8418	13.0	38.5	92	2620	14.0	12.0	99	1110	13.5	5.1	96
METRO CENTRAL CITY	47722	21213	31.4	44.5	102	19216	29.6	40.3	97	5681	31.4	12.3	102	3098	37.6	6.5	123
METRO SUBURBAN	67114	28504	42.2	42.5	98	29021	44.8	43.2	104	7975	42.5	11.9	99	3153	38.3	4.7	89
NON METRO	40959	17888	26.5	43.7	101	16599	25.6	40.5	97	4899	26.1	12.0	99	1988	24.1	4.9	92
HSHLD INC $35,000 OR MORE	17217	7858	11.6	45.6	105	6730	10.4	39.1	94	1764	9.4	10.2	85	654	7.9	3.8	72
$25,000 OR MORE	41274	18565	27.5	45.0	104	17155	26.5	41.6	100	4719	25.2	11.4	95	1930	23.4	4.7	88
$20,000 - $24,999	20306	9013	13.3	44.4	102	6624	13.3	42.5	102	2538	13.5	12.5	104	1038	12.6	5.1	97
$15,000 - $19,999	23109	10725	15.9	46.4	107	10760	16.6	46.6	112	3129	16.7	13.5	112	1379	16.7	6.0	113
$10,000 - $14,999	33677	14214	21.0	42.2	97	14713	22.7	43.7	105	4585	24.4	13.6	113	2031	24.7	6.0	114
$ 5,000 - $ 9,999	22314	8938	13.2	40.1	92	8582	13.2	38.5	92	2343	12.5	10.5	87	1242	15.1	5.6	105
UNDER $5,000	15115	6151	9.1	40.7	94	5000	7.7	33.1	79	1441	7.7	9.5	79	•620	7.5	4.1	78
HSHLD OF 1 OR 2 PEOPLE	68122	25556	37.8	37.5	86	22079	34.1	32.4	78	5962	31.8	8.8	73	2689	32.6	3.9	75
3 OR 4 PEOPLE	59843	28404	42.0	47.5	109	28606	44.0	47.6	114	8135	43.4	13.6	113	3413	41.4	5.7	108
5 OR MORE PEOPLE	27829	13646	20.2	49.0	113	14249	22.0	51.2	123	4658	24.8	16.7	139	2137	25.9	7.7	145
NO CHILD IN HSHLD	86593	33872	50.1	39.1	90	28446	43.9	32.9	79	8148	43.4	9.4	78	3676	44.6	4.2	80
CHILD(REN) UNDER 2 YRS	11451	5804	8.6	50.7	117	6562	10.2	57.5	138	1940	10.3	16.9	141	•731	8.9	6.4	121
2 - 5 YEARS	21779	10743	15.9	49.3	114	12496	19.3	57.4	138	3565	19.5	16.8	140	1175	14.3	5.4	102
6 - 11 YEARS	31760	16177	23.9	50.9	117	17324	26.7	54.5	131	5388	28.7	17.0	141	2143	26.0	6.7	128
12 - 17 YEARS	35811	17438	25.8	48.7	112	17695	27.3	49.4	119	5362	28.6	15.0	124	2563	31.1	7.2	135
RESIDENCE OWNED	105243	45454	67.2	43.2	100	43026	66.4	40.9	98	12772	68.1	12.1	101	5244	63.7	5.0	94
VALUE: $40,000 OR MORE	53331	22347	33.1	41.9	97	21481	33.1	40.3	97	5940	31.7	11.1	93	2582	31.3	4.8	92
VALUE: UNDER $40,000	51912	23106	34.2	44.5	103	21546	33.2	41.5	100	6833	36.4	13.2	109	2661	32.3	5.1	97

there are separate Simmons books for all major product categories. Table 6-3 deals only with all adults and shows usage of categories of soft drinks for the past month broken down by various demographics. SMRB further provides usage information on particular brands of products. Table 6-4 shows, for the same demographic categories as illustrated in the preceding table, the usage levels for particular brands of cola. The important point to note, however, is that in addition to those data types illustrated in these tables, Simmons provides media usage data broken down by the same demographic categories as used for product and brand usage information. This enables market segment and media vehicle matching.

Additional information, broken down by geographic areas, is provided by such services as A.C. Nielsen Retail Store Audits, MRCA (Market Research Corporation of America) panel data, *Editor and Publishers'* "Market Guide," and *Marketing and Sales Management's* "Survey of Buying Power." The "Survey of Buying Power" is particularly useful in helping to determine the sales potential of market segments defined geographically. Retail store sales for given years are reported as shown in Table 6-5. An example of the "Effective Buying Income" data is provided in Table 6-6. The "Buying Power Index" shown in that table is based upon census measurements and has projections for updating. The survey is a multiple-factor index for every major metropolitan area of the United States. The index consists of three factors: population size, disposable income, and the total retail sales of the geographic area. The Buying Power Index data can be combined with the data from Simmons, for example, to produce good market analysis in terms of industry sales, competitors' sales, company sales, and the potential for particular areas.

This brief survey of syndicated segmentation data is not in any way intended to be exhaustive. There are many additional sources available of this nature. And it should be noted that, say in the case of Simmons, the important point is the existence of the data-type and not this particular organization. The information provided by such a company is likely to always exist whether or not it is provided by Simmons. This is a good point to keep in mind since tradition shows that many services have started and then gone out of business over the years.

Table 6-5   Survey of Buying Power

ILL. ESTIMATES — METRO AREA County City	POPULATION—12/31/78 Total Population (Thousands)	% Of U.S.	Median Age of Pop	18-24 Years	25-34 Years	35-49 Years	50 & Over	Households (Thousands)	RETAIL SALES BY STORE GROUP 1978 Total Retail Sales ($000)	Food ($000)	Eating & Drinking Places ($000)	General Mdse ($000)	Furniture/ Furnish / Appliance ($000)	Auto- motive ($000)	Drug ($000)
BLOOMINGTON - NORMAL	124.9	.0569	26.4	21.2	14.6	13.8	23.6	42.1	486,366	86,147	54,595	57,494	23,780	101,030	12,700
McLean	124.9	.0569	26.4	21.2	14.6	13.8	23.6	42.1	486,366	86,147	54,595	57,494	23,780	101,030	12,700
• Bloomington	43.3	.0197	29.1	17.1	15.5	13.6	27.2	16.6	337,480	55,966	33,185	51,555	18,459	78,272	10,567
• Normal	34.5	.0157	22.8	41.4	12.1	12.0	13.0	8.7	48,741	10,442	6,863	2,989	2,918	2,528	1,604
SUBURBAN TOTAL	47.1	.0215	30.9	10.1	15.6	15.3	28.2	16.8	100,145	19,739	14,547	2,950	2,403	20,230	534
CHAMPAIGN - URBANA - RANTOUL	172.0	.0782	24.0	28.6	17.7	12.8	15.6	56.9	650,079	88,754	69,715	99,578	37,793	142,823	24,820
Champaign	172.0	.0782	24.0	28.6	17.7	12.8	15.6	56.9	650,079	88,754	69,715	99,578	37,793	142,823	24,820
• Champaign	60.6	.0276	24.0	33.1	16.2	12.1	17.0	20.7	313,650	31,689	36,019	50,270	23,170	88,378	13,558
• Rantoul	28.0	.0127	22.4	32.3	19.7	11.9	6.2	7.1	81,555	9,258	7,722	7,139	4,975	32,060	1,534
• Urbana	35.8	.0163	23.9	38.0	17.2	10.4	16.2	11.6	91,587	16,435	14,929	18,283	5,339	2,657	3,875
SUBURBAN TOTAL	47.6	.0216	26.9	13.7	19.0	15.8	18.8	17.5	163,287	31,372	11,045	23,886	4,309	19,728	5,853
CHICAGO	7,016.5	3.1927	29.9	12.5	16.6	16.9	24.6	2,422.9	30,392,865	5,378,122	2,862,781	3,914,484	1,503,521	5,776,156	1,074,559
Cook	5,285.7	2.4051	30.5	12.5	16.4	16.7	26.0	1,895.8	22,100,118	3,992,320	2,165,082	2,561,094	1,103,393	3,665,083	806,168
Arlington Heights	69.9	.0318	27.9	9.3	17.2	21.7	16.0	21.3	280,533	54,236	20,913	13,100	14,864	96,905	14,391
Berwyn	46.5	.0212	41.7	10.6	13.1	15.4	41.5	19.6	224,154	32,849	15,512	30,433	11,660	47,627	14,899
• Chicago	2,962.7	1.3481	31.1	13.0	16.2	15.7	27.9	1,160.9	11,429,853	1,986,171	1,196,032	1,227,585	596,634	1,423,997	422,370
Chicago Heights	38.9	.0177	27.9	12.4	16.6	16.3	21.9	12.6	230,346	28,675	24,574	29,810	9,200	84,852	6,923
Cicero	60.4	.0275	35.2	12.8	15.7	15.5	34.6	24.6	187,184	37,874	23,734	8,050	4,562	49,871	4,866
Des Plaines	55.6	.0253	29.7	10.6	17.5	19.3	21.4	18.0	243,129	62,913	28,864	17,039	4,734	34,700	10,988
Evanston	73.9	.0336	32.1	16.9	16.8	14.3	30.8	27.7	320,801	50,571	14,916	25,402	18,497	116,012	8,275
Oak Lawn	63.6	.0289	30.0	10.1	13.6	19.7	23.6	19.2	377,152	67,897	24,107	52,182	17,434	127,519	10,857
Oak Park	58.9	.0268	35.2	11.7	14.8	14.2	36.0	23.8	278,555	45,784	10,655	25,550	17,637	92,063	11,375
Park Ridge	42.4	.0193	35.1	9.0	11.4	20.0	30.2	14.2	184,077	40,395	5,449	792	6,988	83,270	6,687
Skokie	68.9	.0314	33.6	10.6	13.2	20.4	27.8	23.2	545,583	76,429	38,069	111,304	30,709	95,383	14,082
Du Page	583.7	.2656	28.6	10.8	18.1	19.1	19.3	174.3	3,635,339	467,330	300,268	838,745	210,748	962,943	106,159
Elmhurst	44.5	.0202	31.6	10.7	13.8	19.4	25.9	13.8	304,784	40,869	17,598	26,269	4,498	156,689	11,808

Table 6-6   Buying Power Index

ILL. ESTIMATES — METRO AREA County City	EFFECTIVE BUYING INCOME 1978 Total EBI ($000)	Median Hsld EBI	% of Hslds by EB Group (A) $8.000-$9.999 (A)	(B) $10.000-$14.999 (B)	(C) $15.000-$24.999 (C)	(D) $25.000 & Over (D)	Buying Power Index
BLOOMINGTON - NORMAL	866,865	17,966	5.5	15.2	32.2	27.8	.0593
McLean	866,865	17,966	5.5	15.2	32.2	27.8	.0593
• Bloomington	320,476	16,702	6.5	16.2	3.2	24.3	.0275
• Normal	216,304	21,015	4.5	15.3	30.1	37.0	.0124
SUBURBAN TOTAL	330,085	17,890	5.0	15.6	34.5	26.5	.0194
CHAMPAIGN - URBANA - RANTOUL	1,146,369	16,355	6.5	17.4	31.0	23.8	.0793
Champaign	1,146,369	16,355	6.5	17.4	31.0	23.8	.0793
• Champaign	423,096	16,546	5.8	14.0	30.6	24.2	.0317
• Rantoul	141,564	13,787	10.0	30.1	29.5	14.0	.0105
• Urbana	232,947	14,819	6.4	17.8	25.3	24.1	.0147
SUBURBAN TOTAL	348,362	18,154	5.9	16.3	36.0	26.9	.0224
CHICAGO	54,252,265	20,101	4.4	13.2	31.7	34.2	3.6380
Cook	40,761,459	19,259	4.7	14.0	31.3	32.1	2.7076
Arlington Heights	666,135	29,187	1.5	4.8	23.7	65.0	.0398
Berwyn	398,585	19,240	4.3	13.5	34.0	30.5	.0263
• Chicago	21,140,781	15,990	6.1	17.1	30.7	22.8	1.4230
Chicago Heights	258,164	19,052	4.5	15.3	34.3	29.7	.0210
Cicero	468,926	18,285	4.5	15.5	37.5	24.6	.0287
Des Plaines	497,657	25,942	2.0	7.5	30.1	53.8	.0313
Evanston	731,946	21,867	4.6	13.2	26.6	41.5	.0439
Oak Lawn	513,738	25,224	2.2	7.2	31.5	50.8	.0375
Oak Park	613,891	22,073	3.9	12.1	28.8	41.4	.0369
Park Ridge	476,783	30,030	2.2	6.2	21.1	63.6	.0272
Skokie	764,776	28,939	1.6	6.2	24.4	61.5	.0509
Du Page	5,067,074	26,812	2.0	6.4	28.3	56.5	.3626
Elmhurst	424,538	27,514	2.2	6.2	25.4	59.0	.0300
Kane	1,999,897	21,148	3.9	11.9	36.1	35.2	.1375
Aurora	581,161	19,220	4.9	14.5	36.9	28.7	.0416
Elgin	483,975	20,035	4.6	13.3	34.6	31.6	.0378

ILL. ESTIMATES — METRO AREA County City	EFFECTIVE BUYING INCOME 1978 Total EBI ($000)	Median Hsld EBI	% of Hslds by EB Group (A) $8.000-$9.999 (A)	(B) $10.000-$14.999 (B)	(C) $15.000-$24.999 (C)	(D) $25.000 & Over (D)	Buying Power Index
Lake	3,466,277	22,829	3.5	10.8	31.0	43.0	.2326
North Chicago	196,242	18,297	4.2	19.5	35.7	28.1	.0112
Waukegan	468,854	18,695	5.5	15.2	35.7	27.4	.0392
McHenry	964,584	20,508	4.2	12.5	35.8	33.2	.0645
Will	1,992,974	19,241	3.7	13.5	40.9	27.0	.1332
Joliet	567,225	17,893	4.7	14.9	34.7	25.9	.0442
SUBURBAN TOTAL	33,111,484	23,560	2.8	9.5	32.5	45.0	2.2148
CHICAGO - GARY CONSOLIDATED AREA	58,802,499	20,165	4.3	13.0	32.0	34.3	3.9542
△ DANVILLE	763,560	18,277	5.1	12.8	31.7	28.6	.0491
Vermilion	763,560	18,277	5.1	12.8	31.7	28.6	.0491
• Danville	351,903	18,178	5.2	12.2	29.6	29.4	.0253
SUBURBAN TOTAL	411,657	18,351	5.1	13.3	33.3	27.8	.0238
DAVENPORT - ROCK ISLAND - MOLINE	2,740,308	19,026	4.6	13.0	34.8	29.3	.1843
Henry	399,131	17,838	5.5	13.6	34.3	25.9	.0249
Rock Island	1,290,992	19,864	4.3	12.2	34.0	32.6	.0841
• Moline	393,159	20,185	4.4	12.4	31.6	34.8	.0287
• Rock Island	397,230	19,090	5.0	12.1	29.8	32.6	.0247
Scott, Iowa	1,050,185	18,557	4.7	13.7	36.0	26.8	.0753
• Davenport	688,558	17,754	5.1	14.4	34.8	25.0	.0517
SUBURBAN TOTAL	1,260,331	19,414	4.3	12.6	37.3	29.2	.0798
DECATUR	958,618	18,271	5.3	13.3	34.6	26.8	.0664
Macon	958,618	18,271	5.3	13.3	34.6	26.8	.0664
• Decatur	713,708	17,750	5.7	13.3	32.5	26.6	.0535
SUBURBAN TOTAL	244,910	19,417	4.0	13.1	41.6	27.3	.0128
KANKAKEE	598,955	18,014	4.5	14.4	35.6	25.1	.0431
Kankakee	598,955	18,014	4.5	14.4	35.6	25.1	.0431
• Kankakee	224,107	17,388	4.8	14.5	33.0	25.5	.0270
SUBURBAN TOTAL	374,848	18,394	4.3	14.3	37.1	25.0	.0231

QUESTIONS AND PROBLEMS

1. Give a definition of market segmentation. Show its meaning by describing how it might be useful to the advertiser of lawn furniture.
2. Describe the difference between product differentiation (aggregation) and market segmentation strategies. Why would a blending of these strategies often be effective? Provide a specific product-related example.
3. One of the benefits ascribed to market segmentation in this chapter was that it helps in setting more precise market objectives. Give an example which illustrates why this is the case.
4. What are the relative advantages of segmentation strategies which rely on customer self-selection versus controlled coverage? Give an example of each strategy.
5. What is meant by operational market segment? How does the definition of an operational segment relate to the availability of data?
6. Give an illustration of the way in which the "majority fallacy" might operate for a particular brand of video-tape recorder.
7. How could it be determined ahead of time which of two or three market segments might be the most profitable for the firm to concentrate its resources?
8. Under which circumstances might situation-specific segmentation variables be more appropriate than general segmentation variables? Give an example using a particular brand of product.

ENDNOTES

1. David A. Aaker and John G. Myers, *Advertising Management* (Englewood Cliffs, N.J.: Prentice-Hall, Inc., 1975), p. 31.
2. Adapted from J.F. Engel, H.F. Fiorello, and M.A. Cayley, *Market Segmentation: Concepts and Applications* (New York: Holt, Rinehart and Winston, Inc., 1972), pp. 2-3.
3. Arnold M. Barban, Stephen M. Cristol, and Frank J. Kopec, *Essentials of Media Planning: A Marketing Viewpoint* (Chicago: Crain Books, 1976), pp. 28-29.
4. Engel, *et al., op cit.,* pp. 1-2.
5. R.W. Kotrba, "The Strategy Selection Chart," *Journal of Marketing* (July 1966), pp. 22-25.
6. This discussion is adapted from R.E. Frank, W.F. Massy, and Y. Wind, *Market Segmentation* (Englewood Cliffs, N.J.: Prentice-Hall, Inc., 1972), pp. 9-10.
7. Alfred A. Kuehn and Ralph L. Day, "Strategy of Product Quality," *Harvard Business Review* (November-December 1962), pp. 100-110.
8. Frank, Massy and Wind, *op cit.,* pp. 27-28.
9. Barban, *et al., op cit.,* p. 31.
10. For an example of this segmentation approach, see Russell J. Haley, "Benefit Segmentation: A Decision Oriented Research Tool," *Journal of Marketing* (July 1968), pp. 30-35.
11. Barban, *et al., op cit.,* pp. 29-30.
12. R.E. Frank, "Is Brand Loyalty a Useful Basis for Market Segmentation," *Journal of Advertising Research* (June 1967), pp. 27-33.
13. Joseph T. Plummer, "Application of Life Style Research to the Creation of Advertising Campaigns," in William D. Wells (ed.), *Life Style and Psychographics* (in press).
14. W.D. Wells and D.J. Tigert, "Activities, Interests, and Opinions," *Journal of Advertising Research* (August 1971), pp. 27-35.
15. Ruth Ziff, "Psychographics for Market Segmentation," *Journal of Advertising Research* (April, 1971), p. 3.
16. "Psychographics: OK in Some Cases, But There Are Weaknesses," *Madison Avenue* (September 1973), p. 24.
17. James F. Engel, Hugh G. Wales and Martin R. Warshaw, *Promotional Strategy,* rev. ed. (Homewood, Il.: Richard D. Irwin, Inc., 1971), Ch. 9.

MANAGEMENT OF THE ADVERTISING BUDGET

- Importance of the Advertising Budget
- Definition of the Advertising Budget
- Traditional Budgeting Approaches
- Advertising Investment and Payout Planning
- Marginal Analysis Concepts in Budgeting
- Overview of Budgeting Models

Decision Making Organization of This Text

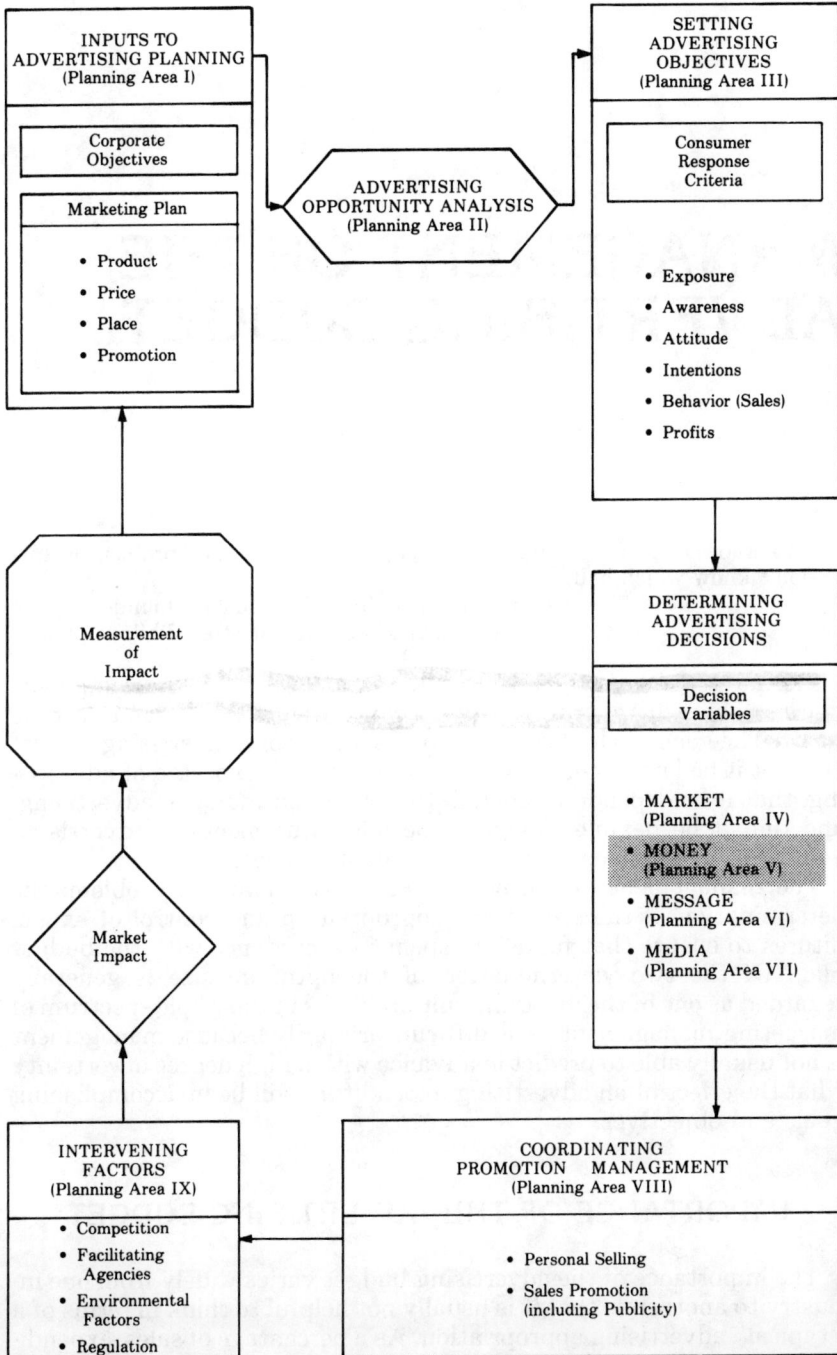

INPUTS TO ADVERTISING PLANNING
(Planning Area I)

- Corporate Objectives
- Marketing Plan
  - Product
  - Price
  - Place
  - Promotion

ADVERTISING OPPORTUNITY ANALYSIS
(Planning Area II)

SETTING ADVERTISING OBJECTIVES
(Planning Area III)

- Consumer Response Criteria
  - Exposure
  - Awareness
  - Attitude
  - Intentions
  - Behavior (Sales)
  - Profits

Measurement of Impact

DETERMINING ADVERTISING DECISIONS

- Decision Variables
  - MARKET (Planning Area IV)
  - MONEY (Planning Area V)
  - MESSAGE (Planning Area VI)
  - MEDIA (Planning Area VII)

Market Impact

INTERVENING FACTORS
(Planning Area IX)

- Competition
- Facilitating Agencies
- Environmental Factors
- Regulation

COORDINATING PROMOTION MANAGEMENT
(Planning Area VIII)

- Personal Selling
- Sales Promotion (including Publicity)

MANAGEMENT OF THE ADVERTISING BUDGET

"I know half of my advertising budget is wasted. The problem is I don't know which half."

—Attributed to John Wanamaker, founder
Wanamaker's Department Store, Philadelphia

The advertising budget is a systematic plan of determining how much, when, where, and for what purposes advertising funds will be spent. The general characteristics of a satisfactory advertising budget are that it be large enough to accomplish the job expected of advertising, that it be dependable enough to permit continuity of advertising, and that it be flexible enough to permit adjustments in advertising volume to meet changing problems and situations.

The management of the budget involves a two-fold problem: the determination of the size of the appropriation and control of expenditures to ensure that funds are spent in accordance with the budget plan. Of the two, determination of the optimum size is generally regarded as one of the most difficult problems in the whole spectrum of marketing management. It is difficult primarily because management is not usually able to predict in advance with a high degree of certainty what the effect of an advertising expenditure will be in accomplishing goals and objectives.

IMPORTANCE OF THE ADVERTISING BUDGET

The importance of the advertising budget varies widely from one industry to another so that it is usually not helpful to think in terms of a "typical" advertising appropriation. As a percentage of sales, expenditures may range from a fraction of 1 percent to over 50 percent. In the mining industry, budgets may vary between .1 percent to .3 percent of sales; in appliance and automobile industries (durable goods industries), the budget might be between 2 and 5 percent of sales; in foods, this figure would be higher, in the range of 5 to 15 percent; in cleaning products, it might be between 10 and 20 percent; and in the cosmetics industry, where the highest percentage of sales is spent on advertising, the figures will range between 20 to 50 percent.

Within industries, the importance of the advertising program in the overall marketing plan varies considerably. For example, in 1977 the ratio of advertising expenditures to net income was 60 percent for Eastern Air Lines while this same ratio was 143 percent for United Air Lines. It might be noted that, in that same year, 24 of the top 100 advertisers in the United States spent more money on advertising than the net income for their company.[1] Fully one fourth of some of the largest corporations in this country spend more money on advertising than they make in profits. Clearly, it would seem that there would be some temptation on the part of the corporate management of these companies to reduce the advertising expenditure so that this might increase profits. That such companies continue to spend such large amounts on advertising must indicate their belief that advertising expenditures are absolutely necessary to the performance of the company in the marketplace, even if they are not certain that the amount they are spending is absolutely correct.

This lack of certainty on the part of business people was demonstrated in a study conducted by Greyser and Reece.[2] In their study, about half of all the business people studied believed that too much money was being spent by companies on their advertising programs. This response was about 15 percentage points higher than the response found when the same questions had been asked nine years earlier; that is, there appears to be an increase in the number of business managers who believe too much money has been spent on advertising. This same study also showed, however, that managers did not believe that the money spent on advertising should be reduced and transferred to other marketing activities; seven out of ten respondents believed such marketing activities would cost more than advertising to do the comparable job.

The ambivalence demonstrated in the above study regarding management's view of the importance of advertising is also reflected in the way advertising budgets are commonly determined. There is a marked tendency for managers to first set some sales objective for a fiscal time period for the company. Then the manufacturing, administration, direct selling costs, and desired profit levels are set; after these are subtracted from sales revenue, the amount left over is allocated to advertising. This seems to suggest that managers are uncertain about the role of the advertising expenditure in creating sales yet just as certain that advertising is necessary to create those sales. This state of affairs is not far-removed from that described by John Wanamaker at the top of this chapter.

The general reasons for such a situation are clear. The optimum size of advertising expenditure is directly connected with advertising productivity and contributions to company net profits. The problem of budget size is complicated by the fact that a variety of factors other than mere size may have a direct effect on the accomplishment of the advertising objective. Many advertising practitioners and researchers believe the quality of the advertising has a more important effect on advertising results than the number of dollars spent. For example, a spokesperson for AdTel, a split-cable market testing system which deals with 80 or 90 tests of advertising variables a year, says that of the several different kinds of tests, advertising spending tests with no copy changes are the type of test with the greatest failure rate. That is, advertising spending tests (often called "advertising-weight tests") are the ones most likely to show no differences in sales levels across different advertising spending levels.[3] In addition to the quality of advertising, the quality of the product, activities of competitors, and the economic climate are to be included among the important factors influencing advertising results.

DEFINITION OF THE ADVERTISING BUDGET

As indicated at the beginning of this chapter, the advertising budget is defined as a systematic plan of determining how much, when, where, and for what purposes advertising funds will be spent. The general characteristics of an adequate budget are that it be large enough to accomplish the job expected of advertising, that it be dependable enough to permit continuity of advertising, and that it be flexible enough for expansion or contraction of the advertising effort to meet changing problems and situations. The flexibility factor is usually met through an advertising reserve.

ITEMS INCLUDED IN THE ADVERTISING BUDGET

From the standpoint of advertising management, it is essential that the items going into the budget be related directly to the objectives of the advertising and promotion effort so that they are logically explained as an advertising expense. Furthermore, once it is agreed what elements fit into the advertising and promotion budget, this agreement should not be voided by any of the management parties involved in the planning and decision-making process.

Sound financial practices must be followed in handling advertising and promotion funds, once classifications have been set up. These matters cannot be left to chance. An adequate system of records should be set up and maintained, and this system should give a complete picture of the advertising financial situation.

In some companies there is a tendency to treat the advertising account as a catchall. It is important that those in charge of managing the advertising appropriation check carefully all items and activities which are charged to advertising. Such activities as the printing of manuals and reports, community chest and welfare activities, and charity contributions, are not part of the advertising investment. The advertising appropriation may be dissipated if such non-advertising activities are included in the budget because, when this is done, it may well leave an insufficient amount for use in trying to achieve the tasks set for the advertising program. Certainly, if corporate management persists in the practice of charging non-advertising items to the advertising account, the advertising manager has every right to increase the appropriation request by an amount equal to the sum of these extraneous items.

There is still great variation in the way different companies set up their budget form, particularly in connection with the items included in it. For example, there can be two advertisers whose total appropriation for "advertising" is publicized at $1 million. In the case of Company A, however, this $1 million can represent expenditures exclusively for advertising media. In the case of Company B, only $300,000 (or 30 percent) might be allocated for the actual purchase of media, and the remainder could cover a host of other items ranging from packaging costs to the salaries of people in the advertising department.

There are also many variations in the breakdown of budgets and classification of items, even in companies that use the same kind of budgeting procedure. For example, in some companies, direct mail to the trade is an advertising cost; in other companies, it is carried as a promotion cost, despite the fact that in both companies the item, *per se*, is included in the total advertising and promotion budget.

A typical budget form is shown in Figure 7–1. This form essentially breaks the appropriation into two major segments: advertising and sales promotion. It represents the budget form used by some packaged goods manufacturers. Within such a budget operation, the relationship of advertising to sales promotion allocation is influenced critically by the overall promotion strategy; this relationship is discussed in some detail in Chapter 16.

It should be noted under the sales promotion section in Figure 7–1 that there is room for a "reserve." This company, for some reason, happens to prefer the reserve in this category, although it would generally be more desirable to classify this separately or as part of the advertising budget. An adequate reserve, however, is essential in sound budgeting operations.

THE ADVERTISING RESERVE

It is frequently impossible in planning advertising to anticipate all future conditions and resulting financial needs. Situations change, and sales and advertising opportunities sometimes develop during the fiscal period. An element of flexibility in the program is needed. A

Figure 7-1 Example of a Budgeting Format

BRAND FORECAST AND BUDGETS

LINE CLASSIFICATION _____
BRAND _____
BRAND CLASSIFICATION _____

1. Detailed Breakdown (6 months)

Estimated Sales	Advertising Budget	Advertising as % of Sales	Sales promotion Budget	Sales Prom. as % of Sales	Total Adv. & Sales Prom.	Combined Adv. & S.P. as % of Sales
_____	_____	_____	_____	_____	_____	_____

A. ADVERTISING: Account # _____ Account Name & Description _____

	Appropriation	Percent of Total
Magazines	_____	_____
Newspapers	_____	_____
Broadcast Production	_____	_____
Radio	_____	_____
Television	_____	_____
Professional Publications	_____	_____
Trade Journals	_____	_____
Print Production	_____	_____

B. SALES PROMOTION:

Reserve	_____	_____
Sampling	_____	_____
Book Matches	_____	_____
Direct Mail	_____	_____
Display Materials	_____	_____
Special Incentives: Consumer	_____	_____
Special Incentives: Trade	_____	_____
Sales Promotion Material	_____	_____
Gift Set Adjustment	_____	_____
Publicity	_____	_____

Product Manager _____ (signature) _____ (date)

Merchandising Mgr. _____ (approved) _____ (date)

reasonable reserve should be established to permit adjustments to changing conditions and opportunities. Needs arise from a variety of sources. They may stem from increases during the fiscal period in such costs of advertising as media rates or production costs, or from the promotion costs of introducing a newly developed product released ahead of schedule by company laboratories. No rigid amount can be suggested for this reserve. A reasonably good estimate is ordinarily the best that can be done in this respect. The important thing for planning is that provision be made for a reserve of this type. It is a necessity if the company is to be assured of a continuous advertising program.

It might be well to point out that management is under no rigid obligation or commitment forcing it to spend this reserve. These funds are available for use when and if they are needed. They should not be spent if there is no need for them, and advertising expenditures made under such conditions would probably not be justified.

Suggestions have been made from time to time for the establishment of an advertising reserve with a slightly different objective. One of the earlier suggestions of this nature was an *Advertising Age* editorial of 1951.[4] This proposal urges that advertising be used in an attempt to introduce more stability into the business cycle. The aim is to reduce the tendency on the part of advertisers to overspend in periods of high business activity and underspend in other periods in which business conditions are generally poor. This practice tends to accentuate the extremes of the cycle. Through this plan an advertising reserve would be set up in one business period, but actually spent during some later period. If part of the high advertising budgets in overactive business periods could be deferred and spent during periods of business recession, the effects of this promotion might materially aid in stimulating demand. This would be one factor in helping to level out the peaks and hollows of the business cycle. It would aid in stimulating demand on the part of the consumers who have adequate purchasing power, but who may be hoarding or otherwise postponing expenditures through fear of losing their jobs, the hope that prices will soon fall to lower levels or other factors of a psychological nature. Such a deferment in expenditures can reach proportions sufficient to cause a significant decline in current consumption. As goods begin to accumulate and back up in marketing channels, the result can be unemployment and declines in consumer purchasing power. While this is only one factor causing business fluctuations, advertising could, if properly timed and widely utilized within industries in this manner, be of material aid in reducing the influence of this factor.

TRADITIONAL BUDGETING APPROACHES

Traditional methods of developing the advertising budget have usually been categorized into four general sets of methods: (1) The percentage-of-sales approach; (2) The all-you-can-afford approach;

(3) The objective-and-task approach; and (4) The competitive-parity approach. Each of these basic methods is briefly described below.

PERCENTAGE OF SALES

Percentage of sales is one of the most widely used of all budgeting methods. In its basic form, a fixed percentage is arrived at, and this percentage is then multiplied times *last year's* sales to arrive at the budget size. Sometimes, this percentage figure is allowed to vary depending upon business conditions.

Another version of the percentage-of-sales method applies the fixed percentage to *next year's* sales to arrive at the budget figure. Thus, the method either deals with *past* or *future* (projected) sales. In addition, advertisers sometimes use a combination of past and future sales to which the percentage is applied. Reference to the past provides some stability while reference to the future presumably offers the opportunity to take advantage of market potential.

It is not clear how the fixed percentage is arrived at in the percentage-of-sales method in any given situation. Presumably the manager examines the industry percentage of sales spent on advertising as well as those for the competitors in relation to the historical trend of such percentages for the manager's own company or brand.

A variation of the percentage-of-sales method is often termed the "unit of sale" method or the "case rate" approach. Here, a particular dollar amount for advertising is allocated for each case which the company expects to sell of its product in the upcoming time period. This approach is often used by manufacturers of durable goods such as automobiles, washing machines, televisions, and so forth. It is also used in association or cooperative advertising where the unit production is fairly well known in advance, such as in the canning industry.

ALL YOU CAN AFFORD

This approach is utilized by nearly as many companies as is the percentage-of-sales approach. The "affordable" approach usually means that advertising will be appropriated after all other unavoidable investments and expenditures have been allocated. The following example illustrates the procedure in a simplified manner.

Example 7-1. Suppose the operating statement for a company is as shown below (in abbreviated format as described in some detail in Example 3-3 of Chapter 3):

Year t

Net Sales	$1,000,000
c.g.s.	600,000
Gross Margin	400,000
Admin/Mktg	200,000
Adv	100,000
Net Profit	$ 100,000.

Suppose that this firm has made a sales forecast for the following year, year t+1, which indicates that sales will be in the neighborhood of $1,250,000. If this forecast holds true, there will clearly be an additional $250,000 available which must go to cover the additional cost of goods sold, administrative/marketing expenses, and net profit, as well as advertising. Following the affordable approach, this additional $250,000 would first be allocated to these factors in accordance with production costs and executive judgment. After a reasonable amount is also allocated to profits, the residual amount would be allocated to advertising. This would be all the company could afford to spend on advertising.

Suppose, in this example, that it is assumed that cost of goods sold will increase in proportion to sales increases. Using the approach shown in Chapter 3, Example 3–3, the "new" cost of goods sold for year t+1 would then be $750,000:

$$\frac{1,000,000}{600,000} = \frac{1,250,000}{X}$$

$$X = 750,000.$$

Profits in the preceding year, t, were 10 percent of sales (100,000/1,000,000 = .10); if profits are maintained at this percentage level in year t+1, they should become $125,000 (.10 × 1,250,000 = 125,000). Suppose that management decides to allocate $50,000 additional to provide salary increases for administrative employees as well as to cover additional marketing expenses. Prior to the inclusion of advertising expenditures, year t+1 statement would appear as follows:

Year t + 1

Net Sales	$1,250,000
c.g.s.	750,000
GM	500,000
Admin/Mktg	250,000
Adv	?
Net Profit	$ 125,000.

Clearly, the amount left over in the above statement is $125,000; this is all the company can afford to spend on advertising next year (assuming they do not wish to borrow funds to pay for such advertising). This $125,000 (500,000 − 250,000 − 125,000 = 125,000) would be the advertising budget using this simplified version of the all-you-can-afford method.

OBJECTIVE AND TASK

In this approach, objectives are developed (these might be only short-run objectives or a combination of short- and long-run objectives) for the brand or company. Of the many types of objectives which could be developed, in practice these are often very closely related to media objectives. A determination is made as to which combination of vehicles (the media schedule) should be used to reach the target market and provide the frequency of exposure desired to get the message across to consumers in this market. The cost of this schedule is then determined; this cost is the advertising budget for the time period. If the cost is greater than the money available for advertising, then either the objectives need to be reduced in scope or additional money must be found. This general approach has been outlined by Frey:[5]

(1) Determine the dollar sales goal for the period ahead.
(2) Identify the potential market and delineate its segments—whose awareness and favorable attitudes are worth striving for.
(3) Measure the present level of unawareness, awareness, favorable attitudes and purchasing among the individuals in these segments.
(4) Calculate any increase in awareness and favorable attitudes necessary to produce the indicated sales increase.
(5) Decide the number of effective message deliveries—conscious impressions—necessary to produce the increase in awareness and attitudes.
(6) Calculate the number of actual message exposures necessary to produce the desired quantity of effective message deliveries, or conscious impressions.
(7) Calculate the number of potential message exposures necessary to produce the desired actual exposures.
(8) Decide which media and which schedules in the media produce the desired total number of potential message exposures at the lowest cost.
(9) This cost is the advertising appropriation.

Clearly, emphasis is put upon a thorough study of the market and product if implementation of the above approach is to be carried out.

COMPETITIVE PARITY

Determining an advertising appropriation by the competitive parity or "competitive comparison" method may take several different approaches. The advertiser may appropriate an absolute dollar amount or a percentage of sales patterned closely after the company's chief competitor or several industry leaders. Or the manager might attempt to approximate the industry spending average. In either approach, the size of the advertising budget is directly influenced by the volume of competitive advertising.

J. O. Peckham, of the A.C. Neilsen Company, has developed a "rule of thumb" for advertising spending based on the competitive comparison concept:

To a product with a good, strong consumer-plus—and this is the basic essential ingredient—add sufficiently skillfully applied advertising over a twenty-four-month period to produce a share of advertising about one and one-half times that of the share of sales you plan to attain.[6]

In other words, Peckham's Rule would suggest that if a company desires to attain a 10 percent market share (that is, 10 percent of all the sales in the company's industry), then the advertising budget should be set so that it is at the 15 percent share of advertising level (that is, the company's spending on advertising is 15 percent of all money spent by all advertisers in the company's industry) during a 24-month period.

With respect to this rule, Peckham has presented such evidence as shown below:[7]

	Market Share	Advertising Share	Ratio of Market Share to Adv Share
Brand A:	19.5%	29.9%	1.54
Brand B:	16.5	24.6	1.50
Brand C:	16.2	20.1	1.24.

This experience is primarily in the food and drug industries where advertising is a very important factor in producing sales, if the size of advertising expenditures as a percentage of sales is any indicator of this.

CRITICISM OF TRADITIONAL METHODS

One of the first to point out the logical fallacies in the traditional methods of budget determination was Joel Dean, an economist. The following analyses are excerpted from his classic discussion of advertising found in his 1951 text, *Managerial Economics.*

The Percentage-of-Sales Approach. This general approach to the problem is hard to support analytically. The purpose of advertising is to increase demand for the company's products above what it would be otherwise—advertising should be viewed as the cause, not the result of sales.

... It would appear even less rational to base the budget on the volume of sales the company expects to get. Sales will be the result of the level of national income, the accumulated effects of past advertising, and the advertising that is currently being decided upon. To the extent that sales are determined by forces other than current advertising, the criterion of expected sales is irrelevant. To the extent that they are determined by future advertising, the criterion is based on circular reasoning.

The All-You-Can-Afford Approach. In practice, this amount is sometimes a predetermined share of the profits, though sometimes it is gauged by the amount of liquid resources and borrowable funds. . . . Used uncritically, the all-you-can-afford method is unsatisfactory, largely because there is no relation between liquidity and the richness of advertising opportunities. If another $1,000 of advertising will bring in $2,000 of added profits, it is hard to say it cannot be afforded. A management that limits advertising to liquid funds or to a percentage of profits may forego money-making opportunities. (On the other hand) . . . spending money on advertising up to the limit of all-you-can afford spending may at times go far beyond the point at which the added earnings from advertising equal their cost.

Objective-and-Task Approach. Under this approach the advertising budget is the amount estimated to be required to attain predetermined objectives. . . . In its bald form, the objective-and-task approach begs the question. The important problem is to measure the value of objectives and to determine whether they are worth the probable cost of attaining them. . . . Objective-and-task assumes that the candle is always worth the cost.

The Competitive-Parity Approach. The size of the optimum outlay is affected by rivals' advertising, since competitors' advertising influences the productivity of the firm's . . . advertising. But it cannot be determined by merely matching competitors' appropriations. Hence, what rivals choose to spend does not in itself provide any valid measure of what the firm's advertising budget should be.[8]

These basic criticisms were first made in 1951, as noted above, and have been repeated for many years in basically the same form. The following observations were made by advertising practitioners and researchers between 1932 and 1953:

All budget factors are important, but the advertiser's own experience with advertising and what it did for him is probably the most influential guide in budget determination.[9]

It is not of the least importance what accounting methods are used to determine what constitutes advertising costs so long as management realizes that one company's methods may require a larger or smaller proportionate appropriation than those of another company.[10]

Few firms have a valid theoretical or research basis for deciding upon the level of advertising expenditures: e.g., whether they should spend $100,000 or $200,000 a year.[11]

The purpose of this article is to list fourteen reasons why any mechanical technique of budget determination (including percent of sale and fixed sum per unit) is utterly unrealistic.[12]

It would not be difficult to find a number of advertising practitioners and others who might make the same comments today regarding the budgeting problem. Despite dissatisfaction with traditional methods over such a long period of time, it is clear that even today advertising managers rely primarily upon one version or another of the four basic traditional methods outlined above.

The most recent survey of advertisers to see which methods were actually used by them in setting the appropriation was conducted in

1975.[13] The authors of this study interviewed, among others, advertising executives of 25 of the 100 leading national advertisers dealing in consumer advertising. The results of their interviews with these executives showed that 92 percent of these 25 firms utilized one variation or another (percent of past or future sales, unit past or future sales) of the percentage-of-sales method. Specifically, the most often used of the percentage-of-sales approaches was percentage of future or anticipated sales; 52 percent indicated they used this approach. The next-most-often-used approach was the all-you-can-afford method; 28 percent indicated they utilized this approach. Twelve percent of the respondents in the study indicated their firms utilized the objective-and-task approach (these figures sum to greater than 100 percent since some firms use several of the different approaches). Only four percent of the executives indicated their firm used any of the newer approaches of a quantitative nature (these approaches are discussed in some detail in Chapter 8).

If, in the above study, only those firms using percentage of past or future sales are included in the percentage-of-sales category, the proportion of firms using this method would be 68 percent. It is interesting to contrast this figure with the survey of this same matter conducted in 1935 by the then National Industrial Advertisers Association.[14] This study showed that 54 percent of companies advertising consumer goods stated that their budgets were set by using the percentage-of-sales method, either past or future. Clearly, despite the criticism of this traditional method, it appears that its usage has not declined; possibly the method might be used more now than in the past.

To put all of this in perspective, the observations made by three advertising practitioners in 1957 are even more valid today than at that time:

> ... Perhaps it is a fair question, then, to ask why further discussion is necessary, since the determination of the advertising budget is, of necessity, a matter of rough executive judgment? The answer is that in order to aid executive thinking effectively, the advertising person and the marketing person must possess a solid background in the best available thinking in this field. The fact that there is a broad area for final executive judgment under conditions of present-day knowledge does not mean that viewpoints and methods of thought do not differ from company to company; nor does it mean that the best results are due primarily to the operation of chance or "good fortune."[15]

It is with this perspective that the remainder of this chapter and Chapter 8 attempt to develop advanced approaches to the budgeting problem.

ADVERTISING INVESTMENT AND PAYOUT PLANNING

In advertising, different companies in different phases of industry have varying policies with respect to the concept of an advertising investment. Beyond the scope of year-to-year budget considerations, there exist advertising appropriation decisions involving management participation which go substantially beyond the annual, semi-annual, or quarterly budget review.

These longer-term advertising decisions, essentially advertising investment decisions, occur both in the case of established as well as new products. More often than not, however, they are of the greater importance in connection with new product introduction or major shifts in advertising and marketing policy.

Advertising, it is recognized, has two effects: (1) It increases sales today; and (2) it builds goodwill to increase sales tomorrow. The first involves primarily problems of selecting the best output rate for maximizing short-run profits. The second has to do with selection of the pattern of investment of capital funds that will produce the best scale of production and maximum long-run profits. Advertising could, therefore, be treated primarily as a capital investment rather than as a current expense. Determination of the amount of advertising expenditures then becomes a problem of capital expenditure budgeting. Advertising investment must then compete for funds with other kinds of internal investment on the basis of prospective rate of return.

Essentially, the philosophy of what is called *payout planning* embraces the idea of investing advertising dollars ahead of sales. In this sense, the idea parallels the investment policy a corporation might undertake in connection with new plant and equipment. With respect to physical items such as plant and equipment, the costs of such capital investment are charged off through the accounting mechanism of the depreciation allowance. Nevertheless, the company has to put out substantial sums of money accounted for in a business sense over more than an annual period.

In a case of advertising dollars (particularly in the case of new product introduction), a corporation must sometimes invest in advertising in an analogous fashion; that is, to allocate dollars on more than an annual basis in order to meet the marketing necessities of a given marketing problem. It may be necessary to invest ahead of sales in order to provide the advertising and promotion weight necessary to introduce a new product, or for a major new marketing posture that a given brand may assume.

Not all corporations can feasibly implement this investment philosophy. Such a philosophy requires that extensive liquid capital be available if positive results of its application in a test market are to be extended on a broad national basis. Furthermore, beyond the money problem, in certain kinds of markets where advertising is not a prime mover in the marketing mix but simply a backdrop to the marketing effort, this kind of philosophy may be neither applicable nor a wise marketing maneuver. Even in packaged goods, where payout planning is frequently undertaken by many of the larger companies, it is often unrealistic to underwrite such a plan when dealing with segmented markets; that is, relatively narrow and small markets where the potential payoff in absolute dollars is not very large.

Beyond the marketing ingredients that must be inspected, the very nature of a corporation's philosophy can frequently influence their attitudes. Some companies (Procter & Gamble is an outstanding example) are vigorous supporters of the philosophy of advertising investment and payout planning. On the other hand, other equally large and successful corporations believe that a product should pay for itself immediately, and stand on its own rather than gain its market hold on the basis of an initial outpouring of extensive advertising effort.

Payout planning, which in a sense is a measurement of demand expansibility, is normally undertaken first through the medium of the test market concept rather than the corporation's moving in on an overall national basis immediately. While some companies have chosen to move in swiftly on a total national basis without the intermediate market test, as normally carried out, market testing of the advertising investment program is the method most frequently utilized. That the investment approach involves complex test market measurement procedures makes its usage and implementation somewhat difficult. This should not be allowed to obscure the basic desirability and integrity of the approach, as described by Dean:

> These measurement difficulties . . . do not invalidate the investment approach itself. For other kinds of investments, e.g., research laboratories and department store escalators, it is equally impossible to estimate the return precisely. Yet few would, for this reason, kick out such items from the capital expenditure budget. Institutional and cumulative advertising should be analyzed in the intellectual setting of the capital budget, viz., long-range strategic and profit objectives, competition of alternative investments for limited company funds, and balancing of risks against prospective return on investment in rationing capital. This kind of investment perspective should be an integral part of an intelligent approach to the advertising budget.[16]

The following discussion provides a simplified example of the use of the advertising investment and payout planning approach.

Example 7-2. Suppose that the Bantin Company is introducing a new line of cameras. This company, say in the past, has always used the percentage-of-sales method for determining advertising budgets. Given their experience with their other brands and their knowledge of competitors' spending on advertising, suppose the Bantin advertising manager decides that the company will spend 12 percent of sales on advertising for the new camera line. Further, suppose the marketing research people for this company have developed a forecast of the sales expected for the camera line over the first three-year period after introduction. At a 12 percent spending rate, ordinarily the situation would appear as below:

Year	Sales Projection	Advertising Budget (12%)
t	$1,000,000	$120,000
t+1	1,300,000	156,000
t+2	1,750,000	210,000
Total	$4,050,000	$486,000.

Over the three-year planning period, Bantin would spend a total of $486,000 on the new camera line. Under the above one-year payout plan, the advertising budget generated by applying the 12 percent to each year's sales projection is spent within that year. This is in contrast to a three-year payout plan. A typical three-year payout plan might call for 60 percent of the total dollars calculated above ($486,000) to be spent in the first year, 25 percent in the second year, and the remaining 15 percent in the third year. This would create a situation as shown below:

Year	Sales Projection	Advertising Budget	Percent of Three–year Budget
t	$1,000,000	$291,600	60%
t+1	1,300,000	121,500	25
t+2	1,750,000	72,900	15
Total	$4,050,000	$486,000	100%.

Clearly, a three-year payout plan provides considerably more funds for advertising at the beginning of the introductory period for this new product. The idea is to provide sufficient funds to get the new Bantin cameras off to a flying start, even if this might mean foregoing some profits on this line until after the third year of its introduction.

MARGINAL ANALYSIS CONCEPTS IN BUDGETING

There is little question about how the advertising budget ought to be set from the standpoint of theory and logic. The theoretical solution to this perplexing advertising problem was stated long ago by economists. Joel Dean brought the ideas of marginal analysis to the forefront in this area of advertising in 1951.[17]

THE MEANING OF MARGINAL ANALYSIS

It is very simple to state the basic idea of marginal analysis. The optimal amount of money to spend on advertising is at the point where the marginal cost of an additional unit of advertising equals the marginal revenue from the sale of an additional unit of product. A firm should continue to add money to the advertising budget as long as these incremental expenditures are less than the marginal revenue they generate. The reaction of many advertising practitioners to the concept of marginal analysis as stated above is summed up aptly in a "talk piece" put together on the subject of budgeting by a major advertising agency:

An economist can say, "Find the intersection of marginal cost and marginal revenue. That's how to set your budget. When additional advertising expense returns only an equal amount of additional revenue, that's when to stop increasing advertising spending, that's your budget level." We advertising people blink, not because we don't understand, but because we don't yet have that data that will let us watch those lines neatly intersect.[18]

The application of the concepts of marginal analysis is indeed fraught with difficulties. The primary issue concerns the development of the relationship between advertising expenditures and sales results. This is the area of advertising dealing with response functions which will be taken up in detail in Chapter 8. For the moment, an examination of marginal analysis in somewhat greater detail will make it clear why the fundamental issue in the development of logically pleasing budgeting procedures hinges almost entirely upon the issues inherent in the building of response functions, that is, in understanding the relationship between advertising and sales.

Figure 7-2 shows the elements involved in the use of marginal analysis. Before examining this chart in Figure 7-2, it is well to keep in mind the basic accounting relationships discussed in Chapter 3 in connection with Example 3-3:

$$GM = S - c.g.s.$$
$$NP = GM - Admin/Mktg - A$$

where: GM = Gross Margin
S = Sales in $
c.g.s. = cost of goods sold
NP = Net Profit
Admin/Mktg = Administration and Other Marketing Costs
A = Advertising Expenditures (Costs).

The sales response function is shown in Figure 7-2 as the top curve which is labeled "Sales"; this curve shows the relationship between advertising expenditures and sales and will be of different shape and position for different brands and products. For illustration purposes, the response function shown here is one for which advertising "causes" increases in sales when it is increased but such increases are of a diminished nature; that is, this response function exhibits diminishing returns throughout its range. Notice that the function intersects the vertical axis at $1,000,000; this would indicate that even without media expenditures of advertising there will still be some sales for this company. In fact, there will be $1,000,000 worth of sales in the absence of advertising activity; these sales are generated presumably by other marketing and economic factors.

The next curve below the response function is labeled "Gross Margin" and represents a scaled-down version of the sales response function above it. It is scaled down because gross profit or margin is equal to sales revenue minus the cost of goods sold (cost of production); in this example, all other costs are also assumed to be subtracted from sales revenue (including Admin/Mktg) to produce Gross Margin.

Figure 7-2 Using Marginal Analysis to Find The Best Advertising Expenditure

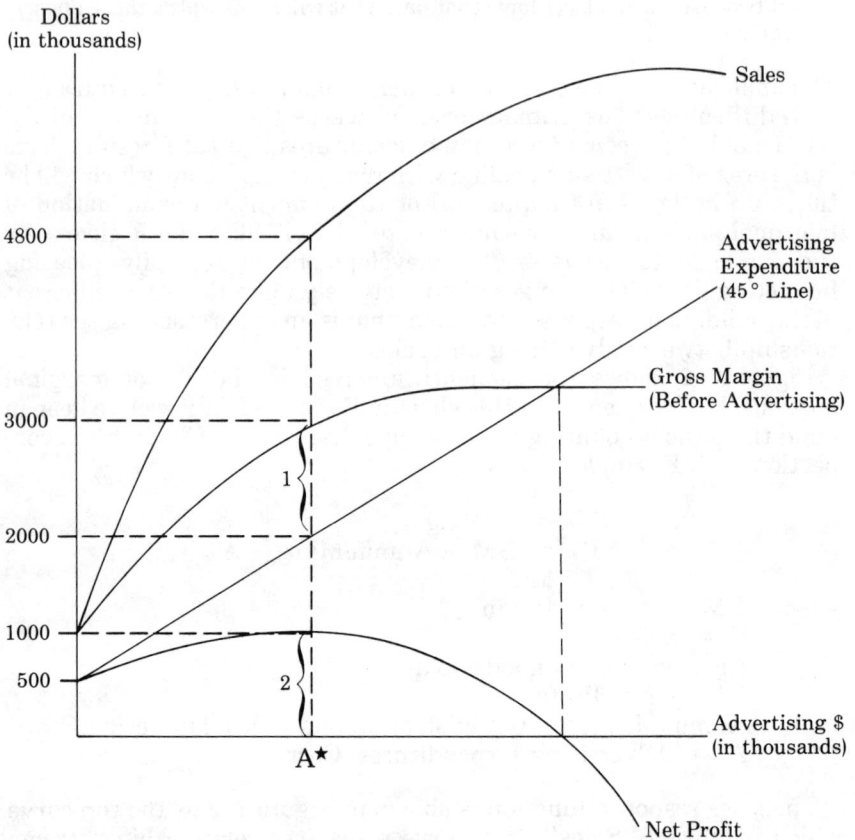

The only cost not already subtracted at this point is the advertising cost. The "Advertising Expenditure" is represented in Figure 7-2 by the 45 degree line. Notice that when advertising equals zero, that is, it is at the origin, the 45 degree line is at $500,000. This indicates that even without media advertising expenditures, there are fixed costs of advertising (salaries of advertising department employees and other overhead such a department might entail). In this example, such fixed costs amount to $500,000 per year, even when there are no media expenditures. This line is drawn at 45 degrees so that advertising expenditures on the horizontal, advertising axis can be "projected" onto and read off the vertical axis.

The curve under the 45 degree line in Figure 7-2 is the "Net Profit" function. It is found by subtracting the advertising expenditure from the gross margin curve which already has all expenditures subtracted from sales revenue with the exception of advertising. Notice that somewhere around an advertising expenditure of $4,000,000 net profits become negative, that is, the firm will lose rather than make money. Notice also that this point corresponds to the point directly above where the gross margin curve intersects the advertising expenditure 45 degree line. In fact the distance between the 45 degree line and the gross profit curve represents the amount of profits to a firm at a given level of advertising spending. The task in marginal analysis is to find the advertising spending level where the vertical distance between the 45 degree line and the gross margin curve is at its greatest. That advertising spending level is the "optimal" spending level and represents the point at which marginal cost of advertising is equal to the marginal gross profit. Net profit is at the maximum at this point and is represented in Figure 7-2 by the number "1". This point on the gross profit curve is also the point at which the tangent to the curve will be parallel to the 45 degree advertising expenditure line. This is the geometric equivalent of the fact that marginal cost of advertising is equal to the marginal gross profit at that point.

Notice that this point on the gross profit curve which provides the maximum net profits corresponds to the highest or maximum point on the net profit curve below it. Notice that the distance labeled number "2" in the figure is the identical distance as that labeled "1" above it. Finding the greatest vertical distance between the gross profit function and the advertising expenditure line is equivalent to the process of finding the maximum of the net profit function. When marginal analysis ideas are applied in practice, the attempt is made to find an advertising expenditure is at the point indicated by "A*" and is in the amount of $2,000,000 per year. At this optimal level of advertising expenditure, $2,000,000, the marginal gross profit obtained from the last dollar invested is $1.00 and the slope of the profit function at A* is zero. Above the level of spending represented by A*, an additional dollar spent on advertising will result in less than $1.00 in additional gross profit. Notice that at $2,000,000 expenditure on advertising (A*), the sales generated would be expected to be $4,800,000 with gross profits of $3,000,000 and net profits of $1,000,000.

Again, it should be noted that this and all similar types of analysis depend on and are derived from the sales response function. It is this recognition that has motivated a great deal of advertising effectiveness research since marginal analysis makes clear the essential and basic nature of the advertising/sales relationship to the development of logically- and theoretically-based budgeting approaches.

Finally, it is worth noting that, from a theoretical point of view, marginal analysis would be applied to each of the factors in the marketing mix, not just advertising. If, for example, the last dollar put into distribution produced $2.00 in additional revenue while the last dollar put into advertising produced $1.50, then it might be wise to take some money from the advertising function into the distribution function. In this manner, an attempt would be made to optimize the entire marketing mix.

OVERVIEW OF BUDGETING MODELS

The concepts of response functions and budgeting models will be examined in some detail in Chapter 8. At this point, however, a brief overview of the nature of such approaches to the advertising budgeting problem will be presented.

USE OF BUDGETING MODELS

As indicated earlier in this chapter, only a small proportion of manufacturers dealing in consumer goods utilize budgeting models; in fact, the most recent study of these matters estimated that only four percent of consumer advertisers use quantitative models in the budgeting process for their firm.[19] When this issue was put to the advertising executives responding in this same study, four percent indicated they used quantitative models heavily, eight percent used them moderately, 12 percent said they used them sometimes, 20 percent used them rarely, and 56 percent said they never used them at all. The conclusion from this is that as the primary process for budgeting in their own firms, only four percent use quantitative models exclusively. But some 24 percent, or almost one-fourth, of these large consumer advertisers make some use of quantitative models in their budgeting process.

When a company decides to make use of budgeting models, it can either develop them or purchase them from companies which market and develop models as their primary business. One of the most popular models in recent years which firms may purchase is the Hendry model. The acceptance by large corporations of this model has apparently been very high. B.F. Butler, President of the Hendry Corporation, has said the following:

> A quantitative method of advertising expenditure analysis, known as HendroGraphics, determines for individual brands of consumer goods the relationship between varying levels of advertising expenditures and the resulting share of market and contribution to profits. Since its development in 1962 it has been successfully utilized by large advertisers in over 60 different consumer product classes in several thousand cases with outstanding overlay with the real world.[20]

This model has been popular enough for the Ogilvy & Mather, Inc. advertising agency to run full-page advertisements in *Advertising Age* extolling the virtues of the Hendry Model as the agency had used it for its various clients; the purpose of such ads, of course, was to inform potential clients that this agency had access to sophisticated tools to help them in their budgeting process.

Counts by knowledgeable people have recently indicated that there are at least fourteen models of the Hendry variety which are available for companies to utilize.[21] Most of these are proprietary in nature so that little is known publicly about them. The basic notions, however, of all models are clear, and these follow closely the ideas set forth in marginal analysis.

ELEMENTS OF BUDGETING MODELS

Budgeting models must have at least four elements. These elements can be generally described in the following steps:

I. Development of a sales response function;
II. Definition of a net profit function for the firm;
III. Substitution of the sales response function in place of sales in the net profit function;
IV. Location of the maximum or near maximum of the net profit function into which sales response has been substituted through either optimization methods or numerical analysis.

These four steps or elements of budgeting models are illustrated in a simplified manner in the following example. Each of these elements is explored in further detail and complexity in Chapter 8.

Example 7-3. The step numbers in this example correspond to the step numbers of the outline above of budgeting model elements.

(1) Suppose a non-linear sales response function is developed and can be represented in the following way:

$$S = 200,000 + 700 \ \sqrt{A}$$

where: S = sales in \$
A = advertising in \$.

The square root sign over advertising in this response function results in a picture of this function somewhat similar to that shown in Figure 7-2 rather than a straight-line or linear function. That is, this function provides for the diminishing returns for sales to advertising expenditures. (This issue is discussed in detail in Chapter 8.)

(2) Suppose, further, that the net profit relationship for a particular company can be stated as follows:

$$NP = S - c.g.s. - Admin/Mktg - A.$$

These symbols are the same as those used in conjunction with the discussion of Figure 7-2 in this chapter.

(3) When the sales response function is substituted into the profit function, the result is:

$$NP = 200,000 + 700 \ \sqrt{A} - c.g.s. - Admin/Mktg - A.$$

(4) Suppose that management has estimated the cost of goods sold to be \$148,000 in the neighborhood of sales (an additional complication is that these costs would usually be variable, depending upon sales levels, and this matter will be taken up in Chapter 8) which are expected in the next planning period. Sup-

pose that marketing and administrative expenses have been set at \$92,000. Under these conditions, the net profit function becomes:

$$NP = 200,000 + 700 \sqrt{A} - 240,000 - A.$$

A numerical analysis of this function (substituting in various levels of advertising expenditures to figure the accompanying net profit figures) provides the following results:

Advertising $	Net Profit
$ 90,000	$80,000
110,000	82,163
120,000	82,487
130,000	82,380

Clearly, the maximum of this net profit function is somewhere in the area of \$120,000 expenditures on advertising. Further values could be tried to more specifically locate the most desirable advertising expenditure, but around \$120,000 advertising expenditure should produce the highest profits under the above given conditions.

This example clearly points out the areas in which refinement is required for the successful implementation of such approaches. The sales response function must be an accurate or acceptably accurate indicator of the effect of advertising, in conjunction with all other important factors, on sales response. The net profit function must be accurately set up to reflect the true conditions under which the firm operates. Net profit can mean many different things to different companies in terms of its definition. It is also not clear that numerical analysis will locate the global maximum of the net profit function. These and other issues are taken up in Chapter 8.

QUESTIONS AND PROBLEMS

1. Talk with a local retail establishment about their advertising program. Specifically, ask them how they go about setting their advertising budget for some time period. Is their approach a logical one?
2. Why do so many large advertisers rely on the percentage-of-sales approach in setting their budgets? Analyze the pros and cons of applying the percentage in this method to past or future sales.
3. How is the percentage figure arrived at when the percentage-of-sales method is utilized by a firm? Describe a specific instance of how this might work for a company selling an aspirin-type product to consumers.
4. How does advertising quality fit into the budget planning system when such methods as percentage of sales, competitive comparison, all-you-can-afford, and similar methods are used to set the budget figure?
5. What does it mean to say that profits are greatest at the point at which marginal revenue equals marginal cost? Provide an example of this where advertising is the cost involved. Use actual numbers in your example.

6. What is said about how advertising works when the response function is similar in nature to that illustrated in Figure 7–2 in this chapter or of the type illustrated in Example 7–3 in this chapter?

7. Can the advertising budget be set without reference to the overall financial situation of the firm? Why or why not?

8. Why might it be difficult for the advertising manager to acquire an amount for advertising from management which is to be used exclusively for the advertising reserve? Why should this be any more difficult than obtaining funds that definitely will be spent on advertising in the current time period?

9. The criticism has been made that advertising managers, by and large, do not set the amount to be spent on advertising on a logical and rational basis. Give two examples of other business functions where appropriation by the firm for that business activity may also not be set entirely on a rational, logical basis.

10. Are sales caused by advertising or is advertising caused by sales? Explain.

11. Why do some advertisers spend more on advertising in any given year than they make in net profits in a year? Give the names of industries in which this tends to be the case, and explain why these industries and not others.

12. Under what conditions would payout planning be desirable for a firm? For what types of firms? If advertising is viewed as an investment, how would the accounting department go about depreciating this investment over the life of the investment? Give an example.

ENDNOTES

1. William M. Weilbacher, *Advertising* (New York: Macmillan and Company, 1979), pp. 38-39.
2. Stephen A. Greyser and Bonnie B. Reece, "Businessmen Look Hard at Advertising," *Harvard Business Review* (May/June 1971), pp. 18-26.
3. *How Much Advertising Is Enough* (Chicago: Foote, Cone & Belding Communications, Inc., 1979), p. 13.
4. *Advertising Age* (April 16, 1951), p. 12.
5. Albert W. Frey, "The Advertising Appropriation," *Proceedings of American Marketing Association Conference,* 1961.
6. James O. Peckham, "Can We Relate Advertising Dollars to Market Share Objectives?" in Malcolm A. McNiven (ed.) *How Much to Spend for Advertising* (New York: Association of National Advertisers, 1969), p. 30.
7. James O. Peckham, speaking to Grocery Manufacturers of America, New York, New York, November 9, 1965.
8. Joel Dean, *Managerial Economics* (Englewood Cliffs, N.J.: Prentice-Hall, Inc., 1951), pp. 364-375.
9. C.A. Kirkpatrick, "12 Factors that Influence the Size of Advertising Budget," *Advertising Agency and Advertising Selling* (May 1953), p. 84.
10. "Four Dangers in Setting Up the Advertising Budget," *Printer's Ink* (December 7, 1945), p. 36.
11. H.E. Agenew, *Advertising Media* (Princeton: D. Van Nostrand Co., 1932), p. 351.
12. C.A. Kirkpatrick, "14 Reasons Why a Formula Can't Sell Your Ad Budget," *Printer's Ink* (April 3, 1953), p. 53.
13. Andre J. San Augustine and William F. Foley, "How Large Advertisers Set Their Budgets," *Journal of Advertising Research* (October 1975), p. 12.

14. J.C. Aspley (ed.), *Sales Management Handbook* (National Industrial Advertisers Association, 1947).
15. Lyndon O. Brown, Richard S. Lessler, and William M. Weilbacher, *Advertising Media* (New York: The Ronald Press, 1957), p. 267.
16. Joel Dean, "How Much to Spend on Advertising," *Harvard Business Review* (January 1951), p. 71.
17. *Ibid.*
18. "How Much Advertising Is Enough?" *op.cit.*, pp. 1-2.
19. San Augustine and Foley, *op.cit.*
20. B.F. Butler, P.M. Thompson, and L.A. Cook, "Quantitative Relationships Among Advertising Expenditures, Share of Market, and Profits," in Malcolm A. McNiven (ed.), *How Much to Spend for Advertising* (New York: Association of National Advertisers, 1969), p. 67.
21. Niles Howard, "Advertising's Holy Grail," *Dun's Review* (September 1978).

8

RESPONSE FUNCTIONS AND BUDGETING

- Application of Marginal Analysis
- Development of Response Functions
- Carryover Effects
- Implementation of Budgeting Models

Decision Making Organization of This Text

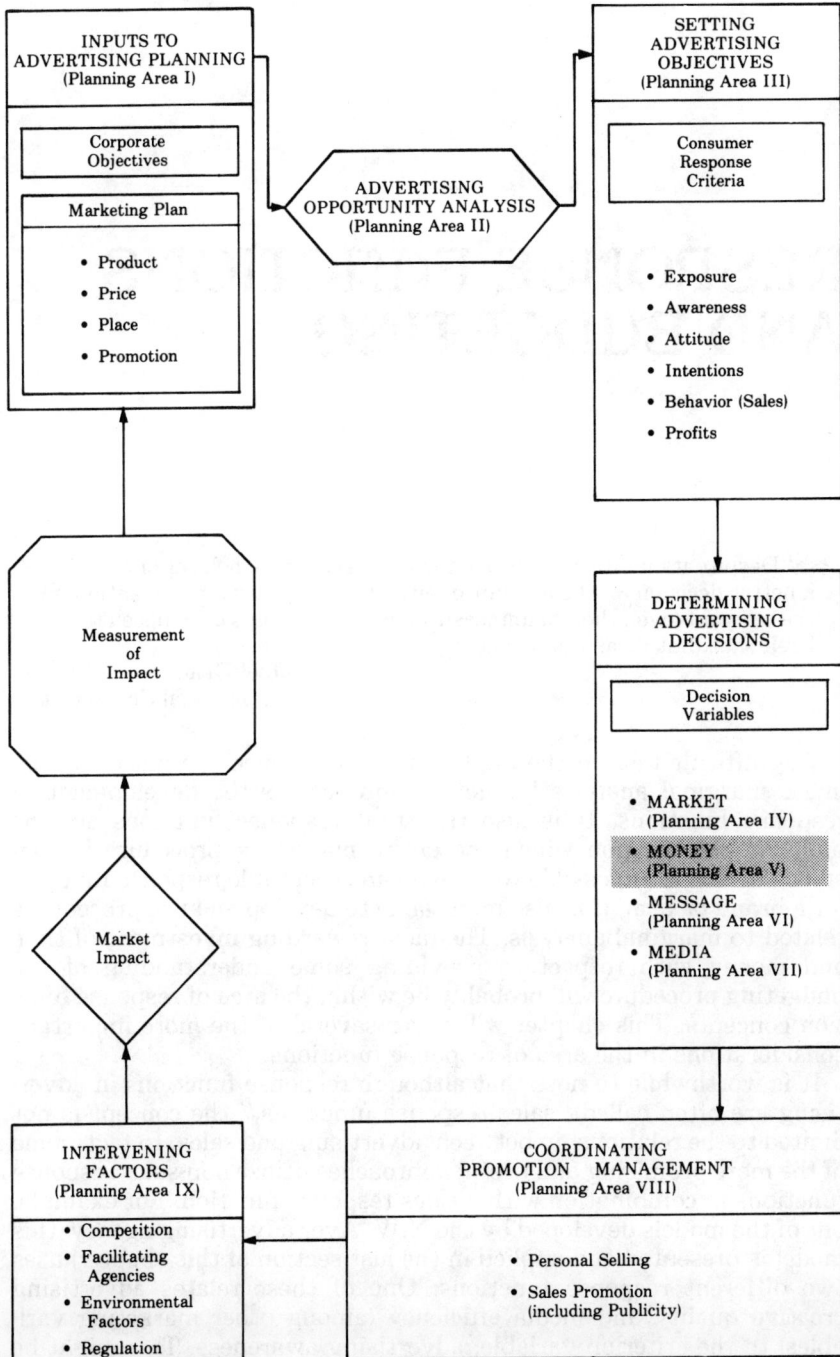

```
┌─────────────────────────┐                          ┌─────────────────────────┐
│      INPUTS TO          │                          │        SETTING          │
│  ADVERTISING PLANNING   │                          │      ADVERTISING        │
│   (Planning Area I)     │                          │       OBJECTIVES        │
│                         │                          │    (Planning Area III)  │
│  ┌───────────────────┐  │     ┌─────────────┐      │  ┌───────────────────┐  │
│  │     Corporate     │  │    ╱ ADVERTISING   ╲     │  │     Consumer      │  │
│  │    Objectives     │  │   ╱ OPPORTUNITY     ╲    │  │     Response      │  │
│  ├───────────────────┤  │   ╲  ANALYSIS       ╱    │  │     Criteria      │  │
│  │   Marketing Plan  │  │    ╲(Planning Area II)╱   │  └───────────────────┘  │
│  │                   │  │     └─────────────┘      │                         │
│  │  • Product        │  │                          │   • Exposure            │
│  │  • Price          │  │                          │   • Awareness           │
│  │  • Place          │  │                          │   • Attitude            │
│  │  • Promotion      │  │                          │   • Intentions          │
│  │                   │  │                          │   • Behavior (Sales)    │
│  └───────────────────┘  │                          │   • Profits             │
└─────────────────────────┘                          └─────────────────────────┘
```

ADVERTISING OPPORTUNITY ANALYSIS (Planning Area II)

Measurement of Impact

Market Impact

DETERMINING ADVERTISING DECISIONS

Decision Variables

- MARKET (Planning Area IV)
- MONEY (Planning Area V)
- MESSAGE (Planning Area VI)
- MEDIA (Planning Area VII)

INTERVENING FACTORS (Planning Area IX)

- Competition
- Facilitating Agencies
- Environmental Factors
- Regulation

COORDINATING PROMOTION MANAGEMENT (Planning Area VIII)

- Personal Selling
- Sales Promotion (including Publicity)

8

RESPONSE FUNCTIONS AND BUDGETING

"Despite its limitations, economic analysis can be helpful in reaching a better decision on the amount of advertising by focusing attention on the relevant (even though unmeasurable) relationships as opposed to the irrelevant (but measurable) ones."

—Joel Dean
Managerial Economist

The difficult task in the implementation of even the most approximate marginal analysis budgeting approach is the development of response functions. It is also true that response functions are the building blocks upon which the entire budgeting procedure is constructed; if it is impossible to develop an acceptable response function for a brand or firm, it is also impossible to develop and use procedures related to marginal analysis. The most rewarding investment of time and money with respect to providing some understanding of the budgeting procedure will probably lie within the area of response function concepts. This chapter will cover several of the more important considerations in the area of response functions.

It is worthwhile to note that although response functions in advertising are often called "sales response functions," the concept is not limited to the relationship between advertising and sales. In fact, some of the more promising and useful approaches utilize non-sales response functions in combination with a sales response function. For example, one of the models developed by the N.W. Ayer advertising agency (this model is presented and applied in the last section of this chapter) uses two different response functions. One of these relates advertising creative quality and media efficiency (among other marketing variables) to the criterion variable, advertising awareness. This might be called an "awareness response function." The second response function relates advertising awareness (among other factors) to a sales-type, behavioral criterion, initial purchase. It is a basic principle in this type of analysis, however, that even though advertising decision variables, such as message and money, might be connected to intermediate criteria in a response function, the intermediate criterion must then be related to some sales-type criterion in a sales response function. The reason for this is obvious; in order to relate advertising input (market, money, message, and media) to financial output (profits or the present value of profits), some measure must be used which can easily be interpreted in terms of *dollars*. It is fine to note that spending $2,000,000 on advertising resulted in brand awareness levels of 48 percent. But the issue concerns how many dollars will accrue to the company from this 48 percent awareness level. For this purpose, awareness must be functionally related to some sales-related criterion. From this standpoint, then, whether advertising objectives are stated in terms of intermediate criteria or not, it is desirable to understand the methods by which sales response functions can be developed.

APPLICATION OF MARGINAL ANALYSIS

In the preceding chapter, a modified example of the application of marginal analysis concepts was presented. The reader could, even in that example, see some of the potential problems which might arise in the actual application of the ideas of marginal analysis. To more clearly delineate the several specific problems which arise, it is worthwhile at this point to look at an example which follows more closely the ideas in marginal analysis than that example illustrates. The example can then be used as a basis for discussion of some of the typical problems which arise in actual implementation and the means by which such problems can be solved.

MARGINAL ANALYSIS AND OPTIMIZATION

The following example shows the use of classical optimization methods as these relate to marginal analysis.[1] There are at least ten major problems illustrated by this example in terms of actual implementation of the ideas shown. These will each be discussed after the example is shown.

Example 8-1. Suppose a company believes that its sales volume is largely determined by the amount of money it spends on advertising, and that there is little or no interaction of advertising with price in the determination of sales volume. No interaction of price and advertising simply means the effectiveness of advertising does not vary when the product price is changed. Suppose this company examines its weekly sales volume records and finds a diminishing returns response function as follows:

$$S = .7\sqrt{A}.$$

This response function, with its parameter set at .7, would indicate, for example, that if advertising dollars spent in a given week were $1600, the number of units sold in that week would be 28 (28 = .7$\sqrt{1600}$). Notice that "S" refers to sales in units here and not sales in dollars as this symbol has been previously used in this book. Below are the definitions of the symbols to be used in this and subsequent examples in this chapter:

S = sales in units (quantity sold)
S$ = sales in dollars
P = price per unit charged for the product
TC = total costs including fixed and variable production costs as well as Admin/Mktg expenses
NP = net profit
A = advertising expenditure in dollars.

The company then defines its total costs as follows:

$$TC = 7000 + 60S.$$

This total cost function says that total costs include $7,000 of fixed costs, which in this example are taken to include administration and other marketing costs as well as plant costs. Total costs also include variable costs of $60 per unit of product sold. Variable costs are "variable" in the sense that the overall cost of raw materials that are used to make the product will depend on the number of units which are to be produced in the weekly time period considered here. Total costs consist, then, of $7,000 in fixed costs (which do not change in relation to the number of units produced) and $60 times the number of units sold (S).

Net profits for this company are defined as:

$$NP = P(S) - TC - A.$$

That is, net profits are equal to total sales revenue (the price charged for each unit times the number of units sold) minus total costs as defined above and minus advertising expenditures. Suppose the company decides price will be $170 per unit. Given this information, the optimal (from the mathematical point of view) advertising expenditure for a given week can be determined. The procedure is outlined step-by-step below.

(1) The first step in the classical optimization procedure is to substitute the total cost function (TC = 7000 + 60S) into the net profit function (notice price of $170 in place of the symbol P):

$$NP = 170S - (7000 + 60S) - A.$$

This can then be simplified to:

$$NP = 170S - 7000 - 60S - A.$$

Collecting together the sales (S) terms above (170S − 60S = 110S) gives:

$$NP = 110S - 7000 - A.$$

(2) Now, the sales response function defined earlier (S = $.7\sqrt{A}$) can be substituted into the last equation form for net profits found in step #1 above:

$$NP = 110 (.7\sqrt{A}) - 7000 - A.$$

This function can then be simplified by multiplying .7 times 110 to yield:

$$NP = 77\sqrt{A} - 7000 - A.$$

(3) This and the following step are actually the points at which the classical optimization procedure is employed. Classical optimization is conducted through the use of differential calculus. (Though the reader may not have studied calculus, the actual mathematics are not important to an understanding of what the calculus application really does.)

To differentiate a function is to find the rate of change of that function, that is, to find the slope or "tilt" of the function at any given point. Figure 7–2 in Chapter 7 showed that the optimal advertising expenditure was at the point where the net profit function was at a maximum (the top of the function). The slope of a function such as that shown for net profit in Figure 7–2 is 0 (zero) at its peak; that is, at its exact peak, the function is neither going up nor going down. Therefore, in this step the rate of change or differential of the function from step #2 will be found. In step #4 to follow, the point at which this rate of change or slope is zero will be found.

$$\frac{d(NP)}{d(A)} = \frac{1}{2}(77)A^{-\frac{1}{2}} - 1.$$

The above equation can be read as follows: "The derivative of the net profit function (as shown on the last line of step #2) with respect to advertising is (or equals) one-half times 77 times Advertising raised to the negative one-half power minus one."

This can be simplified to the following form (77 times ½ equals 38.5):

$$\frac{d(NP)}{d(A)} = (38.5)A^{-\frac{1}{2}} - 1.$$

(4) By setting the derivative in the last line of step #3 above equal to zero and solving for the value of A, the optimal advertising expenditure level is found:

$$0 = \frac{38.5}{\sqrt{A}} - 1.$$

Notice that $A^{-\frac{1}{2}}$ is equivalent to $1/\sqrt{A}$. By adding one to both sides of the above the following results:

$$1 = \frac{38.5}{\sqrt{A}.}$$

Multiplying this equation on both sides by $\sqrt{A}$ gives:

$$\sqrt{A} = 38.5 \text{ and}$$

squaring both sides of this gives the final result:

$$A^* = 1482.25.$$

That is, the company should spend $1,482.25 per week on advertising.

The expenditure on advertising by this company of $1,482.25 per week would be expected to produce extra sales units (compared to the situation where the company did not advertise at all) of:

$$S = .7\sqrt{1482.25} \text{ or}$$

$$S = 26.95 \sim 27 \text{ units per week.}$$

This additional amount of unit sales would produce an additional profit of:

$$NP = 77\sqrt{A} - A \text{ or}$$

$$NP = 77\sqrt{1482.25} - 1482.25 \text{ or}$$

$$NP = \$1,482.25.$$

Notice that fixed costs of $7000 were not subtracted in figuring net profits since these would be incurred whether there was advertising or not, and therefore do not figure in the calculation of profits due to advertising activity.

APPLICATION PROBLEMS

There are possibly ten major problems which will often be encountered when the above approach is attempted in practice. Each of these problems will be examined below. The remainder of this chapter will then attempt to show the methods by which these problems can be resolved so that the general ideas contained in marginal analysis can be applied to practical benefit.

Direction of Causality. In the sales response function used in Example 8-1, it is assumed that sales is a function of advertising; that is, the direction of assumed causation goes from right to left in response functions. It is assumed that advertising causes sales in such a model. But in a model of advertising and sales there are three possible specifications of the relationship between these two things: (1) advertising determines sales; (2) sales determine advertising; or (3) both advertising determines sales and sales determine advertising. Suppose, for example, that the advertising manager for a company has used percentage-of-sales methods in setting the advertising budget in the past. Clearly, there is a likelihood that sales cause advertising in this company's situation rather than vice versa; the level of sales determines the amount to be spent on advertising. This issue can be resolved in a number of ways. First, if some method for setting the budget in the past other than percentage-of-sales method has been used, the idea that sales cause advertising becomes very much less plausible. Second, even in those instances where a method such as percentage of sales has been used, if monthly data on advertising and sales are used in the response function analysis while the advertising budget has been set on an annual basis, it is plausible to assume that causality goes from advertising to sales. Finally, the following two formulations could be tested:

$$(1) \quad S_t = a + bA_{t-1}$$

$$(2) \quad A_t = a + bS_{t-1}.$$

The first relationship specifies that sales in a given time period, say January, are a function of advertising in the preceding time period, say December. The second relationship says that advertising in January is a function of sales in December. If the first relationship is considerably stronger than the second, it is quite likely that causation is in the direction of advertising "causing" sales rather than the other way around. This reasoning is based upon the thinking that something can be "caused" by something else which occurred in time before it but not something occurring in time after it occurs.

Form of Relationship. In Example 8-1, the response function was formulated as diminishing returns in nature; in addition, it was assumed that taking the square root of advertising expenditures would adequately "fit" the actual advertising/sales curve. The number of functional forms which might be used is almost limitless in response function building. Which of the several is the correct one to use? For example, rather than the form $S = a + b\sqrt{A}$ used in Example 8-1, it may be that a function of the form $S = a(\log A)$ would be more appropriate. Such decisions as this must be made in building usable response functions; this issue will be discussed further in the subsequent section of this chapter. For now, it is sufficient for the reader to understand that there are many different equation forms which might represent the relationship between advertising and sales.

Carryover Effects. This issue is of sufficient importance in the advertising budgeting problem that a section will be devoted to it in this chapter. For now, it is important to understand that advertising has effects which are felt immediately as well as those which cannot be observed for some length of time beyond the immediate time period in which the advertising is done. This idea is expressed in the notion of carryover effects: the effect of advertising is "carried over" from the time period in which it is done into subsequent time periods. Many consumers undoubtedly remember "Elsie the Borden Cow" in spite of the fact that no advertising has occurred for this trademark character by this dairy for many years. The reader can supply many other examples of this phenomenon. The point to be made is that if the effect of a certain amount of spending on advertising in a given time period is to be understood, this effect must not only include the effect on the current time period but also that which occurs in all future time periods. There is thus considerable effort made to understand and develop methods for assessing the carryover effect of advertising. Several of these will be discussed in this chapter.

Creative Quality. The response function used in Example 8-1 says nothing at all about the impact of the messages used by the company in their advertising program. Clearly, company A might spend $2,000,000 on advertising while company B spends $1,500,000 and still have an inferior advertising program to company B. Part of this could stem from the quality of the creative work which company B's agency does versus that of company A's agency. Superior creative quality can "make up" for the lack of advertising dollars. This factor can be observed in the beer industry among the three major competitors, Anheuser-Busch, Schlitz, and Miller. The Anheuser-Busch case in Chapter 9 provides some data relating to this issue. The point to be made here, however, is that a response function should include some indicator of the nature of the creative work used in the company's advertising program.

Media Efficiency. Clearly, with the same amount of money spent on advertising the efficiency of the media schedules used can vary fairly dramatically. An efficient media schedule is one which reaches primarily a large majority of the target audience, but not other consumers. An efficient media schedule also provides high enough frequency of exposure to the message that the message "gets across." Reach and frequency are the primary measures of media schedule efficiency, and the manner in which these are "traded off" for a fixed amount of advertising spending will have a great effect on the final results of the advertising program. Accordingly, response functions should include an indicator of the schedule efficiency.

Other Marketing Variables. The response function in Example 8-1 assumes that the only factor causing sales for the given company is the amount of money spent on advertising. In addition to nonmonetary advertising factors, it is clear that, for many consumer products and particularly for industrial goods, other marketing factors may be just as important or more important than advertising in the generation of sales for the company or brand. Sales may, for example, be very sensitive to price changes as in some grocery products. It is often thought that one reason why Schlitz could very often spend considerably more money on advertising than did Anheuser-Busch in the late 1970s and early 1980s while not catching that competitor in terms of sales was due largely to distribution (many other problems developed toward the end of the 1970s with Schlitz in addition to distribution). The point to be made, however, is that if the product is not available in outlets for consumers to buy, no amount of excellent advertising can increase or in any way be related to sales. If the product is judged by consumers to be poor relative to the competitors' products, then advertising will have a tough time producing sales on its own. It is sometimes thought that part of the Schlitz problem in the late 1970s concerned the poor formulation of its brewing process. In such situations, it is doubtful if a response function which includes only advertising would adequately explain the behavior of sales for the company. A response function, under such circumstances, should include other marketing variables in addition to advertising if these marketing factors vary for the particular company or brand.

Competitive Effects. As suggested above, the sales results for one company, for example Jos. Schlitz Brewing Company, are not independent of the marketing and advertising activities of competitors. Even if one company has the excellent mix of marketing factors implemented for a brand, competitor actions could render this program ineffective. Some factor to represent the effect of competition is usually desirable to include in a response function.

Data Definition. Such variables as "sales" can be defined for any given company in many different ways. Sales could be defined, for example, as sales per 1000 people in the target market population. Or market share might be used rather than sales. Sales might be defined as sales in dollars or sales in units. Even advertising can be defined in many different ways. The advertising dollars might be adjusted to constant dollars so that inflation effect is removed from them. These dollars might be divided by the number of target market consumers before being used in response function analysis. Profit can be defined before or after taxes, for example. Decisions must be made as to how to express each of the variables to be included in the response function. For example, it might be that a response function for Schlitz would include advertising dollars which were expressed in terms of thousands of consumers in the legal or otherwise-defined beer-drinking age rather than in terms of the entire population. Since the beer industry is highly competitive, advertising dollars could be expressed as a percentage of the total industry advertising dollars; this is usually termed "advertising share" for a given company.

Present Value of Future Profits. The profits projected from the optimal spending level in Example 8-1 are profits which will accrue to the company at some point in the future. Considering that money has a value over time as any other commodity and that there is risk involved in the consideration of money to be received tomorrow based on decisions made today ("A bird in the hand is worth two in the bush."), it is undoubtedly wise to discount these future profits in terms of the value of money. A budgeting model should, therefore, have provision to determine the "present value" of profits the model projects will accrue in the future (as for example, from the carryover effects of advertising).

Optimization. Finally, the mechanism used to find the advertising expenditure in Example 8-1 was that of classical optimization (differential calculus). Very often, and largely because of the preceding nine factors, the response function becomes very much more complicated than that used in the example. Such functions are often not easily susceptible to the straight-forward application of calculus. Though there are other methods available, it is usually desirable to use a less elegant and formal approach called "numerical analysis" or numerical evaluation of a response function. An example of this was illustrated in Example 7-3 in Chapter 7. Simply put, various levels of advertising spending which are considered feasible are "plugged" into the profit function. After several trial and error substitutions, the maximum or near maximum profit might be found; the advertising expenditure accompanying this profit level would be the most desirable advertising spending level. There are, in fact, some fairly sophisticated methods of conducting numerical analyses, but the trial and error approach is usually acceptable for advertising applications.

Methods of developing response functions are discussed in the following section.

DEVELOPMENT OF RESPONSE FUNCTIONS

The development of response functions follows a process similar to any other model-building process. This process consists of four steps which are briefly described in the next section.

STEPS IN MAKING RESPONSE FUNCTIONS

Any attempt to formally build response functions will go through each of the following processes:

I. Specification
II. Estimation
III. Verification
IV. Prediction.

A brief discussion of each of these steps will make it clear how the model-building process evolves.

Specification. Before anything else is done in this process, it first must be determined what the general nature of the response function will be. Will the function include, for example, the effect of creative quality as this relates to amount of money spent on advertising in generating sales? Will the *dependent* variable (the variable which is to be "explained") be defined as sales or market share? Is the relationship one of diminishing returns between advertising and sales? In other words, specification is the process of deciding upon the functional form which will describe the relationship between advertising (and possibly other marketing variables) and sales. The general nature of these alternative forms will be discussed subsequently in this chapter. But whatever the functional form, specification is the process by which the manager's theory of how advertising works for a particular brand or company is put into testable form. For example, a very naive and simple-minded theory of how advertising works might be stated as: S = a + b(A) where sales in units is said to be a linear function only of advertising dollars.

Estimation. In the above example, S = a + b(A), the letters "a" and "b" are called the parameters of the response function. In order for the specified response function to be of use in budgeting analysis, these parameters must be replaced with actual numbers which show, for the given brand or company in a given unit of time, what the relationship between advertising and sales is within certain degrees of risk. These parameters can be estimated based upon a variety of information about the brand or company (these types of data are discussed below) using the manager's judgment or, more often, using methods of curve fitting such as regression analysis.

Verification. Once the parameters of the response function have been estimated based upon data about the brand, these parameter values must be tested in such a way that the manager can have some assurance about their validity. The usual way of determining the extent to which the parameters actually describe the relationship between advertising and sales is to use statistical significance testing. In this way, it is possible to say with a certain risk level how representative of the advertising/sales relationship the particular parameter values are. For example, in the example S = a + b(A) suppose "a" was estimated as 300 and "b" was estimated as .7 in the preceding step. In the verification step, it might be possible to make a statement such as, "We can be sure that "a" is between 290 and 310 about 85 samples out of every 100 samples of data we use to figure out what "a" really is." The same type of statistical significance statement could be made about parameter "b." The "significance level" in the preceding statement about parameter "a" was .15 (1 − .85 = .15). The significance level often used in commercial work such as the development of response functions is about 15 percent.

Prediction. The final step in building initial response functions is prediction. The response function, in order to be believed, must be able to make fairly or acceptably accurate predictions about future sales or market share behavior of the brand relative to the *independent* or explanatory variables in the response function (the variables such as advertising spending which are supposed to "explain" how sales react). This phase of model-building would actually be more accurately called "prediction and postdiction." One way to get some idea of how well the response function will behave in the future (prediction) is to see if it can predict events which have already occurred (postdiction). The risk inherent in this procedure of postdiction is much less than in waiting for data to accrue so that predictive power of the model can be assessed. In the postdiction process, values for the independent variables are inserted into the response function and the sales or dependent variable measure is calculated; the value for the independent variable is chosen so that the accompanying dependent variable result in reality is already known. For example, a response function might be built to be used after December. How much was spent on advertising in December and what the resulting sales in December were will be known before the model is to be used. Suppose the model is as illustrated in the verification section above, that is, $S = 300 + .7(A)$, and sales in December were $448 per capita in the target market while the advertising expenditure in December was $200 per capita. Using the function for postdiction would provide a sales estimate for December of:

$$S = 300 + .7(200)$$
$$S = 440.$$

The postdicted sales of $440 is $8 in error of the actual December sales per capita; this represents an error of less than two percent ($8/448 = .018$) and may be acceptable in the given circumstance. If the model postdicts this well, there is some faith that it might predict well into the future. Postdiction, of course, might take place for many time periods into the past. But the "acid test" of the model's validity will still remain with predictive tests into the future. How well does the model predict events which have not yet occurred? If a response function can fairly or acceptably predict sales figures which have not yet occurred, then this function will be useful in the budgeting process.

An overall scheme, in terms of data type used to estimate the response function, has been described by an executive from the J. Walter Thompson advertising agency.[2] Dhalla suggests a three-fold process for response function development. First, a preliminary model should be developed using the four-stage process described above and using historical (time-series) data on the brand. Second, the validity of this model ought to be tested, if there is serious question about its accuracy, using data from test market experiments. Finally, the parameters of the response function should be updated over time by using the results of minitests. Only a few markets need be used in this last, updating process since the information will be used not to establish the basic nature of the response function but only to check to see if the parameters of the function have changed. The role of time-series, experimental data and other types of data is discussed in the next section.

DATA BASES

Four types of data upon which response functions can be built will be discussed briefly below: (1) Experimental Data; (2) Time-series Data; (3) Cross-sectional Data; and (4) Judgmental Data.

Experimental Data. Experimental data in advertising and marketing are usually collected with respect to marketing areas or districts. It is not uncommon for a large manufacturer to have 100 districts or more for which sales (and other types of information) are tracked individually. These districts might be "stratified" with respect to some variable such as per capita income. Districts might be selected randomly from within the strata to form experimental clusters. During the experiment, advertising expenditure levels would be assigned randomly to each of the districts within a cluster. For some period of time the sales results or market share results would be observed in these markets. In such experiments, it is difficult to decide just how long the experiment should run. Media-weight or spending tests are widely known for their inability to show differences in sales results for different levels of advertising spending. Dhalla believes that this is due to the advertising treatment receiving too little time to work or show its effects in the markets. He advocates running spending tests for fourteen months or more.[3] He believes an adequate spending experiment should possess the following four characteristics:

(1) Different media weights are assigned to the test areas in a purely random manner rather than on a selective basis. This is a guarantee against bias in favor of one advertising level over another.

(2) The spread between the light and the heavy media weight is sufficiently great. This wide range is necessary to cancel the effects of random factors and to indicate the level where the sales response curve (function) changes from linear to curvilinear.

(3) A sufficient number of markets is selected to permit the replication of the test at least once, if not more, times.

(4) Proper care is exercised to eliminate the influence of external factors which can be controlled. For example, if the company is operating in an oligopolistic market, it is imperative to track competitive advertising in the areas where the test is run. Without this information, the researcher may wrongly conclude that the sales gain is not significant, while in actuality it may be highly so.

Time-Series Data. Most companies have data on their sales and advertising expenditures broken down by sales districts or regions as well as other types of marketing data. These data can be organized by time periods to provide a data base for the development of response functions. These types of data should be examined and utilized first, if available, since they are available without additional expenditures; experimental data can become very expensive to obtain as well as taking a long time to fully develop. An example of a time-series data set is shown below for a given brand:

Quarter	Advertising $	Sales in Units
Winter 1980	$201,000	21,100,000
Spring 1981	322,000	24,050,000
Summer 1981	318,100	25,000,000
Fall 1981	330,000	26,000,100
Winter 1981	320,300	26,100,000
Spring 1982	341,400	28,900,000

Notice that in a time-series, each time period, in this case a quarter, is one observation. Ordinarily, when time-series data are utilized as the basis for the development of response functions, it would be desirable to have at least 18 or so observations upon which to estimate the parameters of the response function. Of course, time-series data on variables other than advertising and sales might be required, for example, on price charged for the brand in each time period or how much competitors spent on advertising in each time period, if the specification of the function called for such information. Ordinarily, the first step in response function analysis would be to attempt to estimate the parameters using such time-series data.

Cross-Sectional Data. Data can be developed for use in response function analyses by taking a "cross section" of the brand's markets *at one point in time;* each market then serves as an observation for the estimation process. This should not be confused with an experiment where the advertising expenditure is systematically varied from market to market in order to observe the response of sales. Here the data are simply available as they occurred due to "normal" ongoing decision processes in each of these markets.

As a data base for the development of the N.W. Ayer New Product Model (which is discussed at the end of this chapter), a cross-sectional sample of brands which had been introduced as new products in the relatively recent past was taken. In this case, each brand serves as the unit of observation, and the advertising (as well as other marketing variables) and sales or other behavioral criteria are recorded for each brand. A sample size of 18 or so brands (observations) would be required to build a response function which might then be applied to the budgeting problems of a new product.

A cross-section of individuals from the target market might also serve as the data base for the development of a response function using individual difference data rather than aggregate data. In this case, individuals serve as the unit of observation, and, of course, the sample size of such individuals should be considerably larger than that required when aggregate data are utilized (perhaps around 200 or so individuals would be adequate).

Judgmental Data. The final type of data which might serve as the basis for estimation of response function parameters is that of judgment. The seasoned advertising program manager obviously must have some "feel" for the brand's responsiveness to advertising activities after dealing with a particular brand or product category for some time. This experience can be the basis for sound estimation of the sales response to advertising. An example of using judgment to estimate response function parameters is provided at the end of this chapter.

FUNCTIONAL FORMS

Part of the problem involved in response function specification is the selection of a functional form to "fit" the actual data upon which the response function will be based. The first step in the selection of functional forms is the drawing of a scatterplot to get a general idea as to the shape of the underlying response function.

A scatterplot for some time-series advertising/sales data is shown in Figure 8-1. Below the figure are listed seven observations on advertising and sales for a hypothetical brand. Notice the figures are "scaled down" by one thousand units or dollars (the actual numbers are simply divided by 1000); this process of scaling down the data is a usual one since it is difficult to deal with large figures when it comes time to fit the response function curve in the estimation process. So, $70,000 of advertising expenditure is represented by the number 70 after scaling down, for example. Each observation is plotted on the graph in Figure 8-1. Each "X" in the picture represents a pair of advertising and the accompanying sales figure. There is one "X" for each of the seven

Figure 8-1   Scatterplot of Time-Series Data

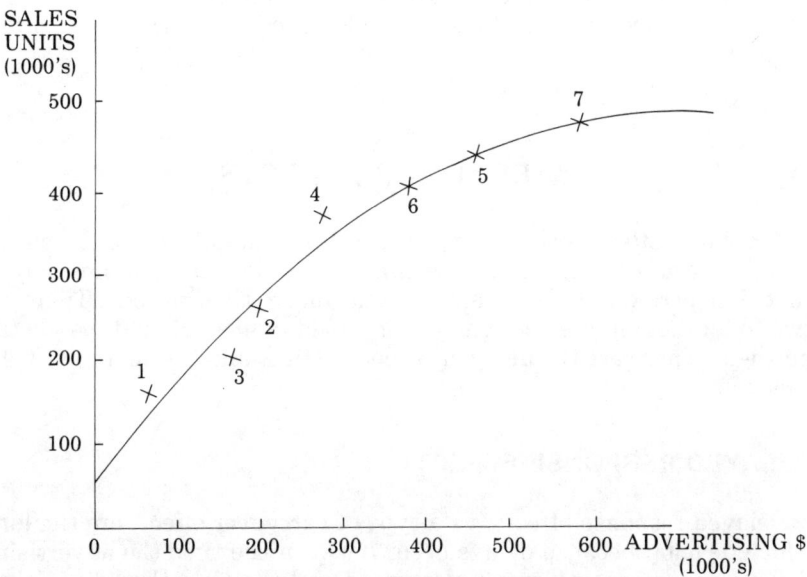

Time-Series for Above Scatterplot

Quarter	Observation Number	ADV$/1000	SALES UNITS /1000
Fall 1980	1	$ 70 (70,000)	150 (150,000)
Winter 1981	2	200	250
Spring 1981	3	190	200
Summer 1981	4	280	360
Fall 1981	5	490	410
Winter 1981	6	390	380
Spring 1982	7	600	450

observations listed below the graph. So, for example, the observation labelled "7" on the graph is the point at which advertising dollars is at 600 on the horizontal advertising axis in combination with 450 on the vertical sales axis.

Clearly, a straight line would be difficult to draw through all of the seven points in the graph in Figure 8-1. Drawing a curve which is closest to each of the seven points, yet is a smooth curve, is analogous to the process of "fitting" a response function to available data. A straight-line response function would not clearly represent the relationship of the seven data points in this graph. Probably a non-linear, concave-downward function such as that drawn in the figure would come much closer to representing all seven of the points than would a straight line. This inspection of a scatterplot is one way which can be helpful in the selection of functional forms. But the selection also depends on many other matters such as the way in which variables which interact are to be represented and so forth. It is also difficult to "draw a picture" of a response function which has more than one independent variable since an axis must be added to the picture for the addition of each independent variable. Issues in the selection and fitting of response function forms are addressed in Appendix A to this chapter.

CARRYOVER EFFECTS

Carryover effect is the term given to the situation where the advertising program conducted in one time period has an effect not only in that time period but also in subsequent, future time periods. There are two major categories of carryover effect which should be distinguished.[4] These are the delayed response effect and the customer holdover effect.

DELAYED RESPONSE EFFECT

Delayed response effects, as a type of carryover effect, are the kind which develop because delays occur between the time the advertising dollars and programs are implemented and the time the advertising-generated purchases occur. There are four types of delayed response effects which can be examined.

Execution Delay. The first type of delay which might occur between the time of advertising expenditure and customer purchase due to these expenditures is that due to executional delay. A company might spend $40,000 on space for a magazine advertisement in March but the advertisement does not actually run until April. Under this kind of circumstance, it would not make much sense to attempt to relate that $40,000 expenditure on advertising in March to the sales which develop in March.

Noting Delay. Some, but not all, advertising activity is subject to a second type of delay called noting delay. For example, an advertisement might appear in a given magazine in April, but a potential customer might not notice the advertisement until May. This type of delay could not occur, of course, in the case of radio and television advertising.

Purchase Delay. A potential customer may be exposed to a magazine advertisement which appears in March but not be motivated to make the purchase of the product until May. Another potential customer may see the advertisement in March and make the purchase in April. There is, therefore, due to purchase delay a distributed lagged impact of the March advertising expenditure on future month's sales.

Recording Delay. The final type of time-delayed impact of advertising on sales is the delay due to the recording system used to track sales of the product. This type of recording delay can work in two different directions. A company might put the product in the distribution pipeline in advance of orders for specific quantities; the product is not yet sold to the final customer but is recorded as a sale on the company's books. On the other hand, the company may have backlog orders in which the orders have been received but are not counted as a sale until the product is shipped. Ideally, the company should date sales as of the time orders are placed if the attempt to relate advertising activity to sales is to be successful.

CUSTOMER HOLDOVER EFFECT

The second major type of carryover effect is termed the customer holdover effect. Suppose that none of the above delayed response effects take place. That is, the advertising is paid for in March, it runs in the media in March, the potential customer notes the advertisement in March, and, finally, the customer makes a purchase of the product in March. Still, there can be an effect of the March advertising in April, May or subsequent months. This customer may have made a purchase of the brand in March, after exposure to the advertisement for the brand, and decided to re-purchase the brand in subsequent months. This scenario would suggest that advertising should be credited, in some part, for holding the customer to the brand in future time periods. Some proportion of the customers generated for a brand by a given time period's advertising will be retained in each future time period. The implications of this for budgeting are clear. If, for example, the carryover effect of the advertising for a particular brand is found to be very strong, it might be the case that less rather than more advertising would be a profitable avenue to pursue. If, on the other hand, the carryover effect is a weak one, the brand may need more money spent on its advertising program.

In order to make use of the concept of carryover effect in budgeting practices, the degree of carryover effect must first be determined. This carryover rate is then incorporated into the response function explicitly. There are two primary means by which the carryover effect of the advertising can be assessed: (1) Experimental determination; and (2) Analytical determination.

EXPERIMENTAL DETERMINATION

The problem in the determination of carryover effects is to determine the rate at which sales carry over from a preceding period into one in which *no advertising* has been conducted during this period. A simple experiment can be developed to measure carryover effect in this manner.

Example 8-2. The Calgar Company manufactures and sells a line of household detergents. It is interested in finding out the carryover effect of its advertising program for its dishwashing liquid, Calclean. Calgar first selects 12 sales districts from around the country in which it is possible to do some testing. It then makes up four separate samples from these 12 districts by randomly assigning each district to one of the four samples, three districts per sample. In one of these samples, in order to determine carryover effect, Calgar will spend no money on advertising for Calclean. It decides to spend different conceivably useful levels of expenditures in the other three testing samples so that some idea of the desirable level of advertising can be obtained for Calclean relative to carryover effects.

Table 8-1 shows the data which were collected for each of the four samples for the purposes of calculating the carryover rate. (What is here called "carryover rate" is sometimes referred to as the retention rate since the idea is to determine the rate at which customers are retained from one time period to the next.) Notice that the experiment is conducted during the winter quarter. Column 1 shows the sales per 10,000 people (called per capita sales) in the target market population in the time period preceding the experiment, fall, for each of the four samples. Sample I was randomly selected from the four sample sets to receive the "no advertising" treatment, as shown in column 2. Per 10,000 target market population, Calgar decided to test $2,000, $4,000, and $6,400 on advertising in the remaining three sample sets (these treatments were assigned randomly to the three test samples).

Column 3 shows the total sales per capita which resulted in each of the four samples at the end of the winter quarter. Notice that in sample I where advertising during the winter was $0 that sales dropped from $10,000 to $5,000 per capita. This is all the information necessary to calculate a carryover rate for Calclean. This calculation is shown in the box in Table 8-1. The sales retained in the absence of advertising, $5,000, amount to one-half of the preceding quarter's sales of $10,000; the carryover rate (noted "c") is, therefore, .5 or 50 percent. Table 8-1 shows the application of this information about carryover to the other three samples to determine the sales in winter due to advertising since some sales would have resulted in those samples even if there had been no advertising during the test period. To determine sales due only to

Table 8-1 Current Effects of Winter Advertising on Winter Sales for Calclean Detergent

Sample	Districts	Sales $ per 10,000 Target Market Population (Fall)	Adv $ per 10,000 Target Market Population (Winter)	Sales $ per 10,000 Target Market Population (Winter)	Sales $ per 10,000 Target Market pop. with no Adv (Winter)	Sales $ per 10,000 Target Market pop. due to Adv (Winter)
I	1,2,5	$10,000 (a)	$0	$ 5,000 (b)	$$- \$5,000\ (.5 \times 10,000) =$$	$0
II	3,7,8	10,000*	2,000	7,000	$$- 5,000\ (.5 \times 10,000) =$$	2,000
III	6,9,10	10,000*	4,000	11,000	$$- 5,000\ (.5 \times 10,000) =$$	6,000
IV	4,11,14	10,000*	6,400	14,000	$$- 5,000\ (.5 \times 10,000) =$$	9,000

$$\text{Carryover Rate} = \frac{\$5,000\ (b)}{\$10,000\ (a)}$$

$$c = .5 \text{ or } 50\%$$

*It is assumed in this analysis that sales in the fall were equivalent across all test markets.

winter advertising, it is necessary that the preceding time period sales (fall) be about the same for all samples to be compared with each other. This could be accomplished by selecting districts for inclusion in the test which had similar *per capita sales* or, if this is not possible, by making the *assumption* that per capita sales were similar (or the same) for all samples. This assumption is made in making the calculations in Table 8-1.

First, the carryover rate (.5) is applied to the total sales in each sample for the preceding (fall) time period. This is the result shown in column 4 and provides an estimate of the sales level in each sample if there had been *no advertising* during winter in the samples. The amount of sales due to advertising is shown in column 5 and is the difference between the total sales during winter (column 3) and the expected sales if no advertising had been done in winter (column 4).

Suppose for Calclean the production costs are about 55 percent of sales and "Admin/Mktg" costs are about 33 percent of sales. If only current effects of advertising on sales are considered, then, in the case of sample IV in Table 8-1, the cost of goods sold is $5,000 (5000 = .55 × 9000) and administrative/marketing expenses would be $3,000 (3000 = .33 × 9000). Since NP = S$ − c.g.s. − Admin/Mktg − A, then the net profits for Calclean (on a per capita basis) would be − $5,400 (− 5400 = 9000 − 5000 − 3000 − 6400). That is, it appears $5,400 has been lost per 10,000 customers due to advertising in the winter in sample IV. But the $6,400 spent on advertising in winter in sample IV has carryover effects which undoubtedly last into subsequent quarters, and, therefore, to calculate its contribution to profits the effects on sales must be calculated for these subsequent quarters and added into the winter quarter sales before advertising expenditures for winter are subtracted to yield the profit estimate. This basic idea that carryover lasts longer than one quarter can be incorporated into the analysis and is illustrated in the next example.

Carryover Rate Application. Given the carryover rate, c, the total sales which should be attributed to advertising in a given time period can be stated as:

$$\overset{(1)}{} \qquad \overset{(2)}{} \qquad \overset{(3)}{}$$
$$TS_t = (S_t - cS_{t-1}) + c(S_t - cS_{t-1}) + c\{c(S_t - cS_{t-1})\} + \ldots$$

where: TS_t = Total Sales in time period "t"
  c = carryover rate
  S_t = sales in period "t"
  S_{t-1} = sales in the preceding time period.

In the above formulation, the total sales for a given period which can be attributed to advertising in that period consist of that period's sales minus the portion of the preceding time period sales which was carried over into the current period (the carryover rate times preceding period sales). Some portion of the current period sales which can be attributed to advertising in the current period will be carried over into the next future period, some portion of these sales carried into the period after that, and so on. This is why the carryover rate is multiplied times the current sales effect of advertising (the first term in the above formulation) on a repeated basis indefinitely into the future (as indicated by the three dots after the formulation). In the above, the term labeled 1 shows the sales in period t (current period, say May) which result from advertising in t. The second term (labeled 2) shows the sales in t+1 (June) which can be attributed to the advertising in May; the term labeled 3 shows the effect of May advertising on sales generated in t+2 (July) and so forth. If in the third term, and all subsequent terms, of the formulation, the "c's" are multiplied together, the following results:

$$TS_t = (S_t - cS_{t-1}) + c(S_t - cS_{t-1}) + c^2(S_t - cS_{t-1}) + \ldots + c^\infty(S_t - cS_{t-1}).$$

All terms in this formulation beyond the first term concern the effect of advertising on *future* time period sales; these future sales have not actually yet occurred at the time period in which the advertising money is spent. Money due to these sales in the future is not the same as money obtained by current sales due to the cost of money, inflation of dollars and so forth. The dollar value of these future sales should therefore be "discounted" to the current time period based upon the prevailing interest rate of money. The discount rate which should be used to make comparable the expected future sales dollars with today's dollars is found by subtracting the interest rate from one (if the discount rate is noted by "r," then r = 1 − interest rate). The discount rate can be included in the above formulation as follows:

$$TDS_t = (S_t - cS_{t-1}) + rc(S_t - cS_{t-1}) + r^2c^2(S_t - cS_{t-1}) + \ldots + r^\infty c^\infty(S_t - cS_{t-1})$$

where: TDS_t = Total Discounted Sales in period t
r = discount rate.

This formulation is really the "sum of an infinite geometric series" and can, fortunately, be simplified greatly. Mathematically, the above formulation is equivalent to:

$$TDS_t = \frac{1}{1 - cr}(S_t - cS_{t-1}).$$

This approach can be used to estimate the sales revenues in a given period which include the present and future sales impact of advertising. Using this approach to determine the budget can be shown by way of the following example.

Example 8-3. This example continues with the Calgar Company and uses some of the information contained in Example 8-2. Suppose that total sales over all districts for Calclean in fall were $3,200,000 based upon a target market population of 5,000,000. The data in Table 8-1 can be projected from the 10,000 per capita basis up to the total 5,000,000 target market size. For example, the $2,000/10,000 population spent on advertising in Sample II would be $1,000,000 on the basis of 5,000,000 target market size (1,000,000 = 5,000,000 ×

2,000/10,000). If the advertising expenditures and resulting sales (column 3) in Table 8-1 are projected in this fashion, this results in the following:

Alternative	Adv\$ (A_t)	Sales \$ (S_t)
A	\$1,000,000	\$3,500,000
B	2,000,000	5,500,000
C	3,200,000	7,000,000.

The three spending levels used in the experiment in the three samples which received advertising in Table 8-1 will be considered as alternative spending levels for Calclean. The issue involved is: What should Calgar spend on advertising in the next time period for its Calclean detergent?

Suppose the carryover rate is as calculated in Table 8-1, that is, 50 percent, and the prevailing interest rate at which Calgar could borrow funds is 12 percent ($r = 1 - .12$ or $r = .88$). The total discounted sales volume for Calclean for each of the three alternative spending levels on advertising is first calculated for:

$$A \quad TDS_t = \frac{1}{1 - .5(.88)} \{3,500,000 - (.5)3,200,000\} = \$3,392,857$$

$$B \quad TDS_t = \frac{1}{1 - .5(.88)} \{5,500,000 - (.5)3,200,000\} = \$6,964,286$$

$$C \quad TDS_t = \frac{1}{1 - .5(.88)} \{7,000,000 - (.5)3,200,000\} = \$9,642,857.$$

Finally, suppose that all costs except advertising expenditures amounted to about 60 percent of sales revenue. The net profits projected for each of the three alternative spending levels can then be calculated as follows:

	Plan A		Plan B		Plan C
S	\$3,392,857	S	\$6,964,286	S	\$9,642,857
TC	2,035,714	TC	4,178,572	TC	5,785,714
GM	1,357,143	GM	2,785,714	GM	3,857,143
A	1,000,000	A	2,000,000	A	3,200,000
NP	\$ 357,143	NP	\$ 785,714	NP	\$ 657,143.

Clearly, alternative B (spending \$2,000,000 on advertising) is the preferable alternative since it provides the largest net profits of any of the three alternative expenditure levels. Notice that this result does not necessarily indicate that alternative B is the "optimal" advertising expenditure but merely that it is the "best" of the three alternative spending levels which were included in the analysis.

ANALYTICAL DETERMINATION

One of the most frequently used methods of finding the carryover effect of advertising is through application of the "Koyck" model.[6] This method uses time-series data rather than experimental data as illustrated in the previous examples. Regression analysis is performed on the time-series data to estimate the parameters of the Koyck functional form; one of these parameters can be interpreted as the carryover rate. The Koyck model can be formulated in either a linear or nonlinear manner. This approach was applied by Kristian Palda in his classic study on the Lydia Pinkham Company.[7]

Linear Koyck Model. That sales in the current time period depend on advertising expenditures in previous periods as well as in the current period can be stated as follows:

$$S_t = a + bA_t + bcA_{t-1} + bc^2A_{t-2} + \ldots$$

where: a = intercept term
b = regression coefficients
c = carryover rate.

Notice that a geometric decline in advertising's effect is postulated in a manner similar to that illustrated in the previous section dealing with experimental methods of determining the carryover rate.

Koyck, a Dutch econometrician, developed a modification of the above through the use of some algebra which overcomes the difficulty of knowing how far back in time the terms in the above formulation should go; that is, the question of how long advertising's effect lasts. The linear Koyck model is:

$$S_t = (a-ac) + bA_t + cS_{t-1}.$$

The parameter associated with the "lagged" sales term (S_{t-1}) is the carryover rate. This model hypothesizes that the effect of advertising conducted in all preceding time periods on current sales in period "t" can be "captured" or summarized in one term, lagged sales. Sales are thus assumed in this formulation to be a function of advertising and sales in the preceding time period. One problem which sometimes occurs in the use of this approach is that, where strong sales trends are noted, the effect of previous time period sales on current sales is so strong that the effect of current advertising on sales can hardly be detected. When such results occur in application, the use of the Koyck model must be examined very carefully.

It should also be noted that in the above formulation advertising is related in a linear way to current sales. This clearly would not be the case in many or, indeed, most advertising applications. For this reason, the Koyck model can be formulated in several non-linear ways. One of these is shown below.

Exponential Koyck Model. The Koyck model can be cast in a nonlinear framework by considering the following formulation of the geometrically declining effect of past advertising on current sales:

$$S_t = \{1 - e^{a - (bA_t + bcA_{t-1} + bc^2A_{t-2} + \ldots)}\}.$$

After the algebra developed by Koyck is applied to this non-linear formulation of current and past advertising on current sales, the exponential Koyck model can be stated as:

$$\ln\{1 - (S_t - a)/\overline{S}\} = bA_t + (c) \ln\{1 - (S_{t-1} - a)/\overline{S}\}.$$

There are many other functional forms which could be used to provide a non-linear relationship of advertising and sales in the Koyck model. This response function is in linear form and can be fitted through regression analysis. Notice that the term on the left-hand side of the equation can be considered as one number (this number can be calculated for each sales observation once "a" or the intercept term is estimated by judgment) and the same can be done for the far-right-hand term in the equation. The model then becomes basically a linear model where the intercept term is taken to be zero as in: $S_t = b(A)_t + c(S)_{t-1}$.

At this point, it should be clear to the reader that, regardless of the method used to determine the actual carryover rate for a particular brand, it is paramount that the carryover rate be known so that the budgeting process can be carried out with this knowledge. Without an understanding of the delayed effects of advertising and its holdover effects it is not possible to determine a logical spending level for the brand. The possible exception to this lies in the area of direct mail advertising.

PRESENT VALUE OF CARRYOVER EFFECTS

When carryover effects of an advertising expenditure are considered as part of the budgeting planning process, certain amounts of returns are estimated for each of a certain number of time periods following the expenditure; these returns are estimated in such a manner that it will be reasonable to attribute the returns to the action of the advertising program in the one time period only. These returns are those estimated to be returned to the company over some *future* time periods which have not yet occurred. Because all planning involves uncertainty, these estimated returns should be *discounted* back to the current planning time period prior to evaluating the worth of the advertising expenditure from which it is assumed the returns can be attributed. "A bird in the hand is worth two in the bush" so that, generally speaking, two dollars to be obtained one year from today cannot be considered of the same value as two dollars in the pocket today. The reason for this is clear; it is not certain that the two dollars expected to be received one year from today will, in fact, actually be received. Two dollars in the pocket today, on the other hand, is a sure thing. The *Net Present Value* concept, along with several derived ideas, is the usual method financial people use to evaluate the comparative worth of several investments which are expected to produce returns over their life span. If advertising can be viewed as an investment in the brand, then the carryover effects of this investment over time should be evaluated using investment concepts such as NPV. Three methods of evaluating alternative investments are illustrated in Example 8-4.

NET PRESENT VALUE AND EVALUATION OF CARRYOVER EFFECTS (EXAMPLE 8-4)

In this example, it will be assumed that $20,000 will be invested in an advertising program; for sake of simplicity in illustrating the financial concepts, it will be assumed that an analysis of carryover effects indicates that an equivalent amount of profit ($5,000) is estimated to be derived from this expenditure for each of the following ten years after the expenditure (this is indeed an example of "high" carryover). Three means of evaluating this investment will be illustrated: (1) the Payback Year Method; (2) the Net Present Value Method; and (3) the Discounted Rate of Return Method.

Payback Year Method. Suppose a $20,000 investment is made in advertising and this advertising is estimated to produce annual returns (profits) of $5,000 for each of the next 10 years. The payback year for this investment is calculated as follows:

$20,000/$5,000 = *4-Year Payback Period.*

This is equivalent to a rate of return (undiscounted) of:

5,000/20,000 = 25% rate of return (RoR) on the investment.

Net Present Value Method. Assume that $121 is to be received two years later with a 10% interest rate (value of money) in effect. How much money must be invested today to get $121 at the end of a two-year time period? By definition,

$$\text{Present Value of } \$1 = 1/(1 + i)^n$$

where: i = interest rate
n = number of years or time periods.

$$\text{Present Value of } \$1, 2 \text{ years, } 10\% \text{ interest} = 1/(1 + .10)^2$$
$$= \$.826444.$$

This can be interpreted to mean that 82¢ invested today at 10% compounded interest rate will return $1.00 two years from today. Now, if the present value of $1 is computed above to be 82¢, then the present value of $121 of these dollars is:

Present Value of $121, 2 years, 10% interest = $121 × .826444
$$= \$100.$$

That is, $100 must be invested today to get $121 at the end of two years at a 10% rate of interest.

The present value of $1 must be distinguished from the related concept of the present value of a $1 *annuity*. Annuity means that $1 will be received annually in *each* year of the operation of the annuity or investment as opposed to receiving only $1 at the *end* of the investment period as in the above example. The present value of a $1 annuity can be defined as follows:

$$\text{Present Value of \$1 annuity} = \sum_{x=1}^{n} \{1/(1+i)^x\}$$

where: i = interest rate
n = number of years.

For example, calculate the present value of a $1 annuity over a two-year time period with a 10% interest rate in effect:

$$\text{Present Value of \$1 } \textit{annuity,} \text{ 2 years, } 10\% = \sum_{x=1}^{n} \{1/(1+.10)^x\}$$

$$= 1/(1.10)^1 + 1/(1.10)^2$$

$$= 1.736.$$

The present value of a $1 annuity received for each of two years with a 10% interest rate in effect is approximately $1.74.

Now, suppose that a company's minimum acceptable RoR (rate of return as defined above under Payback Year Method) is 18% for any investment. What is the *net* present value (NPV) of a $20,000 investment which is expected to provide carryover returns of $5,000 for each of the next 10 years?

$$\text{Present value of a \$1 annuity, 10 years, } 18\% = \sum_{x=1}^{10} \{1/(1.18)^x\}$$

$$= 4.494.$$

Then, $5,000 × 4.494 = $22,470 (the present value of annual returns) and

$$\text{NPV} = \$22,470 - \$20,000 \text{ (cost of the investment)}$$
$$\underline{\text{NPV} = \$2,470.}$$

Discounted Rate of Return Method. Assume a $20,000 investment in advertising with carryover returns estimated to be $5,000 annually for each of the next 10 years. The discounted rate of return can be calculated using the following steps:

(1) Find the payback year.

This has already been done in the section of this problem above entitled *Payback Year Method* and was found to be 4.

(2) Find the present value of $1 at any interest rate for 10 years which is closest to 4 (the payback year from step (1) above). Use present value tables in the back of financial texts to find 3.923 is the closest to 4 in 10 years. The interest rate associated with this present value is 22% (for 10 years, 24% = 3.682 and the next closest in the tables is 22% = 3.923). This could also be found, rather than by using tables, by solving the following equation for "i":

$$4 = \sum_{x=1}^{10} \{1/(1 + i)^x\}.$$

(3) $5,000 (annual return) × 3.923 = $19,615 (present value of returns at 22%).

Since $20,000 − $19,615 ≈ $0 Net Present Value, 22% is *defined* to be the Discounted Rate of Return. *By definition,* Discounted RoR is the rate of return (always a percentage) at which the NPV of the investment is equal to *zero* dollars.

IMPLEMENTATION OF BUDGETING MODELS

Three examples are provided below which point to the methods by which budgeting models of different varieties may be implemented and used in practice. First, the N.W. Ayer New Product model will be presented and applied. Following this a judgmental model and a model utilizing time-series data will be examined.

CROSS-SECTIONAL EXAMPLE (EXAMPLE 8–5)

The N.W. Ayer advertising agency developed a new product model involving a two-equation response function for use in the development of advertising programs for its clients' new products.[8] The developers of the model first worked with Ayer advertising executives to develop the following model specification:

$$AR = a_1 + b_1(PP) + b_2\sqrt{(AHI)(CE)} + b_3(CP^*) + b_4(CI)$$

$$IP = a_2 + b_5(\hat{AR}) + b_6(DN)(PK) + b_7(FB) + b_8(CP) + b_9(PS) + b_{10}(CU)$$

where: a_i = intercept terms

b_i = regression parameters.

After this specification, data were collected on 60 new products which the Ayer agency had introduced to the market over some time period. Among these brands were Apple Jacks cereal, Scope mouthwash, Cool Whip, Ultra-Brite toothpaste and so on. Some data were obtained by direct consumer measurement by Ayer, others were from syndicated services such as Starch, and much of the data came from judgment by Ayer advertising people. The variables in the above functional specification were defined as:

AR: Percent of housewives able to recall advertising claims at the end of 13 weeks after introduction

PP: Uniqueness of product positioning

AHI: Average household impressions of media schedule

CE: Creative quality of advertising

CP*: Value of consumer promotion which includes advertising material

CI: Product category interest by consumers (Starch scores)

IP: Percent of housewives making one or more purchases of the product during the first 13 weeks (initial purchase)

$\hat{AR}$: Recall of advertising predicted by first equation

DN: Adequacy of distribution

PK: Packaging quality

FB: Closeness of name of product to family brand name

CP: Consumer promotion quality (excluding advertising materials)

PS: Satisfaction of consumers with product on trial tests

CU: Percent of consumers who use the product category.

After the data on all the above variables were assembled for the 60 brands to serve in the analysis, regression analyses were conducted to find the following parameters of the response functions:

$$\hat{AR} = -35.88 + .76(PP) + 2.12 \sqrt{(AHI)(CE)} + .04(CP^*) + .39(CI)$$

$$\hat{IP} = -16.01 + .37(\hat{AR}) + .19(DN)(PK) + 9.24(FB) + .09(CP) + .02(PS) + .07(CU).$$

Notice that the two advertising explanatory variables, AHI and CE, are dependent on each other (are multiplied times each other) and are under the square-root sign, indicating diminishing returns or a concave-downward relationship with the response criterion, advertising awareness.

These two response functions have been extended by a third to produce an estimate of market share:[9]

$$MS = 1.05 (IP) \{1 + e^{(-3.9486 + .35375P)}\}^{-1}$$

where: MS = market share
IP = initial purchase rate
P = price/unit.

The logistic portion of this share response function (the part in brackets) represents the repeat purchase rate as a function of price charged per unit. The parameters of this function were selected using judgment regarding the particular application to be illustrated here, Maxim coffee. The parameters allow the repeat rate to vary as a function of price between 45 and 55 percent. The assumption is also made that the trial rate of Maxim will be expected to be 150 percent of what it was at the end of the first 13 weeks (initial purchase rate, IP). It was judged that 70 percent of repeat buyers would become loyal purchasers which would finally serve to establish the market share:

$$MS = 1.5 \ (IP) \ (RR) \ (.7) \quad or$$
$$MS = 1.05 \ (IP) \ (RR)$$

where: RR = repeat purchase rate function in brackets above.

Suppose two alternative advertising and marketing plans are to be evaluated using this model. Suppose the two plans are represented by the following values for each of the advertising and marketing response function variables:

Variable	Alternative 1	Alternative 2
Adv $ year 1	$12.8 million	$9.5 million
Adv $ year 2	9.6 million	6.0 million
Adv $ year 3	9.6 million	6.5 million
Price	$12/unit	$11.50/unit
PP	52	52
AHI	9.63	7.28
CE	64	64
CP*	135	108
CI	38	38
DN	70	70
PK	60	60
FB	.3	1.0
CP	123	108
PS	80	80
CU	90	90.

To provide an idea as to how this model works, the calculations, in part, are shown for alternative #1; then the final results for both alternatives are presented for decision making purposes.

Alternative 1:

$$\hat{AR} = -35.88 + .76(52) + 2.12\sqrt{(9.63)(64)} + .04(135) + .39(38)$$
$$\hat{AR} = 40.26\%$$

$$\hat{IP} = -16.01 + .37(40.26) + .19(70)(60) + 9.24(.3) + .09(123)$$
$$+ .02(8) + .07(90)$$

$$IP = 28.17\%$$

$$MS = 1.05 \ (28.17) \ \{1 + e^{[-3.9486 + .35375(12)]}\}$$
$$MS = 12.72\%$$

The total industry market for freeze-dried coffee such as Maxim was estimated at 56,000,000 units (a unit is defined as several jars of several different sizes). The expected first-year unit sales for Maxim would, therefore, be estimated as 7.067 million units (.1262 × 56,000,000 = 7.067). Based upon estimated gross margin per unit for Maxim of $5.72, plant cost of $5.00 per unit, the use of straight-line depreciation of the plant, and a 12 percent interest rate, the following criteria were calculated for the two alternative plans:

Criteria	Alternative 1	Alternative 2
Awareness	40.26%	37.03%
Initial Purchase	28.17%	32.60%
Market Share	12.62%	15.88%
Sales (units) Year 1	7.067 million	8.892 million
Profit over 3 years	$21.96 million	$22.13 million
Net Present Value @ 12%	$9.58 million	$10.78 million.

Clearly, alternative 2, which involves lower spending levels on advertising than alternative 1, is the preferable advertising and marketing plan for the introduction of Maxim of the two plans considered here. Notice that the discounted profits of alternative 2 are $10,780,000 compared to $9,580,000 for alternative 1.

JUDGMENTAL EXAMPLE (EXAMPLE 8-6)

Table 8-2 shows a time-series data collection for the Rollo Paper Company, a manufacturer of paper towels; Rollo believes that advertising plays a very important role in producing sales volume for the paper towel portion of their business. Advertising expenditures and sales in units (cases of 12 rolls of paper towels) are shown for 19 business quarters. Also, in Table 8-2 are three abbreviated financial statements for the last three quarters for the paper towel portion of Rollo's business.

A response function for which it is relatively convenient to estimate the parameters of this function through the use of executive judgment is shown below:[10]

$$S = Min + (Max - Min) \left[\frac{A^b}{a + A^b} \right]$$

where: Min = the minimum sales might become in the absence of advertising

Max = the maximum sales might become if a great deal of advertising is used

a = parameter to be fitted through judgment

b = parameter for function shape (concave: $0 < b < 1$ and S-shaped: $b > 1$).

Table 8-2   Advertising, Sales and Financial Data
for Rollo Paper Company

Quarter	Adv$	Sales (case units)
Summer 1977	$ 590,000	510,000
Fall 1977	400,000	500,000
Winter 1978	800,000	706,000
Spring 1978	680,000	950,000
Summer 1978	975,000	895,000
Fall 1978	1,180,000	1,460,000
Winter 1979	1,351,000	1,987,000
Spring 1979	1,579,000	2,396,000
Summer 1979	1,498,000	2,501,000
Fall 1979	1,600,000	3,602,000
Winter 1980	1,800,000	3,721,000
Spring 1980	1,698,000	3,264,000
Summer 1980	1,880,000	3,380,000
Fall 1980	2,250,000	4,419,000
Winter 1981	2,100,000	4,186,000
Spring 1981	2,410,000	4,421,000
Summer 1981	2,600,000	4,519,000
Fall 1981	2,660,000	4,815,000
Winter 1982	2,700,000	4,770,000

Abbreviated Statements

	Summer 1981	Fall 1981	Winter 1982
Sales	$25,758,300	$27,927,000	$29,097,000
	@$5.70/case	@$5.80/case	@$6.10/case
c.g.s.	18,030,810	19,828,170	20,995,803
GM	$ 7,727,490 (30%)	$ 8,098,830 (29%)	$ 8,029,133 (28%)
Admin/Mktg	3,968,366	4,126,261	3,779,056
Adv	2,600,000 (10%)	2,660,000 (9.5%)	2,700,000 (9.6%)
Net Profit	$ 1,159,124 (4.5%)	$ 1,312,569 (4.7%)	$ 1,622,141 (5.5%)

If the executive can answer four questions, then it is possible to use the above response function:
(1) If advertising is increased to far above its current level, at what level would sales be expected to peak (Max sales)?
(2) If advertising is discontinued altogether, to what level would sales be expected to decline (Min sales)?
(3) What amount of advertising is required to maintain (Maintenance Advertising) sales at a level about 25% of current sales (Initial Sales)?
(4) If 50% more is spent on advertising than that required to maintain the initial sales level (+50% Advertising), what sales level would probably result from this advertising (+50% Sales)?

Figure 8-2 shows a possible picture of such a judgmentally-determined function.

Figure 8-2   Judgmental Response Function

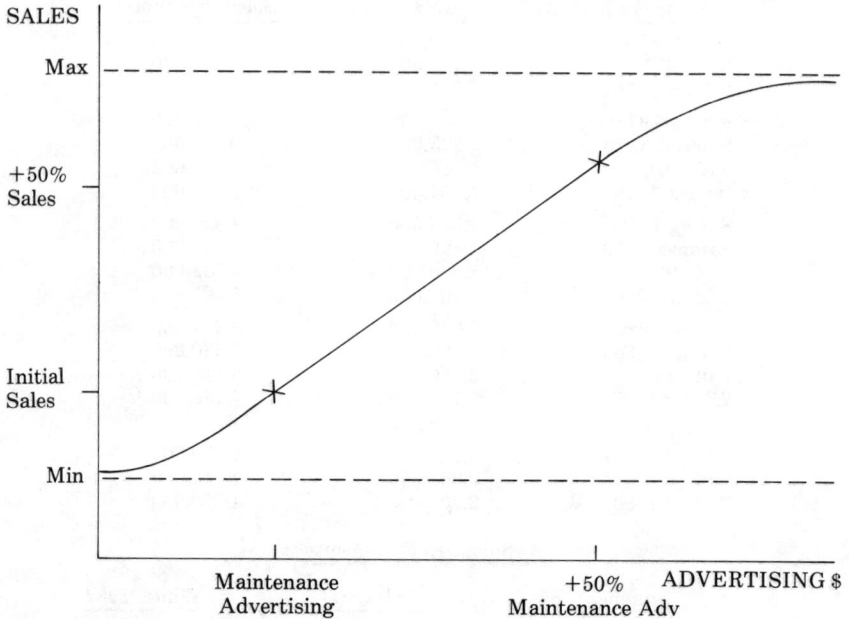

Suppose the Rollo advertising manager, after examining the relationships between quarterly advertising and sales in Table 8-2, answers the above four questions so that the following values result:

>Max Sales: 5.2 million units
>Min Sales: .5 million units
>Initial Sales: 1.4 million units
>+50% Sales: 3.6 million units
>Maintenance Adv: $1.2 million
>+50% Adv: $1.8 million (.5 × 1.2 + 1.2 = 1.8).

The two parameters of the response function, a and b, are estimated using the following:

$$a = \left[\frac{\text{Max} - \text{Initial}}{\text{Initial} - \text{Min}}\right] \qquad a = \left[\frac{5.2 - 1.4}{1.4 - .5}\right] \qquad \underline{a = 4.22}$$

$$b = \frac{1}{\log + 50\% \text{ Adv}}\left[\log\left(\frac{+50\% \text{ Sales} - \text{Min}}{\text{Max} - +50\% \text{ Sales}}\right)\left(\frac{\text{Max} - \text{Initial}}{\text{Initial} - \text{Min}}\right)\right]$$

$$b = \frac{1}{\log(1.8)}\left[\log\left(\frac{3.6 - .5}{5.2 - 3.6}\right)\left(\frac{5.2 - 1.4}{1.4 - .5}\right)\right]$$

$\underline{b = 3.58}$ (the function is, therefore, S-shaped since b > 1.)

The response function for Rollo, based on these judgments, would then be:

$$S = .5 + (5.2 - .5)\{A^{3.58}/(4.22 + A^{3.58})\}.$$

The Rollo advertising manager wishes to evaluate three alternative levels of advertising expenditures using this response function: $2.68 million, $2.78 million, and $2.90 million. For $2.68 million on advertising, the calculations are:

$$S = .5 + 4.7\{2.68^{3.58}/(4.22 + 2.68^{3.58})\}$$
$$S = 4.68 \text{ million units.}$$

Rollo plans to raise the price in spring of 1982 to $6.40/unit (price was $6.10/case in winter 1982). It also estimates the spring 1982 production costs at $4.50/case, up from $4.40/case in winter 1982. Given this information, the advertising manager for Rollo calculated the expected net profit relative to the expenditure of $2.68 million on advertising in spring of 1982:

Sales (units)	4.680,000	
	@ $6.40/case	
Sales	$29,952,000	
c.g.s.	21,060,000	(4.50 × 4.68 million)
GM	8,892,000	
Admin/Mktg	4,044,000	
Adv	2,680,000	
NP	$ 2,168,000.	

The Admin/Mktg costs in the above were estimated as 7 percent over the cost for administrative and other marketing expenses for winter 1982 (4,044,000 = .07 × 3,779,056 + 3,779,056).

After the advertising manager conducted similar analyses for the other two advertising expenditure alternatives, the following information was available for decision making purposes:

	Advertising $	Estimated Sales (units)	Estimated Profits (millions)
Alternative A:	$2.68 million	4.68	$2.168
Alternative B:	$2.78	4.74	$2.182
Alternative C:	$2.90	4.80	$2.176.

Clearly, the Rollo advertising manager would, on the basis of this analysis, select Alternative B and choose to spend $2.78 on advertising in spring 1982. This would be in the amount of $80,000 over advertising in the preceding quarter ($2,700,000 was spent on advertising by Rollo in winter 1982).

TIME-SERIES EXAMPLE (EXAMPLE 8–7)

The manager for advertising at Rollo Paper Company also developed a response function using the time-series/regression analysis approach.

Two functional forms were examined: (1) a power function; and (2) a logistic function. The parameters for the power function were determined through the use of regression analysis as (for a discussion of this process, see Appendix A):

$$S = .0896(A)^{1.391}.$$

The coefficient of determination for this relationship showed that about 94 percent of the variance in Rollo's 19 quarterly sales figures was accounted for by this function of advertising expenditures in those 19 quarters. Each of the two parameters of the function was significant at the .15 level of significance. (The parameters in the above function are a = .0896 and b = 1.391). There was, however, a significant amount of autocorrelation present in the formulation. In addition, it is noted that paramater "b" is greater than 1 which would indicate a curve of a concave-upward nature (the power function is concave-downward showing diminishing returns only when parameter "b" is less than 1). Since a scatterplot of the actual 19 quarters of advertising and sales (units) for Rollo looks as though it is either concave-downward or S-shaped, this function does not seem practicable. This is demonstrated when it is used to "postdict" for winter 1982:

$$S = .0896(2700)^{1.391} \quad \text{or} \quad S = 5533.174$$

where: 2700 = winter 1982 advertising scaled down by 1000.

The predicted winter 1982 sales of 5,533,174 units is in error of actual winter 1982 sales (4,536,000) by 22 percent ({5,533,174 − 4,536,000}/4,536,000 = .22).

The parameters of the logistic function were fitted for an upper asymptote (maximum sales) estimate of 5,250,000:

$$S = \frac{5250}{1 + e^{-(-3.166 + .002029A)}}.$$

The coefficient of determination for this function was 95.5 percent; this function is S-shaped and shows a postdiction error of 6.7 percent for winter 1982. The parameter "b" in this function (b = .002029) was just significant at the .15 level; this was due largely to the presence of significant autocorrelation. This means that this particular function, though it is of an appropriate or acceptable shape and does have a "high" r^2 (coefficient of determination), must be used with caution. Of the two functions fitted by Rollo's advertising manager, this logistic function is preferable.

When the above function was used by Rollo's advertising manager to evaluate the same three alternative advertising spending levels used in Example 8-5, the following information for decision making was developed:

	Advertising $	Estimated Sales (units)	Estimated Profits (millions)
Alternative A:	$2.68 million	4.76 million	$2.318
Alternative B:	$2.78	4.84	$2.376
Alternative C:	$2.90	4.92	$2.414.

Using the time-series/regression analysis approach for the development of the response function, Alternative C (spend $2,900,000 on advertising in spring 1982) would be preferred since the estimated net profits are greatest for this alternative of any of those examined. It should be noted that the same price per unit and production cost per unit as well as administrative and other marketing costs were used in determining the profit estimates above as were used in the preceding example, Example 8–5. These two examples together indicate the importance of the response function in budgeting; depending upon the method used in building the function, the budget recommendation can differ greatly.

APPENDIX A

SPECIFICATION OF RESPONSE FUNCTIONS

The discussion below is intended to give some idea to the reader of the variety of functional forms which are available for use in building the response function. Each represents a way of handling the different problems in response function analysis which were outlined earlier in this chapter. Many of the different forms to be discussed can be combined with each other in a single response function. It should also be noted that "simultaneous equation" forms will not be illustrated below. However, such simultaneous forms can be very helpful, indeed necessary, in the cases where it is not at all clear whether advertising "causes" sales or vice versa. A limited example of two-equation response functions was illustrated at the end of this chapter through the N.W. Ayer model.

Linear. Linear response functions have been encountered in Appendix B in Chapter 1 as well as previously in this chapter. Linear or straight-line functions are represented algebraically as:

$$S = a + b(A)$$

For example, a function where "a" is assumed to be zero (that is, the function intersects or crosses the vertical axis at point zero) might be $S = .6(A)$. This function states that for every one dollar spent on advertising, six-tenths units of sales will result. A linear function is one in which the returns to advertising are proportionate regardless of the amount spent on advertising. In the preceding example, six-tenths of the amount of money spent on advertising is equivalent to sales regardless of the absolute amount spent on advertising; if $20 is spent on advertising, six-tenths of this would result in sales or if $200,000 is spent on advertising, six-tenths of this amount would result in sales. In linear functions, in other words, returns to scale are constant throughout the range of the function. Figure 8–3(a) shows a generalized linear response curve which can be represented by the general form, $S = a + b(A)$.

Figure 8-3 Response Function Forms

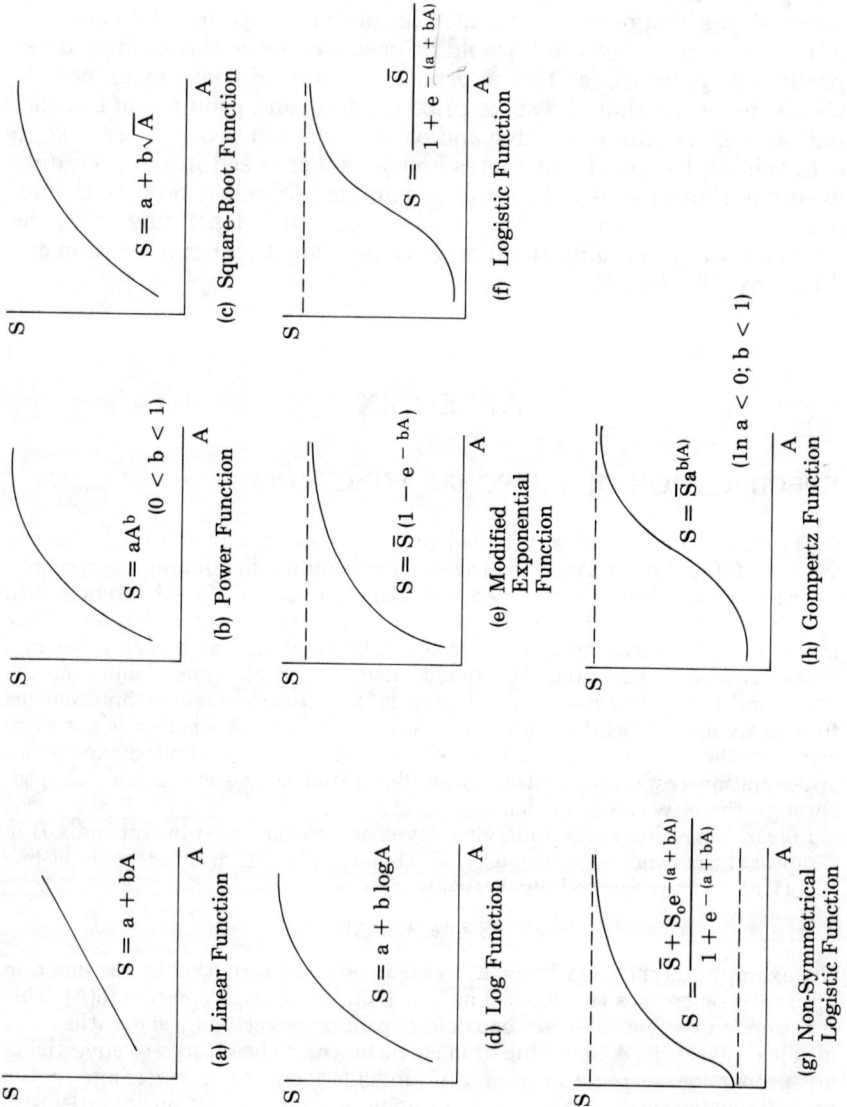

(a) Linear Function
$$S = a + bA$$

(b) Power Function
$$S = aA^b \quad (0 < b < 1)$$

(c) Square-Root Function
$$S = a + b\sqrt{A}$$

(d) Log Function
$$S = a + b \log A$$

(e) Modified Exponential Function
$$S = \bar{S}(1 - e^{-bA})$$

(f) Logistic Function
$$S = \frac{\bar{S}}{1 + e^{-(a + bA)}}$$

(g) Non-Symmetrical Logistic Function
$$S = \frac{\bar{S} + S_0 e^{-(a + bA)}}{1 + e^{-(a + bA)}}$$

(h) Gompertz Function
$$S = \bar{S} a^{b(A)} \quad (\ln a < 0; b < 1)$$

Each of the functional forms discussed below has the characteristic that the function can be "transformed" through the application of some algebra to a linear form. This is important since the most common method of estimating the parameters of a response function is to use a method called regression analysis (this method is discussed generally subsequently in this chapter). In order for regression analysis to be used to fit functions to data, the function must be of a linear form. Thus, prior to the application of regression analysis, the response function is transformed to linear format.

Concave. A concave-downward response function is shown in Figure 8–3(b). There are several types of functions which have the general shape of that shown in Figure 8–3(b). One of the more flexible of these is the power function:

$$S = a(A)^b \quad \text{where } 0 < b < 1.$$

When $b = \frac{1}{2}$, the power function becomes similar to one illustrated earlier in this chapter (the square-root function): $S = a\sqrt{A}$. This is similar except the intercept is assumed to be zero in the power function. This can be seen in comparison to the square-root function: $S = b\sqrt{A}$. Here "a" is the intercept term (the point at which the curve crosses or intercepts the vertical or sales axis), and it is assumed to be zero. Figure 8–3(c) shows a square-root function.

For fitting purposes, the power function can be transformed to linear form so that it becomes:

$$\log(S) = \log a + b \log(A).$$

Prior to fitting the sales and advertising data using this function, the sales figures and the advertising figures for each observation would be "transformed" by taking the log to base 10 of each of the figures. Curve fitting would then be conducted using the transformed values of the observed sales and advertising figures.

The log function shown in Figure 8–3(d) also provides a response function with the concave-downward shape. Notice it differs from the transformed version of the power function only in that the dependent variable (sales) is not transformed through the taking of base 10 logarithms:

$$S = a + b \log(A).$$

Another functional form providing the concave-downward shape is illustrated in Figure 8–3(e) and is called the modified exponential function:

$$S = \bar{S}\{1 - e^{-b(A)}\}$$

where: $\bar{S}$ ("S Bar") = upper asymptote
e = the natural number 2.718 . . .

The $\bar{S}$ in this function represents the upper asymptote or the maximum size that sales could become in the particular brand or firm situation which is being analyzed for a certain time period. It is represented by the dashed line above the function in Figure 8–3(e). The number "e" is similar to the number "π" (pi) in the sense that 2.718 . . . is a number which often occurs in natural phenomena. For fitting purposes, this function can be transformed to:

$$\ln\left[1 - \frac{S}{\bar{S}}\right] = -b(A)$$

where: ln = natural logarithm (log to base e).

The concave-downward representation of the response function assumes that there is no such thing as increasing returns to scale for a particular brand or firm. Over the entire range of the function, each successive dollar spent on advertising produces proportionately less returns in sales; the first dollar spent on advertising is the most efficient dollar. When more money is spent on advertising, sales go up but they do not go up proportionate to the increase in advertising. Suppose, for example, a response function for a brand might be developed as $S = .6\sqrt{A}$. If \$400 is spent on advertising, this response function would indicate that 12 units of sales would result $(12 = .6\sqrt{400})$. If advertising expenditure is doubled from \$400 to \$800, the sales results do not double but go up only about 40 percent $(16.9 = .6\sqrt{800})$. This issue will be examined more carefully after discussion of the "S-shaped" functions below.

Sigmoidal. Figure 8–3(f) shows the shape of the logistic function; this function presents a symmetrical S-shaped picture. The function is symmetrical in the sense that the upper part of the curve could be turned over, and it would correspond perfectly to the lower portion of the curve. That is, the two portions of this curve are mirror images of each other. The curve is represented in functional form as:

$$S = \frac{\bar{S}}{1 + e^{-\{a + b(A)\}}}.$$

After some algebra is conducted on this function, for fitting purposes it can be transformed to the following linear form:

$$\ln \left[\frac{S}{\bar{S} - S}\right] = a + b(A).$$

In order to fit this function to sales and advertising data, for each observation the sales figure must be divided by the quantity of the upper asymptote of sales minus the sales figure itself; then the natural log is taken of this number. The entire expression on the left-hand side of the function then serves as the dependent variable (transformed); clearly, this is a linear function since the "S" in $S = a + b(A)$ is simply replaced by a transformed version of sales: $\ln\{S/(\bar{S} - S)\}$.

Another function which produces the S shape and is another version of the logistic model but does not have to be symmetrical at the inflexion point of the curve (the point at which the function changes from concave-upward to concave-downward) is:

$$\ln \left[\frac{\bar{S} - S}{S - S_o}\right] = a + b(A)$$

where: S_o = lower asymptote.

The lower asymptote in the above function is the point at which sales can go no lower and is represented by the lower dashed line in Figure 8–3(g).

The Gompertz function also displays an S-shaped curve similar to the logistic and is represented by the following functional form:

$$S = \bar{S} \, a^{b(A)} \qquad \text{where: } \ln(a) < 0 \text{ and } b < 1.$$

This, for fitting purposes, can be transformed to linear format in the following manner:

$$\ln(\ln\bar{S} - \ln S) = \ln(-\ln a) + \ln b(A).$$

More detailed discussion of the Gompertz and related curves can be found in the text by Gilchrist.[11] The Gompertz function is shown in Figure 8–3(h).

The use of an S-shaped curve implies that there is a range of expenditure levels on advertising for which there are increasing returns to scale (the concave-upward or lower portion of the curve). The implication of the S-shaped curve is that there is a "threshold" which must be reached for the effect of advertising to "take-off" and produce an effect; below this threshold there will be little or no influence of advertising. Joel Dean put the case for increasing returns in the following way:

> Larger appropriations may make feasible the use of expert services and more economical media. More important than specialization usually are economies of repetition. Each advertising attack starts from ground that was taken in previous forays, and where no single onslaught can overcome the inertia of existing spending patterns, the hammering of repetition often overcomes skepticism by attrition.[12]

In disagreement with the idea that there is such a thing as increasing returns to scale (and thus an S-shaped curve) is Julian Simon. After his study of several specific advertising/sales situations, he concluded:[13]

> There is not one single piece of strong evidence to support the general belief that increasing returns exist in advertising. A very few studies suggest that there are increasing returns, but their evidence is weak. . . . But there are a great many of them that show diminishing marginal returns, and I feel their collective weight is much greater than that of the evidence supporting increasing returns.
> . . . Threshold effects and increasing returns to repetition and size constitute a monstrous myth, I believe, but a myth so well entrenched that it is almost impossible to shake.[13]

Many advertisers, indeed, believe that there is such a thing as increasing returns to scale. David Berger, National Research Director for Foote, Cone & Belding (a large Chicago-based agency) has argued in favor of the S-shaped curve.[14] Others (many times these are agency clients) have argued just as persuasively against the idea of increasing returns to scale inherent in the S-shaped curve. For example, Gus Priemer, Manager of Advertising Services for S.C. Johnson Company, has suggested that if increasing returns exist it might be in the situation where a weak tv commercial is being used. If viewers do not fully grasp the product's promise on the first exposure, he suggests the advertiser has created a delay in consumer response which shows up as an S-shaped curve. On the acceptance of the concave-downward curve, Priemer says:

> The existence of a convex (concave-downward) response curve appears to frighten many people. *Agencies see the potential of fewer dollars spent behind advertising campaigns, or more new ads needed during the year.*[15]

Since the concave-downward curve embodies diminishing returns throughout its entire range, it suggests that fewer advertising dollars would be preferable to more.

The point that should be made here is that, despite the strong views held on this matter by advertising people and others, any one of many different shapes may most realistically represent a given brand's response function in a given situation. The functional form should be selected which most adequately fits that situation.

Lagged Terms. One of the ways in which the lagged or carryover effects of advertising can be represented in a response function is through the use of "lagged terms." An example of such a function is shown below:

$$S_t = a + b(A_t) + c(A_{t-1}).$$

In the above example, the time period "t" might, for example, refer to winter quarter 1982 while time period "t-1" would then refer to the preceding time period, fall 1981. The function shows that sales in winter 1982 would be a function of advertising in winter 1982 as well as the advertising conducted in fall 1981. This is a way, then, of showing how the effect of preceding time period advertising relates to the current time period sales. One of the problems in the use of lagged term functions lies in the decision as to how many lagged terms to include in the function. How far back does the effect of advertising go for the individual brand or firm? It might be, in the example, that summer 1981 advertising might also have an effect on winter 1982 sales; if so, then another lagged term should be added to the response function. Notice that the "c" in the above is a third parameter of the function which is associated with the effect of the lagged term.

Variable Interaction. The variables on the right-hand side of a response function are called explanatory variables, as indicated earlier. When explanatory variables on the right-hand of the equation are not independent of each other, they should not be separated by a "+" sign in the function but rather should be multiplied together to form one term of the function. For example, suppose creative quality (as measured on a 1 to 10 copytesting scale on a sample of target market consumers) and media schedule efficiency (as measured by the frequency to the target market reached by the schedule) are to be included as explanatory variables in a reponse function. Clearly, using an excellent commercial in conjunction with a poor media schedule which provides low frequency will probably result in a poor effect on sales; likewise, a schedule which provides high frequency of exposure for a commercial which is very poor in quality will also probably have undesirable impact on sales. In other words, these two factors "interact" to produce the outcome, sales. These factors should be represented in the response function as follows:

$$S = a + b\sqrt{(M)(F)}$$

where: M = message quality (creative)
F = frequency of media schedule.

Notice in this function message quality and media efficiency are not utilized as two independent variables but are combined (by multiplying them by each other) into one independent variable. This procedure should be followed any time explanatory variables are believed to interact with each other in producing the impact on the dependent variable. Notice that this example above has been formulated using the square-root sign over the advertising variables so that the functional form is concave-downward.

Creative Quality. Consider the following functional form:

$$S = a(P)^b c(A)^d$$

where: P = price.

First, this function shows price and advertising in interaction through use of a power function illustrated earlier. The parameter "b" above can be interpreted as the elasticity coefficient while "d" can be considered the advertising response coefficient (these were discussed and illustrated in Chapter 3). Second, the parameter "c" can be viewed as a factor to show the importance of creative quality in relation to dollars spent on advertising (A) in the response function. Suppose the parameters of this function were determined to be:

$$S = 100,000P^{-2}cA^{1/4}.$$

Price elasticity is shown as -2 and advertising response coefficient is one-fourth. Suppose the company which is developing this response function tests the copy or commercials which are to be used in the campaign in a testing system such as the theatre system used by ASI, Inc. Suppose the testing results show that 15 percent of those tested preferred the company's brand before exposure to the commercials for the brand while 25 percent preferred it after exposure. This is a gain of 10 points pre- and post-exposure for the company's brand preference. Suppose the company also arranges to test, on the same ASI system, its major competitor's commercials and finds they gain only 6 percentage points pre- and post-exposure. Parameter "c" in the response function could then be set at 1.67 ($1.67 = 10/6$). This would indicate that the company's advertising dollars go 67 percent further than those of the major competitor because of the edge it has in its creative quality. The final functional form would then look as follows:

$$S = 100,000P^{-2}(1.67A^{1/4}).$$

This is one manner in which the effect of creative quality can be incorporated into response functions so that the effect of advertising is represented by factors other than simply the amount of money spent on advertising.

Competitive Effects. One way in which competitive effects can be built into response functions was illustrated by creative quality indices shown above. Another method is to express the dollars spent by the company on advertising relative to those spent by the entire industry in which the company competes. Using the power function again:

$$S_t = S_{t-1}\left[\frac{A_t}{I_t}\right]^a$$

where: I_t = sum of all companies' advertising $ in time period "t" (the industry advertising $ in t).

Notice that "a" is the only parameter to be estimated in this power function, and it can be interpreted as the advertising response coefficient as presented and discussed in Chapter 3.

PARAMETER ESTIMATION

The usual method of developing the parameters of a response function is to use the statistical technique of *regression analysis*. This technique cannot be considered in detail here, but a few points can be simply made which will illustrate how it is determined that a particular response function is adequate or inadequate for budgeting purposes.

There are three primary measures which can be examined in regression analysis to determine the statistical adequacy of response function parameters: (1) The coefficient of determination or R^2 (usually called "R-squared"); (2) Multicollinearity; and (3) Autocorrelation. In order for a response function to be useful for further analysis in the budgeting context, it should show a high R^2, little multicollinearity and little autocorrelation.

The meaning of R^2 is illustrated by the example of a scatterplot in Figure 8-4. The dashed line in Figure 8-4 represents the mean sales for the observations illustrated by the dots in the scatterplot. It is helpful to think of a single observation when conceptualizing the meaning of the coefficient of determination. For this purpose, observation noted "A" in Figure 8-4 can be used (any other dot would just as easily do in the explanation). The regression equation or function (a linear response function is shown here) is, of course, represented by the straight line which goes through point B. Notice that point B is directly below point A and lies right on the regression line; point B is the sales value "predicted" for or given to point A by the regression analysis or equation. The relation of the actual observation (point A) to the predicted value for point A (point B, that is) compared to point C (the mean sales value over all observations or dots) defines R^2. The coefficient of determination is defined as the ratio of explained variance (the distance between B and C) to total variance (the distance between A and C). In statistics, variance is a concept dealing with the distance single observations or dots are away from the average of all observations; that is, it is a measure of the dispersion or spread of the observations around the mean score. Since explained variance is part of the total distance between A and C, this distance represents a *percentage* of the total distance:

$$R^2 = \frac{\text{Explained Variance}}{\text{Total Variance}}$$

Figure 8-4   Variance in Regression Analysis

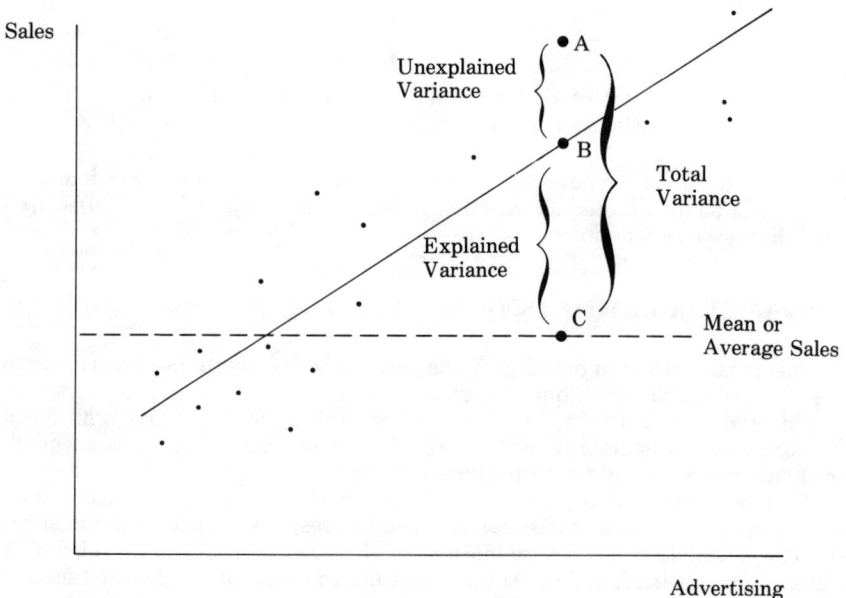

It can be seen from Figure 8-4 that if point A was right on the regression line (that is, point A and point B were the same) then explained variance would equal total variance, and thus R^2 would be 100 percent. That would mean that all of the variance in sales was "explained by" advertising. The higher the R^2 percentage, the more the sales is explained by or accounted for by the advertising.

If a functional form, as stated before, has a high amount of explained variance (high R^2) and low autocorrelation and low multicollinearity, then it may be an adequate function to use in budgeting analyses. Briefly, multicollinearity refers to the situation in which variables which are specified as independent variables in a function are not really independent at all. For example, if message quality and media efficiency were used as independent variables (connected by a plus sign rather than multiplied by each other) in a response function for a firm that had high quality advertising programs (they knew how to develop both good commercials and good media plans), it is likely that these two variables would be highly correlated with each other; that is, they would not be independent variables. This situation would be one in which the response function exhibited multicollinearity.

Autocorrelation refers to the situation in which, if it is present, the parameters of a response function cannot be trusted to really represent the actual relationships between the variables in the function. Autocorrelation is the correlation of the residuals (unexplained variance) for each observation with each other. Autocorrelation can occur because of the lagged effect of advertising over a number of time periods; because an incorrect functional form was specified in the first place; or because an important explanatory variable or variables were left out of the function.[16] For example, suppose only advertising expenditure was used as an explanatory variables in a function in a situation in which price was also very important in producing sales; it is likely that autocorrelation would result. This problem could be "cured" by the inclusion of price in the specification of the function.

QUESTIONS AND PROBLEMS

1. Draw a scatterplot for the data for Rollo Paper Company shown in Table 8-2. How could you draw a scatterplot for Rollo if both advertising and price were to be included?

2. Contrast the strengths and weaknesses which you see in the judgmental method versus the time-series/regression method of developing response functions.

3. Develop a judgmental response function along the lines of that used in Example 8-5 in this chapter for the scatterplot and accompanying data in Figure 8-1.

4. What factors could be major contributors to the changing value of response function parameters over time for a given brand?

5. Which of the two carryover effects (customer holdover effect or delayed response effect) do you think is more important? Why?

6. Examine the response function developed by the J. Walter Thompson advertising agency for one of its client's brands. (This can be found in N.K. Dhalla, "How to Set Advertising Budgets," *Journal of Advertising Research* [October 1977], p. 15). Does this response function appear adequate to the task for which it was intended? Does it include the most im-

portant explanatory factors for the type of product illustrated? Why are the data measured on a per capita basis?

7. Do you agree with Joel Dean or Julian Simon about the existence of increasing returns to scale in advertising? Why is this issue of any importance from a practical point of view? Why would advertising agency people, in particular, be very concerned about this issue?

8. What characteristics of the N.W. Ayer New Product Model in Example 8-4 in this chapter do you find desirable and which undesirable? Why in each case?

9. When two response function methods provide different results and these point to different decisions about how much to spend for advertising, how is one approach selected over the other? What factors would be considered in this selection process? Why do such differences occur in the first place?

10. In what ways is the use of the response function and marginal analysis-like approach more logical than traditional budgeting "rules of thumb" such as percentage of future or anticipated sales?

ENDNOTES

1. This example is adapted from Philip Kotler, *Marketing Decision Making: A Model Building Approach* (New York: Holt, Rinehart and Winston, 1971), pp. 46-48.
2. Nariman K. Dhalla, "How to Set Advertising Budgets," *Journal of Advertising Research* (October 1977), pp. 11-17.
3. *Ibid.*, p. 13.
4. This characterization has been suggested by Kotler, *op.cit.*, Ch. 5.
5. This approach has been suggested by Julian L. Simon, *Advertising Management* (Englewood Cliffs, N.J.: Prentice-Hall, Inc., 1971), among others.
6. Darral G. Clarke "Econometric Measurement of the Duration of the Advertising Effect on Sales," Working Paper No. 75-106, Marketing Science Institute, April 1975.
7. Kristian S. Palda, *The Measurement of Cumulative Advertising Effects* (Englewood Cliffs, N.J.: Prentice-Hall, Inc., 1964).
8. The original Ayer model is presented in H.J. Claycamp and L.E. Liddy, "Prediction of New Product Performance: An Analytical Approach," *Journal of Marketing Research* (November 1969), pp. 414-420.
9. G.S. Day, G.J. Eskin, D.B. Montgomery, and C.B. Weinberg, *Cases in Computer and Model Assisted Marketing: Planning* (Palo Alto: Hewlett-Packard, 1977).
10. This model is adapted from John D.C. Little, "Models and Managers: The Concept of Decision Calculus," *Management Science: Applications* (April 1970).
11. Warren Gilchrist, *Statistical Forecasting* (New York: John Wiley & Sons, 1976), Ch. 9.
12. Joel Dean, *Managerial Economics* (Englewood Cliffs, N.J.: Prentice-Hall, Inc., 1951), p. 357.
13. Julian Simon, *op.cit.*, pp. 75-76.
14. David Berger, "How Much to Spend," paper presented to Advertising Research Foundation Conference, New York, New York, March 18, 1980.
15. Gus Priemer, "Are We Doing the Wrong Thing Right?" *Media Decisions* (May 1979), p. 152.
16. Leonard J. Parsons and Randall L. Schultz, *Marketing Models and Econometric Research* (New York: North-Holland Publishing Company, 1976), p. 104. See this reference also for a discussion of some econometric approaches in the determination of response functions.

CASES IN ADVERTISING BUDGETING AND CONTROL

- Fox Lines, Inc. (A)
- American Food and Beverage Company
- The Reneé Farver Company
- The Oron Paper Company (A)
- The Agen Company
- Commonwealth Food Products Grocery Company
- Atwood Company
- The Anheuser-Busch Company

9

CASES IN ADVERTISING BUDGETING AND CONTROL

Case 9–1—Fox Lines, Inc. (A)[1]

DETERMINATION OF APPROPRIATION SIZE

Company officials developed a plan of marketing and promotional strategy for Fox Lines, Inc., a subsidiary of the Fox Corporation, based upon the general objective of building greater revenue for the company. The strategy defined the target as:

1. The current bus rider who could be persuaded to continue to ride the bus and to take more and longer bus trips.
2. The automobile traveler, especially the lone automobile traveler—the research has shown that the latter group was most amenable to a change in transportation form. In addition, the continuous increase in fuel prices will motivate the private automobile traveler to convert to the bus.
3. The rail traveler—a group which considers bus a possible alternative mode of transportation more than the users of other modes of transportation.

The plan also included the long-range objective of enhancing the prestige and social status of the bus as a mode of intercity travel. In attempting to determine the size of the advertising appropriation for 1980, management considered the following four methods to arrive at the final decision:

1. Percentage of Last Year's Sales (Method A):
   (Sales in 1979 × Average Percentage)

2. Percentage of Last Year's Sales (Method B):
   (Sales in 1979 × Average Advertising-Sales Ratio)
3. Percentage of Future Sales:
   (Projected Sales Based on the Average Rate of Increase in Sales
   × Average Advertising-Sales Ratio)
4. Percentage of Future Sales:
   (Projected Sales Based on the Company Potential × Average
   Advertising-Sales Ratio)

FOX LINES SALES AND ADVERTISING EXPENDITURES

Fox Lines has nearly 60 percent of the total intercity bus market.
Trailways, Inc., the second largest bus company, has approximately
15 percent of the market. These two companies operate three-quarters
of the country's 8,300 long-distance buses. Fox Lines sales and
revenues in the last 10 years and its estimated advertising expenditures in the last 6 years are shown in Figure 9-1.[2]

Figure 9-1   Sales and Advertising Expenditures of
Fox Lines

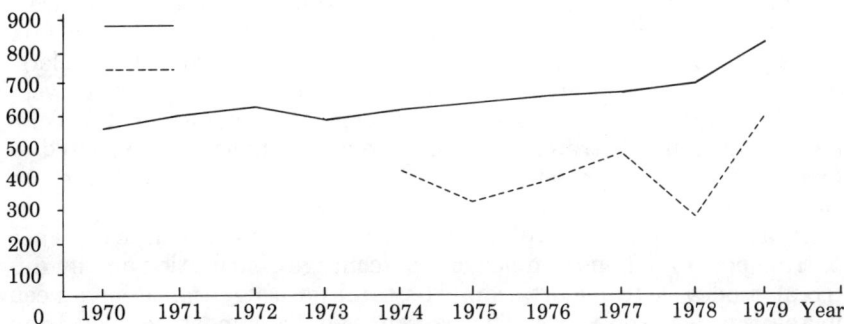

SOURCE: The Fox Corporation Annual Reports, 1974, 1977, 1979.

———— Sales & Revenues
       ($ Million)

------------ Advertising
       (# Thousand)

The Fox Lines sales and revenues have been increasing steadily over
the period from 1970 to 1979, except they dropped from $614,895,000
to $568,543,000 in the years 1972-1973. Sales and revenues increased

most from 1978 to 1979, a 16.46 percent increase in this period. On the other hand, advertising expenditures, which include advertising for Fox Sight-Seeing Tours, Travelpass, chartered bus travel, and Fox Lines general promotion, fluctuate without showing any consistent pattern for the years 1974-1979.

Although Trailways has a much smaller share than Fox, Trailways started an aggressive advertising campaign for its reduced fares. In the summer of 1977, for example, Trailways started running TV commercials for a new coast-to-coast fare, which was supposed to be the lowest fare from Los Angeles to New York. In 1978, Trailways' new advertising campaign specifically named its competitor, saying that "Trailways is cheaper than Fox on most lines." In response to Trailways' challenge, Fox offered a new $69 maximum one-way fare on all interstate routes.

FOX LINES POTENTIAL

One of the initial tasks facing the Fox Lines management group concerned a satisfactory definition of company potential, since the greatest volume increases obviously would come from those areas which had most potential. In many industries potential is defined as the volume of the entire industry, and this is viewed as the maximum business attainable. Since Fox had such a substantial share of existing intercity bus volume, however, some executives believed that a potential objective based upon total industry volume would only constrict the company's opportunities and confine them to a too-narrow area. True expansion, they claimed, required adoption of the view that Fox Lines potential consisted not only of all present intercity bus travelers, but also of other intercity travelers. These were people who were specific targets of Fox Lines advertising, as described in the company's advertising strategy, and who could reasonably be expected to transfer from their present modes of transportation to bus travel. In this category, for example, were train travelers.

Exhibit 9-1 shows the volume of intercity passenger traffic by types of transport in billions of miles and percentage distribution among different modes of transportation. The total passenger-miles have been increasing over the years: The passenger-miles almost doubled from the 784 billion miles of 1965 to the 1,450 billion miles of 1977. The passenger-miles traveled by buses have been almost constant since 1950, at around 25 to 26 billion miles, except the figures dropped to 19 billion miles in 1960 and they increased to 28 billion miles in 1974. Railroads also show a stable pattern after the volume of traffic decreased from 18 billion miles to 11 billion miles in the years 1965-1970. Railroads, which had more than 6 percent of the total intercity traffic in 1950, have been keeping less than 1 percent of share in the 1970s, when the government started subsidizing the railroad industry. Airways are the only sector that has been growing both in passenger-miles and in percentage shares. The share of airways increased, on the average, by .30 percent during the period 1971-1977, whereas the average percentage distribution of private automobiles decreased by .21 percent, and those of buses and railroads decreased by .07 and .04 percent respectively during the same period.[3] The passenger-miles traveled by private automobiles decreased slightly, from 1,286 billion miles to 1,234 billion miles, in 1977. It is likely that some portion of automobile travelers is moving to more economical modes of transportation such as buses or railroads, considering that fuel prices have been continuously increasing.

The research showed that the most important characteristics influencing bus travel were:

1. Income—there is a distinct tendency for lower income people to prefer the bus.
2. Age—the bus market draws relatively heavily from the upper and lower age groups.
3. Sex—women tend to use the bus more frequently than men.
4. Marital Status—single people favor bus travel.

FOUR ALTERNATIVES FOR THE ADVERTISING APPROPRIATION

A problem facing the management in deciding the size of advertising appropriation was a lack of relationship between advertising and sales (see Figure 9–1 again). First of all, the "responsiveness" of sales to advertising expenditures, i.e., advertising elasticity, was calculated based on the following formula:

$$\text{Advertising Elasticity} = \frac{\% \text{ change in \$ sales}}{\% \text{ change in \$ advertising}}$$

The average advertising elasticity for the years 1975-1979 was .083, that is, sales increased only by .083 percent with a 1 percent increase in advertising, on the average. This figure led a group of executives to propose that next year's appropriation should not exceed certain percentages of last year's sales—average figure of the percentages of previous year's sales, or the percentage of average advertising expenditures to the average sales volume. On the other hand, another group of executives, who proposed to expand the Fox Lines market by redefining its potential, was in favor of a more aggressive advertising program. In addition, it was also considered that a certain proportion of future sales would be spent on advertising by projecting next year's sales based upon the average rate of increase in the past years' sales.

Then, the management's task was to calculate alternative advertising appropriations based on the above four methods.

Exhibit 9-1 Volume of Intercity Passenger Traffic by Types of Transport

Billions of Passenger-Miles

Types of Transport	1950	1955	1960	1965	1970	1971	1972	1973	1974	1975	1976	1977
Private Automobiles	438	637	706	818	1,026	1,071	1,129	1,174	1,143	1,164	1,286	1,234
Domestic Airways	10	23	34	58	119	120	133	143	146	148	165	176
Bus	26	25	19	24	25	26	26	26	28	26	25	26
Railroads	32	29	22	18	11	9	9	9	10	10	10	10
Inland Waterways	1.2	1.7	2.7	3.1	4.0	4.1	4.0	4.0	4.1	4.0	4.0	4.0
Total	508	716	784	920	1,185	1,230	1,300	1,356	1,331	1,352	1,440	1,450

Percent Distribution

Types of Transport	1950	1955	1960	1965	1970	1971	1972	1973	1974	1975	1976	1977
Private Automobiles	86.20	89.01	90.10	88.86	86.60	87.11	86.82	86.58	85.88	86.09	85.83	85.10
Domestic Airways	1.98	3.18	4.33	6.31	10.01	9.76	10.24	10.55	10.97	10.95	11.46	12.14
Bus	5.20	3.56	2.47	2.58	2.14	2.07	1.97	1.92	2.10	1.92	1.74	1.79
Railroads	6.39	4.01	2.75	1.91	.92	.73	.66	.67	.75	.74	.69	.69
Inland Waterways	.23	.24	.34	.34	.34	.33	.31	.29	.30	.30	.28	.28
Total	100.0	100.0	100.0	100.0	100.0	100.0	100.0	100.0	100.0	100.0	100.0	100.0

SOURCE: U.S. Commerce Commission, Annual Report; Intercity Ton- Miles, 1939-1959; and Transport Economic Quarterly. Adapted from Statistical Abstract of the United States, 1979.

Year	Sales ($'000)	Advertising ($'000)	(1) % increase in sales	(2) $ Adv. as % of last year's sales
1970	553,182	—	—	—
1971	576,262	—	? %	—
1972	614,895	—	?	—
1973	568,543	—	?	—
1974	629,634	4,115.6	?	? %
1975	638,463	3,502.8	?	?
1976	660,853	3,916.4	?	?
1977	694,009	5,001.3	?	?
1978	727,965	2,996.0	?	?
1979	847,803	6,036.8	?	?

(3)
Average = ?%

(4)
Average = ?%

where: (1) Percentage increase in sales

$$= \frac{(Sales_{t+1} - Sales_t)}{Sales_t} \times 100$$

(2) Advertising as a percentage of last year's sales

$$= (Advertising_{t+1} / Sales_t) \times 100$$

(3) Average rate of increase in sales

= [Sum of percentages in column (1)] /9

(4) Average percentage of last year's sales

= [Sum of percentages in column (2)] /6

Note: "t" refers to a particular year such as 1970, and "t+1" is the next year. In this example, "t+1" is 1971.

Average Advertising-Sales Ratio

$$= \frac{\text{Average \$ Advertising from 1974 to 1979}}{\text{Average \$ Sales from 1974 to 1979}}$$

$$= \underline{\quad ? \quad} \text{ (5)}$$

Having obtained the above five percentage figures, the final task of calculation was to get four appropriation figures using these percentages.

1. Percentage of Last Year's Sales: Using Average Percentage of Sales (4)

$Advertising for 1980 = Sales in 1979 × (4)

= $ _____?_____

2. Percentage of Last Year's Sales: Using Average Advertising-Sales Ratio (5)

$ Advertising for 1980   = Sales in 1979 × (5)

                            = $ _____?_____

3. Percentage of Future Sales: Using the Average Rate of Increase in Sales (3)

Projected sales for 1980   = Sales in 1979 × [1 + (3)]

$ Advertising for 1980   = Projected sales × (5)

                            = $ _____?_____

4. Percentage of Future Sales: Based on the Company Potential
   a. Increase in the total bus market in 1980   = __?__ %
   b. Fox Lines share in the 1980 bus market   = __?__ %
   c. Increase in the Fox Lines sales from 1979 to 1980   = __?__ % (6)
      (based on the above two estimations)

Projected sales for 1980   = Sales in 1979 × [1 + (6)]

$ Advertising for 1980   = Projected sales × (5)

                            = $ _____?_____

QUESTIONS FOR DISCUSSION

1. Conduct the calculations required to fill in the blanks in this case at all points where a question mark appears.
2. What opportunities do you see for Fox Lines advertising programs?
3. Conduct a competitive analysis of the transportation market opportunities.
4. What appropriation method of the four outlined in the case do you believe to be the most appropriate for the Fox Lines situation? Are any of the methods adequate to the problem? If no, what other methods would you *specifically* suggest be implemented by Fox Lines?

ENDNOTES

1. For the company background and promotional plans, students are encouraged to read the case, Fox Lines, Inc. (B).
2. Advertising expenditures include newspaper supplements, magazines, network and spot TV, network and spot radio, and outdoor advertising. For 1978, spot radio expenditures are available only for the first half of the year: Spot radio expenditures during this period were $56,200. Spot radio expenditures for 1979 are not available.
3. These figures are the averages of the annual rate of change for the period 1971-1977.

Case 9-2—American Food and Beverage Company

COMPANY BACKGROUND

American Food and Beverage Company (AF&B)[1] manufactures a variety of cake mix and frostings as well as instant coffee. These products are sold at popular prices and distributed nationally. AF&B entered the instant coffee market in the early 1950's and achieved national distribution of the product by the end of 1961. American Breakfast[2] was one of the leading national brands of instant coffee at that time. However, its market share started declining in the mid 1960's facing the keen competition from Maxwell House instant coffee made by General Foods and Nescafe made by Nestle. American Breakfast's market share declined to less than 2% in 1977 from the all-time high of 12.8% in 1963.

TECHNOLOGICAL INNOVATIONS

AF&B did not adopt any technological innovations in instant coffee during the 1960's although the company executives had recognized that the ordinary spray-dried coffee was becoming obsolete and less attractive to consumers. The most common production method of instant coffee in the 1960's was to spray brewed coffee in a fine mist into a very high tower at very hot temperatures; the coffee dries and becomes a soluble powder as it falls. This production method, because of its use of the heating process, was known to have an effect on the aroma, which is a very important attribute of coffee. Two major improvements have recently been added to this ordinary spray-dry method. One was the use of a vacuum during the process of spray drying, which more effectively preserves the aromatics of coffee. The other new method was agglomeration: In this process, the original fine powder is formed into larger particles and the moisture component is evenly distributed within a particle. Therefore, agglomerated coffee is more soluble in water than the ordinary spray-dried coffee. In the early 1970's most of the major manufacturers switched to agglomeration, and more than 70% of the instant coffees in the market were agglomerated types.

While agglomerated coffee was a modification of the ordinary spray-dried coffee, freeze-dried coffee was introduced as a significant innovation in instant coffee before the advent of the agglomerated. In the freeze-dried process, brewed coffee is directly transformed into dried particles without heating in a hot temperature. Therefore, the freeze-dry process is considered to be superior to other methods in preserving aroma. For this improved method, it is more costly to change plant equipment from manufacturing of the ordinary spray-dried to freeze-dried coffee than to the agglomerated coffee.

Having carefully studied such technological innovations, the company's executives decided to remodel its plant for the production of freeze-dried coffee in 1972. This decision was not a mere attempt to follow an already-developed innovation. AF&B's research and development department had found a less expensive method of the freeze dry process by that time. Also, the management considered that freeze-dried coffee was the fastest-growing sector in the instant coffee market. AF&B started the distribution of a freeze-dried coffee in several test markets in 1975, and the company is now considering its introduction into the national market.

FREEZE-DRIED MARKET

The total consumption of coffee, including both regular grind coffee and instant coffee, has been gradually decreasing since the mid 1960's. However, the consumption of instant coffee continuously increased from the early 1950's up until the mid 1970's. In 1976, 1.48 cups of regular coffee were consumed per person per day, and .63 cup of instant coffee was consumed on the same basis. The downward shift of the total coffee consumption in the mid 1970's was attributed to the increased price of coffee beans and to the increased usage of soft drinks. In 1977, the average retail price of regular coffee in 16-oz. cans rose 85.3% and that of instant coffee increased 52.2%.

Exhibit 9-2 Percentages of Persons Drinking Coffee and Other Beverages

	1950	1975	1976	1977
Coffee	74.7%	61.6%	59.1%	57.9%
Milk and milk drinks	51.0	51.1	50.1	48.9
Fruit and vegetable drinks	32.8	44.0	44.3	46.2
Soft drinks	29.1	46.9	48.6	46.4
Tea	24.0	26.9	26.3	30.7
Cocoa, hot chocolate	5.4	2.8	3.8	NA

NA = not available
SOURCE: *Advertising Age*, June 26, 1978.

While the size of the total coffee market has been shrinking over time, the consumption of freeze-dried coffee has increased in the mid 1970's. The consumption of spray-dried, on the other hand, decreased dramatically from 1969 to 1975 as indicated in Exhibit 9-3.

Exhibit 9-3 Instant Coffee Consumption by Freeze-Dried and Spray-Dried
(cups per person per day)

	1969	1975	1976
Freeze-Dried	.11	.29	.25
Spray-Dried	.58	.39	.38
Total Instant	.69	.68	.63

a: Includes all persons of age 10 and over.

SOURCE: Pan-American Coffee Bureau, *Coffee Drinking in the United States*, 1976.

The major reason for the increased consumption of freeze-dried coffee is deemed to be the increased consumption of decaffeinated coffee in both spray-dried and freeze-dried forms.

COMPETITION BETWEEN MAXIM AND TASTER'S CHOICE

The freeze-dried market was evenly divided by Maxim, the first national brand of freeze-dried coffee produced by General Foods, and Nestle's Taster's Choice; each had 10.5% market shares in 1970.

General Foods introduced Maxim in an Albany test market in 1964, then they expanded the market into New York, Arizona, and Indianapolis. In 1968, Maxim achieved its all-time high, 13% of the total instant coffee market. However, Maxim lost its lead to Taster's Choice in only two years. Taster's Choice had only 4% of market share in 1969, but its share was more than doubled in the following year. It became the top brand among the freeze-dried coffee brands in 1971 with 11% of the total instant coffee market. The total share of freeze-dried achieved 30.9% of the instant coffee market in 1974 when Taster's Choice had 11.7% of the share and the newly introduced Taster's Choice Decaffeinated increased its share from 2.5% to 5.1%.

It was believed that one of the causes for Maxim's failure was its cannibalization from the same company's Maxwell House sales. Maxwell House instant coffee, however, maintained about 27% of market share in 1971 and 1972, although it declined from 27.5% to 23.5% in 1969. Brim and Freeze-Dried Sanka, the other freeze-dried decaffeinated brands of General Foods, appear to have been complementing Maxim's lost share.

While Maxim suffered from its resemblance to Maxwell House due to its use of family brand name, Nestle took full advantage of the unique features of freeze-dried coffee by positioning Taster's Choice as an entirely new form of coffee. The copy approach for Taster's Choice emphasized that it "looks, tastes, and smells like real coffee." This strong product differentiation and, in addition, its unique square glass contributed a great deal to the rapid growth of Taster's Choice. The estimated advertising expenditures for Maxim totaled approximately $24,000,000 in the years 1966 to 1970, while the expenditures for Taster's Choice during the same time period were about $19,000,000. Advertising Expenditures for freeze-dried coffees in recent years are shown in Exhibit 9-5.

ENTRY TO THE NATIONAL FREEZE-DRIED MARKET

AF&B's freeze-dried coffee, Mocha,[3] has a unique, mild flavor derived from mocha coffee. Also, it is priced lower than the other premium-priced freeze-dried coffees: Mocha's retail price is approximately 20 cents lower than that of Taster's Choice for a 4-oz. jar, and

Exhibit 9-4   Percentage Share of Freeze-Dried Brands

	1969	1970	1971	1972	1973	1974	1975	1976	1977	1978	1979
Maxim	13.0	10.5	8.2	7.5	7.3	7.0	5.5	5.3	4.5	4.0	3.7
Freeze-Dried Sanka	2.5	4.5	4.7	4.2	3.6	3.6	3.2	3.1	2.5	2.5	2.5
Brim[a]	—	—	—	1.9	3.3	3.5	3.5	3.5	3.5	3.0	2.8
Taster's Choice	4.0	10.5	11.0	12.6	11.9	11.7	11.7	11.8	12.5	12.5	12.7
Taster's Choice Decaffeinated	—	—	—	—	2.5	5.1	5.4	5.5	5.6	5.1	4.8
Freeze-Dried Total	19.5	25.5	23.9	26.2	28.6	30.9	29.3	29.2	28.6	27.1	26.5

a: Brim and International after 1974
SOURCE: *Advertising Age*, Sept. 11, 1972; July 11, 1977; April 14, 1980.

Exhibit 9-5   Estimated Advertising Expenditures of Leading Brands of Freeze-Dried Coffee (in $'000)

	1976	1977	1978	1979
Maxim	$3567.3	2806.9	3710.6	6417.5
Freeze-Dried				
Sanka[a]	201.2	477.6	1209.8	1581.4
Brim[b]	5416.4	379.3	1440.3	8979.9
Taster's Choice[c]	8395.8	7439.1	7415.4	12157.7

a: These figures include the joint advertising for Freeze-Dried Sanka and other brands of Sanka. Expenditures spent solely for the other products of Sanka in 1976 to 1979 were: $10,764.4, 6,421.0, 12,752.2, and 19,120.9. (in thousands).
b: These figures include joint advertising for regular Brim and freeze-dried Brim. Expenditures spent solely for regular Brim in 1976 to 1979 were; $1,864.1, 2,498.5, 2,661.8, and 3,611.9. (in thousands).
c: These figures are combined expenditures for Taster's Choice 100% Coffee and Taster's Choice Decaffeinated.

SOURCE: Leading National Advertisers; Radio Expenditures Report.

30 cents lower for an 8-oz. jar. These prices are also lower than those of Maxim and Brim. AF&B can sell Mocha at lower prices with comparable product quality to that of the leading brands because of their improved production methods.

The brand manager of Mocha proposed that they should advertise this product to the younger market, 18 to 29 years old, for two reasons.

(1) Since the generic demand for coffee has been declining for more than 10 years, the total market size must be expanded by inducing young consumers to switch from soft drinks to coffee.

(2) Mocha's mild flavor will be liked by young people who are used to the sweet flavor of soft drinks.

The brand manager also presented coffee usage data by age groups to the management.

Exhibit 9-6   Coffee Consumption by Age (cups per person per day)

Age Groups	1970	1971	1972	1973	1974	1975	1976
10 — 14	.13	.12	.12	.09	.11	.10	.11
15 — 19	.77	.60	.55	.54	.46	.57	.42
20 — 24	1.82	1.68	1.48	1.65	1.35	1.38	1.15
25 — 29	2.68	2.71	2.47	2.44	2.70	2.23	2.08
30 — 39	3.61	3.72	3.51	3.28	3.02	2.94	2.76
40 — 49	3.93	3.93	3.72	3.75	3.68	3.79	3.44
50 — 59	3.75	3.44	3.35	3.44	3.49	3.21	3.34
60 — 69	2.96	3.07	2.85	2.70	2.72	2.77	2.93
70 and over	2.39	2.39	2.49	2.30	2.22	2.29	2.44

SOURCE: Pan American Coffee Bureau, Coffee Drinking in the United States, 1976.

The management estimates that Mocha will achieve national distribution within the next three years with the aid of an effective advertising program. The company goal is set as follows:

Exhibit 9-7   Market Share Goals for Three Years

Year	Percentage share of instant coffee market
1980	3%
1981	5
1982	8

QUESTIONS FOR DISCUSSION

1. Estimate the size of freeze-dried market for 18-to-29-year-olds. (It is estimated that approximately 20.8% of the total U.S. population was 14 to 24 years old in 1978.) Evaluate the opportunity to advertise this company's product to this segment. Also, suggest any other possible target audience, and provide reasons.

2. What size appropriation do you recommend for this company for each of the 3 years indicated in Exhibit 9-7? Explain fully how you arrived at your recommended figure and justify your method.

ENDNOTES

1. Fictitious company name.
2. Fictitious brand name.
3. Fictitious brand name.

Case 9-3—Reneé Farver Company[1]

Reneé Farver, Inc. is one of the country's large cosmetics companies, producing and selling millions of dollars of products each year. Like all successful cosmetics firms, Reneé Farver relies heavily upon sales promotion methods to cultivate their market. Advertising plays a prominent part in their sales promotion program, with expenditures of $14,000,000 to $15,000,000 representing 19 to 20% of sales in a typical year.

RETAIL DISTRIBUTION POLICIES

The company attempts to sell its products as prestige items and appeals to customers on the basis of fashion and exclusiveness. In attempting to carry out this plan, Reneé Farver carefully screens all retailers and selects only those who indicate a willingness to cooperate with its campaigns, who have appropriate facilities, and who appeal to a fashion-conscious clientele. About 2,000 retail outlets are used, including 725 department stores, several hundred women's specialty shops and approximately 1,200 drugstores.

SPECIAL PROMOTION METHODS

To increase its share of the highly competitive cosmetic market, the Farver Company makes use of a variety of sales promotion methods in addition to the national advertising program mentioned above. The company sells its products directly to retailers through a field force of personal salesmen. It is the direct responsibility of these salesmen to open new accounts and to work with retailers to make certain that retail outlets stock adequate inventories of Farver Brand products; display these brands attractively; and give them adequate advertising support at the local level.

In order to encourage retailers to expand their advertising support for the Farver branded products, the company sets up a quite liberal, cooperative advertising program. Farver agrees to pay 50% of a store's newspaper advertising for Reneé Farver products. The company, however, stipulates certain conditions which should be met before the allowance will be paid.

The advertising charges must be invoiced to Farver at the store's lowest contract rate, less all discounts and rebates to the store. Farver's amount of financial cooperation with each retailer is determined by the total amount of store net purchases of Farver products during a calendar year. These cooperative funds are to be paid on a graduated percentage scale of 5% on the first $5,000 up to a maximum of 8% on purchases over $25,000.

Bills for cooperative advertising must be accompanied by tear sheets of the actual ad. No payments will be made for production or layout costs.

Direct mail handled through the retailers plays an important part in the Farver sales promotion program. Elaborate and expensive direct mailings are developed by the Farver sales promotion department and sent out to selected retailers, who mail the material to their customers. The mailing list is usually taken from charge accounts.

These mailings are usually tied directly to the promotion of some specific product; frequently this is a new addition to the line. Some special inducement to buy in the form of free merchandise is common practice with the direct mail promotion. Farver customarily pays all costs including postage. Because of the expense involved, this program is restricted to the larger, more profitable accounts.

Farver management recognizes that personal sales efforts of store employees can be very effective in promoting the sale of one brand of a product over another. As a means of encouraging retail sales personnel to favor the sale of their products, Reneé Farver management pays special bonuses to store employees. The amount of these payments varies with the volume of merchandise purchased. In some cases, payments of this type account for as much as one-third to one-half of the entire personal selling costs of the department.

As another device for increasing the amount of personal sales effort devoted to their products at the retail level, Reneé Farver also employs special demonstrators. These demonstrators work in selected retail stores throughout the country and are generally more effective sales people than regular store employees, because they are better trained and are able to concentrate all of their sales efforts on the Reneé Farver line of products.

This method is so effective that sales of Farver products frequently double or triple in outlets where demonstrators are used. There are about 250 of these demonstrators working in various areas throughout the country. Demonstrators are supplied only to those retail outlets which will reciprocate in such ways as carrying representative stocks, maintaining adequate counter displays and mentioning the product in fashion shows. Outlets which receive demonstrators account for about 40% of Farver's total sales volume and consist primarily of department and specialty stores.

QUESTIONS FOR DISCUSSION

1. Appraise the promotion program for Reneé Farver.
2. What relationship should in-store demonstration programs play relative to advertising in the promotion program for Farver?
3. Could Farver reduce its expenditures on advertising?

ENDNOTES

1. Company name is fictitious.

Case 9–4—The Oron Paper Company (A)

The Oron Paper Company manufactures paper napkins, toilet tissue, facial tissues and towels. These products are branded under the Oron label and sold to the consumer market. Sales for the paper towel part of their business are given below for six recent years:

1982	$5,750,100
1981	5,763,300
1980	5,581,200
1979	4,953,400
1978	4,651,000
1977	4,335,600.

Two elements in the sales trend for towels should be noted. In 1980, Oron introduced an improved version of the towel that made it stronger and more absorbent than the old towel. This was backed by an appropriation of about $300,000 in 1980. There have not been any significant changes in the towel product since that time.

In 1982, company management had to contend with a plant strike which lasted three weeks. In order to reduce expenses from this unanticipated event, the advertising manager was forced to reduce the usual 6% appropriation to about 5½% for 1982.

Because of the lag in 1982 sales, the advertising manager suggested a major push in 1983 to offset the decline in 1982. The advertising manager recommended an advertising appropriation of 9% of 1982 sales.

The abbreviated statement for 1982 is given below (paper towels only):

Sales	$5,750,100
c.g.s.	4,025,100
GM	1,725,000
Admin/Mktg	1,123,019
Adv	316,981
NP	$ 285,000.

QUESTIONS FOR DISCUSSION

1. Evaluate the advertising manager's recommendation for the 1983 appropriation using break-even analysis.
2. On what basis do you determine 1983 sales potential for Oron Paper?

Case 9-5—The Agen Company

In U.S. homes there is an annual consumption of frozen foods of 30 lbs. per capita. Regional consumption of this product, however, is subject to considerable variation and differs significantly from the national average.

The management of the *Agen Company*, a regional distributor of frozen foods, believed that these differences should be utilized in allocating advertising expenditures if the company is to promote in line with market potentials and opportunities.

Statistics are given below for three important Eastern markets in which the Agen Company was particularly interested and in which they planned to spend an advertising appropriation of $1,000,000.

In his zeal to maximize the effectiveness of his budget, the advertising manager began work on the table which you see below. Before he could complete his calculations, however, he suffered a heart attack.

Market	Population	Variation in Consumption of Frozen Food	Adjusted Area per Capita Consumption	Total Area Consumption	% of 3-Market Region	Recommended Share of Budget
New York	15,000,000	10%+				
Phila.	4,000,000	30%+				
Cleveland	2,000,000	20%+				

QUESTIONS FOR DISCUSSION

1. Assuming that you were promoted to the position of advertising manager of the Agen Company, complete the calculations which your predecessor was unable to finish.

Case 9-6—The Commonwealth Food Products Grocery Company

The executives of the Commonwealth Food and Grocery Company,[1] one of the country's largest food processors, were engaged in evaluating the promotion of individual products in the company's line.

For many years the company had followed a policy of product diversification, so that many products, while distributed through food stores, were not food products. One of these non-food products came under the scrutiny of the executives engaged in this evaluation of advertising and promotion programs. This product, which carried the brand name Zorina,[2] was an ironing aid product which had been on the market for many years. Zorina, when rubbed on the iron, acted as a facilitating agent in reducing friction and made the iron glide more easily. One or two other, virtually identical, branded products are also on the market.

Zorina is a relatively inexpensive product, selling in the 39-49¢ bracket. It is an unique product in that it had never had a budget for advertising. Over the years Zorina sales have been good, although during the past six to eight years sales have been declining. In spite of this decline in sales, also shared by the other brands, Zorina's rate of contribution to profits was considerably above the average of most of the other company products. The favorable profit picture was, of course, attributable principally to the fact that no advertising expenditures were charged to Zorina. Zorina produced a 30% gross margin for the company.

During the course of the review, one member of the group proposed that an advertising appropriation be allocated to Zorina in the amount of $1.25 million. He supported his suggestion by pointing out that few, if any, other of the company's products were expected to produce sales and profits without the benefit of advertising. It was his belief that, if adequate advertising support were given Zorina, there was a better than reasonably good opportunity for both sales and profits to be increased. The most reasonable estimate for next year's sales was agreed upon by Zorina executives to be $7,239,750. Other members of the evaluation group, however, were skeptical of the proposal.

Abbreviated Statement for Last Year

Sales	$6,895,000
c.g.s.	4,826,500
GM	2,068,500 (30%)
Admin/Mktg	750,000
Adv	1,000,000
NP	$ 318,500.

QUESTIONS FOR DISCUSSION

1. What policy would you recommend for Zorina? Support your recommendation adequately.

2. Given the level of gross margin for Zorina, what level of advertising activity might be supported by the brand (relatively speaking as a percentage of sales)?

3. Is the opportunity for advertising spending on Zorina an excellent one? Why or why not?

ENDNOTES

1. Fictitious name.
2. Fictitious name.

Case 9–7—The Atwood Company: Cyclical Variation in Advertising and Sales Promotion Expenditures

The Atwood Company, in 1981, adopted an advertising and sales promotion policy that was somewhat different from that usually followed by American business. This involved varying advertising and sales promotion efforts inversely with the business cycle instead of the more conventional approach of increasing these expenditures in periods of peak business activity and cutting back during periods of recession or depression.

The company used a diversified sales promotion program which included advertising to consumers and to dealers through trade papers; personal selling both to wholesalers and retailers; and some additional sales promotion activities. These included catalogues, direct-mail campaigns to dealers, publishing a house organ, preparation of window displays and other dealer helps, operating four retail stores in which new products and new sales promotion methods were tested, and providing instructors to work in other retail stores as demonstrators to show final purchasers the various uses for Atwood products.

The Atwood Company manufactured and sold a line of paper products and gift wrappings. It had three manufacturing divisions: gift boxes, paper novelties, and special holiday merchandise. Sales volume in 1981 amounted to $16,100,000. The company distributed about 50% of its products directly to chains and retailers and 50% through wholesalers. Company salesmen were paid a combined salary and bonus.

Prior to the inauguration of the counter-cyclical policy, company management had never given serious consideration to the budgeting of its sales promotion expense in relation to the business cycle. The sales promotion expenses had increased during periods of prosperity and decreased during periods of depression. In 1981, the company experienced a decline in sales and the board of directors expressed a wish that some of the appropriations spent in 1980 were available for sales promotion work in 1981. This situation induced the company to adopt the program of setting a tentative five-year budget for sales promotion work; the actual budget for the next calendar year was to be fixed during the latter part of the existing calendar year in accordance with the forecast of general business conditions and the probable production during the next calendar year. The amount to be expended on sales promotion work would increase when business conditions were poor and decrease in periods of general business prosperity.

The aim of this policy was to keep the company factory operating at or near capacity without selling beyond production limits in times of general business prosperity. In expediting this policy, the company increased both consumer and trade advertising and size of the salesforce during dull periods and decreased these efforts during periods of large sales volume when orders up to the capacity of the factory could be secured without intensive sales effort.

The Atwood Company considered it an economic waste to carry on intensive sales promotion activities during the periods of business prosperity when it had more orders than it could handle; during periods of business depression or recession, however, when added stimulus was needed to keep the plant manufacturing at capacity, the company did not hesitate to increase the amount spent in sales promotion work.

Since its heaviest sales came at the holiday season, national magazine and spot TV advertising were made to correspond to this. While the company did not consider a large amount of consumer advertising in magazines practical, it was of the opinion that a certain amount was necessary to help create consumer demand and to convince retailers that the company was helping them to sell its products.

At the time the company decided to follow a regular program of national advertising, the question was raised as to how closely the expenditures for advertising could be made to agree with the company's policy of varying sales promotion expenses inversely with the business cycle. It would not be possible to vary the national advertising step by step perfectly inversely to general business conditions, because national advertising in some media had to be contracted for several months in advance and because it was necessary to advertise to the final purchasers some months before an improvement occurred in general business.

The Atwood Company decided, therefore, to vary the expenditure for national advertising inversely with the business cycle as far as it could forecast cyclical changes and as far as its space contracts permitted space revision.

While the amount expended in trade-paper advertising was small, it was a sensitive index of the application of the company's budgeting policy; insertions could be varied within a month of the time a cyclical change appeared in general business conditions. Changes were not made for seasonal differences; these were provided for in the advertising schedule itself. The inverse relation maintained between sales effort and business conditions in the case of fluctuations of a cyclical nature did not apply in the case of seasonal variations in the company's own sales. The Atwood Company planned its advertising schedule a year in advance, and varied the trade, magazine, and spot TV advertising directly with the seasonal sales volume.

After several years of experience with the new program, company management recognized the desirability of utilizing all facets of the marketing program, instead of just sales promotion, in order to get maximum response from this policy. New products and new uses for Atwood products were introduced in periods of recession in order to increase sales. Occasionally prices were cut in order to spur lagging sales.

The company's advertising manager recommended that the policy could be furthered by setting aside, in years when profits were normal or above normal, a reserve fund for advertising during subsequent periods of less prosperity. It was the advertising manager's purpose to use this fund for increasing the company's advertising in years when business conditions were unpromising. At such times, it was represented, expenditure of the desired additional amount out of current income might not appear financially sound. As soon as business prosperity returned, the fund would be built up again.

While the appropriations for advertising and for sales promotion were fixed during the latter part of the year preceding that in which they were to be used, they were subject to revision during the year to which they applied, in so far as cyclical changes in business conditions made revision necessary.

QUESTIONS FOR DISCUSSION

1. Describe the cyclical variations in Atwood sales.
2. Do you agree with Atwood's spending policy? Why or why not?
3. Do you believe in the idea of a reserve fund set aside in years when company profits are normal or above normal? Could this money be put to work for the company and still be in reserve? How?

Case 9-8—The Anheuser-Busch Case: Advertising and Sales Results in the Brewing Industry

THE PROBLEM OF OPTIMUM SIZE OF ADVERTISING APPROPRIATION

For most companies in most industries in the United States, the problem of "How Much to Spend for Advertising" is a perennial and pervasive one. This is true for the brewing industry which is characterized by different approaches to the determination of size and by a lack of uniformity in size of the advertising appropriation. Estimates indicate that expenditures for advertising, both in total dollars spent and cost per barrel or case of beer, vary widely between companies in this industry.

To illustrate this, Table 9-1 below contains sales figures and advertising expenditures for 1977 for the ten largest companies in the brewing industry.[1] This table shows sales by companies; advertising expenditures for these companies in total, per barrel, and an industry ranking for advertising expenditures per unit—per barrel in this case.

Looking at the figures in Table 9-1, there is some correspondence between the total advertising expenditures and sales. For example, Anheuser-Busch was in first position both in sales and advertising expenditures. On the other hand, Adolph Coors shows the greatest discrepancy between the rank in sales and the rank in advertising expenditures: Coors was in fifth place in sales but in the ninth place in advertising expenditures. Also, this table indicates that per-barrel expenditures of advertising vary largely by company. The top three brewers, Anheuser-Busch, Miller Brewing Company, and Joseph Schlitz, spent relatively more for advertising: their per-barrel expenditures were \$1.60, \$1.78, and \$1.98, respectively. Another interesting observation is that The Carling Brewing Company spent \$2.18 per barrel, the highest rate on a per-barrel basis in the industry, while their sales ranked in 10th place. It might be of some interest to note that, among leading brewers, Carling has been spending for advertising much more than the industry average and Coors has been spending much less on a per-barrel basis over the years.

ADVERTISING/SALES RELATIONSHIPS FOR ANHEUSER-BUSCH, SCHLITZ AND MILLER

The total beer consumption in the United States increased, on the average, by 3 to 4% annually in the 1970s. However, as indicated in Figure 9-2 and Table 9-2, much of the growth in the industry sales has been taken up by the top three brewers, Anheuser-Busch, Miller, and Schlitz, who accounted for 56.5% of the industry sales of 175 million bbls. The growth of beer consumption has been attributed to the growing population in the legal drinking age, the rapid rise of the low-calorie beers, and a steady increase in disposable income. In addition, the increased advertising has been regarded to foster the sales of beer. This may be true at an aggregate industry level, but increased advertising is not always followed by increased sales of individual companies.

Table 9-3 and Figures 9-3 to 9-5 below give an overview of the relationships between advertising and sales for Anheuser-Busch, Schlitz and Miller for the thirty-year period, 1950-1979.

Anheuser-Busch and Schlitz were the giants of the U.S. brewing industry until Miller Brewing Company, which was acquired by Philip Morris in 1970, increased its sales in the mid 1970s. For the first half century, Schlitz led the brewing industry in sales. Schlitz lost its lead to Anheuser-Busch temporarily in 1953 when Schlitz production was reduced sharply as a result of a lengthy employee strike during the summer of that year. Schlitz regained the lead during the last half of 1954, retained a narrow advantage for several years, and lost it to

Table 9-1 Sales & Advertising Expenditures of Top Ten Brewers 1977

Company	Sales by Bbls.	Market Share	Adv. Expend.	Adv. Exp. per Bbl.	Rank in Sales	Rank in Adv. Exp.	Rank in Adv/Bbl.
Anheuser-Busch	36,600,000	23.3%	$58,687,200	$1.60	1	1	4
Miller	24,200,000	15.4	43,283,400	1.78	2	3	3
Jos. Schlitz	22,130,000	14.1	43,928,800	1.98	3	2	2
Pabst	16,003,000	10.4	10,969,789	.68	4	4	11
Adolph Coors	12,830,000	8.2	4,355,333	.33	5	9	12
Olympia	6,831,000	4.4	8,830,050	1.29	6	6	5
G. Heilman	6,245,000	4.0	4,736,473	.75	7	8	10
Stroh	6,114,000	3.9	7,310,516	1.19	8	7	6
F. M. Schafer	4,700,000	3.0	4,325,193	.92	9	10	9
Carling	4,350,000	2.8	9,524,792	2.18	10	5	1

SOURCE: *Advertising Age, October 9, 1978, p. 122. Standard and Poor's Industry Surveys, July 1979, Vol. 1, p. B68.*

Figure 9-2   Sales of Leading Brewers

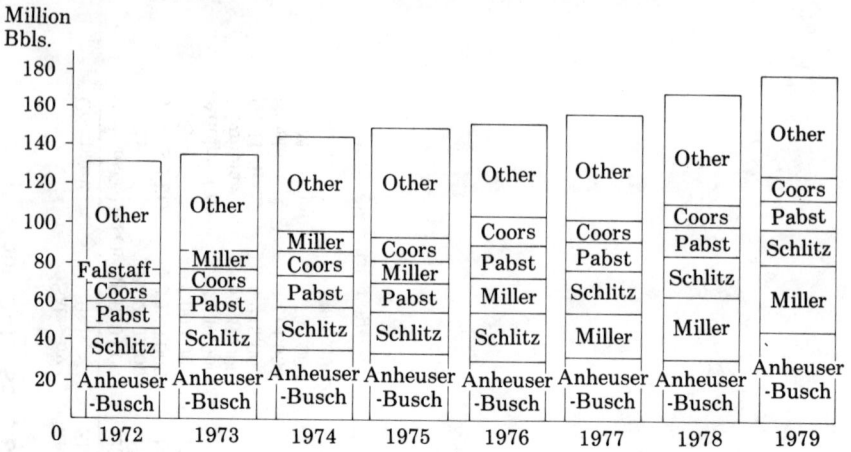

Million Bbls.

| | 1972 | 1973 | 1974 | 1975 | 1976 | 1977 | 1978 | 1979 |

Table 9-2   Market Shares of Anheuser-Busch, Schlitz and Miller

	1972	1973	1974	1975	1976	1977	1978	1979
Anheuser-Busch	20.1%	21.6	23.4	23.7	19.3	23.3	25.1	26.4
Schlitz	14.3%	15.4	15.6	15.7	16.1	14.1	11.8	9.6
Miller	4.1%	5.0	6.3	8.7	12.1	15.4	18.8	20.5

SOURCE: *Standard and Poor's Industry Surveys*, 1974-1980; *Advertising Age*, September 6, 1979, p. 24 and p. 147.

Anheuser-Busch in 1958. Anheuser-Busch has been in first place in sales since that time.

Figures 9–3 to 9–5 indicate that sales of beer do not always respond positively and quickly to changes in volume of advertising; these figures show that inverse relations are found in many of these periods.

As an example of this, Schlitz increased its advertising from $3,733,430 in 1953 to $7,319,025 in 1954—a dramatic increase of 96%. This resulted in a very modest 2.8% increase in Schlitz sales, from 5,255,000 bbls. to 5,406,000 bbls. During the period 1955-1959, Schlitz increased advertising sharply for two years and then cut back to the original level during the next two years. Sales, however, did not follow these variations in advertising effort; they continued on an almost even level during the entire four-year period. In 1959 Schlitz again began an expansion in advertising spending beginning with a budget of $7,461,000 and reaching a high in 1964 of $18,311,319. This increase seemed almost certainly to have been triggered by the fact that Anheuser-Busch took over first place in sales of beer in the U.S. during this period.[2] Even though Schlitz made what might be considered an all-out effort through advertising to regain first place, they did not

Table 9-3

Year	ANHEUSER-BUSCH Expenditure (Advertising)	ANHEUSER-BUSCH Sales (Bbls.)	JOSEPH SCHLITZ Expenditure (Advertising)	JOSEPH SCHLITZ Sales (Bbls.)	MILLER Expenditure (Advertising)	MILLER Sales (Bbls.)
1950	$ 1,486,292	4,889,000	$ 1,749,321	5,097,000	$ 665,841	2,105,000
1951	1,887,227	5,479,000	2,347,578	5,716,000	1,035,675	2,612,000
1952	1,681,096	6,034,000	2,341,768	6,347,000	1,227,687	3,043,000
1953	3,041,609	6,711,000	3,733,430	5,255,000	1,327,696	2,138,000
1954	6,820,379	5,829,000	7,319,025	5,406,000	3,430,691	2,096,000
1955	5,493,665	5,617,000	7,450,861	5,780,000	1,683,523	2,191,000
1956	6,816,889	5,864,000	8,605,134	5,941,000	3,683,764	2,246,000
1957	9,438,976	5,864,000	10,682,254	6,024,000	3,200,547	2,221,000
1958	10,263,530	6,982,000	7,741,692	5,893,000	3,219,304	2,220,000
1959	11,197,036	8,065,000	7,461,781	5,863,000	3,114,585	2,359,000
1960	11,856,556	8,480,000	10,070,397	5,640,000	3,794,492	2,376,000
1961	12,492,371	8,507,000	12,710,220	5,764,000	2,382,590	2,700,000
1962	13,165,812	9,015,000	14,223,960	6,880,000	2,737,365	2,805,000
1963	15,883,188	9,397,000	16,159,959	7,834,000	3,170,761	2,917,000
1964	16,608,927	10,379,000	18,311,319	8,266,000	5,512,112	3,284,000
1965	16,365,540	11,800,000	15,577,474	8,607,000	5,848,395	3,667,000
1966	13,366,805	13,699,000	17,162,777	9,450,000	7,563,715	4,150,000
1967	16,980,767	15,500,000	16,311,026	10,200,000	8,829,471	4,575,000
1968	14,609,872	18,400,000	17,566,628	11,602,000	8,901,219	4,850,000
1969	16,057,638	18,700,000	16,423,556	13,700,000	9,483,172	5,190,000
1970	18,686,798	22,202,000	16,703,792	15,129,000	10,927,735	5,150,000
1971	23,715,800	24,309,000	17,165,900	16,708,000	13,468,300	5,200,000
1972	25,025,606	26,522,000	20,699,446	18,906,000	11,014,600	6,353,000
1973	20,522,602	29,887,000	19,722,864	21,343,000	10,914,623	6,919,000
1974	17,839,935	34,100,000	20,910,940	22,661,000	13,556,133	9,066,000
1975	27,354,000	35,200,000	26,530,000	23,279,000	21,252,000	12,862,000
1976	28,535,300	29,060,000	34,131,400	24,162,000	29,114,700	18,403,000
1977	58,687,200	36,600,000	43,928,800	22,130,000	43,283,400	24,200,000
1978	79,786,500	41,600,000	44,743,100	19,580,000	64,036,300	31,274,000
1979	112,768,700	46,200,000	54,110,100	16,804,000	75,003,000	35,774,225

SOURCE: *Advertising Age*, February 3, 1958, p. 52; October 9, 1961; September 9, 1968, p. 106; September 20, 1970, p. 31; October 30, 1972, p. 145; September 23, 1974, p. 41; October 9, 1978, p. 122; September 6, 1979; September 11, 1980.

NOTES: Advertising expenditures for 1971 do not include newspaper advertising. Advertising expenditures by Miller in 1978 and 1979 were compiled from figures supplied by *Leading National Advertisers*.

achieve this goal as Anheuser-Busch remained in first place and increased their lead during the next decade. In 1965 Schlitz cut back their advertising expenditures to $15,577,474—a reduction of almost 15%. The increase in Schlitz sales, however, which had begun in 1960, continued with an increase of 843,000 bbls.—almost 10%—between 1965 and 1966. Part of the cut in advertising was restored in 1966—$17,162,777—and was continued at about the same level until 1972-1973 when it was increased to about $21,000,000. Schlitz sales (see Figure 9-4 again) have continued to increase at a very substantial rate each year, reaching an all-time high of 24,162,000 bbls. in 1976. After this year, however, Schlitz sales started declining sharply, and they decreased to 16,804,000 bbls. in 1979—approximately a 30% reduction from 1976. During this period, Schlitz's market share declined from 16.1% to 9.6%. On the contrary, Schlitz's advertising expenditures have been continuously increased in these years. As Figure 9-4 shows, their advertising expenditures have been almost linearly increasing up to $54,110,000 in 1979. Yet, no positive responses in sales have been observed by 1979.

In 1976 Anheuser-Busch met a 95-day employee strike. In this year Schlitz increased its sales by 883,000 bbls. and Miller gained as much as 5,541,000 bbls., while Anheuser-Busch lost more than 7 million bbls. Miller's dramatic expansion was seen around this time period. As Figure 9-5 indicates from the 1950s through 1963, Miller's sales curve was almost flat, staying at under 3 million bbls. Miller's advertising expenditures in these years fluctuated between $665,841 and $3,794,492. From 1963 to 1964, Miller increased advertising 74%, from $3,170,761 to $5,512,112. In this period sales increased by 13%, from 3,667,000 bbls. to 4,150,000 bbls., with a 29% increase in advertising. However, sales increased only by 1% in 1971, when advertising was increased from $10,927,735 to $13,468,300, a 23% increase. As Figure 9-5 clearly shows, Miller's sales started to show a more positive and quick response to the increase in advertising after 1974. Advertising and sales curves appear to be almost parallel in the mid 1970s. For example, advertising was increased by 57% in 1975 and sales followed it with an increase of 42% in that year. Miller gained the third position with 12.1% of market share in 1976, and it has been in second place since 1977, outselling Schlitz and gradually approaching Anheuser-Busch.

The lack of positive response of sales to force of advertising seems to be true, to some extent, in the Anheuser-Busch experience. In 1953, for example, Anheuser-Busch advertising expenditures were $3,041,609. During 1954 they were increased to $6,820,379—an increase of 124%. Anheuser-Busch sales, however, decreased from 6,711,000 bbls. in 1953 to 5,829,000 in 1954 and dropped further in 1955 to 5,617,000 bbls. In 1955 Anheuser-Busch began a steady ten-year expansion in size of advertising effort, reaching a high of $16,608,927 in 1964 and then decreasing slightly to $16,365,540 in 1965. In the years 1966, 1967, and 1969, Anheuser-Busch varied their advertising appropriation, cutting back to $13,366,805 in 1966, increasing to $16,980,767 in

1967, cutting to $14,609,872 in 1968.[3] In 1969, they began an upward trend in spending which has continued up to the present, except for a cutback in 1974. Anheuser-Busch sales (see Figure 9-3) seemed not to be directly affected by these variations. Sales continued on an upward climb, reaching an all-time high in 1975 of 35,200,000 bbls. Their sales were seriously affected by the employees' strike in 1976. However, sales recovered promptly in the following year, from 29,888,000 bbls. to 34,100,000 bbls. Advertising expenditures have also been increased in large scale since 1977. From 1976 to 1977, advertising was increased by 106%, and it has reached $112,768,700 in 1979.

THE ANHEUSER-BUSCH APPROACH TO THE PROBLEM

During the period 1962-1964, Anheuser-Busch conducted two major experiments on advertising expenditures. Budweiser was selected as a test brand for these experiments. The management was especially concerned with the effects of advertising upon sales. Management wanted to know if they were spending too much for advertising, too little, or the right amount. Because of the effects on company sales and profits, these are vitally important questions. Over-spending directly reduces company profits; under-spending may act directly to reduce sales and profits. The Anheuser-Busch people decided to study the problem in considerable depth through a program of marketing testing and experimentation, working with their advertising agency, the D'Arcy Advertising Company.

THE FIRST EXPERIMENT: 1962

The researchers responsible for this experiment developed the following hypotheses about the relationship between advertising and sales.[4]

1. There is a "threshold" in the response: a small amount of advertising has almost no effect upon sales, but as the amount is increased, it produces an increasing effect upon sales.
2. Then, sales continue to respond to the increase in advertising at a decreasing rate until the effect of advertising reaches the "saturation" point, that is, no further increase in sales.
3. Response to further increase in advertising remains relatively unchanged until sales reach "supersaturation," a point beyond which sales respond negatively to advertising, that is, sales decrease with the increase in advertising.

Three levels of advertising and marketing factors—(1) sales effort (salesmen), (2) amount spent for point-of-sales, and (3) advertising expenditures—were tested in the following manner.

Treatment	#1	#2	#3
Sales Effort	decrease	no change	increase
Point-of-Sales	decrease	no change	increase
Advertising Dollars	-25%	no change	$+50\%$

Each test market was assigned to one of the three levels of each treatment. For example, some markets were assigned to the combination of "decrease" in sales effort, "no change" in point-of-sales, and "50% increase" in advertising expenditures. Monthly sales in each test market were measured for 12 months during 1962.

Results of this experiment showed that different levels of sales effort and point-of-sales had no differentiating effects. Also, contrary to the expectation, a 25% reduction of advertising generated a 14% increase in sales, whereas a 50% increase in advertising produced only a 7% increase in sales and a 0% change in advertising (same amount of expenditures as before the experiment) caused no change in sales. The results are shown below.

Change in Advertising	Average Percent Change in Sales
-25%	$+14\%$
no change	0
$+50\%$	$+7\%$

THE SECOND EXPERIMENT: 1963-1964

In order to account for the unexpected results of the above experiment, the researchers proposed a modified hypothesis that different segments of consumers had different response patterns: they assumed that heavy users were more sensitive to advertising than moderate and light beer drinkers; so, when these segments' response functions are combined into an aggregate function, there would be three peaks, which represent the peak of each segment's response function.

Anheuser-Busch has divided the United States market for beer into 200 geographical areas. The second experiment called for different levels of spending in seven groups of markets with several market areas in each group. One group was utilized as a control group, six groups as test markets, with under-spending in two groups and over-spending in the other four. In the control areas, a so-called "normal" level of spending was continued. This was the rate at which the company had been spending prior to the experiment. The seven levels of spending were: -100% of normal, -50% of normal, control-normal, $+50\%$ of normal, $+100\%$ of normal, $+150\%$ of normal and $+200\%$ of normal.

Tests were continued for two years and monthly sales were measured for 6 months in 1963 and for another 6 months in 1964. The sales results are summarized below.

Group #	Change in Advertising	Average Percent Change in Sales
1	−100%	0%
2	− 50	+15
3	control	0
4	+ 50	+ 7
5	+100	+ 6
6	+150	+ 3
7	+200	−13

There were two major findings from this experiment. First, only two peaks, not three, were observed; one at the +50% level and the other at the −50% level of spending. Secondly, complete elimination of advertising (Group 1) did not decrease sales; sales stayed the same.

Since the management was interested in the second result, that is, no negative effect of the complete elimination of advertising upon sales, they conducted further tests on the eliminations of advertising in order to find out the deterioration rate of advertising. Advertising expenditures were cut by 15% in the 25 smallest markets, then the reduction rate was increased to −25% in 50 markets. The total sales of Budweiser increased from 7.5 million bbls. to 14.5 million bbls., with its market shares from 8.1% to 12.9% over the period 1962-1968. But, a small decline in sales was observed about one and a half years later in the test markets where advertising expenditures were reduced. Sales in these markets were restored to normal growth rate when advertising was restored to normal rate.

AN OVERVIEW OF ADVERTISING/SALES RELATIONSHIP

Figures 9-3 to 9-5 show a relatively long time period of trends in volume of advertising and volume of sales of beer. Historical advertising and sales data were taken each year over 30 years. In the Anheuser-Busch experiments, sales were observed in relatively short periods, one to two years. And, in these experiments, positive relationship between size of advertising expenditures and sales was not observed.

QUESTIONS FOR DISCUSSION

1. Using the time-series data given in Table 9-3, draw sales response functions for Anheuser-Busch, Schlitz, and Miller for the period 1950-1979. Define "advertising" and "sales" in your response functions: You might consider total advertising dollars, advertising dollars per barrel, or advertising dollars per capita in the total U.S. population or in the target market, for example. Plot each year's observation, with advertising on the X-axis and sales on the Y-axis. Also, draw sales response functions for Bud-

Figure 9-3

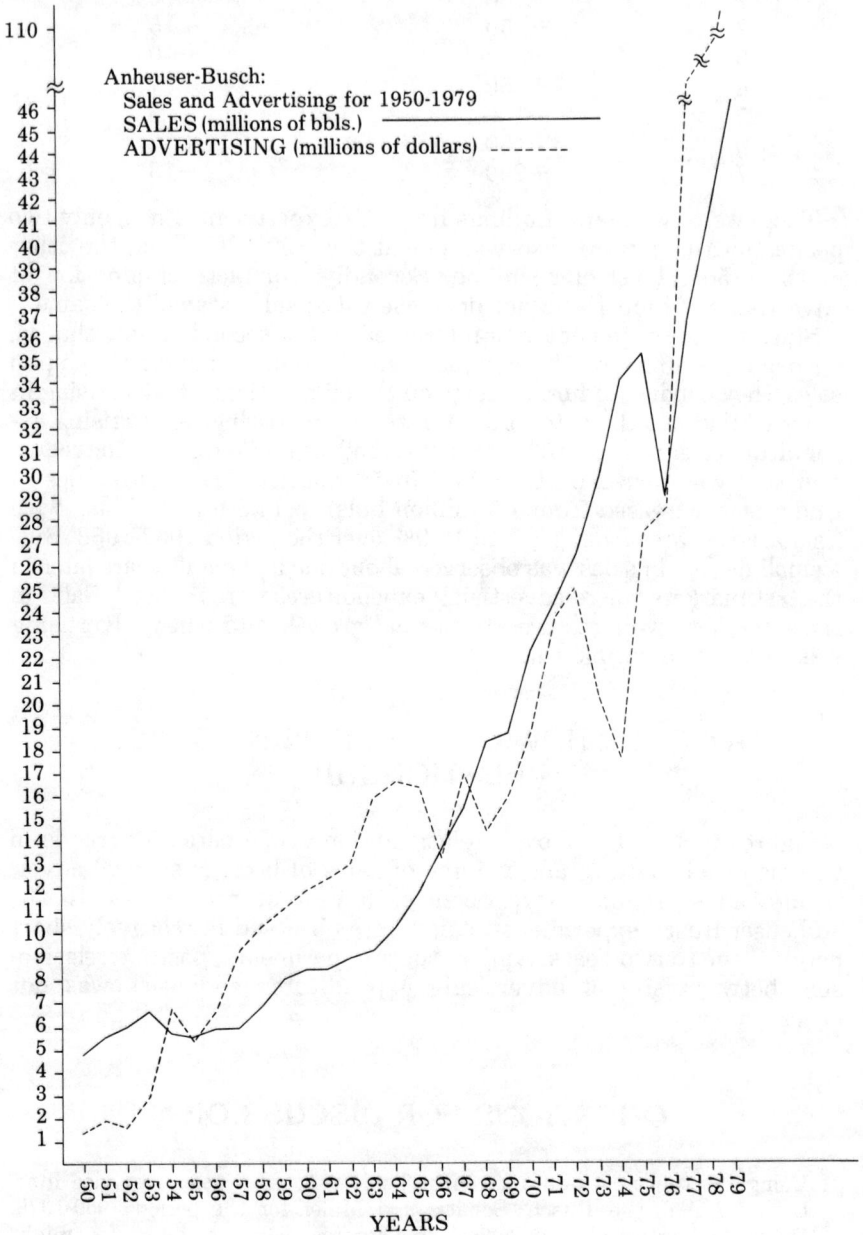

Anheuser-Busch:
Sales and Advertising for 1950-1979
SALES (millions of bbls.) ————
ADVERTISING (millions of dollars) - - - - - -

YEARS

Figure 9-4

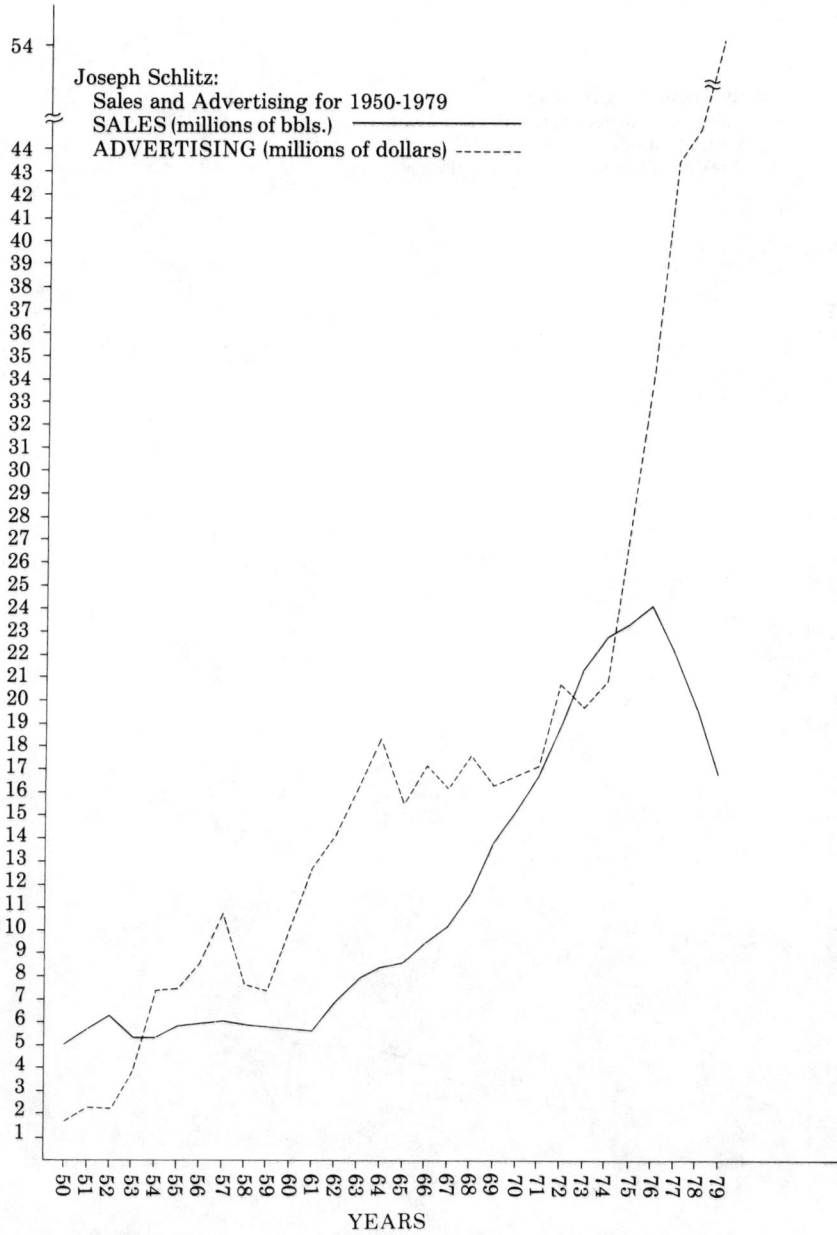

Joseph Schlitz:
Sales and Advertising for 1950-1979
SALES (millions of bbls.) ——————
ADVERTISING (millions of dollars) -------

YEARS

Figure 9-5

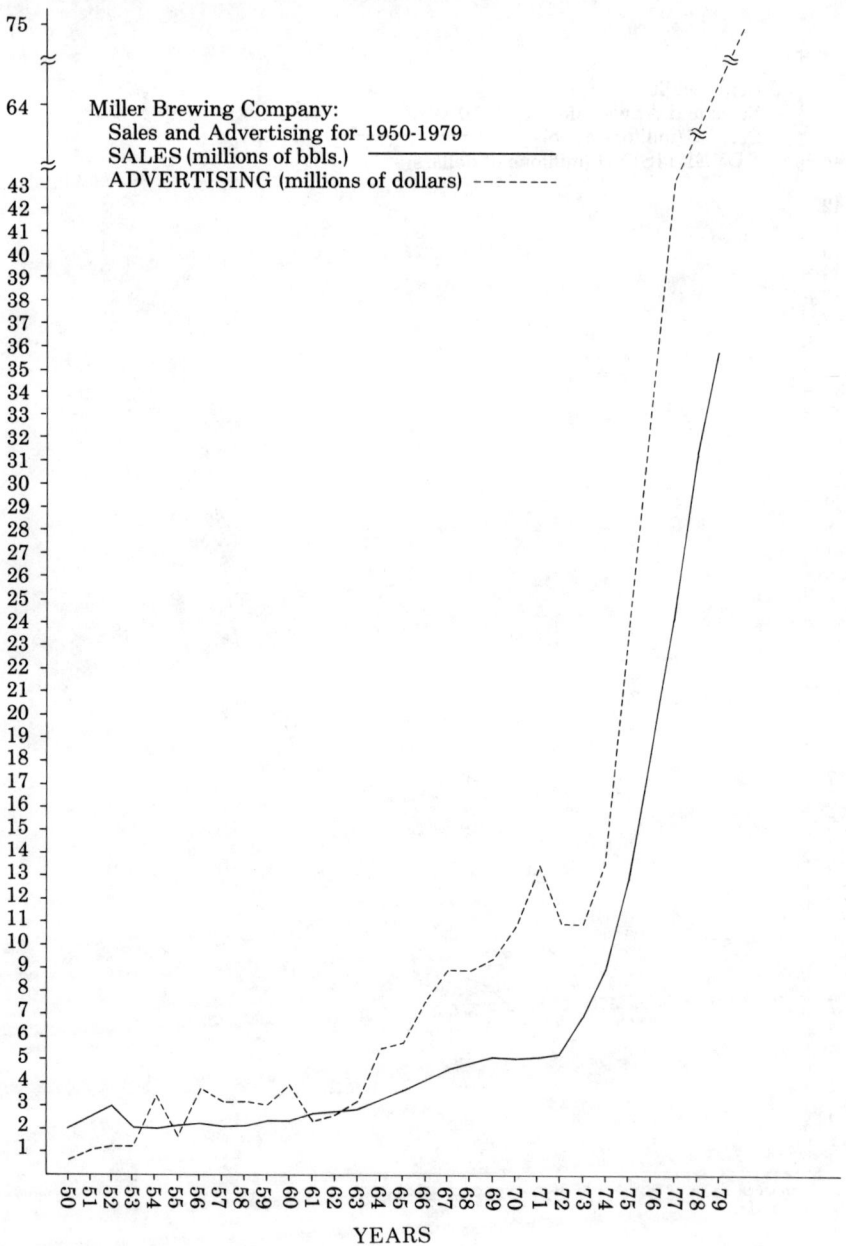

Miller Brewing Company:
Sales and Advertising for 1950-1979
SALES (millions of bbls.) ——————
ADVERTISING (millions of dollars) ‒‒‒‒‒‒‒

YEARS

weiser using the results of the experiments for the years 1962 and 1963-64. Use the percent changes in advertising and sales given in the summary tables.

2. Interpret the sales response functions you have drawn considering what kind of "shapes" are found for each company and Budweiser: are they linear, concave-downward, or S-shaped? Considering the different nature of time-series data and experimental data in terms of the time periods of observation and control of other factors (for example, in the 1962 experiment, the levels of sales effort and point-of-sales were determined by the experimenter), what are the implications of these functions for the relationship between advertising and sales?

3. Suppose you are the advertising manager of Anheuser-Busch, Schlitz, or Miller. Do you think you should spend more, less, or the same for advertising in 1980? Why?

ENDNOTES

1. Sales by barrels were originally taken from *Beer Wholesalers' News,* the monthly bulletin of the National Beer Wholesalers' Association of America, copyright 1978. Advertising expenditures were compiled from figures supplied by *Leading National Advertisers* and *Advertising Age* estimates. These figures include estimates of expenditures in measured media—general magazines, spot radio, network and spot television, newspapers and outdoor. The ranking of advertising expenditures were obtained among the 14 breweries with annual sales of one million or more barrels. In addition to these expenditures, many of these companies are spending sizable amounts on point-of-purchase materials, promotions, sporting events, local advertising, etc. For Anheuser-Busch these expenditures for 1977 have been estimated at $20,483,800 (*Advertising Age,* September 6, 1979, p. 28.).

2. Schlitz, seemingly, did not consider their temporary loss of first place in 1953 of great significance. Schlitz production was reduced sharply that year by a lengthy employee strike, and Schlitz was unable to meet consumer demand for their product.

3. The Anheuser-Busch experiments on advertising expenditures are described in some detail below.

4. For the description of the Anheuser-Busch experiments, see Ackoff, Russell and Emshoff, James, "Advertising Research at Anheuser-Busch, Inc. (1963-68)," *Sloan Management Review,* Winter 1975, pp. 1-15; Rao, Ambar, *Quantitative Theories in Advertising,* New York, John Wiley & Sons, 1970.

10

ADVERTISING CREATIVE STRATEGY

- The Concept of Creative Strategy in Advertising
- The Marketing Mix and Creative Strategy
- Distinguishing Creative Strategy and Tactics
- Communication Objectives
- Communication Approaches
- Market Data and Creative Strategy

Decision Making Organization of This Text

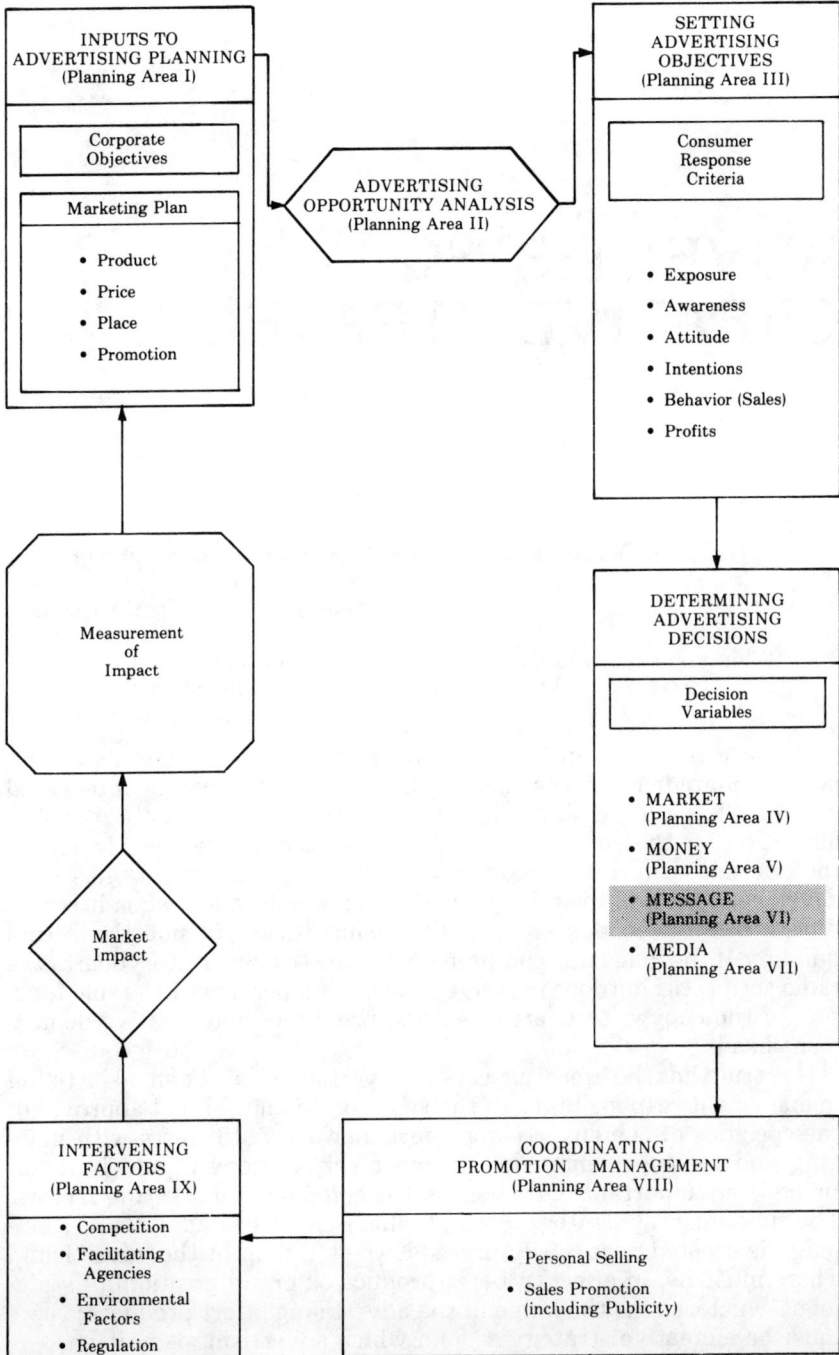

INPUTS TO
ADVERTISING PLANNING
(Planning Area I)

Corporate
Objectives

Marketing Plan

- Product
- Price
- Place
- Promotion

ADVERTISING
OPPORTUNITY ANALYSIS
(Planning Area II)

SETTING
ADVERTISING
OBJECTIVES
(Planning Area III)

Consumer
Response
Criteria

- Exposure
- Awareness
- Attitude
- Intentions
- Behavior (Sales)
- Profits

Measurement
of
Impact

DETERMINING
ADVERTISING
DECISIONS

Decision
Variables

- MARKET
  (Planning Area IV)
- MONEY
  (Planning Area V)
- MESSAGE
  (Planning Area VI)
- MEDIA
  (Planning Area VII)

Market
Impact

INTERVENING
FACTORS
(Planning Area IX)

- Competition
- Facilitating
  Agencies
- Environmental
  Factors
- Regulation

COORDINATING
PROMOTION   MANAGEMENT
(Planning Area VIII)

- Personal Selling
- Sales Promotion
  (including Publicity)

ADVERTISING CREATIVE STRATEGY

"It is more important to do the right thing than to do things right."
—Peter Drucker
Analyst of Corporate Structure

"What you say is more important than how you say it."
—David Ogilvy
Advertising Practitioner

Suppose the decision has been made to use advertising as an important ingredient in the marketing mix; the concept of integrated planning has been embraced and understood; the estimate of dollar allocation for the advertising budget has been determined. In effect, the critical backdrop preceding the creation of advertising has been developed. What is the role of advertising management when it comes to the basic decisions of the advertising itself? Is not the actual building of the magazine comprehensive, the television storyboard, the radio script, the outdoor poster, or the newspaper layout the sole function of the copywriters, art directors, producers and creative department heads?

It is true that the literal aspects of advertising are not an advertising management responsibility in the sense of "doing." Final approval of the specifics of the advertising effort, however, still rests with planning and management people in most corporations in which advertising is an important ingredient in the complex of marketing factors. The fundamental strategy around which any basic advertising campaign is created necessarily precedes the building of the advertising. There must be, in effect, a basic product or brand positioning statement which acts as the hinge of the advertising effort produced; there must be a creative strategy around which advertising is written.

THE CONCEPT OF CREATIVE STRATEGY IN ADVERTISING

Creative strategy indicates *what* advertising will say but does not specify *how* it will be said. According to Weilbacher, there are two distinct aspects of advertising copy strategy formulations:[1]

(1) An advertising copy strategy states, in general terms, what information the advertising will convey and why this product can make these assertions of benefit to the consumer.

(2) An advertising copy strategy specifies the information to be conveyed but not the form in which it will be conveyed. A sound advertising copy strategy should lead to numerous acceptable advertising executions.

Weilbacher, an advertising practitioner for many years, clearly recognizes the utility of defining creative strategies in distinction to executional factors.

Advertising creative strategy can be conceived most satisfactorily in specific terms as the building of the *purchase proposition*. This involves a study of the uses and want-satisfying qualities of the product and selecting the specific use, or uses, which seem to offer the best opportunities for promotion, and then guiding the advertising effort in this direction. The establishment of this purchase proposition should flow naturally from a marketing posture, and management people as well as the creators of advertising should be involved.

Several successful advertising practitioners have commented on the value of selecting and concentrating on a single purchase proposition. Rosser Reeves, at one time the head of the creative function at the Ted Bates agency, defined this process as "the unique selling proposition:"[2]

> Each advertisement must make a proposition to the consumer, not just words, not just product puffery, not just show window advertising. The proposition must be one that the competitor either cannot, or does not, offer. It must be unique—either a uniqueness of the brand or a claim not otherwise made in that particular field of advertising . . .

Leo Burnett, founder of the famous Chicago advertising agency after his name, has said the following:[3]

> My technique, if I have one, is to saturate myself with knowledge about the product. I believe in good depth interviewing where I come realistically face to face with the people I am trying to sell. I try to get a picture in my mind of the people they are—how they use the product, and what it is—they don't often tell you in so many words—but what it is that actually motivates them to buy something or to interest them in something.

And William Bernbach, the noted copywriter and co-founder of the Doyle Dane Bernbach advertising agency, says:[4]

> You've got to get saturated with it. You must get to the heart of it. Indeed, if you have not crystallized into a single purpose, a single theme what you want to tell the reader, you cannot be creative.

And David Ogilvy, creator of such advertising legends as the Hathaway Shirt "eye-patch man" and co-founder of the Ogilvy & Mather agency, listed as commandment number two among his eleven advertising creative commandments:[5]

> "Unless your campaign is built around a great idea, it will flop."

THE MARKETING MIX AND CREATIVE STRATEGY

The mix of marketing decision variables provides the backdrop against which the creative strategy is developed. The decisions which are made about positioning, product, packaging, pricing, and other promotion in addition to advertising will have a great impact on the nature of the creative strategy.

POSITIONING

Just how a product is positioned in the competitive market can have a tremendous influence on the creative posture assumed by the advertiser. For example, the "do-it-yourself" carpet cleaning business has traditionally been dominated by the liquid carpet cleaners such as Bissell Rug Cleaner and liquid cleaners sold in conjunction with rental cleaning equipment. Airwick Industries then introduced a new product called Plush to this market which quickly pre-empted an important share of the market. This product is called a "dry cleaner and conditioner" and provided the basis for the creative strategy: "Steam clean without wetness or waiting." If a competing company brings out another dry cleaner-type carpet cleaner which it wishes to use to extend its representation in the carpet cleaner market, this company can position the cleaner in one of two basic ways:

(1) Either compete *generically* with all kinds of carpet cleaners and feature the more general fact that it, too, has a dry cleaner entry and, in effect, act to compound Plush's influence by shifting more people away from other types of cleaners to dry cleaners.

(2) Or, it can attempt to feature some reason why its particular dry cleaner is better than Plush, thus concentrating its creative advertising power against Plush specifically.

The fact is that the competitive position assumed will critically influence advertising strategy and hence, advertising tactics. The decision on what competitive position to take is an important advertising management decision.

As an additional example of the impact of competitive positioning on creative strategy, suppose a company wishes to market a high-quality frozen doughnut. This doughnut has a slight premium price and an unusually crisp taste. It is made with whole wheat flour and an unusual group of spices and possesses a "nutty" overtone. It has been sold through a leading inexpensive restaurant chain for years, to be eaten, of course, at the point of purchase. Available data on the doughnut market indicate that a sizable minority of the population consumes doughnuts of any kind on a regular basis. Furthermore, while doughnuts are eaten at all meals, there is somewhat disproportionate consumption for breakfast and in-between snack times.

A basic question of creative strategy to be answered is will the new frozen doughnut take a competitive position as just another doughnut, competing with all other doughnuts presently being sold, or as a general "sweet good" designed to cater to all elements of the market on the assumption that its inherent differences are such that it can broaden the doughnut consumption pattern? The manufacturer says it is a doughnut only because it is shaped like one. In terms of other marketing variables, it is unlike similarly shaped products in many more ways than it is like them.

PRODUCT

It is widely recognized in the advertising business that one of the basic jobs of the copywriter is to determine which product value can be featured most effectively from both consumer and laboratory product research.

In this situation, it should be clear that production people and management people who understand their products can make an important contribution to creative strategy. Any potential creative posture assumed can frequently be importantly modified when additional product values are developed, and when these values either have been or can be built into recognizable assets from the consumer point of view. For example, putting lemon and/or borax into such products as laundry detergents and toilet bowl cleaners was a common practice and has had a tremendous impact on the creative orientation for such products.

Another example of the role product values play in the development of creative strategy is illustrated by Comet cleanser, a Procter & Gamble brand. The introduction of chlorinated bleach through the Comet brand not only had an effect on the creative strategy for this brand, but actually forced a change, as a consequence of market-share inroads made by Comet, in the creative strategy of Ajax, the leading competitor. Before the introduction of Comet, Ajax had to a great extent built its position as a market leader on the basis of the fact that it was the first cleanser on the market that had visible foaming action, which provided the product-value basis around which the creative story could be built.

PACKAGING

There is an old saying in advertising that the purpose of the container is to carry the product. And while it should have all the assets inherent in good packaging, it should not be the feature of the advertising story at the expense of the product itself.

In many instances in a competitive economy, however, one manufacturer, particularly in the packaged goods industry, cannot hope to build and retain a satisfactory share of market on a product's formulation alone. While product differentiation is the principal basis for building brand control of markets, these product qualities may be duplicated by competitors rather easily and quickly, unless the innovator is protected by patents. A considerable amount of manufacturing ingenuity is expended in imitating product qualities for which consumer preference has been demonstrated in the market. This duplication, at a lower price, has formed much of the basis of keen competition between manufacturer brands and distributor brands. This has tended to direct competitive activities through all available avenues, so that packaging developments in recent years have assumed significantly greater importance in the marketing scheme and, hence, in the advertising framework. It might be noted that a recent use of packaging has been to justify a price reduction and to provide the basis for the advertising of so-called "generic" food items in many grocery chain stores.

An excellent example of the use of packaging as the foundation for the creative strategy development is the Clorox entry in the room deodorant or freshener market. Their product, Twice as Fresh, was packaged in such a way that it can be left open for continuous freshening, as in the case of solids, or it can be closed and opened only when the power of a spray is required. This is accomplished by opening the product package all the way and waving it through the air in much the same manner as a spray would be used. Though the product is essentially similar to a solid, the packaging device used made it possible to differentiate the product from other room fresheners. The copy strategy developed on this packaging basis was: "Better than a solid, more than a spray."

Another example of the impact of packaging on creative strategy is provided by Ty-D-Bol toilet bowl cleaner by the Knomark company. Though this product initially contained the same ingredients as liquid and crystal bowl cleaners, the package made it unique. It was placed in a package which, when inserted in the tank of the toilet, automatically released cleaning agents on flushing. This package improvement provided the basis for creative strategy. Later, when other companies entered with competing package designs, Knomark turned to the product itself and differentiated it further by adding lemon and borax; these additions then served as the copy platform or strategy.

The use of packaging in the strategy and concept formation for nonpackaged goods products can be seen in the campaign developed for Sheaffer Eaton. Figure 10-1 shows the use of different pen styles around which the copy strategy is built. The package, rather than the writing characteristics of the pen itself, serves as the focus of the creative strategy in this example. While this is not, in technical parlance, a package innovation, it may be considered the facsimile for what packaging is in the packaged-goods industry.

In assessing the potential influence of packaging on advertising creative strategy, the *uniqueness* and *dramatic aspects* of the packaging and the field in which the strategy is to be applied are vital influ-

Figure 10-1   Sheaffer Eaton "Eight Chances"
Advertisement

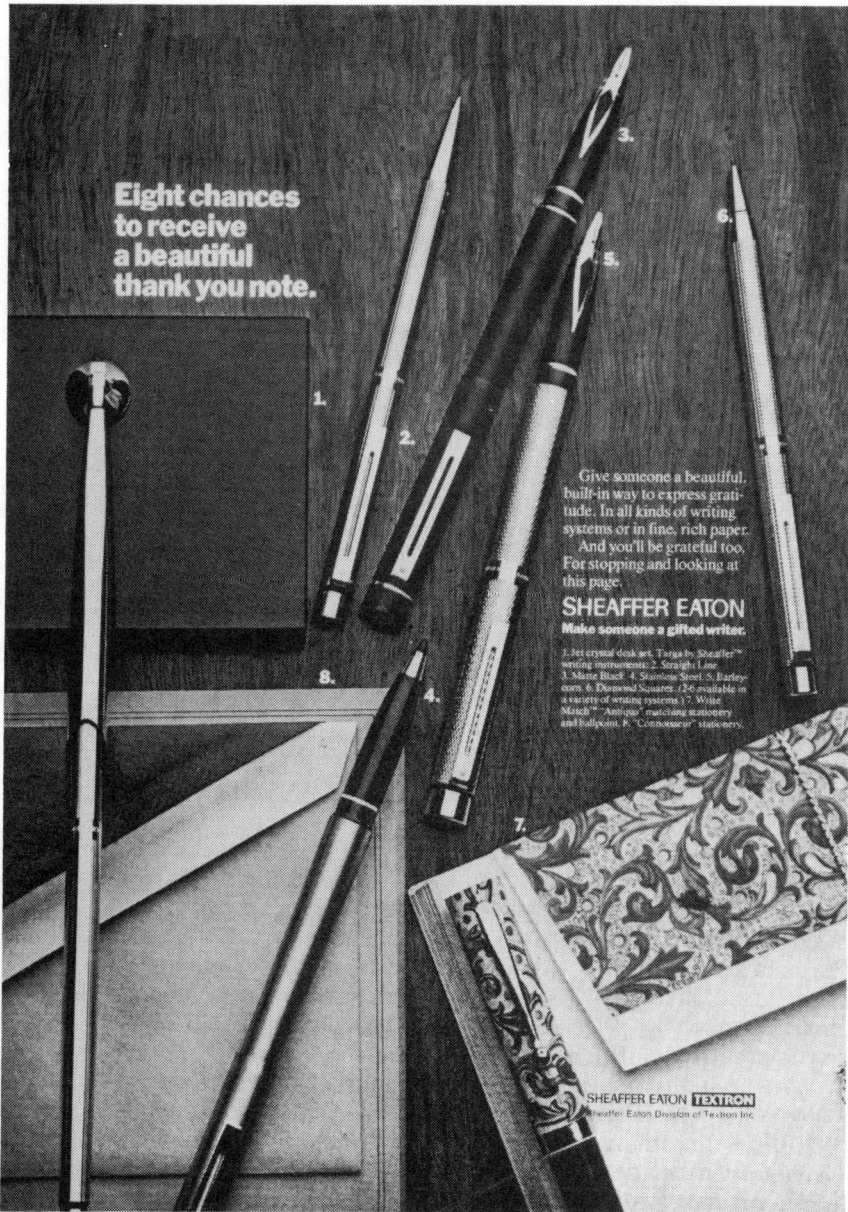

ences with respect to whether or not the featuring of packaging assets is a wise stance to adopt.

PRICING

In many categories of packaged-goods products, price differential between competing brands is not significant and, therefore, may have little to do with creative strategy. However, for advertisers who follow a market segmentation strategy, price competition may be an important method of reaching specific target markets. It has been recognized by small manufacturers who have wished to carve out a market of significant size for themselves in a given area. Since brand representation in many primary markets is so large and variegated, the possible importance of price competition is also recognized by larger manufacturers with multiple-brand operations, such as Procter & Gamble. Corporate growth for such companies probably will come from the introduction of new products into markets which have historically been regarded as secondary in importance.

One of the general types of markets which such manufacturers might pursue is the so-called "quality" market. Examples of such markets can be seen in many businesses such as gourmet foods, watches, writing instruments, and even automobiles. These markets normally carry premium-priced merchandise. In a number of instances, a premium price in and of itself not only influences advertising budget availability and media selection, but also can influence the creative strategy. Figure 10-2 shows another advertisement by Sheaffer Eaton, a division of Textron, which emphasizes price in the creative strategy and execution. This advertising has, in effect, utilized the price as a prima-facie indication of overall superior quality and acceptance.

The reverse of this situation also exists; that is, where a lower-priced item attempts to carve out its own segment at the opposite end of the price scale. An example of this is easily observed in the strategy followed by the Purex Corporation in the advertising for their dry laundry bleach, Purex. The creative strategy involves a comparison of the price of Purex relative to Clorox II and Snowy dry bleaches since Purex is significantly lower in price than are these competitive brands. Figure 10-3 also shows the strategy pursued for No Nonsense Panty Hose. Clearly, low price relative to other types of clothing items serves as the creative platform or strategy for this brand.

There are many instances where the market fact of price positioning must be inspected carefully by management in considering market opportunities and market potential. It is a very important management decision whether or not this fact of marketing life should be used by the advertising practitioner as a specific and important aspect in campaign planning. The possible benefits of demand elasticity on sales volume enter the picture here. A premium-priced brand which has been held on a relatively stable sales plateau for some time may experience a considerable increase in sales if the price is lowered to permit competi-

Figure 10-2 Sheaffer Eaton "Targa" Advertisement

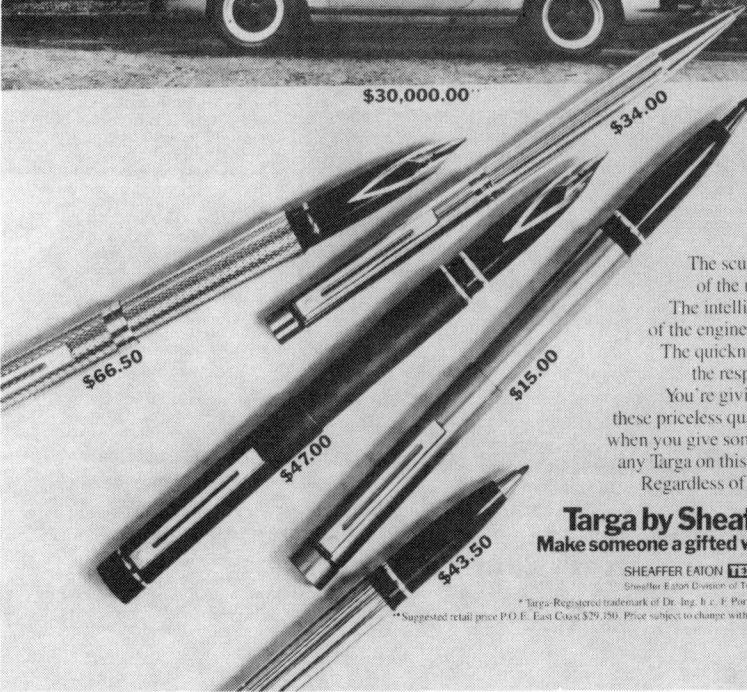

Figure 10-3 No Nonsense Advertisement

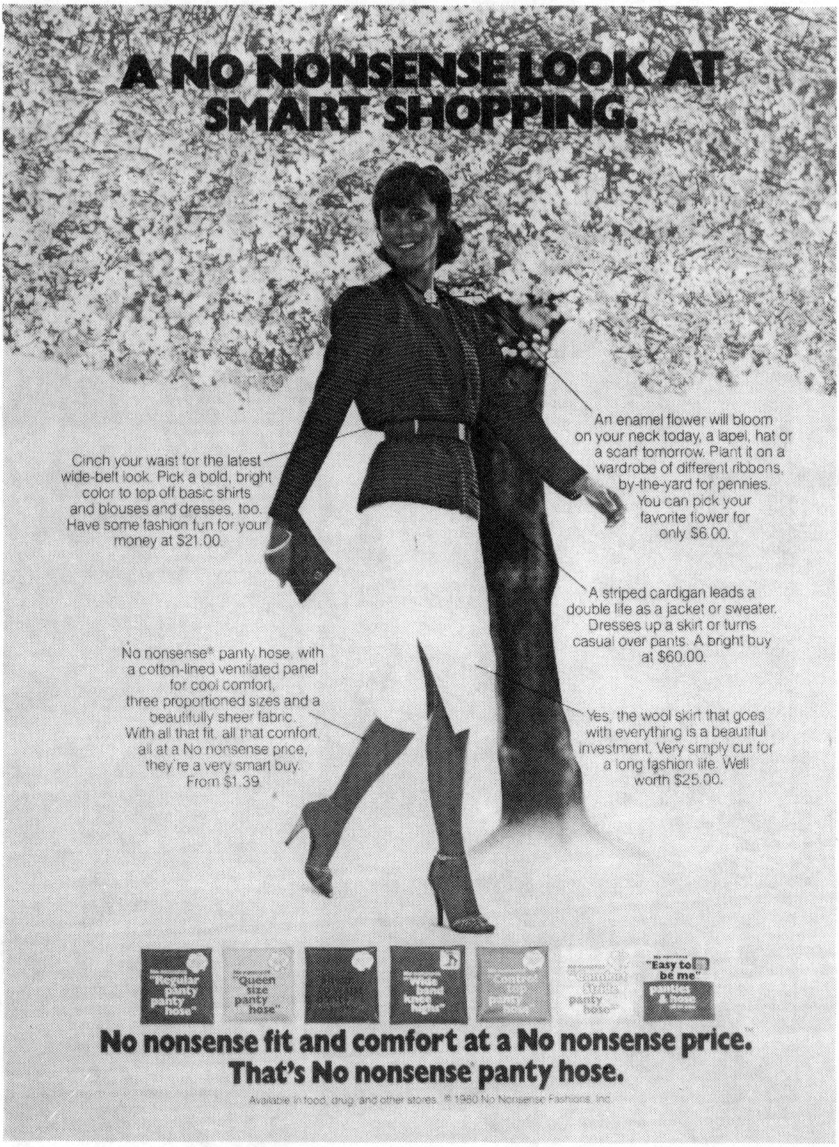

tion with the so-called popular-priced brands in the field. This strategy was used several years ago when Blatz beer was changed from a premium-priced beer to a popular-priced brand. The Ford Motor Company also pursued this policy with their Thunderbird automobile. Such "trading down" may offer attractive opportunities for broadening the market for some brands. Such strategy should be used only after quite careful deliberation since the freedom of choice to management is usually quite limited. Such price adjustments are usually one-way streets in that, once made, management is virtually committed to keep the brand in the new price class.

SALES PROMOTION

In many instances of promotion planning and management, promotion implementation follows the building of advertising strategy. There are, however, situations in which the creation of the advertising strategy is importantly contingent on the merchandising and promotion aspects of the situation. The creative strategy decided upon may have to have, inherent in it, a promotion "hook" which furnishes an important part of the material for planning the sales promotion.

For example, this type of situation is very important in the fine china industry. Practically all specific items in a relatively long line of products are featured at various points in a campaign because the typical retailer who sells china thinks, buys, and promotes on an item basis. Consequently, for companies such as Wedgwood, Ltd., an important part of the advertising strategy is related to item selection; the items selected depend primarily upon their promotability at the retail level. Figure 10–4 shows the manner in which item selection serves as the basis for Wedgwood's creative strategy.

This approach is also seen very clearly in the fashion industry. It would be rare for an advertisement for Hathaway Shirts, for example, not to feature a basic item around which the sales promotion program is built. In such cases as this, the annual advertising budget is divided into basic periods of sales promotion, and during each period certain key items, judged to have prospective fashion acceptance and high seasonal integration, are featured. This particular merchandise must be shown during that period in the tactical translation of the advertising.

OTHER ADVERTISING DECISION VARIABLES

In addition to the non-advertising marketing decision variables such as those discussed above, advertising factors such as media and money and market have an influence in very clear ways on the determination of the creative strategy. The impact of these factors on the decision regarding creative strategy is discussed below.

Market Segmentation. The market target is one of the critical determinants of creative strategy. For instance, a radio and television set

Figure 10-4   Wedgwood China Advertisement

manufacturer has information to indicate that general purchase as well as specific brand decisions are influenced equally by both the man and the woman in the family. After considering the situation, this manufacturer comes to the conclusion that the most satisfactory approach will be through a selective target market. The advertising manager decides that if the company identifies itself closely with the female half of the household and directs all advertising effort toward women, it will be possible to carve out a more important segment of the market than if the company appeals equally to both men and women. The result of this situation is that the product should be designed to please women, and the advertising should be directed at women with a creative orientation which will be effective with women. This obviously affects the literal aspects of the copy as well as the art aspects of the treatment of the product values.

Media Planning. In many situations, creative decisions precede media decisions; that is, creative strategy comes before media strategy. For example, if the creative strategy and the tactical needs of the advertiser require the use of color, then the media department should adhere to this qualification in setting up their media planning structure. The converse is generally not true; that is, the media department does not tell the copywriters and management personnel that they can buy more black and white pages, and that the greater frequency more than compensates for the lack of color. The creative needs should govern the situation. While this may be the ideal atmosphere in which media and copy decisions should be made, it is not unusual in actual practice for the media aspects of the situation to critically influence a creative strategy.

If a given television vehicle is available to a manufacturer at an unusual cost efficiency and with program values psychologically compatible with the manufacturer's brand, it may well be that advertising management might ask copywriters if the advertising copy strategy agreed upon can be as effectively implemented in the television medium.

The decision on the integration of these two basic advertising factors (copy and media) is an important advertising management decision which goes beyond the scope of the making of advertising, per se. It might well be that the relationships among the strategic elements of the creative platform would need to undergo some change if the television broadcast medium were to be selected rather than a printed medium. The adding together of the additional positive media values an' ombining them with what may be regarded as some negative aspects in the changing of creative emphasis is part of advertising management's decision-making process, but one which very much has a firm influence on the final advertising itself.

Advertising Budget. The advertising budget can have far-reaching impact on the setting of creative strategy. The most common illustrations are manufacturers with limited money in highly competitive fields. They must often incorporate a "daringness" in their advertising strategy in order to try to compensate for their burial under the avalanche of competitive dollars. This is not to say that any manufacturer, regardless of the funds available, should not attempt to have the most creative, exciting advertising that can be developed. It can be said, however, that the "radicalism" with which an advertiser tends to approach the problem can be importantly influenced by the market share for the brand as well as the advertising share relative to the major competitors in the market. Thus, the smaller-budget advertiser might well consider taking a chance in advertising a bit more seriously; this attitude could influence the way in which creative strategy is developed.

One of the most famous campaigns of all time was developed by David Ogilvy for the Hathaway shirt company, then a small manufacturer with little money to spend on advertising. Ogilvy created "The Man in the Hathaway Shirt," advertising strategy which was, at the time, an unusual approach for the shirt industry. The small budget with which Hathaway was required to conduct its advertising program probably encouraged the somewhat "radical" approach of symbolizing the company through use of a man with an eye patch.

DISTINGUISHING CREATIVE STRATEGY AND TACTICS

Once the purchase proposition is agreed upon, it is then the job of the advertising "doer" to implement such a proposition, thus building the basic campaign for final submission and approval to the client. This latter job is tactical and is a job in which advertising management does not need to get intimately involved. Such involvement may foster the destruction rather than the building of fine advertising.

It should be noted that analysis of these matters sometimes forces an artificial breakdown of a process into elements which are fundamentally in an unbreakable liaison. It is sometimes difficult to separate creative strategy from creative tactics because the two are so interwoven; it is possible for an extraordinary layout and visualization concept or a very intriguing television product value to modify a going-in strategic outlook.

To further clarify the distinction between creative strategy and creative tactics, a few examples are presented and analyzed below.

COMPARISON OF COMPETITIVE STRATEGIES

The following example analyzes the different strategies utilized by four different camera companies. Each has developed a different strategy which has been interpreted in the print advertising.

Example 10-1. The basic strategy followed by Leitz in the advertisement shown for Leica cameras, was to position the Leica as a quality camera. Not only was it the first 35mm camera, but it has also maintained a tradition of excellence in craftsmanship. Leitz advertising strategy does not hinge on any specific product feature. Instead, Leitz distinguishes its current camera as the Leitz descendant in a long line of superior mechanical and optical achievements. Figure 10-5 shows a tactical implementation through magazine advertising of this strategy for Leica.

Mamiya 35mm cameras, a relatively new camera line, developed a product-related creative strategy which relies upon technological developments. The strategy for Mamiya was to emphasize the development of a computerized shutter system which automatically set the shutter speed. The tactical translation of this is shown in Figure 10-6 where the advertising illustrates how this new product feature makes the camera simple to operate.

Figure 10-7 shows a print advertisement for Minolta 35mm cameras. Here the strategy is also product-related; in fact, the product feature is very similar to that of Mamiya, an automatic shutter-speed system. Rather than emphasizing simplicity of taking pictures with the camera, however, Minolta strategy concerns the ability of the product-related feature to take a particular type of picture, action pictures, in a better manner than a camera without the feature. Clearly, there is some important overlapping as far as strategic posture is concerned between Mamiya and Minolta. It is in the area of basic translation where the creative advertising people have made an attempt to differentiate further the two brands. Though the product feature underlies the strategy for both cameras, this strategy is interpreted in two quite different ways.

Yashica 35mm cameras use price as the basis for strategy development and thus set the camera line apart from the competitors. Since the camera line is somewhat expensive, Yashica uses a strategy whereby price must be interpreted in a positive manner to consumers. Figure 10-8 shows an interpretation where reasons are provided why consumers can afford Yashica cameras. In this case, price of the product has dictated creative strategy.

It is important to recognize that in these examples the strategic alternatives are not many, and it is, therefore, difficult for a camera manufacturer to turn itself around and mirror different strategic faces. In such cases, differences are due as much to tactical implementation as to strategic emphasis and differentiation.

UNIQUE STRATEGIES

Below is an example where the strategy developed sets the product completely apart from the competitors due to the differentiation of the product.

Example 10-2. An inspection of the Cycle Dog Food point of view clearly shows a clean strategic approach. Cycle has said that their dog food is made for different stages of a dog's life. Cycle 1 is for young puppies which need a great deal of protein at that stage of life; Cycle 2 is for dogs in their middle years, when activity is greatest; and Cycle 3

Figure 10-5   Leica Camera Advertisement

Figure 10-6   Mamiya Camera Advertisement

Figure 10-7   Minolta Camera Advertisement

If you can see it happening, you can take a picture of it with the dependable Minolta XG-1.

Because the XG-1 measures light in a way that makes action photography just about foolproof.

Even if your subject is moving from sunlight to shadow, Minolta's Continuous Automatic Exposure System changes the exposure for you. Automatically.

That means after you focus, the compact, lightweight XG-1 does all the work. And you take all the credit.

As for value, the reliable XG-1 is the least expensive automatic 35mm SLR Minolta has ever made.

Add to your range of creative ideas by adding a Minolta Auto Winder, Auto Electroflash, or any of the more than 40 computer designed Minolta lenses.

For more information about the Minolta XG-1, write Minolta Corporation, 101 Williams Drive, Ramsey, N.J. 07446. In Canada: Minolta, Ontario, L4W 1A4. Or see your photo dealer. He'll show you why the Minolta XG-1 is the camera that lets you take the pictures you never thought you could take.

minolta XG-1

The automatic choice for action photography.

Figure 10-8   Yashica Camera Advertisement

Take it ...easy

Yashica's three major reasons why you can afford to own a top-quality 35mm SLR camera.

REASON # 1: The ideal foundation for a growing camera system is Yashica's top-of-the-line, yet reasonably priced FR-I.* This FR-I offers both professional control and automatic ease, including more than 300 highly sophisticated accessories plus a full line of famous Carl Zeiss and Yashica lenses.

REASON # 2: Perfect for those who want a fully automatic SLR offering superior quality results is Yashica's popular-priced FR-II. This top-quality 35mm camera, like the FR-I, offers auto winder capability and accepts all the other Yashica accessories.

REASON # 3: Now you can step-up to 35mm photography at an economical size and price with Yashica's compact FX-3. Featuring all of Yashica's most advanced electronics and stylish design, this most affordable SLR accepts many of the accessories available to Yashica's FR-I and FR-II models.

See these "reasons why", today, at your local Yashica dealer.

YASHICA

411 Sette Drive, Paramus, New Jersey 07652

*FR is a licensed trademark of Cine Magnetics, Inc.

is for maturing dogs, whose exercise is limited. This strategic outlook represents a creative marketing decision, and apparently Cycle was the first to recognize and exploit this marketing opportunity.

In contrast with the camera examples in Example 10-1, there is a relative *uniqueness* in strategic outlook in the Cycle case.

In essence, the Cycle situation demonstrates a completely different strategic posture for a given brand in addition to those differences that can be translated in the advertising itself. On the other hand, in the camera instances, with a less severe difference in strategy, there is consequently greater reliance on tactical translation. As a matter of fact, the difficulty of differentiating a brand puts a further premium on strategic orientation in the making of advertising. This is particularly true when there is a general equality of production facilities of different manufacturers and the consequent ability of firms to copy each other quickly in the product development area.

Figure 10-9 illustrates this point graphically. If the differentiation of the brand is low relative to the product features of the competitors, then the reliance of the brand's advertising program on creative strategy will likely be low and reliance on differentiation through the use of creative tactics will necessarily need to be high. On the other hand, a brand which is clearly differentiated from the competitors' brands in terms of product features can easily serve as the basis for a differentiated creative strategy which is highly different than the competitors' strategies. The use of creative tactics to provide for differentiation in the advertising for the brand may be high or low, but creative tactics are of secondary importance for such a differentiated brand.

Figure 10-9   Role of Product Differentiation in Advertising Differentiation

	Creative Strategy Differentiation	Creative Tactics Differentiation
Low Product Differentiation	LOW	HIGH
High Product Differentiation	LOW	LOW/HIGH

PRICE VERSUS PRODUCT FEATURES

The following automobile examples provide a clear indication of the relative roles which price and product features can play in the development of strategy.

Example 10-3. The Mercedes print advertisement shown in Figure 10-10 shows the strategic decision to identify with the history of quality which this company has built in America throughout recent years. Mercedes is essentially positioned as *the* quality automobile due to the 94-year history of making quality automobiles. This history is the strategic "hook" in Mercedes advertising.

Figure 10-11 shows a Volvo print advertisement which takes direct competitive aim at Mercedes. The strategic "hook" for this comparison is the price of Volvo, which is considerably lower for the Volvo model featured (though Volvo does have a very expensive, hand-made model) than most Mercedes models. The Volvo strategy here relies upon price.

Both the Saab strategy shown in Figure 10-12 and the Peugeot strategy shown in Figure 10-13 rely upon product features and so, in this way, very much overlap. But the Saab strategy is interpreted in a tactically different manner than Peugeot. Saab tactics involve a comparison of its product features to almost all of its main competitors; Peugeot simply states its features and makes no mention in any specific way of its competitors' features. Here there are no strategic differences, so the differentiation of advertising must fall to the tactical level. In comparison, price provides a product differentiation basis for the development of a distinct creative strategy for Volvo in relation to Mercedes.

Clearly, advertising management has a lot to do with and a good deal to contribute to advertising *strategy*. This does not mean that management should not evaluate and contribute to *tactics* as developed by the copywriters, art directors and producers. However, advertising management's major contribution is to creative strategy, and such strategy emanates from marketing strategy. In sound advertising planning, a fundamental point of view *precedes* the making of the advertisements themselves.

COMMUNICATION OBJECTIVES

Communication objectives are those which have been identified as involving "intermediate criteria" as these were discussed in Chapter 4. Communication objectives can be classified along two dimensions: (1) With respect to the three dimensions of effectiveness (cognitive, conative, and affective); and (2) with respect to their global versus operational nature. The type of communication objective which is agreed upon by advertising management sets the stage for the development of specific advertisements. It is important that a clear and explicit connection be made between global and operational objec-

Figure 10-10   Mercedes Advertisement

For 1980, Mercedes-Benz introduces the most relentlessly efficient automobiles in its history.

Stringent efficiency is no sudden demand to the engineers of Mercedes-Benz. For 94 years they have built cars with little else in mind. And for 1980 they have inched the standards up another notch. Without down-sizing bodies or engines, without slashing weight or cutting corners in quality or safety or comfort, they have created the most relentlessly efficient Mercedes-Benz automobiles yet.

Diesels—and more power to them

In any ordinary year, it would be major news that Mercedes-Benz engineers had boosted the performance of their Diesel-powered cars.

And boost it they did—to a healthy degree. The muscular 300 SD Turbodiesel is even more muscular. The five-cylinder 300 TD Station Wagon, 300 CD Coupe and 300 D Sedan move more briskly. The 240 D Sedan enjoys new punch.

But 1980 is no ordinary year. The best news is that the legendary Diesel fuel efficiency remains legendary.

The pleasant shock of efficiency

All six Mercedes-Benz gasoline models remain on the leading edge of automotive technology for 1980.

In these cars for 1980, fuel efficiency gains some makers might be pleased to achieve in two, three or five years have been achieved in one. Advances ranging from a 14.3* percent increase in fuel mileage for the 280 CE Coupe, 280 E and 280 SE Sedans, to a 33.3 percent gain in the 450 SEL Sedan, the 450 SL Roadster and the 450 SLC

Coupe. Compare this to other cars. Your mileage may differ depending on speed, weather conditions and trip length.

In 1980 as in 1886

Every car maker today speaks of its products as being "right for the times." Mercedes-Benz is no exception.

But there is one difference. Making its cars more efficient does not loom only as the challenge of the eighties at Mercedes-Benz. It has always been the challenge.

Engineered like no other car in the world

*California emission cars.

Figure 10-11   Volvo Advertisement

"ANYONE WHO'S THINKING OF SPENDING $24,000 FOR A LUXURY CAR SHOULD TALK TO A PSYCHIATRIST."

— Dr. John Boston, psychiatrist and Volvo owner, Austin, Texas

John Boston, a Texas psychiatrist, owns a '73 Volvo. He bought that Volvo because, as he puts it: "I had admired what Volvo had done in the area of safety. The car seemed well-built. It offered solid European craftsmanship without the inflated price."

We wanted Dr. Boston's opinion of the new Volvo GLE, which has a full assortment of luxury features as standard equipment — and a price tag thousands of dollars below that of the well-known German luxury sedan.

"It's an excellent value. In my opinion, the individual buying this car would have a strong, unsuppressed need to get his or her money's worth. He or she would probably also have a strong enough self-image not to need a blatant status symbol."

When we told him that some people were actually paying five to ten thousand dollars more for a luxury car, Dr. Boston's response was characteristically succinct. "That's not using your head."

Finally, we asked Dr. Boston if, when he was ready for a new car, he'd consider the Volvo GLE for himself. "I'd be crazy if I didn't."

VOLVO

A car you can believe in.

Figure 10-12   Saab Advertisement

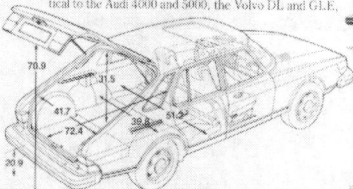

Figure 10-13   Peugeot Advertisement

505. THE ONLY CAR IN ITS CLASS "THAT MAY STILL BE IN TUNE WITH THE TIMES TEN YEARS FROM TODAY." —Autoweek

The new 505 from Peugeot is truly a car that doesn't require any compromises.

From the sleek lines outside, to the brilliant planning inside, the 505 is designed for today as well as tomorrow.

Everything about the car is built for the driver. The perfectly natural angle of the steering wheel. The expansive windshield that offers you a view of the road instead of a view of the hood.

The appointments are superb. An international dashboard (with simple symbols rather than words) lets you "read" everything at a glance.

The placement of the controls is so efficient that the driver has merely to gesture, rather than move.

For the driver and his favorite passenger, there are orthopedic bucket seats with back headrests.

The seats adjust to any position. The headrests adjust as well.

There is more than enough room —head room, leg room and seat room—for the driver and four passengers. And the kind of interior space that doesn't make you feel like you've been "downsized."

The ride itself is outstanding. Compliments of a European suspension system that protects you from the imperfections of the road. And thanks to Peugeot's patented extra large shock absorbers which soften the bumps.

The handling is effortless. In this case, the tightness of the car lending itself to the ease of the driver. (Power-assisted rack-and-pinion steering helps, of course. So do power-assisted disc brakes on all four wheels.)

The 505 Diesel is equipped with a 4 speed manual transmission and delivers an impressive EPA estimated 35 mpg highway, and an estimated 29 mpg.†

The 505 gasoline version is equipped with a 5-speed manual transmission (combined with a Bosch K-Jetronic fuel injection system) to make it one of the most responsive automobiles you've ever driven.

Add to all that the fact that at Peugeot a car is built, not merely assembled. And tested individually.

And what you get is a car that isn't just right for ten years from now. It's right for all the years in between.

†Peugeot 505D, manual 4-speed transmission. Estimated mpg of other cars. You may get different mileage depending on how fast you drive, weather conditions, trip length and condition of your car. Actual highway mileage will probably be less than the highway estimate.

PEUGEOT
PROGRESS IN MOTION

tives so that message strategy is consistent with the overall advertising strategy set at the level of global objectives.

GLOBAL OBJECTIVES

The creative strategy must be directly related to the overall advertising strategy. The overall advertising strategy will usually be stated in terms of *global objectives*. Table 10-1 shows examples of global objectives and their connection with specific, operational objectives for message development. Global objectives must be stated in quantitative form, must be measurable, and must specify some given time period in which the objective is to be reached. Notice that global objectives can be categorized by which of the three dimensions of effectiveness is assessed. Such an objective as "increase brand awareness from the current level of 34% to 50% in the next quarter" is used to guide not only the message strategy development but also the media strategy and the budget setting process. In this sense, global advertising objectives guide the entire campaign development, and message, media, and money strategies follow from them.

OPERATIONAL MESSAGE OBJECTIVES

Table 10-1 also illustrates some examples of operational objectives. Again, specific, operational message objectives can be categorized by each of the three dimensions of effectiveness (cognitive, conative, and affective). Operational objectives of a cognitive nature have to do with teaching, showing, or reminding a specific target market about various aspects of the brand. Conative operational objectives are set for copy which attempts to move consumers to some action, such as sending in a coupon from a magazine advertisement. Affective operational objectives deal with attitudinal changes which are desired. For example, it may be the case that consumers of the target market of "Clean" toothpaste have an unfavorable attitude toward this brand of toothpaste because they believe that it removes enamel from teeth, that is, it is highly abrasive. An operational affective objective might be set for Clean as follows: "To convince consumers in our target market that Clean is less abrasive than the leading brand of toothpaste." Other general examples are shown in Table 10-1.

It should be noted that *multiple objectives* of either a global or an operational nature might be set in a given instance for a particular brand. These multiple objectives might be set *within* a particular dimension of effectiveness, for example, cognitive, or *between* dimensions of effectiveness, for example, cognitive and conative. Problems which arise in the setting of multiple objectives, when multiple criteria (dimensions of effectiveness) are involved, are discussed in Chapter 11.

Operational Objective Problems. According to researcher Steuart Henderson Britt, operational objectives must meet four criteria:[6]

(1) They must indicate the basic message to be sent.

**Table 10-1 Communication Objectives
(Intermediate Criteria)**

	COGNITIVE	CONATIVE	AFFECTIVE
Global Objectives	To increase *Brand Awareness* from the current level of 34% to 50% in the next quarter.	To increase *Purchase Consideration* from the current level of 27% to 35% in the next quarter.	To increase favorable *Brand Evaluation* from the current 36% to 45% in the next quarter.
Operational Objectives	1. To show consumers how the brand can satisfy a need. 2. To remind consumers of a slogan they already know. 3. To teach consumers about an important brand attribute.	1. To induce consumers to buy at a different season of the year. 2. To obtain inquiries that will be followed up by personal calls. 3. To induce consumers to use the brand in some new way.	1. To convince consumers they can avoid something distasteful by owning the brand. 2. To convince consumers that the brand will provide a reward more effectively than a competing brand. 3. To associate the brand with a desirable symbol.

(2) They must descriptively detail the intended audience of the basic message.

(3) They must explicitly state the intended effect(s) of the message on the audience.

(4) They must mention, prior to measurement of success, the evaluative criteria for the determination of success (or failure) of the campaign down the road.

Britt examined 135 so-called "successful" campaigns developed by 40 advertising agencies. He discovered that 64 percent of these campaigns fulfilled the first three of the above criteria, but only two campaigns (less than one percent of the sample) fulfilled all four criteria. This means that 36 percent of the campaigns did not, at minimum, state the basic message to be delivered, the audience to be reached, and the intended effects. Clearly, there is room for improvement in the use of objectives in the development of creative strategy statements.

COMMUNICATION APPROACHES

Once the strategy has been developed and the creative objectives have been determined as part of this strategy, the communication approach must be considered. That is, the development of particular appeal strategies which will be used in specific advertisements needs to be determined. There has been a great deal of work conducted in social psychology, advertising and marketing on the question of appeal effectiveness. Communication approaches will be examined from the standpoint of: (1) message principles; and (2) the creative mix.

MESSAGE PRINCIPLES

The basic findings from many studies on the effectiveness of message strategies have been conveniently summarized by Delozier; these are provided below as a means of compactly presenting the wealth of information which might be examined on this topic.[7]

(1) *One-sided versus two-sided messages*

    (a) A one-sided message is more effective when (1) the audience initially agrees with the communicator's position, (2) the audience is poorly educated, and (3) the audience is unlikely to hear counter-arguments.

    (b) A two-sided message is more effective when (1) the audience initially disagrees with the communicator's position, (2) the audience is well-educated, and (3) the audience is likely to hear counter-arguments.

(2) *Climax versus anticlimax order*

    (a) Neither a climax nor an anticlimax order is generally superior to the other.

    (b) Where audience interest is low for the material presented, the anticlimax order is superior to the climax order.

(c) Where audience interest is high for the material presented, the climax order is superior to the anticlimax order.

(d) The pyramidal order is the least effective order of presentation.

(3) *Recency-primacy*

(a) Neither a recency nor a primacy order is generally superior to the other.

(b) Controversial topics, interesting subjects, and highly familiar issues favor the primacy order.

(c) Uninteresting subjects and moderately unfamiliar issues favor a recency order.

(4) A message arrangement which first arouses a need and then provides information relevant to the satisfaction of the need is superior to an arrangement which is opposite in order.

(5) A message which presents highly desirable material followed by less desirable material is better in changing opinions than a message which arranges these components in an opposite order.

(6) A highly credible source induces more opinion change when he or she presents his or her pro arguments first, followed by his or her con arguments, rather than vice versa.

(7) Generally, a communicator is more effective in changing opinions in the desired direction by drawing a conclusion.

(8) For less intelligent people, the communicator will achieve greater opinion change in the desired direction if he or she draws a conclusion; for highly intelligent people, drawing a conclusion or leaving the conclusion to the audience is about equally effective in changing opinions.

(9) If people perceive that the communicator has an intent to manipulate by stating a conclusion, or if people might feel an insult to their intelligence by having a conclusion drawn for them, a communicator is more effective by leaving the conclusion to the audience.

(10) In a communication dealing with highly personal or ego-involving issues, the communicator may be more effective by allowing receivers to draw a conclusion themselves; for impersonal topics, stating a conclusion is generally more effective.

(11) For highly complex issues, the communicator is more effective if he or she states a conclusion for his or her audience; for simple issues, the approach makes little difference.

(12) *Fear appeals*

(a) Sometimes a mild fear appeal is more persuasive than a strong one; at other times a strong fear appeal is better than a mild one.

(b) In general, strong fear appeals appear to be superior to mild ones when they "pose a threat to the subject's loved ones; are presented by a highly credible source; deal with topics relatively unfamiliar to the subject; aim at subjects with a high degree of self-esteem and/or low perceived vulnerability to danger."

(13) "It seems that fear appeals are most effective when (1) immediate action can be taken on recommendations included in the appeal; and (2) specific instructions are provided for carrying out recommendations included in the appeal."

(14) "Pleasant forms of distraction can often increase the effectiveness of persuasive appeals."

(15) Active participation can increase the effectiveness of the persuasive appeal.

(16) *Emotional appeals* are enhanced by:
  (a) Using highly effective language to describe a situation
  (b) Associating the proposed idea with either popular or unpopular ideas
  (c) Associating the proposed idea with visual or nonverbal stimuli that might arouse emotions
  (d) The communicator displaying "nonverbal emotional cues."

(17) Arousing feelings of aggression, followed by suggestions of how to reduce those feelings, may be an effective appeal in certain situations.

(18) In general, *humor* appears to be a very effective means of attracting attention and aiding in recall and comprehension; however, its effectiveness in persuasion is doubtful.

(19) In persuasive communications, "emotionally charged" language is more effective on an audience who already agrees with a communicator; however, it may produce effects opposite to those intended, especially on an audience who initially disagrees with the communicator.

(20) In general, when highly favorable words are associated with a concept, an audience will view the concept as favorable; when associated with unfavorable words, the concept will be generally viewed as unfavorable.

(21) Nonverbal communication is often more important in communicating an idea than the verbal message it accompanies.

(22) The nonverbal code is primarily instrumental in eliciting feelings and emotions within an audience.

Nonverbal communication, mentioned in the last two items above, is one element of the "communication mix." This mix is discussed below.

COMMUNICATION MIX

The "Communication Mix" refers to the tactics by which the creative strategy is carried out. The communication mix deals with the relationships in given messages between: (1) the *sender* (advertiser); (2) the *message* (such as the factors described in the preceding section); (3) the *channel* (the efficacy of the various mass media types, for example, radio, television, and so on); (4) the *receiver* (the definition of the target market); and (5) the *feedback* (the assessment of the effect of the message on the receiver). The development of an advertisement involves the "juggling" of each of these five elements of the communication mix. Relationships across these five communication mix variables can be examined in terms of the usage of "verbal" versus "nonverbal" elements in the message.

Dunn and Barban have summarized a considerable amount of research findings in the following guidelines regarding the usage of verbal and nonverbal elements in message construction:[8]

(1) *Where the appearance of a product is important in the ultimate purchase, the visual should be emphasized.* A good example is the fashion advertisement. No words can re-create the exact design of a dress—the buyer wants to know just how it looks.

(2) *The more important it is to make emotional associations with the product, the more we should emphasize the visual.* Note how few words are used in perfume copy.

(3) *The more important the facts are in accomplishing the advertising objective, the more important the verbal will be.* Consider the purchase of an expensive machine tool by a firm's purchasing agent: he or she will want facts and plenty of them. Most of the factual data he or she needs will be in verbal form—specifications, operating instructions and so forth.

(4) *The more important narrative is in making the point of an advertisement, the more important the words will be.* Words are essential here to develop interest in the characters, the situation, and the outcome.

(5) *The newer the product, the more likely you are to emphasize the copy.* People naturally will have many questions in their minds. What does the product look like? How does it operate? Who is likely to use it? They may not verbalize these questions, but they are there all the same; and often they are questions that demand verbal answers.

(6) *Words are generally preferable for emphasizing action to be taken.* Mail order advertising usually includes a great amount of copy. This copy is partly to provide answers to questions consumers have no opportunity to ask in person, and partly to outline the action.

Whatever the communication approach taken in the tactical translation, the creative strategy or creative platform is the central element. This is summarized by Hafer and White in their "crude creed for copywriters:"[9]

Start with a
basic selling idea or concept
which succeeds in
linking consumer benefit   stay on track
and *product exclusive*   strive for the unexpected
then   seek a recurring theme
think visually   be yourself.
talk friendly
keep it simple
prove your point

MARKET DATA AND CREATIVE STRATEGY

It has been shown how creative strategy is related to marketing strategy, how important a creative point of view is to the building of advertising, management's involvement in the development of such a point of view, the relationship between creative strategy and other basic advertising and promotional decisions, and the distinction between creative strategy and creative tactics.

At the same time, it has been shown how many of the factors in the total marketing mix can and do actively influence the actual creative strategy itself. The basic insight which normally provides the welding ingredient that results in the final strategic expression frequently comes from the thoughtful consideration and imagination of one person or a couple of people. These people do not reach conclusions in a blind vacuum. They inundate themselves with vital information about a given brand, product group and industry; relevant information which can act as an idea stimulant to the establishment of creative strategy; information which, when digested, can act as a catalyst for creative thinking; and information which can be molded into many forms of interpretation. Then they act to provide direction and guidance.

This information has many dimensions, ranging from the attitude of the vice-president in charge of sales to newspaper reproduction values of the given brand or type of merchandise. From a practical point of view, however, it would appear that there are three fundamental areas of exposure which deal with the informational needs as far as the establishment of basic creative strategy is concerned. They are listed and briefly discussed below. Two provisos, however, must be kept in mind:

(1) Information can frequently be submitted with a point of view. It is unreasonable to presume that a market research person does not, cannot, or should not have a point of view with respect to the meaning and implication of basic data which are collected.

(2) Most information can reflect different perspectives in interpretation. A fact is really not a fact until it has been given meaning within the environment in which it operates. It is this very difference of perspective, reflected via insight, combined with what may be best termed a contemporary awareness, which indeed acts to separate the top advertising professionals from their less sensitive counterparts.

These three basic factors are listed below, together with brief commentary and explanation where relevant.

MARKET ANATOMY DATA

This is information which provides insight into basic marketing prospects for a given product group or specific brand. For example, in the beer business a disproportionate amount of beer is consumed by people between the ages of 21 and 35. Decaffeinated coffee has a disproportionate amount of consumption among older people. Diet soft drinks have a disproportionately high consumption among employed women. All these findings have either direct or indirect relevance to the building of a marketing strategy, and the marketing strategy represents one of the firm foundations on which the creative strategy is constructed.

MARKET PHYSIOLOGY DATA

Information in this category goes beyond the simple description of what people are, and offers some insight into the complexities and the nature of their habit patterns. Consider a few instances gathered from research:

(1) There is an equal influence exerted by both men and women in the purchase of a TV set.
(2) Car owners are not specifically aware of how much it costs to maintain an automobile over a given year.
(3) Brand loyalty in the shampoo business is almost non-existent whereas there is a very high brand loyalty in the baby products business.

These kinds of market data reflect activity rather than a description of consumer characteristics and most of the time do have an effect on creative strategy. Life style data developed for segmentation purposes can play a valuable role in the development of creative strategy by uncovering the physiology of the market.

MARKET PSYCHOLOGY DATA

This represents a third layer of the market description process and deals with attitudes and opinions rather than basic facts or actual behavior patterns. For example:

(1) People do not generally drink whisky because they like its taste but despite the taste.
(2) People are reluctant to think about death and its consequences.
(3) Speed of relief is the most important factor in which people are interested when taking a patent remedy to counteract headaches.

These types of psychological generalizations have a tremendous effect on any creative posture. An awareness of the socio-psychological make-up of consumers is highly essential in the structuring of advertising creative strategy. The tools of the social scientist, properly employed and interpreted, are of great use in this area.

These market facts, of course, must be inspected, analyzed and interpreted in the light of what is known about market segments, budgets, product characteristics, pricing, packaging, competitive advertising strategies, and promotion orientation. Furthermore, all these factors must realistically be considered within the framework of corporate philosophy, which can also influence creative orientation. The Miles Laboratories people, for example, have a policy which involves the actual participation of physicians not only as technical consultants with respect to the claims made in advertising, but also as screens through which the advertising is filtered with respect to taste and general treatment. The classic Alka Seltzer series, featuring "Speedy," partially represented a corporate attitude which reflected a desire not to sell over-the-counter medicines in the rugged, overt, hard-sell fashion followed successfully by many other manufacturers.

Marketing and advertising research play an important role in narrowing the area of decision making for advertising management. But the fact remains that after all the organized thinking, research, and logic are applied, the problem of selecting a useful creative strategy remains very much an art, an art which should be tempered by the scientific approach yet not hampered by undue intrusion of science.

QUESTIONS AND PROBLEMS

1. Pick four magazine advertisements from a magazine such as *Newsweek*, *People* or *Better Homes & Gardens*. Analyze the advertisement in each case to isolate the strategy behind the advertisement. Describe the tactical translation of the strategy in each case.

2. Find an advertisement which, you believe, makes an effective use of fear appeal concepts. Why does it make effective use of fear appeals?

3. In what ways do Reeves, Bernbach, Ogilvy and Burnett seem to agree about the nature of creative strategy? Contrast the Bernbach approach to creative development (as illustrated by Hathaway Shirt advertising).

4. Briefly describe the reasoning behind making a distinction between creative strategy and tactics. Of what possible benefit is such a distinction?

5. Develop a creative strategy for a new brand of soft frozen yogurt called YoFreeze which comes in 16 flavors and is eaten from cones.

6. Describe a brand in any product category where you believe that a two-sided appeal in the creative approach would be the better tactic than a one-sided approach. Why do you believe this is so in your example?

7. Why is it important to develop operational message objectives as part of the creative strategy? Give an example for a well-known toothpaste of an operational objective you feel would be beneficial for the brand to pursue.

8. In this chapter, Britt's ideas of meaningful objectives were set forth. Do you agree with his characterization of useful objectives? How were the advertising campaigns which Britt studied successful yet did not follow his guidelines for useful objectives if his guidelines are meaningful?

ENDNOTES

1. William M. Weilbacher, *Advertising* (New York: MacMillian and Company, 1979), p. 174.
2. Rosser Reeves, *Reality in Advertising* (New York: Alfred A. Knopf, Inc., 1968), pp. 47-48.

3. Leo Burnett, quoted in Denis Higgins, *The Art of Writing Advertising* (Chicago: Advertising Publications, Inc., 1965), p. 43.
4. William Bernbach, "Advertising's Greatest Tool," in John S. Wright and Daniel S. Warner (eds.) *Speaking of Advertising* (New York: McGraw-Hill Book Company, 1963), p. 313.
5. David Ogilvy, *Confessions of An Advertising Man* (New York: Atheneum, 1964), pp. 93-103.
6. Steuart Henderson Britt, "Are So-Called Successful Advertising Campaigns Really Successful?" in R.D. Michman and D.W. Juggenheimer (eds.), *Strategic Advertising Decisions* (Columbus, Ohio: Grid, Inc., 1976), p. 127.
7. M. Wayne DeLozier, *The Marketing Communication Process* (New York: McGraw-Hill Book Company, Inc., 1976), pp. 110-112.
8. S. Watson Dunn and Arnold M. Barban, *Advertising: Its Role in Modern Marketing* (Hinsdale, Illinois: The Dryden Press, 1978), pp. 331-332.
9. W. Keith Hafer and Gordon E. White, *Advertising Writing* (St. Paul: West Publishing Co., 1977), p. 89.

CREATIVE STRATEGY AND COPY RESEARCH

- Copy Research Perspectives
- Hierarchy of Effects and Copy Research
- Measurement of Recall and Attitude Change
- The Multiple Criteria Dilemma
- Selection of Copy Research Methods

Decision Making Organization of This Text

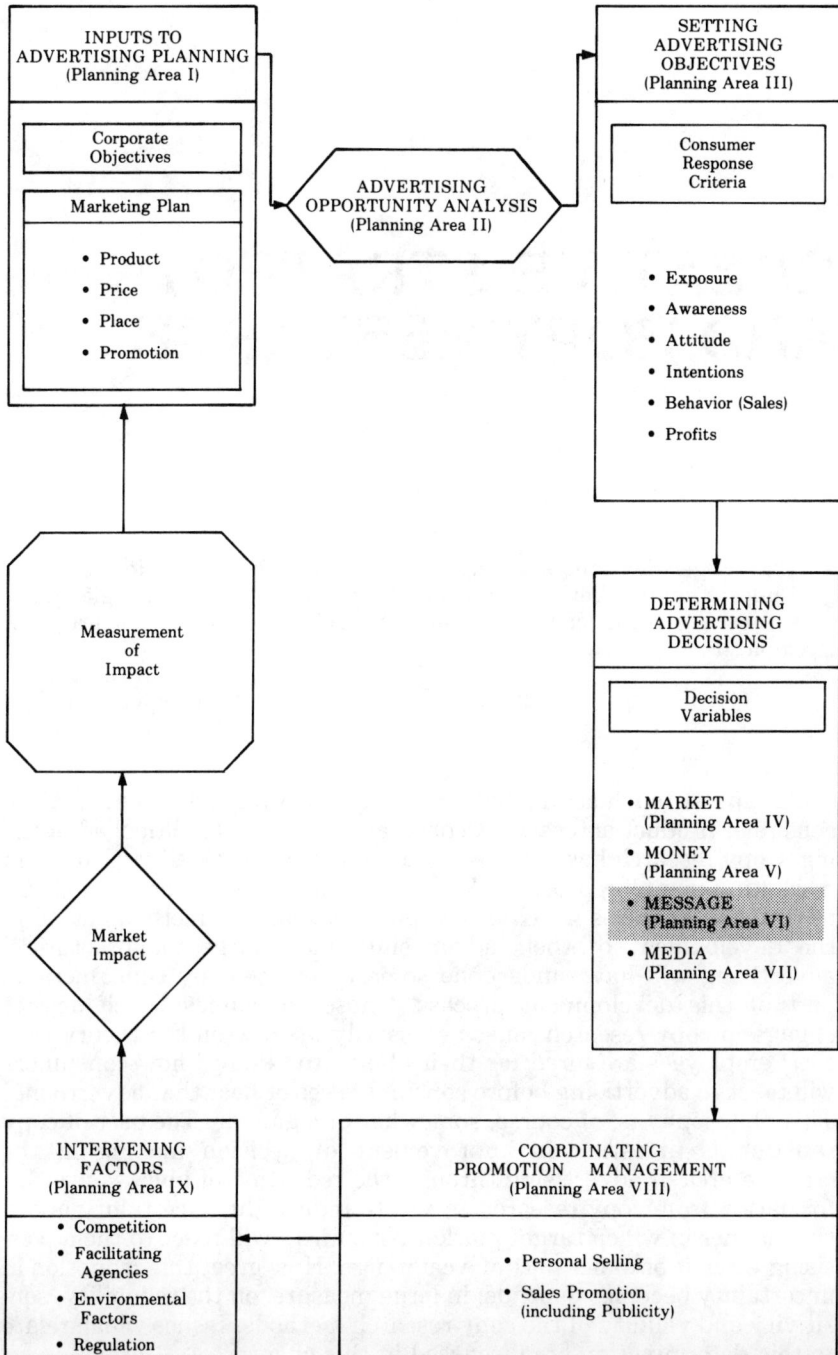

CREATIVE STRATEGY AND COPY RESEARCH

"... A genuine understanding of the effects of communications on attitudes requires both survey and experimental methodologies ... Neither is a royal road to wisdom, but each represents an important emphasis."

—Carl I. Hovland
Social Psychologist

Perhaps as much as $95 million will be spent in 1980 on evaluating consumer product and service, corporate image, and political advertising. Copy research has become a standard part of the advertising and marketing planning process. While it is true that there are some large advertising agencies which utilize no copy research methods at all in the development of their advertising, most large manufacturers' advertising will have undergone some assessment by consumers as part of this development process. Those companies which do not engage in copy research must necessarily operate on the theory that their employees are hired for their ability to "know" how consumers will react to advertising before consumers see or hear that advertising. This philosophy is, of course, somewhat of a gamble. The user of copy research is investing in improvement of decision making in the creative area of advertising through the reduction of uncertainty. Information from copy research serves to reduce the uncertainty about the manner in which target market consumers will react to the advertising when it becomes part of a campaign. How great this reduction in uncertainty becomes depends, in large measure, on the reliability, sensitivity and validity of the copy research methods. Issues which relate to this determination are discussed in this chapter.

COPY RESEARCH PERSPECTIVES

There are practically as many views on the value and role of particular copy research methods as there are users of such research. At one point, Robert Mayer of Young & Rubicam advertising agency estimated that there were about 33,000 different ways to test copy.[1] Some of the ingredients in copy research methods are: buying intention, coupon redemption, simulated sales response, attitude toward the brand, attitude toward the advertising, skin response, brain waves, eye movement, pupil dilation, unaided recall, aided recall, recognition, recall of copy points, recall of slogan, visual recall, pre/post measurement, post only measurement, single exposure, multiple exposure, projectable samples, non-projectable samples, natural exposure, forced exposure, in-home exposure, theatre exposure, trailer exposure, group testing, individual testing, distraction, and competitive advertising. Clearly, the number of combinations of these ingredients can become very large. With all these possibilities, it should be no surprise that there is no single universally agreed upon copy research method.

COPY RESEARCH VERSUS COPY TESTING

In an important article which appeared in 1972, Shirley Young, Director of Research at Grey Advertising in New York, examined the use of copy research. She found that all too often copy research was being used as a "test" to generate a single number (which she called "magic numbers") which would tell whether one ad was better than another. A copy research procedure can generate one or both of the following measures: (1) *global measures* which provide a summary of the advertisement's effectiveness; and (2) *diagnostic measures* which provide detailed information about various dimensions of the advertisement. A global measurement is like a test in the sense that, based upon the single number, it is possible to tell *which* of the several ads tested is superior. This does not tell *why* a particular advertisement was better than another, only that it was better.

The situation is somewhat analogous to that in which a student takes an essay-type examination. A letter grade or number grade may be assigned by the professor without any additional comments. The student, when the exam is returned, will understand how well he or she did compared to classmates or some normative level of performance. But the question will usually arise as to *why* the essay answers were good or *why* they were poor. This "why" can only be discovered by the student if the professor discusses the answers or provides comments which explain the nature of the single-number grade. If a student performs poorly on an exam, the "why" becomes quite important since only through this information can the student expect to make changes so that performance can be changed in the future. This is very much like the situation in which the copywriter operates.

The purpose of copy research should be *to provide a basis for making better advertising*. As will be seen below, single numbers are needed by account managers for decision making purposes about particular advertisements; but copywriters, the people who make the advertising, need to know why a particular advertisement was deemed effective and why it was not. Diagnostic information must be a part of a copy research procedure for the purpose of providing this information to copywriters and other "makers" of the advertising. For example, a copywriter may want to know what consumers thought about the models used in one ad versus an alternative ad. Or the writer may want to know if consumers believed one claim more so than another. If the writer only finds out, after copy research has been conducted, that his or her particular ad had very high recall, it may remain a mystery to this person why this was the case. How will this person repeat this performance? Learning about effective advertising through only single number research is a "trial and error" process. Something is tried, a number is generated, and, if the number is poor, something else is tried. This something else could be determined in less of a trial-and-error manner if diagnostic information were provided in the research output. Clearly, the desirable copy research method provides both global and diagnostic information which can be of use to both account managers and copywriters.

In the past, copy research was usually referred to as "copy testing." This term is not descriptive of the acceptable copy research procedure because it implies a test, after the fact, of a finished product. The emphasis should be placed on the use of copy research *during the development* of advertising so that it can be of help in building good advertising. In addition, a single-number test can very easily lead to a situation where "the tail wags the dog." That is, if a copywriter, for example, understands that the advertising he or she develops will be "tested" on a recall system in which the only important outcome is the percentage of consumers who accurately recalled the advertisement, this knowledge on the part of the writer will produce, in all likelihood, some interesting behavior. The writer will then concentrate on making an ad which will produce "high" recall scores; the writer should be concentrating on producing the best advertising possible, not on producing high recall scores. The "test" comes to dictate the writer's frame of mind. From this standpoint, it is preferable to think of "copy research" rather than of "copy testing." The terminology used by a particular firm reflects its philosophy about the development of advertising, and such terminology is more than an argument in mere semantics. The terminology used in conjunction with copy research sets the tone for the manner in which brand managers at the client company, account managers at the agency, and the creative people will view the advertising development process in the particular case. In summary, it is preferable to have a "copy research" method which provides global measures to managers and detailed diagnostic measures for the creative people.

VIEWS OF COPY RESEARCH

There have been several studies done over the years about the value of copy research in the advertising process as a whole. One of the most important of these was the study done by the American Association of Advertising Agencies conducted in 1977 and headed by Shirley Young of the Grey advertising agency.[2] The results of this survey of large advertisers and agencies are discussed below along with those of a study conducted in 1980 on related matters.

Measures Used. In the 4A study reported by Young, 47 corporate (client) research directors, 30 agency research directors, and 50 creative directors representing 38 advertising agencies participated. The companies represented by the respondents were responsible for developing and evaluating in excess of one-third of all national advertising in the United States. The sample was drawn from the 100 Leading National Advertisers and the top fifty largest advertising agencies.

The responses indicated that commercial playback was a measurement used by the highest proportion of companies; commercial playback refers to immediate recall of the message after exposure to it. This measure was followed by commercial recall (such as day-after recall) and overall persuasiveness and persuasiveness based on specific brand attributes (attitude change based upon a global, single measure or based upon an attitude model). Commercial recall as an element included in their copy research methodology was reported by 49 percent of the respondents; attitude change was reported as a method used by 39 percent of the respondents. Since commercial playback (mentioned by 78 percent of the respondents) can mean many different types of measurements, it can be concluded that the two *single* measurement systems used most often by advertisers are recall and attitude change. It might also be noted that 30 percent of the respondents indicated they measured attitude toward the commercial (the attitude object in attitude change measurement is necessarily the brand).

These results can be compared with a 1980 survey which included responses from 42 of the 100 Leading National Advertisers and 27 of the top 100 advertising agencies.[3] Responses in this survey indicated that 42 percent used on-air recall testing methods while 32 percent used forced-exposure attitude-type methods. Though somewhat lower than in the 4A study, these figures are quite close to the 49 percent and 39 percent reported, respectively, in that study. Clearly, as the authors of the 1980 study point out, on-air recall-type methods and forced-exposure attitude-type measures are the most commonly used by the top advertisers and agencies in this country.

It might be noted that when the respondents in the 4A study were asked which measures *should* be included, 87 percent believed recall should be included, 76 percent believed global attitude change should be included, 76 percent believed attitude change based upon brand attributes (attitude scale or model) should be included, and 61 percent indicated commercial attitude should be included. In other words, most of the respondents believed that both recall and attitude measures should exist in the copy research method utilized.

Users of Copy Research. The respondents in the 4A study were asked who benefits most and least from copy research. By far, they believed that brand managers at the client company benefited most (61 percent mentioned them) while about half as many respondents believed "creatives" benefited most (34 percent), and 24 percent believed account managers at the agency benefited most. A large proportion of the respondents (48 percent) indicated that creative people benefited least from copy research. When asked which group of advertising people *should* benefit most from copy research, it was extremely clear that the respondents believed creative people, the people who make the advertising, should benefit most from copy research (70 percent indicated this). The implication is that more emphasis needs to be put on the diagnostic values of copy research and perhaps somewhat less emphasis on the "magic number" aspects.

Purposes of Copy Research. The 4A study investigated how copy research was utilized by advertisers and agencies. The responses showed that most often (51 percent of respondents mentioning) copy research results serve as a "go/no-go" report card for decision makers about whether or not an advertisement should be used in a campaign. Other reasons mentioned considerably less frequently were: helps to sell a point of view, serves as an aid to judgment, just one of several means used to evaluate copy, and provides creative guidance. It is interesting to note that only 22 percent of the respondents indicated this last item, use of copy research results to provide creative guidance in the development of advertising. When asked how copy research *should* be used, only 18 percent mentioned "Go/No-Go report card" usage while almost three-fourths (74 percent) mentioned "to provide creative guidance." Clearly, practice and ideal do not coincide in the copy research area of advertising.

4A Recommendations. The American Association study reported above made the following recommendations regarding copy research perspectives:[4]

(1) There should be a range of copy research techniques used which are matched to a specific copy problem.
(2) Multiple rather than single criteria should be measured.
(3) Copy research should be primarily designed to help the creative people.
(4) Copy research should be designed to provide creative guidance on how to create more effective copy.

HIERARCHY OF EFFECTS AND COPY RESEARCH

Figure 11-1 shows the relationship between effectiveness dimensions (for example, affective), criteria (for example, attitude), and copy research method (for example, attitude change in a laboratory environment). Advertising objectives should be set in terms of well-defined criteria, and then these criteria should be accurately linked to some copy research method. This linkage is important. In the past, people have confused the relationships between dimensions of effectiveness, criteria, and copy research method. For example, in one of the most famous, and by now classic, studies in the use of criteria, entitled "Attitude Measures That Predict Purchase" by Joel Axelrod, several of the measures in no way could be viewed as attitude measures.[5] One of the measures he examined was brand awareness. If this measure is taken to be an indicator of attitude (like or dislike of a brand, for example) then it will not be possible to untangle the effects of a commercial on the different dimensions of effectiveness since these all become confounded with each other. It is best to keep these categories distinct if objectives are to be of any help in the development of solid advertising programs. Different copy research methods *should not* be viewed as different measures of the same thing (in general) but as different measures of different things (criteria). It should be noted, however, that there are, *within* a given criterion, many different ways to measure this criterion. For example, the exposure criterion might be measured both by the "glue-seal" technique or the recognition technique in magazines.

Figure 11-1   Hierarchy of Effects and Copy Research

Effectiveness Dimension	Criterion	Example of Copy Research Method
COGNITIVE	Exposure	Recognition
	Awareness (Conprehension)	On-Air Day-After Recall
CONATIVE	Intention	Forced Exposure Pre/Post Consideration
AFFECTIVE	Attitude	Forced Exposure Constant-Sum Scale Attitude Change

SELECTION OF CRITERIA

The "conventional wisdom" in copy research followed the idea that criteria should be selected according to the objectives of the advertising program of which a given execution may be a part. For example, if the brand is new to the market, the objective would be to promote brand awareness through the advertising, and brand awareness, therefore, should serve as the criterion in copy research. This might be the case for new Twice As Fresh air freshener, for example. The thinking is that it is enough of a job for advertising to just let people know the product exists, let alone stimulate consumers to like the brand or to purchase the brand.

A new feature may be added to a brand so that the objective of the advertising may become one of communicating this addition; accordingly, advertising comprehension may serve as the criterion for the copy research. For example, lemon might be added to Mr. Clean so that it is important to determine if consumers perceive from the advertising that "Mr. Clean is lemon-refreshed." It is assumed, then, that it is too much to expect that, in addition to communicating this product addition, the advertising also will stimulate consumers to like the brand more as a result of this addition as well as moving them along the purchase intention continuum.

It may be the case that the brand suffers from unfavorable evaluation on the part of target market consumers because of some improper belief linkage. The criterion, in this case, might become attitude change. "I don't like Macleans' toothpaste because it is highly abrasive," is an example of an improper belief linkage of this type since Macleans has been shown, in standard government tests, to be relatively low in abrasion compared to its competitors. The advertising might supply this information, and it seems reasonable, therefore, for the impact of this information to be assessed on the attitude change criterion of effectiveness.

There are at least four major problems with this "conventional" approach to objective setting and criterion selection in copy research:

(1) A brand may need help in many areas of the advertising province in order to succeed.

(2) Singling out one objective leads to the "tail wagging the dog" syndrome discussed earlier in this chapter (copywriters concentrate on achieving a "high" score on the single criterion rather than on making excellent, overall advertising).

(3) As a practical matter, it is extremely difficult in many cases to pin down one criterion in an empirical manner as the factor of overriding importance relative to the other criteria.

(4) It is now generally agreed that effectiveness of advertising consists of three dimensions, not one (see Chapter 4 on this point).

Finally, it should be noted that the 4A discussed previously in this chapter showed fairly conclusively that practitioners of advertising employed by large advertising agencies and client corporations generally believe that several measures should be taken in a copy research method rather than any given one.

The lack of recognition of the above multiple-criteria proposition on the part of some has promoted a continuing debate over the relative merits of different copy research systems. This debate has usually concerned itself with the relative reliability, sensitivity, and validity of the different methodologies. The classic work of Axelrod mentioned previously was of this nature as well as the more recent work of Ostlund, Clancy and Sapra.[6] It should be possible to develop measurements of all criteria which are reliable, sensitive, and valid within acceptable limits for such commercial work. The debate should not be one, for example, of whether on-air, day-after recall measures are less reliable than forced-exposure, attitude-change measures but rather on how DAR (day-after-recall) methods can be improved with respect to reliability.

COPY RESEARCH METHODS

Though there are many factors upon which copy research methods can be distinguished from each other, the two factors of overriding importance are: (1) dimensions of effectiveness which are measured; and (2) the method of exposure. To illustrate the range or variety of approaches which copy research can take, some syndicated services which offer copy research procedures to agencies and advertisers will be discussed. These methods are categorized in Figure 11-2 for television and in Figure 11-3 for print. Figure 11-2 shows the categorization of 16 selected, syndicated copy research methods by a number of dimensions of effectiveness measured (cognitive, conative, and affective) and the method of exposure (on-premise or on-air exposure). Figure 11-3 shows a similar categorization for nine selected print syndicated services. It should be recognized that many advertising agencies (though not as many now as, say, about ten years ago) develop and implement on an on-going basis their own copy research systems; they may also utilize a syndicated service for particular clients in addition to their self-developed system. The discussion below, then, is in no way intended to be exhaustive of the possibilities but merely suggestive of the possibilities. The illustrative methods will be discussed by the number of dimensions of effectiveness which they attempt to measure.

Uni-dimensional Methods. One of the most-often used services is that provided by the Burke Marketing Research Corporation for the measurement of 24-hour delayed recall of television commercials (Day-after Recall or simply DAR). The attraction of this method rests largely in the completely natural manner in which respondents are exposed to the advertising. The "test" commercial is aired on a local station in three markets selected by the agency and advertiser in so-called Burke cities (cities where they conduct telephone interviews). Respondents are selected randomly from the directory of each city and called 24 hours after the broadcast. A fairly elaborate coding system

Figure 11-2 Broadcast Syndicated
Copy Research Methods

	TRI-DIMENSIONAL METHODS	BI-DIMENSIONAL METHODS	UNI-DIMENSIONAL METHODS
On-Premise Exposure	*Tele-Research* (Trailer) • DAR • Pseudo-purchase • Attitude *ASI* (Theatre) • 24/48-Hour Recall • Pre/Post Intention • Attitude *McCollum/Spielman* (Theatre) • Brand Awareness • Intention • Attitude	*ARS* (Theatre) • 72-Hour Recall • Pre/Post Intention *Burgoyne "Pace"* (Trailer) • Immediate Recall • Pre/Post Intention *Sherman Group* (Trailer) • Immediate Recall • Intention	*Ostberg* (In-Home Projector) • Brand Awareness • Immediate Recall
On-Air Exposure	*Mapes and Ross* (UHF-Recruit) • DAR • Buying Intent • Attitude Change *Starch INRA Hooper CRT* • 1 thru 5-Day Recall • Brand Awareness • Intention • Attitude (control group)	*Gallup & Robinson In-View* (UHF-Recruit) • DAR • Attitude *Audits & Surveys TTC* (Cable TV-Recruit) • DAR • Attitude *Sherman Group* • DAR • Intention *Gallup & Robinson TPT* • DAR • Attitude	*Burke Marketing Research* • DAR *ASI* (Cable-Recruit) • DAR *Ostberg* • DAR

has been developed by Burke for the establishment of the possibility that the respondent was in the "commercial audience." Commercial audience is the term used to define those people who could have seen the commercial and is determined from a series of questions asked respondents about their activity around the time the commercial was aired. Questions are asked of those deemed to be in the commercial audience regarding the commercial (both aided and unaided formats are used). The verbatims elicited by telephone interviewers are recorded (verbatims are all the comments made by the respondent about the brand and commercial) and later analyzed to determine various categories of recall. These categories will be discussed below when DAR is more specifically discussed. The point to be made here, however, is that DAR conducted in the manner which Burke utilizes has the virtue of measuring impact of commercials in a completely natural-exposure environment. This is its primary attraction and accounts for the popularity of the method. Recall of commercial content is the only measure.

In contrast to this method, Ostberg uses an in-home exposure method by showing commercials at the respondent's home on a projec-

Figure 11-3 Print Syndicated Copy Research Methods

	TRI-DIMENSIONAL METHODS	BI-DIMENSIONAL METHODS	UNI-DIMENSIONAL METHODS
On-Premise Exposure	*McCollum/Spielman* (Special Magazine) • Brand Awareness • Recall • Intention • Brand, Ad Attitude	*Sherman Group* (Tip-In and Folio) • Immediate Recall • Intention	*Burke Marketing Research* (Tip-In) • DAR
At-Home Exposure	*ASI* (Tip-In) • Immediate Recall • Pre/Post Intention • Attitude *Mapes and Ross* (Tip-In) • Immediate Recall • Pre/Post Intention • Attitude	*Gallup & Robinson* (In-Magazine, Tip-In) • DAR • Brand Awareness • Attitude *Sherman Group* (Tip-In and Folio) • Recall • Intention	*Starch INRA Hooper* (In-Mazazine) • Recognition

tor. The respondent is first asked on an unaided basis for brand awareness in the test brand product category. The respondent then sees the test commercial embedded with several other control commercials for brands in other product categories. After exposure, the respondent is asked to name brands in four product categories, one of which is the test brand category and three of which differ from those asked prior to exposure. Immediate recall of commercial points is assessed by asking respondents to describe the test brand through rating scales on several attributes, some of which were the subject of the commercial. Notice, in this system both brand awareness and immediate recall of commerical content are measures of only one dimension of effectiveness, the cognitive dimension.

In the magazine advertisement area of assessment, Burke also offers DAR service very similar to the one utilized by them in television commercial measurement. The method uses on-premise exposure (respondents look at the advertisement in a shopping center location) to a magazine in which the test brand ad is "tipped-in" a regular magazine. This means that, of course, the ad did not appear originally in the magazine when it was published. The respondents are asked to look through the magazine and are told that 24 hours later someone will call them to ask them about the content of the magazine. When the respondent is called, he or she is asked general questions about the magazine itself, if he or she recalls certain product categories (test and control are mentioned), and, if he or she remembers specific brand names of products advertised in the product categories, what the advertisements showed and said. If specific brands are not remembered, a brand name cue is given (aided recall). Burke also uses, if the client desires, the "folio" method rather than the tip-in method where the ad to be tested is one of several ads for other products contained in a portfolio which the respondent is then asked to examine.

The classic example of "at-home" exposure in magazine advertising copy research is the Starch Recognition Method conducted by Starch INRA Hooper. Randomly selected respondents across the United States are interviewed in their homes regarding the magazine issues being tested (all ads one-half page or larger are tested by Starch). This method applies only after the advertisement has actually run nationwide in a magazine tested by Starch. The exposure method is not "natural" in the sense that, after it has been established that the respondent read part of the magazine and, therefore, could conceivably have been exposed initially to the ads in the issue, the interviewer shows the magazine to the respondent and goes through it page by page while asking questions about each ad. The respondent is asked if he or she "recognizes having seen the ad the first time the magazine was read." The percentage of respondents who say "yes" to this type of question constitutes the "noted" score for the ad in question. The interviewer subsequently points to each major element in the print ad and asks if the respondent remembers seeing it before. Each element (illustration, logo and so forth) is thus given a noted score. A "seen-associated" percentage score is developed which is based upon the proportion of respondents who indicate they saw the part of the ad with the advertiser's brand name. The "read most" score is the percentage of respondents indicating they initially read half of the copy or more. This method has been criticized severely over the years in terms of its validity (there is no way to check on the veracity of the interviewee's responses since the ad is shown at the time of interview), but it is still widely purchased because of the history (it has been used since the 1920's by some advertisers) of usage and its inexpensiveness (the cost is shared by many advertisers).[7]

Bi-dimensional Methods. Audits & Surveys has a service for television commercial research called TTC (Television Testing Company) which utilizes on-air exposure. In this system, the test commercial is aired on cable television (CATV) in markets selected from the 10-12 which are available. Three commercials (one of which is the client's) are shown in a 7-15 minute movie short. Respondents are pre-recruited; that is, using sample specifications provided by the agency or client, TTC calls respondents and requests them to watch CATV at the time the commercial will be shown. Two dimensions of effectiveness are assessed: recall of commercial content 24 hours after exposure (cognitive dimension); and attitude toward the commercial (affective dimension). If the client desires, respondents can be telephone-interviewed immediately after the exposure rather than 24 hours later (DAR).

ARS (Research Systems Corporation) conducts on-premise exposure in which two dimensions of effectiveness (cognitive and conative) are measured. Respondents are randomly selected from the directory and invited by phone to attend the testing premises. Respondents are exposed in a theatre (called "theatre testing" frequently) to a half-hour pilot program which was rejected by networks for programming purposes; respondents have, therefore, not seen this program previously. The program contains test commercials as well as control commercials. Before viewing, respondents are asked which brand in certain product categories they "intend" to select if they win a prize "attendance drawing" at the end of the session. After viewing, this question is asked again and serves as the pre/post intention measure (conative measure). Respondents are called 72 hours after the exposure to measure delayed recall (cognitive measure).

In magazine measurement, Gallup & Robinson uses either the "tip-in" or "in-magazine" method (the ad actually is run in a "real" magazine). Under either method of exposure, the respondent is selected randomly from the directory and visited at home; a magazine (either actual or tipped-in version) is given to the respondent. The respondent is told he or she will be called back 24 hours later regarding the magazine's contents. At the time of call-back, the interviewer first asks general questions about the magazine to establish readership. The interviewer then reads a list of brands and asks the interviewee if there were ads in the magazine for each brand (90 percent of the brand names appeared in the magazine while 10 percent did not). For each brand answered in the affirmative by the respondent, he or she is asked to describe the ad and what his or her attitudes were toward the brand after reading the ad. Thus both the cognitive (brand recall and advertising recall) as well as the affective (attitude toward advertisement) dimensions are measured.

The Sherman Group, Inc. uses an on-premise, bi-dimensional copy research procedure to test print advertising. Either the "tip-in" approach or the folio approach to exposure can be used. The respondents are mailed the magazine containing the test ad; one week after the mailing, respondents are interviewed in their homes. Respondents are asked whether or not they remember seeing a particular ad for a particular product category; if they do remember, they are then asked to describe the ad. Then, all respondents are given an opportunity to see the ad, and then they are asked what was worth seeing about the product in the ad. Finally, they are asked if they would mention something about the product described in the ad to a friend. The method, therefore, assesses the cognitive dimension (recall) and the conative dimension (intention to mention the ad to a friend). This latter measure is termed the "buy test" by the Sherman group.

Tri-dimensional Methods. The Mapes and Ross Company utilizes an on-air exposure method which measures all three dimensions of effectiveness (cognitive, conative, and affective). In this procedure, respondents are recruited on a random basis to watch a program (which varies from test to test) on a UHF station (in one of three cities) which contains the test commercial. Prior to exposure, respondents are asked which brand they like best in the test brand product category (this is done in an unaided fashion). This is accomplished on the phone at the same time respondents are asked to watch the program. The day after exposure, respondents are called back and asked the brand liking question again (post-exposure measure). Then the interviewer asks the respondent if he or she recalls seeing commercials the day before for six brands (all of which were in the program viewed). For each commercial recalled in this general way, the respondent is requested to describe each commercial specifically. Finally, each respondent is asked to rate the test brand as well as the other five brands for which commercials appeared on 4 to 16 statements using a 10-point attitudinal scale; respondents are also asked if the commercial in each case increased their interest in buying the brand. Thus, there is a cognitive measure (24-hour recall), a conative measure (buying interest), and two affective measures (pre/post attitude change and attitude based upon specific attribute scales) in the Mapes and Ross method.

Figure 11–4 describes the method developed by Jenssen and used by his Tele-Research Corporation to conduct tri-dimensional on-premise television commercial copy research.[8] At a shopping center site, consumers are invited to participate before going into a store. They are given cents-off coupons for 10 products (among which is the test brand). The respondents are told they can use the coupons at a designated store on the test day only. Another sample is recruited and given the coupons; this sample serves as the "control group." The test group is taken into trailer facility (called the trailer exposure method) located at the shopping center and is exposed to TV material with test brand commercial in it as well as commercials for other products. After exposure, respondents are asked about the effect of the commercial on interest in buying the brand on a five-point scale. Respondents are called 24 hours later to assess recall. Pseudo-purchase behavior is indicated by the proportion of coupon redemptions in the "test" group versus those in the "control" group.

In the print area, ASI-Market Research, Inc. conducts a procedure in which all three dimensions of effectiveness are measured. The at-home exposure method involves the "tip-in" approach in which the test magazine with the client's ad is tipped-in and left at the respondent's home. The respondent is asked to read the magazine and is told the interviewer will return to ask questions the following day. The respondent is told there will be a prize for his or her participation and asked which brand would be preferred if he or she is selected as a prize winner. At the next interviewing session, the respondent is asked if he or she recalls reading specific ads in the magazine and what the ads showed or said (nine ads are specified by the interviewer; four ads for test brands, four other ads in the magazine and one ad which was not in the magazine). In addition, after the ad is shown by the interviewer to the respondent, the interviewee is asked about reactions to the ad and the effect the ad had on the respondent's interest in buying the product. Thus, the method measures cognitive (recall), conative (buying interest), and affective (pre/post attitude change) dimensions of effectiveness.

The McCollum/Spielman Company offers an on-premise, tri-dimensional copy research method for print advertising. In this system, the testing is done at semi-permanent facilities of the company (they are moved when too many respondents are interviewed from the same area over a period of time). Television commercials are also measured in conjunction with the print assessment (these commercials would be from different advertisers than those using the print facilities). A special magazine called *Prevue Studio Review,* which is written by McCollum/Spielman and is similar to a theatre playbill, contains four full-page ads (two test and two control). Respondents are first asked about brand usage in several categories. The playbills are then distributed while the respondents are waiting for the TV program to begin; respondents are urged at this time to read the playbill magazine. While the tapes are being changed for a second TV program/commercials, respondents are urged to look at the playbill again. At the end of the second program, respondents are questioned about the TV material followed by questions about brand awareness and advertisement recall for the print ads which appeared in the playbill. Respondents are also asked to open the magazine and look at the ads; at this time product and advertisement attitudes are elicited. Respondents are also asked which brand they would prefer to have for the product category tested; the proportion of those who are not test brand users (as determined by the usage questions at the beginning) who say they would choose the test brand is an intention measure. Thus, brand awareness and recall

Figure 11-4   Impact of TV Commercials:
Example of After-Only With Control Design

The purpose of this experiment was to measure the effectiveness of two different TV commercials.

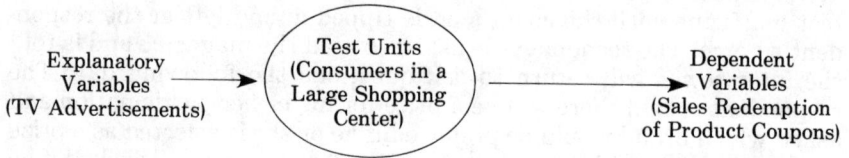

Explanatory Variables (TV Advertisements) → Test Units (Consumers in a Large Shopping Center) → Dependent Variables (Sales Redemption of Product Coupons)

Three different groups of shoppers were interviewed in a shopping center just before entering a large Los Angeles supermarket. Two of the groups then viewed certain TV commercials which included one advertisement in each group for the product which was to be evaluated. All three groups were given a gift packet of ten different cents-off coupons redeemable for various items that the supermarket carried, including the test product. All three groups of shoppers were randomly selected, so the sales redemption rate of coupons in the supermarket was assumed to measure the effectiveness of the two different commercials.

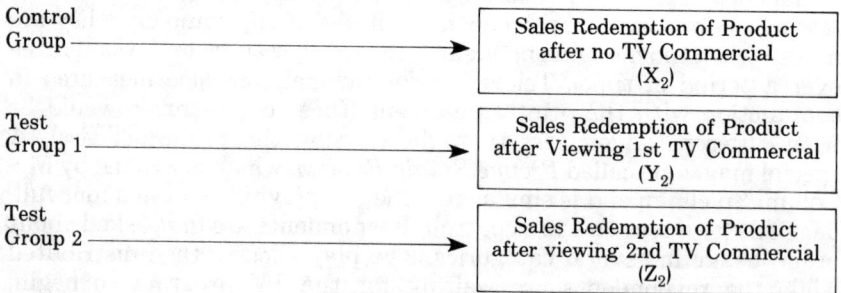

Control Group ——→ Sales Redemption of Product after no TV Commercial (X_2)

Test Group 1 ——→ Sales Redemption of Product after Viewing 1st TV Commercial (Y_2)

Test Group 2 ——→ Sales Redemption of Product after viewing 2nd TV Commercial (Z_2)

Treatment Effects = $(Y_2 - X_2)$ and $(Z_2 - X_2)$

The actual sales redemption rates were:

Test Units	Sales Redemption Rate	Treatment Effect
Control Group	14.5%	
Test Group 1	21.7	7.2%
Test Group 2	30.0	15.5

SOURCE: Ward J. Jenssen, "Sales Effects of TV, Radio, and Print Advertising," *Journal of Advertising Research* (June 1966), pp. 2-7. Reprinted from *Marketing Research Process* by Keith K. Cox and Ben M. Enis, Goodyear Publishing Co., 1972, p. 316.

(cognitive measures), an intention (conative measure), and attitude toward brand and print ad (affective measures) are assessed in the single procedure.

It should be noted that in the copy research industry, as in the media data research industry, companies go out of business over time and new ones begin. So, in the above discussion the examples using company names should not be construed as the important factor. The methods are likely to survive over time even if particular companies go out of business. This fact is illustrated by the demise of the Schwerin Organization which was famous for its theatre testing for many years. The ASI Market Research Company uses almost the identical procedure today, including the use of reaction profile indicators which are developed for each respondent in the theatre; the profiles are derived, as were the Schwerin profiles, by respondents' pushing buttons at their seats when they see something pleasing or displeasing.

Another view of various available copy research methods is provided in a text which reports on work in this area by the Marketing Science Institute.[9] Additional overviews on work in copy research may be found in the two articles by Holbert entitled, "Key Articles in Advertising Research" and "More Key Articles in Advertising Research."[10] The Advertising Research Foundation also has published annotated bibliographies on copy research.[11]

MEASUREMENT OF RECALL AND ATTITUDE CHANGE

The two most important methods in copy research are the on-air and forced (on-premise) exposure methods.[12] The most-often used on-air method is one in which recall is assessed the day after exposure in several markets; the "pure form" of this method is represented by the Burke DAR procedure discussed in the preceding section. The most-often used on-premise exposure method is the theatre method; this is represented in "pure form" by the ARS or ASI procedures discussed previously. It should be noted that the term "persuasion" is often used by practitioners in conjunction with forced exposure methods. The use of this terminology is unfortunate since persuasion can mean many different things to different people. Persuasion could mean pre/post-exposure brand choice change, brand preference change, change in simulated purchase, brand consideration change, brand intention-to-buy change, or attitude change, among others. Attitude means favorableness or unfavorableness toward some object (brand or commercial) and is, most likely, what is meant in forced-exposure testing more often than not. It would be preferable to refer to pre/post attitude change in conjunction with on-premise testing than to "persuasion." The term, persuasion, as used in the great deal of communication research work conducted at Yale after World War II inevitably meant "attitude change" or "attitude shift."[13] Contemporary work in communication research also uses the term "attitude change."

Because these two methods are dominant in the copy research field, they will be considered in some detail in the following sections.

METHODOLOGY

Though in the preceding section general descriptions of DAR and attitude change methods were provided, a complete understanding of the dynamics of each method and the issues involved in each is required before the controversy which surrounds the two most popular methods can be comprehended. Detailed examples of each method are presented below.

Recall (Example 11-1). Suppose two different commercials for Glow toothpaste are tested on the standard DAR system. These two commercials should represent two alternative strategies which are being considered for the Glow campaign. Each is tested in three cities, and the tests are about a month apart. Table 11-1 shows the data which result from these tests after verbatims have been coded. Verbatims are the responses of interviewees given to the telephone interviewers and recorded by them during the interview.

Table 11-1 DAR Copy Research Results for Glow Toothpaste

	February 3, 1982 Glow Commercial A		March 11, 1982 Glow Commercial B	
Total Dialings	5,250		6,314	
Dialings by City	Davenport:	1701	Milwaukee:	2104
	Grand Rapids:	1860	Dayton:	3009
	Omaha:	1689	Denver:	1201
% and (number) Completed Interviews (Program Audience)	4.0% (210)		3.5% (221)	
Commercial Audience (Base Number)	57.2% (120)		59.3% (131)	
Unrelated Recall	14.2% (17)		9.3% (12)	
Aided Related Recall* (General and Specific)	25.3% (30)		34.2% (45)	
Unaided Related Recall (General and Specific)	18.4% (22)		10.9% (14)	
Unaided Related Recall* (Specific Only)	16.0% (19)		8.3% (11)	

*Statistically significant differences across commercials, $\alpha = .15$

The first item which is shown in Table 11-1 concerns the number of telephone dialings which were required, using the randomly generated sample of numbers, to obtain around 200 or so respondents who watched the television program in which the commercial appeared. Notice that in the case of Commercial A more than 5,000 dialings were required before 210 people who watched the program and would agree to the interview were accumulated. This is not an uncommon situation and has prompted various agencies to attempt procedures to lessen the number of dialings required in DAR so as to reduce the cost and time involved in the overall procedure. One system is called the "pre-alert" method whereby a random sample is contacted by phone and asked to watch the channel on which the commercial will appear at the time it will appear on the following day. Typically, this procedure would save about 75 percent of the dialings typically required under the standard DAR system. For example, suppose it is desired to have about 120 respondents in the commercial audience for a particular test. Assuming that about 75 percent of those contacted will not participate in the research for whatever reasons and that only about 70 percent of those pre-alerted who say they will watch the program, in fact, do watch it, about 684 dialings would be required to conduct the pre-alert process:

Number of Initial Dialings:	684	
25% Participation Rate:	171	(.25 × 684 = 171)
Number of DAR Call-Backs:	171	
30% Attrition Rate:	120	(171 × .70 = 120)
Total Initial + Call-Backs:	855	(684 + 171 = 855).

This pre-alert would yield the same number of respondents in the commercial audience as shown for Commercial A in Table 11-1 but would require only 16 percent as many dialings (855 compared to 5,250).

A large advertising agency recently studied the effect of pre-alerting on recall scores for several commercials tested under the standard DAR format and under the pre-alert format. The commercials used in the research were for such packaged goods products as margarine and the like. The scores are shown below:

	Standard DAR Related Recall	Pre-Alert Related Recall
Commercial #1	16%	14%
Commercial #2	7%	10%
Commercial #3	15%	16%
Commercial #4	13%	14%
Commercial #5	18%	14%
Commercial #6	29%	18%
Average of All Six Commercials:	16.3%	14.3%.

In only one of the above six tests of pre-alert versus standard DAR is there probably a statistically significant difference between the related recall scores generated under each approach (Commercial #6). Overall, the scores look quite close. Though further investigation would be required, initially it appears that one way of reducing costs in DAR might be to pre-alert respondents. It is recognized, however, that for some this distortion of the standard DAR format would, prima facie, destroy the validity of the method. Contrary to the above results, "common sense" would seem to indicate "hyped-up" recall scores under the pre-alert system. It should be recognized, too, that recruiting is a common feature (as shown in Figure 11-2) of many syndicated services which measure DAR. Recruiting is the same thing as pre-alerting.

Notice that, in Table 11-1, about 60 percent of those in the program audience are classified as belonging to the "commercial audience" in the case of both commercials. The standard DAR format utilizes a series of questions to determine if the respondent was concentrating on the television at the precise time the commercial appeared. The interviewer asks for program content, given some prompts, for the 60-second period immediately before the commercial and the 60-second period immediately following the commercial. In addition the interviewer reads a prompt of the commercial itself. For any of these three parts of the television content which the respondent does not remember seeing, the respondent is asked (1) whether he or she was in or out of the room at the time, (2) whether he or she changed channels or not, and (3) if he or she was in the room, what he or she was doing at that time. Commercial audience consists of those people who had an opportunity to see the commercial; that is, those who remember seeing at least two of the three program segments or those who were in the room, awake, and watching the channel on which the commercial was aired. Ordinarily, between 35 percent and 95 percent of the program audience is in the commercial audience. The commercial audience size provides the base number of people upon which all other figures in Table 11-1 are percentaged.

All the remaining items in Table 11-1 refer to the categorization of the verbatims. Some sample verbatims are illustrated in Table 11-2 for a Colossal Laundry Starch commercial; the first five were categorized or coded as related recall while the remaining five were coded as unrelated recall.

The usual categories for coding of DAR verbatims are presented below:

(1) *Unaided Recall* refers to a verbatim elicited without prompting with respect to either the brand name or commercial content;
(2) *Aided Recall* is a verbatim which results from prompting with respect to either the brand name and/or general content;
(3) *General Recall* refers to verbatim comments which describe the commercial under test but which could also accurately describe, in a general manner, other commercials which have aired for the brand.

(4) *Specific Recall* refers to a verbatim which could come only as a result of viewing the particular test commercial; that is, the verbatim describes specifically the detailed content of the commercial;

(5) *Unrelated Recall* is an elicited verbatim which has nothing to do with the message under test;

(6) *Related Recall* refers to verbatim comment which is associated with the commercial under test in either a general or specific manner.

Table 11-2   Sample DAR Verbatims for Colossal Laundry Starch "Ironing Demonstration" Commercial

---

1. *There was a lady ironing, and she held up a blouse. NMR. It gives clothes body. It's economical and good enough to use in a laundry. NMR. Makes clothes look fresh. NMR.

2. *A woman was putting a white blouse in the starch. She ironed it and showed how pretty it looked after it was starched. Makes your ironing go smoother. NMR. At the end of the commercial, they showed the box of starch.

3. *A woman was standing by her ironing board. She was ironing clothes. NMR. There was a whole bunch of clothes by the ironing board and she was telling about how good this new Colossal Starch was. She said it makes your clothes nice and fresh looking.

4. *Someone said Colossal Starch was economical. NMR.

5. *A woman was pouring starch into a sink. then she ironed a dress and talked about the starch. Oh, she said, I wish I had found this starch before. This new starch is so much better than my other one. It makes the clothes firm and not too stiff. My old one used to leave the shirts so stiff they could stand up by themselves.

6. It was the one about the washing machine test. They said it could be used in your washing machine. The woman poured it right in her washing machine. NMR. Gives clothes a good finish, not sticky.

7. You can spray it on and it won't clog the spray nozzle. Clothes look nicer and have body. Just spray it on and make your iron glide. They showed how it worked.

8. There was a little boy telling his mother to use the Colossal Starch. NMR.

9. It was a woman standing in her garden by a clothesline discussing starches with her neighbor. She advised her neighbor to use Colossal.

10. They have this big display of irons and an announcer says that Colossal is recommended by the manufacturer. NMR.

NMR indicates "no more recall" at the particular point in the interview probe.

*indicates the verbatim was coded as related recall.

SOURCE: Sample report of Burke Marketing Research Inc. for Colossal Laundry Starch "Ironing Demonstration" 30 second commercial, 1977.

Clearly, the most stringent test, from the standpoint of respondent memory, is specific, unaided, related recall. As the last line in Table 11-1 indicates, this number of people can become very small (19 for

Commercial A and 11 for Commercial B) from the standpoint of the number of dialings made (5250 and 6314, respectively). Using this criterion, Commercial A is superior to Commercial B. Notice that if the aided related recall measure is used, the opposite conclusion would result.

With respect to the coding system described above, Russell I. Haley, a prominent advertising researcher, criticized this usual method before the annual meeting of the Advertising Research Foundation:[14]

> ... We need a new way of coding recall. We need to code the types of feedback we are getting by their nature. As I mentioned earlier we're getting additions, distortions, put-downs, replays of past advertising, and probably a lot more besides. We need a structure for organizing this sort of information.

Such a structure which takes into account the depth of recall in a particular verbatim as well as making use of the "inferences" contained very often in recall material is described in the next section; it is termed the Personal Product Response method. Even this method, however, does not quantitatively account for the number or bits of information which a particular respondent plays back accurately. A respondent who remembers six of the information bits in a commercial certainly has greater "recall" than a person who remembers only one bit of information accurately.

Though the aided, related recall figures shown in Table 11-1 may appear quite small, these figures are quite in line with usual occurrences. The Burke Marketing Research Company has reported DAR norms for all commercials tested between 1975 and 1977.[15] Of the 1,692 commercials tested during that period on female samples, the average related recall score was 24 percent (the range was from 0 to 57 percent). These were all 30-second commercials for products such as OTC (over the counter) drugs, beverages, branded food products, and toiletries. A related recall score of 23 percent would put a commercial in the top 50 percentile of the nearly 1700 commercials tested. This 23 percent would ordinarily be about 30 people in the test; if two commercials are being compared, this would mean that about 12,000 dialings were made by interviewers to get down to about 60 or so people upon which the decision as to which commercial is better will be made.

The cost of the standard DAR test should be noted. Finished commercials are required in the standard DAR format (though rough commercials can be used in an altered format, this method is not equivalent to standard DAR). In the beer industry, it would not be uncommon for the finished commercial to entail $50,000 in production costs. If two commercials are to be tested, as in the example in Table 11-1, and the cost of the test itself is around $7,000 per commercial (excluding TV air time), then the cost would be somewhere around $114,000. Though as a proportion of the media expenditures over a given period of time this may not be very large, the cost of standard DAR is above that of many other testing methods.

Attitude Change (Example 11-2). Suppose respondents are invited to a theatre for the screening of a pilot (which is usually one which has been rejected by networks or syndicates) television program. Prior to the screening, respondents are asked to divide up 10 points among three brands of toothpaste (Glow and its two major competitors, Ultran and Dreen) according to how much they like each brand. The question might appear as follows:

"We'd like you to rate 3 brands of toothpaste according to how much you like each brand."

"Please give us your rating by dividing 10 points among the 3 brands. The more you like a brand of toothpaste, the bigger the number of points you would give it. The less you like a brand, the smaller the number of points you would give it."

"You can give any brand as many points or as few points as you like. And you don't have to give a brand any points if you don't want to. Remember that the total number of points you give the 3 brands must add up to 10."

BRANDS OF TOOTHPASTE

NAME OF BRAND	NUMBER OF POINTS
GLOW	_____
ULTRAN	_____
DREEN	_____
TOTAL	10

One-third of the total sample of respondents would then see the pilot with several commercials embedded in it, among which would be Glow Commercial A and a commercial for each of the two competitors (Ultran and Dreen). Another third of the sample would see the same pilot and commercials except that the order would be rotated so that the Ultran commercial was seen first followed by the Glow and Dreen commercials; the final third of the sample would see the Dreen commercial first followed by the Ultran and Glow commercials. This rotation would be conducted to control for any possible serial or order effects which might occur.

Following the exposure, respondents are asked to divide up 10 points again according to how much they like each brand of toothpaste. In addition, the "hype" statement might be added:

"The commercials you've just seen may have reminded you of one or two things about these toothpastes or told you something new about them. Will you please rate the three brands of toothpaste according to how much you like them *RIGHT NOW.*"

Diagnostic questions about individual brand and commercial attributes would probably be assessed next. Suppose that about 210 respondents are processed through this type of theatre procedure for the Glow Commercial A; this sample size is very common in this type of copy research work. Then suppose another 210 respondents are recruited to come to the theatre to see the same pilot and the same commercials for Ultran and Dreen as well as the same non-toothpaste commercials used in the test above. But this time the second commercial for Glow is inserted in place of the Glow Commercial A so that this is a test of the Glow Commercial B against the same competitive and program context as that used for Commercial A. These two procedures produce results based upon the use of the constant-sum scaling device (dividing up 10 points among the brands) as shown in Table 11-3.

Table 11-3   Constant-Sum Scores for Glow and Competitors (Overall Scores and by Direction of Shift)

		Average Post Score −	Average Pre Score =	Average Change Score
Glow Commercial A:				
	GLOW	3.01	1.82	+1.19
	ULTRAN	4.37	4.96	− .59
	DREEN	2.62	3.22	− .60
Glow Commercial B:				
	GLOW	3.52	2.06	+1.46
	ULTRAN	3.64	4.72	−1.08
	DREEN	2.84	3.22	− .38

		Positive Shift	Negative Shift	No Change
Glow Commercial A:				
	GLOW			
	People	41%	11%	48%
	Shift	3.41	1.85	—
	ULTRAN			
	People	11%	38%	51%
	Shift	2.31	2.20	—
	DREEN			
	People	18%	30%	52%
	Shift	1.86	3.08	—
Glow Commercial B:				
	GLOW			
	People	47%	8%	45%
	Shift	3.52	2.20	—
	ULTRAN			
	People	14%	48%	38%
	Shift	2.65	3.07	—
	DREEN			
	People	18%	28%	54%
	Shift	1.95	2.67	—

Notice in Table 11-3 that the scores from this procedure are presented in two different ways. At the top of the table the mean or average scores for each test are shown for the scores given by the 210 respondents to, for example, Glow in the Commercial A test before seeing the pilot and commercials (pre-score) and after seeing the pilot and commercials (post-score). The pre-score is subtracted from the post-score to give the average amount of shift or change pre- to post-exposure; these scores are ordinarily called "change scores." Notice that within a test, say the test for Commercial A, the three change scores for Glow, Ultran and Dreen must add up to zero. In this example, Glow Commercial B (mean change score of +1.46) was statistically significantly different (α = .15) from Glow Commercial A (mean change score of +1.19). Commercial B would be the better commercial using this overall or "global" attitude change measure.

The constant-sum measure of attitude change is an abstract measure in the sense that it does not refer to numbers or percentages of people, as in the DAR system. Therefore, users of this system often prefer to present the results of such tests as shown in the bottom of Table 11-3. Here the overall scores are broken down by the direction of movement or shift pre- to post-exposure. For example, in the case of the test for Glow Commercial A, 41 percent of the 210 respondents moved up (gave more points to Glow after exposure than they did before exposure) while 11 percent moved down pre- to post-exposure. Almost one-half (48 percent) remained the same, that is, gave Glow the exact same number of points before and after exposure. Notice that about one-third to one-half of the total respondents tend to stay the same over all brands in both tests. This is a common finding in such testing where only one exposure to the commercial is utilized.

There is no control group used in the procedure just described; in this sense the testing system is a "pseudo experiment." Though scientific considerations would seem to dictate the use of a control group, this is not usually employed in copy research work. In addition to the practical reasons of time and money, there is some "practical" evidence that control groups are not particularly useful in such copy research work. For example, Van de Sandt indicates that in the type of design used in most commercial effectiveness research the results are usually examined in terms of a comparison of pre-post differences or a comparison of post scores for each test group with control-group scores.[16] He points out that it is an empirical fact that the pre-post differences are almost always positive when test groups are compared to control groups (test groups tend to have the more positive scores). This is due in large part, he believes, to an experimental situation with a liberal degree of acquiescence and goodwill. This goodwill is further heightened because the sample is generally selected from a population defined as the specific target group for the product category, and the target group as often as not is composed of subjects favorable to the product, if not necessarily the brand. Van de Sandt concludes that it is useless to utilize a control group in such research (that is, a group which receives no exposure to the commercials) because it is almost a certainty, given past findings, that such a comparison between that group and the test group will lead to an exaggerated favorable conclusion.

Several observations can be made regarding the use of this constant-sum, forced-exposure system for measuring global attitude change. First, it can be noticed in Table 11–3 that Glow shows unequal pre-scores across the test for Commercial A and that for Commercial B (1.82 and 2.06, respectively). This creates a problem in comparing the change scores for Glow across the two commercials. It is not entirely fair to judge the two commercials based upon the size of the change scores when the brand started out differently between the two groups. In fact, the difference between the Glow change scores across the two commercial tests (1.46 − 1.19 = .27) is only slightly larger than the difference between the pre-scores for Glow across the two commercial tests (2.06 − 1.82 = .24). When the brand starts out at the low end of the constant-sum scale, there is a great deal of room for improvement after exposure to the commercials. For the case in which the brand starts out at the high end of the continuum, there is little room for upward movement after exposure. This gives rise to a spurious degree of relationship (inverse correlation) between the movement potential on the constant-sum scale and the amount of change pre-post exposure.

The point at which a respondent starts out (pre-exposure) on the constant-sum scale is very highly related to the usership pattern of the respondents. Figure 11–5 shows the "S-shaped" relationship of pre-score points on the constant-sum scale for "Brand A" (a toiletry product) to usership (define as brand last bought in the product category). Clearly, for the 960 respondents upon which this relationship is based, the higher the points attributed to Brand A on the pre-exposure constant-sum scale, the higher the probability that the respondent is a user of Brand A. For example, only 4.5 percent of the respondents who give Brand A one point on the pre-score are users of Brand A while 26.7 percent of those who give Brand A ten points on the pre-score are users of Brand A.

There are three ways in which the unequal-starting-point problem can be attacked. One method would be to recruit a quota sample of one-third users of Glow, one-third users of Ultran, and one-third users of Dreen. This is costly and time-involving and will not provide perfectly matched pre-scores since the relationship between brand usage and point allocation is not a completely certain one. Another method is to apply a statistical tool called "covariance analysis" in which the differential effect of pre-scores is removed from the post-scores (the pre-scores are statistically "held constant"); these adjusted post-scores are then tested for significant differences between two different commercials for a given brand.[17] Another approach is to use an adjustment mechanism based upon the numerical relationship of pre-scores to the potential amount of movement possible for the given starting point. For example, suppose a given respondent allocates two points to Brand A prior to exposure and four points after exposure for a change score of two points. This respondent has a potential movement up for

Figure 11-5   Relationship Between Allocation of
Constant-Sum Scale Points and Brand Usage

Brand A Users As
Proportion of All
Brand Users

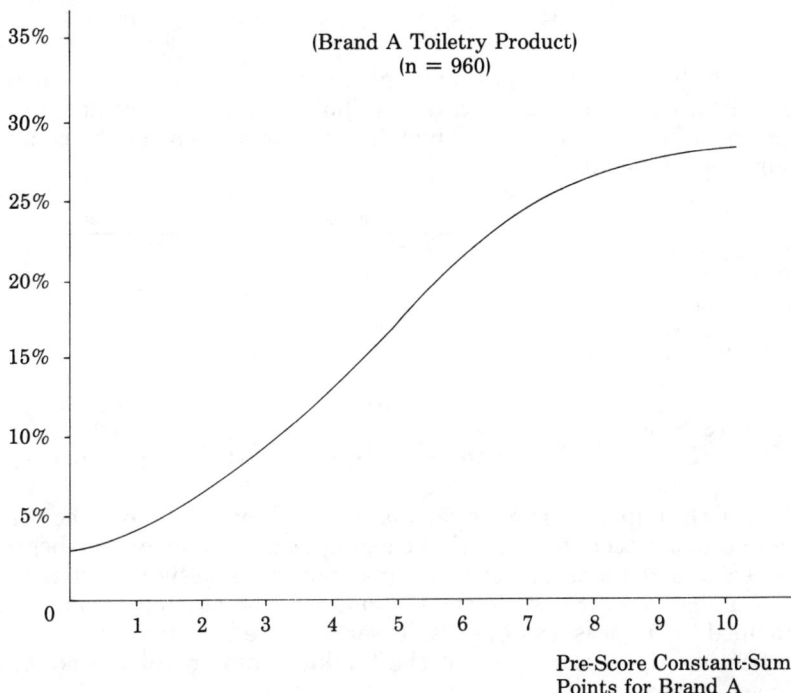

(Brand A Toiletry Product)
(n = 960)

Pre-Score Constant-Sum
Points for Brand A

Overall Sample Usership Composition:
     18% Brand A
     33% Brand B
      7% Brand C
     42% All Others

Brand A for eight points; the actual movement up for this respondent is one-fourth the potential movement (2/8 = .25). Now, if all three brands started at equal levels (equal pre-scores) they would begin at 3.33 on the 10-point scale. This would leave a potential movement up of 6.67 (10 − 3.33 = 6.67). The respondent actually moved up 25 per-cent of the potential amount; when this movement rate is applied to the equal-starting point potential movement, the change score ad-justed for unequal starting points is obtained as 1.66 (.25 × 6.67 = 1.66). Some further examples are shown below:

	Respondent #1	Respondent #2	Respondent #3
Pre-Score	2	5	3
Post-Score	4	4	2
Change Score	+2	−1	−1
Change Potential	+8	−5	−3
3.33 Potential	6.67	−3.33	−3.33
Adjusted Change	+1.66	− .67	−1.11
	(6.67 × 2/8)	(1/5 × −3.33)	(1/3 × −3.33).

For the change of scores of zero, an adjustment can also be made to account for the idea that an ad which "holds" a respondent at seven pre and post is superior to one which holds a respondent at the constant-sum scale level of 1:

	Respondent #4	Respondent #5
Pre-Score	7	1
Post-Score	7	1
Change Score	0	0
+1 Adjusted Change	+2.22	+ .74
−1 Adjusted Change	− .48	−3.33
Difference +1 and −1	2.70	4.07
	{2.22 − (−.48) = 2.70}	{.74 − (−3.33) = 4.07}
Adjusted Score	+ .87	−1.29
	{(2.70/2) + (−.48) = .87}	{(4.07/2) + (−3.33) = −1.29}.

Notice the adjusted score is calculated as mid-way between the +1 and −1 adjusted scores. In the above example, a respondent who begins at seven and remains at seven after exposure is assigned an adjusted change score of .87 while the respondent who started at one and remained there was assigned a lesser adjusted change score, −1.29, reflecting the lesser value of the "holding power" of the ad at this lower level.

A final issue which might be noted in conjunction with this global attitude-change example concerns the pinpointing of the commercial which "caused" the change in constant-sum points from pre- to post-exposure. Did the respondent really "dislike" Brand B's commercial a great deal, and, therefore, decide to take some points away from Brand B on the post-exposure measurement? In the constant-sum system of measurement, the points taken away from one brand must necessarily be given to at least one other brand; in this example, these other brands would be receiving points "by default" rather than because their commercials prompted the respondent to like the brands more after exposure. This problem is not easily overcome, but one large agency used the following question in an attempt to pin down the brand which starts the "chain reaction" in point allocation:

"Was there anything in any of these commercials that you just saw that made you feel differently at all toward any of the brands?

(___) YES   (___) NO

If "yes":

Which brand did you feel most differently about?

Did you feel more favorable or less favorable toward it?"

RELIABILITY/VALIDITY/SENSITIVITY

A great deal of academic and practical work has been conducted in recent years regarding the reliability, validity, and sensitivity (the degree to which a copy research method can detect differences between commercials when these actually exist) of the DAR and Attitude-Change methods. Because of the overwhelming importance of these two methodologies in copy research, the available evidence on these issues will be examined with respect to each of these two methods. Before this, however, it is helpful to understand the general meaning of reliability and different types of validity in the context of a procedure call the "Multitrait-Multimethod Matrix."[18] The ideas contained in this method are presented below.

Example 11-3.[19] The basic idea of the multitrait-multimethod matrix is illustrated by the data shown in Table 11-4. Suppose that 20 or so commercials for a given brand are tested on three effectiveness dimensions using recall, attitude and intention criteria. Furthermore, these 20 commercials are tested on these three criteria by three different measurement methods. In one instance, suppose a group of five copywriters familiar with the product category are asked to rate each of the 20 commercials on recall, attitude and intention criteria; for each criterion, the five copywriters' ratings are averaged into a composite rating for each commercial.

Next, suppose the same 20 commercials are tested in an on-premise exposure system such as the theatre approach. Finally, the 20 commercials are tested on a recruited-sample, on-air system. Notice, that to measure recall in the on-premise system the recall score would be generated in each instance through call-backs to those attending the theatre screening. In the on-air system, respondents would need to be recruited since pre-exposure attitude would need to be measured. Thus, the recall and attitude measures generated under the on-premise and on-air approaches would not be expected to be the same.

The figures presented in Table 11-4 are correlation coefficients which can, of course, range between -1.00 and $+1.00$. These data illustrate two types of validity assessment. First, *convergent validity* can be assessed by examining the coefficients for the same criterion across different assessment methods (judgment, on-premise, and on-air). For example, there is a fairly strong relationship between copywriters' judgments on the recall criterion and on-premise consumer recall measurement ($r = .68$); there is an even stronger relationship between consumer on-premise recall and consumer on-air recall ($r = .76$). The fact that, in this hypothetical example, the same

Table 11-4 Hypothetical Multitrait-Multimethod Matrix of Correlations for Copy Research Methods

	Copywriter Ratings			Consumer Ratings (On-Premise)			Consumer Ratings (On-Air)		
	R_1	A_1	I_1	R_2	A_2	I_2	R_3	A_3	I_3
Copywriter Ratings									
Recall R_1	1.00								
Attitude A_1	.42	1.00							
Intention I_1	.34	.45	1.00						
Consumer Ratings (On-Premise)									
Recall R_2	.68	.18	.22	1.00					
Attitude A_2	.10	.67	.20	.44	1.00				
Intention I_2	.09	.19	.60	.22	.50	1.00			
Consumer Ratings (On-Air)									
Recall R_3	.76	.19	.22	.86	.39	.34	1.00		
Attitude A_3	.14	.69	.15	.29	.90	.24	.35	1.00	
Intention I_3	.19	.08	.58	.33	.33	.95	.23	.44	1.00

ADAPTED FROM: David A. Aaker and John G. Myers, *Advertising Management* (Englewood Cliffs: Prentice-Hall, Inc., 1975), p. 452.

criterion measured in different ways produces comparable results points to the convergent validity of the criterion. In Table 11-4, the correlations seem to point to rather high convergent validity of all three criteria.

Another type of validity is called *discriminant validity*. If the three criteria used in Table 11-4 are supposed to measure different aspects of the effectiveness of commercials, then the correlations between the criteria should not be high, that is, they should show divergence as opposed to convergence. This is clearly the case for the hypothetical data in Table 11-4. For example, the relationship between on-premise recall and on-premise intention is only .22; the relationship between on-premise recall and on-air intention is only .33. If these types of cross-criteria correlations were high, this would indicate that the criteria are not measuring different dimensions of effectiveness. Since these three criteria are accepted as indicators from a conceptual point of view of the cognitive, affective and conative dimensions of effectiveness, it would be expected that acceptable measures of these three criteria would show *high* divergent or discriminant validity. This is the case for the measures in Table 11-4.

There is a third type of validity which cannot be assessed by the data shown in Table 11-4. This is called *face validity* and refers to the extent to which it appears reasonable, from a description of the method involved, that it will accurately measure what it is supposed to measure. For example, the face validity of DAR measured through an on-premise, forced-exposure procedure or through a pre-alert or recruit-type on-air procedure would appear to most people familiar with copy research methods to be considerably lower than that for the standard on-air DAR system. This is largely due to the fact that respondents do not know they will be respondents until after they have been naturally exposed to the commercial in the standard DAR approach; in the other two systems, respondents are aware they are a part of some type of research procedure prior to exposure.

Reliability is the extent to which a measure gives the same answer for the same commercial when the measure is applied more than once. The usual method for assessing copy research reliability is to test the same commercial twice; when this experience has been accumulated for a respectable number of commercials, a correlation coefficient can be calculated between the test and retest commercial scores. Table 11-5 shows the constant-sum attitude change scores for ten different commercials for the same brand of toothpaste (data are hypothetical). The correlation between these ten commercial test and retest scores is .96, statistically significant at the .01 level. This correlation-type information is usually the only information developed in test-retest studies which have been reported in copy research. But Silk has noted that when the correlation coefficient computed between tests and retest is utilized as a reliability coefficient there are two possible interpretations which could be drawn from low test-retest correlations.[20] First, it could be said that reliability is low due to the large random component in the test and retest scores. Alternatively, it could be said that the low correlation coefficient really indicates a systematic change in the test/retest scores due to events occurring between the test and retest; the testing system would be considered reliable under the latter interpretation. In order to determine which interpretation should properly be placed on the correlation coefficient in test/retest studies, additional analyses must be conducted. If the mean difference between test/retest scores is insignificant and if the variances between the test and retest scores are roughly equivalent, then the correlation coefficient can properly be interpreted as an indication of reliability. On the other hand, if there is a significant difference in test/retest means and variances, the interpretation of the correlation coefficient in terms of reliability of the copy research system is ambiguous; no conclusion can be drawn about reliability. In the example shown in Table 11–5, the correlation coefficient is high and there are no significant differences between test/retest means and variances: therefore, the conclusion can be drawn that the particular constant-sum attitude change procedure used to generate the data in Table 11–5 is a reliable one.

Table 11-5   Hypothetical Test-Retest Constant-Sum
Attitude Change Scores

Commercial #	Mean Test Scores	Mean Retest Scores
1	3.12	3.19
2	− .44	−1.57
3	1.23	1.13
4	2.20	1.56
5	.09	.13
6	−1.10	−1.04
7	2.01	2.46
8	1.33	1.56
9	1.00	.89
10	− .88	−1.05
Mean over 10 Commercials:	.856	.726
Variance:	1.96	2.50
Standard Deviation:	1.40	1.58

Note: There is no significant difference ($\alpha = .05$) between the mean test and retest scores (.856 and .726) or between the test and retest variances (1.96 and 2.50).

The study of reliability in copy research has not as yet taken the above considerations into account. It is, therefore, unclear whether one criterion is more or less reliable than another despite the number of reliability studies which have been undertaken in copy research. This problem may explain the disparate findings on reliability to be discussed below.

Recall. There are a number of factors which have been uncovered which affect the magnitude of DAR scores which are extra-content in nature (have nothing to do with the content of the commercial under test). Clancy and Kweskin examined tests of 25 commercials on the standard DAR system.[21] They found the most important factor which explained the difference between DAR scores for different commercials was the proportion of the commercial audience which indicated they found the program in which the commercial appeared to be one of their "favorites."

Young found an impact of the city in which the DAR test is conducted on overall DAR scores.[22] She uncovered systematic differences for 15 commercial tests by the cities in which each commercial was tested. Her analysis of variance of these data showed that city variability was about as large a determinant of recall as was the creative content of the commercial. In another study reported by Young, an examination of 128 commercial tests showed that a given city's related recall score varied +4.6 to −4.3 percentage points from the mean of all cities, suggesting both a systematic bias on scores in certain cities and a large range of unknown error in any single city. The problem here is illustrated by the hypothetical data below (remember from Example 11–1 that the overall recall score is derived from testing in three, many times four, different cities):

Test City	Commercial Audience Size	Commercial A Related Recall	Commercial B Related Recall
Davenport	35	9%	8%
Milwaukee	35	10%	25%
Grand Rapids	35	8%	8%
Overall Related Recall Score (Average over three cities)		9%	14%.

Clearly, the three-percentage point difference between these two commercials for the same brand is due to the difference found only in Milwaukee (the other two cities show the same or about the same recall for both commercials). This is what is meant by "differences due to cities" as opposed to differences between the content of the commercials themselves. Even if the difference between 9 percent and 14 percent is statistically significant in the above data, it is not at all clear that the two commercials are different in terms of impact on recall.

Shulman found variation in recall scores by the day-part in which the DAR interviewing takes place.[23] He found that for both 30- and 60-second commercials the average recall score was higher for the morning than for the afternoon interviews. In about 80 percent of the tests of the 60's and 68 percent of the 30's, morning interviews yielded higher recall levels than afternoon interviews. This suggests that the later in the day that the test commercials are shown, the more likely they are to be recalled since the shorter will be the time period between exposure and interviewing.

Appel studied advertising wear-out using DAR and further delayed measurements of recall on 96 retests representing 81 different 60-second television commercials for 31 different brands. Expected recall scores were generated for commercials based upon the correlation of test with retest. The difference of the actual retest score from the predicted or expected score was the measure used to assess the effect of elapsed time on recall scores; elapsed time was considered an indicator of the amount of interim exposure of the test copy between test and retest. The analysis confirmed changes in recall scores over time. There was an increase in score (which was attributed to learning) followed by a fairly regular decline (which was attributed to wear-out of the advertising message). This would seem to point to the reliability of DAR since the difference in scores appears due to the true shift in scores due to lapse of time between test and retest rather than measurement error.

Barclay, Doub, and McMurtrey studied recall as a function of time and program slot.[24] Among tuned-in homes, housewives recalled daytime commercials just as well as nighttime commercials. In-program commercials were better recalled than spots. At night, recall was substantially higher in more highly rated programs. In daytime, serial programs generated higher recall than other types of programs. Clearly, this would seem to indicate that recall scores will differ, not only between cities, but also depending upon the surrounding program content; if this is not held constant across the test cities, the recall scores will contain this non-content impact in addition to the commercial content impact.

The commercials presented by Heller were found to have a test/retest correlation of .68, only a moderate level.[25] Although Heller did not calculate the correlation (this was later done by Silk), he did present the recall scores showing the consequence of using a method of low reliability. The commercials presented by Heller generated test and retest DAR scores of a difference such that different conclusions were implied as to which commercial should be run, depending on whether the test or retest scores were used.

Clancy and Ostlund examined 106 test/retest pairs of on-air recall tests.[26] The commercials for television covered many convenience goods as well as some non-convenience products such as automobiles. The time interval between test/retest varied from one to 11 weeks. The test/retest correlation was .67; the average difference between the test/retest scores was 6.4 percentage points; this difference was statistically significant eight out of ten times. There was a clear product category effect with correlations ranging from −.69 for soaps and cleansers to .98 for cigarettes. When the correlation coefficient was weighted for the number of pairs in each category, it dropped from .67 to .29.

Clancy and Ostlund also examined another set of 32 television commercial test/retest pairs; these were developed by a commercial testing service rather than by the agency itself. The test/retest correlation for these commercials was .76; there was an average difference between test/retest scores of 5.6 percentage points, significant seven out of ten times. The correlations ranged from .12 to .83 for soups and toiletries, respectively. When the number of pairs of commercials in each product category was taken into account, the test/retest correlation dropped from .76 to .59. On the basis of these investigations, the researchers concluded that reliability was not sufficiently high for on-air tests to make fine distinctions concerning the relative effectiveness of alternative commercials in a single product category.

The same 106 commercials examined by Clancy and Ostlund were utilized by Kahn and Light to examine the reliability of on-air, DAR testing.[27] Kahn and Light first examined the distribution of 633 commercials tested on this system; the average related recall score was 33.4 percent. As indicated in the Clancy and Ostlund study, there was an average difference of 614 points between test and retest scores for the 106 commercials of the total of 633 which were tested twice. Adding and subtracting this difference from the average for all commerials of 33.4 provided an "unreliability zone" of 27.0 and 39.8 for unreliable scores. If a commercial yielded a score between these upper and lower bounds, it was considered to be an unreliable score. Fifty percent of the commercials tested on the agency's on-air system (the agency was Batten, Barton, Durstine & Osborne) fell outside the unreliability zone, 61 percent of recall scores fell outside using a second on-air system, and 72 percent fell outside using a third on-air recall system. Kahn and Light also examined the predictive validity of six commercials on the DAR system. They found that level of recall was highly related to subsequent sales levels and, thus, endorsed the validity of the DAR system.

Hodock has recently provided evidence that DAR scores are very sensitive to the composition of the sample used in the testing procedure.[28] For example, he found, in the case of a commercial for a skin-conditioning product, that the related recall score was 14 percent for the entire commercial audience while it was 59 percent for those individuals who had purchased a skin conditioning product within the past month. For a new drug product, those who used the product category had a related recall score of 23 percent while the entire commercial audience related recall score was only 6 percent. Clearly, the nature of the audience composition in the test would have a great impact on the reliability of test/retest scores.

With respect to sensitivity of recall measures, Young found in the application of statistical criteria (significance levels) to recall scores for two brands that these scores could reject or accept commercials in only 24 percent of 17 tests for one brand and 14 percent of 28 tests for a second.[29] This is probably one result of the generally low reliability levels of DAR scores. The underlying problem seems to be that DAR is sensitive to many factors external to the advertising content being tested, as pointed out above. In his examination of some 80 DAR tests, Heller concluded that over the narrow range of scores obtained for a single brand, recall cannot discriminate sufficiently for making copy-research decisions.[30] He suggests that "under these conditions recall measures should be used only as a disaster check."

Attitude Change. Clancy and Ostlund, in the above study, also investigated attitude shift reliability and validity. There were 42 pairs of commercials for which test/retest data were available; pre/post buying interest was utilized as a surrogate measure of attitude shift. The ten-point constant-sum scale was the measuring instrument used. Test/retest correlations of .84 and .64 were found for post-only buying interest and pre/post shift, respectively. The researchers concluded that forced-exposure scores were more reliable than on-air scores. They also made the argument that forced-exposure scores had greater validity than on-air recall testing. Though there was an absence of data to relate each of the criteria to some measure such as sales, they found that merely administering the 0-to-10 constant-sum scale twice in succession for a given product without including the test commercial exposure on the reel did not itself cause any plus or minus change in buying interest scores for the product. The correlation of these scores exceeded .90. This is in line with the classic study on copy research validity conducted by Axelrod discussed earlier which showed constant-sum scales to be superior in predicting brand-choice behavior when compared to recall methods.

Kahn and Light, in the previously mentioned study by them on recall, also investigated pre/post attitude shift measures in copy research. They looked at the proportion of times three different attitude-shift measures fell outside the "unreliability zone" which was constructed in a similar manner to that described above for recall scores. They found that 50 percent of the tests under one attitude-change measure, 53 percent under a second measure, and 48 percent under a third measure of attitude change fell outside the unreliability zone; that is, only about 50 percent of the attitude shift scores were reliable. These two researchers from BBDO then examined the validity of attitude-shift measures in relation to sales for six commercials for which the validity was also examined relative to recall scores. The relationship between attitude shift and sales levels for the six commercials was inverse; that is, the higher the attitude shift, the lower the sales and vice versa. Kahn and Light concluded that the validity of recall was higher than that of attitude-change measures.

In contrast to this conclusion regarding reliability by Kahn and Light, Silk examined the attitude shift scores for ten commercials tested in a theater system; he concluded that the reliability of the attitude-change measure generated in that system was acceptable.[31]

The sensitivity of attitude shift measures has not been the subject of a great deal of published material. However, in Axelrod's aforementioned study, the sensitivity of 14 different measuring instruments was examined by exposing 150 housewives to print advertisements and taking a pre- and post-exposure measurement for each instrument. A control group of 50 respondents received no advertising stimulus between the pre and post measurements. The pre/post difference was significantly different between the test and control groups for the constant-sum scale (α = .15). Axelrod concluded that the constant-sum pre/post measure was one of the most sensitive of the 14 measures he examined.

A large advertising agency investigated the sensitivity of an attitude-change measure using the constant-sum scale and found that, for some 200 commercial tests, there was approximately a 33 percent chance of detecting differences between any two commercials tested at the α = .15 level of significance. This level of sensitivity to discriminate between commercials is very much a function of the sample size used in the test; in this instance, the sample size utilized in the test for each commercial was 210 respondents.

Practitioner Views on Reliability/Validity. A survey of top advertisers and agencies was recently conducted by Ostlund, Clancy and Sapra.[32] The results of this survey showed that the issue of copy research reliability is not the important issue which it should be if practical results are to be usable from copy research. About 90 percent of agency respondents in the survey indicated that they test the same commercial twice on the same testing system less than five percent of the time. In other words, for these practitioners reliability is rarely examined.

On the question of validity assessment, about 70 percent of the agency respondents indicated they test the same commercial on two different copy research methods 25 percent of the time or less. That is, discriminant validity does not appear to be an issue of great interest to users of copy research. Agency respondents also indicated that suppliers of copy research services do not generally provide evidence to them on the reliability, validity, and sensitivity of their methods. For the agency respondents in the study, 11 percent said reliability information is always provided, 15 percent said sensitivity information is always provided, and only 7 percent said validity information is always provided by the supplier. The authors concluded their study with this observation:[33]

> Advertisers and agencies are spending a great deal of their money on copytesting services for which they receive no assurances that the testing method possesses validity. Moreover, given the relative simplicity with which test/retest reliability can be assessed, it is strange that there has not been greater demands for full documentation on at least the reliability of alternative copy-testing methods in widespread use.

MULTIPLE CRITERIA DILEMMA

All of this discussion and worry about the relative reliability, validity, and sensitivity of on-air recall versus on-premise pre/post attitude change copy research systems stems from a very practical problem. There is a very low relationship between what these two approaches tell about a commercial's worth; the consequence of this is that one system says Commercial A is better than Commercial B for a given brand while the other system says Commercial B is better than Commercial A. This has been termed the "multiple criteria dilemma" since use of the two testing systems will invariably produce this type of decision making problem or dilemma for the advertising manager.

RECALL/ATTITUDE CHANGE RELATIONSHIP

There appears to be a moderate relationship between recall of commercial content and the commercial's effect on attitude change. This relationship, unfortunately, is most often a negative or inverse one. Kahn and Light reported a correlation between a theatre pre/post attitude change measure and on-air DAR for eight commercials of −.60.[34] For another 11 commercials and a different attitude change measure they found a correlation between that measure and DAR of +.26. Young found a correlation of DAR and attitude shift of +.05 for 15 commercials. Table 11–6 shows scores for eight commercials for a leading shampoo brand on DAR and a 10-point constant-sum scale measure of attitude change; the correlation found by a large agency handling this brand was −.41. For eleven laundry detergent commercials tested on the same systems as the shampoo commercials, the correlation was similarly negative. For the commercials shown in Table 11–6, there are 28 possible combinations of two commercials compared to each other on the criteria (commercial 1 with commercial 2, commercial 1 with commercial 3 and so forth). In 17 of these 28 comparisons, the DAR and attitude shift measures point to a different one of the pair as the better commercial; this is about 60 percent of the time and concerns only statistically significant differences ($\alpha = .15$). For example, in Table 11–6 when commercial 1 is compared to commercial 2, it is better than commercial 2 on DAR while commercial 2 is significantly better than commercial 1 on attitude change. Which is the better commercial? This is the *multiple criteria dilemma*. Kahn and Light similarly note that 77 percent of the time an advertiser who was a BBDO client would have come to a different conclusion about the effectiveness of a commercial, depending upon the system chosen to aid in the decision making process: DAR or a theatre attitude shift measure.[35]

RESOLVING THE DILEMMA

The first point which should be made is that, from a conceptual point of view, and as discussed in Chapter 4 of this text, recall and attitude change are intended as measures of two *different* underlying dimensions of the effectiveness of advertising messages. Recall is supposed to tap the cognitive dimension while attitude is intended to assess the affective dimension. It is, therefore, fortunate that there is generally a lack of high correlation between the two measures. This simply shows that they measure different aspects of the commercial's effectiveness. If they were highly correlated, this would mean that the two mea-

Table 11-6   DAR and Attitude Shift Constant-Sum Scores for Eight
Shampoo Commercials

Commercial #	DAR Score	Attitude Shift Score
1	40%	+ .02
2	31%	+ .12
3	26%	+1.05
4	11%	+ .60
5	32%	+ .72
6	34%	+ .50
7	15%	+1.18
8	18%	+ .10
Average	26%	.54

$$r = -.41$$

sures were essentially tapping the *same* underlying dimension of effectiveness.

To the extent that it is deemed by the advertising manager to be important to assess the impact of a commercial or advertisement on consumers on more than one dimension of effectiveness, no dilemma exists at all between these two criteria. The advertising manager should simply have copywriters and producers develop advertising which is effective on all dimensions. That is, the better commercial is the one which performs better than another on both criteria (if only two criteria are involved). It is difficult to make good advertising if this is defined as advertising which performs in a superior manner on all three dimensions of effectiveness (cognitive, conative, and affective). For example, it is easier for a copywriter to develop an ad which is a "grabber" and gets attention through some highly unusual device which will stimulate recall than it is to both stimulate recall and produce favorable attitudes; the unusual is not often immediately "liked" on initial contact. Since it is difficult to create good advertising which works on all three dimensions, it should not be surprising that low correlations are found more often than not between the two criteria, attitude and recall. But it should be recalled that long ago such writers as Clyde Bedell understood that a good advertisement was one which got attention, created interest, developed conviction, promoted desire, and led to action on the part of consumers (AICDA). These elements, as noted in Chapter 4, represent three different underlying dimensions of communication effectiveness.

This point of view is also buttressed by the differences in the nature of on-air versus on-premise or forced exposure research designs. Carl Hovland, the famous communication researcher who did great volumes of research studies on communication effects at Yale University after World War II, concluded that, even though survey (on-air) designs and experimental (pseudo-experimental on-premise) designs produced greatly different results for the same communication issue, both were needed.[36] He believed that they simply were not comparable but one was no better than the other, though a great deal of his own work was in the experimental area, since each methodology produced different information about the effectiveness of communications.

Nonetheless, even though the above is recognized, the dilemma still will remain in a great many decision making situations where multiple criteria are employed in the assessment of commercial effectiveness in copy research. Several approaches have been suggested to ease the difficulty of decision making in such circumstances, but these generally can be categorized as primarily of an *empirical* nature or of a *conceptual* nature.

Empirical Approaches. Wind and Denny have proposed that several intermediate criteria would be measured in the copy research procedure and analyzed using the multivariate analysis of variance statistical technique (MANOVA).[37] In their application of MANOVA to the copy research problem, Wind and Denny obtained several measures for the same commercial (overall or global attitude, intention-to-buy, and evaluation of the brand on five different attributes). Through use of these data in MANOVA for several commercial executions for the same brand, they were able to make a decision as to which of the commercials was superior given the several criteria applied to each commerial simultaneously. MANOVA is, therefore, an analytical scheme which provides for a decision on commercial effectiveness, given a significance level chosen by the decision maker and data on several criterion variables.

Leckenby conducted a study to further explore the application of MANOVA to the copy research decision problem.[38] In this study, two particular problems were treated in some detail: (1) the development of a single design for the measurement of two of the more popular criteria, recall and attitude change, in print copy research situations; and (2) the analysis of data generated by such a research design. A design was developed which provided a compromise to the usual forced-exposure conditions of attitude shift tests and the natural exposure environment of recall testing. Three main effect factors were specified in the study (it is the objective of MANOVA to see if effects of any of these factors can be detected in the several criterion variables): (1) competitive brands (three brands for a product category were selected); (2) test brand execution (two different advertisement executions were tested for one of the three brands); and (3) rotation for first-position order effects (to see whether or not sequencing in the exposure of the ads to subjects would have an effect).

Respondents completed pre-exposure and post-exposure attitude measures toward each of the three brands. The next day, respondents completed recall questions (specific recall of execution content) using a scaled rather than a verbatim procedure.[39] These two criteria, as expected, pointed toward the superiority of different executions for the test brand. This dilemma was resolved through the use of MANOVA and discriminant analysis (DISCRIM). Discriminant analysis indicates which of the criteria is more affected by the factors when a main effect on the criterion variables is detected. This is important in the situation where recall is higher than attitude shift for test brand execution A, but attitude shift is higher than recall for test brand execution B. DISCRIM indicates the relative importance of the criterion variables in this situation and alleviates the problem described above.

Conceptual Approaches. Plummer, as well as others, have described a system developed at the Leo Burnett advertising agency which combines recall and attitude in a conceptual manner; this approach is called the Personal Product Response (PPR) system.[40] In this system, air time is purchased on an independent television station, and a panel of viewers is recruited to watch the program. The day after the test commercials are run, the recruited viewers are telephoned from a central location. The respondents are asked four questions: (1) "Would you describe the commercial for me?" (2) "What did this commercial make you think of?" (3) "What was the main idea the commercial was trying to get across?" and (4) "Which brand of (product category name) was advertised?"

In addition to the usual type of recall score, the PPR score is developed as an attitudinal measure. The Personal Product Response measure is the proportion of the proved recallers who spontaneously mentioned favorable personal experience with the advertised brand (past, current, or anticipated experience is included). Each commercial tested in the approach receives an overall score called the Commercial Performance Score (CPS). The CPS indicates the proportion of viewers in the commercial audience who both prove commercial awareness (recall) and give a Personal Product Response (an attitude-related response). Plummer reported on extensive studies conducted by the Burnett Company with respect to the reliability, validity, and sensitivity of the approach; these investigations produced satisfactory results from their point of view.

Leckenby and Tinkham conducted a study designed to test the proposition that attitude toward a "new" brand is a function of beliefs and evaluation of cognitive material which is *recalled* as well as that which is *inferred* from an advertisement for that brand.[41] The inferential portion of the approach is similar, from a conceptual viewpoint, to the Personal Product Response discussed above. The approach can be summarized as:

$$A_B = w_1(A_R) + w_2(A_I).$$

The above approach suggests that attitude toward a brand (A_B) is a function of attitude based upon recall of commercial content (A_R) as well as attitude based upon inference (A_I). Each of these two attitudinal bases is more or less important than the other, and this is indicated by the weights attributed to each underlying component of brand attitude (w_i).

The model considers recall of advertising messages to be one of the bases upon which consumers can form an attitude about the brand.

Consumers may like or dislike what they remember from advertising. In addition, however, individuals develop an attitude toward a brand from sources other than the advertising for that brand. Inferences can be drawn about the brand through usage of the brand, talking with friends about the brand, and so forth. On the basis of this inferred information, an attitude can be formed about the brand. Also, and this would be particularly important in the case of a new brand introduction, individuals can make inferences about the brand based upon the information given in the advertising for that brand. For example, they might recall that the advertising for Sony Betamax says that cassettes tape up to four hours of programming but infer from this message element that four hours is not long enough to tape more than one evening's programming. Inference, as the basis for brand attitude formation, can come from advertising and non-advertising sources. Inference can be viewed as a mediator of the attitude/recall relationship.

When the above concept was tested in a copy research design by Leckenby and Tinkham, substantial evidence was uncovered which supported the basic idea. The utility of the approach for resolution of the multiple criteria dilemma was also addressed. The recall and inferential attitude components can be combined into a single indicator of the overall effect of the commercial on the respondents, thus alleviating the problem of the different decisions which might be indicated by several criterion measures.

SELECTION OF COPY RESEARCH METHODS

Plummer has suggested the use of the following seven criteria to determine which of several alternative and available copy research methods is preferable:[42]

(1) Reliability
(2) Validity (construct validity)
(3) Sensitivity
(4) Independence of Measures (Discriminant Validity)
(5) Comprehensiveness (global and diagnostic measures)
(6) Relationships to Other Tests (Convergent Validity)
(7) Acceptability (Commitment to the Method)

A more detailed list of elements which need consideration during the copy research method selection process would include the following factors which summarize many of the copy research issues discussed in this chapter.

(1) Examine rough or finished ads?
(2) How many ads to examine?
(3) Is the ad examined in context (magazine, TV program, etc.)?
(4) Examine executions or strategies?
(5) Use single or multiple exposure?

(6) Use single or multiple criteria?
(7) Which criterion/criteria to measure?
(8) Use single number of diagnostic measures?
(9) Use on-air or on-premise methodology?
(10) Use experimental or survey design?
(11) Reliability, validity, and sensitivity of measures?
(12) How much does the method cost?

If these questions can all be answered in a satisfactory manner for a number of alternative copy research methods, then it will be a relatively easy matter to select the approach which best meets the needs of the individual advertiser. The above questions are not likely to receive equally satisfactory answers when applied to any given copy research method. And, in the final analysis, the copy research method which is selected by a particular advertising manager or agency personnel will be a reflection of their "theory" of how advertising works. Krugman has summarized two main approaches which he sees people using as their "theory" of how advertising works:[43]

Hard In/Easy Out

Attention requires effort
The eye is a gate keeper to the brain
One must compete intensely for attention
One must spend a lot of $$ to get into perception
Messages are easily "forgotten," easily fall out of storage
One must then spend a lot of $$ to get back in

Easy In/Hard Out

The brain sees much more than the eye can attend to and
    selects anything of interest for retention
It's easy to get into storage for later use
It's easy to get into storage with relevant audiences
Even much useless stimuli are recognized when later triggered,
    when reminded, when a later use develops
Things in storage are never completely forgotten
One can spend less $$ to get in, or to remind

QUESTIONS AND PROBLEMS

1. List some reasons why commercials differ in effectiveness. What do you mean by effectiveness?
2. Indicate some of the advantages and disadvantages of using a copy research method which involves multiple exposure to the message. How might multiple exposure be accomplished in a copy research method based on the on-premise approach yet have high external validity?
3. List ten reasons why it is difficult for copywriters to develop television commercials which perform equally effectively on all three dimensions of effectiveness (cognitive, conative, and affective).
4. What reasons can you give which would explain the lack of interest on the part of practitioners in the issues of reliability, validity, and sensitivity in

copy research (as indicated by the Ostlund, *et al.* study reported in this chapter)?

5. How can strategies rather than executions be tested? How can rough advertisements be tested, maintaining validity, rather than finished ads? Why, if validity, reliability, and sensitivity can be maintained at acceptable levels, would it be preferable to test strategies and roughs (say animatics or photomatics instead of finished TV commercials)?

6. Is the multiple criteria dilemma a dilemma? Explain and provide some examples.

7. What is the "bottom-line" reason for advertising management's use and attraction to copy research methods? How would you determine if the cost of a copy research method is worth the benefit received from the method as an advertising manager charged with the selection of a copy research procedure?

8. You are an account manager at an agency working for the K&G Company on its Crinkle's Potato Chip product. K&G directs you to evaluate representative campaign executions on the basis of DAR. You find that your market share is dropping, yet the executions being utilized in the campaign for Crinkle's have gotten very high DAR scores when copytested. You decide that maybe you should, contrary to the thinking at K&G, begin to assess the impact of your executions on more than just the DAR measure. You know that sales will not be a sensitive indicator of execution superiority in a one-exposure copytesting situation; you also do not believe in the validity of the recognition method of copytesting. So you decide to track each execution on two criteria: Awareness (comprehension) and Attitude. You wish to operationalize these criteria through DAR and attitude shift or change measures. Develop a design to measure DAR and attitude change measures on one sample of respondents; that is, for each execution tested, you would measure DAR and attitude change relative to the execution using only one group of respondents. You should describe the design by addressing the twelve questions regarding copy research method selection posed at the conclusion of this chapter.

ENDNOTES

1. Kenneth A. Longman, *Advertising* (New York: Harcourt Brace Jovanovich, Inc., 1971), pp. 318-319.

2. Shirley Young, "Copy Testing: For What? For Whom?" paper presented to Annual Conference of the Advertising Research Foundation, New York, New York, October 1977.

3. Lyman E. Ostlund, Kevin J. Clancy, and Rakesh Sapra, "Inertia in Copy Research," *Journal of Advertising Research* (February 1980), pp. 17-24.

4. Young, *op.cit.*, pp. 10-13.

5. Joel N. Axelrod, "Attitude Measures that Predict Purchase," *Journal of Advertising Research* (March 1968), pp. 3-17.

6. Ostlund, *et.al.*, *op.cit.*

7. Lee Adler, Allan Greenberg, and Darrell B. Lucas, "What Big Agency Men Think of Copytesting Methods," *Journal of Marketing Research* (November 1965), pp. 339-345.

8. Ward J. Jenssen, "Sales Effect of TV, Radio, and Print Advertising," *Journal of Advertising Research* (June 1966), pp. 2-7.

9. Homer M. Dalbey, Irwin Gross, and Yoram Wind, *Advertising Measurement and Decision Making* (Boston: Allyn and Bacon, 1968).

10. Neil Holbert, "Key Articles in Advertising Research," *Journal of Advertising Research* (October 1972), pp. 5-13 and Neil Holbert, "More Key Articles in Advertising Research," *Journal of Advertising Research* (August 1977), pp. 33-42.

11. *An Annotated Bibliography of Copytesting: 1960-72* (New York: Advertising Research Foundation, 1972). See also the special issue of the *Journal of Advertising Research* (October 1973) which lists 48 firms which provided copy research services at that time.

12. Ostlund, *et.al.*, *op.cit.*, p. 18.

13. See, for example, C.I. Hovland, I.L. Janis, and H.H. Kelly, *Communication and Persuasion* (New Haven: Yale University Press, 1953).

14. Russell I. Haley, "How Advertising Works," Proceedings of Advertising Research Conference, January 1975, New York, New York, p. 10.

15. *Day-After Recall Television Commercial Testing Technique*, Burke Marketing Research, Inc., Cincinnati, Ohio, 1978.

16. Udolpho Van de Sandt, "Pretesting with Competition," *Journal of Advertising Research* (September 1969), pp. 17-20.

17. See, for example, Lionel C. Barrow, Jr., "New Uses of Covariance Analysis," in D.A. Aaker, *Multivariate Analysis in Marketing: Theory and Application* (Belmont, California: Wadsworth Publishing, 1971), pp. 195-205.

18. Donald T. Campbell and Donald W. Fiske, "Convergent and Discriminant Validation by the Multitrait-Multimethod Matrix," *Psychological Bulletin* (March 1959), pp. 81-105.

19. This example is adapted from D. Aaker and J.G. Myers, *Advertising Management* (Englewood Cliffs: Prentice-Hall, Inc., 1975), p. 452.

20. Alvin J. Silk, "Test-Retest Correlations and the Reliability of Copytesting," *Journal of Marketing Research* (November 1977), pp. 476-486.

21. Kevin J. Clancy and D.M. Kweskin, "TV Commercial Recall Correlates," *Journal of Advertising Research* (April 1971), p. 18.

22. Shirley Young, "Copy Testing Without Magic Numbers," *Journal of Advertising Research* (February 1972), p. 3.

23. Art Shulman "On-Air Recall by Time of Day," *Journal of Advertising Research,* (February 1972), p. 11.

24. W.D. Barclay, R.M. Doub, and L.T. McMurtrey, "Recall of TV Commercials by Time and Program Slot," *Journal of Advertising Research* (June 1965), p. 41.

25. Harry E. Heller, "The Ostrich and the Copy Researcher—A Comparative Analysis," Paper presented to the New York City Chapter of the American Marketing Association, December 1971.

26. Kevin J. Clancy and Lyman Ostlund, "Commercial Effectiveness Measures," *Journal of Advertising Research* (February 1976), pp. 29-34.

27. Fran Kahn and Larry Light, "Copytesting: Communication vs. Persuasion," *Advances in Consumer Research: Volume 2*, Association for Consumer Research, 1975, pp. 595-605.

28. Calvin Hodock, "Copytesting and Strategic Positioning," *Journal of Advertising Research* (February 1980), pp. 33-38.

29. Young, "Copytesting Without Magic Numbers," *op.cit.*

30. Heller, *op.cit.*

31. Silk, *op.cit.*, p. 485.

32. Ostlund, Clancy and Sapra, *op.cit.*

33. *Ibid.*, p. 22.

34. Kahn and Light, *op.cit.*

35. *Ibid.*

36. Carl I. Hovland, "Reconciling Conflicting Results from Experimental and Survey Studies of Attitude Change," *The American Psychologist* (October 1959), pp. 8-17.

37. Y. Wind and J. Denny, "Multivariate Analysis of Variance in Research on the Effectiveness of TV Commercials," *Journal of Marketing Research* (May 1974), pp. 136-142.

38. John D. Leckenby, "An Empirical Approach to the Multiple Criteria Problem in Copytesting Research," *Journal of Advertising* (Winter 1978), pp. 19-27.

39. Recall was measured in the manner described by J. Jaccard and M. Fishbein,

"Inferential Beliefs and Order Effects in Personality Impression Formation," *Journal of Personality and Social Psychology,* Vol. 16, No. 6, pp. 1031-1040.

40. Joseph T. Plummer, "Evaluating TV Commercial Tests," *Journal of Advertising Research* (October 1972), pp. 21-27.

41. J. Leckenby and S. Tinkham, "Recall, Inference and Attitude in Copytesting Research," paper presented to Association for Education in Journalism, Advertising Division, Madison, Wisconsin (August 1977).

42. Plummer, *op.cit.,* p. 21.

43. Herbert Krugman, "Opportunities in Advertising Research of the Future," Proceedings of the Advertising Research Foundation Conference (New York, New York, January 1975), pp. 35-40.

CASES IN CREATIVE STRATEGY DECISIONS

- Sunkist Growers, Inc. (B)
- Oron Paper Company (B)
- Gold O'Roast Corporation (A)
- Nu-Dye Products, Inc.
- Sears, Roebuck and Company
- Gulf Oil Company—U.S.
- Glade Glass Ovenware Company
- Metro Transit District

CASES IN CREATIVE STRATEGY DECISIONS

Case 12-1—Sunkist Growers, Inc. (B)

The primary marketing objective of the Sunkist growers organization is the profitable sale of their members' citrus fruit. To expedite the accomplishment of this objective, a separate sales organization has been established for each of the three fruits—one for oranges, one for lemons, and one for grapefruit.

Chief responsibility for sales of lemons rests with the Lemon Sales Manager who reports to the Vice-President of Fresh Fruit Marketing. The fresh fruit sales organization includes district sales offices throughout the United States. The registered trademark "Sunkist" is used on all first-grade fruit, and the "SK" trademark is used on second-grade fruit.

Distribution of lemons is through direct buying retailers, wholesalers and jobbers and also through auction markets in six principal cities. Export sales are made throughout the world. The company has a direct sales force calling on these distributors. During the past few years, Sunkist, like many other marketers in the food industry, has encountered increased concentration of buying power among its retail customers.

PRODUCTION OF LEMONS

Since World War II, the United States has become the principal lemon-producing country in the world, with 35-40 percent of total world supply; Italy ranks second with a share of world market of 20-25 percent. The California-Arizona climate is perfect for lemon production and is the only region in the United States where lemons are produced on a commercial basis, although efforts were made to do so in Texas. The production of lemons in Florida was an industry of considerable importance prior to the freeze of the 1894-95 season, but this freeze brought about the complete destruction of the lemon industry at the time, and since then it has not been reestablished on a commercial basis.

The average lemon tree bears commercial crops by the fifth year after planting and yields about 1400 lemons annually. Although in Southern California the lemons are picked from the tree 12 months a year, over 55 percent is harvested during the 4 months from February through May.

The better quality production is set aside for the "fresh" market. The balance of the crop is used for processing. The grower is vitally interested in the division of the crop between fresh and processed, since fresh fruit yields a considerably higher return. One of the major problems of the industry is the growing trend toward increased use of processed lemon products at the expense of fresh usage. Exhibit 12-1 shows the trend in the division of the crop between these two alternatives.

Exhibit 12-1   Lemon Production and Utilization—1971-1980

Year	Production (in 1,000 tons)	Utilization of Prodn (in 1,000 tons) Fresh	Processed	Value of Prodn 1,000 Dollars
1971-72	634	365 (57.6)	269 (42.4)	80,266
1972-73	844	419 (49.6)	425 (50.4)	97,302
1973-74	676	422 (62.4)	254 (37.6)	109,851
1974-75	1,118	438 (39.1)	680 (60.1)	113,226
1975-76	670	416 (62.1)	254 (37.9)	101,949
1976-77	988	497 (50.3)	491 (49.7)	92,500
1977-78	991	463 (46.7)	528 (43.3)	110,635
1978-79	745	455 (61.1)	290 (38.9)	134,573
1979-80	789	407 (51.6)	382 (48.4)	161,319

Figures in brackets are percentages

SOURCE: Crop Reporting Board—U.S. Dept. of Agriculture.

Annual changes may not be meaningful since the fresh product gets first call on available supply, and a small crop, such as in 1975-76, will induce a higher percentage of share for the fresh market. The reverse also holds true during large crop years as in 1974-75. Of more than passing interest in this exhibit is the fairly consistent and rapid increase in the value of production in the last four years despite falling volume of production. In 1971-72, lemon production utilized as fresh fruit was approximately $46,000,000 with $34,000,000 of processed products. By 1979-80, these figures had increased to $83,000,000 and $78,000,000, which shows the increasing usage of lemons for processing.

PRODUCT QUALITIES AND CONSUMPTION FORMS

Lemons, or their direct derivatives are offered to consumers in a variety of physical forms. They are:

1. Fresh, i.e., whole lemons.
2. Fresh lemon juice (properly called pure, or whole, lemon juice since it is not necessarily fresh). This is generally claimed to be superior to that of processed forms.
3. Concentrated Lemon Juice—made by evaporating the water content of the juice until the remaining portion is six times as strong as fresh juice.
4. Reconstituted Lemon Juice—made by diluting concentrated juice with water to the strength of average, fresh juice.
5. Concentrated Lemonade—either frozen (developed in the mid 1940s) or regular, which is lemon juice and sugar and used as a base for making lemonade.

In addition to these forms, lemon is also used as a garnish, and because of its tartness is considered valuable to cut grease taste. Lemon is also used as a substitute for vinegar where mildness is preferred.

The lemon's most important vitamin content is Vitamin C, also called ascorbic acid. Lemons also have small amounts of vitamins A, B1, B2, and calcium. Fresh lemons are ideal for low sodium diets, as they are low in sodium content and high in potassium.[2]

Juice	Calories in 1 cup juice quantities
Apple	121
Blackberry	66
Blueberry	111
Crab Apple	96
Grapefruit	83
Grape juice	140
Lemon	61 (USDA #456 Handbook)
Lime	64
Loganberry	86
Orange	112 (for all varieties)
Pineapple	108

Lemon juice is an especially valuable source of vitamin C. It has 30-70 milligrams of vitamin C per 100 grams, while the edible portion of fresh lemons has 30-65 milligrams of vitamin C per 100 grams. This is higher on an equivalent weight than for any other fruit. Historically, lemons have been used to combat scurvy, which is caused by a vitamin C deficiency. A shortage of vitamin C may also be the underlying cause for hemorrhages anywhere in the body, changes in the structure of teeth and gums, bone deformities, enlargement of the heart and damage of the heart muscles, anemia, degeneration of the sex organs.[3]

It is also claimed that a shortage of vitamin C lowers the resistance of the body to bacterial toxins.[4] In turn, bacterial infections, even from a slight cold, cause depletion of the vitamin C in the body. The recommended daily allowance of vitamin C is 60 milligrams for adults and 45 milligrams for children.

MARKET SIZE, CONSTITUTION, AND TRENDS

Production influences, rather than sales requirements, are the important determinants of the annual quantity of lemons produced. Since annual yields are subject to the vagaries of weather conditions, however, differences in crop sizes alone on a year to year basis do not usually reflect consumption patterns. Over the longer term, production can, of course, be adapted to marketing requirements through more extensive as well as intensive land usage.

As indicated in Exhibit 12-2, lemon production has increased over threefold during the past 55 years. Actual per capita production doubled during this period, even though lemon acreage declined. From 1945 through 1954, production remained static at 6.9 lbs. per capita. During the next 25 years there has been a constant fluctuation.

Exhibit 12-2   Lemon Production—55 Year Trend in 5 Year Averages

Year	Production (million lbs)	Production (index)	Production Per Capita lbs	Production Per Capita index
1919-24	391	100	3.5	100
1924-29	523	134	4.4	126
1929-34	565	144	4.5	129
1934-39	739	189	5.7	163
1939-44	1,057	270	7.8	223
1944-49	1,003	256	6.9	197
1949-54	1,047	268	6.8	194
1954-59	1,211	310	7.3	209
1959-64	1,236	316	6.2	177
1964-69	1,232	315	6.5	186
1969-74	1,341	342	6.4	183

SOURCE: U.S. Department of Agriculture

California-Arizona production dropped 24.8% from 52.0 million carton equivalents in 1977-78 to 39.1 million in 1978-79.

Yield averaged 512 cartons per acre on 76,423 bearing acres compared to the 1977-78 yield of 710 per acre from 73,258 acres. Some 2.7 million cartons equivalents are certified as left on-tree due to economic abandonment.

In 1978-79, freeze loss was significant in the lemon crops of Central and Southern California.

Exhibit 12-3 represents an attempt to measure the trend of lemon production for use in the United States. It appears that the increase in

416

per capita production is not a reflection of increased domestic usage, but rather that a substantial portion of the yearly crop is exported.

Exhibit 12-3   Lemon Production for Domestic Consumption

Year	Production (1,000 tons)	Million Boxes
1971-72	634	16,680
1972-73	844	22,200
1973-74	676	17,800
1974-75	1,118	29,400
1975-76	670	17,620
1976-77	988	26,000
1977-78	991	26,100
1978-79	745	19,600
1979-80	789	20,750

SOURCE: U.S. Department of Agriculture

In fact, as a result of the increased use of frozen concentrates, consumption of all fresh citrus fruits has declined by one-fourth since 1950. (See Exhibit 12-4)

Exhibit 12-4   U.S. Per Capita Consumption of Fresh Lemons

Year	Fresh Lemons in lbs	% Change	All Fresh Citrus
1965-66	2.3		29.1
1966-67	2.3	—	31.6
1967-68	2.2	− 4.3	26.2
1968-69	2.1	− 4.5	28.2
1969-70	2.1	—	28.6
1970-71	2.2	4.8	29.2
1971-72	1.8	−18.2	27.2
1972-73	1.9	5.6	27.3
1973-74	2.0	5.3	27.3
1974-75	2.0	—	29.8
1975-76	1.8	−10.0	29.2

As seen in Exhibit 12-4, this decline took place on a straight line basis and shows no sign of reversal. Coincident with the decrease in consumption of fresh lemons, the use of frozen concentrate for lemonade advanced sharply. (Exhibit 12-5)

The abatement of the decline during the last year in the table can be attributed to the warm summer that year. A similar occurrence took place in 1979, when the warm summer stimulated volume movements in many markets, with demand holding strong despite rising prices.

Exhibit 12-5   U.S. Per Capita Consumption of Frozen Concentrate for
Lemonade & Single Lemon Juice Over 15-yr Period

Year	Frozen Concentrate for Lemonade Base	Single Strength Lemon Juice
1960	.56	.35
1961	.45	.13
1962	.36	.13
1963	.33	.16
1964	.38	.15
1965	.38	.13
1966	.33	.09
1967	.36	.13
1968	.30	.09
1969	.29	.09
1970	.24	.06
1971	.26	.06
1972	.28	.09
1973	.35	.06
1974	.32	.06
1975	.45	.14

THE REVENUE PICTURE FOR LEMON GROWERS

This has presented a bleak picture for the growers. The "on-tree"
price which Sunkist growers receive for their lemons has shown a
severe decline. (Exhibit 12-6)

Exhibit 12-6   California and Arizona on-tree Prices 1973-77,
in Dlrs. Per Packgd Box

California:

Year	Fresh	Processed	All
1973-74	7.05	.58	4.66
1974-75	6.43	−.62	2.43
1975-76	5.85	−.95	3.32
1976-77	3.80	−.95	1.58

Arizona:

Year	Fresh	Processed	All
1973-74	7.60	.70	4.83
1974-75	5.30	.25	1.60
1975-76	9.15	−.95	4.79
1976-77	4.35	−.95	1.27

The wide discrepancy in income yields between fresh and processed
lemons is the reason why Sunkist advertising and promotions efforts
are concentrated upon including increased consumption of the product

in fresh form. The price obtained for the crop depends not only upon its quality and quantity but also upon its ends use. Declining prices combined with increasing costs of cultivation have almost eliminated the industry's profits.

The oversupply of lemons in the 1957-58 crop year combined with a mild summer made the marketing of the lemon crop extremely difficult. As a result of these difficulties, some new marketing practices were introduced, among which was a new method of pricing. Prior to the new system of pricing, buyers were frequently faced with price increases on lemon purchases in the midst of a promotion. As a result, many refrained from promoting the item.

ADVERTISING AND SALES PROMOTION OF LEMONS

A separate advertising plan each year is developed for the lemon growers of Sunkist. As is the case with each of the other products of the cooperative, this plan is developed through the joint efforts of the advertising committee and the advertising department. This plan must be approved by the Sunkist Board of Directors. The advertising committee may approve recommendations of the advertising manager for deviations from the plan unless there are major changes in policy or strategy. If major changes are involved, approval must be obtained from the Board.

Funds for the advertising appropriation are acquired by assessments to growers on a per-case basis. The size of this assessment depends on the estimates of the size of the lemon crop and requirements for advertising funds.

In 1979, the steep fall in lemon production due to the freeze led to the immediate reduction of advertising and other postponable administrative and marketing expenses. These expenses were $16.2 million in 1978-79 compared to $23.1 million in 1977-78, a reduction of 29.9%.

The sharp drop in funds available for fresh fruit advertising forced cancellation of all major national campaigns, but small scale programs were used in key markets as needed to stimulate demand for specific fruit sizes and grades.

There were incentives given to the trade to accelerate movement and to reduce the accumulation in mid-summer.

The themes for most of the promotions, focused on traditional seasonal events, such as lemon-with-fish for Lent and lemonade in the summer.

These programs received enthusiastic support from the retailers, as they were able to co-ordinate their own advertising efforts with Sunkist's promotions.

A four-week test promotion was conducted in Cleveland, by Sunkist and the California Avocado Commission. Food preparation specialists introduced shoppers to the idea of using lemons with avocado for a unique taste. This resulted in a 25 percent increase in sales of fresh lemons in Cleveland despite rising FOB prices.

In the absence of national advertising exposure for Sunkist citrus, a lot of other promotional efforts were undertaken:[4]

— Releases with crop condition information, recipes and photographs were distributed regularly to more than 8,000 consumer communicators, including newspaper and magazine food editors, producers of radio and TV talk and feature shows, and supermarket consumer specialists;

— A special lemon/fish press kit with full-color photos was prepared for food editors' use during the Lenten season. The material was developed by Sunkist and the Canned Salmon Institute, Alaskan Crab Institute, and Halibut Association of North America.

— Sunkist and the California Avocado Commission co-hosted a group of influential supermarket consumer specialists on an educational tour of California-Arizona agricultural areas.

The theme of the Sunkist lemon ad is "Ain't Sunkist Tart," very similar to the one for oranges "Ain't Sunkist Sweet" sung to the tune of the oldie "Ain't She Sweet."

In 1955, Sunkist copy talked about "Time For A Lemonade Life—refreshes, quenches thirst, ready in seconds, picks you up." Newspaper ads carried recipes for the "Perfect Lemon Pie" with Sunkist lemons being the prime ingredient.

By 1957, the approach was a "flu preventive" copy. And in 1958 it was a "Beat the Heat" promotion. Copy style has changed over the years to keep pace with changes in advertising trends.

With this knowledge of the lemon business, and consumer use patterns, the advertising agency was able to develop a suggested advertising campaign.

QUESTIONS FOR DISCUSSION

1. For what purposes should fresh lemons be advertised?
2. When should fresh lemons be advertised?
3. Develop a copy platform for fresh lemon advertising.

Your answers to these questions should be incorporated in presentation form as if you were a member of the advertising agency soliciting the Sunkist account. Support your recommendation with the facts provided in the case. The estimated budget to be used is $1 million.

Case 12-2—Oron Paper Company (B)

The management of the Oron Paper Company was deeply concerned over company sales and the competitive position of Oron's consumer products division, and undertook a program of research and reappraisal to aid in formulation of long-term promotional strategy. Although the consumer products division represented less than one-third of Oron's total sales of over $64 million, management directed special attention to this division with the objective of expanding sales and share of market. The principal products in this market are paper napkins, facial tissue, toilet tissue, and paper towels. Even as early as 1958, the market for these totaled over $500 million. (Exhibit 12-7)

Exhibit 12-7   Annual Market Size of Individual Consumer
Paper Products

Product	Annual Retail Volume
Toilet Tissue	270,000,000
Facial Tissue	120,000,000
Napkins	70,000,000
Towels	55,000,000

SOURCE: Company Estimates for 1958.

Management was especially interested in the consumer products division because of the opportunity of achieving better sales stability through this area of company operations. The pulp and paper industry has often been called the "prince and pauper" of industry because it is characterized by high fixed costs and periods of overexpansion. At these times many operators slash their prices in order to keep their operations going, because of the extraordinarily high expenses incurred by a closed plant. Since the products of Oron's industrial division were undifferentiated and fell within a broad generic class, they were at the mercy of erratic cyclical behavior of the industry's prices. In order to achieve a continuity of sales and profits, it was management's objective to build consumer demand for their branded consumer goods products which would enable them to hold an adequate price level and maintain sales despite competition and adverse economic conditions.

PRODUCT INTRODUCTION

The family which controlled the company saw an opportunity for the marketing of a quality paper napkin. The paper napkins available on the market were rather flimsy. The management felt that it was time to introduce to the market a paper napkin with greater durability and absorbency. They, therefore, began to pay a great deal of attention to quality controls. In an effort to promote this new paper product, Oron resorted to a consistent merchandising and advertising program.

MARKETING METHODS

Oron's sales area was confined to the section of the United States east of the Rockies since high freight rates on bulky items such as paper made it prohibitively costly to sell at distances farther from the plant. The company distributed principally through food outlets, employing its own sales force to sell to grocery wholesalers, grocery co-operatives, and directly to chain stores. In addition to this sales force, Oron maintained a group of missionary salesmen who called directly on retail stores in order to obtain better shelf position and displays at the point of sale.

THE COMPETITIVE PICTURE

Despite its prominence in the napkin field, Oron was barely represented in the larger markets which existed for facial tissue, toilet tissue, and paper towels. The Scott Paper Company dominated the toilet tissue and towel business, while Kimberly-Clark's Kleenex facial tissue accounted for over 50 percent of the volume in this field. By the middle of the 1970's, however, Oron maintained a 10 to 80 percent share of the napkin business in the markets in which it operated. The company's leading seller was the Oron Table Napkin which contained 80 single-ply napkins per box.

By 1979, one of the competitors introduced its brand of an improved quality of napkins. This product was made by a new technological process which gave it a crisp appearance with a luster-like attractive finish. This product was test marketed very successfully. It received public acceptance and began eating into Oron's share of the paper napkins' market.

This caused Oron to reappraise its own objectives. With the size of the market being small and faced with extremely powerful competition, the resulting market size was too small to warrant the type of advertising expenditure required to support a full-scale competitive brand effort.

PRODUCT LINE EXPANSION

All this gave the impression that *even* Oron's napkin business would soon disappear unless vigorous action was undertaken to develop a full-line of consumer paper products. The company first undertook a long-range strategic program to produce and market a quality product. Starting with the New York market, which accounted for approximately 30 percent of Oron's napkin sales, the company embarked upon an aggressive merchandising venture to establish its toilet tissue on a market-by-market basis. These activities included such direct-action promotional methods as sampling, couponing, and cents-off sales. Since paper items are relatively bulky and space-consuming, some difficulty was encountered in this promotion as retailers were reluctant to find the room for additional products. It took a fair amount of convincing to secure distributors in a group of fourteen key markets in its distribution area.

This expansion of product line, while essential from a long range viewpoint, was accompanied by certain undesirable repercussions on sales of the principal product of the consumer division—paper napkins. During this period the company's major promotional efforts were concentrated on their toilet tissue program at the expense of their paper napkin business.

But this expansion of product line merely slowed down the process of declining sales. This was realized by the management at Oron. They subsequently decided that they had to enter the market with a revolutionary product if they did not want to lose out to the competition. They, therefore, decided to manufacture a paper towel product with much greater absorbency and at the same time not bulky in size. This implied a new manufacturing technology.

The immediate implication was the new investment necessary by way of equipment. It also implied the introduction of a type of paper product which was normally bought only by the relatively better off segment of the population. Oron wanted to price the product so as to get the lower income segment.

To investigate the possibility of such a move, Oron got its advertising agency to conduct a survey on the qualities which people most sought in paper towels as well as on the price they were willing to pay for it. The "guesses" of Oron management proved right when over 90 percent of those sampled said that the quality they most looked for was absorbency. A majority also said they would like a paper towel which they could use for at least two to three wipes. The survey also indicated that the appropriate price for the product would be $0.80 for a roll.

With this information, Oron went ahead with its plan. Its only problem was with the pricing of the product. Since the new paper required heavy capital investment, the product had to be priced so as to give a reasonable rate of return to justify the investment. But at the same time, since Oron wanted the lower income segment of the population as well, the paper could not be priced too high. Therefore, management decided to initially price their roll of paper towel at $0.75 which was a couple of cents cheaper than the price of its competitors. Since the industry was highly competitive, Oron decided not to do any test marketing. Instead they introduced the product with a big burst of advertising, primarily through television, promotions and cents-off coupons, catching the competition off guard.

QUESTIONS FOR DISCUSSION

1. If you were responsible for Oron's marketing and advertising program, would you agree with the Oron paper towel decision? Explain why or why not.
2. Make recommendations on the selling strategy you would adopt.

Case 12–3—Gold O'Roast Corporation (A)

COMPANY BACKGROUND

The Gold O'Roast Corporation[1] is one of the country's leading regional coffee brewers. The company started and still bases its business in the metropolitan New York area. Gold O'Roast started business in the early 1920's by opening retail outlets specializing in the sale of groceries. The company has been aggressive in expanding its market and entering new businesses since that time. In the early 1930's, Gold O'Roast entered the restaurant business. In 1959, the company operated 28 chain restaurants in the metropolitan New York area. The revenue from the restaurant operation accounted for 40% of the total sales. The restaurants, featuring counter-style, fast service, low prices and no tipping, were concentrated in busy business and shopping areas. The company also entered the business of roasting, packing and distributing of ground coffee under the label of Gold O'Roast Coffee in 1953.

HISTORY OF MARKET EXPANSION

The Gold O'Roast Coffee, the company's premium-priced coffee, became the New York metropolitan area's third largest selling brand behind regular-priced Maxwell House and Savarin, excluding grocery chains' private labels, within a few years after its introduction. The revenue from the coffee business accounted for 60% of the company's sales. In 1958, Gold O'Roast introduced its coffee into new markets such as Washington, D.C., Baltimore, Richmond, Norfolk, Rochester, Buffalo, and Toronto. In these markets, Gold O'Roast Coffee was distributed through food brokers, but local sales were also backed by an aggressive advertising program.

The company's financial condition was sound in the 1960's. The company had $37.7 million sales and $2 million profits in 1965. The company acquired three regional coffee roasters in 1964, two of which were combined with the Old Judge Coffee brand. Meanwhile, Gold O'Roast expanded its restaurant operation and also started selling frozen baking goods. Some of their new ventures, such as frozen donuts, were not very successful.

In 1961, Gold O'Roast Coffee was sold in 17 states. Also, instant coffee had been introduced by that time. The company expanded its market into a total of 22 markets by 1965, from Miami to Montreal and Toronto. A more recent move of the company was its entry to North and South Carolina in 1977. And, the company started the sales of coffee in Chicago and Los Angeles shortly after 1977. In addition, decaffeinated regular grind coffee was added to the product line.

Gold O'Roast yielded approximately $163.1 million revenue in 1976. The revenue from coffee sales accounted for 75% of the total, with the remaining 20% from the restaurant operation, and 5% from frozen cakes. Although the company has expanded its coffee market over the past 20 years, 35% of the total coffee sales are still made in the New York metropolitan area, where the company has 13% of the market share today. However, the company is planning to introduce Gold O'Roast Coffee in the national market within a few years.

NATIONAL COFFEE MARKET

Competition has been very keen in the national coffee market. Competition may become more intense in both regular and instant coffee markets since the total consumption of coffee has been decreasing over the years.

Exhibit 12-8   Rate of Coffee Consumption (cups per person per day)[a]

	1960	1970	1971	1972	1973	1974	1975	1976
Regular	2.21	1.91	1.83	1.67	1.61	1.50	1.52	1.48
Instant	.56	.66	.67	.68	.69	.75	.68	.63
Total	2.77	2.57	2.50	2.35	2.30	2.25	2.20	2.11

a = Includes all persons of age 10 and over

SOURCE: Pan American Coffee Bureau, *Coffee Drinking in the United States*, 1976.

The total coffee industry sales including both regular and instant coffee were approximately $1.5 billion in 1972, $2 billion in 1977, and increased to $4.5 billion in 1980. These figures reflect the increased prices of coffee beans. The total instant coffee market was estimated to be about $450 million in 1968, $550 million in 1971, and $650 million in 1973. The average margin in the regular coffee industry is about 1%, and that of the instant coffee industry is about 5%.

In the national regular coffee market, General Foods had been holding more than 30% of the total market. However, the Company's total market share has been decreasing from 35.2% to 31.5% in the late 1970's. Although General Foods' Maxwell House had been the leader in regular coffee market until recently, Procter & Gamble's Folger's brand gained a larger share of 26.5% in 1978, and 27.3% in 1979. General Foods and Procter & Gamble account for almost 50% of the total market. Another remarkable feature in the regular coffee market is that other small brands not listed in Exhibit 12-9, including private labels such as A&P, have been holding nearly 30% of the share.

In the instant coffee market, General Foods had a market share of 47.5% in 1979, although the company's total market share had been gradually decreasing in the late 1970's. Nestle has increased its total

Exhibit 12-9   Regular Coffee Market Shares

	1974	1975	1976	1977	1978	1979
General Foods						
Maxwell House[a]	25.3	24.9	24.1	24.9	22.3	22.3
Sanka	4.0	4.0	4.0	3.5	2.0	2.1
Yuban	2.2	2.2	2.2	2.0	2.0	2.0
Max-Pax & Brim	3.7	4.1	4.5	4.0	3.5	3.5
Mellow Roast	—	—	—	.8	1.8	1.6
Company Total	35.2	35.2	34.8	35.2	31.6	31.5
Procter & Gamble						
Folgers	20.7	21.0	21.4	21.4	26.5	27.3
Hill's Brothers						
Hill's Brothers	7.7	7.6	7.5	7.0	6.9	6.6
Standard Brands						
Chase & Sanborn	3.8	3.7	3.5	2.9	1.6	1.0
Coca Cola						
Merryland Club	1.6	1.8	1.9	1.8	1.4	1.2
Butternut	2.5	2.7	2.8	2.7	2.7	2.5
Company Total	4.1	4.5	4.7	4.5	4.1	3.7
Subtotal	71.5	72.0	71.9	71.0	70.7	70.1
All Others	28.5	28.0	28.1	29.0	29.3	29.9

a: Electra-Perk is roughly 6% in all years
SOURCE: *Advertising Age*, July 11, 1977; April 14, 1980.

Exhibit 12-10   Instant Coffee Market Shares

	1974	1975	1976	1977	1978	1979
General Foods						
Maxwell House[a]	25.5	24.9	24.5	24.0	24.0	23.4
Maxim	7.0	5.5	5.3	4.5	4.0	3.7
Sanka	11.2	11.6	11.1	10.0	10.0	9.8
Yuban	2.0	2.0	2.0	1.3	1.3	1.3
Freeze-Dried						
Sanka	3.6	3.2	3.1	2.5	2.5	2.5
Brim[a]	3.5	3.5	3.5	3.5	3.0	2.8
Mellow Roast	—	—	—	1.5	3.5	4.0
Company Total	52.8	50.7	49.5	47.3	48.3	47.5
Procter & Gamble						
Folgers	6.8	8.0	7.0	7.0	8.0	8.5
Hill's Brothers						
Hill's Brothers	1.0	.9	.8	.5	.3	.2
Nestle						
Taster's Choice						
100% Coffee	11.7	11.7	11.8	12.5	12.5	12.7
Nescafe	11.0	11.0	12.6	12.0	10.5	10.0
Decaf	1.4	1.4	1.0	1.0	1.0	1.0
Taster's Choice						
Decaffeinated	5.1	5.4	5.5	5.6	5.1	4.8
Sunrise	—	—	—	—	3.0	4.0
Company Total	29.2	29.5	30.9	31.1	32.1	32.5
Borden						
Kava	.8	1.1	1.3	1.2	1.0	1.0
Subtotal	90.6	90.2	98.5	87.1	89.7	89.7
All Others	9.4	9.8	10.5	12.9	10.3	10.3

a: Brim and International
SOURCE: *Advertising Age*, July 11, 1977; April 14, 1980.

company's share in the past 10 years since its introduction of Taster's Choice. The company's share increased from 14% to 32.5% during the years from 1968 to 1979. Procter & Gamble's Folger's Brand has been maintaining approximately 7 to 8% of share over the past 10 years. The other companies are competing for the rest of the 11.5% of the market.

PRODUCT DIFFERENTIATION IN THE COFFEE MARKET

There has been more segmentation within the coffee market since the late 1960's with respect to caffeine content, product forms, price, and other features such as packaging.
(1) Caffeine Content
Decaffeinated coffee is available both in regular and instant coffee.

Exhibit 12-11   Cunsumption of Decaffeinated Coffee (cups per person per day)[a]

	1958	1962	1975	1976
Decaffeinated	.04	.10	.31	.30
Non-decaffeinated	2.83	3.02	1.89	1.81
All Coffee	2.87	3.12	2.20	2.11

a: Includes all persons of age 10 and over
SOURCE: Pan American Coffee Bureau, *Coffee Drinking in the United States*, 1976.

The consumption of decaffeinated coffee increased from .10 cup per person per day to .30 cup per person per day in the years from 1962 to 1976. In 1976, nearly three-quarters of the total consumption of decaffeinated coffee originated in the instant coffee sector. Decaffeinated coffee accounts for more than 20% of the total instant coffee market in the 1970's, and more women drink this type of coffee than men.
(2) Product Forms
Freeze-Dried: In addition to the ordinary spray-dried coffee, freeze-dried coffee, such as General Foods' Maxim and Nestle's Taster's Choice, was introduced in the mid 1960's. In 1976, about .25 cup of freeze-dried coffee was consumed per person per day, while .38 cup of spray-dried coffee was consumed per person per day.
Blend of Spray-Dried and Freeze-Dried: Two brands of coffee were introduced on a trial basis as a new blend of spray-dried and freeze-dried coffee; General Foods' Master Blend and Proc-

ter & Gamble's Epic were introduced into test markets in the early 1970's.

Grain Blends: General Foods' Mellow Roast is a mixed blend of coffee and grains such as wheat and bran. This brand is priced lower than the regular-priced instant coffee.

(3) Price

In addition to the traditional regular-premium distinction, some other forms of price reduction have been introduced.

Economy Brand: Lower-priced regular grind coffee is sold in 13- and 26-oz. cans. These brands are advertised as yielding a larger number of cups of coffee than others. Procter & Gamble's Folger's Flaked, General Foods' Maxwell House Master Blend, Hill's Brother's High Yield, and Coca Cola's Maryland Club and Butternut Extra Measure are of this type. Most of these brands, except Folger's, were distributed locally in the late 1970's.

Bonus Jars: Many brands of instant coffee are now sold in a 10-oz. jar size at a lower price per pound.

ADVERTISING STRATEGIES FOR GOLD O'ROAST

Gold O'Roast Coffee was long advertised as "Heavenly Coffee" with an emphasis on its premium quality in the early 1960's. The recent advertising also features an economic advantage as well as its quality. "Richer and Stronger" and "One-Third More Cups" are emphasized in a print advertisement for the company's regular coffee. "Darker and Richer" are featured in an advertisement for the instant coffee.

The company added spot TV recently to spot radio and print media for the advertising of its coffee products. The advertising expenditures for the years 1974 to 1980 are shown in Exhibit 12-12.

Exhibit 12-12   Advertising Expenditures for Gold O'Roast Coffee: 1974-1980 ($'000)

		News paper	Magazine	News paper sup.	Net work TV	Spot TV	Out- door	Spot radio	Total
'74	R,I	NA				142.6		16.8	159.4
'75	R	NA		16.5	14.1			20.6	51.2
'76	R	113.554				78.0		80.8	272.354
'77		70.839							70.839
'78	R	NA	38.9			.4		106.2	145.5
'79	R	NA				341.4		NA	341.4
'80	R, I	NA				656.3		NA	656.3

Note:
R: regular coffee   I: instant coffee   NA: data not available
'77: no advertising in measured media other than newspapers
'78: spot radio only for the first 2 quarters
'80: January-September
Newspaper expenditures are available only for 1976 and 1977.

SOURCE: Leading National Advertisers, Radio Expenditures Report, *Advertising Age*, June 26, 1978.

QUESTIONS FOR DISCUSSION

1. Appraise the opportunity to advertise Gold O'Roast Coffee in the national market.
2. Evaluate the advantages and disadvantages of Gold O'Roast coffee products in light of the competition in the regular and instant coffee markets.
3. Which Gold O'Roast brand(s) do you recommend for aggressive advertising backing in the national market? State how you would position the brand(s) and define the target audience.
4. Develop creative strategies for the Gold O'Roast brands for the target audience you defined.

ENDNOTE

1. Company name has been disguised.

Case 12-4—Nu-Dye Products, Inc.[1]

COMPANY BACKGROUND

The T. & P. Company produces and distributes a line of household dyes which have been on the market for over 60 years under the brand name of Nu-Dye. Nu-Dye is the biggest brand in the market and it holds more than three-quarters of the country's dye market at present. Products are distributed in every type of retail outlet such as variety stores, drugstores, and large grocery chains.

In 1980, a new management team headed by a new president assumed control of T. & P. Company operations. One of the moves initiated by the new president was a re-examination of a wide range of company policies and operations. Included in this review was a complete reappraisal of advertising and promotion strategy. A new advertising agency was appointed and asked to assist in this study by submitting suggestions for an advertising program. Since very few housewives are assumed to dye faded, old clothes and household items today, the first task assigned for the agency was to examine new uses of home dye products and to suggest a new product positioning which would appeal to contemporary consumer needs.

THE NU-DYE PRODUCT LINE

The line of Nu-Dye fabric dye is packaged in a $2\frac{1}{8}$ oz. size, which is available in fifty-four colors and retails for 99 cents. This line of products is made in forms of powder and liquid. In addition to this complete line of tints and dyes, Nu-Dye also produces and markets a color remover and a bluing called Glisten. This color remover is used to remove colored material from a fabric to facilitate redyeing it. The product can also be used to remove stains from white materials.

Although new products and product modifications are infrequent in this industry, T. & P. introduced a new type of dye in 1959. This dye could be used in a washing machine and was known in the industry as a washing machine dye. Prior to the introduction of this new product, home dyeing had to be done in a pot of boiling water, constantly stirred. There were obvious hazards and inconveniences connected with this method. By reducing the dependence upon boiling water and by permitting dyeing to be done simply and conveniently in a washing machine, it was made possible to dye larger items such as draperies, sheets and bedspreads. This new product contributed to the company's increased sales by increasing the number of dye users and by increasing the occasions for dyeing.

THE MARKET TRENDS FOR DYES

There were two peaks in the sales of home dyes: The first one occurred in the early 1950's and reached its highest in the late 1950's; the second one appeared in 1969, when tie-dye fashion was spread among young people, fostered by the trend of "do-it-yourself" as well as by an aggressive mass merchandising of the textile industry.

PHASE I   REDYEING OF OLD ITEMS

Retail dollar sales of tints and dye increased by 28.6 percent from 1953 to 1958 (see Exhibit 12–13), compared to a population increase of 9.0 percent during the same period. In a mature industry, such as dyes, where product innovations are infrequent, this should be considered quite satisfactory growth, indicating more extensive or intensive use of the product.

Exhibit 12-13   Retail Sales of Tints and Dyes

Year	Retail Sales (000)	Per Cent Change from Prior Year
1958	$16,550	+ 5.6
1957	15,680	+ 6.5
1956	14,720	+ 4.3
1955	14,110	+ 3.2
1954	13,670	+ 6.3
1953	12,860	
1958/1953		+28.6
Population 1958/1953		+ 9.0

SOURCE: Topics Publishing Co.

The basic consumer utility of dyes at this time was that redyeing could extend the useful lives of clothes and household articles when such items began to look faded before fabrics were worn. Since the cost of commercial dyeing was more expensive, and since dyeing was essentially an economy measure, many housewives undertook to do the job at home.

Although many housewives were engaged in home dyeing over the years, sales of dyes started declining in the early 1960's. There were several reasons for this decline in dye sales:

1. There was an increased availability of low-price household items, such as bedspreads and slip covers, and other soft goods that were once dyed at home. Also, there were more varieties in color and design in such items. These factors motivated consumers to repurchase commercially produced items more frequently.
2. There was an increased use of synthetics especially for items such as bedspreads and draperies on which dyes did not work. Dyes worked very well on all natural fibers, rayon, and nylon, but not on many other synthetics.
3. The higher standard of living discouraged women from redyeing their old clothes and household items: the increased discretionary income of households and the increased employment for women permitted them to purchase frequently changing new fashions.
4. Since color has become a less important element of new fashion, redyeing was a less attractive way for women to update their clothes.

PHASE II   TIE-DYE BOOM

The fad of tie-dyeing spread among young people from 1969 to the early 1970's. This boom was propelled by the unique atmosphere of that time: Campuses were crowded with student activists until the late 1960's. There were "hippies" and "flower children," and "psychedelic" was the name of the game in music, art, and fashion. Tie-dyeing started among the flower children in California, and then it was promoted on a commercial basis to young people. While ready-made tie-dye fashion was available at both popular-priced stores and high-fashion boutiques, tie-dyeing also had creative appeals for self-expression and originality which could be easily enjoyed at relatively low costs.

T. & P. Company was one of the major promoters of tie-dyeing. Before the company started an extensive tie-dye campaign, it had tried to appeal to the young consumers. In 1968, T. & P. ran a tie-in campaign with several manufacturers of jeans and sneakers to promote brush painting on clothes, hats, and sneakers using the company's dyes. Compared to this initial campaign, tie-dyeing was promoted far more extensively. In promoting tie-dyeing, T. & P. and its advertising agency defined the following objectives:

1. Reposition Nu-Dye from the "then" image of redyeing to the "now" image of fashion leader.

2. Communicate to young audience who love color in the age of color.
3. Keep traditional customers, primarily housewives and older women.
4. Generate heavy sales volume through many and varied uses.

T. & P.'s print advertising which was carried in many women's fashion magazines showed "after" scenes of various tie-dyed items such as T-shirts and tights accompanied with illustrated instructions for tie-dying. Since T. & P. had no major competitors, advertising concentrated on promoting the usage of dye rather than the brand. In addition to advertising, T. & P. commissioned a young fabric designer to create tie-dye fabrics, which were subsequently purchased by leading designers. By 1970, the company mailed as many as 500,000 instruction booklets to consumers.

Besides the company's direct advertising efforts, tie-dyeing was also introduced to housewives as a new handicraft in women's magazines. Tie-dyeing was also featured in special interest magazines such as *School Arts* and *Design* in the early 1970's.

T. & P. Company's sales increased by 35 percent from 1968 to 1969. The company held as much as 85 percent of the 24 million-dollar dye market at this time. Well behind T. & P., Tintex had a 10 percent share, and Putnam Dyes, Inc. had a 3 percent share.

PRESENT MARKET FOR DYE

By early 1970, T. & P. had succeeded in improving its product quality. Its dyes are now applicable to most non-metallic materials, except glass fiber and acrylic fiber. However, the total population of dye users has declined significantly since the tie-dye fad disappeared before 1975. Then, the research department conducted a consumer survey in order to investigate the actual usage of dyes and consumer perceptions of this product.

The current dye users were classified into two groups. One was the users of traditional redyeing. More than 60 percent of this segment consisted of women over 50 years old. The other segment was considered a growing population of handicraft lovers, whose average age was 36. The first segment accounted for less than 5 percent of the sample of 2,000 women, and the second accounted for 18 percent. Some of the women in the second group were still trying tie-dyeing with more elaborated techniques, in combination with stitching and different methods of tieing, using several different colors. The survey found that such women applied tie-dyeing for household decoration such as wall hanging and cushions rather than for clothes. Another use of dyes was to color yarns for knitting and weaving. Among the users of dyes for this purpose, it was found that some women preferred using natural dyes made from plants and vegetables to obtain earth colors. The third type of handicraft persons was occasional users of dyes for painting small household items such as napkins and luncheon mats.

The survey also revealed that most of the non-users were reluctant to use dyes for the following reasons:

Dyeing is old fashioned and is associated
with stinginess 45%
Dyeing is time-consuming 28
Clothes might be colored unevenly 17
Colors would come out and spread
into other things when dyed
items are washed together 10
I cannot find my favorite colors 7
It reminds me of the crazy tie-dye fashion 1

In spite of these negative perceptions about dyeing, more than 40 percent of these non-users indicated that they were interested in trying dyeing for creative purposes if they were provided with adequate instructions.

CREATIVE STRATEGIES FOR NU-DYE

Based upon the above consumer survey, T. & P. Company's advertising agency suggested that creative uses of dyes for handicraft and home decoration should be emphasized in the Nu-Dye advertising. The agency recommended two segments of audience:
1. Current users of dyes for handicraft, and women with semi-professional skills in other handicrafts than tie-dyeing.
2. Female non-users of dyes who are interested in using dyes to decorate their households.

The agency eliminated the current users of dyes for redyeing purposes since Nu-Dye has already achieved well-established brand acceptance among these women. T. & P.'s executives opposed the idea of eliminating the redyeing segment, since this segment accounted for more than 50 percent of the company's sales volume. Besides, they suggested that the current inflation would motivate even younger housewives, as well as older women, to redye their clothes and household items. The executives pointed out that home sewing has been becoming more popular among women of various ages for economic reasons. On the other hand, the brand manager agreed with the agency's recommendation. And, he proposed that new uses of Nu-Dye could be promoted through booklets and through art and craft courses for housewives at community high schools and colleges.

QUESTIONS FOR DISCUSSION

1. Evaluate the agency's recommendations with regard to the product positioning and the definition of target audiences for Nu-Dye.
2. Prepare creative strategies for Nu-Dye advertising (print media). In your creative strategies, state your advertising goals in terms of effectiveness criteria and your definition of target audience.

ENDNOTE

1. Company name is disguised.

Case 12-5—Sears, Roebuck and Company

ANALYSIS OF A NEW ADVERTISING POLICY

In early 1960 the executives of Sears, Roebuck and Company were involved in a discussion of company advertising policies. Sears, one of the country's largest merchandisers, is also one of the largest advertisers with an annual budget exceeding $100 million.

For many years Sears advertising, aside from their catalog, had been almost completely local in nature. The principal advertising objective was to promote sales of Sears' own brands of merchandise through their retail stores. All advertising funds, other than costs of the catalog, were spent for this purpose, although the Public Relations department did make extensive use of publicity as a means of communicating company policies.

BACKGROUND INFORMATION ON SEARS' OPERATIONS

In 1963 Sears was an international merchandising operation with a combined retail and mail order sales volume of $5,155,766,391, the major part of which was done through their retail stores. By 1970 sales volume reached nine billion two hundred sixty million.

Sears was established as a mail order company in 1886 and was operated exclusively as a mail order business for many years. The first retail store was opened for operation in 1925, and the retail phase of the business was continuously expanded until the company now operates 1057 stores, 859 in the United States and 198 in foreign countries.

MERCHANDISING POLICIES

The great bulk of Sears' sales volume is done is Sears' own brands of merchandise. As a general rule, brands of merchandise owned by other companies were distributed through the Sears organization only when the marketing opportunity was considered inadequate to develop and market one of Sears' own brands.

From the inception of the company, price factors have been of great concern to management. Sears' policy has been to try to give the customer a product of satisfactory quality at a price below that of competition. In referring to company policies during the mail order phase of the company, Emmet and Jeuck, in their history of Sears, Roebuck & Company say:

> "In a real sense the cornerstone of the business was a low-price policy. Richard Sears would exercise great ingenuity in pushing down his buying price so that he might advertise lower selling prices on items whose potentialities he thought great. Long before Nourse, Sears banked on demand elasticity.
>
> "Though experience must have taught him that his low prices would be followed by competition, he depended on getting there first! He held firm convictions about the virtues of enjoying the initial advantage.
>
> "To depend upon radical price reduction without risking inferences of inferior quality, Sears early adopted the guarantee and a liberal returned-goods policy, which served to endorse the quality of the merchandise as well as to coax customers into experimenting with a not-thoroughly familiar method of buying. (Mail order)."

Procurement of merchandise of satisfactory quality at satisfactory low prices was a difficult problem for the company in many periods of its history. When it proved to be impossible to secure the quality of merchandise at satisfactory prices from independent producers, Sears & Roebuck entered into factory ownership, wholly or partially, in the merchandise lines in question. Richard Sears' early policy was to enter factory ownership only when compelled to and to restrict his interest to 50% or less whenever feasible. The firm wanted to do as little of its own manufacturing as reasonably possible. Company management still adhers generally to this policy.

ADVERTISING POLICY

Sears, Roebuck has been a heavy advertiser throughout the entire history of the company. Richard Sears, the co-founder, was primarily concerned with sales promotion. He believed so strongly in the power of consistent advertising and promotion that he spent huge sums to build the Sears-Roebuck reputation throughout rural America.

In the early stages of the mail-order business, Sears bought prodigious quantities of advertising space in periodicals with circulation to farm homes. Sears was also a very able copywriter and he filled this space with copy that captivated his readers. He recognized the importance of integrating merchandise selection, price, advertising and promotion into one consumer package.

The available data indicate that advertising expenditures in 1898 were approximately $400,000, or 13% of sales for that year. In 1902, the advertising budget was $1,500,000, or 9% of sales. Total operating expense in this year was 18.39%. Advertising was the largest single item of expense during this period.[2]

The expansion of Sears' sales through retail stores and the relative decline in importance of the mail order side of the business brought changes in company advertising policy. Local sales through local retail stores, to Sears management, meant local advertising. Local news-papers became the principal media and continued so for many years. Local, direct-action advertising expenditures continued to grow and since 1965 have exceeded $100,000,000 each year.

The review of advertising policy by Sears' executives, referred to above, was a broad-gauge discussion which covered an evaluation of the effectiveness of the present local advertising program. In addition, it included an appraisal of the total consumer awareness of Sears' advertising and its effect on the Sears "image," and of the attitude of people in general toward the company and Sears' merchandise.

This appraisal resulted in recommendations for a drastic modifica-tion and expansion of Sears' advertising and promotion program to in-clude national advertising which would in no way supplant or in any way interfere with the local advertising effort. Proceeding on these recommendations, as expeditiously as possible, Sears engaged an advertising agency and launched an advertising campaign in national media. This campaign was a rather substantial one with a budget in 1965 of $15,000,000. In 1970 reliable estimates put the figure above $45,000,000.

The objective of the new campaign was to: "Build a better image of the company and of Sears' merchandise by interpreting and explaining company policies and services to the public. In these advertisements we are telling millions of existing and potential customers many things about Sears they never dreamed of. We want them to say: 'I never knew that. *How interesting.* Sounds good . . . I must shop at Sears more often.'

"Today, millions of Americans know a good deal more about Sears than they knew a year ago: About its low profit margin, for instance. About its telephone shopping service. About its Fashion Board, its Service Fleet, and the famous Sears laboratory for testing merchan-dise. About the range of goods Sears sells, including fabulous mink."[3]

There were some changes in company policies and operations which accompanied, or in some cases, slightly preceded the national cam-paign; one of the very important of these was an upgrading of Sears' merchandise in both quality and price. A number of advertisements in such media as *Life* featured merchandise items in price lines not associated with the usual consumer image of Sears as a "price," economy retailer, e.g., mink coats at $3,500 and up. The campaign is to be continued indefinitely.

QUESTIONS FOR DISCUSSION

1. Do you agree or disagree with Sears' advertising program adopted in 1965?
2. Evaluate the creative strategy employed in this advertising program.
3. How is this creative strategy related to the overall marketing strategy of Sears?
4. Suggest a creative strategy for Sears in light of current marketing developments in their retailing area and the current situation of the company.

ENDNOTES

1. Emmet & Jeuck, *Catalogues and Counters,* University of Chicago Press, 1950, p. 173.
2. *Ibid.,* p. 6.
3. From a statement by Charles H. Kellstadt, Chairman of the Board, Sears, Roebuck and Company.

Case 12-6—Gulf Oil Company—U.S.[1]

In April, 1974, Mr. Charles Swinson, advertising and sales promotion manager of Gulf Oil, was attempting to develop his recommendations to top management with respect to promotional activities of the firm during the coming fiscal year. Unprecedented developments in the energy market in the previous nine months had resulted in a complete turnabout in the promotional objectives and strategies of the entire oil industry. As a result of the energy crisis, Mr. Swinson was under pressure to design a promotional communications plan to cope with a concerned and hostile public, and sagging morale within the advertising department, which had found it extremely difficult to adjust its thinking to the new environment.

BACKGROUND

Gulf Oil, based in Houston, Texas, is a subsidiary of a diversified petroleum company, Gulf Oil Corporation, which was in its 73rd year of operation. Gulf Oil ranked as the fifth largest gasoline marketer in the United States preceded by Texaco, Shell, Amoco and Exxon, in that order. In recent years, the company had retained about a 6 percent share of market relative to its competitors. Table 12-1 presents data on total sales and advertising media expenditures by the six largest oil company advertisers during 1972.

In addition to gasoline, motor oil, tires, automotive lubricants and related automotive products produced by Gulf Oil, other divisions and subsidiaries of Gulf Oil Corporation were engaged in a wide variety of ventures. These ventures include a number of energy-related activities—coal mining, atomic power, petrochemicals and other resource extraction. The parent corporation had enjoyed a lucrative eleven-year alliance with Holiday Inns, Inc. Furthermore, the Gulf Oil Real Estate Development Co. was established in 1972 and among other projects was developing a residential, industrial and commercial complex on a 2,700-acre site in Orlando, Florida, near Disney World.

Consolidated net income of Gulf Oil Corporation for 1973 was $800 million compared with $447 million in 1972, an improvement of 79 percent (see Table 12-2). Higher earnings were attributed primarily to higher refined product prices and sales volume, a broadening plastics and chemicals market, elimination of marginal operations, and an expanded tanker fleet. Gulf Oil Corporation's worldwide profits were up 75 percent in the first quarter of 1974. The earnings from Gulf Oil Cor-

Table 12-1 Sales & Media Expenditures—Six Largest Oil Company Advertisers 1972

Company	Total Sales ($ mil.)	Total Advertising Expenditures ($ mil.)	% of Measured Media Dollars								
			Genl. Mags.	Farm Pubs.	Bus Pubs.	Spot TV	Net. TV	Spot Radio	Net. Radio	Out-door
Exxon Corp.	22,438	34	4.8	0.9	—	44.3	20.3	22.2	—	7.5
Shell Oil Corp.	4,817	31	7.9	4.8	1.5	42.5	34.8	5.2	2.9	0.4
Texaco Inc.	8,693	27	4.5	0.3	3.6	4.2	66.3	13.8	6.8	0.5
Standard (Indiana)	5,401	26	2.9	4.2	3.7	39.9	22.0	26.2	—	1.1
Mobil Oil Co.	10,295	24	5.3	4.1	2.7	17.2	40.9	22.9	6.4	0.4
Gulf Oil Corp.	7,624	23	1.9	—	4.0	13.8	66.3	10.6	2.1	1.3

SOURCE: *Advertising Age.*

Note: Media expenditures percentages are based on total expenditures in measured media only.

poration's U.S. petroleum operations increased 14 percent in 1973. This increase was attributed to increased prices for crude oil produced and to a 12.3 percent increase in refined product sales volume. Gulf maintained that product price increases received by the corporation reflected the recovery of increased costs as approved by the Cost of Living Council, and that by far the greatest increase in earnings was realized by overseas operations rather than by Gulf Oil.

In the first quarter of 1973 the future looked extremely promising for Gulf Oil, whose 20,000+ service stations were servicing six to eight million people *per week* in thirty-five states. Numerous factors were combining to create a record demand for gasoline (and other fuels as well). 1971-72 car years were banner sales years. The average size and weight of the new cars was quite large. The new cars used 30-35 percent more gasoline, a fuel penalty resulting from strict federal auto emission standards. As the cars aged, the fuel penalties sometimes rose to 40 and 50 percent. The economy was such that it stimulated a maximum number of miles traveled—business was booming and income levels were high. Finally, research showed that 72 percent of the people who had bought a 1972 car had another car; over 35 percent became three-car families. Old cars weren't being retired and the demand for automobiles was growing at 8-10 percent. Not only did all these statistics forecast record sales of and demand for gasoline; more ominously, they portended an inevitable fuel crisis when this vast demand outstripped refining capacity of the oil companies. In the second quarter of 1973, talk of a fuel crisis or "energy crunch" began, and in the 3rd and 4th quarters, the frightening effects of the energy crisis were initially felt. When it became clear that fuel oil would be in short supply in the U.S. that winter, the gasoline companies were allocated crude oil and their supply began to run short of demand by 2-3 percent.

PRODUCT ADVERTISING—GULFTANE

At the time the energy crunch hit, Gulf Oil was undertaking a large-scale advertising campaign for its low-lead, medium-priced Gulftane gasoline. Normally product-specific advertising was not characteristic in the oil industry. Research had shown 95 percent awareness of the Gulf logo, and very high aided and unaided recall of Gulf advertising. Product-specific advertising had not been found to alter awareness—awareness resulted from point-of-sale promotions and transaction impressions. Advertising could have an effect on market share, however, and Gulftane was a 91-octane, low-lead product, cheaper than competitors' low-leads. Low-leads were being specified in new-car owners' manuals, and the demand for such products had increased 50-60 percent in a year. All in all, Gulf Oil felt Gulftane had tremendous competitive potential.

Unfortunately, with the onset of the energy crisis, intensive product advertising of Gulftane—in fact, *any* advertising campaign which would increase driveway traffic at Gulf service stations—was con-

Table 12-2　Five-Year Financial Summary
Gulf Oil Corporation

	1973	1972	1971	1970	1969
		(Dollar Amounts in Millions)			
STATEMENT OF INCOME					
Revenues					
Sales and other operating revenues (includes consumer excise taxes)					
United States	$ 4,626	$ 3,944	$ 3,841	$ 3,881	$ 3,703
Foreign	5,217	3,680	3,364	2,716	2,407
	9,843	7,624	7,205	6,597	6,110
Dividends, interest, equity earnings and other revenues	164	109	167	123	128
	10,007	7,733	7,372	6,720	6,238
Deductions					
Purchased crude oil, products and merchandise	2,833	1,763	1,651	1,656	1,431
Operating expenses	1,618	1,447	1,330	1,182	1,089
Selling, general and administrative expenses	944	921	935	810	796
Consumer excise taxes	1,426	1,381	1,265	1,201	1,156
Sales, use, ad valorem and other taxes	265	228	211	203	175
Income taxes					
United States	23	12	31	12	4
Foreign	1,341	800	724	423	372
Deferred	12	11	17	49	66
Depreciation, depletion, amortization and retirements	610	576	510	522	451
Interest on long-term debt	135	147	137	112	87
	9,207	7,286	6,811	6,170	5,627
Income before extraordinary item	800	447	561	550	611
Extraordinary item	—	(250)	—	—	—
Net income	$ 800	$ 197	$ 561	$ 550	$ 611
Estimated losses from discontinued operations charged to net income					
Net (loss)	$ —	$ (27)	$ (32)	$ (26)	$ (19)
Per share	$ —	$ (.13)	$ (.15)	$ (.12)	$ (.09)
Per share data					
Income before extraordinary item	$ 4.06	$ 2.15	$ 2.70	$ 2.65	$ 2.94
Extraordinary item	—	(1.20)	—	—	—
Net income	$ 4.06	$ .95	$ 2.70	$ 2.65	$ 2.94
Cash dividends	$ 1.50	$ 1.50	$ 1.50	$ 1.50	$ 1.50
Shareholders' equity	$ 28.61	$ 26.04	$ 26.59	$ 25.42	$ 24.28

SOURCE: 1973 Gulf Annual Report.

sidered by Gulf Oil management to be imprudent. Since Gulf could *not* satisfy the additional demand, it was feared that intensive advertising for products in *very* finite supply would serve no purpose but to evoke hostility from the consuming public. It would be a needless expenditure of advertising dollars with possible negative consequences. Thus, in May of 1973, Gulf Oil began phasing out Gulftane advertising (spot TV and radio plus newspapers) in its seventy-five market areas.

With the premature demise of the Gulftane campaign, the company was left with an advertising vacuum. Gulf Oil executives and the subsidiary's ad agency Young & Rubicam felt they had to hit on new promotional tactics which would preserve the firm's market share and reputation without creating additional demand. The immediate strategy was no advertising at all. Studies showed that public opinion was beginning to run very strongly *against* the oil corporations who were advertising the most—namely Exxon and Amoco. These firms were suggesting that consumers should drive slower, drive less, and use small cars in attempts to conserve fuel—tactics which some marketers call "demarketing," or attempting to manage a too-high level of demand for a scarce product.

Gallup polls and other studies indicated that 62 percent of the public did not really believe there was an energy crisis and 73 percent believed the oil companies were "rigging" the crisis so they could justify higher prices. By fall of 1973 Congress had picked up on the public discontent; certain members of Congress had accused the oil companies of conspiracy and the newly-created Federal Energy Office was investigating the industry leaders. Gulf Oil and the other oil companies stepped up their lobbying on Capitol Hill, because there was a growing fear that increasing consumer concern would result in a movement to nationalize the oil industry.

The fuel situation was exacerbated considerably in late fall of 1973 when the Arab oil countries embargoed oil shipments to the U.S. and drastically hiked the price of crude oil to *all* buyers. The fact that the embargo was visible proof of a real energy crisis could have helped the oil companies' credibility, except that published oil company profits were at a record high. Congress was talking of cutting oil company profits by taxing, cutting oil depletion allowances, or putting price ceilings on gasoline. The oil industry was rapidly becoming everybody's scapegoat.

THE AGENCY'S POSITION

During the advertising hiatus which began with the demise of the Gulftane campaign, Gulf Oil and Young & Rubicam developed a series of ad campaigns which were subjected to consumer panels and other tests of advertising effectiveness. These consumer education ads—which attempted a logical, unemotional presentation of the facts on the energy crisis—were tested, but fell through because viewers perceived them as self-serving rather than objective. Ads suggesting that the consumer take measures to conserve gasoline were perceived as an attempt by the oil companies to shift the burden of responsibility to the consumers.

Young & Rubicam had come to the conclusion that an item-by-item refutation of all the charges made against Gulf Oil and the industry would do more harm than good. Consumer panel reaction to such "refutational" advertising had been quite negative. On the basis of their research, Young & Rubicam concluded that the refutational ads apparently made Gulf Oil appear defensive and paranoid, and only added fuel to the fire by focusing on controversial issues. Any facts invoked by Gulf Oil in its own defense were immediately suspect. In addition, the creative talent at Young & Rubicam felt that the educational but long-winded ads required in a consumer education or refutational campaign were an aesthetic washout. They lacked eye appeal and the reader tended to lose interest halfway through. Perhaps more important, the ad executives at Young & Rubicam were appalled at the thought of writing off the large investments Gulf Oil had made over the years to increase driveway traffic and market share. Young & Rubicam had worked hard to project an image of Gulf as a service-oriented gasoline retailer marketing high-quality petroleum products. The agency felt that the company could not afford to forfeit this image, *especially* at a time when oil companies were struggling for credibility and public acceptance.

Young & Rubicam pointed out that although Gulf Oil had drastically reduced their expenditures on advertising during 1973, in 1972 the subsidiary spent approximately $3.2 million to advertise Gulf dealer service. Advertising expenditures during 1972 promoting gasoline for network and spot TV were $1,597,000 and $1,578,000 respectively. During the year Gulf auto tires advertising expenditures on network TV were $45,000. The subsidiary also benefited from the parent corporation's general promotional expenditures of $3,735,000 during 1972.

Young & Rubicam was not opposed to all advertising. Indeed they felt that aggressive, large-scale product advertising was in order, particularly since Gulf Oil had developed a lead-free gasoline—Gulfcrest—with excellent market potential.

GULFCREST

Late in 1973 Gulf Oil announced that Gulfcrest was ready for marketing. The product was to replace the popular Gulftane low-lead. Gulfcrest was to be phased gradually into all market areas in which Gulf Oil operated, with the product available in all areas by July 1, 1974. July 1 was the deadline set by the Environmental Protection Agency for the availability at most gasoline stations of a lead-free gasoline of at least 91 octane rating for use in the 1975 model automobiles.

During the final quarter of 1970, Gulf Oil began making plans for the manufacturing and marketing of a lead-free gasoline to replace

Gulftane. The firm had begun developing the new gasoline at that time after becoming convinced that it would eventually be necessary to produce a lead-free product to satisfy the Clean Air Act of 1970. Gulfcrest met or exceeded all EPA requirements for an unleaded product.

Consistent with their low profile promotional strategy, Gulfcrest was introduced without fanfare. Little publicity and no consumer advertising was utilized or planned to introduce the new gasoline.

Gulf's Marketing Department's research indicated demand for Gulfcrest at 5 percent of the firm's total gasoline production, or about one million gallons a day. The firm's research projected demand growth to range from 7-10 percent per year, thus by 1980 Gulfcrest should account for 50-65 percent of total gasoline sales.

RESEARCH DEVELOPMENTS

In recent months Gulf Oil researchers had developed two promising items relevant to the gasoline shortage. The first was a catalyst that decomposes oxides of nitrogen in auto exhaust and thus may help make unleaded gasoline unnecessary. The catalyst had been sent to various automobile manufacturers and others for road testing. The researchers had tested the unit on an engine test stand and found it effective for the equivalent of 50,000 miles of normal driving.

Second, through improvements in existing equipment and techniques, Gulf Oil research had developed an easily portable device for checking and evaluating the efficiency of an automobile engine in only thirty seconds. The device was an infrared exhaust gas analyzer used to measure an engine's combustion as it relates to gasoline economy in two areas—hydrocarbon and cabon monoxide. Hydrocarbon parts per million are related to the engine's mechanical functions, e.g., ignition, timing, spark plugs, etc. The percentage of carbon monoxide in engine exhaust relates to the air/fuel mixture in the carburetor.

Two attendants are required for operation of the system. A long flexible tube connected to the device is attached to the exhaust pipe of the auto for a quick test which does not require raising the hood or asking the driver to get out of the car. The test suggests if the engine is performing efficiently or if maintenance work is in order. If the test indicated an unsatisfactory condition on either or both of the readings a number of likely causes were identified to the motorist.

ECONO-CHECK PROGRAM

The second research development had led the company's marketing department to develop and test market a pilot project named Econo-Check Program. The auto-exhaust analyzer was installed in Ford Econoline vans and two attendants performed the service for motorists in shopping center parking lots in two test markets—Corpus Christi, Texas and Baton Rouge, Louisiana. In both test markets the program had been well publicized through advertising. Exhibit 12–14 shows a newspaper ad promoting the service.

The Econo-Check Program was tested for three-week periods during November and December 1973 in both markets. In-depth consumer research was conducted immediately after performing the service and one month later to explore consumer attitudes concerning the value of the program and their perception of the company providing the service. The results were extremely positive (see Table 12–3).

Table 12-3 Consumer Attitudes Towards Econo-Check Program

	Corpus Christi (n = 496)	Baton Rouge (n = 288)
1. *How would you rate this Econo-Check service?*		
Immediately after taking test		
Excellent	49%	44%
Very good	34	24
Good	13	23
Fair, Poor	2	3
Don't Know	2	6
Telephone survey—one month later		
Excellent	32	
Very good	36	
Good	26	
Fair, Poor	4	
Don't Know	2	
2. *How do you feel about Econo-Check testing this car again or another car you might own? How likely are you to do this?*		
Extremely likely	55	48
Very likely	25	24
Probably likely	13	19
Unlikely	6	9
Don't Know	1	
3. *In general how do you feel about a major oil company furnishing this Econo-Check service?*		
Extremely good idea	56	46
Very good idea	33	24
Good idea	9	28
Fair, poor, bad idea	2	2

On the basis of the test market results, the members of Gulf Oil's marketing department responsible for evaluating the program recommended that Gulf:

1. Equip and staff six Econo-Check vans.
2. Conduct Econo-Check in twenty-two markets with a minimum of two vans per market for a minimum of two weeks each.
3. Offer the service to the consumer on a free basis.
4. Support the program with television and newspaper advertising.

Exhibit 12-14   Gulf Oil Newspaper Ad

LOOK FOR GULF'S FREE ECONO-CHECK

The test that tells you in minutes if you're getting the most out of your gasoline.

These days you want to be sure you're getting the most out of the gasoline you buy. And Gulf wants to help you do it.

So, we're bringing the Gulf ECONO-CHECK™ to you, right in your own neighborhood.

Gulf's ECONO-CHECK is a scientifically-designed and specially-equipped mobile van that will test your engine's performance—and tell you whether or not you're wasting gasoline through inefficient operation.

This is a test only. Not a tune-up. But it's FREE, and it's easy to take. Simply drive up to Gulf's ECONO-CHECK van when you see it in a shopping center parking lot. In just minutes, you get the test results for your car. Without raising the hood, or getting out from behind the wheel.

So take advantage of Gulf's FREE ECONO-CHECK in your neighborhood, soon. If your car has an engine problem, your test result will suggest possible causes.

For the little time it takes, you could save a lot of money in the months ahead!

Gulf
GULF OIL CORPORATION

ECONO-CHECK SCHEDULE
November 11th through November 22nd

Highland Mall • Westgate Mall

SEE IF YOUR ENGINE IS WASTING GASOLINE

10:00 AM to 6:00 PM, except on Sundays and during rainy weather.

5. Conduct consumer surveys on the Econo-Check and evaluate the program after four months.

Estimated cost to implement recommendations 1 through 4 were as follows:

Six Econo-Check vans	$ 60,000
Staff expense	99,200
Literature, maintenance, and miscellaneous	7,800
Advertising	275,000
	$442,000

OVERALL PROMOTIONAL OBJECTIVES: GULF OIL COMPANY—U.S.

As a result of a series of task force meetings of the top management and planners of both Gulf Oil Corporation and Gulf Oil and their advertising agency, a general statement of objectives and strategy for future promotional efforts had been developed. The objective of any proposed promotional effort would be to provide a positive consumer communication by offering an easily recognized consumer benefit which the public would perceive as having true value and would be competitively unique. Ideally the program would protect brand loyalty of current customers and strengthen Gulf's service image with potential customers without adding to service station problems where shortages existed. Further, the promotion should build a service capacity reputation and a favorable consumer attitude that would assist Gulf Oil and its dealers in capturing a larger share of the automotive service market on a continuing basis.

Finally, the promotional program should contribute to Gulf's credibility with the public and help foster renewed faith in the company as a responsible corporate citizen.

The major objectives and strategy guidelines were summarized as follows:

1. Offset customer's negative perception of Gulf and other oil companies.
2. Provide a positive consumer communication during the gasoline shortage.
3. Strengthen Gulf's service image without adding to service station problems where shortage situations exist.
4. Increase recognition of Gulf as a service oriented company.

Although Young & Rubicam realized that promotion of a gasoline product was somewhat incompatible with Gulf's low profile approach, the agency was in favor of promoting the introduction of Gulfcrest. In addition, at these meetings the agency reiterated their opposition to refutational advertising as an answer to Gulf's problems.

QUESTIONS FOR DISCUSSION

1. Develop recommendations for the firm's promotional activities with respect to the agency's position and the desirability for a refutational campaign.
2. Suggest alternative strategies for the firm's promotional activities during the coming fiscal year.

ENDNOTE

1. This case was prepared by John H. Murphy and Catherine C. Bently, The University of Texas at Austin.

Case 12-7—Glade Glass Ovenware Company

USE OF TEST FOR APPRAISING OVENWARE ADVERTISING

The sales manager of the Glade Glass Ovenware Company in a recent year approached Andrew Dorchester, a sales and advertising consultant, for advice on setting up a test to determine what copy approach to adopt for the magazine advertising of its glass ovenware.

The company sold a complete line of glass ovenware for the home, including casseroles, pie dishes, baking pans, frying pans, custard cups, and so on. The utensils were sold through hardware stores, department stores, and houseware specialty stores throughout the nation. There were two retail sales peaks—one during the latter part of November and in December before Christmas and the other during April and May.

For some years the company had carried on a consistent program of indirect-action advertising in national magazines, primarily women's service magazines. This was considered by the company as reminder-type advertising, the general of. which was to keep the Glade Glass name before the country.

From time to time, the company's advertising agency had carried out surveys among consumers in order to determine consumer usage and opinions regarding kitchen wares. At the time the sales manager approached Mr. Dorchester, the agency had developed three different copy approaches, based on different copy ideas advanced within the agency and the Glade Company. One copy theme stressed the cleanliness of the ware; another featured the convenience and attractiveness of serving food directly from the utensils in which the food was baked; and the third approach centered on the claim of better baking results from Glade ovenware.

Members of the advertising staff and the agency representatives had suggested that several types of tests might be employed to determine which of these various copy themes to adopt. One executive favored a consumer opinion test. Another favored split-run inquiry tests. The sales manager, however, expressed a strong preference for a sales test as the only type that would really show what advertising was doing.

QUESTIONS FOR DISCUSSION

1. What advice would you give the people at Glade Glass Ovenware Company if you were in Mr. Dorchester's position?
2. What role should copytesting play in the development of creative strategies in a company such as Glade?
3. Are any of the tests suggested by members of the advertising staff and agency representatives up to the task at hand?
4. What role might recall copy research play in the development of creative strategy at Glade?

Case 12-8—Metro Transit District

BACKGROUND

The Champaign-Urbana Mass Transit District (MTD) was founded in August, 1971. Before 1971, bus service had been provided by National City Lines. NCL had been losing money for a number of years and wanted to give up the Champaign-Urbana market. A group of concerned citizens banded together and as a result of a referendum vote, MTD was born. The objective of MTD is to provide safe and inexpensive public transportation. Public transportation is now viewed as a public service rather than a profit-making venture. For every dollar MTD receives in fares, it spends three dollars to provide service. MTD receives funding from four sources: fares, local property tax, state subsidy, and federal subsidy through the DOT.

In the beginning, MTD was plagued by inefficiency and high turnover among management. The current management team has been in office for only two years. The amount of recovered costs has risen from 31% in 1971 to 34% in 1975. In the last two years, there has been a 100% increase in ridership. MTD expects to carry 1.45 million riders in 1976. Business is very good during the winter, but slows down a great deal during the summer. December through March are the busiest months. MTD currently has 25 buses, 17 of which are in regular use during a given day. The other eight are used for special promotions, are being overhauled or are on standby in case of a breakdown. The busiest part of the day is early morning and late afternoon.

PRODUCT

List of Schedules in Order of Number of Riders

Green	Orchard Downs—This is the route used
Blue	most frequently by students
Lavender	Yellow
Orange	Grey—(These last two have the most
Red	potential)

CUSTOMER PROFILE

There are a lot of people that usually ride the bus regularly (e.g., senior citizens, poor people, etc.). Therefore, advertising and marketing efforts are aimed at the "choice rider." By definition, a "choice rider" is a person who is currently using an alternative form of transportation. Approximately 60% of MTD riders are students. The other forty percent is made up of a variety of people. In most other cities, school age children and people from lower socioeconomic groups make up the largest group of riders. A significant number of riders are business people. The groups with the largest potential in terms of increased ridership are the children and poor people.

Profile of MTD Riders

				Under 18	8.8%
				18-34	75%
SEX	Male	48.6%	AGE	35-49	9%
	Female	51.4%		50-64	4.9%
				over 65	2.4%

COMPETITION

MTD does not try to compete with the car in the family. A car is more convenient and is available seven days a week; MTD only runs on Monday through Saturday. However, MTD does try to compete with the second car in the family. In a recent survey of MTD riders, the following question was asked:

If you could not ride the bus, what form of transportation would you use?

Car	31.3%
Walk	20.3%
Get a Ride	19.5%
Bicycle	10.8%
Wouldn't Go	6.5%
Taxi	6.0%
Carpool	2.5%
Other	2.8%

78.9% had a valid driver's license.

MTD feels that they pick up a significant number of walkers and bicyclers during the winter. There was a survey of people who do not ride MTD, but due to methodology problems, the results were inconclusive.

ADVERTISING AND SALES PROMOTION ACTIVITIES

When MTD was formed, an advertising agency was used for about a year and creative work is now prepared by MTD. The current creative thrust is toward helping people remember the MTD telephone number. MTD has five lines for incoming calls and there are times when all five lines are busy. MTD had Illinois Bell conduct a survey of the lines to make sure that no calls were being missed. MTD wants to encourage people to ride the bus as much as possible. Therefore, MTD makes information as accessible as possible. Schedules are distributed in many locations across town. Schedules are even available in car dealership service departments for people who are leaving their automobiles. Since MTD is supported in part by a referendum, it is important for them to keep a good image in the twin cities.

Advertising is concentrated during times when ridership is down and also during the following promotional periods:

Christmas Promotion—trying to encourage people to do their Christmas shopping on MTD. Also trying to promote a light, good-hearted image. Give away free rides and buttons. May try to coordinate it with local merchants this year. Also had free buses running on certain routes during various parts of the day. The routes having the free buses varied during the day and ran on the days when ridership is slowest (Thursday, Friday, Saturday).

Summer Promotion—to try and stimulate ridership among school kids and other people in the community. This is run when the students have left for the summer and ridership is down.

Welcome Back Promotion—September—to welcome back university students and faculty with MTD.

In addition, MTD offers school children an opportunity to learn about the bus system by having field trips for any fifth or sixth grade class that asks for one. It is this age of children that are beginning to go around town on their own. The trip consists of picking up the children at school in an MTD bus, taking them to MTD headquarters in Urbana, conducting a tour, and returning them to school. MTD estimates that over 60% of fifth and sixth graders took a field trip last year. This program is not advertised because the teachers now know about MTD and all they have to do is call MTD and ask for a trip.

Complaints are handled quickly and every complaint receives a written reply within eight days.

MTD's media mix consists primarily of radio, because of its high reach and low cost. Newspapers are used for two week periods only during promotions because they are too expensive. The following radio stations are used:

WDWS— opinion leader station and senior citizens. MTD is concerned about reaching people who may not ride but who are influential in the community.
WLRW
WCCR

The "Back Seat Driver's Club" is a promotional item for senior citizens.

PROBLEMS

— During August, 1973, MTD went to a "GRID" system. Under this system, the buses ran either North-South or East-West. This made it virtually impossible for a person to get across town without making at least one transfer. This caused a lot of negative public reaction and ridership dropped. In December, 1973, MTD went back to a loop system which it uses now.

— MTD is always working on ways to become more dependable.

— MTD has a large education job to do in the poor sector of town where illiteracy exists and people cannot read the schedules. MTD has talked to ministers and other opinion leaders in these areas to encourage people to try MTD.

BUDGET

$25,000 for one year. This is strictly for advertising. Schedules cost another $15,000.

QUESTIONS FOR DISCUSSION

1. Develop two alternative creative strategies for MTD.
2. Which do you believe is better for MTD to use? Why?

ADVERTISING MEDIA STRATEGY

- Management and Media
- The Marketing Mix and Media Strategy
- Elements of Media Planning
- Overview of Media Models

Decision Making Organization of This Text

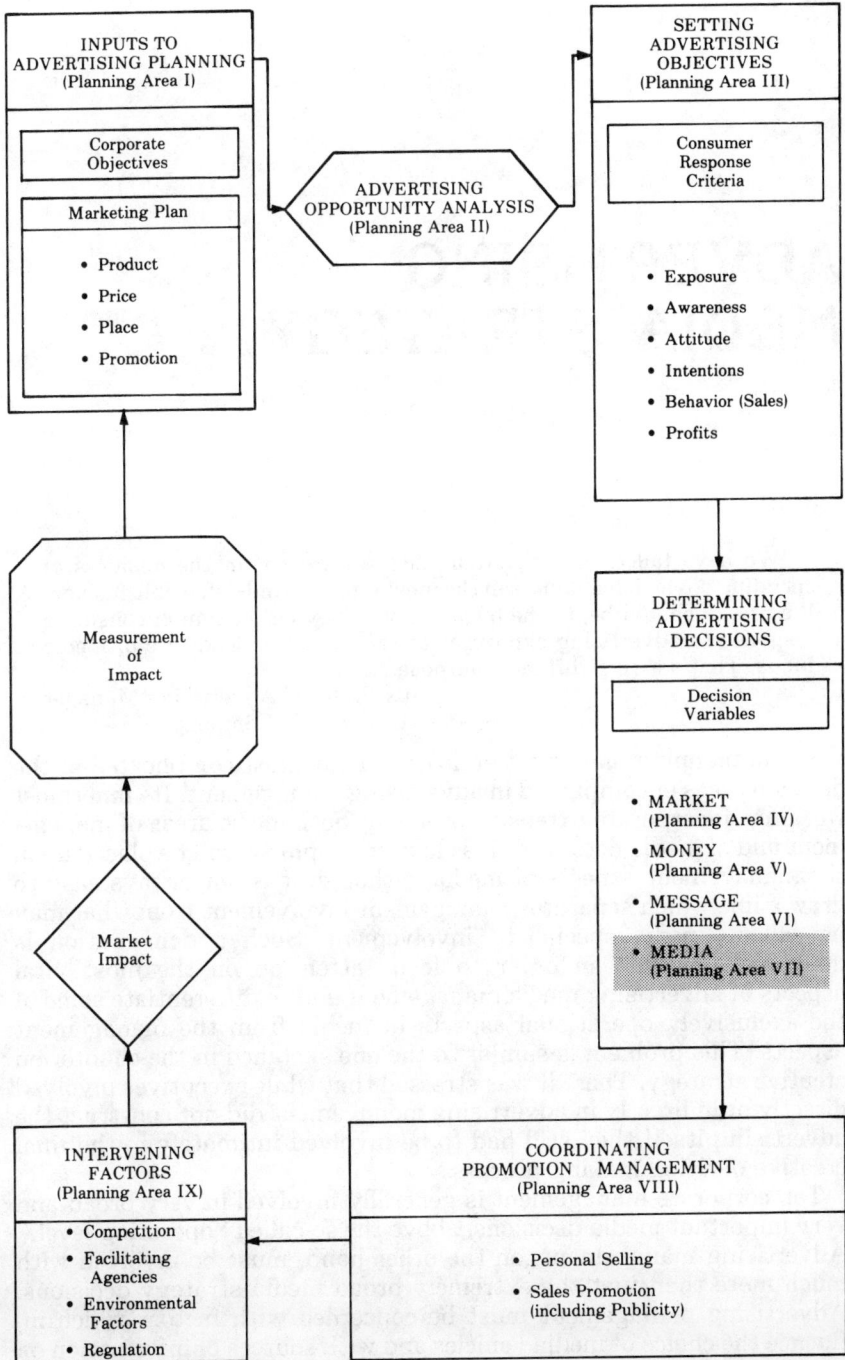

13

ADVERTISING MEDIA STRATEGY

"We have failed to understand that we are *not* in the business of spending advertising dollars in the most efficient and defensible fashion. We are, or should be, in the business of achieving maximum consumer response to advertising exposures at the lowest expenditure of media funds. That's a very different purpose."

—Gus Priemer, Advertising Manager
S.C. Johnson Company

Media planning and selection is one of the most complicated of the decision areas encompassed in advertising management. Its innermost workings incorporate extensive problems both in the areas of management and of media detail. In this chapter, emphasis will be placed upon the management aspects of media, although it is not always easy to draw a line which separates management involvement from what may be called "media specialist" involvement. Such a demarcation is desirable, however, in order to focus attention on the most vital aspects of advertising media management and to differentiate some of the exclusively operational aspects of media from the management aspects. This problem is similar to the one sketched in the chapter on creative strategy. There it was stressed that while executives involved directly or indirectly in advertising management did not construct the advertising itself they still had to be involved intimately in the final creative decision making process.

Top corporate management is generally involved in very broad and very important media decisions, above the so-called "operating level." Advertising management, on the other hand, must be involved with much more than just the extremely broad media strategy decisions. Advertising management must be concerned with factors which influence the choice of media vehicles and with sources of information on media qualities and characteristics. This is necessary if management is to do an adequate evaluation of media recommendations by the advertising agency. At the same time, advertising management is not generally concerned with the daily operating details of advertising media.

MANAGEMENT AND MEDIA

In the broadest terms, the media decision area can be divided into two parts: (1) media planning and strategy; and (2) administration of the media plan. For example, a decision on seasonal media investments regarding whether or not a hiatus should be taken during the summer is the kind of decision which must necessarily involve people at a relatively important level both in the advertiser's company and at the advertising agency.

On the other hand, whether Erie, Pennsylvania, is scheduled in a spot television buy for the advertiser is not normally a decision of sufficient import to involve any but lower echelon people, such as a time buyer at the advertising agency.

At times, the issues are not quite that clear. Clearances of a major market on a prime-time program buy can critically concern management people, particularly when there are sales management overtones to the decision. If such cities as Baltimore, Maryland, or Richmond, Virginia, are not getting a given television show or are getting it at a different or less effective hour, this can have an indirect effect upon advertising policy because of a disproportionately negative effect on the attitudes and morale of the sales people responsible for those sizable markets, as well as a direct effect upon consumer advertising coverage and impact.

It is helpful, nevertheless, to inspect the functioning of media organization to understand the degree of involvement that the non-media expert would have in any given phase. The expert on media, as the expert in any field, must be concerned with the entire structure of advertising media. The objective, however, is to position the executive in advertising management in terms of involvement in important media decisions. Once the media areas of greatest concern to the advertising management executive are established, those selected areas can be discussed in some detail.

THE MARKETING MIX AND MEDIA STRATEGY

The influences which serve as the backdrop for media decision making can be categorized as follows:

(1) Characteristics of the Market Segments
(2) Characteristics of the Product and Price
(3) Characteristics of the Distribution System
(4) Characteristics of the Promotion System
(5) Uncontrollable Variables.

These factors are the limits within which both the media planner and the media operator (buyer) must work. In one sense, they represent a removal of "degrees of freedom" from the media planner. They are the benchmarks that general advertising management must supply to the media people, and they must be kept in mind constantly as the media plan is developed. They represent additional evidence of the importance of understanding the continuing relationship between all advertising decisions and the total marketing structure.

In order to bring this concept of interaction into focus more effectively, a brief example of how each of these basic elements can critically affect media planning and operations is needed.

CHARACTERISTICS OF THE MARKET SEGMENTS

A product geared to sell to teenagers creates an automatic direction on the part of the media planner and buyer, in orienting the space and time purchases toward young people. A market such as this which has a sharply diverse geographic development obviously provides another directional arrow for the media planner. A product that is premium priced and designed to sell to the upper income groups, or a product selling exclusively to men, or a product with other basic market characteristics, all provide criteria for media selection.

While information describing the nature and profile of the market is essential for media decision making, the mature planner must understand that in actual practice matching product markets and media audiences closely, using mass media, is frequently not easy.

All the basic mass media tend to reach a diversified group of consumers. While it is true that certain media or certain vehicles tend to place disproportionate weight against a given market segment, it is not possible in many instances to select media or media vehicles which match markets that closely. For example, in the area of spot television, certain properties will tend to show a greater concentration against given audience areas. *The Lawrence Welk Show*, a syndicated television program, has a much higher rating among older women in small families than among younger women who tend to have burgeoning larger families. Such a property might well be a better selection than another program which does not put maximum weight against the older market. However, the purchase of *The Lawrence Welk Show* only reflects a degree of relative influence; a large number of messages will still be geared, by the very nature of the broad mass aspects of the medium itself, against market segments which do not necessarily reflect the most exploitable sales potential.

McCall's magazine tends to reach a proportionately younger audience than does *Good Housekeeping*, one of its many competitors in the women's service book field. If a product's market characteristics tend to skew just a bit towards younger women, then, other things being equal, the media planner and buyer would tend to use *McCall's* in the print list. However, a magazine with a basic circulation of

8,000,000 and a total readership of almost twice that figure, naturally reaches a broad mass market covering *all* age groups.

Carrying this logic a step further, an advertiser, in the magazine print medium, could purchase space in *Seventeen,* and would be assured that the prospective advertising exposure would number almost exclusively teenage girl readership. However, the cost *efficiency* of reaching this market segment, almost exclusively, tends to be somewhat higher as the medium becomes highly selective. Sometimes (and rather paradoxically) an advertiser may spend money more efficiently, when wishing to reach a relatively narrow market segment, by simply using mass vehicles even though, in a marketing sense, the advertiser may be paying for waste circulation and exposure simply because of the greater inherent efficiency of the broadest mass media.

The advertiser must have available these data on market characteristics for his product or, at the very least, a point of view with respect to whom the product is to be sold. But the practical aspects of mass-media operations are such that the narrowing of media decision making as a consequence of analysis of such information is frequently not that sharp primarily due to the pervasive nature and large audience potential of most mass media. There is generally a large area of media choice left, particularly with products that have broad mass markets, and which demonstrate only marginal movements toward certain market characteristics rather than reflecting highly segmented markets. Ideally, the isolation of prospects, which is the objective of market segmentation and media interpretation of market data, is a continuing objective of the mature media planner. Insofar as the planner can match the media selection to the market segment selected as the target market, the planner generally increases dollar efficiency. The planner must strive for such congruence wherever feasible. Market and media matching will be discussed in further detail later in this chapter.

CHARACTERISTICS OF THE PRODUCT AND PRICE

The second marketing factor which can have a very important influence on media decisions comes from the inherent product characteristics. There are certain kinds of products which cannot tastefully employ certain types of media. Occasionally legal restrictions inhibit the use of certain kinds of broad exposure media by advertisers of given items. Liquor, for instance, cannot now be advertised in the broadcast media.

Direct product influences of the type above, however, have declined in force as new ways of using the different media have developed. Products for which there were severe media restrictions have bypassed these roadblocks through new advertising approaches. In television, for example, feminine hygiene products are now able to be advertised in certain time slots. The tone of the advertising was developed in such a way so as to overcome any media or audience negative reactions. In newspapers, the increasing use of photo-offset printing processes has made the reproduction of ROP color much more appealing than in the past. This increased capability of newspapers has opened up the medium to advertisers who require excellent color reproduction. The DelMonte Campaign which relied upon the excellent reproduction of the color of various vegetables could not have run in the newspaper medium several years ago.

The more creative use of sound and musical values for communicating ideas opened up radio broadcasting as a possibility to advertisers who have not previously been interested in that medium. The ability to use the true-to-life vignette in radio broadcasting has been an important contributory force. Thus, while physical product and product personality influences have to be considered, they are not overpowering as far as "leading" the media decision is concerned.

Pricing policy influences the media plan in basically three ways.[1] First, the pricing policy affects profit margins, which in turn affect the amount of money which is available to be spent on the purchase of media time and space. As has been observed in Chapter 7 on budgeting, advertising expenditures must come out of gross margin which is itself a function of sales revenues (price times quantity sold).

Second, margins within the distribution channel may affect the amount of dealer support that the advertiser can expect from wholesalers and retailers. When the margin to wholesalers and retailers is small, these organizations have less incentive to provide aggressive promotional support to the manufacturer. If pricing policy results in large margins for channel members, this may result in a lesser need for media expenditures on the part of the manufacturer, since promotional activity on the part of channel members can be expected to supplement the manufacturer's advertising activity.

The third influence of pricing policy on media planning is the result of the interaction between pricing policies and product characteristics. Since price is sometimes perceived as an indicator of product quality, many high-quality products also carry high price tags. The prestigious image that must be carried by the advertising for such a product cannot be conveyed through the creative execution alone. The media schedule used will also serve to give an indication of the quality level of the advertising and the product. An advertisement in the *New Yorker* magazine will provide a different quality image than will the same advertisement in *True Story*.

CHARACTERISTICS OF THE DISTRIBUTION SYSTEM

Influences of the distribution system on media planning are of two types.

First, a simple physical influence reflecting the fact that a product may only be distributed in certain areas is clear. Restricted distribution may obviously inhibit the purchase of certain types of media. For example, an advertiser distributing within a local market, or within a narrow regional area cannot economically employ national magazines unless a regional edition is utilized. On a national basis, the advertiser would be investing in too much waste circulation, and even on a regional basis the advertiser would need to determine to what degree the magazine's regional edition conformed to the advertiser's distribution makeup.

Sometimes, even within a given local market, automatic media restrictions are imposed. For example, certain broadcast stations (either radio or television) may deliver advertising messages in important quantities to the outskirts of the market's area where the advertiser in question may not have effective distribution. Therefore, the actual cost efficiency of a local broadcast investment may be much greater than the theoretical cost efficiency computed on the basis of the total coverage achieved by the station, which presumes brand distribution throughout the station's coverage area.

Sometimes, products have distribution on a broad national basis, but this national distribution is restricted primarily to large cities. Clearly, the media plan should be such as to reach primarily urban rather than rural areas throughout the entire country.

One of the age-old questions that always has to be considered by the decision maker is whether distribution is sufficient to be supported by advertising. For example, in the case of a given drug item, when does a national advertising investment seem feasible? Would the investment be feasible if the distribution system covers 40 percent of all commodity sales in drug outlets? Would the investment be feasible if this distribution coverage was only 20 percent? This is frequently a difficult question to answer, particularly in the non-packaged goods fields where it is believed that one of the functions of advertising is to help gain the very distribution against which the advertising dollars are supposed to operate.

The second area of distribution influence is psychological more than physical. Sometimes the choice of consumer media may be importantly affected by the desire to influence specific units in the distribution chain. In these kinds of situations, retailers are often an extremely vital factor in the marketing structure and their influence on the consumer may strongly overshadow the advertising. This has historically tended to be the case in the soft goods business and is in sharp contrast to the marketing concept orientation of the packaged goods manufacturers. Even a regional advertiser may spend what appears to be inefficient money on national magazine advertising only to provide the sales tool and prestige overtone required to impress given retailer outlets. Beyond the scope of catering to retailer influence on the consumer, there is frequently a need or a desire to use media values solely to create a rallying point for distributor units. The Hallmark Card Company presents television spectaculars or specials so that some excitement will be felt by the retail outlets which carry their products; this excitement may contribute to the continued association of the retailer with Hallmark rather than with other card companies. Thus, distribution geography as well as distribution psychology must be considered a critical influence on media decision making.

CHARACTERISTICS OF THE PROMOTION SYSTEM

Advertising, sales promotion, and personal selling combine in varying degrees to form a promotion mix for every product. Each of these elements of overall promotion strategy has an impact on media planning.

The Importance of Sales Promotion Strategy. Sales promotion decisions also tie in with media planning. The activities included in sales promotion may affect media plans because of the need to communicate to consumers detailed information about some particular promotion. If it is necessary to present, in some detail, a permanent record of contest rules, lists of prizes, and methods of entering the promotion, some type of print medium would have obvious advantages.

Other special promotions may be inspired by a medium, such as a particular broadcast program, a particular magazine, or newspaper. In this type of promotion, the medium may try to interest the advertiser by pledging editorial support and activity at the dealer level. This additional support may be the decisive factor in the final media choice. The so-called "shelter books," such as *Better Homes & Gardens,* frequently have "do-it-yourself" and "home improvement" issues, and advertisers whose products are closely related to the subject may very profitably participate in the promotion.

The Nature of Advertising Creative Strategy. Some advertising copy is better adapted to some advertising media than to others. Food advertising, in color, is uniquely suited to magazines since the quality of reproduction is generally superior to newspapers, even when the newspapers use photo-offset printing processes. Television is the medium ideally suited for products which lend themselves well to demonstration and to a personal sales touch. Newspapers' timeliness and newsworthiness have made the medium highly successful for new-product introductions. Advertising effectiveness is increased if the copy requirements are included as an integral part of the media selection.

UNCONTROLLABLE VARIABLES

It is clear that many factors which the media planner must keep in mind when developing the overall media strategy are beyond direct control. Yet these factors will definitely have an impact on the final effectiveness of the media plan and must, therefore, be considered explicitly by the planner. Uncontrollable variables are of two types: (1) internal uncontrollable factors; and (2) external uncontrollable factors.[2]

Internal Uncontrollable Variables. It is clear that most of the marketing mix factors discussed above are usually beyond the control of the media planner. Beyond the marketing mix variables and the advertising appropriation itself, there are other factors internal to the company which have an impact on the media planning process. These factors can be subsumed under company policy and corporate image.

For example, a company which prides itself on a "wholesome" family image would probably not choose to advertise in a magazine which contained sexually explicit material even though this magazine's audience profile conformed very closely with the target market profile for its product. The media planner may be required to sacrifice some efficiency in the media schedule because of such uncontrollable factors.

External Uncontrollable Variables. These factors can be classified into five primary categories: (1) competitive efforts; (2) economic conditions; (3) legal and cultural environment; (4) weather and other natural phenomena; and (5) media environment.

Competition becomes a factor primarily in terms of the volume of advertising which competitors conduct in the various media types and vehicles. If several competitors advertise in a single issue of a publication, it may not be in the best interest of the advertiser to also advertise in that publication if the advertiser's product is relatively undifferentiated from the competitors' products. This is so since the impact of the message for a "me-too" brand will be diluted in the context of several similar messages. In addition, in the broadcast area, the clutter introduced by many competing advertisers may dilute the impact of the advertiser's message. If a competitor advertises frequently on television in a given "daypart," this cluttered environment may not give a chance for one or two spots of the advertiser to gain attention of the viewer or may lead to confusion of the advertiser's message with that of the competitor's message.

General economic conditions have an impact on media planning and decision making. Media prices are greatly affected by inflation as are other commodities. Some media may become so expensive relative to others that they are ruled out as possibilities for certain advertisers. During a recession, it may be the case that paper production declines to a point where newspapers must pay highly increased prices for newsprint relative to supply; this will be reflected in higher costs to the advertiser. Relative to newspapers, the broadcast media, which are not subject to such expenses, may become more of a bargain.

In addition, the economic conditions in a certain geographic market area may be considerably poorer than in the general economy as a whole. It may not be profitable to purchase advertising time or space in these spot markets since the per capita income is too low to support purchase volume sufficient to cover the advertising expenditures for that area and still provide reasonable profits for the company.

Such statutes as the Public Health Cigarette Smoking Act of 1971 have had a great effect on the nature of media planning. Media planners cannot consider the broadcast media for cigarette advertising because this law bans the advertising of cigarettes from radio and television. Illegal products, such as fireworks, cannot be advertised. Voluntary restraints imposed by the media themselves are even more important than the legal codes; the Television Code of the National Association of Broadcasters prohibits member stations from accepting liquor advertising. The cultural standards are also reflected in the individual policies of vehicles. *Good Housekeeping* magazine will not sell space to advertisers whose products are of questionable utility to consumers.

Weather and other natural events have an impact on the media planning process also. For example, the seasonal timing of the buys for a media schedule may be quite different for snowmobiles than for golf clubs. Many such products have sales curves which are higher in one season than in another; the advertiser will usually make a decision as to when it is desirable to have the heavy push in advertising based upon this fact.

The media environment can have a definite impact on the media planner's work. For example, a bank would not wish to have its print advertisement run in the newspaper next to an editorial piece about a bank robbery. In general, the media planner will prefer those media vehicles which provide a favorable "editorial" context for the product to be advertised. This factor, however, is not under the control of the media planner but rather under the control of those who own or run the medium.

ELEMENTS OF MEDIA PLANNING

Media thinking begins, as must all good advertising thinking, with marketing thinking. Essentially a media strategy, as a copy strategy, should emanate from the basic marketing outlook taken by a brand. There are three basic elements in every properly formulated strategy. First, the available data are collected and analyzed. Second, these data are combined with the existing marketing situation to determine the alternatives from which media decisions may be made. And third, executive judgment is then applied to these alternatives and from them is selected the most desirable alternative media strategy and the most desirable media alternatives.

Three simple examples will clarify this outlook on the media planning process. Suppose a decision is made not to use network television programming because the expense involved in carrying program costs may not be considered worthwhile; such expense would mean sacrificing the buying of additional advertising weight that could be gained if a spot television operation was underwritten. In other words, the strategic decision here is that the qualitative association of the brand with a program structure was not sufficient to overcome the quantitative values (in terms of advertising weight) which could be achieved by investing the same dollar amount in spot television buys. This is a media strategy decision.

A decision made to use national magazine print advertising because it permits the use of color rather than daytime radio is stating that the creative value and resultant advertising impact in the use of color more than compensates for the broadcast values in daytime radio (including such a positive factor as a very high cost efficiency). This is not to say, of course, that there are not manifold considerations involved in such a basic media decision, but it is to say that in the specific sense stated it represents a *strategic* decision.

Sometimes, a media strategy outlook stems completely, and without even the possibility of modification, from the marketing strategy. For example, if the marketing strategy states that the product positioning posture of the brand is to sell the brand to younger women in the middle and lower income groups, then this automatically becomes part of the media strategy statement. In other words, one aspect of the media strategy must be to reach women in such a fashion that the particular groups on which the marketing strategy focuses are featured in the final media selection.

In this particular instance, an isolated element within the total structure of media strategy is being examined in order to make the principle of media strategy more lucid. It must again be emphasized that the interactive aspects of media strategy nearly always involve a management selection of alternatives which are not always pointed in the same direction. In the example just noted above, in order to reach women in certain income groups, some other sacrifice may be necessary in carrying out the media plan. It is a rationalization and cohesion of these diversified factors that is the basic function of top media planning and advertising management.

Figure 13-1 illustrates the various stages of the media planning process which will be discussed briefly below. Though there are many ways in which the media planning process might be conceived, the conceptualization in Figure 13-1 shows a process consisting of seven basic stages:

Stage I: Marketing Mix Backdrop
Stage II: Selection of Target Markets
Stage III: Selection of Reach Criteria
Stage IV: Determination of Media Objectives
Stage V: Explication of Constraints
Stage VI: Determination of Market/Media Match
Stage VII: Selection of Vehicles.

The issue of the marketing mix backdrop has been previously addressed above while selection of target markets is covered in detail in Chapter 5 on market segmentation. Only Stages III through VII will, therefore, be discussed below.

STAGE III: SELECTION OF REACH CRITERIA

The Media Audience Concepts Committee of the Advertising Research Foundation developed in the late 1950's the basic criteria upon which reach of a media schedule or an individual vehicle might be viewed.[3] They basically arrived at the definition of six levels upon which reach *might* be viewed. It should be noted that the term "might" is used here since a report of this committee at the 1978 Advertising Research Foundation annual conference by Seymour Banks pointed out that little progress had been made toward implementation of the overall model reported by Paul E.J. Gerhold in

Figure 13-1   The Media Planning Process

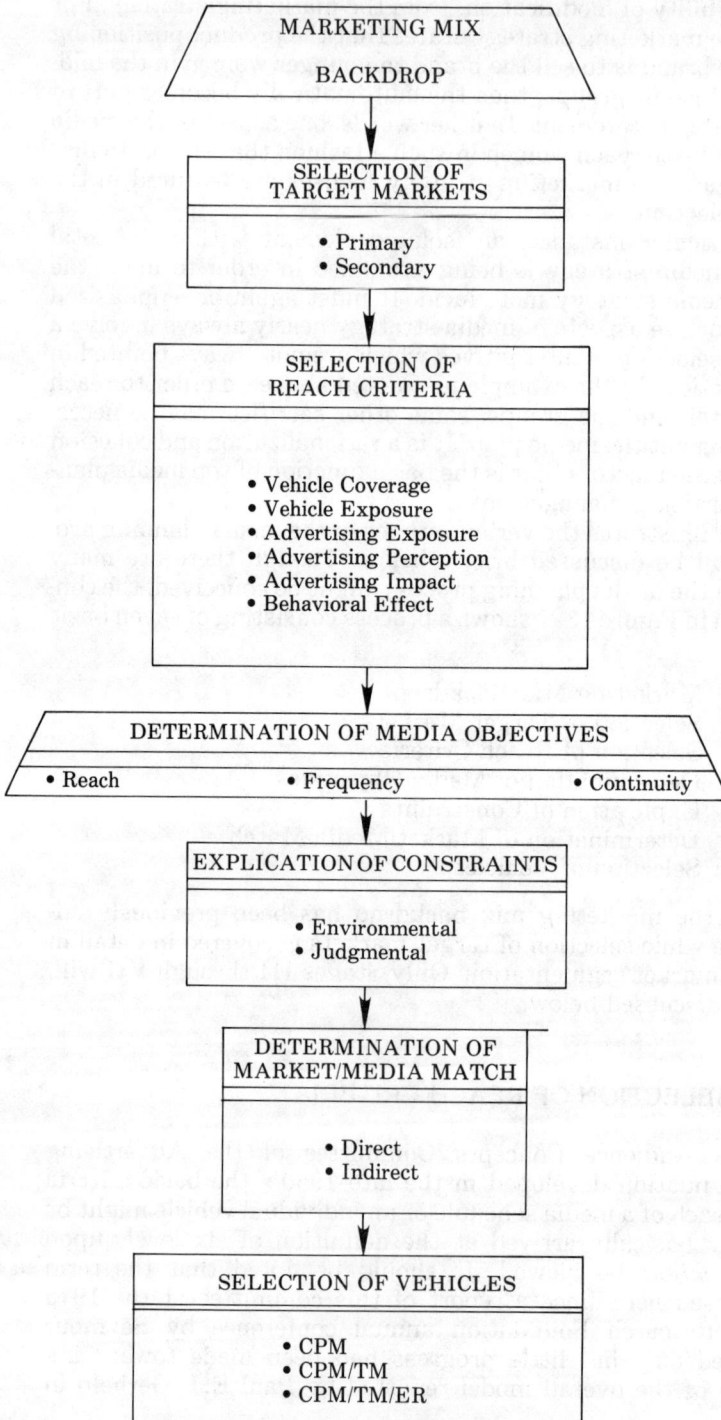

```
                    ┌─────────────────────────┐
                   /    MARKETING MIX          \
                  /     BACKDROP                \
                 /_____  \
                              │
                              ▼
                   ┌─────────────────────┐
                   │   SELECTION OF      │
                   │   TARGET MARKETS    │
                   ├─────────────────────┤
                   │   • Primary         │
                   │   • Secondary       │
                   └─────────────────────┘
                              │
                              ▼
              ┌───────────────────────────────┐
              │     SELECTION OF              │
              │     REACH CRITERIA            │
              ├───────────────────────────────┤
              │                               │
              │   • Vehicle Coverage          │
              │   • Vehicle Exposure          │
              │   • Advertising Exposure      │
              │   • Advertising Perception    │
              │   • Advertising Impact        │
              │   • Behavioral Effect         │
              │                               │
              └───────────────────────────────┘
                              │
                              ▼
        ┌─────────────────────────────────────────────┐
       /        DETERMINATION OF MEDIA OBJECTIVES       \
      /────────────────────────────────────────────────  \
     / • Reach          • Frequency          • Continuity  \
    /_____\
                              │
                              ▼
                   ┌─────────────────────┐
                   │ EXPLICATION OF CONSTRAINTS │
                   ├─────────────────────┤
                   │   • Environmental   │
                   │   • Judgmental      │
                   └─────────────────────┘
                              │
                              ▼
                   ┌─────────────────────┐
                   │  DETERMINATION OF   │
                   │ MARKET/MEDIA MATCH  │
                   ├─────────────────────┤
                   │                     │
                   │   • Direct          │
                   │   • Indirect        │
                   └─────────────────────┘
                              │
                              ▼
                   ┌─────────────────────┐
                   │ SELECTION OF VEHICLES │
                   ├─────────────────────┤
                   │                     │
                   │   • CPM             │
                   │   • CPM/TM          │
                   │   • CPM/TM/ER       │
                   └─────────────────────┘
```

1959.[4] Nonetheless, the levels of criteria suggested for the viewing of *effective reach* (levels 4, 5, and 6 below) have utility for media planning since they involve the concept of differential effects of certain combinations of vehicles and messages. The concept of effective reach will be taken up in some detail in Chapter 14. At this point, the distinction should be made clearly between the import of the six levels of criteria upon which reach might be viewed:

Level 1: Vehicle Coverage
Level 2: Vehicle Exposure
Level 3: Advertising Exposure (Pre-Cognitive Criteria)
Level 4: Advertising Perception (Cognitive Criteria)
Level 5: Advertising Impact (Affective Criteria)
Level 6: Behavioral Effect (Conative Criteria).

It should be noted that for these levels to be useful in media planning and selection, each must be measured in terms of the number *or* proportion of the target market of people involved. For example, vehicle coverage means "how many people" are covered by the vehicle or schedule in question. Advertising impact would need to mean, in general, "how many people" had favorable attitudes toward the brand or advertising with respect to a given message in a given vehicle or schedule. Clearly, it would be expected that the *number* of target market people would decline for a given vehicle as the reach is figured from the lowest to the highest level number above; that is, Level 1 would have the largest number of people for a given vehicle while Level 6 would probably have the smallest number of people for that same vehicle. The reach criteria, therefore, become more stringent as the level number increases. Each of these levels will be generally addressed below. It should be noted that each level was discussed in some detail in Chapter 4 on advertising objectives, though not with respect to the media question specifically. The reader may find it helpful to refer back to Chapter 4 at this point since the following discussion of each of the above criteria levels will necessarily remain brief. Declining reach levels are shown in Figure 13-2.

Level 1: Vehicle Coverage. In the broadcasting business the unit of measurement, with respect to physical distribution or coverage, is the number of radio and/or television sets owned. Obviously, ownership is essential to eventual exposure in broadcast media; in addition, the geographical area to which the station signal can be received must be considered. In actual practice, ownership can be viewed in two ways. It can be viewed in terms of homes having one or more sets, regardless of the number of sets owned, and it can be viewed in terms of the total number of sets owned. Here, multiple ownership is taken into consideration. As multiple ownership has increased in the broadcast media, the number of sets owned rather than the families simply qualifying by owning at least one set has been the reference criterion. With radio and television having almost universal ownership, the only critical quantitative variable which the media planner has to keep in mind is the multiple ownership factor.

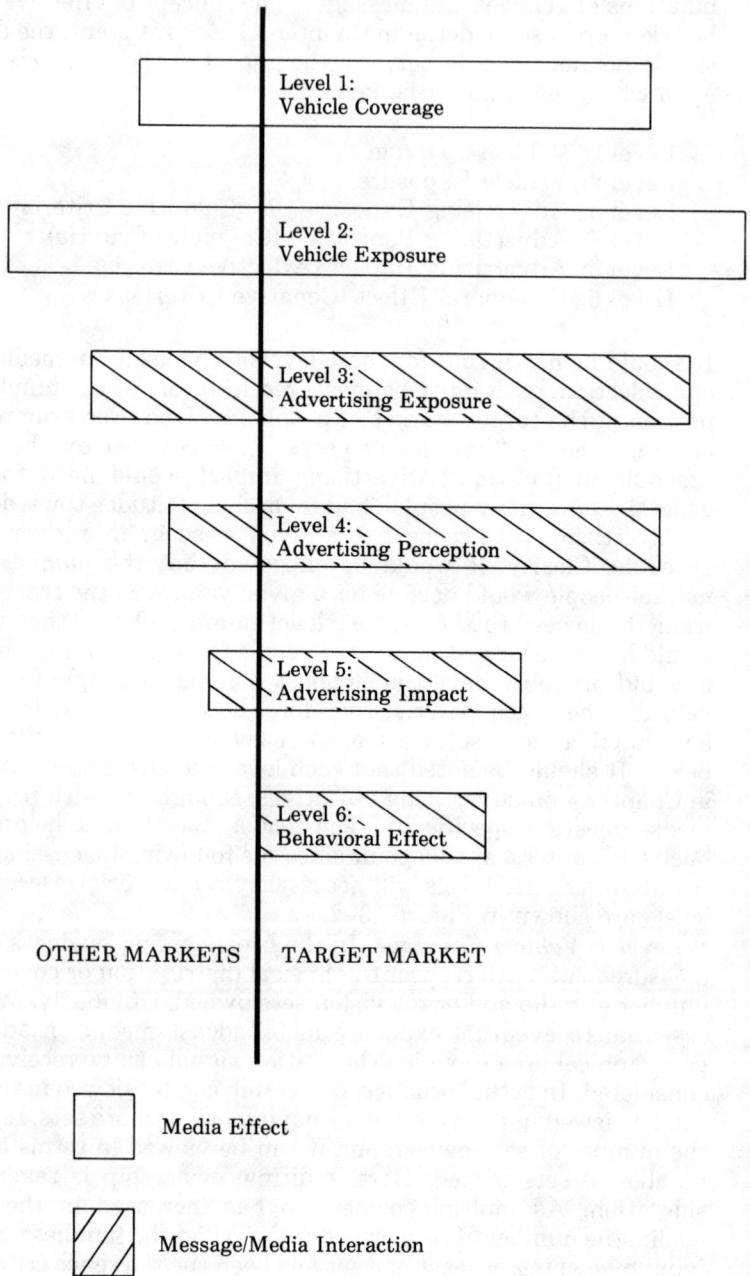

Figure 13-2 Declining Number of People in Successive Reach Levels

Level 1:
Vehicle Coverage

Level 2:
Vehicle Exposure

Level 3:
Advertising Exposure

Level 4:
Advertising Perception

Level 5:
Advertising Impact

Level 6:
Behavioral Effect

OTHER MARKETS   TARGET MARKET

Media Effect

Message/Media Interaction

For example, the radio industry has rightfully emphasized this point because the typical home has two to three radio sets in working order. This means, unlike the majority of television viewing, that radio listening has become primarily a matter of individual listening rather than family viewing. This prospective exposure to multiple sets, particularly during certain seasons of the year such as summertime, when portable radios take on added significance, and when increased automobile travel mirrors a greater importance for the automobile radio, has restressed the vitality of the radio medium and provided a significant extension of audience. A knowledge of ownership statistics is vital as a first step in media evaluation and planning on a broadcasting basis.

In print, the unit of measurement, in terms of physical distribution or coverage, is represented by the familiar circulation figure which magazines and newspapers show. This is knowledge that is audited by the Audit Bureau of Circulations (ABC) and furnishes the media planner with reliable data in terms of the purchase of print vehicles.

While the ownership of radio or television sets (except for the extension of multiple ownership) tends to vary little, the prospective variation of circulation (reflecting ownership) in the print media can be substantial. Basic circulation data, over the short term, tend to be fairly consistent in reflecting the standing of different publications. Circulation changes do occur, however, and the media planner has to keep continually abreast of prospective changes in circulation dynamics for all magazines of any consequence and for newspapers in major markets.

For example, *Cosmopolitan* magazine, as a consequence of new and vigorous editorial treatment, became the leader in the women's service book field. With a swiftly rising circulation, *Cosmopolitan* came to be regarded as a "hot" book in the field.

The non-specialist must rely on the media specialist for details on circulation patterns, changes in circulation movement, major changes in print media standing, and other types of detailed information.

Level 2: Vehicle Exposure. In the broadcasting industry, the total audience potential is expressed in terms of tuners or viewers (listeners, in the case of radio) at a given time of day or night. Tuning, as a statistic, simply reflects the fact that a television or radio set is on; it does not guarantee viewing or listening. Viewing (or actual listening), on the other hand, reflects some kind of attention being paid at a given time. Many services are available which measure, in different ways, this prospective audience exposure; some of the services rely exclusively on a tuning measurement while others claim they reflect some degree of viewing. Some of these services were briefly discussed in Chapter 4 on objectives.

For media planning purposes, the best available measurement of exposure is generally considered to be whether or not a given set is on, be it a radio or television set. Since the editorial framework of broadcasting is in terms of programming, audience is usually thought of with reference to a given program or portion of a program. In the case of advertisers who are spot advertisers, that is, they buy time between programs, for practical purposes they are normally identified with the exposure of the programs surrounding the spot buy.

The A.C. Nielsen Company is noted for its development of program exposure ratings through use of devices attached to individual television sets from a selected sample of homes around the United States. The rating developed from such measurement is really a measurement of prospective market penetration and does not indicate in any way exposure to a given advertising message. Even within a given program there are significant variations on a minute-by-minute basis so that a given commercial can have a varying exposure depending upon the exact time at which it appears. The same logic naturally applies to spot advertising which, appearing between programs, is subject to more dial movement and station switching than the typical within-program message.

Again, the specific use of ratings data is the province of the media department. Whether a property gets a 15 rating or a 25 rating (prospectively reaches 15 percent or 25 percent of the total television homes) is not a management issue generally. Providing this information through research services, evaluating its reliability and validity, and how it should be used is primarily the job of the media and media research personnel. From the standpoint of advertising management, however, an understanding of such a statistic from the media planning point of view is essential. Media decisions in broadcasting cannot and should not be made exclusively on the basis of ratings. For example, a given program may have a sizable advantage over a contending program in overall rating, but within a given market segment, the lower rated program may actually be more efficient. The advertising management personnel do not have to become experts on broadcast ratings but must understand how they fit into the media planning framework.

In the print area, increasing attention has been given to the idea that total audience potential is best expressed in terms of total readers (circulation multiplied by the number of readers per copy) rather than in terms of circulation alone. The magazine industry has accentuated the idea of total readership; this includes readership of all people within the home and those outside the home who read the vehicle. Even when circulation figures are relatively comparable, total readership figures can differ markedly from magazine to magazine. When they are available (as they are in the case of larger magazines), this additional readership factor is very important. This importance is indicated not only in a more realistic reflection of total audience potential, but also in the provision of more information about the audience; such additional information concerns the product usage and demographic profiles of vehicle readers.

Total readership data from newspapers has not generally been available. This is primarily due to the fact that underwriting a major study is an expensive proposition, and for many newspapers to do this independently does not seem practical. Advertising management need not be concerned with the research aspects of gathering this type of information. Management should, however, understand the importance of the total readership concept and ensure that media specialists exploit such information in their work.

Level 3: Advertising Exposure (Pre-Cognitive Criteria). Advertising exposure represents the number of prospects reached with the advertising message. Advertising exposure should not be confused with the actual communication of an advertising message since this entails effectiveness of the message.

In broadcasting, advertising exposure is indicated by the people exposed to commercials, that is, those people with sets turned on and tuned to a specific channel which carries the message at the time of such tuning. Essentially, this measurement in broadcasting represents the *opportunity* for communication rather than actual impact of communication. Data measuring broadcast advertising exposure are available from many sources, particularly through the A.C. Nielsen organization.

Because the print media (particularly magazines) have felt at a disadvantage when compared with the broadcast media concerning exposure, many vehicles have undertaken research to measure the people exposed to the advertising page. The so-called "glue seal" technique is an example of such research.

Level 4: Advertising Perception (Cognitive Criteria). This is the first measurement step which indicates not only the power of the carrying vehicle, but also the power of the advertising which it carries. In broadcasting, the measurement used is normally the minimum commercial recall; that is, recall of some specific aspect of the advertising message. Recall is discussed in detail in Chapter 11 on copy research.

Within a medium such information can be very valuable if confidence can be placed in the research on which the information is based. For example, in terms of both the total audience potential criterion and advertising exposure criterion, it might well appear that a one-minute spot announcement is as effective a buy as a participating minute in an hour show. Or the 30-second spot may be more than one-half as effective as a 60-second spot. The additional value in terms of perception of the 60 over the 30 may not be worth the additional cost involved.

In the print area, there are measurements analogous to those in broadcasting in terms of the recognition or recall of advertising. Here, too, there are service organizations which provide continuous data in this area in addition to data gathered through custom-designed research sponsored by advertisers and agencies. For example, there might be some question as to whether a certain creative approach requires large space or can attain certain objectives without the attendant large space costs. In general, however, these measurements tend to show such extensive variation that the ability to apply overall principles is restricted.

The evaluation of advertising copy effectiveness may reveal factual data regarding media which may prove to be helpful in media evaluation and selection. These are, in the main, highly sensitive tests which tend to show considerable variations in copy effectiveness. If they are used on copy of uniform quality and fluctuations appear in the scores, then such fluctuations may be an indication of variations of some internal media factor such as size, location, and use of color. Such conclusions, of course, must be based upon carefully controlled experiments in which the advertising copy is held constant and variables are introduced through the media.

Level 5: Advertising Impact (Affective Criteria). Impact represents a step beyond perception as noted in Chapter 4 with respect to the discussion of the hierarchy of effects notions. In the broadcast media and in the print media it represents communication in terms of change in attitudes and emotional involvement on the part of the prospective purchaser. Although there are continuing services available to provide some indication of the degree of such impact, there is no uniform agreement among the top advertising practitioners on the validity, reliability and sensitivity of such measures with respect to media applications. In contrast, the use of DAR (Day-after Recall) methods for the assessment of advertising perception has become a fairly standardized and agreed-upon procedure.

Nonetheless, the attitude-change type of information for the assessment of advertising impact can have an important influence on certain programming decisions in which advertising management is involved. Whether management utilizes Level 4 or Level 5 data in the calculation of effective reach figures will often depend upon their viewpoints on on-air versus on-premise testing of copy with respect to its reliability, validity, and sensitivity; those who take the multiple criteria viewpoint would utilize both in the development of effective reach figures for alternative media vehicles or schedules.

Level 6: Behavioral Effect (Conative Criteria). Essentially, the final decision which reflects the combined effect of the complete interaction of media and copy decision making should be based upon data measured on consumers at the check-out counter. At the present time, advertising management is some distance from having adequate data of this type upon which to make media decisions. However, the advent of computerized check-out in a great many supermarkets in the United States makes such data development on an on-going basis more nearly feasible than in the past.

Some corporations have found it effective to run market tests involving different media mixes, although the widespread success of media-weight tests is not common. Market tests are more frequently done in the case of new-product introductions than in the case of established brands (although, as noted in Chapter 8, some of the more successful market tests have been conducted by such established brands as Budweiser). However, for the typical media plans and decisions confronting an advertiser or an agency, market testing is not practicable on a continuing basis for most manufacturers since it is time consuming and very costly as a general rule.

The above six levels of measurement for the purpose of estimating the reach of a vehicle or a schedule represent a stairway of media values which conclude with the three dimensions of effectiveness of the hierarchy of effects notions: Cognitive, Affective, and Conative. As noted in Chapter 4 on objectives, it is not clear that such a one-way, linear conception of the operation of advertising (both media and copy) is always apparent; in fact, in most low-involving purchase situations (convenience goods) it has been demonstrated that the "stairway" actually is ordered as: Cognitive (awareness), Conative (behavior), and Affective (attitude). The application of such ideas to the media area is clearly the way in which advertising decision making can become *integrated* in nature since both copy and media measurements are involved in the last three of the suggested six levels of measurement above. The manner in which integration can take place in decision making will be examined in some detail in Chapter 14 when the *Message/Media Response Value* concept is introduced.

STAGE IV: DETERMINATION OF MEDIA OBJECTIVES

After the marketing backdrop has been explicated, the target market has been defined, and a decision has been made about level of reach criteria to be employed in subsequent reach analyses, objectives must be set for the media planning process, as in any planning process.

Though a media plan may be based on many specific types of objectives, in general there are three basic factors which serve in the statement of quantifiable media objectives: (1) Reach; (2) Frequency; and (3) Continuity. *Reach* refers to the number of households or individuals who will be exposed *at least once* in a given time period (usually a four-week period is employed); the way in which such exposure is defined depends upon the level of reach criteria employed as discussed in the preceding section. *Frequency* refers to how often households or individuals will be exposed within a given time period. And *continuity* concerns the number of weeks and in what sequence throughout the budgeting year the brand will be advertised.

There are two general points which should be noted regarding the relationship of these three objectives. First, as illustrated in Figure 13-3, the three factors of reach, frequency, and continuity can be viewed in a triangular relationship; the size of this triangle is governed by the size of the advertising budget. The larger the budget, the larger can be the reach, frequency and continuity factors in the overall media plan.

The second aspect of the relationship between these three media objectives is shown in Figure 13-4. Since, for a given budget, the area of the triangle connecting the three objectives is fixed, it follows that for one of the three to be increased, at least one of the remaining two factors must be decreased. For example, if greater reach is desired in the selected schedule, this can be achieved for the given budget level only if the frequency involved in the schedule is reduced. Three alternative configurations of reach, frequency, and continuity are illustrated in Figure 13-4; it is clear that though the shape of the triangle may change, the overall area of the triangle cannot change for a given

Figure 13-3   Budget Level and Media Objectives

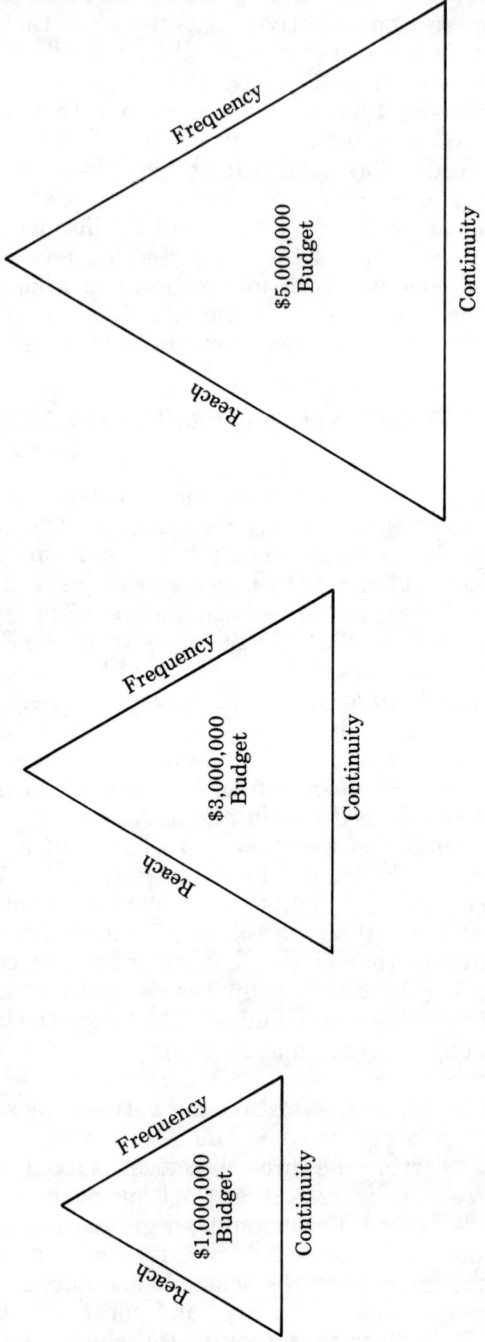

budget level. In Figure 13-4, the central triangle represents the size of the budget while the three surrounding triangles represent different allocations of this budget to the media objectives of reach, frequency, and continuity. Each of these three media objectives is discussed briefly below.

Figure 13-4   Trade-Off Between Media Objectives

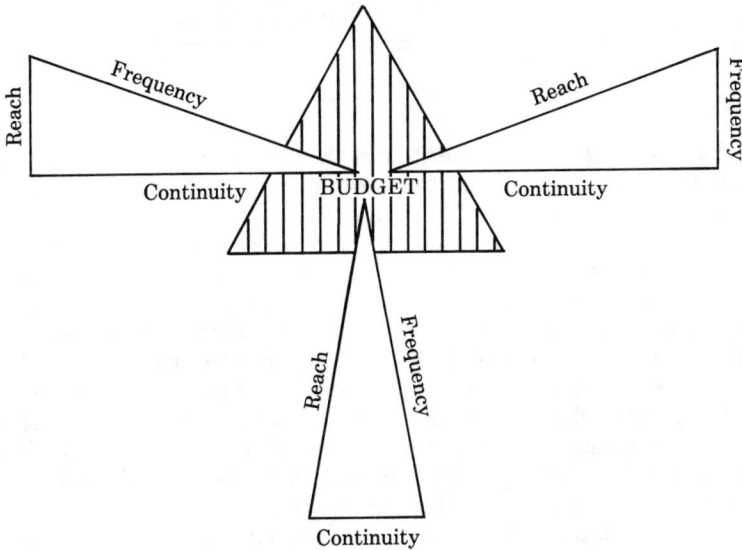

Reach and Frequency. The relationship between reach and frequency is most easily visualized in terms of the concept of *gross rating points* or gross reach. Gross rating points (usually referred to as "GRP's") is the sum of the individual audiences of the vehicle insertions used in a schedule. Though the concept originated in television media scheduling (the "rating" in GRP's comes from the Nielsen rating of a program), it is widely used now as a general concept applying to all media types. Suppose Magazine A has 29 percent of its audience in the target market profile definition for the brand in question while Magazine B has 57 percent of its audience contained in the product's target market. The GRP's for a schedule consisting of two insertions in Magazine A and two insertions in Magazine B would be 172 [172 = (2 × 29) + (2 × 57)]. It should be noted that gross rating points or gross reach aspects of a schedule counts some of the audience members twice since the same person, for example, may be exposed to the first insertion in Magazine A and also to the second insertion in Magazine A or multiple exposures to some other combination of the four insertions in the schedule. Gross reach or GRP's are sometimes referred to as *duplicated reach* for this reason. Suppose that the *unduplicated reach* (the number of *unique* individuals exposed to the entire schedule at least once) for the above schedule is determined to be 80 percent of the target market for the brand (how this is determined is, in large measure, the subject of Chapter 14 on exposure estimation). The average frequency of this schedule can, therefore, be calculated in the following manner:

$$\text{Average Frequency} = \frac{\text{Gross Reach (GRP's)}}{\text{Reach (Unduplicated)}}$$

$$2.15 = \frac{172}{80}$$

Note that the frequency calculated in the above manner is an *average* frequency and means that, on the average, it can be expected that the average member of the target market will be exposed to the vehicles in the hypothetical schedule about 2 times; some people will be exposed more than two times while some will be exposed fewer than 2 times. But the above relationship between gross reach, reach and average frequency should make it clear to the reader that there is a trade-off relationship between reach and frequency relative to gross reach. Gross reach is often taken as a surrogate indicator of the size of the budget since it depends solely on the number of insertions purchased and the audience size of each insertion. For a given GRP level representative of a given budget level, frequency can be increased only if the denominator above (unduplicated reach) is decreased.

Table 13-1 illustrates the reach and frequency relationship in some detail. In this table, a sample of 5 viewing homes has been selected (of course, the samples which such organizations as A.C. Nielsen utilize are in the neighborhood of 1,000 households) and analyzed for viewing behavior over two four-week viewing periods. Comparison of period two with period one shows how reach can decline for these five households while frequency rises. It might be kept in mind that media personnel very frequently utilize proportions or percentages in their calculations (as in the above example) rather than the actual number of households or individuals involved; though the results are the same (except for rounding error) using percentages makes such calculations considerably easier, as will be observed in the following chapter.

Continuity. Continuity can be viewed from the standpoint of two categories: (1) *Massed* advertising insertions in the media schedule and (2) *Spaced* advertising insertions in the schedule. Spaced continuity involves the continuous use of advertising spaced over the planning time period whereas massed continuity refers to the "pulsing," "waving," or "flighting" of the insertions. A spaced advertising media schedule, for example, might have one insertion every four weeks for one year while a massed schedule might use the same budget to purchase one insertion every week for thirteen weeks; no advertising would be con-

Table 13-1 Inverse Reach/Frequency Relationship

(X = HH (household) exposure to Program A)

Sample HH#	Period One Week #				Period Two Week #			
	1	2	3	4	1	2	3	4
1	X			X	X	X	X	X
2								
3		X	X					
4	X	X	X			X	X	X
4	X		X	X	X		X	

Rating	60%	40%	60%	40%	40%	60%	60%	40%

	Over Four-Week Period:	Over Four-Week Period:
GRP's	200 = (60 + 40 + 60 + 40)	200 = (40 + 60 + 60 + 40)
Reach	80% = 4/5	60% = 3/5
Average Frequency	2.50 = 200/80	3.33 = 200/60

ducted during the rest of the year after the initial thirteen-week "burst."

There is very little published evidence on which of these two continuity strategies is more effective. One of the first psychologists to study learning and forgetting, which is the basic issue in continuity questions, was Ebbinghaus. In a series of experiments in which he was his own subject, he would attempt to learn a series of nonsense syllables by oral repetition. Despite such an experimental setup's limitations, his findings have subsequently been confirmed in psychological as well as advertising settings. Ebbinghaus found that *spaced* repetitions were more effective than repetitions *massed* together in terms of recalling the nonsense syllables.[5] These 1902 experiments were first replicated in advertising contexts by Strong and reported in 1912.[6] Using a laboratory setup, Strong used four dummy magazines and a wide number of advertisements; controlling for advertisement size, he found that four weekly exposures (*spaced* exposures) was superior in generating recall of the ads than was either one exposure in each of four days or four exposures all at one experimental sitting (*massed* exposures). He also found that most of the forgetting of the advertising content occurred within two days of exposure.

The now classic study in this area of continuity was conducted in 1958 by Pomerance and Zielske of Foote, Cone & Belding advertising agency in Chicago.[7] The results of the study were reported by Zielske in 1959 and the data generated have come to be known as Zielske's Curve.[8] The study is a classic because of the ingenious design and the elaborateness of the study. Twenty-six groups of women, randomly selected from a telephone directory in Chicago, were mailed from one up to thirteen different advertisements for a food brand drawn from a single newspaper campaign for the product. One group received an advertisement weekly for thirteen weeks while the other group received the same thirteen mailings at intervals of four weeks during the year. Recall was measured by telephone interviews where only mention of the product class was used as an aid to the recall process. The results were based upon analyses of some 3,684 respondents who completed the study. No single person was interviewed more than once since this might destroy the validity of the recall measurements by hyping the recall in subsequent time periods unnaturally. The results are shown in Figure 13–5 as adapted from the reanalysis of the original data which was recently conducted by Simon.[9] Though Figure 13–5 shows that the massed schedule produced the highest levels of recall (62 percent recall for those receiving thirteen ads as measured during the fourteenth week), the *spaced* schedule produced the largest number of recall-weeks (total area under the curve) during the year. Recall-weeks refers to the recall level multiplied by the number of weeks in which this recall rate was observed. So, though the highest level of recall was obtained from a massed schedule, the overall greatest impact during the entire year was obtained from the spaced schedule (2130 recall-weeks as compared to 1076 recall-weeks for the massed schedule).

Though others indicate that massed schedules perform better than spaced schedules, no evidence is provided to substantiate such assertions.[10] Studies which have made the data public upon which the studies were based all point toward the general superiority of the *spaced* media schedule. As Simon has noted, there is no published evidence that the massed schedule is superior to the spaced schedule, but the reverse is true.[11] Though flighting remains popular in media practice, the evidence at the moment does not recommend such a continuity strategy in media scheduling.[12]

STAGE V: EXPLICATION OF CONSTRAINTS

Constraints on the decision making process of the media planner are of two types: (1) Environmental; and (2) Judgmental. Factors which fall into these two categories of constraints have already been set forth above under the discussion of uncontrollable variables so they will simply be listed here to remind the reader that such factors act as constraints on what is feasible in the development of the media plan.

Environmental Constraints. Constraints of the environmental nature are those which are beyond control of either the advertising personnel or those within the corporate structure in any direct way. Environmental constraints include the following factors:

(1) General Economic Conditions
(2) Competitive Efforts
(3) Legal and Cultural Environment
(4) Natural Phenomena (Weather, etc.)
(5) Media Environment (Qualitative Factors).

Figure 13-5   Zielske's Original Data Points and
Smoothed Curves

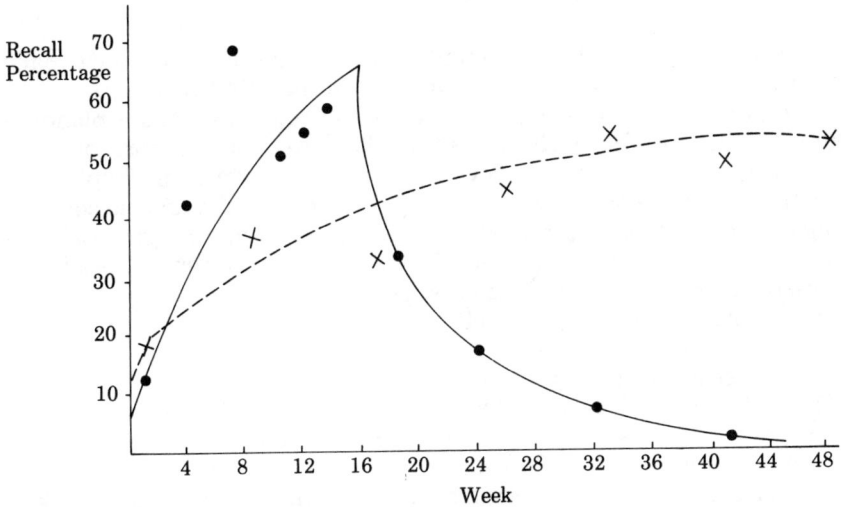

Recall
Percentage

- = observation for *massed* schedule (one ad each of 13 weeks)
X = observation from *spaced* schedule (one ad every four weeks for year)
——— = smoothed curve for *massed* schedule
- - - - = smoothed curve for *spaced* schedule

SOURCE: Adapted from Julian L. Simon, "What Do Zielske's Real Data Really Show About Pulsing?" *Journal of Marketing Research* (August 1979), p. 418.

This last factor, Media Environment, deals with such concepts as mood, excitement, atmosphere, prestige, permanence, reputation, and many other "intangible" elements of this nature. These factors can be regarded as intangibles when compared with measures such as reach, frequency, and continuity which are more easily quantified. Because of the difficulty of measuring these kinds of elements, it might appear that they are of secondary importance. However, from the standpoint of advertising management's involvement in media:

It should be clear that in the area of qualitative factors there is a broad field in which media judgment and creative thinking can operate. It does not mean that because there may not be clear, concise *definition*, simple, direct *measurement*, or straightforward, prima facie *correlation*, these factors are not important, or that the information provided on these factors is not valuable and useable. It does mean that the blending of these factors and the available data on them is the responsibility of the advertising executive. It is the media person with the greatest creative insight and the most competent judgment who will, in the long run, most effectively wed advertising copy to the media choice to achieve maximum effectiveness.[13]

The critical point to keep in mind is that media planners must make creative use of the media environments as they find them.

Judgmental Constraints. Some constraints on the media planning process are alterable in the sense that they are under the control of the corporate personnel at some level other than that of the media planner. Refusal to allow company advertising to appear in a magazine containing explicit sexual material would be an example of a judgmental constraint on the media planner. These constraints can generally be classified under the following categories:

(1) The Advertising Budget
(2) The Marketing Mix
(3) General Corporate Policies.

The upholding of a particular corporate image through the media types and vehicles used in the advertising would fall under the latter category of corporate policies.

After definition of marketing backdrop, definition of target market, selection of reach criteria, setting of media objectives, and explication of the constraints, the next step in the general media planning process is that of matching the markets and media availabilities in preparation for the actual media selection process.

STAGE VI: DETERMINATION OF MARKET/MEDIA MATCH

The matching of markets and media vehicles is one of the most important steps in the overall media process. There are two general approaches which might be followed in this process: (1) Direct Matching; and (2) Indirect Matching. Each of these two approaches is illustrated in Figure 13-6.

Direct Matching. There are two ways in which direct matching might be conducted. Figure 13-6 shows the direct matching of demographic profiles of the target market with the demographic profiles of the media vehicles *without* respect to product usage levels of these demographic groups being taken explicitly into account. Below are shown two magazines' demographic profiles on age in comparison to the demographic profile of the brand's target market (which presumably has been selected because it is believed these particular individuals represent the *prime prospects* for purchase of the brand):

Age Category	Target Market Profile (Age)	Magazine A Profile (Age)	Magazine B Profile (Age)
18-34	20%	34%	17%
35-49	42	19	45
50-64	31	26	24
65+	7	21	14
	100%	100%	100%

Figure 13-6   Direct and Indirect Market/Media Matching

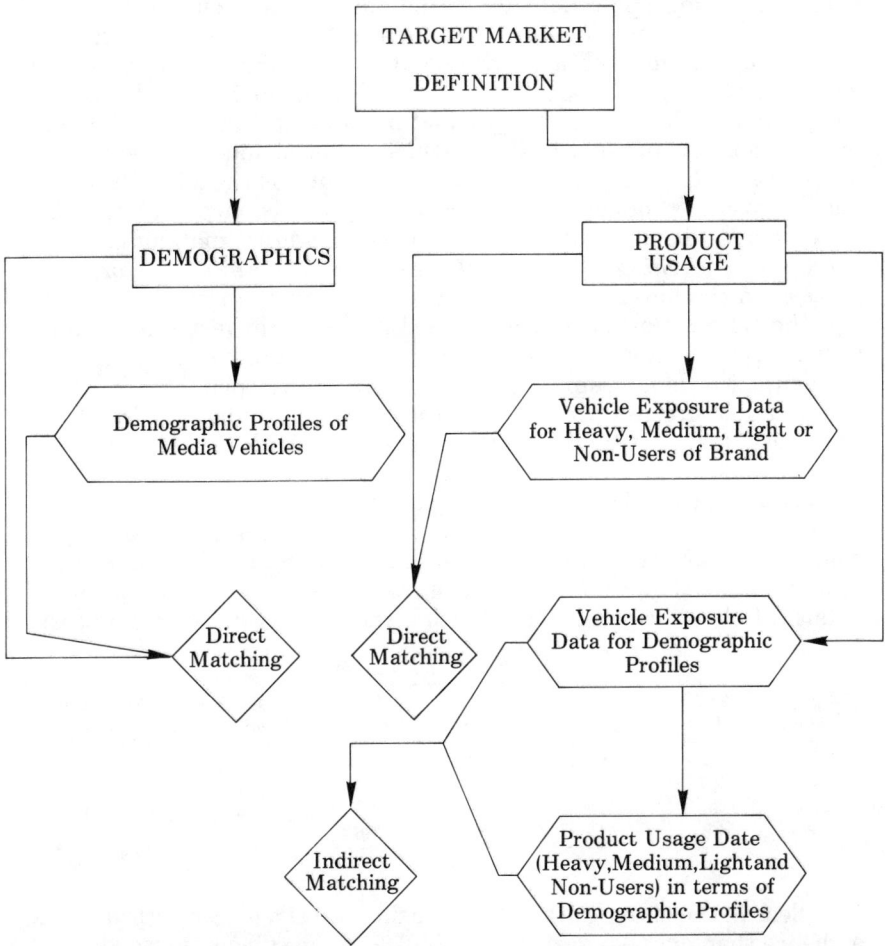

SOURCE: Adapted from A.M. Barban, S.M. Cristol, and F.J. Kopec, *Essentials of Media Planning: A Marketing Viewpoint* (Chicago: Crain Books, 1976), p. 45.

Clearly, the demographic profile of Magazine B more closely "matches" the demographic profile of the target market for the brand than does that of Magazine A. If this were the only criterion involved (it would ordinarily not be since *cost efficiency* has not been examined), Magazine B would be the better selection in terms of *matching efficiency*. This same direct matching process might be carried out, as illustrated on the right-hand side of Figure 13–6, with respect to product usage variables (heavy, medium, light, and non-users) rather than with demographics. It should be noted, in any case, that the data upon which the direct matching takes place come from the same sample base. At the moment, the only service which provides product usage data and demographic data for brands and media vehicles from the same sample of individuals is that of the W.R. Simmons Company through its Simmons Market Research Bureau (SMRB) which is an amalgam of Target Group Index (formerly Axiom Market Research) and Simmons Reports. If the product involved in the media planning process is a new product or is one which is not included in the SMRB survey data, direct matching is not possible unless the advertiser conducts a custom product-media usage study for this purpose. Since this is expensive, the alternative is often that of indirect matching.

Indirect Matching. Figure 13–6 also shows the indirect matching process on the lower right-hand side of the figure. In indirect matching, the target market is first defined *explicitly* in terms of product usage levels (heavy, medium, light, and non-user); for each of these segments, the demographics profiles are then developed. Finally, these demographic profiles are matched to the demographic profiles of the candidate media vehicles. This process is indirect inasmuch as demographics represent a mediating factor between the way in which the target market is initially defined and the way in which the audiences of the vehicles are defined. For this purpose, the data upon which the target market is defined might come from a different sample of individuals than that upon which the audiences of the vehicles are defined. Below are some data showing the indirect matching process:

		Profiles of Usage (Age)				
Age Category	(21%) High	(40%) Medium	(34%) Light	(5%) Non-User	Magazine A Profile (Age)	Magazine B Profile (Age)
18-34	42%	54%	12%	10%	34%	17%
35-49	20	16	32	14	19	45
50-64	30	12	43	20	26	24
65+	8	18	13	56	21	14
	100%	100%	100%	100%	100%	100%

It is clear in the above data that Magazine A has a larger portion of its audience than does Magazine B in the 18-34 age sub-category which is the most important age sub-category for high and medium users of the brand in question; the high and medium usage level individuals account by far for the largest portion of the brand's market (61%) and probably should be the most important categories of usage in the matching process for this brand. Magazine A would, therefore, be selected under this indirect matching approach over Magazine B when *matching efficiency* is the only criterion utilized in the selection process.

The indirect approach may be desirable under the following conditions: (1) information on product users' media exposure is not available; (2) creative strategy relies heavily on a knowledge of the target market's demographic characteristics; (3) demographics significantly influence other marketing elements, such as distribution; or (4) frequency of use is unknown as in the introduction of a new product, in which case the planner would focus on total usage of the product category as a basis for media/market matching.[14]

Efficiency of Direct Versus Indirect Matching. The available evidence makes it clear that direct rather than indirect matching is the more efficient method. Efficiency in market/media matching is defined by media planners using a standard *index of target market selectivity.* This index is obtained by dividing the proportion of a media vehicle's audience who are target market members by the target market membership of the population as a whole. Therefore, an index of 1.50 would indicate that the media vehicle was 50 percent more efficient in reaching the target market than if its audience had been selected randomly from the population as a whole. On this basis, Assael and Cannon found a 62 percent drop in efficiency from direct to indirect matching.[15] In another study, Cannon and Merz found an average efficiency index of 1.86 using direct matching for 25 vehicles, 1.29 for indirect matching using psychographics from TGI data, and 1.27 for indirect matching using demographics on the same 25 vehicles.[16] The available evidence on this question clearly favors the use of *direct* matching wherever this is possible.

After the development of matching information, the media personnel are in a position to carry out the actual selection of vehicles for the media schedule.

STAGE VII: SELECTION OF VEHICLES

The media vehicle selections are ordinarily the responsibility of media buyers at advertising agencies; as such, and strictly speaking, the selection of media vehicles for the media schedule is not within the proper province of advertising management and the media planner. However, the development of the *general process* through which media buyers are expected to conform in their selection of vehicles is properly the responsibility of the media planner and is, therefore, considered here as part of the media planning procedure. Once the planner or manager of media activities for the firm has set up the selection process, the routine operation of media selection according to this process can be carried out through media buyers.

The position of vehicle selection within the market/media matching process previously discussed is illustrated by the outline shown in Figure 13–7. This figure shows that media evaluations and selections take place after media usage analysis is conducted in relation to direct (Target Market Definition by Behavioral Categories such as product usage) and indirect (Multivariate or Subjective Target Market Definition and Surrogate Definition) matching. The primary element which enters into the selection process after the market/media matching procedure is that of *cost.*

Traditionally, magazines were compared to each other in terms of the measure, cost per thousand reached or CPM. Today, this measure can be and is applied to all media types. The reach upon which this cost of insertion is based becomes a major issue in the selection process.

Figure 13-7   Selection of Media Vehicle Alternatives

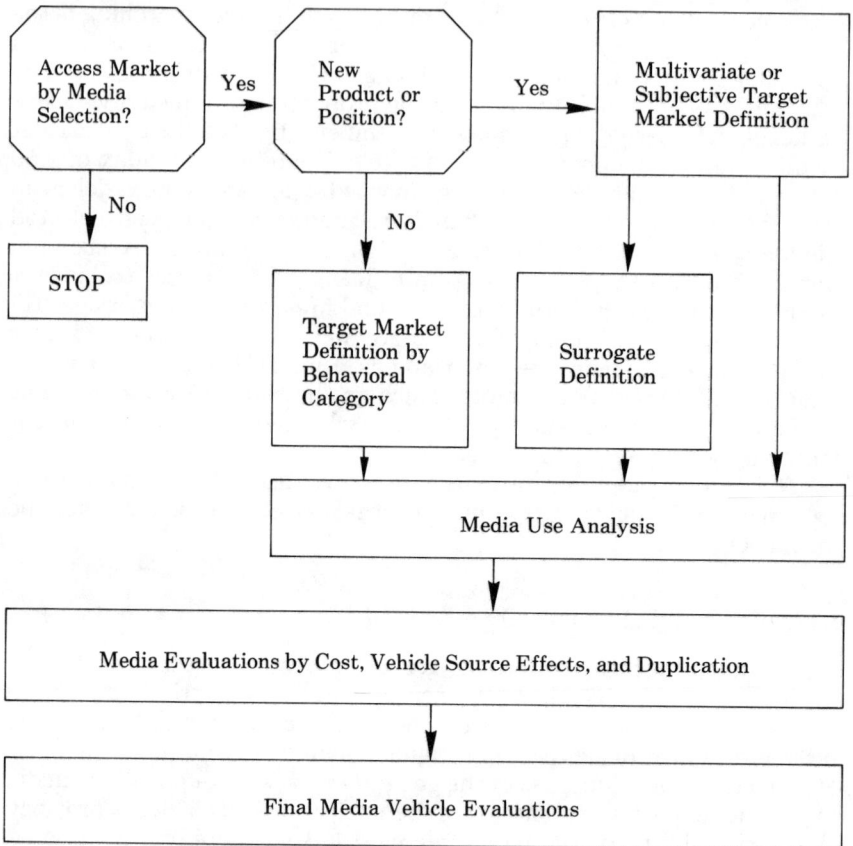

SOURCE: Adapted from Hugh M. Cannon and G. Russell Merz, "A New Role
for Psychographics in Media Selection," *Journal of Advertising*
(vol. 9, no. 2, 1980), p. 34.

Three general levels of CPM figures should be distinguished: (1) CPM
per total vehicle audience (noted simply as CPM); (2) CPM based upon
the vehicle's reach only to the target market population (noted
CPM/TM); and (3) CPM per target market population *reached effectively* (noted CPM/TM/ER). As noted in Figure 13-7, the reach figure
upon which CPM is based must also take account of the duplication
provided in the overall schedule if the vehicle is added to the schedule;
the reach figure utilized, therefore, regardless of the level above,
should be an *unduplicated reach* rather than gross reach figure. The
determination of unduplicated reach is problematic and is the subject
of the following chapter on exposure estimation; here it will be as-

sumed the figures on each are net or unduplicated. In terms of the above three CPM levels of reach, it is clear that CPM/TM will be larger than CPM for a given vehicle while CPM/TM/ER will be still larger than CPM/TM. An example will make this clear.

Example 13-1. Suppose the Glower Corporation is developing a media schedule for its brand of floor polish called Sunglow. Among the many vehicles to be included as possible selections for the schedule are Magazine A and Magazine B. The TM (target market) size is defined directly through high and medium brand usage and consists of 24,000,000 households. Data are then developed for all vehicles along the lines illustrated for Magazine A and Magazine B below:

	Magazine A	Magazine B
Cost per Insertion:	$22,000	$26,000
Total Coverage:	10,000,000	13,000,000
Coverage to TM:	6,000,000	6,000,000
Effective Coverage Rate:	24%	35%
(Discussed Below)		

Three CPM calculations are then made for each magazine based upon different definitions of the vehicle coverage or reach. These three calculations are shown for Magazine A below:

$$CPM = \frac{Cost}{Coverage} \times 1000$$

$$CPM_A = \frac{\$22,000}{10,000,000} \times 1000 = \underline{\$2.20}$$

$$CPM/TM = \frac{Cost}{Coverage\ to\ TM} \times 1000$$

$$CPM/TM_A = \frac{\$22,000}{6,000,000} \times 1000 = \underline{\$3.67}$$

$$CPM/TM/ER = \frac{Cost}{Coverage\ to\ TM \times Effective\ Coverage\ Rate} \times 1000$$

$$CPM/TM/ER_A = \frac{\$22,000}{(6,000,000)(.24)} \times 1000 = \underline{\$15.28}$$

The calculated CPM values based upon different coverage definitions are given below:

	Magazine A	Magazine B
CPM:	$2.20	$2.00
CPM/TM:	$3.67	$4.33
CPM/TM/ER:	$15.23	$12.38

Clearly, though Magazine A has the lowest CPM in terms of reach to the target market, Magazine B is preferable if CPM in terms of total vehicle coverage is utilized in the selection process or if CPM in terms of effective reach to only target audience members is used. Notice also that the CPM figures become progressively larger for each of the magazines as the definition of coverage or reach becomes more rigorous.

Effective reach will be discussed in some detail in the following chapter in conjunction with the Message/Media Response Value concept. Generally, effective reach differs from "plain" reach inasmuch as it takes into account the effective interaction of the copy in the particular media vehicle to produce variations in effectiveness of the advertising overall. Effective reach is a concept which takes account of the *interactive* nature of copy and media in advertising. In terms of the effective reach of an entire media schedule, J. Walter Thompson media personnel have defined this concept as the proportion of target market individuals or households who receive between three and ten exposures to the advertising contained in the media schedule.[17] For example, suppose the exposure distribution (a concept to be treated in detail in Chapter 14) for a media schedule showed the proportions of people exposed to the vehicles in the schedule 1 time, 2 times, 3 times, and so forth as follows:

Number of Exposures	Unduplicated Reach to TM
0	18%
1	10
2	6
3	8
4	9
5	10
6	8
7	6
8	5
9	4
10	2
11+	14
	Total: 100%

The rate of effective coverage for this media schedule, according to the Thompson agency definition of effective reach, would be 52 percent $(52 = 8 + 9 + 10 + 8 + 6 + 5 + 4 + 2)$.

In this present example for Sunglow polish, Magazine A's effective coverage rate was 24 percent while Magazine B's was 35 percent. These effective coverage rates were defined for the vehicles using the recognition measure of *advertisement exposure* as the criterion of effective reach. Starch recognition scores (say the average over the past five years for all full-page floor polish ads which were inserted in Magazine A) were used as the basis for estimating that 24 percent of those target market households exposed to Magazine A would also be exposed to the Sunglow print advertisement for floor polish. Clearly, in the ultimate sense, the particular Sunglow advertisement which is actually to be used in the campaign should be tested in Magazine A if this measure of effective coverage is to be more precise. But just as clearly, and unfortunately, it would be impracticable to test every ad in every vehicle before it is run; the number of combinations of potential vehicles for inclusion in the media schedule with, say, two or three alternative advertisements which might be placed in these vehicles becomes rather large. In addition, it might be noted that effective reach can be defined in terms of any one or some combination of the six levels of reach criteria discussed earlier in this chapter. Any useful development of the effective reach concept will depend heavily upon the manager's knowledge of copy research methods and their application in the media context.

Preparations for Buying. Preparations for buying media are essentially *operating* preparations; they involve the contact of the appropriate media representatives, discussions of possible scheduling, agreement on merchandising support provided by the media themselves, and other areas of a similar operating nature. Negotiations at a *managerial* level most frequently involve the commitment of dollars for major television broadcasting buys. Here, the relatively complex discount structure of broadcasting, combined with the fact that the supply and demand of major television time vary from period to period, frequently makes advertising management involvement in this area a necessity.

Negotiating operations, even at a higher level, are so dependent on the intricacies of broadcast pricing and time structure, that no procedural rules can be laid down. But an intimate knowledge of broadcast market operations is required, and at least one major executive with the advertiser and/or agency must be an informed expert in this area and up to date with the constant market changes. In purchasing television and radio spots, negotiations are normally the province of the broadcast buyer, in contrast to the network situation described above. It is up to the buyer to maximize the efficiency in the given market by the most propitious combination of time, ratings, frequency, and available discounts. In print media where there is a much less flexible discount structure and no real ceiling on availabilities since space can be expanded and time cannot, negotiations take place at a much lower level in the form of position negotiations and similar requests.

Actual Purchasing. The purchase is in the hand of the Media Department of the agency and involves a detailed knowledge of the media complex. For example, in major network program commitments so-called order letters dispatched to confirm the purchase of a given property are quite complicated in construction and require a coverage of many specific points which, if not carefully covered, can lead to difficulty at a later date. In essence, a management-oriented executive has only the obligation to see that the most efficient and knowledgeable people at the buyer level are fulfilling the purchase requirements.

The Accounting Function. This involves an estimate of billing on a proposed buy. Media accounting is needed because when advertising is purchased the exact dollars of a given buy or in a given market are never available until *after* the advertising has run. For example, it is possible that a station blackout in a given market on a given night would require that the advertiser be recompensed either with another spot or a refund. The estimate is, then, an approximation of a given investment. There is, of course, no direct involvement of advertising management in this process.

Media Checking. Because of the complexity of advertising media, particularly in the spot broadcasting area, procedures have been set up to at least spot check the advertising which has been committed to run. Sometimes in the broadcast area, for example, a given commercial is not run and this omission not reported to either advertiser or the agency. The checking procedure is designed to provide a limited police force in order to furnish at least a reasonable guarantee that an advertiser is receiving value for dollars spent. In the print area, for example, in the use of color, sometimes reproduction is poor and the advertiser wishes to request a "make-good" of the medium in question. In order to do this, a copy of the advertisement as it finally ran in a given newspaper or Sunday supplement needs to be checked by the agency in order to keep abreast of production inequities.

With this outline of the media planning process in mind, it is worthwhile to examine the area of media models and their contribution to media planning ideas and executions. One type of media model, exposure distribution, will be examined in detail in the following chapter because of the overriding importance of this type of model in practical media planning and selection processes. However, the reader should be aware of the developments in the comprehensive media model area; for this purpose, the following section briefly provides some history on the development of this area and an overview of the types of procedures which have been developed.

OVERVIEW OF MEDIA MODELS

Media models have become an integral part of some portion of the media operation at large advertising agencies. Such models can be classified into two very general categories: (1) Comprehensive Media Planning and Selection Models; and (2) Exposure Estimation Models. The comprehensive media models have a complete procedure for the specification by the planner of media objectives and most other elements of the media planning process as well as a system for the application of these elements in the screening and selection of individual media units for the media schedule.[18] Exposure estimation and exposure distribution models, on the other hand, deal primarily with the issue of the calculation of unduplicated reach and the frequency distribution by number of exposures of a given media schedule. Unfortunately, most comprehensive media models do not treat exposure estimation in the detail with which individual exposure estimation models deal with this important and basic issue in media evaluation.

The exception to this pattern can be found in the simulation variety of comprehensive media models; here the exposure distribution issue is treated explicitly and is modeled in detail. Since exposure estimation models will be examined in the following chapter, only comprehensive models will be examined at this point.

SOME USEFUL TERMINOLOGY

Four quite general terms appear frequently in connection with media models: (1) Algorithm; (2) Heuristic; (3) Iteration; and (4) Monte Carlo Simulation. The understanding of media models requires some understanding of each of these terms in a general way. These terms can be briefly described in the following manner:[19]

Algorithm. An algorithm is a procedure (or set of rules) for solving a problem by following a specific number of steps in a certain manner. If the steps are followed carefully, they guarantee a solution. Writing algorithms is an important part of the general procedure of writing computer programs, although they usually precede actual program construction. Algorithms (and flow charts) include steps for knowing where to start a process and where to stop. Almost all mathematical formulae can be reproduced in algorithmic form.

Heuristic. The algorithm method of solving problems is direct. If one follows the instructions, an answer is obtained. But sometimes, and especially in the case of media strategy planning, an algorithm cannot be devised because the problem is too complex to understand. A heuristic might then be substituted for an algorithm; a heuristic is an empirically based aid or decision rule-of-thumb to follow when the problem cannot be placed in algorithmic form. The answers obtained by heuristics may not be a perfect solution to problems. An example of a heuristic decision rule in media planning might be to state that attention value of any advertisement is the direct function of an advertisement's size. The model will then give more weight to people who read large ads than those who read small ads. While this heuristic may be true, it is not always true; yet without such a heuristic, ad size might be ignored entirely.

Iteration. Some algorithms execute the same series of instructions to the computerized model over and over again with slight modifications until an optimum solution is reached (The High Assay Model of the Young & Rubicam agency is of this type and will be discussed shortly). The process could require that the next time an operation is executed, the last estimate could become the next input so a better estimate is obtained each time the computer repeats the instructions. This process is repeated until the best solution is found. An iteration could also be based on a heuristic in the sense that it may require some rules-of-thumb in carrying out its calculations. Iteration includes the repetition of instructions and a set of rules to identify the best solution.

Monte Carlo Simulation. The Monte Carlo simulation procedure is used to obtain approximate evaluations of a solution by using random numbers. The random numbers are applied to empirically observed or measured probability distributions (the Leo Burnett procedure to be discussed shortly follows this approach). Like heuristics, the Monte Carlo method may be used in place of strict algorithms. An example of

Monte Carlo technique applied to media planning is in the estimation of probabilities that a certain individual in the target market will watch television or read a magazine. Through the Monte Carlo method, it is possible to estimate media exposure through searching a table of random numbers. Suppose SMRB data show that the proportion of the target market viewing a program is 40 percent. Using this as a probability that a given individual will view the program, the computer is used to generate a two-digit number. If the random number is between 00 and 39, the person is called a viewer; if the number is between 40 and 99, the person is called a non-viewer.

These terms will become somewhat more clear when they are used in the following discussion of comprehensive media models.

Four comprehensive media model types will be examined: (1) Mathematical Programming models; (2) Stepwise Analysis models; (3) Simulation models; and (4) Decision Calculus media models.

MATHEMATICAL PROGRAMMING

The first comprehensive media models developed were of the mathematical programming variety; these were developed in the late 1950s and early 1960s by such advertising agencies as Batten, Barton, Durstine and Osborn.[20] The most common application in the mathematical programming area was, specifically, through the use of the mathematical methods of linear programming.[21] In general, the linear programming model consists of two distinct portions: (1) the objective function; and (2) sets of constraints. Though linear programming, because of the many difficulties which will be enumerated below, is not used today in media applications, it is instructive to examine the general procedure of the approach; much of the basic thinking, including the concept of objective function and constraints, has served as the basis for contemporary approaches to media models.

The basic LP (linear programming) approach will be formally stated below; then each element of the procedure will be examined:

(1) $\quad \max \text{REU} = E_1 X_1 + E_2 X_2 + \ldots + E_n X_n$

s.t.

(2) $\quad C_1 X_1 + C_2 X_2 + \ldots + C_n X_n \leq B$

(3) $\quad C_2 X_2 + C_4 X_4 + C_{10} X_{10} \geq .25(B)$

(4) $\quad X_i \leq 52 \quad X_i \geq 0.$

The above statements represent a complete specification of a linear programming problem. However, this is an abstract statement since the coefficients in the objective function (the E's) and in the constraints (the C's) must be replaced by actual numbers for the given media situation before this is a concrete problem for which a solution can be found.

Statement (1) above is the *objective function* in the model. It indicates that values of X (number of insertions in each media unit in the pool of "candidate" or feasible vehicles and units for the particular schedule) should be selected through the linear programming procedure such that REU's (total rated exposure units) will be at a maximum amount. One of the major problems in the application of linear programming was in the development of these rated exposure units for each media unit. For each X or vehicle, the REU had to be developed (noted by each E alongside the X in statement 1). In general, this was attempted through a four-step process involving four adjustments to exposure data for each vehicle. These levels are:

I. Vehicle Audience
II. Vehicle Coverage to Target Market
III. Target Market Exposure to Advertising
IV. Media Environment Adjustment (Qualitative Factors).

The above adjustments can be understood in the context of Example 13–1 presented earlier in this chapter. There, the total coverage of Magazine A was 10,000,000 while the coverage to the defined target market was 6,000,000 (Levels I and II above, respectively). The effective coverage rate in the example was 24 percent for Magazine A. Since, in that example, effective coverage was defined as recognition of advertising based upon Starch scores (an indicator of exposure to advertising), the target market exposure to advertising for Magazine A would be 1,440,000 (6,000,000 × .24 = 1,400,000). Finally, this figure must be modified for the impact of the media environment of Magazine A on the eventual effect of the copy included in that vehicle. Suppose on a scale of 0 to 100, the media planner perceives Magazine A to rate at 70 in terms of its suitability in terms of intangible factors for the particular advertising which might be placed in the vehicle. At level IV above, then, the final "E" or rated exposure value for Magazine A would be 1,008,000 (1,440,000 × .7 = 1,008,000). For purposes of calculations in the computer program, this E value would probably be scaled down in the case of all the vehicles by 100,000 or so; the final E value for Magazine A would then become 1.008 (1,008,000 divided by 100,000). If Magazine A is called candidate vehicle number one, the number 1.008 would be put in statement (1) above in place of E_1. This would similarly be done for all candidate vehicles which might possibly be included in the final media schedule.

Statement (2) above is called the *budget constraint* because it puts an upper limit on the number of insertions which can be purchased in terms of the budget level with which the media planner is working. The "C's" in statement (2) refer to the cost per insertion in each of the candidate vehicles. In Example 13–1, Magazine A cost $22,000 per insertion; C_1 would, therefore, be replaced by the number .022 (22,000 scaled down by 100,000). Notice that the cost of one insertion in a vehicle multiplied by the number of insertions in that vehicle will be the cost of advertising in that vehicle; when this is done for each vehicle included in the schedule and all these values are added together, the total cost of the schedule is obtained. Statement (2) says that this total schedule cost should be less than or equal to the budget size (B dollars).

Statement (3) is a *judgmental* rather than an *environmental* constraint like statement (2). Statement (3) incorporates the media planner's belief or judgment that enough insertions must be purchased in vehicle numbers 2, 4, and 10 so that such purchases account for at least one-fourth of the total advertising budget for the media schedule in question. The C's, again, stand for the cost per insertion in vehicle 2, 4, and 10, respectively. A linear programming problem statement may have as many constraint inequalities as the media planner desires.

The final constraints shown in statement (4) are environmental constraints. It is assumed in the example that all vehicles are weekly magazines so that not more than 52 insertions in any one vehicle is possible. Also, the number of insertions cannot be less than zero (called the non-negativity constraint); this is indicated by the final constraint indicated in statement (4) above.

Figure 13-8 shows the graphical solution of a linear programming problem of a very simple form; as a practical matter, linear programming problems are solved using the "Simplex" algorithm.[22] But for illustrative purposes, the ideas can be observed in Figure 13-8; what is accomplished in pictorial form there is accomplished mathematically in the Simplex method. The simplified problem solved in Figure 13-8 is stated as follows:

$$(1) \quad \max REU = 2X_1 + X_2$$

s.t.

$$(2) \qquad X_1 + 4X_2 \leq 24$$

$$(3) \qquad X_1 + 2X_2 \leq 14$$

$$X_1, X_2 \geq 0.$$

The above problem includes only two "vehicles" and the first is twice as effective as the second in terms of producing rated exposure units. This objective function is subject to (s.t.) two formal constraints and the usual non-negativity constraint. The two constraints are first plotted as lines labeled (2) and (3) in Figure 13-8. Points A, B, and C are called "corner points" and represent three possible or feasible solutions to the linear programming problem. Line (1) is then plotted in the figure; this is the objective function where an arbitrary value of 10 has been used in place of REU in (1) so that the function can be plotted. This line is then moved parallel to itself as far as possible to the right in Figure 13-8 but still remain in the space bounded by points A, B, C and the origin (0 point); this is at point C in Figure 13-8. Point C is, therefore, the point at which the values at that point for X_1 and X_2 will produce the largest REU in the objective function and also conform to the two constraints in the problem. The optimal values of X_1 and X_2 for this problem are shown to be $X_1 = 14$ and $X_2 = 0$. No other values of these two variables will produce as large an REU (REU's are at a maximum) yet stay within the two constraints.

The straight-forward application of linear programming methods in the manner described above has all but been abandoned now in prac-

Figure 13-8   Graphical Solution of Linear
Programming Problem

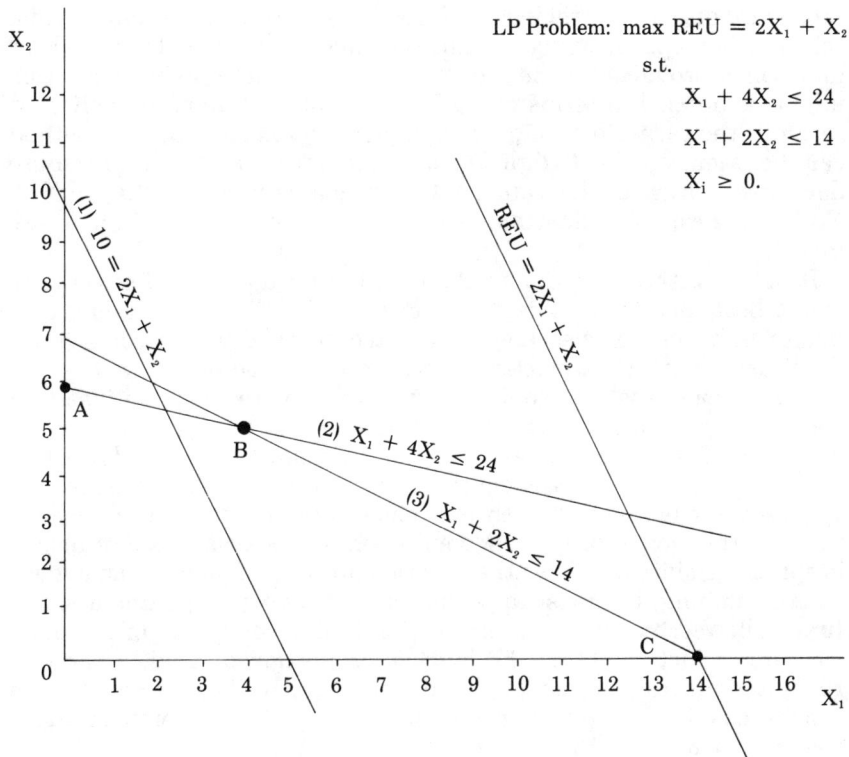

LP Problem: max REU $= 2X_1 + X_2$

s.t.

$X_1 + 4X_2 \leq 24$

$X_1 + 2X_2 \leq 14$

$X_i \geq 0.$

tice. There were four primary problems which are associated with the method which could not be resolved:

(1) LP assumes that each exposure has a constant effect which does not change with additional exposures (the E's remain the same).

(2) LP assumes constant media costs (this ignores the fact of volume discount structures in media buying and is represented by constant C's in the structure of the model).

(3) LP cannot handle the problem of audience duplication within and across vehicles.

(4) LP does not include any factor which deals with seasonality (it does not tell when to schedule the insertions over time).

Though some of these problems have been addressed at one time or another, in practice, media planners have turned to other tools such as stepwise procedures, simulation models, and decision calculus approaches.[23]

STEPWISE ANALYSIS

Stepwise analysis is utilized in models which employ an iterative procedure discussed previously. Stepwise analysis constructs a media schedule in steps, bringing into the schedule at each step the vehicle or unit which provides for the greatest increase in net effectiveness (this might be defined in terms of a CPM figure based upon unduplicated reach to the target market, for example). An example of this method can be seen in the "High Assay" incremental search procedure developed for use at the Young & Rubicam advertising agency in New York.[24] Figure 13-9 illustrates the steps involved in the High Assay model.

It starts with the media available in the first week and selects the single best buy. After this selection is made, all the remaining candidate units or vehicles are reevaluated to take into account their duplication with the vehicles already in the schedule, as well as the media discounts which would be involved if more than one insertion was purchased in a vehicle. Then a second selection is made for the same week if the *achieved* exposure rate is below the *optimal* rate (see Figure 13-9). This process continues until the optimal exposure rate for the week is reached; then new choices are considered and cycled through the model for the following week. High Assay, as a principle, is appealing since it follows the general approach of physical analogues such as mining; the most appealing as "easy-to-get" gold is assayed first, followed by the less accessible and more costly to "mine" gold. The area which contains the highest proportion of gold in the surrounding mineral base should be mined first; it will assay higher than other areas. In this light, four possible strengths can be pinpointed for the approach:

(1) The procedure handles the audience duplication issue.
(2) It develops a schedule over time (tells when to schedule the insertions which are purchased).
(3) It handles the media discount structures.
(4) It incorporates important explanatory factors in the development of the definition of *Optimal* exposure rates (though the final schedule may not be optimal because of the stepwise rather than simultaneous nature of the approach).

SIMULATION

Simulation, in general, has been briefly described above. Here an example of the procedure which the Leo Burnett Company utilizes called Mini-Compass System will be illustrated.[25] The Burnett system is a scaled-down version of the COMPASS system which was developed by the Diebold Group (a consulting firm) for a consortium of several advertising agencies in the late 1960's. Since the full-blown model proved to be too "data demanding" in terms of the cost and unavailability of much of the required data, Burnett scaled down the original model to a more manageable and practical format. In 1977, for

Figure 13-9 High Assay Media Selection Procedure
(Young and Rubicam Agency)

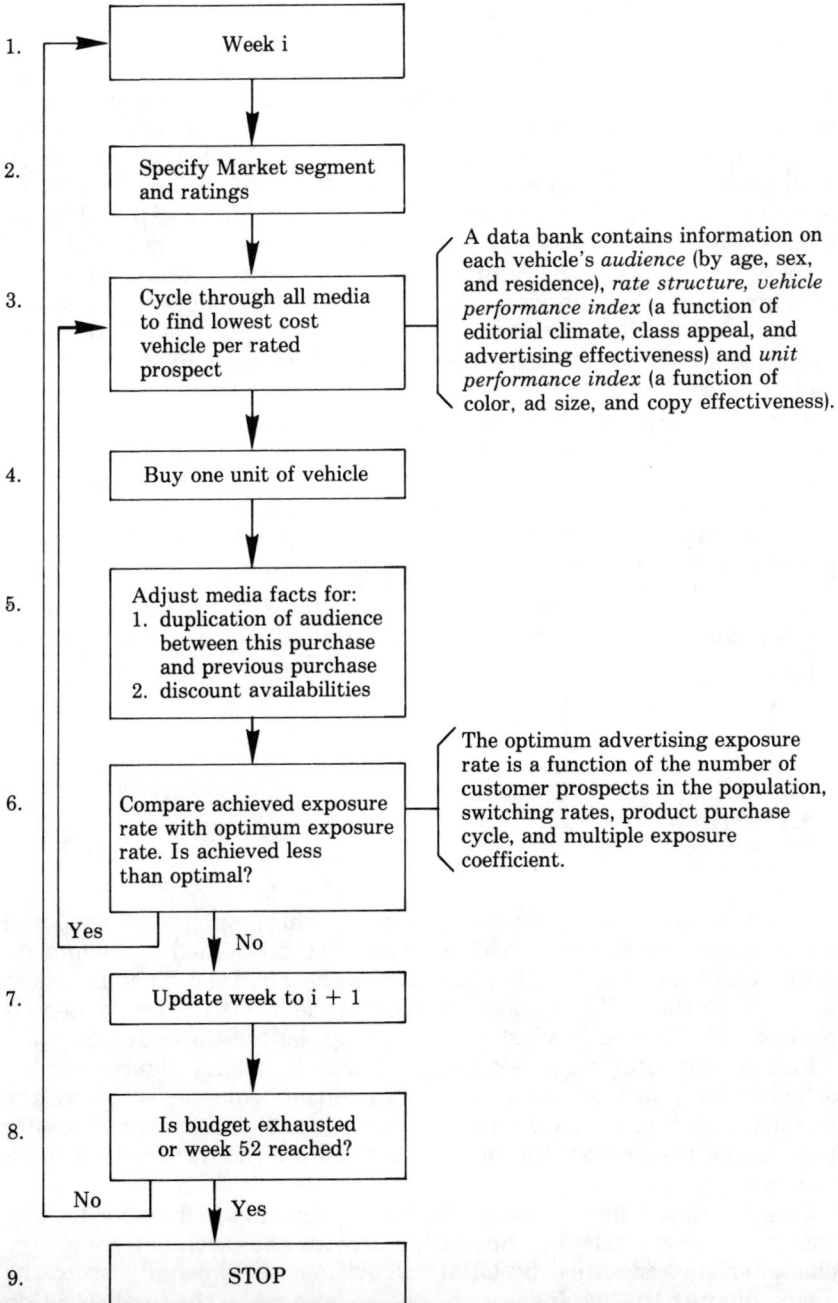

1. Week i

2. Specify Market segment and ratings

3. Cycle through all media to find lowest cost vehicle per rated prospect

A data bank contains information on each vehicle's *audience* (by age, sex, and residence), *rate structure, vehicle performance index* (a function of editorial climate, class appeal, and advertising effectiveness) and *unit performance index* (a function of color, ad size, and copy effectiveness).

4. Buy one unit of vehicle

5. Adjust media facts for:
   1. duplication of audience between this purchase and previous purchase
   2. discount availabilities

6. Compare achieved exposure rate with optimum exposure rate. Is achieved less than optimal?

The optimum advertising exposure rate is a function of the number of customer prospects in the population, switching rates, product purchase cycle, and multiple exposure coefficient.

Yes | No

7. Update week to i + 1

8. Is budget exhausted or week 52 reached?

No | Yes

9. STOP

SOURCE: Philip Kotler, *Marketing Decision Making: A Model Building Approach* (New York: Holt, Rinehart and Winston, 1971), p. 457.

example, Burnett evaluated a total of 5,000 different media schedules using the system; the system can handle up to ten plans at a time containing up to 40 TV or magazine vehicles.

The system produces output giving size of the target market, total impressions, GRP's, CPM's, reach, average frequency, the frequency distribution, and impressions by frequency level; these figures can all be broken down by individual target groups on a weighted or unweighted basis. The system utilizes data from SMRB reports and TV audiences conformed to national Nielsen levels to estimate the probability that a given individual in the simulation will be exposed to the vehicle. In addition to this probability of exposure to each vehicle, the 15,000 individuals in the Simmons data base also are defined by their demographics and product use levels. For each respondent, the system determines whether a person is exposed based upon the respondent's probability versus chance. This can be illustrated by the example shown below.

Example 13-2. Suppose a schedule is being considered which includes five insertions in *Better Homes & Gardens* magazine and three commercials in M*A*S*H. Suppose the respondent's probability of exposure to BH&G (as determined by Simmons audience base) is .60 while the exposure probability to M*A*S*H is .80. The process would proceed as follows in the Monte Carlo simulation:

Insertion	Respondent Probability	Computer Random No.	Exposed if $p \geq$ Random No.
BH&G 1	.60	92	NO
BH&G 2	.60	17	YES
BH&G 3	.60	48	YES
BH&G 4	.60	57	YES
BH&G 5	.60	73	NO
M*A*S*H 1	.80	24	YES
M*A*S*H 2	.80	83	NO
M*A*S*H 3	.80	61	YES

In the above simulation for one respondent, this respondent is exposed to the schedule a total of *five* times; therefore, 5 is added to the impression level of the schedule, 1 is added to the reach of the schedule, and 1 is added to the "5" frequency of exposure level. If the respondent is part of a "weighted" target market group, before these numbers are added to the total impressions, reach, and frequency figures for the schedule they are weighted by the weighting value selected by the media planner for the target market group of which the respondent is a part. Table 13-2 shows the sample output from the Leo Burnett Mini-Compass system.

In general, simulation models lack an optimizing feature for finding the "best" media schedule but rather provide the reach and frequency characteristics modified by CPM calculations; it is usually up to the media planner to then inspect the output and make the final selection among the alternative schedules which were processed by the model. Notice, however, that simulation models do go beyond just the calcula-

Table 13-2 Sample Output of Leo Burnett Company's Mini-Compass Media Selection Model

Vehicle Name	Vehicle Weight	Unit Cost	Number of Insertions in Plan Number									
			1	2	3	4	5	6	7	8	9	10
Reader's Digest	100	$60,439	1	1	2	2	2	1	1	1	1	1
Natl. Geo.	100	$56,850	1		1	1	1	1	1	1	2	2
Fam. Circle	100	$38,470	1	2	1			1	2			
Gd. Housekeeping	100	$29,930	1	2			1	2	1	1	1	
McCall's	100	$37,125	1	1		1				2		1
Family Health	100	$12,600	1	1	1	1	1	1	1	1	1	1
Total Insertions per Plan			6	7	5	5	5	6	6	6	5	5
Total Cost per Plan (M = 1000's)			$235	$247	$229	$227	$220	$228	$237	$234	$217	$224
Demographic Population (M)			5,874	5,874	5,874	5,874	5,874	5,874	5,874	5,874	5,874	5,874
Reach (M)			4,458	4,665	4,119	4,054	3,965	4,650	4,595	4,369	4,053	3,909
Reach (%)			75.90	79.42	70.12	69.07	67.51	79.16	78.23	74.39	69.01	66.56
Average Frequency			2.04	2.46	2.10	2.18	2.07	2.03	2.05	2.20	1.79	1.89
GRP's			155.1	195.1	147.0	150.3	139.9	160.6	160.7	163.4	123.7	126.1
Total Exposures (M)			9,107	11,460	8,636	8,826	8,217	9,436	9,441	9,598	7,268	7,407
CPM Gross Impressions ($)			25.85	21.55	26.49	25.77	26.80	24.18	25.08	24.39	29.81	30.22

Frequency Distribution (Sum = % Reach)

Number of Exposures	1	2	3	4	5	6	7	8	9	10
1	25.50	26.39	23.10	18.57	19.97	32.78	30.23	27.09	35.56	28.53
2	30.69	20.62	22.86	24.79	27.33	23.41	25.43	18.04	16.72	19.92
3	11.69	13.15	19.29	20.76	16.03	13.34	13.37	19.13	12.38	15.18
4-5	7.81	16.28	4.87	4.90	4.18	9.63	8.92	9.78	4.34	2.93
6-8	.21	2.98	0	0	0	0	.47	.35	0	0
9-12	0	0	0	0	0	0	0	0	0	0

tion of reach and frequency; in this sense, then, they are comprehensive media planning and selection models because they allow target market weighting and the costing analyses to be conducted in conjunction with the basic reach and frequency calculations.

DECISION CALCULUS

The models in this category are the most recent developments in the area of comprehensive media planning models. The model to be examined briefly here is that developed by John D.C. Little, the originator of the decision calculus concept in model building (another of Little's models was encountered in the judgmental application in Chapter 8 dealing with budgeting models). Little's MEDIAC model will be examined to show the basic concepts involved; however, the reader should be aware that other developments have taken place in this area. For example, a model named ADMOD is a general improvement upon MEDIAC in the sense that it incorporates advertising response linkages between advertising exposure and cognitive criteria rather than the rather gross linkage in MEDIAC between exposure and sales.[26] It might be noted that MEDIAC has been available for some time now in interactive computer mode; it is used, for example, by Telmar Communications Corporation in New York, a service firm which does work primarily for advertising agencies.

The structure of the MEDIAC model will now be described in a general way. The model assumes an advertiser is seeking to buy media for a one-year time period with a certain budget (called B in symbolic form here). The advertiser is able to identify different market segments and estimate the sales potential (or maximum sales) which might obtain in each of these segments. The sales potential of a market segment in MEDIAC can be stated as:

$$\bar{S} = ns$$

where: $\bar{S}$ = sales potential of market segment in a given time period
n = the number of people in the segment
s = sales potential of a given person in the market segment.

The sales potential ($\bar{S}$) represents the maximum sales that could be obtained in a market segment if the company uses its marketing and advertising resources in the best possible way; in the language of Chapter 8 dealing with response functions, it is the upper asymptote on sales. The more dollars the company spends on advertising in media reaching a market segment, the higher the per capita exposure level, and the higher the percentage of this maximum sales potential which will be achieved. This percentage of maximum sales potential is, therefore, a function of per capita exposure level:

$$r = f(E)$$

where: r = percent of sales potential of a market segment that is realized in a given time period

E = exposure level of an average individual in the market segment in a time period.

In MEDIAC, of course, a specific functional form must be used to represent this relation between exposure and proportion of sales potential realized. One such relationship which produces a diminishing returns (concave downward) relationship between percent of sales potential realized and number of exposures is the modified exponential function discussed in the Appendix to Chapter 8:

$$r = a(1 - e^{-b(E)})$$

where: a and b are parameters of the function to be determined for a particular brand's situation

e = the natural number 2.178 . . .

The total sales for the planning year can be stated as:

$$\begin{array}{cc} & \text{Time} \\ \text{Segments} & \text{Periods} \\ S = \Sigma & \Sigma \ nsf(E) \end{array}$$

where: S = total sales over one year by summing (Σ) over market segments and time periods (weeks).

The next thing MEDIAC does is to determine how the per capita exposure level (E) is developed. In the absence of new advertising reaching a particular market segment in time period "t," the per capita exposure level will be some fraction, p, of last time period's exposure level, period "t − 1":

$$E_t = pE_{t-1}.$$

This fraction, p, represents the percentage of the advertising that is remembered from one time period to the next by an average person in the segment. If there is new advertising in the time period t, then the exposure level for this period will be given by:

$$E_t = pE_{t-1} + \Delta E_t$$

where: Δ = increase or change in per capita exposure level in a market segment in time period t due to advertising new to this time period reaching the segment.

This increase in per capita exposure value, ΔE, must be related to the purchase of vehicles to be included in the schedule. MEDIAC assumes this relationship is a function of three things:

$$\Delta E = vkx$$

where: v = exposure value of one exposure in a particular media vehicle to a person in the market segment

k = the expected number of exposures produced in a market segment by one insertion in this media vehicle in the time period

x = the number of insertions in this vehicle in the time period.

The exposure value in MEDIAC is assumed to be a function of four main factors:

(1) Media Class: such factors as the potential of the vehicle for demonstration, believability, color, etc.
(2) Editorial Climate: The addition or subtraction from the ad's effect due to the editorial matter in the vehicle.
(3) Media Option: Such factors as ad size, use of color, etc.
(4) Market Segment: Exposure value may vary by the segment to which the vehicle is addressed.

The expected number of exposures produced in a market segment by one insertion in the vehicle (variable "k") is an adjustment to coverage figures obtained in the following way:

$$k = hgna$$

where: h = probability of exposure to an ad in the vehicle, given the person is in the audience of the vehicle (advertising exposure)

g = the fraction of people in a market segment who are members of the vehicle's audience

n = number of people in the market segment

a = seasonal index of audience size for a vehicle.

Finally, the above description of how the media process works must be embodied in some heuristic designed to find the best media plan. The problem can be viewed, as it is in one version of MEDIAC, as one of finding the x's (number of insertions in each vehicle) which will maximize the objective function stated as:

$$\max \text{REU} = \Sigma \, \Sigma \, nsf(E)$$

s.t.

(1) $E_t = pE_{t-1} + \Sigma\Delta E$ (summed over all vehicles)

(2) $L \leq x \leq U$
where: L = minimum number of insertions to be allowed in a given vehicle
U = maximum number of insertions to be allowed in a given vehicle

(3) $\Sigma\Sigma \, cx \leq B$
where: c = cost per insertion in a given vehicle
B = total size of the budget

(4) $x, E \geq 0$.

Constraint (1) above is the current exposure value constraint which contains the decision variables (x's or the number of insertions to be selected in each vehicle are included in $\Delta E = vkx$). The second constraint allows the planner to indicate the environmental constraint of 52 maximum or upper limit on weekly magazines for the number of insertions and 0 or some judgmental level for the minimum number of insertions. Constraint (3) is the usual budget constraint so that more money is not spent on a schedule than is available in the budget. And constraints in (4) are the non-negativity constraints as discussed in linear programming previously.

Though it is possible that this functional arrangement can be solved using piecemeal linear programming methods, this has proved too cumbersome in practice so that a heuristic has been developed and is now used in MEDIAC to provide a good but not necessarily "optimal" solution to the selection problem. Table 13–3 shows a sample of the printout from MEDIAC for four fictitious media vehicles listed as AAA, BBB, and so forth in the sample printout. Notice that only average frequency, rather than the complete frequency distribution, is provided by MEDIAC.

QUESTIONS AND PROBLEMS

1. What is the relationship between the three dimensions of effectiveness (cognitive, conative, and affective) to media planning and selection?
2. Which of the three Starch Recognition scores discussed in Chapter 11 on Copy research (noted, seen-associated, or read-most) would be most appropriate to use as the basis for estimating exposure to the advertisement in magazines?
3. In what ways might the editorial climate of a magazine affect the resulting impact of the vehicle on exposure to an advertisement carried in the magazine?
4. Of what importance is the work of Zielske discussed in this chapter with respect to the development of media models of a comprehensive nature? How might the information developed by Zielske be utilized or incorporated into a media planning and selection model?
5. In what ways might *coverage* be defined for the various media types such as TV, radio, outdoor, direct mail, magazines, and newspapers? Is the figure generated by Nielsen audiometers to generate network program ratings comparable to Starch Recognition figures for magazines? Why or why not?
6. The noted advertising practitioner and researcher, Herbert Krugman, says that three exposures to advertising is enough. Do you agree with Krugman? Why or why not? What theory of advertising would lead one to conclude that three exposures is the ideal number in general?
7. What impact would consumer's perceptions of newspaper reporters' credibility have on the advertising of products in that newspaper? Should advertisers be concerned about news credibility?
8. Construct a flow chart model which would conduct the media selection process using the stepwise approach outlined in this chapter. Assume only magazines would be candidate vehicles in your work.

Table 13-3 Sample Printout for MEDIAC Model

TELMAR BENCHMARK SYSTEM II   2-MAY-73   06:05

BRAND X — MAXIMIZE REACH FOR $500,000 BUDGET

MEDIA OBJECTIVES

BUDGET GOAL: $ 500,000

OPTIMIZATION
BASED ON: REACH

SELECTION PROCESS VIA MEDIAC MODEL

MEDIA	COST	CUME % REACH	AVG. FREQ	GRP
1 BBB	48000	28.85	1.00	28
1 BBB	96000	36.99	1.56	57
1 AAA	150000	49.68	1.67	83
1 GGG	180000	53.15	1.73	92
1 AAA	234000	58.14	2.02	117
1 FFF	257000	59.79	2.03	121
1 BBB	305000	62.80	2.39	150
1 AAA	359000	65.40	2.68	175
1 BBB	407000	67.17	3.04	204
1 GGG	437000	68.32	3.12	213
1 FFF	460000	69.21	3.13	216

***BUDGET GOAL REACHED

MARKET SEGMENT SUMMARY

BENCHMARK II SUMMARY
AND ANALYSIS

USES	MEDIA	COST
3	AAA	162000
4	BBB	192000
2	FFF	46000
2	GGG	60000
11		460000

DEMO NAME	ABCD
POPULATION	50833
GROSS IMPRESSIONS	110282
CPM GROSS IMPRESSIONS	4.17
GROSS RATING POINTS	216
NET REACH	35181
PERCENT NET REACH	69.21
CPM NET REACH	13.08
AVERAGE FREQUENCY	3.13
DEMO WEIGHT	1.00

SOURCE: Telmar Communication's Corporation (Copyrighted) and reprinted in Jack Z. Sissors and E.R. Petray, *Advertising Media Planning* (Chicago: Crain Books, 1976), p. 284.

ENDNOTES

1. Arnold M. Barban, Stephen M. Cristol, and Frank J. Kopec, *Essentials of Media Planning: A Marketing Viewpoint* (Chicago: Crain Books, 1976), pp. 1-10.
2. This categorization has been suggested by Barban *et al., op. cit.,* pp. 20-25.
3. Audience Concepts Committee, "Toward Better Media Comparisons: A General Survey" in A.M. Barban and C.H. Sandage, *Readings in Advertising and Promotion Strategy* (Homewood, Il: Richard D. Irwin, 1968), pp. 194-200.
4. Paul E.J. Gerhold, "Better Media Planning: What Can We Do Now?" in *Better Media Measurements of Advertising Effectiveness: The Challenge of the 1960's* (New York: The Advertising Research Foundation, 1959).
5. Hermann Ebbinghaus, *Grundzuge der Psychologie* (Leipzig: Viet, 1902).
6. Edward K. Strong, "The Effect of Length of Series Upon Recognition," *Psychological Review* (January 1912), pp. 44-47.
7. Eugene Pomerance and Hubert Zielske, "How Frequently Should You Advertise?" *Media/Scope* (September 1958).
8. Hubert Zielske, "The Remembering and Forgetting of Advertising," *Journal of Marketing* (January 1959), pp. 239-243.
9. Julian L. Simon, "What Do Zielske's Real Data Really Show?" *Journal of Marketing Research* (August 1979), pp. 415-420.
10. See, for example, the assertions made by Ambar G. Rao, *Quantitative Theories in Advertising* (New York: John Wiley & Sons, 1970) and Russell Ackoff and James R. Emshoff, "Advertising Research at Anheuser-Busch, Inc. (1963-1968)," *Sloan Management Review* (Winter 1975a), pp. 1-15 as well the follow-up article by the same authors in the Spring 1975 issue of *Sloan Management Review* which covers the research at Anheuser-Busch conducted during 1968 and 1974.
11. Simon, *op. cit.,* p. 419.
12. See the discussion on this matter in Jack Z. Sissors and E.R. Petray, *Advertising Media Plannning* (Chicago: Crain Books, 1976), pg. 165.
13. Lyndon O. Brown, Richard S. Lessler, and William M. Weilbacher, *Advertising Media* (New York: The Ronald Press, 1957), p. 225.
14. Barban, *et al., op. cit.,* p. 46.
15. Henry Assael and Hugh M. Cannon, "Do Demographics Help in the Media Selection Process?" *Journal of Advertising Research* (December 1979), pp. 7-11.
16. Hugh M. Cannon and G. Russell Merz, "A New Role for Psycholographics in Media Selection," *Journal of Advertising* (Vol. 9 no. 2, 1980) and Hugh M. Cannon and Patricia S. McMonagle, "Matching Media with Markets: What Does it Contribute to Media Selection?" in James E. Haefner (ed.) *Proceedings of the Annual Conference of the American Academy of Advertising,* 1980, pp. 98-101.
17. J. Walter Thompson Company, *The Concept of Effective Reach* (November 6, 1973), p. 6.
18. Media planners have generally adopted the following definitions with respect to media: (1) *Media Type* refers to a particular class of media such as radio, television and newspapers; (2) *Media Vehicle* refers to a particular carrier within a media type such as WPGU-FM, WABC-TV, and *The New York Times;* and (3) *Media Unit* refers to a particular space or time specification within a vehicle such as 60" spot in drive time on WPGU-FM, 30" spot in prime time on WABC-TV, and one-half page, B/W *The New York Times.*
19. This discussion is adapted from that given in Sissors and Petray, *op. cit.,* pp. 272-274.
20. Robert D. Buzzell, *Mathematical Models and Marketing Management* (Boston: Division of Research, Gradute School of Business, Harvard University, 1964), Ch. 5.
21. See, for example, Ralph L. Day, "Linear Programming in Media Selection," *Journal of Advertising Research* (June 1963), pp. 40-44.
22. F. S. Hillier and G. Lieberman, *Introduction to Operations Research* (San Francisco: Holden-Day, Inc., 1967) Chs. 5, 6, and 15.
23. For further examples of this approach see the discussion in Chapter 11, "Media Selection and Allocation Methods," in Anthony F. McGann and J. Thomas

Russell, *Advertising Media: A Managerial Approach* (Homewood, Illinois: Richard D. Irwin, Inc., 1981), pp. 275-308.

24. The High Assay procedure is described in William T. Moran, "Practical Media Decisions and the Computer," *Journal of Marketing* (July 1963), pp. 26-30. The Ogilvy & Mather advertising agency also developed a procedure of this type, among others.

25. The Leo Burnett Company, "A Non-Technical Outline of Mini-Compass," 1977.

26. See a discussion of ADMOD in David A. Aaker and John G. Myers, *Advertising Management* (Englewood Cliffs, N.J.: Prentice-Hall, 1975), pp. 483-490. A discussion of MEDIAC can be found in John D.C. Little and Leonard M. Lodish, "A Media Planning Calculus," *Operations Research* (January-February 1969), pp. 1-35. This discussion of MEDIAC is adapted from that given in Philip Kotler, *Marketing Decision Making: A Model Building Approach* (New York: Holt, Rinehart, and Winston, 1971), pp. 460-464.

MEDIA STRATEGY AND EXPOSURE ESTIMATION

- Importance of Exposure Estimation
- Using Exposure Distributions
- Overview of Exposure Estimation Methods

Decision Making Organization of This Text

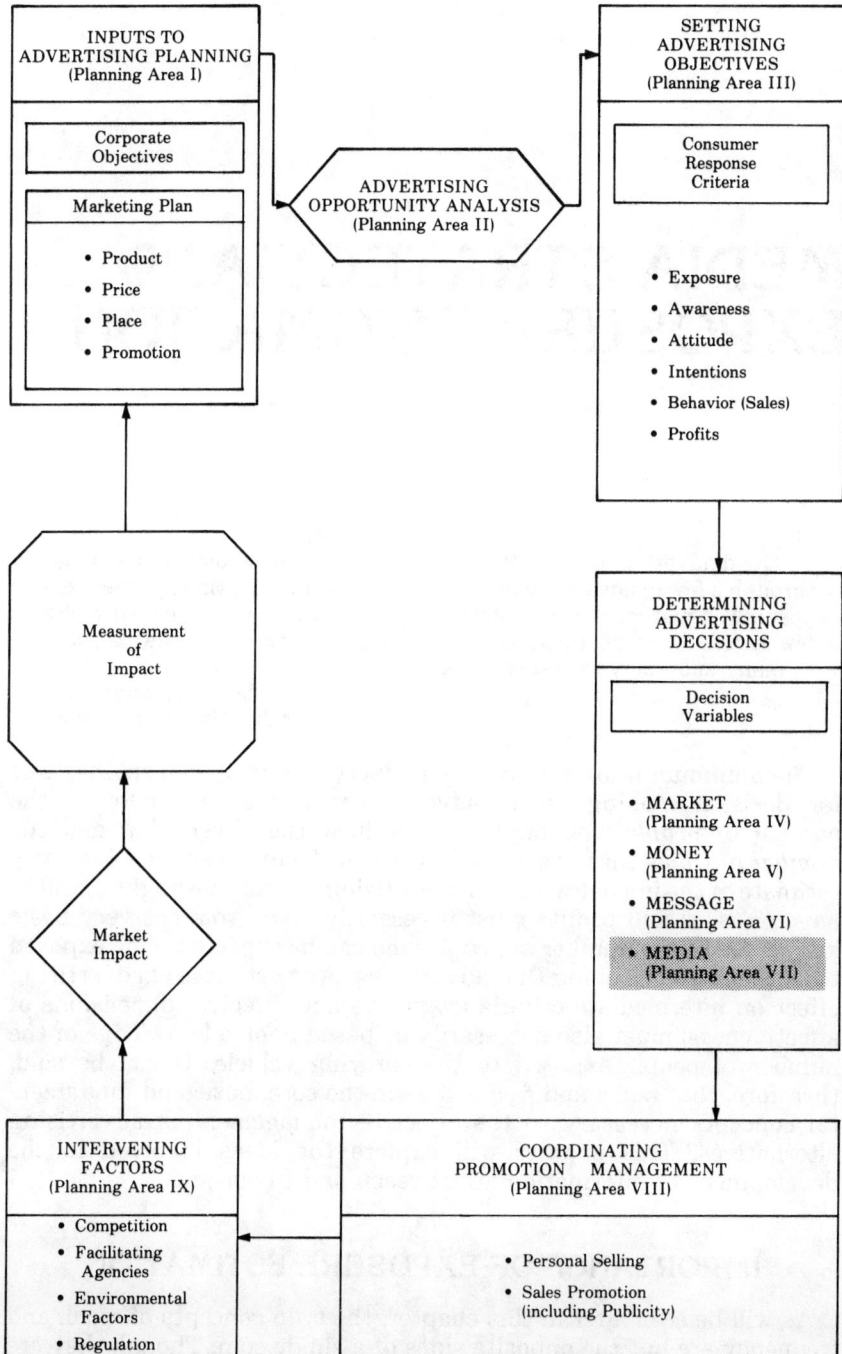

INPUTS TO ADVERTISING PLANNING
(Planning Area I)

- Corporate Objectives

- Marketing Plan
  - Product
  - Price
  - Place
  - Promotion

ADVERTISING OPPORTUNITY ANALYSIS
(Planning Area II)

SETTING ADVERTISING OBJECTIVES
(Planning Area III)

- Consumer Response Criteria
  - Exposure
  - Awareness
  - Attitude
  - Intentions
  - Behavior (Sales)
  - Profits

Measurement of Impact

DETERMINING ADVERTISING DECISIONS

- Decision Variables
  - MARKET (Planning Area IV)
  - MONEY (Planning Area V)
  - MESSAGE (Planning Area VI)
  - MEDIA (Planning Area VII)

Market Impact

INTERVENING FACTORS
(Planning Area IX)

- Competition
- Facilitating Agencies
- Environmental Factors
- Regulation

COORDINATING PROMOTION MANAGEMENT
(Planning Area VIII)

- Personal Selling
- Sales Promotion (including Publicity)

MEDIA STRATEGY AND EXPOSURE ESTIMATION

"Good advertising gets attention, and its message lasts long enough through a few exposures to make one or two points. Optimally, these exposures should reach the target audience with an effective balance of a few exposures to most persons in the audience, rather than one exposure to many and many exposures to a few.

—Herbert Krugman
Advertising Researcher

The minimum information which advertising management requires for decision making about advertising alternatives involves the *number of people* who might see or hear the advertising and the *number of times* these people might see or hear the advertising. Any estimate of the impact which an advertising alternative might possibly have on sales and profits must necessarily stem from the very basic knowledge of the number of people who can be expected to be exposed to the vehicle containing that advertising. Any estimate of advertising effect on intermediate criteria (cognitive and affective dimensions of effectiveness) must also necessarily be based upon a knowledge of the number of people exposed to the carrying vehicle. It can be said, therefore, that *reach* and *frequency* are the core, basic and fundamental concepts necessary to the effective management of advertising alternatives. This chapter will explore the ideas involved in the development of information about reach and frequency.

IMPORTANCE OF EXPOSURE ESTIMATION

As will be seen later in this chapter, the twin concepts of reach and frequency are but the opposite sides of a single coin. Though they are highly related to each other, the type of information for decision making which they provide is quite different. Reach is necessary information for the purpose of making estimates of the potential profitability of an advertising program. For example, suppose a target market consists of 1,000,000 households and advertising Alternative A will reach 15 percent of these households with the advertising message while Alternative B will reach 30 percent. This means that Alternative A is expected to yield a *potential* audience size (since reach means reach to the vehicle carrying the advertising and not necessarily the advertising itself) of 150,000 households and Alternative B a potential audience size of 300,000 households. Suppose this company has estimated, for the time interval involved, that 25,000 units of the brand must be sold to simply break even. The marketing and advertising managers estimate that, based on past experience, about 15 percent of the potential audience will buy the product. This would imply that under Alternative A, 22,500 purchases would result while under Alternative B 45,000 purchases would result; clearly, on the basis of this information, Alternative B would be preferred. All estimates of the sales potential and profit potential of a brand due to the advertising for that brand must necessarily involve a knowledge of the *reach* of that advertising program.

Frequency provides another type of essential information for decision making. If the advertising manager wishes to arrive at some reliable estimate of the translation of potential audience size (reach) into actual sales (getting a figure such as the "15 percent" figure in the above example), this estimation process must rest on the determination of frequency as the starting point. The effect of advertising on the cognitive and affective dimensions of effectiveness is directly related to the number of exposures to the advertising which consumers receive in a given advertising campaign (though this relationship will differ dramatically from brand to brand and campaign to campaign). The cognitive and affective dimensions are related in some way to the conative dimension (behavioral or sales dimension). In one way or another, the effect of advertising on either sales or some intermediate criterion begins with an understanding of the relationship of these to number of exposures or *frequency* of the advertising.

The noted advertising researcher, Herbert Krugman, indicated the importance of reach and frequency in advertising planning as stated at the top of this chapter. He has also given some more specific information on the desirable frequency levels in advertising in order to obtain the desired sales or other criterion-level results. Based upon his work with eye cameras which track the eye movement in response to exposure to print advertising, Krugman suggested that three exposures were enough.[1] Others have conducted work in laboratory (artificial advertising exposure) situations as well as in the field and concluded that three to four exposures appeared to provoke the optimal response on selected intermediate criteria.[2] In his famous article entitled, "Why Three Exposures May Be Enough," Krugman asserted that the first exposure, like the first exposure to anything, was something new and dominated by the consumer reaction, "What is it?"[3] The second exposure, he suggested, was characterized by the response, "What of it?" That is, having fully appreciated just what is the nature of the new information on the first exposure, the consumer shifts to a question of whether or not the advertising has any personal relevance. Another element for the second exposure is the startled recognition response, "Ah ha, I've seen this before!" Such recognition permits the consumer to pick up where he or she had left off without the necessity of doing the "What is it?" all over again. Finally, on the third exposure, the consumer knows he or she has been through the "What is it's?" and the "What of it's?" and the third exposure then becomes a reminder, that is, if there is some consequence of the earlier evaluations yet to be fulfilled. It is also the beginning of withdrawal of attention from the completed task, or as Krugman puts it, of disengagement from the advertising. He further asserts that all exposures beyond the third serve the same basic function as the third:

> . . . this pattern holds true for all larger numbers of exposures. That is, most people filter or screen out TV commercials at any one time by stopping at the "What is it?" response, without further personal involvement. The same person months later, and suddenly in the market for the product in question, might see and experience the 23rd exposure to the commercial as *if it were the second.* That is, now the viewer is able to go further into the nature of his or her reaction to the commercial—and then the 24th and probably the 25th might finish off that sequence with no further reaction to subsequent exposures.[4]

Regardless of how many exposures may be enough in a given situation (this will depend on such factors as the criterion involved, the type of product, the appeal, the audience, the media vehicles, and the exposure setting, among others), a decision must be made as to what the appropriate number of exposures should be for the advertising campaign.[5]

USING EXPOSURE DISTRIBUTIONS

Before examining various methods which can be used to estimate the extent and nature of exposure to a media schedule's vehicles, the primary purposes and uses of exposure distributions will be discussed. First, the definition of exposure distribution will be given, followed by a discussion of the measures of media objectives which are derived from exposure distributions. Then an operational view of effective reach in relation to exposure distributions will be presented.

DEFINITION OF EXPOSURE DISTRIBUTION

An exposure distribution in advertising media provides basic information essential to sound media planning and selection processes. The *exposure distribution concept* can be defined as a description of how many times (0, 1, 2, 3, and so forth up to the total number of insertions in the schedule) a certain number or proportion of people or households in the target market will see or hear the vehicle in which the advertisement will be placed. A sample exposure distribution is shown below for a schedule consisting of six insertions:

Number of Times Exposed	Number of TM HH's	Percentage of TM HH's
0	4,400,000	25.1
1	3,900,000	22.3
2	2,300,000	13.1
3	1,800,000	10.3
4	2,600,000	14.8
5	1,900,000	10.9
6	600,000	3.5
Total	17,500,000	100.0%.

For the above exposure distribution, notice that 4.4 million households would be expected to *not* be exposed at all to the schedule; this means that 25.1 percent of the target market households would *not* be reached by this particular schedule. Notice also that no one in the target market can be exposed seven or more times since the schedule only calls for six insertions. These insertions might all be in the same vehicle or different vehicles. Typically, however, the exposure distribution does not mix media types, for example, radio and magazines, but rather is estimated separately for each media type. This stems from the lack of uniform audience data across media types, and, in particular, the lack of duplication data across these types. In addition, due primarily to the cost difference between such types as radio and television, it is extremely difficult to consider one exposure to radio and television as equivalent. Subjective weighting of such inter-media differences is required but is not particularly desirable since these introduce an abstract dimension into exposure distributions. In general, it can be said that it is desirable to produce separate exposure distributions for each media type; a possible exception to this general rule is in the area of *simulation* of exposure distributions as illustrated by the Leo Burnett agency Mini-Compass system in the previous chapter.

It might be noted that quite often the exposure distributions which media planners actually use are *truncated* distributions. A truncated distribution is shown below for a schedule which consisted of 22 insertions in total:

Number of Times Exposed	Percentage of Target Market
0	22.1%
1	14.3
2	12.4
3	10.5
4	7.9
5	13.8
6+	19.0
Total	100.0%.

Notice that "6+" above stands for all those people who were exposed *six or more* times to the media schedule; some individuals or households (this is not specified above) will be exposed 7 times, 8 times, 9 times, and up to 22 times. Since many of these categories become very small as the size of insertions in the schedule increases, it is common practice to compress them into an "or more" category. This process is called truncating the distribution.

Such exposure distributions as shown above must be *estimated* and are not actually known in any absolute sense. Such distributions are actually "double estimations" since they are estimated from media data from such sources as SMRB which are themselves estimates of the population audiences of vehicles based upon sample data. Since no one individual knows for certain what the correct distribution in all cases actually is, there have been a variety of methods developed to estimate the distributions. They usually all provide somewhat comparable answers although for certain types of schedules the answers can vary dramatically depending upon the method used. Most advertising agencies of any size have their own estimation methods on their computer or use a service such as Telmar, Inc. of New York to do the estimation.

The primary reason why exposure distributions must be estimated for particular combinations of media vehicles in a schedule is due to the problems of vehicle *duplication*. Duplication refers to the situation in which a given member of the target market is exposed to the advertisement in more than one vehicle *(within-vehicle duplication)* or is exposed to the advertisement more than one time within the same vehicle *(between-vehicle duplication)*. Figure 14–1a illustrates audience duplication for three vehicles where one insertion is placed in Magazine A, one in Magazine B, and one insertion in Magazine C. The center triangle is called the "triplication" or third-order duplication and represents the people who are exposed to all three magazines. Area AC represents the number of people who are exposed only to Magazine A and Magazine C. If a fourth magazine were added to this schedule, then the fourth-order duplicated audience size would need to be determined. Since services such as SMRB only measure among their sample members the duplicated audiences between magazine pairs, any duplication of an order above two (pair-wise duplication) must, therefore, be estimated in order to produce an exposure distribution.

In Figure 14–1a, suppose Magazine A has an audience among the target market of 1.1 million households, Magazine B's audience is 1.3 million HH's, and Magazine C's audience is 1.4 million HH's. These total audiences are distributed across the various areas in Figure 14–1a. Notice that the unduplicated reach for one insertion in each of the three vehicles would be 2.9 million households and not 3.8 million (3.8 million is the sum of the individual magazine audiences and would be the gross reach). Reach refers to the number of *unique* individuals exposed one or more times. This can be found by adding up each individual area in Figure 14–1a to arrive at 2.9 (2.9 = .5 + .7 + .9 + .3 + .2 + .2 + .1); it can also be found through the application of the Inclusion/Exclusion formula (as in Boolean Algebra). The Inclusion/Exclusion Principle states that the probability of exposure to Magazine A or Magazine B or Magazine C is equal to the sum of the probabilities of exposure to each of them minus the three pair-wise duplication probabilities (for example, as between Magazine A and Magazine B) and, finally, plus the probability of triplication. Though probabilities have not been used in this illustration, the same thinking applies: 2.9 = 3.8 − (.4 + .3 + .3) + .1. Notice, for example, that .4 is the duplication between Magazine A and Magazine B in Figure 14-1a (.4 = .1 + .3).

Audience accumulation is also illustrated in Figure 14-1b for Magazine A. Each circle, in this case, now represents an insertion in Magazine A, so three insertions are shown for the same vehicle, Magazine A. The reach of three insertions in Magazine A is 2.5 million households (2.5 = .5 + .6 + .7 + .3 + .1 + .2 + .1); or through Boolean Algebra, 2.5 = 3.3 − (.4 + .3 + .2) + .1. Accumulation, in other words, removes the duplication which takes place *within* a vehicle rather than across or *between* vehicles (to which the term *net audience* is ordinarily applied).

When a media schedule calls for insertions in several vehicles and/or several insertions in the same vehicle, the process of estimating the exposure distribution amounts to a process of removing the double counting, triple counting and so forth from the *sum* of the individual audiences of the insertions.

MEASURES DERIVED FROM EXPOSURE DISTRIBUTIONS

Most of the important measures utilized in the process of selecting a schedule in conformance with media objectives are derived from the estimated exposure distribution. These measures include: reach, GRP's (gross reach, or gross impressions), average frequency, effective reach, and various CPM (cost per thousand) measures. The derivation of each of these important measures will be illustrated in the following example.

Example 14-1. The brand manager of Kelso detergent at the Caspen Company is faced with the problem of selecting a television media schedule to be used in the next quarter for Kelso. The choice has been narrowed to two media schedule alternatives. Below are the exposure distributions for the two TV media schedules:

Exposure #	Media #1	Media #2
0	22%	30%
1	35	25
2	30	20
3	7	25
4+	6	0
Total	100%	100%.

Figure 14-1 Audience Duplication and Accumulation for Three Magazines

Vehicle Audiences:

Magazine A—1.1 million households
Magazine B— 1.3 million households
Magazine C— 1.4 million households

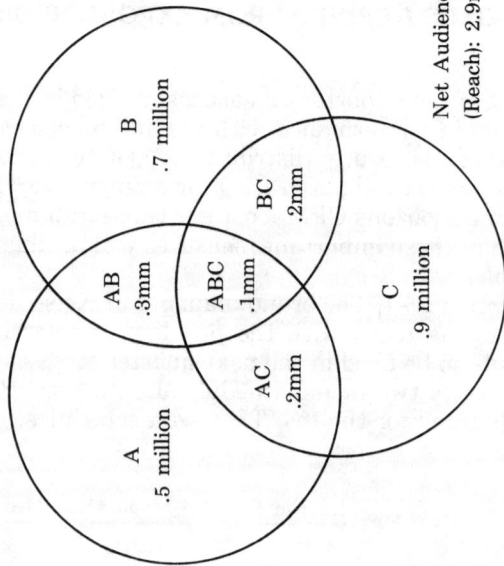

A
.5 million

AB
.3mm

B
.7 million

AC
.2mm

ABC
.1mm

BC
.2mm

C
.9 million

Net Audience
(Reach): 2.9m

(a) Audience Duplication

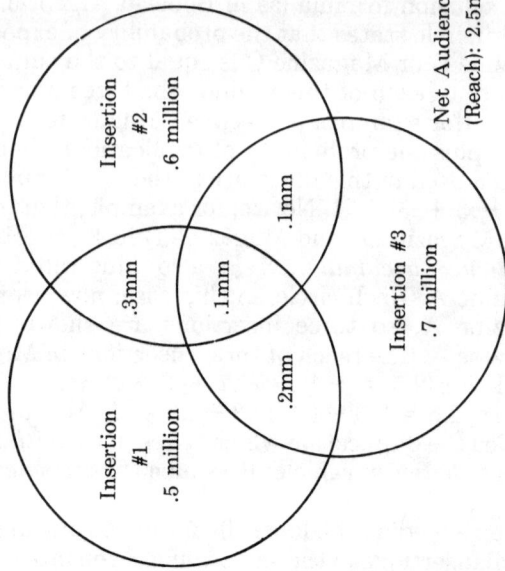

Insertion
#1
.5 million

Insertion
#2
.6 million

.3mm

.1mm

.1mm

.2mm

Insertion #3
.7 million

Net Audience
(Reach): 2.5m

(b) Audience Accumulation

The size of Kelso's target market is estimated as 35 million HH's. Media schedule #1 above will cost a total of $155,000 while schedule #2 will cost a total of $139,000.

By applying the percentages in the above distributions to the target market size, the household distributions can be examined:

Exposure #	Media #1	Media #2
0	.22 × 35 = 7.7m	.30 × 35 = 10.5m
1	.35 × 35 = 12.25	.25 × 35 = 8.75
2	.30 × 35 = 10.5	.20 × 35 = 7.0
3	.07 × 35 = 2.45	.25 × 35 = 8.75
4	.06 × 35 = 2.1	.00 × 35 = 0.0
Total	35.0m	35.0m.

Reach (unduplicated reach) can then be calculated for each schedule in a number of ways:

	Media #1	Media #2
Reach (%)	78% = 100% − 22%	70% = 100% − 30%
Reach (HH's)	.78 × 35 = 27.3mHH's (27.3=12.25+10.5+2.45+2.1)	.70 × 35 = 24.5mHH's (24.5=8.75+7.0+8.75+0).

In other words, reach is the sum of those individuals reached 1 time, 2 times, 3 times and 4 times or more; this is equivalent to subtracting the number not reached (or percentage) from the total number of people in the target market (or 100%).

GRP's (gross rating points) are calculated as follows as are gross reach or gross impressions (the non-percentage counterpart of GRP's):

	Media #1	Media #2
GRP's	140=(35×1)+(30×2)+(7×3)+(6×4)	140=(25×1)+(20×2)+(25×3)+(0×4)
Gross Reach	140% × 35 = 49m	140% × 35 = 49m.

GRP's and gross reach are measures, therefore, of the total percentage or number of exposures delivered by the media schedules; the term gross reach is sometimes called *duplicated reach* to indicate that the measure includes the same person or household counted more than once.

Average frequency is then calculated for each schedule:

	Media #1	Media #2
Average Frequency	140/78 = 1.8 (49m/27.3m = 1.8)	140/70 = 2.0 (49m/24.5m = 2.0).

Schedule # 1 would be expected to deliver an average of 1.8 exposures to the vehicles included in the schedule while schedule #2 would deliver an average of 2.0 exposures to the vehicles.

CPM/TM (cost per thousand to the target market) can be calculated as follows:

	Media #1	Media #2
CPM/TM	($155,000/27,300,000)×1000=$5.68	($139,000/24,500,000)×1000=$5.67.

In other words, it will cost \$5.68 for every one thousand target market members reached by schedule #1 while this cost will be \$5.67 for schedule #2, almost identical.

Finally, the effective reach and cost per thousand in terms of effective reach to the target market can be calculated. Suppose effective reach is defined in the manner used by the media department at the J. Walter Thompson advertising agency (as discussed in Chapter 13); this agency defines effective reach as the number of people in the target market reached between 3 and 10 times. In the current example, effective reach would be:

	Media #1	Media #2
ER(%)	13% = 7% + 6%	25% = 25% + 0%
ER(HH's)	4.55mm = 2.45 + 2.1	8.75mm = 8.75 + 0
CPM/TM/ER	(\$155,000/4.55mm)×1000=\$34.06	(\$139,000/8.75mm)×1000=\$15.88

Clearly, in terms of this particular definition of effective reach, schedule #2 is more cost efficient.

MESSAGE/MEDIA RESPONSE VALUES

As noted in Example 14-1 above, effective reach can be defined as the number of exposures a target market individual or household receives. It might also be defined in terms of criteria higher in level (as these levels of reach were defined in Chapter 13) of reach such as in the cognitive, conative, or affective dimensions. Measures of commercial or advertisement effectiveness for the message to be used in the media schedule might be copy researched on criteria such as advertising awareness, attitude change, or intentions-to-buy. This information could then serve to define the meaning of "effective reach" as it is used in the media process.

Only one criterion might serve in the definition of effective reach or some combination (multiple criteria) might serve in the definition. If multiple criteria are employed, however, it might be noted that the criteria would often be combined for decision making purposes using *subjective weights* which reflect the decision maker's attribution of importance of these criteria as indicators of commercial effectiveness. If subjective weighting is employed in the effective reach, it should be noted that an abstraction is then introduced into the reach values; the resulting reach figures should, accordingly, be used only in a relative sense to be compared from one media schedule to the next. An example of the calculation of Message/Media Response Values as an indicator of effective reach is given below.

Example 14-2. This example is a continuation of that begun in Example 14-1. Suppose that Kelso's brand manager believes only in testing commercials on the recall measure of the awareness criterion. The distribution of correct Day-after Recall (DAR) scores for two commercials being considered for possible use in the media schedules given in Example 14-1 are shown below:

Exposure #	Commercial A	Commercial B
0	0%	0%
1	7	8
2	15	25
3	20	20
4	24	20.

As can be seen from the above, each of the two commercials has been tested over four exposures (multiple exposure copy testing) to a representative sample drawn from the target market for Kelso detergent. The following will illustrate how the four Message/Media Response Values (MMR's) are calculated for the four possible combinations of two media schedules and two commercials. For example, in the case of Media #1 and Commercial A:

Exposure #	HH Distribution		DAR Distribution		Effective Reach
0	7.7mm	×	0.00	=	.00
1	12.25	×	.07	=	.86
2	10.50	×	.15	=	1.58
3	2.45	×	.20	=	.49
4+	2.10	×	.24	=	.50
				MMR Value	3.43.

The Message/Media Response value is the sum of the effective reach figures calculated for each level of exposure. It is, therefore, a measure indicating the expected number of households to result with correct day-after recall of Commercial A when carried in Media schedule #1. It would be expected that 3,430,000 HH's would be effectively reached using this particular combination of media and commercial. The MMR values for all four combination of schedules and commercials are given below:

Media #	Commercial	MMR Value	CPM/TM/ER (based upon MMR values)
1	A	3.43	$45.19=(155/3430)×1000
1	B	4.52	$34.29=(155/4520)×1000
2	A	3.41	$40.76=(139/3410)×1000
2	B	4.20	$33.10=(139/4200)×1000.

In terms of cost efficiency based upon the effective response defined in the MMR manner, the combination of schedule #2 and Commercial B is the best alternative. In terms of MMR values alone without regard to cost, Schedule #1 and Commercial B would be superior since that combination delivers the largest number of effectively reached households, 4,520,000 compared to only 4,200,000 for Media #1 and Commercial B.

Since the exposure distribution provides such basic and important information to the media planner, it is appropriate to examine the methods by which such distributions can be developed. The next section provides an overview and historical perspective on the development of exposure distribution models. The last section of this chapter will show by example how four of the more important methods are applied to actual problems in media.

OVERVIEW OF EXPOSURE ESTIMATION METHODS

There have been many methods developed over the years since Hyett first developed the application of the Beta distribution to the problem of exposure estimation in 1958.[6] It is not possible to discuss here all methods which have been developed and utilized over the past twenty-some years; at any rate, many of these methods are proprietary and nothing has been published in a public way regarding their nature. But several important, published methods will be examined to give some indication of the general nature of exposure estimation methods. These will be discussed by the following categories: (1) Ad hoc models; (2) Stochastic models; (3) Ad hoc/stochastic combination models; and (4) Simulation models. After this general discussion, the application of four useful and important methods of exposure estimation will be examined.

AD HOC MODELS

The methods which will be referred to here as "ad hoc" are those which have been developed with no particular rationale or "theory" purported to underlie the method. The primary criterion which the developers of ad hoc methods employ is estimation *accuracy;* that is, these people search for "formulas" which will accurately and reasonably reproduce actual, known reach estimates for media schedules as well as give reasonable extensions of reach for the schedules. The difficulty with such methods lies in the extent of their generalizability to "new" schedules which were not examined by the developer in the process of building the ad hoc formula. Because the method encompasses no overall theory of how the vehicle accumulation and duplication processes work, it may hold only for the peculiarities of the particular schedules analyzed by the developer or for schedules which are very similar to those schedules. It is difficult to specify the characteristics of media schedules ahead of time for which the method should perform well since the method is not tied explicitly to theoretical assumptions about the duplication and accumulation processes it attempts to represent. With this in mind as a limitation, methods which have, nonetheless, performed quite well in actual tests can be found among the ad hoc formula-type methods. Of the four methods to be discussed here, two (Hofmans' and Morgensztern's formulas) have performed quite well on schedules for which the actual reach and exposure distributions were known.

One of the earliest attempts (after Hyett mentioned above) to systematically estimate unduplicated reach was by Agostini,[7] a

Frenchman. In 1961, he developed the following empirical formula based upon his analysis of French magazine readership:

$$R = \frac{A}{1 + (KD)/A}$$

where: R = the net coverage (reach) of a set of m vehicles
A = the sum of the readership (audience) of each vehicle included in the set
D = the sum of the duplicated readership of all pairs of vehicles in the set
K = 1.125 (Agostini's Constant).

It can easily be seen from the above that the reach (R) of one insertion in Magazine A which has an audience, for example, of 200,000 households and one insertion in Magazine B which has an audience size of 300,000 households, where the duplicated audience between A and B is 50,000, would be calculated as 350,685 (350,685 = 400,000/{1 + 1.125(50,000)/400,000}).

Though the procedure suggested by Agostini produced some close estimates of reach, Claycamp and McClelland eventually demonstrated that Agostini's constant was, in fact, a variable dependent upon the average number of vehicles read per readers and the variation of this statistic over the population.[8] The development of exposure distributions is very importantly linked to this early work (from the above it can be seen that Agostini's formula only produces one number as a result, the total unduplicated reach for the schedule) on reach estimation. The two, reach estimation and exposure distribution estimation, are very closely linked. An exposure distribution will produce the frequencies of a certain proportion of the audience exposed no times, one time, two times, three times, and so forth. Reach can be calculated from this exposure distribution in two ways: (1) Reach can be calculated by subtracting the number of people in the zero-class or no-exposure frequency class from the total number of people in the target market (or the proportion or percentage in the no-exposure class from 100 percent); and (2) by summing up the number or proportion of people in each of the exposure classes other than the zero-class. These two figures are equivalent if the calculations have been conducted accurately.

Another ad hoc method was developed by Young to estimate the reach of radio audiences.[9] Young conducted regression analyses on data for several variables obtained on a sample of 86 radio schedules. For this sample size of 86, Young found a high relationship (R^2 of between .86 and .95, depending upon the demographic group analyzed) between the known reach (the dependent variable) of the 86 schedules and four independent or explanatory variables: GRP's of the schedule, number of radio stations used in the schedule, number of time periods used, and the number of spots per station. Using a modified exponential functional form, regression analysis yielded parameters of the function; this function could then be used to estimate reach for a new schedule (not one of the 86 sample schedules used to build the function) of radio spots. One of the models he developed, with its appropriate parameter values inserted was:

$$R = 85\{1 - (.659)e^{-.51X_1 - .07X_2 - .08X_3 + .04X_4}\}$$

where: R = proportion (percentage) reach of the schedule
   85 = saturation reach (maximum coverage of stations used in schedule)
   e = the natural number 2.718 . . .
   X_1 = GRP's of schedules
   X_2 = number of stations used in schedule
   X_3 = number of time periods used in schedule
   X_4 = number of spots per station.

For example, suppose a radio schedule calls for GRP's of 146, three stations, 1 time period (6-10 a.m.), and 24 spots per station. The reach for this schedule would be calculated as:

$$R = 85\{1 - (.659)(2.718)^{-.51(1.46) - .07(3) - .08(1) - .04(24)}$$

$$R = 33.8 \text{ percent.}$$

Unfortunately, with this model as with most other ad hoc methods, no information has been provided as to the accuracy of the reach projections for actual media schedules beyond the 86 initially used to build the model's parameters as given above. And, of course, since the model was built in 1972, the parameters given above would not hold, in any case, for today's situation. It should be noted also that this model was built specifically for radio schedules. Separate models would be needed for spot television, network television, network radio, magazines, newspapers, and so on. But this is also true of most exposure estimation models.

One of the documented ad hoc models is that developed by Hofmans, another Frenchman, in 1966.[10] This model has been tested quite extensively on magazine schedules and has performed overall quite well. Hofmans' formula can be viewed as a variation of Agostini's formula where Agostini's constant has been replaced by a variable K. In Hofmans' formula, K is a function and varies in relation to the individual audience sizes of the vehicles involved as well as the pair-wise duplications between all the vehicles in the schedule. In one large-scale test of Hofmans' formula, the formula produced an average error of 2.46 percent compared to 3.86 percent error of estimated versus actual reach of magazine schedules for Agostini's formula.[11] A virtue of Hofmans' method is its simplicity for the degree of accuracy provided in its use. Since the application of Hofmans' method is illustrated in Appendix A to this chapter, the explanation of the model will wait until that point.

Another variation of Agostini's method was developed by the Frenchman, Morgensztern in 1970 which takes into account both the duplication within and between vehicles as does the Hofmans Modified method to be applied later in this chapter. Morgensztern's model is, thus, a multi-vehicle, multi-insertion model as opposed to Agostini's formula which can only be used in the multi-vehicle situation where one insertion is used in each vehicle in the schedule. Since the formula for Morgensztern's model is very similar to Hofmans' formula, it will not be given here. It can be noted, however, that on a test of 57 magazine schedules for which the actual reach was tabulated by IMS (Interactive Market Systems, Inc. in New York), the Morgensztern model had an average percentage error in its reach projections of 2.82 percent.[12] This is compared with 2.80 percent error on the same 57 schedules for the Hofmans model. The additional complication introduced by Morgensztern does not appear worth the additional effort required over Hofmans' approach.

STOCHASTIC MODELS

Stochastic models differ from ad hoc approaches inasmuch as they require the explicit statement of hypotheses about the nature of duplication and accumulation processes underlying the development of schedule reach. Such hypotheses can, therefore, be tested and either accepted or disregarded for future work and application. Stochastic models also convey the view that exposure to a media schedule is a probabilistic process and not a deterministic one; that is, it is assumed that exposure is, in some measure, a chance process. Such methods are also to be desired over most ad hoc models because they produce *exposure distributions* from which reach may be calculated whereas the foregoing ad hoc models only produce the reach estimate itself. Exposure distributions, as was pointed out at the beginning of this chapter, provide helpful decision making information which can be masked when only reach and average frequency are employed in this process. Most stochastic methods are also based upon known mathematical probability distributions such as the binomial distribution, the hypergeometric distribution, and so forth. Use of known probability distributions has several advantages. First, a probability distribution is positive everywhere on its interval of definition so that logical errors such as negative reach figures are impossibilities; this sometimes occurs in ad hoc models such as Hofmans' and others. Second, the area under the probability curve of the distribution adds up to 100 percent and, therefore, illogical outcomes such as a reach greater than 100 percent are not possible; this phenomenon also occurs in some ad hoc procedures for certain types of schedules. And, finally, if a known probability distribution is utilized in the exposure estimation process, the way in which the "parameters" can be found is fairly well-known since mathematicians will have studied the distribution for a long time.

As indicated earlier, Hyett developed a procedure in 1958 for estimating the cumulative coverage (reach) of a schedule based upon the Beta distribution. This important development established the procedure used in contemporary stochastic models. In most cases, the procedure for estimating the distribution of exposures begins with the assumption that the pattern of exposure distribution follows one or more well-known theoretical probability distributions. Once the parameters of the theoretical distribution have been estimated from actual data using one of several methods (some of these are the method of moments, maximum likelihood methods, and least squares estimators), the complete estimated exposure distribution is generated by the theoretical distribution.

Another procedure developed in Britain for the purpose of estimating reach, as opposed to the full distribution, is the Sainsbury technique.[13] The Sainsbury method assumes that exposure is a Bernoulli process (that is, that it follows a binomial distribution). The method can be stated as follows:

$$R_m = 1 - (1 - p_1)(1 - p_2)(1 - p_3) \ldots (1 - p_m)$$

where: R_m = reach of "m" vehicles in a schedule with one insertion in each vehicle
p_i = the audience of vehicle "i" expressed as a percentage of the target market size.

For example, suppose three vehicles have audiences of 24 percent, 30 percent, and 20 percent. Using the Sainsbury model, reach would be 57.4 percent ($.574 = 1 - \{(1-.24)(1-.30)(1-.20)\}$). In a test of the Sainsbury model on nine schedules of five magazines each and nine schedules of 11 magazines each, the average percentage error was 18.32 percent and 24.58 percent, respectively.

The Sainsbury method was modified for the case in which duplication data were available between pairs of vehicles in the schedule. In this case, the formula becomes:

$$R_m = 1 - \{(qd_1)(qd_2)(qd_3) \ldots (qd_m)\}$$

where: q_i = $(1 - p_i)$ or the "noncoverage of vehicle i"
dq_i = q_{ij}/q_j or the "adjusted noncoverage" of vehicle i by vehicle j where vehicle j is the vehicle in the schedule with the largest audience size.

For example, suppose the three vehicles used above to illustrate the Sainsbury "normal" method are in a schedule and the net coverage (unduplicated pair-wise audience) of vehicle 1 with vehicle 2 is 40 percent, vehicle 1 with vehicle 3 is 30 percent, and vehicle 2 with vehicle 3 is 45 percent. This information is summarized below:

	Coverage	Noncoverage
Vehicle 1	24%	76%
Vehicle 2	30	70
Vehicle 3	20	80
Vehicles 1 & 2	40	60
Vehicles 1 & 3	30	70
Vehicles 2 & 3	45	55.

Since Vehicle 2 has the largest audience (30%), it will be used to adjust the coverages of the other vehicles. Then:

$$qd_1 = q_{12}/q_2 = .60/.7 = .86$$
$$qd_2 = q_{22}/q_2 = q_2 = .7$$
$$qd_3 = q_{23}/q_2 = .55/.7 = .78 \text{ and}$$
$$R_3 = 1 - \{(.86)(.70)(.78)\} = 53\%.$$

Notice that by inclusion of the information on pair-wise vehicle duplication (the net audiences), the reach estimate was reduced from the 57.5 percent in the preceding example to the 53 percent figure above. In a test of the Sainsbury Modified method on the same schedules of five and 11 magazines reported above, the percentage error was reduced from the 18.32 percent figure to 6.2 percent for the five-magazine schedules and from 24.58 percent to 12.69 percent for the 11-magazine schedules. Thus, the Sainsbury Modified formula is superior to the Sainsbury "normal" method.

In 1964, Richard Metheringham, media director at Foote Cone & Belding advertising agency in Britain, reported his method of exposure distribution estimation which incorporated both the Beta distribution used by Hyett and the Binomial distribution which serves as the basis for the Sainsbury method.[14] It is based on the compound Beta Binomial Distribution, though Metheringham himself described the method as an empirical formula (ad hoc) and thus free of any assumptions inherent in any theoretical probability distribution. The Beta distribution is used to estimate the probabilities that an individual is exposed to any one, any two, any three and up to any number of vehicles included in the schedule. These probabilities are then used in the Binomial distribution to estimate the distribution of exposures, that is, the proportion of the target audience that is exposed to one and only one insertion, two and only two insertions, and so on. The method is attractive since the only data required for the exposure distribution estimate are: (1) the average vehicle audience (vehicle coverage); (2) the two-insertion cumulative audience of each vehicle; and (3) the pair-wise duplicated audience or net audience for each combination of two vehicles. In a test of the method on the 57 IMS media schedules for magazines indicated earlier, the average percentage error of estimated versus actual schedule reach for the Metheringham method was 5.2 percent.[15] This is quite excellent when compared with many other methods.

The final stochastic model to be examined in this overview is that developed by Kwerel in 1969.[16] Kwerel's model is detailed and applied in Appendix A to this chapter so that it will not be discussed in detail at this point. It might be noted, however, that the reach estimates of the Kwerel model were tested on schedules of three, four, and five magazines; the percentage error in the reach estimates for these schedules were 1 percent, 3.3 percent, and 6.8 percent, respectively. When Hofmans' formula was utilized on the same schedules, the reach errors were 2 percent, 4.2 percent, and 6.0 percent, respectively.[17] In general, it has been found that Hofmans' formula performs better on large schedules (those including a large number of vehicles) while

Kwerel's method performs better on small schedules (those with four or fewer vehicles involved).

AD HOC/STOCHASTIC COMBINATION METHODS

The most recent work in the area of exposure distribution estimation shows again that the Beta Binomial Distribution (BBD) is an appropriate basis upon which to model the exposure distribution problem. Headen, Klompmaker, and Teel developed in 1976 an interesting combination procedure for use of the BBD as a model for the problem. The method is really a combination of the approaches utilized by Young and those utilized by Metheringham described earlier in this chapter.[18] There are three parameters which must be estimated in order to use the BBD. One of these parameters can be considered as the numer of insertions in the schedule. The remaining two must be estimated from the first two "moments" of the distribution: the mean and variance. The mean of this distribution can be represented by Gross Rating Points for television schedules. However, the variance is unknown and must be estimated. In this procedure, the variance is estimated as a function of four independent variables: number of insertions in the schedule, number of vehicles used in the schedule, number of vehicles available, and the average audience of the schedule's vehicles. Regression analysis on a sample of schedules is used to estimate the variance. Once this is accomplished, the parameters of the BBD can be calculated through simultaneous solution of the "moment equations" which represent the two parameters as a function of the mean and variance of the distribution. The developers have presented evidence that this procedure works quite well for both network television and spot television media schedules.

SIMULATION MODELS

The general approach regarding the simulation of reach through exposure distributions has been examined in the preceding chapter with regard to the comprehensive media model called Mini-Compass and utilized by the Leo Burnett advertising agency. Several other simulation approaches have been developed over the years. Greene's personal probability assignment method, which is a combination of simulation and probability distribution methods, has been examined closely for performance and is apparently quite acceptable.[19] The performance of most other simulation methods, such as CAM in Britain, the SCAL model in France, and the model developed by the Simulmatics Corporation in the United States has not been well documented publicly.[20] It is interesting to note the SCAL model was supplanted by the Morgensztern model discussed previously in this chapter by a number of large French advertising agencies; this has taken place because of the methodological weakness inherent in the simulation approach. Simulation of exposure distributions is not the most computationally efficient means of reach estimation to include in a comprehensive media planning and selection model, because in the optimization process the computer must sometimes examine as many as 20,000 simulated individuals' exposure probabilities. In "formula" models, such as the ad hoc and stochastic methods discussed above, relatively fewer calculations must be made than in the simulation approach. When a comprehensive model must examine 30 or 40 different media schedules to find the best one, the number of calculations to arrive at the schedule reach in each case can become overwhelming and very time consuming even with the fastest computers. Of all the simulation approaches, the approach of Greene mentioned above is probably most desirable because of its reported accuracy and because it combines the simulation approach with the stochastic approach.

APPENDIX A

SOME ESTIMATION METHODS IN APPLICATION

Four methods of estimating reach will be examined in this Appendix through the use of examples: (1) Hofmans' Model; (2) Kwerel's Model; (3) Metheringham Method (Beta Binomial Distribution); and (4) Multivariate Polya-Eggenberger Distribution (Dirichlet Multinomial Distribution). The latter two produce the complete exposure distribution. While an extension of Kwerel's basic method will produce an exposure distribution, it will not be examined or illustrated here.

The data which will serve as the basis for all computations in the examples in this section are provided below:

Vehicle #	Vehicle Name	Single Insertion Audience (A_i)
1	Better Homes & Gardens	17.44%
2	Family Circle	11.14
3	Ladies' Home Journal	12.76

Two-Insertion Cumulative (R_i)	Duplicated Audience (A_{ij})	Net Audience (N_{ij})
23.21%	1-2: 4.70%	1-2: 23.88%
15.57	1-3: 5.05	1-3: 25.15
17.34	2-3: 3.64	2-3: 20.26.

Hofmans' and Kwerel's Multi-Vehicle, Single-Insertion models will be used to estimate the reach of a schedule consisting of one insertion in each of the three magazines above for a total of three insertions in the schedule. Hofmans' and Kwerel's Multi-Vehicle, Multi-Insertion models as well as the Beta Binomial and Dirichlet Multinomial models will be used to estimate the reach of a schedule consisting of two insertions in each of the three magazines for a total of six insertions in the schedule. In addition, the complete exposure distribution will be calculated for the latter schedule using the BBD and DMD methods.

Hofmans' Multi-Vehicle, Single-Insertion Model (Example 14–3)

In each of the examples in this section, the basic formulas for the models will be given first; then the application of the formula will be shown in a numbered, step-by-step sequence. Hofmans' basic formula is given by:

$$R_m = \frac{(\Sigma A_i)^2}{\Sigma A_i + KD}$$

where: $KD = \Sigma\Sigma K_{ij}A_{ij}$: Total Between-Vehicle Duplication

$K_{ij} = (A_i + A_j) / (A_i + A_j - A_{ij})$: Variable form of Agostini's Constant.

Step 1: Calculate KD (Total Duplication).

	(A_i+A_j)	$A_{ij}/$	$(A_i+A_j-A_{ij})$	$= K_{ij}A_{ij}$
Vehicles 1-2:	(.1744+.1114).047/(.1744+.1114−.0470)			= .0562
Vehicles 1-3:	(.1744+.1276).0505/(.1744+.1276−.0505)			= .0606
Vehicles 2-3:	(.1114+.1276).0364/(.1114+.1276−.0364)			= .0429
			KD	= .1597

Step 2: Calculate R_3 (Reach of One Insertion in Three Vehicles).

$$R_3 = (A_1 + A_2 + A_3)^2/(A_1 + A_2 + A_3 + KD)$$
$$R_3 = (.1744+.1114+.1276)^2/(.1744+.1114+.1276+.1597)$$
$$R_3 = .2982$$

The reach of one insertion in three vehicles is, therefore, according to Hofmans' Method, 29.82 percent.

Hofmans' Multi-Vehicle, Multi-Insertion Model (Example 14–4)

Here it will be assumed that the multi-insertion schedule consists of *two* insertions in each of the three magazines indicated above for a total of six insertions in the schedule.

$$R_{mn} = \frac{(\Sigma n_i A_i)^2}{\Sigma n_i A_i + KD + \Sigma kd}$$

where: R_{mn} = reach of m vehicles with n insertions in each vehicle

$KD = \Sigma\Sigma n_i n_j K_{ij}A_{ij}$ where $K_{ij}A_{ij}$ is as in Example 14–3

$$\Sigma kd = \frac{\Sigma n_i(n_i - 1)^a}{2} (k_i d_i)$$

$$a = \log\left[\frac{R_n(nR_1 - R_n)}{R_2(2R_1 - R_2)}\right] \Big/ \log(n-1)$$

Fortunately, for two insertions maximum in any given vehicle, Σkd reduces to $\Sigma k_i d_i$ where:

$$k_i = 2R_1/R_2$$
$$d = 2R_1 - R_2$$
$$R_i = \text{coverage of ``i'' insertions in a given vehicle.}$$

Step 1: Calculate Sum of Audiences for Insertions.

$$\Sigma n_i A_i = n_1 A_1 + n_2 A_2 + n_3 A_3$$
$$= 2(.1744) + 2(.1114) + 2(.1276)$$
$$\Sigma n_i A_i = .8268$$

Step 2: Calculate Sum of Duplication Between Vehicles.

$$KD = \Sigma\Sigma n_i n_j K_{ij} A_{ij}$$

$$n_i n_j(A_i + A_j) \quad A_{ij}/ \ (A_i + A_j - A_{ij}) \qquad\qquad = n_i n_j K_{ij} A_{ij}$$

Vehicles 1-2: $2(2)(.1744+.1114).0470/(.1744+.1114-.0470) = .2248$
Vehicles 1-3: $2(2)(.1744+.1276).0505/(.1744+.1276-.0505) = .2424$
Vehicles 2-3: $2(2)(.1114+.1276).0364/(.1114+.1276-.0364) = \underline{.1716}$
$$KD = .6388$$

Step 3: Calculate Duplication Within Vehicles.

$$d_i = 2R_1 - R_2$$
$$k_i = 2R_1/R_2$$
$$d_i \quad \times \quad k_i \quad = k_i d_i$$
$$(2R_1 - R_2) \times (2R_1/R_2) = k_i d_i$$

Vehicle 1: $\{2(.1744) - .2321\} \times \{2(.1744)/.2321\} = .1754$
Vehicle 2: $\{2(.1114) - .1557\} \times \{2(.1114)/.1557\} = .0960$
Vehicle 3: $\{2(.1276) - .1734\} \times \{2(.1276)/.1734\} = \underline{.1204}$
$$\Sigma k_i d_i = .3918$$

Step 4: Calculate the Reach of the Schedule.

$$R_3 = \frac{(\Sigma n_i A_i)^2}{\Sigma n_i A_i + KD + \Sigma kd}$$

$$R_3 = \frac{.8268^2}{.8268 + .6388 + .3918}$$

$$R_3 = .3680.$$

The reach of the six-insertion schedule is 36.8 percent using Hofmans' model.

Kwerel's Multi-Vehicle, Single-Insertion Model (Example 14–5)

$$R_m = 2(UB)(LB)/(UB + LB)$$

where: R_m = reach of m vehicles with one insertion each

UB = upper bound on the reach figure = $A - \dfrac{2}{m}$ (D)

LB = lower bound on the reach figure = $(h+1)\overline{A} - \dfrac{h(h+1)}{2}$ $(\overline{D})$

h = minimum number from (m−1) and K where K is the largest integer (whole number) contained in the quantity $\overline{A}/\overline{D}$

$\overline{D}$ = $\dfrac{2D}{m(m-1)}$: average pair-wise duplication

$\overline{A}$ = A/m: average of vehicle audiences

A = sum of audiences = ΣA_i

D = sum of duplications ΣA_{ij}

Step 1: Calculate Average Audience and Average Duplication.

A = .1744 + .1114 + .1276
A = .4134

$\overline{A}$ = .4134/3
$\overline{A}$ = .1378

D = .0470 + .0505 + .0364
D = .1339

$\overline{D}$ = 2(.1339)/3(3−1)
$\overline{D}$ = .0446

Step 2: Calculate Upper and Lower Bounds on Reach.

UB = .4134 − (2/3).1339
UB = .3241

LB = (2+1).1378 − $\dfrac{2(2+1)}{2}$ (.0446)

LB = .2796

The minimum for use in the calculation of the lower bond above is found as

h = min(m−1,K)   where K = .1378/.0446 = 3.08
h = min(3−1,3)
h = min(2,3)
h = 2.

Step 3: Calculate the Reach for the Schedule.

R_3 = 2(.3241)(.2796)/(.3241+.2796)
R_3 = .3002.

The reach of one insertion in each of the three magazines is 30.02 percent using the Kwerel approach.

Kwerel's Multi-Vehicle, Multi-Insertion Model (Example 14–6)[21]

$A = \Sigma n_i A_i$: sum of the audiences for the insertions

$\overline{A} = A/N$: average audience where N is the total number of insertions (N=6)

$\Sigma d_i = \Sigma \binom{n_i}{2}(2R_1 - R_2)$: duplication within vehicles

> where: $\binom{n_i}{2}$ stands for the number of *combinations* of n_i things taken 2 at a time. In general, the number of combinations of n things taken r at a time is given by
>
> $$C_r^n = \binom{n}{r} = \frac{n!}{r!(n-r)!}$$
>
> where n! is read "n factorial" and is equal to:
>
> $$n! = n(n-1)(n-2)(n-3)\ldots 1.$$
>
> For example, $3! = 3(2)(1) = 6$. And $\binom{3}{2}$ is $\dfrac{3!}{2!(1!)}$, for
>
> example, and becomes: $\dfrac{3(2)(1)}{2(1)(1)} = 3$. Zero factorial (0!) is
>
> defined to equal 1 (0! = 1).

$\Sigma d_{ij} = \Sigma n_i n_j A_{ij}$: duplication between vehicles in the schedule

$D = \Sigma d_i + \Sigma d_{ij}$: total duplication (between + within)

$\overline{D}/\binom{N}{2}$: average duplication

UB, LB, h, K, and R_m are as in Example 14–5.

Step 1: Calculate Average Audience.

$A = n_1 A_1 + n_2 A_2 + n_3 A_3$

$A = 2(.1744) + 2(.1114) + 2(.1276)$

$A = .8268$

$\overline{A} = .8268/6$

$\overline{A} = .1378$

Step 2: Calculate Within-Vehicle Duplication.

$\Sigma d_i = \binom{2}{2}\{2(.1744)-.2321\} + \binom{2}{2}\{2(.1114)-.1557\} + \binom{2}{2}\{2(.1276)-.1734)\}$

$\Sigma d_i = .2656$

Step 3: Calculate Between-Vehicle Duplication.

$\Sigma d_{ij} = 2(2).0479 + 2(2).0505 + 2(2).0364$

$\Sigma d_{ij} = .5356$

Step 4: Calculate Total and Average Duplication.

$D = .2656 + .5356$

$D = .8012$

$\overline{D} = .8012/\binom{6}{2}$

$\bar{D}$ = .8012/15

$\bar{D}$ = .0534

Step 5: Calculate Upper and Lower Bounds on Reach.

UB = $.8268 - \dfrac{2}{6}(.8012)$

UB = .5597

LB = $(2+1).1378 - \dfrac{2(2+1)}{2}(.0534)$

LB = .2532

h = $\min(N-1,K)$

h = $\min(6-1,2)$ $K = \bar{A}/\bar{D} = .1378/.0534$

h = 2 K = 2.58

Largest integer contained in K is 2.

Step 6: Calculate the Reach for the Schedule.

R_3 = $2(.5597).2532/(.5597+.2532)$

R_3 = .3487 or 34.87%.

The reach of the six-insertion schedule utilizing the extended Kwerel model is 34.87 percent.

Metheringham Method (Beta Binominal Distribution) (Example 14-7)

The method developed by Metheringham in 1964 is equivalent, as indicated earlier in this chapter, to the application of the Beta Binominal distribution. The calculation approach adopted by Metheringham is considerably more complex than that which is actually required to generate the exposure distribution based upon the BBD. Though the approach shown here is different than that utilized by Metheringham, it can be shown that it produces identical results to his calculation approach; it is adopted here because of its relative simplicity.

$\bar{R}_1 = \Sigma n_i A_i / \Sigma n_i$: average reach of one insertion in each of the vehicles in the schedule

$\bar{R}_2 = \dfrac{(\Sigma(\binom{n_i}{2}) R_{2i}) + (\Sigma\Sigma n_i n_j R_{ij})}{\binom{N}{2}}$: average reach of two insertions in each vehicle

where: m = number of vehicles in schedule

n_i = number of insertions in vehicle i

N = total number of insertions in schedule

R_{2i} = accumulation of vehicle i over two insertions

R_{ij} = net audience of vehicles i and j

A_i = audience of vehicle i.

$a = \dfrac{\bar{R}_1(\bar{R}_2 - \bar{R}_1)}{2\bar{R}_1 - \bar{R}_2 - (\bar{R}_1)^2}$: parameter α of BBD (exposure parameter)

$$b = \frac{a(1 - \overline{R}_1)}{\overline{R}_1} : \text{parameter } \beta \text{ of BBD (non-exposure parameter)}$$

The exposure distribution (BBD) is then generated using the following expansion:

$$P(x: a,b,N) = \binom{N}{x}\left[\frac{a(a+1)(a+2)\ldots(a+x-1)(b)(b+1)(b+2)\ldots(b+N-x-1)}{(a+b)(a+b+1)(a+b+2)\ldots(a+b+N-1)}\right]$$

where: a, b are the BBD parameters
N = number of insertions in the schedule
x = exposure number.

Step 1: Calculate Average Reach of One and Two Insertions.

$\overline{R}_1 = \{2(.1744) + 2(.1114) + 2(.1276)\}/6$

$\overline{R}_1 = .1378$

$\overline{R}_2 = \{\binom{2}{2}.2321 + \binom{2}{2}.1557 + \binom{2}{2}.1734 + (2)(2).2388 + (2)(2).2515 +$

$(2)(2).2026\} / \binom{6}{2}$

$\overline{R}_2 = .2222$

Step 2: Calculate a and b parameters of BBD.

$$a = \frac{.1378(.2222 - .1378)}{s(.1378) - .2222 - .1378^2}$$

$a = .3380$

$$b = \frac{.338(1 - .1378)}{.1378}$$

$b = 2.1148$

$(a+b) = 2.4528$

Step 3: Calculate the Exposure Distribution by Expanding BBD.

Exposure #

0: $.6099 = \binom{6}{0}\dfrac{2.1148(3.1148)(4.1148)(5.1148)(6.1148)(7.1148)}{2.4528(3.4528)(4.4528)(5.4528)(6.4528)(7.4528)} = \text{denominator}$

1: $.1738 = \binom{6}{1}.3380(2.1148)(3.1148)(4.1148)(5.1148)(6.1148) /d$ $d = 9889.0367$

2: $.0951 = \binom{6}{2}.338(1.338)(2.1148)(3.1148)(4.1148)(5.1148) /d$

3: $.0580 = \binom{6}{3}.338(1.338)(2.338)(2.1148)(3.1148)(4.1148) /d$

4: $.0353 = \binom{6}{4}.338(1.338)(2.338)(3.338)(2.1148)(3.1148) /d$

5: $.0196 = \binom{6}{5}.338(1.338)(2.338)(3.338)(4.338)(2.1148) /d$

6: $.0083 = \binom{6}{6}.338(1.338)(2.338)(3.338)(4.338)(5.338) /d$

Total: 1.0000.

Notice that the sum of the proportions for all six exposures must add up to 100 percent of the target market. The zero-class (exposure # 0) above is calculated as .6099; therefore, the reach as figured using the BBD method would be 39.01 percent (1 − .6099 = .3901). The above exposure distribution shows that 17.38 percent of the target market would be exposed one time, 9.51

percent would be exposed two times, 5.8 percent would be exposed three times, and so forth to this schedule consisting of a total of six insertions (two insertions in each of three vehicles). Notice that summing exposure classes 1 through 6 also produces the identical reach figure of 39.01 percent (.3901 = .1738 + .0951 + .058 + .0353 + .0196 + .0083).

Performance of Hofmans, Kwerel, and BBD Models. Use of the Hofmans model produced a reach estimate above of 36.80 percent for the six-insertion schedule, the Kwerel model produced a reach figure of 34.87 percent, and the BBD method yielded a figure of 39.01 percent. Clearly, the method used will have an effect on the reach figure obtained; here the difference at most is 4.14 percent between the methods, but this can become quite large. There are some general ideas about when each method performs best but no hard and fast rules can be stated since not a great deal of evidence is available on the alternative performance of the methods on schedules.

In general, it is known that Hofmans' method performs least well when there is a great deal of overall duplication in the schedule (both within- and between-vehicles; in this situation, the KD term in Hofmans' formula is considerably larger than the sum of the audience, A.

Kwerel's method performs least well when the upper and lower bounds are far apart; this makes intuitive sense since the farther apart these two figures are the "rougher" will be the estimate. Experience is required in working with particular vehicles and schedules in order to "know" what "far apart" might mean in a particular situation since this is a relative idea.

The Metheringham method (BBD) is known to produce a phenomenon called "declining reach" when large and extremely small audience vehicles are mixed in the same schedule. This is an illogical and impossible outcome in reality. For example, a schedule consisting of two insertions in Vehicle A (audience size of 13.5%) and two insertions in Vehicle B (audience size of .8%) where A's two-insertion cumulative audience is 24.8%, B's cumulative audience is 1.33%, and the net audience between A and B is 13.98% produces a BBD reach figure of 41.34%. However, when the four Vehicle B insertions are removed from the schedule and the BBD reach is re-estimated, the reach increases to 42.38%. This, of course, is illogical and a physical impossibility. Reach cannot decline or become smaller when insertions are added to a schedule; even if duplication of the additional insertions with those already in the schedule was 100%, the reach would remain the same and not decline. The BBD method is also known to generally overestimate the true size of the schedule reach; in the above examples, it can be noticed that the BBD reach is larger than either Hofmans or Kwerel reach.

Dirichlet Multinominal Distribution (Example 14–8)

One of the most recently developed approaches based upon a probability distribution utilizes the compound Dirichlet multinomial distribution (DMD).[22] This distribution is a member of the family of distributions called Multivariate Polya-Eggenberger Distributions. This method overcomes the problem of declining reach often observed in conjunction with the Metheringham application of the BBD. As will be seen in the first step below of the application of this method, some ad hoc method must be used first to calculate the reach of one insertion in each of the vehicles. In this illustration, Hofmans' formula is used, but some other approach such as Kwerel's model, for example, could just as well be used in the first step. This method is also the multivariate form of the beta binomial distribution (BBD) so that it will be seen in step 4 below that the method used in Example 14–7 to fit the BBD parameters "a" and "b" in steps 2 and 3 in that example are used in the DMD method here.

It might be noted that although the Metheringham method has been shown to produce acceptably accurate reach estimates (although it usually over-estimates reach), the BBD distribution upon which the method is based is not capable of reproducing multiple peaks or modes of an exposure distribution. The BBD is at most a bi-modal distribution (two peaks) whereas the DMD can exhibit many peaks in the exposure distribution. This will be observed when the distribution generated below using the DMD is compared with that in Example 14–7 which used the same data as those used below.

Step 1: Application of Hofmans' Multi-Vehicle, Single Insertion Formula. This formula was already used on the data for which the DMD will be used (two insertions in each of the three magazines indicated at the beginning of this appendix); the results of that application can be seen in Example 14–3. In Example 14–3, the reach of one insertion in each of the three vehicles was calculated to be .2982 or 29.82 percent.

Step 2: Use of the Inclusion/Exclusion Principle to Find Sum of nth Order Duplications.

S_n = sum of nth order duplications

R_i = reach of one insertion in each of "i" vehicles

R_3 = $S_1 - S_2 + S_3$ which is equal to:

   S_3 = $R_3 - S_1 + S_2$

   where: R_3 = .2982 from Step 1 above

   S_1 = sum of single-insertion audiences (ΣA_i)

   S_1 = .1744 + .1114 + .1276

   S_1 = .4134

   S_2 = sum of duplications (ΣA_{ij})

   S_2 = .047 + .0505 + .0364

   S_2 = .1339

S_3 = .2982 − .4134 + .1339

S_3 = .0187

Step 3: Use Waring's Theorem to Find Exclusive Exposure Probabilities. It should be noted that, when the proportion of a vehicle's audience to the target market is viewed as a probability of exposure to that vehicle by a member of the target market, this probability is not an *exclusive* exposure probability. Exclusive probabilities must sum to unity (100 percent) for all the vehicles involved in a media schedule. Suppose four vehicles are considered for inclusion in a media schedule, and these vehicles have percentage audiences of .34, .29, .45, and .30. Clearly, in this case the sum of the individual audience percentages (exposure probabilities) exceeds 1.00 (.34 + .29 + .45 + .30 = 1.38); this is so because some of the individuals or households included in the 34 percent audience of the first vehicle also are exposed to one or more of the other three vehicles to be included in the media schedule. Thus, such exposure probabilities are not representative of an individual's *exclusive* exposure only to a particular vehicle. In this step, audience proportions are converted to exclusive exposure probabilities.

p_i = exclusive exposure probability for exposure to "i" number of insertions in the schedule assuming *one* insertion in each vehicle.

$p_0 = 1 - S_1 + S_2 - S_3$: $1 - .4134 + .1339 - .087$ = $.7018$

$p_1 = S_1 - 2S_2 + 3S_3$: $.4134 - 2(.1339) + 3(.0187)$ = $.2017$

$p_2 = S_2 - 3S_3$: $.1339 - 3(.0187)$ = $.0778$

$p_3 = S_3$: $.0187$ = $.0187$

Total 1.0000

The exclusive probability of exposure of a member of the target market to *none* (p_0) of the three vehicles in the schedule if only one insertion were put in each of the three vehicles is calculated above to be .7018. The exclusive probability of exposure to *any one* (p_1) is .2017, the exclusive exposure probability for exposure to *any two* insertions (p_2) is .0778, and the exclusive probability of exposure to *all three* (p_3) is .0187. It should be noticed that these are exclusive exposure probabilities since they sum to 1.00.

Step 4: Estimate BBD Parameters for Each Vehicle Separately.

a_i = parameter a for vehicle number "i"

b_i = parameter b for vehicle number "i"

$$a_i = \frac{R_1(R_2 - R_1)}{2R_1 - R_1^2 - R_2}$$

where: R_1 = reach of one insertion in vehicle i

R_2 = reach of two insertions in vehicle i

$$b_i = \frac{a_i(1 - R_1)}{R_1}$$

$$a_1 = \frac{.1744(.2321 - .1744)}{2(.1744) - (.1744)^2 - .2321} = .1166$$

$$b_1 = \frac{.1166(1 - .1744)}{.1744} = .5521$$

$(a_1 + b_1) = (.1166 + .5521) = .6687$

In a similar manner: $a_2 = .0902$ $a_3 = .0892$

$b_2 = .7198$ $b_3 = .6098$

$(a_2 + b_2) = .8100$ $(a_3 + b_3) = .6990$

Step 5: Estimate Dirichlet Multinominal Parameter s.

s = weighted average of $(a_i + b_i)$ from Step 4 above where the weights are the vehicle single-insertion audiences (s is the average of the BBD parameters)

$$s = \frac{.1744(.6687) + .1114(.8100) + .1276(.6990)}{(.1744 + .1114 + .1276)}$$

$s = .7161$

Step 6: Estimate the Exposure Parameters for the DMD.

A_0 = the non-exposure parameter of the DMD

A_1 through A_3 = the exposure parameters of DMD for exposure to one through three exposures, respectively

$A_0 = p_0(s)$: .7018(.7161) = .5026

$A_1 = p_1(s)$: .2017(.7161) = .1444

$A_2 = p_2(s)$: .0778(.7161) = .0557

$A_3 = p_3(s)$: .0187(.7161) = .0134

Total .7161 = s

Step 7: Generate Exposure Distribution Using Dirichlet Parameters. This final step involves viewing a schedule of six insertions such as that for which the calculations are being undertaken here as a two-week schedule in which one insertion is placed in each of the three vehicles included in the schedule in each of the two weeks. Individuals who received the maximum number of exposures to the schedule, six in this case, would then have had to be exposed to all three vehicles on two different occasions, that is, in the two different weeks of the schedule. Since there are many different combinations of exposure to such a two-week schedule, these must be enumerated for inclusion of the calculations for the exposure distribution. This enumeration also serves as the guide as to which DMD parameters are to be used in the calculation for a particular exposure level and how many times (as in the BBD application in Example 14-7, Step 3) the particular exposure and non-exposure parameters should be used. For example, for the case of zero exposures to the schedule, this would mean two non-exposures (one non-exposure to the week-one schedule and one non-exposure to the week-two schedule) so that the non-exposure parameter (A_0) would be used twice in the calculations.

The DMD is generated using the expansion and enumeration process shown in Table 14-1. When the various ways in which two exposures to the schedule can take place as well as the ways in which three and four exposures can take place are summed for their exposure probabilities (for example, the exposure probabilities calculated in Table 14-1 for two exposures were .1345 and .0456; when these are summed the probability of exposure to two of the six insertions in the schedule is obtained as .1801), the final exposure distribution is obtained as:

Exposure #	Proportion of TM
0	.6145
1	.1181
2	.1801
3	.0241
4	.0509
5	.0012
6	.0110
Total	1.0000

The reach of the schedule of two insertions in each of the three magazines is calculated by the DMD method as 38.55 percent (1 − .6145). This compares to the reach calculated by the Metheringham method of 39.01 percent, by the Hofmans method of 36.80 percent, and by the Kwerel method of 34.87 percent. It can also be noted that the above DMD distribution is of two peaks, one at the zero-class or no-exposure level and one at the two-exposure level (61.45%

Table 14-1 Enumeration and Expansion of DMD

$$p(x_i) = \frac{n!}{(k_0!)(k_1!)(k_2!)(k_3!)} \{A_i(A_i+1)/s(s+1)\}$$

where: A_i = appropriate DMD parameter from Step 6

n = maximum number of insertions in any one vehicle

Number of Exposures	k_i(Parameter #) and Exposure Pattern for two-week Schedule				$\dfrac{n!}{(k_0!)(k_1!)(k_2!)(k_3!)}$ $\dfrac{2!}{2!(0!)(0!)(0!)}$	$\times A_i(A_i+1)/s(s+1)$	= Exposure Probability
	0	1	2	3			
none	2	0	0	0	2	$\times$ (.5026)(.5026)/.7121(1.7121) =	.6145
one	1	1	0	0	2	$\times$ (.5026)(.1444)/1.2289 =	.1181
two	0	2	0	0	1	$\times$ (.1444)(1.1444)/1.2289 =	.1345
two	1	0	1	0	2	$\times$ (.5026)(.0557)/1.2289 =	.0456
three	1	0	0	1	2	$\times$ (.5026)(.0134)/1.2289 =	.0110
three	0	1	1	0	2	$\times$ (.1444)(.0557)/1.2289 =	.0131
four	0	0	2	0	1	$\times$ (.0557)(1.0557)/1.2289 =	.0478
four	0	1	0	1	2	$\times$ (.1444)(.0134)/1.2289 =	.0031
five	0	0	1	1	2	$\times$ (.0557)(.0134)/1.2289 =	.0012
six	0	0	0	2	1	$\times$ (.0134)(1.0134)/1.2289 =	.0110
						Total	1.0000

and 18.01%, respectively). An examination of the Metheringham distribution in Example 14-7 shows only one peak at the zero-class level. It is known that the DMD is superior to the BBD approach in reproducing the peaks of the exposure distribution. In a test of the DMD on the 57 IMS media schedules referred to earlier in this chapter, the error of the DMD was 2.14 percent on the average as compared to 5.20 percent for the Metheringham BBD method.[23]

QUESTIONS AND PROBLEMS

1. In what ways might information obtained from an exposure distribution be more helpful to decision makers in advertising than simply reach estimates? Give an illustration of an actual situation for a brand where this would be the case.

2. Do you agree with Krugman's theory that "three exposures are enough?" Why or why not?

3. Why is estimation of reach basic and central to all effective advertising management which is based upon information acquisition? Why is this piece of information any more important than any other bit of advertising information?

4. Develop an example using actual figures of the manner in which the Message/Media Response value concept would be applied where more than one copy research criterion was measured and this information was available for the creative material which was to be run in the schedule.

5. In what way is gross audience or gross impressions a useful analytical tool in the development of media schedules? If unduplicated reach is known, would an advertising manager have any reason to examine gross reach (that is, duplicated reach)?

6. What is the value of keeping the reach figure upon which CPM estimates are calculated as a concrete "people" figure rather than an abstract figure based upon various weightings in a subjective manner by the media planner? Is there any point in having absolute rather than relative figures in media planning?

7. What are the relative strengths of ad hoc models versus distribution models in the estimation of reach in media?

8. How does the media planner determine which method of estimating reach the media department will use on an on-going basis? What criteria might be helpful to keep in mind when making this selection? Why are your criteria important?

ENDNOTES

1. Herbert E. Krugman, "Procedures Underlying Response to Advertising," *American Psychologist* (April 1968).

2. See, for example, Robert C. Grass and Wallace H. Wallace, "Satiation Effects of TV Commercials," *Journal of Advertising Research* (September 1969), pp. 3-8, Herbert E. Krugman, "What Makes Advertising Effective," *Harvard Business Review* (March-April 1975), p. 103, and Michael L. Ray and Alan G. Sawyer, "Repetition in Media Models: A Laboratory Technique," *Journal of Marketing Research* (February 1971), pp. 20-29.

3. Herbert E. Krugman, "Why Three Exposures May Be Enough," *Journal of Advertising Research* (December 1972), pp. 11-14.

4. *Ibid.*

5. Some of these factors, as they impact on the relationship between frequency of exposure to advertising and intermediate criteria, have been systematically explored by Ray and Sawyer, *op. cit.*

6. G.P. Hyett, Paper read to the Statistics Seminar, London School of Economics, February 1958.

7. J.M. Agostini, "How to Estimate Unduplicated Audiences," *Journal of Advertising Research* (March 1961), pp. 11-14.

8. H.J. Claycamp and C.W. McClelland, "Estimating Reach and the Magic of K," *Journal of Advertising Research* (June 1968), pp. 44-51.

9. L.F. Young, "Estimating Radio Reach," *Journal of Advertising Research* (October 1972), pp. 37-41.

10. P. Hofmans, "Measuring the Cumulative Net Coverage of Any Combination of Media," *Journal of Marketing Research* (August 1966), pp. 269-278.

11. J. L. Chandon, *A Comparative Study of Media Exposure Models,* doctoral dissertation (Northwestern University, Evanston, Illinois, 1976), p. 337.

12. *Ibid.*, pp. 534 and 541.

13. J.M. Caffyn and M. Sagovsky, "Net Audiences of British Newspapers: A Comparison of the Agostini and Sainsbury Methods," *Journal of Advertising Research* (March 1963), pp. 21-25.

14. R. Metheringham, "Measuring the Net Cumulative Coverage of a Print Campaign," *Journal of Advertising Research* (December 1964), pp. 23-28.

15. Chandon, *op. cit.*, p. 491.

16. S.M. Kwerel, "Estimating Unduplicated Audience and Exposure Distribution," *Journal of Advertising Research* (June 1969), pp. 46-53.

17. Chandon, *op. cit.*, pp. 374-375.

18. R.S. Headen, J.E. Klompmaker, and J.E. Teel, Jr., "TV Audience Exposure," *Journal of Advertising Research* (December 1976), pp. 49-52.

19. J.D. Greene, "Personal Media Probabilities," *Journal of Advertising Research* (October 1970), pp. 12-18.

20. S.R. Broadbent, "Beyond Cost per Thousand: An Examination of Media Weights," *The Thomson Medals and Awards for Advertising Research,* 1968, pp. 105-140, Simulmatic Corporation, *Simulmatic Media Mix,* 1. General Description, 2 Technical Description, New York, October 1962, and M. Marc, "Combining Simulation and Panel Data to obtain Reach and Frequency," *Journal of Advertising Research*, (June 1968), pp. 11-16.

21. This extension of Kwerel's method has been suggested and developed by Ms. Shizue Kishi, doctoral student, Department of Advertising, University of Illinois at Urbana-Champaign, 1980.

22. This model was originally suggested by Chandon, *op. cit.*

23. *Ibid.*, p. 491 and p. 520.

CASES IN MEDIA STRATEGY DECISIONS

- The Charleston Manufacturing Company
- Tartan Distillers, Inc.
- The Casper Chocolate Company
- Coastal Fisheries, Inc. (B)
- Oron Paper Company (C)

CASES IN MEDIA STRATEGY DECISIONS

Case 15-1—The Charlestown Manufacturing Company[1]

COMPANY BACKGROUND

The Charlestown Manufacturing Company, located in the Midwest, is a medium-sized company with annual sales in the vicinity of $16 to $17 million. The company manufactures and markets through retail outlets a full line of sewing accessories, threads, bindings, embroideries, and patterns for women's and children's clothing.

The success of the Charlestown Company was a post-World War II phenomenon with a heavy reliance on aggressive advertising and promotion. During the war, Mrs. Charles Fredericks, a middle-aged widow, operated a small notions store in her hometown while her only son, Robert, served in the Army. In 1944 Fredericks was discharged with severe injuries sustained in combat. While recuperating from his wounds, he helped his mother in the operation of the store. Robert Fredericks soon recognized the potential in this business but also saw that the real opportunity lay in manufacturing rather than in retailing. He realized that the limited civilian production of clothing, and particularly the absence of style merchandise, had created a vacuum which could be filled by home-produced clothing. Most of the capital for the expansion of the business came from Fredericks' accumulated army pay, separation allowance, and disability payments. In the beginning, company products were distributed through the family retail store and by personal selling on a house-to-house basis.

The venture proved successful, and the company prospered to the point where retail distribution was expanded to other cities. Fredericks began an intensive advertising program with the principal media used being radio and newspapers. As television became more prominent during the postwar period, the company employed this medium with considerable success. Viewers were shown how they could make the attractive clothing demonstrated on television at little cost through the purchase of Charlestown's patterns and supplies.

The company contracted with other manufacturing firms at first for its production and, as sales expanded, finally instituted its own manufacturing operations. At this point, Charlestown abandoned its retail operations in order to concentrate complete efforts on the production and distribution of its full line of home sewing accessories. Distribution was achieved throughout the country through wholesalers to retail variety and notion stores. Television remained the almost exclusive advertising medium used by the company. Despite the fact that the fashion colors could not be shown over television, the tremendous impact of the medium made it an extremely effective selling device. It was particularly well suited to demonstration by professional models illustrating the ease with which the attractive clothing could be made at home.

PROMOTION PROBLEMS

The Charlestown line was expanded until it included about 150 items. During any one year, however, the company was unable to promote the entire line satisfactorily. Not more than a dozen or so leading items could be advertised on television because of the limited budget, the need for national coverage, and the relatively high expense of television use. While the advertised items were demanded by retailer and consumer alike, it was found that the balance of the line tended to be forgotten and, of particular importance, the majority of retailers were reluctant to stock even a representative supply of the company's standard or non-advertised items. Since these standard items did not possess the unique or exclusive characteristics of the advertised items and were often duplicated by the company's competitors at lower prices, the company encountered increasing difficulty in maintaining adequate retail distribution on the bulk of its line. These standard items were quite important since they not only contributed importantly to the company's sales volume but were also quite profitable.

As a result of these problems, the company requested its advertising agency to devise a plan by which this large segment of the line could be advertised effectively. The request indicated that a token budget of $320,000 would be allocated for this purpose as compared to a budget of $1,360,000 which was used to promote the leading or exclusive items in the line.

AGENCY RECOMMENDATIONS

In formulating its program, the agency presented the following as the strategic objectives which should guide the advertising efforts placed behind the standard items:

1. Promote the fact that Charlestown was a producer of a wide variety of sewing accessories for the consumer.
2. Convey to retailers the fact that Charlestown also promoted the standard items and induce the retailer to feature this merchandise.

In light of these objectives, the agency recommended that Charlestown view the problem of advertising the standard items as being one of combined advertising and retail promotion rather than consumer advertising alone. In the opinion of agency representatives, the leverage of funds devoted to merchandising and promotion efforts, when small budgets are used to do a national job, was greater than if those funds had been allocated to consumer advertising alone. Accordingly, it was decided that it was necessary to use a hard-hitting campaign which related the advertising directly to the promotion of the merchandise at the point of sale in order to obtain the necessary retail distribution and displays.

Since the budget was limited and the available funds had to be used to promote a wide variety of products, it was recommended that magazines instead of television be used as the principal medium. To support and implement this recommendation, the agency designed a unique service booklet called the Charlestown Home Sewer's Guide. The booklet contained useful information for the housewife on all phases of home sewing and was designed to serve as a permanent manual. In the booklet interspersed with the information were ads promoting individual items in the company's standard line. The agency recommended that this guide be used as an insert in national magazines.

In order to further coordinate the advertising with the retailer, it was suggested that the guide should contain a contest and that additional copies of the guide should be made available to the retailer free of charge for distribution to his customers. It was further suggested that in order to coordinate the promotion of the standard items with the leading television-advertised items, part of the telecommercials should be used to promote the guide in order to direct the viewer to her notion retailer for a free copy of the guide. If this were done, the company should have a coordinated campaign between all items in the line. Most important, it was believed that by tying in the availability of the guide with the retail store, effective distribution and display of the standard items could be obtained in conjunction with the free distribution of the guide.

MEDIA STRATEGY

The media strategy for the magazine campaign in which the guide would be used was based upon reaching young mothers approximately 18-34 years of age. It was believed that they were the best prospects for home sewing supplies. To accomplish the desired objectives, the agency submitted three alternative media plans for Charlestown's consideration.

Each of these plans attempts to accomplish the stated objectives via the use of different methods of media implementation. Their difference resides in the extent to which merchandising and promotion concentration is employed, as contrasted to extensive advertising coverage.

PLAN I

This plan is based upon the use of an extensive number of magazines to achieve broad scale coverage and circulation. The schedule includes six monthly magazines and one mass weekly. Exhibit 15-1 outlines the recommended schedule, which is based upon the use of black and white pages as the space unit. This schedule will give Charlestown opportunity for the following:

1. To deliver mass circulation and readership within a concentrated 10-week period. These publications have a gross circulation of 48,433,000 and 134,568,000 gross readers.
2. To present the trade with a schedule which consists of a large number of mass books.
3. To present the copy story in a dominant black-and-white, two-page spread.
4. To utilize magazines which enjoy relatively long life in the reader's home plus the mass audience weekly TV Guide.

PLAN II

This plan is based upon the use of a 4 page insert (4 pages in four colors) in *Cosmopolitan* which would represent the previously described Charlestown Home Sewer's Guide, plus a black and white page in *Redbook* and *Parents*. The details are given in Exhibit 15-1.

The basic difference between this plan and Plan I is the use of the Sewer's Guide as a substitute for the allocation of funds to a wider variety of publications. The centrality of importance of the Sewer's Guide as a merchandising device has been covered in detail. However, this plan does not concentrate all of the available funds for the purchase of two supporting publications.

PLAN III

This plan is based upon the concentration of available funds for the purchase of Sewer's Guide inserts in two publications; *Cosmopolitan* and *Redbook*. Cost details are given in Exhibit 15-1.

Exhibit 15-1 Cost, Audience, and Efficiency Analysis, Print Plan

Publication	Circulation (000)	Space Unit	Cost Dollars	Readers Per Copy Total	Men	Women	Total (000)	Men (000)	Women (000)	Women (18-34) Readers %	(000)	Cost Per Thousand Circulation	Total Readers
PLAN I													
Better Homes & Gardens	8,007	1-pg. B/W	47,945	3.1	0.8	2.3	24,743	6,577	18,166	41.6	7,551	5.99	1.93
Redbook	4,451	1-pg. B/W	27,435	2.9	0.5	2.4	12,819	2,050	10,769	50.2	5,402	6.16	2.14
Parents	1,441	1-pg. B/W	14,780	3.0	0.5	2.5	4,375	758	3,617	67.6	2,444	10.26	3.38
Good Housekeeping	5,178	1-pg. B/W	36,045	4.0	0.7	3.3	20,636	3,678	16,959	41.0	6,957	6.96	1.75
Woman's Day	7,536	1-pg. B/W	46,395	2.5	0.2	2.3	18,693	1,635	17,058	40.8	6,963	6.16	2.48
T.V. Guide	19,043	1-pg. B/W	58,800	2.3	1.0	1.3	43,804	19,664	24,140	49.9	12,034	3.09	1.34
Cosmopolitan	2,777	1-pg. B/W	16,585	3.4	0.8	2.6	9,498	2,168	7,330	67.3	4,935	5.97	1.75
Total	48,433		247,985				134,568	36,530	98,038		46,286	5.12	1.84
PLAN II													
Cosmopolitan	2,777	4-4 C	147,839	3.4	0.8	2.6	9,498	2,168	7,330	67.3	4,935	53.24	15.57
Parents	1,441	1-pg. B/W	14,780	3.0	0.5	2.5	4,375	758	3,617	67.6	2,444	10.26	3.38
Redbook	4,451	1-pg. B/W	27,435	2.9	0.5	2.4	12,819	2,050	10,769	50.2	5,402	6.16	2.14
Total	8,669		190,054				26,692	4,976	21,716		12,781	21.92	7.12
PLAN III													
Cosmopolitan	2,777	4-4 C	147,839	3.4	0.8	2.6	9,498	2,168	7,330	67.3	4,935	53.24	15.57
Redbook	4,451	4-B/W	109,740	2.9	0.5	2.4	12,819	2,050	10,769	50.2	5,402	12.33	4.28
Total	7,228		202,709				22,317	4,218	18,099		10,337	28.04	9.08

MAGAZINE DETAILS

Better Homes & Garden. It is an A.B.C. audited monthly publication with an average per issue circulation of 8,007,000. It delivers close to 25 million readers per issue. It also delivers almost 7,551,000 women readers between the ages of 18-34 years.

Redbook. *Redbook* has become one of the most important publications servicing the young married population. It has shown steady circulation increases.

Redbook is an A.B.C. audited monthly publication with a circulation of 4,451,000 per issue and a total readership of almost 13 million—approximately 84 percent women. Of its 10,769,000 women readers, almost 5.5 million are between the ages of 18-34 years.

Parents. *Parents Magazine* is considered to be the authoritative publication in the field of child-rearing. In addition to its exceptionally well-read editorial matter, advertisements in this publication normally achieve better than average "noting" scores, according to recent studies.

While the circulation of this publication is somewhat less than 1.5 million, it is a direct target audience with over 2.4 million women readers between the ages of 18-34. In addition to delivering the much desired audience of lower-age adults, *Parents* is a highly merchandisable publication because of its Commendation Seal of Approval.

Good Housekeeping. *Good Housekeeping*'s vast variety of different editorial categories gives it a vitality enjoyed by few other magazines. A *Good Housekeeping* reader can expect to find helpful articles on almost any subject from fashion and beauty to home care.

This publication's Seal of Approval, which has come to stand for quality in the eyes of both consumers and retailers, has proved itself to be a powerful tool for many merchandising-minded advertisers.

Good Housekeeping has a total circulation of 5.1 million and delivers almost 20 million readers monthly. It reaches over 6.9 million women between the ages of 18-34.

Cosmopolitan. By the very nature of its editorial content, *Cosmopolitan* appeals to a younger adult audience. It not only covers vital human behavior problems, but emphasizes other important factors in the young married home, child care, beauty and grooming, fashions, and home decorations. Because of its superior editorial format, it far outsells its competitors in both circulation and advertising. *Cosmopolitan* delivers a total circulation of 2,770 and almost 9.5 million total readers; 67 percent of its 7.3 million female readers are between 18 and 34 years old.

Woman's Day. *Woman's Day* is a monthly publication distributed through supermarkets. It enjoys a monthly circulation of 7.5 million and delivers 18.5 million readers per issue. Editorially, it concerns itself with articles of interest to the housewife. These articles range from cooking and fashion to beauty and child care.

TV Guide. *TV Guide* is the largest circulated weekly publication in the world. With a total circulation of 19,043,000 per week, *TV Guide* delivers over 43,804,000 readers.

Editorially, *TV Guide* devotes itself solely to the television industry—its problems and leading personalities. The publication is really divided into two sections—national features and local program listings. The listings contain the week's programming—Saturday through Friday. This is not to say, however, that the feature section is not also well read. While it is true that most of *TV Guide*'s readers use the publication to help them become more selective TV viewers, it was believed that almost all *TV Guide* readers read through the national feature section.

QUESTIONS FOR DISCUSSION

1. Offer your evaluation of the effectiveness of the agency's plan in achieving the desired objective.
2. Using the Metheringham method described in the Appendix to Chapter 14, calculate the reach and average frequency for each of the three media plans given in this case.
3. Which of the three media plans should Charlestown use if it is decided to adopt the agency's recommendations? Justify your decision.

ENDNOTE

[1] Company name is disguised.

Case 15-2—Tartan Distillers, Inc.

Tartan Scotch is imported from Scotland by Horowitz Brothers and Kramer, one of the country's leading distributors of distilled products. As part of their franchise agreement with the distillers of Tartan Scotch, H.B. & K. assumed all marketing and advertising activities for the brand within this country. The brand was among the top three in its category. It had national distribution, and was backed by an advertising budget of approximately $5.5 million in 1979. Because of legal restrictions on the usage of radio and television for liquor, roughly 75 percent of the media budget was used for the purchase of magazine space, 19 percent for newspaper space, and the balance on outdoor.

MEDIA POLICY REVIEW

About this time Tartan's advertising agency instituted a review of their media allocation policy. The principal objective of the media revision was to determine whether the expenditure of more funds in magazine at the expense of newspapers would be beneficial to promotion of sales.

The media schedule for Tartan called for publication of newspaper advertisements on a once-a-week basis. *Fortune,* a monthly, and *Time* and *The New Yorker,* both weeklies, were considered as the chief vehicles. There was some concern as to whether or not magazines could provide the breadth and depth of coverage which newspapers had supplied, as well as the required flexibility which was necessary to provide heavy advertising weight in those areas which were responsible for proportionately heavier Scotch consumption.

USE OF READERSHIP STUDIES IN ANALYSIS

For the purpose of comparing magazines and newspapers, the advertising agency used *Fortune, Time,* and *The New Yorker* since it was their opinion that these three leading magazines with their editorial appeal would be appropriate magazines for Tartan Scotch.

On the basis of data available, it was found that each issue of *Fortune* reached 2.5 households, *Time* reached 4.8, and *The New Yorker* 6.4 households (pass-along readership). Thus, every ten copies of each of these magazines reached 25, 48, and 64 homes before being discarded. It was also found that each issue of these three magazines had a combined circulation of 25.482 million, which entered 48.5 million unduplicated households. This was equivalent to one out of every two households in the country.

In addition to the mass population coverage provided by the magazines, it was found that they also reached a high percentage of those families who represented the best purchasers of wines and liquors.

GEOGRAPHICAL CONSUMPTION PATTERN
FOR SCOTCH

The consumption of Scotch is not the same throughout the country. On a per capita basis, the consumption in the East is considerably higher than in other areas. The Tartan sales pattern, though not completely comparable to that of total Scotch consumption, followed the industry pattern closely. One of the principal factors which required careful analysis by the agency was the ability of the three magazines to give adequate coverage to the more important Scotch consumption areas.

Since magazine circulation generally follows the pattern of population residence, some company representatives believed that concentration of the advertising schedule in magazines might take away too much weight from the good Scotch areas and place it in more poor areas. Therefore, the problem was one of getting the desired reach and frequency by manipulating the combination of buys. Exhibit 15–2 will give an idea of the geographical distribution of families and of Scotch consumption.

Exhibit 15-2   Regional Distribution of Families & Scotch Consumption

	Families (percent)	Scotch Consumption (percent)
New England	4	7
Mid Atlantic	21	31
E. Central	13	10
W. Central	16	13
S. East	18	13
S. West	10	8
Pacific	16	16

SOURCE: Target Group Index, 1978.

COMPARISON OF MEDIA

It was believed that the lower relative circulation of the magazines in the more important Scotch consumption areas could be compensated for in a number of ways. It was suspected that further analysis would indicate that the cost-per-thousand male ad-noters delivered by magazines was significantly lower than that delivered by newspapers. This is critical since circulation alone can hardly be taken as a measure of advertising performance without consideration of the extent to which the particular ad is seen. If a dollar spent in magazines could be shown to be more productive in terms of reaching people than a dollar spent in newspapers, then it was possible that a lesser amount of magazine-advertising dollars spent in the lower circulation areas would provide as many ad-noters as a higher budgeted newspaper campaign.

In order to analyze the relationship between magazines and newspaper ad-noters on a cost equivalency basis, it was necessary to select a unit of advertising measurement for comparison. For this reason it was decided to use a 1,000-line, black-and-white newspaper advertisement and a full-page, four-color magazine advertisement. Physically, both are approximately equal in size. The magazine advertisement dominates the page, while the newspaper advertisement covers only about 40 percent of the total space on the page. Furthermore, the use of fine color reproduction gives the magazine advertisement a definite edge.

To determine the relative cost efficiencies of the magazines versus newspapers, the three magazines were compared to the 300 largest circulation newspapers. Since Tartan was advertised in over 300 newspapers annually, the comparison was in order. The total circulation for the three magazines was 25.5 million versus 64.8 million copies for the 300 newspapers. Total circulation figures were multiplied by 2.1 in the case of magazines and 1.1 in the case of newspapers to obtain the total number of male readers. This gives a male readership of 53.6 million for magazines and 71.3 million for newspapers.

It was also found out that the average four color, full-page magazine advertisement for liquor products achieved a 24 percent reader-noting compared to 19 percent for the average 1,000 line newspaper liquor advertisement. When these percentages are applied to the total male readers, an "ad-noters" figure of 12.9 million for magazines compared to 13.6 million for newspapers is obtained. These figures were then divided by the space costs in each of the media to find out which was less expensive on the basis of cost per thousand male ad-noters.

Based on the findings, the agency prepared two media schedules. One was $4.4 million only for newspapers and the other combined newspapers and magazines with $4.13 million for magazines and $270,000 for newspapers. The newspaper coverage in the second schedule was merely to bolster total coverage in the high consumption Eastern Area. By this method, the combination was able to deliver a bonus audience in every one of the country's major regional divisions. On the basis of this analysis the agency recommended that advertising for Tartan Scotch should be concentrated on magazines rather than in newspapers.

When this material was presented to executives of Horowitz Brothers and Kramer, they accepted the superiority of magazines for advertising their product. They were, however, reluctant to accept the agency's recommendations for a number of reasons. They pointed out that retailers and wholesale distributors are key factors in the sale of a bottle of Scotch. These men can literally make or break sales of a brand of liquor, and, traditionally, they have preferred newspaper advertising because of its "local impact." The importance of satisfying the demands of this group was high in the minds of the men who marketed Tartan. Furthermore, it was their opinion that newspapers provided a sense of "immediacy," as a result of their news content, and this immediacy tended to rub off on the advertising.

QUESTIONS FOR DISCUSSION

1. Do you think Horowitz Brothers and Kramer were right in their assumption of the immediacy effect?
2. Should H.B. & K. accept the agency's recommendations to use the three magazines instead of newspapers as their major advertising media?

Case 15-3—The Casper Chocolate Company

The president of The Casper Chocolate Company of Brooklyn, New York, Mr. Art Morgan, was concerned with the determination of advertising strategy and with building a media plan to facilitate its execution. The advertising appropriation for the company was set at $660,000 using the percentage of sales method. Mr. Morgan was keenly aware of the limitations which he faced with this budget as compared to the multi-million-dollar expenditures of other advertisers.

Many small advertisers in similar circumstances recognize the limitations of their funds and their inability to cover properly the entire population with their advertising. As one means of coping with this situation, some advertisers adopt a course of market segmentation. This approach recognizes that a large heterogeneous market, characterized by divergent demand, may be classified into a number of smaller consumer groups on the basis of some mutual factors such as age, sex, income, religion, etc. These smaller population groups may have sufficient homogeneity to make profitable their cultivation on an individualized basis. These groups may respond differently to different product characteristics such as color, taste, smell, or texture; they may respond differently to different advertising appeals, and it may be possible to reach them by different advertising media.

COMPANY BACKGROUND

The Casper Chocolate Company manufactures a line of packaged candies, foremost of which is the "Casper'" line. Casper is a confection made of chocolate candy liberally mixed with raisins, cashews, and Brazil nuts. The product's name describes its unique shape. While much chocolate candy is made in a conventional bar size, Casper is cubelike in shape and almost the size of the ice cube made by the ordinary home refrigerator. The distinctive size appeals to many people as it permits them to take a very liberal bite and taste fully the chocolate flavor. This can be done more effectively, the company maintains, than with a thin bar of chocolate. Casper is available in 25 cents, 50 cents, six pack, party bar, and many other size variations. The 25-cent bar, however, is the company's leading seller.

The Casper Company was incorporated in 1968 when Mr. Jeff Jaffe, the principal stockholder, purchased at auction the plant and equipment of a bankrupt concern. Mr. Jaffe, at the time, had had previous experience as an executive in the candy industry. Company sales grew steadily and by 1978 were in the vicinity of $10 million.

PRODUCT DISTRIBUTION

Casper products are sold widely throughout the country but not on a completely national scale. Distribution is somewhat spotty in some areas. Sales volume, except for the summer months, is relatively steady throughout the year. During the summer months, however, the warm weather melts chocolate and serves as a deterrent to sales.

The product is distributed through wholesalers and jobbers in the confectionary and grocery trades as well as through chain stores. At retail, Casper is sold in candy, grocery, cigar, and variety stores, in fact, over any counter where gum and candy bars are normally available.

One of the trade papers in the industry estimated that total candy sales were distributed among the various types of outlets as follows:

Type of Outlets	Percentage of Total Candy Sales
Independent food stores	21
Drugstores	16
Food chains, supermarkets	15
Cigar, stationery stores	10
Theaters, amusement	9
Vending machines	5
Department, variety stores	3
Military units	3
Restaurants	3
Service Stations	1
All other	14

Casper sales followed this pattern. The best geographical markets for Casper are in the area east of the Rocky Mountains.

DETERMINATION OF ADVERTISING STRATEGY

Mr. Jaffe and his advertising agency recognized the value of the segmentation concept and the advertising advantage of making an adequate impact upon any geographical market or market segment which he reached. It was his belief that it was more advantageous to reach one prospect with ten advertising messages than ten prospects with one message each. The advertising agency concurred in this philosophy, since experience has shown that adequate repetition of a selling message is required until a consumer is motivated to action.

The company sought to capitalize on the shape of their product in their promotion as well as its taste and quality. Casper had pioneered the acceptance of the new chocolate bar shape among consumers and had made this shape peculiarly its own. The Casper bar was one of the first candy bars to be wrapped in foil. This served to help identify the brand in the consumer's mind very closely with silver foil wrapping. The company sought to make the cube shape of the product an important asset in strategy in two ways:

1. By highlighting the shape in all advertising to induce immediate shelf recognition of the product.
2. By attributing taste advantages to the shape—i.e., "thick chocolate tastes better."

After careful consideration of all the facets of the problem, it was determined that the objectives and desired effects could be achieved in one of three ways:

1. Limitation of the markets which received advertising.
2. Market segmentation, i.e., the concentration of advertising upon one segment of the population, such as teen-agers. This would permit Casper to achieve the required advertising frequency among this selected population group. This type of approach is predicated upon the thesis that more extra volume can be obtained via the concentration of advertising effort on the small

group than through the dilution of effort among the larger group.

3. A third means of achieving the desired objective is some combination of the first two.

Assuming that the decision were made to appeal to a limited or segmented group, a medium best capable of reaching this group was required. Thus, Casper was faced with a threefold problem:

1. Audience: Should the company try to reach a limited audience only? If so, which audience would be the most satisfactory?

2. Media: What media should the company use to reach the desired audience?

3. Markets: How many and which markets should the company try to advertise in?

AUDIENCE DEFINITION

Complete data on candy consumption are not available since the company has not sponsored any research on this subject. It was the opinion of company management, however, that almost everyone eats candy, that there is no sharp line separating or distinguishing consumer groups for this product. Through published sources the company was able to obtain some consumption data to bolster their opinions and beliefs. This information was secured through a consumer panel by one of the industry's suppliers and indicated the following:

1. Sales volume of chocolate and candy bars is skewed toward the larger communities.

2. Income groups earning less than $10,000 annually are "poor" consumers of candy, while those earning $25,000 and above eat more candy than the average consumers.

3. In the purchase of chocolates and candy bars the female purchaser is about four times as important as the male.

This information plus the desire to expand the potential for Casper Candy were telling arguments in favor of advertising to a broad market. In addition, this approach provided a great deal of flexibility in selection of media, enabling the company to purchase those media capable of conveying the desired selling message at the most efficient cost without consideration to the necessity of reaching a highly selective audience. On the other hand, this approach did not fit in well with the advertising philosophy of Casper management. Advertising to everybody severely limits the frequency of contact per person reached and dissipates coverage over several audience segments so that no group is covered well. This makes the interest level of the product relatively low in all audience segments.

If the company were to advertise to a selected segment of the market, this would permit significant coverage of the market selected. It would permit greater frequency of message delivery, a minimization of waste circulation and the opportunity to tailor copy to the specific market segment.

In the event that a selective approach were adopted, it was believed that age and sex would be the most realistic alternatives for market segmentation. Advertising to women was considered advantageous since they were the purchasing agents for the family, particularly for the children who consume a great deal of candy. In addition, from an advertising media standpoint, women are not difficult to reach. They also represent the prime shopper in supermarkets, a form of outlet that accounts for over one-third of candy sales of the Casper type and one which is constantly growing in importance. In spite of the relatively large purchases made by women, it was believed that there is a smaller percentage of heavy candy consumers among women than among other market segments because of their weight consciousness.

Another population group worthy of consideration was the teenage group. This segment of the market was growing in numbers. Per capita consumption of this group was believed to be relatively high. This group was also easy to reach as specialized print and broadcast media were available to each the teen-agers. On the negative side for this group, limited experience on another brand of candy had not proved successful when a teen-age appeal was used. While media are available, the choices are quite narrow and, in particular, local television availabilities are limited.

A third alternative was children between 5 and 12. This group not only purchases and consumes candy for themselves, but they also exert an influence on family consumption patterns. Strong selective local media are available to reach them. They represent a significant portion of the total population, and candy is an important and high interest category to them. If they are sold at this age, it is logical to assume that they will carry their candy preferences with them when they grow up. This group is, of course, barraged by commercials from other candy manufacturers, and good media availabilities are subject to intense competitive buying pressure. The purchasing power of this group is limited, and they may not be discriminating enough to appreciate Casper's quality. They may prefer a greater quantity of a cheaper candy product.

MEDIA

The most desirable media available to reach these limited market groups are as follows:

Women	Teens	5-12
Sectional issues of women's magazines	Comic books	Sunday comics
Daytime radio serials	Disc jockeys	Daily newspaper comic pages
Daytime TV	Late afternoon TV of dance-music variety	TV spots in children's programs
a. Spots		
b. Syndicated films		Sponsorship of syndicated children's programs

Each of these media offers advantages and disadvantages and, thus, calls for analysis and evaluation. For example, sectional issues of women's magazines are generally relatively expensive. They cannot be purchased on a market-by-market basis which was of importance to Casper. The various comic sections are good in reaching children and have the further advantage that they may be studied, clipped, or saved. This could be particularly important if a premium offer is to be made. In addition, very few—if any—candy manufacturers were using any form of comics at this time for their advertising. This would give Casper a high degree of exclusiveness in the medium.

On the negative side, comics of all forms were considered to be a relatively inefficient medium from a cost standard. In addition, they were an unproved medium for candy advertising. Their advertising value was suspect, since they were not a major medium for any product class.

Television had many virtues to offer Casper. This medium has a history of success with respect to its ability to motivate women and children to purchase products. Sight, sound, motion, and demonstration give the medium the maximum opportunity for expression. If syndicated shows are to be used, then the prestige factor of program identification can be achieved. With spot television, more frequent message delivery to the selected market segment could be achieved because of the lower cost. With spots the least risk would have to be assumed in terms of contractual commitments.

There are, of course, disadvantages also for television. The medium was virtually saturated with advertising for competitive candies and other items for children. Casper's principal selling season began after the termination of the summer and the end of the heat problem which hampered chocolate sales. It is during this very period that television time directed to children is at a premium because of the pre-holiday toy advertising campaigns. The cost factor is also an important consideration. If syndicated shows are purchased, the Casper budget probably would permit not more than one show a week. This would severely limit the advertising frequency which was considered such an important factor. Use of spot television also lacked program identification, an important impact element. This is, however, freely available to reach any segment of the alternative audience whether they are women, children, or teen-agers.

MARKETS

From a geographical point of view, Casper markets can be divided into three groups as follows:

Basic Markets. These are the markets with sales above $100,000 per year. They are Casper's best markets, accounting for more than 75 percent of the company's volume. There are seventeen such basic markets.

Growth Markets. This group of twelve markets accounts for 4 percent of Casper's volume. Although they are new markets, having been opened recently, they have shown a market response to the investment of advertising funds.

Non-Response Markets. There are markets which, over a number of years, have shown no significant sales progress. The five markets in this group, which account for 8 percent of total Casper sales, have historically high advertising to sales ratios. These specific markets are listed in Exhibit 15-3.

Exhibit 15-3

BASIC MARKETS

Chicago	New Orleans
New York	Dallas
Philadelphia	Minneapolis-St. Paul
Miami	Norfolk
St. Louis	Madison
Champaign	Atlanta
Cincinnati	Kansas City
Altoona	Columbus
Providence	

GROWTH MARKETS

Baltimore	Boston
Cleveland	Detroit
Pittsburgh	Schenectady
Wilkes-Barre	Grand Rapids
Green Bay	Syracuse
Seattle	Indianapolis

NON-RESPONSE MARKETS

New Haven	Portland
Youngstown	Washington, D.C.
Buffalo	

QUESTIONS FOR DISCUSSION

1. Develop an overall advertising strategy for Casper.
2. Construct media objectives for Casper.
3. Develop a complete media plan for Casper based upon these media objectives and advertising strategy.
4. Offer your recommendations as to: Audience, Media, and Markets. How do you support these recommendations with specific back-up evidence?

Case 15-4—Coastal Fisheries, Inc. (B)

THE MARKET FOR CANNED CAT FOOD

As noted in Coastal Fisheries Case (A), Coastal Fisheries were introducing to the market a new canned cat food under the brand "Hep

Cat." One of their major problems concerned the selection of advertising media.

As indicated in Case (A), the market for canned cat food has shown a consistent expansion during the Post-World War II period. From 1976-79 total industry sales had shown a growth rate of 9 percent per year. In 1979 sales at the retailers' level were estimated to amount to $560 million.

On a nationwide basis, about one out of every eight families owns a cat. While this tends to make for a lucrative national market, management of Coastal Fisheries recognized that there are substantial variations in cat ownership by areas. These differences were studied carefully by Coastal management and the advertising agency in preparing media recomendations. Families in rural areas, for example, despite being the smaller part of the overall population of the country, still comprise the majority of the cat owners in the nation. It was also found out that cat ownership alone was not an adequate index of consumer purchases of cat foods. On the farms, where around 50 percent of the cat population is found, the rate of purchase of canned cat food is very low. Such factors made it difficult to select appropriate media and media vehicles.

In order to devise a suitable media strategy it was necessary for the Coastal management to utilize market data on dog and cat ownership.

THE MARKETING PROGRAM

The board of directors of Coastal gave authorization to the marketing department to proceed with the marketing of Hep Cat in an important and aggressive manner. It was decided to enter the market on a staggered regional basis. During the first year the product would be distributed in only one-third of the country. During the second year advertising and distribution would begin in a second third of the country. In this way the entire country would be covered by the end of the third year. This approach was used to enable the company to spend relatively "heavy" funds on advertising without being committed to the full expenditures that would be required for a national undertaking. It was also believed that early efforts in a segment of the market would uncover pitfalls upon which the company could improve when it later entered new markets.

The advertising budget for the first year, for one third of the country, was set at $3 million, which in terms of the sales of the company was very small. It was realized that this was hardly an overwhelming budget in the terms of the job to be done. Furthermore, Coastal had to contend with a heavy barrage of advertising from its competitors.

In preparing their marketing plans, the advertising and sales managers reviewed carefully the distribution of total food store and retail sales in the United States on the assumption that these would parallel the sales of Hep Cat. Their study indicated that approximately

Exhibit 15-4   Characteristics of Purchasers of Cat Foods

Household Characteristics	Percentage Distribution of Households	Percentage Distribution of Pet Food Purchases
All Households	100%	100%
Annual Household Income		
Less Than $5,000	12.0	12.9
5,000— 7,999	11.5	12.1
8,000— 9,999	16.8	5.8
10,000—14,999	17.8	17.2
15,000—19,999	22.0	21.7
20,000—24,999	9.7	9.0
25,000 or more	20.2	21.2
Education of Principal Female		
Did Not Graduate High School	26.7	24.6
Graduated High School	43.5	43.0
Attended College	16.4	17.6
Graduated College	13.4	14.9
Geographic Region		
North East	21.3	25.7
North Central	24.6	20.9
South	29.6	29.0
West	24.5	24.5
Market Location		
SMSA Central City	28.4	33.3
SMSA Suburban	34.6	38.1
Non SMSA	37.0	28.6
Occupation		
Professional/Managerial	13.8	14.0
Clerical/Sales	19.5	20.8
Craftsmen/Foremen	0.9	1.1
Other Employed	14.6	14.0

SOURCE: Target Group Index, '78 p. 13.

30 markets accounted for about 70 percent of the total retail sales for the country. It was estimated that these forty top markets accounted for at least 75 percent of total cat food sales. The decision was made to concentrate the initial efforts of the company in these markets until sales had been firmly established nationally and adequate advertising funds were available to do a proper job in additional markets. In the first year of market introduction and advertising, fifteen markets were selected for Hep Cat distribution.

QUESTIONS FOR DISCUSSION

1. With the information available, suggest a procedure for selecting markets for the introduction of Hep Cat.
2. Indicate how you would allocate available advertising funds among these markets.
3. Develop a media plan for Hep Cat.

Case 15–5—Oron Paper Company (C)

For its 1982 fiscal year, beginning September 1, 1981, the Oron paper company established an advertising appropriation of $5.75 million to advertise its consumer products. Included among these products were paper napkins, toilet tissue, facial tissue, and towels which are listed here in the order of their importance in company sales. The objectives of Oron advertising were threefold:

1. To build consumer sales through direct-action advertising.
2. To expand distribution and improve dealer relations and support.
3. To improve company prestige and the image of product quality in the minds of consumers.

ORON DISTRIBUTION

Oron products were sold only in the area east of the Mississippi River. The company did not, however, have consistently good distribution throughout this entire region. Since paper products are quite bulky relative to their price, retailers are reluctant to devote shelf space to them. A package of paper napkins, for example, retails for 45 cents compared to an 8½ ounce can of peas which takes up one-fifth as much shelf space.

Price competition also causes distribution difficulties. Paper products are readily available from small manufacturers who do not make their own paper. These producers, who are called converters in the trade, undersell branded, advertised paper napkins by 2 cents to 3 cents per package. The same situation prevails with all consumer paper products. As a result, Oron frequently encountered difficulty in obtaining adequate retail distribution for its products throughout the sales territories.

It is axiomatic that advertising is severely handicapped in its efforts to build sales if the consumer cannot find the product when he/she goes shopping. Since paper goods products are relatively undifferentiated, advertising alone is usually inadequate to build sufficient demand over a short period of time to "force" distribution. As a consequence, the company confined its advertising only to those areas in which there was adequate distribution. The top sixteen markets of the company accounted for the following share of its business for various product categories:

Napkins	81%
Toilet Tissue	87%
Facial Tissue	68%
Towels	72%

Oron's total strength was not equal in all of its top markets. Sales in New York, the most important market for the company, were equivalent to those in the last eight of the sixteen markets. Besides the difference in absolute volume, there were also substantial differences in sales by product as the above figures indicate.

In New England for example, the company had no distribution of its facial tissue. In other areas towel distribution was absent. Thus, even in the sixteen top Oron markets only a checkerboard pattern of distribution existed. This pattern was further complicated by the varying degrees of "maturity" of the individual products in the various markets. While adequate distribution for toilet tissue existed in both New York and Providence, the company's share of the toilet tissue market in New York was almost double the one possessed in Providence.

ORON'S MEDIA OBJECTIVES

In 1981 the company had used newspapers, local television newscasts, and television network to carry its advertising. For the following year, the company management issued a statement of objectives which laid down the basic media requirements and the factors which they thought to be important in connection with media. These were:

Advertising Coordination and Timeliness. The ability to tie together the many products made by the company was deemed important. The timing of promotions which required advertising support was not universal in all markets. This required a high degree of coordination among sales, advertising, and sales promotion departments in order to bring the efforts of all of these forces into effect against a common target at the same time.

Company Backdrop for Trade Prestige and Consumer Image. Oron products compete with those of two of the country's largest manufacturers. Although the company believed that Oron's quality compares more than favorably with that of the products of the others, the company must match the prestige value or so-called "quality" image which its competitors have established in the minds of consumers. The choice of media can be crucial in achieving this goal. The same held true with the trade, who tend to promote those brands which in their minds perform the most effective advertising job.

Flexibility. The diversity of Oron's products and problems among its 16 markets required a high degree of flexibility and the ability to make rapid changes. The ability to bring extra weight into one or more markets on specific products was considered an important asset.

Woman Orientation. Women are responsible for the major part of paper-product purchases. Accordingly, the prime target of the advertising should be women, rather than men or children.

Merchandisability. Paper products are strongly subject to unplanned or impulse purchases. Store displays can substantially increase their sales movement. Efforts to obtain these from retailers are predicated to a great extent on the retailers' evaluation of a company's advertising power. Selection of media which appealed to the trade was an important consideration.

Mass Coverage with a Class Emphasis. Although paper product purchases are related directly to population, people in the higher socio-economic groups generally consume more than others. Since these people are also the social leaders whose behavior is emulated by others, their patronage is sought by many advertisers.

Product Demonstration. Strength, size and improved perforations are among the many paper qualities which can physically be demonstrated. One of the company's competitors had been able to enhance its market position substantially by using a very effective means of demonstrating the wet strength of their products in advertising. It was anticipated that, if possible, a physical demonstration should be prepared for Oron's advertising.

Visual Identity. Oron was in the midst of redesigning its logo and packaging and believed that the advertising should be able to present visually the new designs to the public.

Management of the company realized fully that no one advertising medium could fulfill all of their expectations and that a combination of media would probably be required.

AGENCY QUANTITATIVE ANALYSIS

The advertising agency prepared a list indicating the quantity of advertising which could be purchased in the sixteen markets with the available funds. These suggestions, covering five different media types and their variations, are shown in Exhibit 15-5.

The next step was one of reconciling and merging the company objectives and media requirements with the quantitative data compiled by the agency.

Exhibit 15-5   What Oron Budget Would Buy in Basic Media

	Number of Advertisements	Number per Week
In Newspapers (1000 lines B&W)		
10 markets, 10 papers	50	1
4 markets, 4 papers	20	⅓
2 markets, 2 papers	20	⅓
In Radio (60-second spots)		
3 markets	3600	20
2 markets	1500	28
11 markets	750	15
In TV (30-second spots Prime Time)		
3 markets	400	5
4 markets	100	2
9 markets	84	½
In TV (30-second spots Late News)		
4 markets	300	6
4 markets	200	4
8 markets	213	4
	No. of Months, – 100 Showings	
In Billboards		
7 markets	12 months	
6 markets	12 months	
3 markets	12 months	

QUESTIONS FOR DISCUSSION

1. Which media vehicle or combination of media vehicles do you recommend Oron use?
2. Justify this recommendation quantitatively.
3. Evaluate Oron's statement of media objectives. Do you agree with any or all of them? Why or why not?

PART 4:
COORDINATING
PROMOTION
MANAGEMENT

- The Promotion Program
- Cases in Promotion Management

THE PROMOTION PROGRAM

- Selection of Methods of Promoting Sales
- Promotion Selection Factors
- Coordination of the Promotion Program

Decision Making Organization of This Text

INPUTS TO ADVERTISING PLANNING
(Planning Area I)

- Corporate Objectives

- Marketing Plan
  - Product
  - Price
  - Place
  - Promotion

ADVERTISING OPPORTUNITY ANALYSIS
(Planning Area II)

SETTING ADVERTISING OBJECTIVES
(Planning Area III)

Consumer Response Criteria

- Exposure
- Awareness
- Attitude
- Intentions
- Behavior (Sales)
- Profits

DETERMINING ADVERTISING DECISIONS

Decision Variables

- MARKET (Planning Area IV)
- MONEY (Planning Area V)
- MESSAGE (Planning Area VI)
- MEDIA (Planning Area VII)

Measurement of Impact

Market Impact

INTERVENING FACTORS
(Planning Area IX)

- Competition
- Facilitating Agencies
- Environmental Factors
- Regulation

COORDINATING PROMOTION MANAGEMENT
(Planning Area VIII)

- Personal Selling
- Sales Promotion (including Publicity)

16

THE PROMOTION PROGRAM

"One is never entirely without the instinct of looking around."
—Walt Whitman

It should be understood that advertising is not the only way or
necessarily the desirable way to promote sales. Some "looking
around" is required among the methods other than advertising which
might be effectively used in the overall promotion progam. In this
phase of the decision-making process, company management is concerned with the development and management of the complete program of promotion. These functions should be set in a much broader
perspective than the consideration of advertising problems alone. It is
proper to recognize the differences in functions and responsibilities of
top company management and those which belong to the advertising
department and/or brand management in this regard.

Top management should assume responsibility for selecting the
most effective method or combination of methods of sales promotion,
for coordinating these into an efficient, integrated program, and
testing and evaluating the final, overall results of the program. The
choice of an effective combination of methods of promoting sales may
be considered a function of top company management since the task is
directly related to and should be consistent with company marketing
policies and objectives, products, markets, and distribution methods.
These are broad-range factors for which the perspective of top management is essential. Advertising management responsibility, on the
other hand, should be concerned with the relatively narrow sphere of
activities directly related to the areas and the problems of planning
and executing advertising. The type of company organization has an

566

important influence upon the relationships and divisions of responsibility in these functions.

SELECTION OF METHODS OF PROMOTING SALES

A manufacturer may accomplish sales goals by choosing from a wide variety of promotion methods and devices. For purposes of management and control, these methods are frequently grouped under personal selling, advertising, and sales promotion. The term "sales promotion" as used here follows the American Marketing Association's definition of sales promotion in a specific sense since both advertising and personal selling are also forms of sales promotion in the general use of the term.

Sales promotion includes those sales activities that supplement both personal selling and advertising and coordinate them and help to make them effective, such as displays, shows and expositions, demonstrations, and other non-recurrent selling efforts, not in the ordinary routine.

Some examples of the three types of promotion methods given below are intended to be illustrative of the variety of facilities available for the promotion program rather than all-inclusive:

PERSONAL SELLING

1. Creative selling
2. Routine selling, including the "order-taking" type
3. Missionary selling, those efforts by manufacturers to support and supplement personal sales efforts of distributors

ADVERTISING

1. Long-range, indirect-action advertising, the usual objective of which is to create favorable brand image and product reputation
2. Direct-action advertising designed to stimulate some type of immediate action from consumers, including vertical cooperative advertising
3. Advertising to dealers and distributors

SALES PROMOTION

1. Merchandise displays
2. Packaging
3. Point-of-purchase promotion
4. Demonstrations
5. Exhibits at trade shows and conventions
6. Publicity (all types)

7. Quick-response stimuli
   a. Free samples
   b. Premiums
   c. Combination deals (in conjunction with other products)
   d. Contests
   e. One-cent and cents-off sales
8. Miscellaneous promotion materials
   a. Films
   b. Product information folders and pamphlets
   c. Direct mail advertising (if not handled by the advertising department or personnel)

Alternatives include not only the choice of the various basic methods but the *proportions of each* (the weighting given to each of the three promotion elements in terms of their importance in the overall promotion program) which will be used or the relative reliance which will be placed upon each method. The variations in the combinations used by different manufacturers may be illustrated by simple comparisons of the relative amounts spent for each method as measured by percentages of sales. In the case of a producer of heavy industrial goods such as forklift trucks, for example, expenditures for advertising may amount to a fraction of one percent of sales, while ten percent or more may go into personal selling activities. In the case of a producer of proprietary, over-the-counter drugs, these relationships may be exactly reversed; advertising may amount to 30 or even 50 percent of sales in this industry, while personal selling costs may be held to less than one percent. These two cases represent extremes, and the large majority of companies are generally interested in seeking the most favorable combination of several of these methods.

ROLE OF ADVERTISING MANAGEMENT

As has been pointed out above, advertising management has relatively narrower responsibilities than top company management and is concerned with those activities directly related to planning and directing the advertising effort. As a rule, advertising management in a manufacturing concern should assume responsibility for the following areas or types of problems:

(1) Participation in the original decision to advertise
(2) Determination of tasks and statement of advertising objectives
(3) Involvement in the coordination of advertising, personal selling, and sales promotion
(4) Selection of and working with the advertising agency or agencies
(5) Determination of proper themes and advertising appeals
(6) Determination and control of the advertising appropriation
(7) Selection and direction of the use of media
(8) Direction and utilization of advertising research
(9) Test and measurement of the effectiveness of advertising.

PROMOTION SELECTION FACTORS

The forces which direct management decisions toward one or another combination of methods of building sales may be grouped under the following factors: (1) Type of product; (2) Company objectives and marketing policies; (3) Distribution channels and type of retail outlets; (4) Competitive influences. Each of these factors is discussed briefly below. These are illustrated in Figure 16–1.

**Figure 16-1   Factors Influencing Selection of
Promotion Methods**

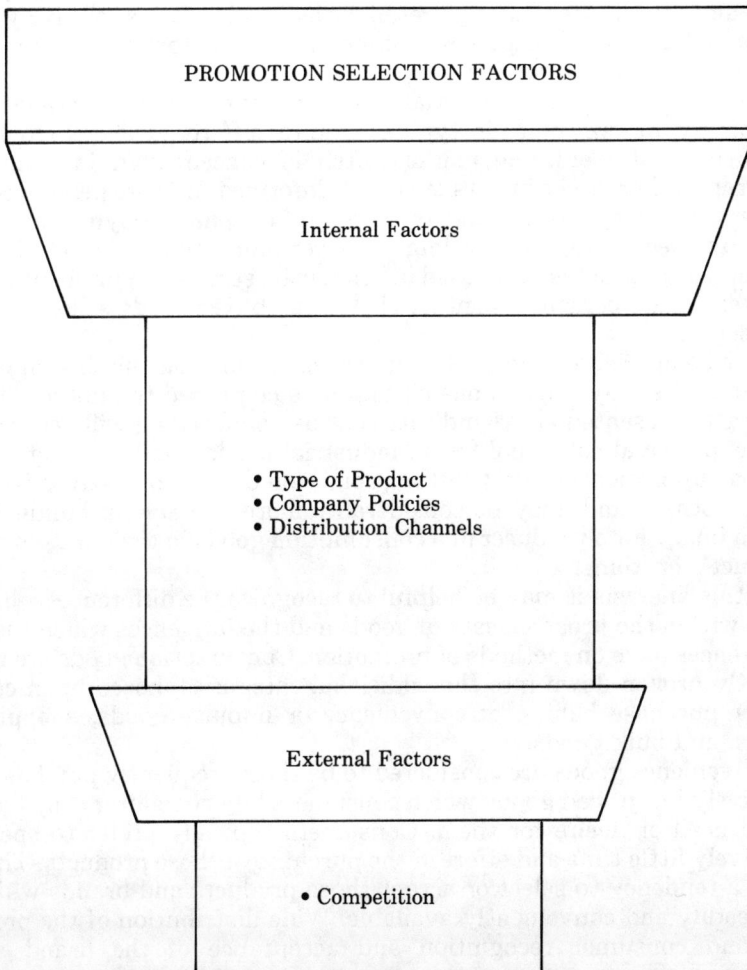

PROMOTION SELECTION FACTORS

Internal Factors

- Type of Product
- Company Policies
- Distribution Channels

External Factors

- Competition

TYPE OF PRODUCT

The type of product, the diversity of product lines, and the markets to which they are beamed make up an important part of the sales problems involved in the selection of promotion combinations. Is the product one which is directed to an industrial goods market, or is it a finished product sold to an ultimate consumer market? This may be an important determinant of the market, the type of customers, and the buying motives and habits of customers in this market and, accordingly, the promotion problems involved.

The market for some types of consumer goods, food and drugs for example, is characterized by a large number of potential buyers, a wide geographical area, buying motives which frequently are emotional, a selling price per unit which is relatively low, a frequent-purchase pattern, and distribution through retail outlets which offers relatively little opportunity for direct sales contact with the customer either by the manufacturer or the retailer.

The market for an industrial goods product, heavy installation machinery for example, is typically quite different. There are few potential customers, the market often is concentrated in a small geographical area, the buyers are better informed than are general consumers, buying motives tend to be more "rational," buying may be done by specification, the selling price per unit tends to be relatively higher, the product is purchased infrequently, service requirements are greater, and personal contact between buyer and seller more necessary.

Such comparisons suggest the advantages which one method of promoting sales may offer in one situation as compared to another. The contrasts presented above indicate that personal selling will generally be the principal sales tool for an industrial product; advertising may play a supplementary part in the promotional program. Advertising, on the other hand, may be considerably more valuable in building a brand image for a producer of a consumption goods in the minds of the product's customers.

In this analysis it may be helpful to recognize the differences which exist within the broad classes of goods and the influences which these differences have on methods of promotion. Consumption goods are frequently broken down into the additional categories, based upon consumer purchase habits, of convenience or impulse goods, shopping goods, and bulk goods.

Convenience goods are considered to be those frequently purchased, relatively low-priced goods which consumers buy soon after they have felt a need or desire for them. Consumers typically prefer to spend relatively little time and effort in the purchase of these products. They have a tendency to select or accept those products and brands which are readily and conveniently available. Wide distribution of the product and consumer recognition and acceptance of the brand are minimum requirements for the manufacturer who hopes to compete successfully in the market for these types of goods. Brands, in some cases, are not of primary importance in product selection.

Shopping goods are those products for which consumers typically "shop around" as a means of making comparisons between products on the bases of price, product qualities, and style features. The shopping goods category is frequently broken down further into fashion and service or durable goods.

Within these groups there may be differing opportunities for use of the various methods of promotion and certain generalizations regarding promotional methods are possible as a result of an analysis of these purchase habits. Advertising and display, for example, are considered to be relatively more appropriate for and to do more of the total selling task for convenience goods than for shopping goods. This is especially true where self-service methods are widely employed in the distribution of convenience goods. In the case of relatively more expensive shopping goods, advertising plays its part in building brand reputation and acceptance, while demonstration and shopping comparisons made with the aid of personal sales people may play a more important part in completing the final sale.

COMPANY OBJECTIVES AND MARKETING POLICIES

The objectives, policies, and marketing philosophy of a firm may exert considerable influence upon the choice of particular methods of cultivating markets. If company management is aggressive, is seeking maximum sales, profits, and a constantly increasing share of market, this may call for marketing and promotional efforts considerably different from those employed by a company whose management is more complacent, less aggressive, and is content with smaller sales and share of market. Both of these corporate outlooks may be appropriate in conditions of shrinking resources and/or the "less is more" attitude. But such differences in outlook would have an impact on the combination of promotion methods used as well as the volume of promotional efforts.

The brand policies of a company may also influence company sales problems and sales methods. The problems of building a consumer demand arise directly from the decision to brand and promote a product. A manufacturer producing unbranded merchandise or placing a distributor's brand on the product chooses to avoid these selling and advertising problems. The influence of brands on marketing and promotion problems increases in almost direct proportion as additional brands are added to a company's product line and may reach maximum complexity when a multi-divisional company produces and distributes brands which compete with other company products as well as those of other companies.

DISTRIBUTION CHANNELS AND TYPES OF RETAIL OUTLETS

The channels of distribution through which merchandise moves also may exert a rather important influence on the methods of promotion which a manufacturer may use. The type of distribution channel used affects both the amount of contact which a manufacturer may have with customers and control over sales efforts. Figure 16-2 illustrates alternative channels of distribution.

Figure 16-2   Typical Distribution Channels for
Consumer Goods

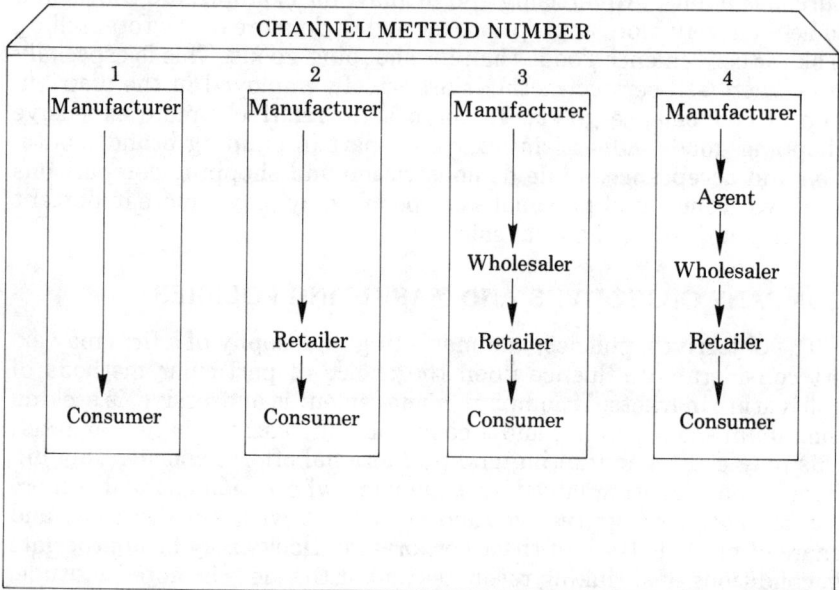

CHANNEL METHOD NUMBER

1	2	3	4
Manufacturer	Manufacturer	Manufacturer	Manufacturer
			Agent
		Wholesaler	Wholesaler
	Retailer	Retailer	Retailer
Consumer	Consumer	Consumer	Consumer

Maximum contact between manufacturer and consumer and control over sales is to be found in Channel 1 in Figure 16-2; this arrangement is typical of house-to-house distribution. Many companies using this method of distribution use no, or practically no, advertising. They rely almost entirely upon personal sales efforts. Channels 2, 3, and 4 represent an increasing separation between the manufacturer and the market. When middlemen are brought into the marketing picture, there generally is need for some increase in non-personal selling efforts on the part of the manufacturer to compensate for the resulting loss of personal selling effort and personal relationship between producer and consumer. Advertising frequently supplies this increased non-personal effort.

The number and types of retail outlets used affect both the amount and quality of sales promotional support which the retailer may contribute to the manufacturer's overall promotion program. This is of primary importance since the amount and quality of retail support given to a brand directly influence the extent of the job which the manufacturer must do.

Whether the product is distributed through service or self-service retail stores has a marked influence upon the type and extent of the promotion task which faces the manufacturer. In the past the promotion efforts of independent retailers have been responsible to a large degree for the success or failure of many brands owned either by manufacturers or wholesalers. In the canned fruits and vegetables industries, for example, there have been instances where the promotion efforts of independent retail grocers have been so effective that a very minimum of advertising by the owner of the brand (either packer or wholesaler) has been necessary in the successful promotion of the brand. When these personal sales efforts have been removed, as a result of the growth of self-service in the food field, the brander usually must expand advertising and other non-personal promotion to compensate for the decline in personal promotion if the brand is to maintain its position in the market.

COMPETITIVE INFLUENCES

So long as business operates within the environment of the competitive economic system, the decisions and activities of competitors should exert tremendous influence upon management decisions. This influence will extend beyond the interest in sales promotion methods alone. It should include modifications and improvements incorporated in products and the rate at which these changes are made. Price policies and channels and methods of distribution of one company are of interest to and will tend to influence decisions of management in competing firms.

Within the area of sales promotion, competitors' actions influence both the type of promotion effort and the volume of this effort. If, for example, one company expands its promotion and attempts to increase its share of market at the expense of competitors, this may mean increased advertising expenditures for other leading firms in the industry. This influence may extend to promotion methods or even to media selection. It may mean using certain advertising media as a defensive move if the use of these media limits what a strong competitor may do.

The influence of competitors' activities in determining the sales promotion program may not be constant from one industry to another or from one time period to another. The influence of this factor in the program depends upon the number of competitors, the quality of competitive action, the size of total industry demand, and the direction of the industry demand trend. If, for example, the total sales of an industry increase each year at a rate faster than capital investment and the formation of new companies, there will generally tend to be an easing of competitive selling pressures in that industry. Sales will be easier to get and individual members may have a greater independence of action in the marketing methods used than would be the case if competition were increasing.

COORDINATION OF THE PROMOTION PROGRAM

The importance of an integrated marketing program involving product, price, product distibution, and methods of promotion has been emphasized earlier. Maximum effectiveness from advertising should not be expected unless it complements and is supported actively by other divisions of the company and by other forms of promotion by the company and by dealers and distributors.

True coordination should be interpreted to include all efforts at brand and company-name promotion: advertising, personal selling, missionary sales efforts, design and distribution of displays and point-of-purchase material, demonstrations, packaging, sampling, and publicity both for product and for company. The objective is to bring maximum sales power to bear upon the market. This can be done only if all forms of sales promotion by the manufacturer and by dealers are working at the same time toward the accomplishment of mutual sales goals.

For purposes of organization and control, the task of coordination may be divided into two phases: (1) internal; and (2) external. The *internal* problems deal with the methods of promoting sales which are used by and are directly under the control of the manufacturer. The *external* phase is concerned with attempts by the manufacturer to motivate dealers and distributors and to integrate the manufacturer's sales promotion efforts contributed by dealers and distributors.

Advertising management should expect to assume direct responsibility for developing machinery for this coordination. While, ideally, this should be a cooperative effort with all interested parties taking an active part, the importance of this management function is far too great to leave to chance, or to assume that someone else may do it. The general conception of the major elements of promotion program coordination are illustrated in Figure 16–3; each of the elements in that illustration are discussed briefly below.

INTERNAL COORDINATION

Efforts at internal coordination should be directed toward integrating advertising with personal sales efforts and all other methods of promotion which are used by a manufacturer.

Primary Groups Within the Company. Within the corporation itself, the main groups toward which coordination efforts should be directed are key company executives, salespersons, sales promotion personnel, and the manufacturing/production personnel.

In the case of top management of the company, these are the people who have responsibility for final decisions for approval of budgets and company programs. This top management group should be well in-

Figure 16-3   Coordination of the Promotion Program

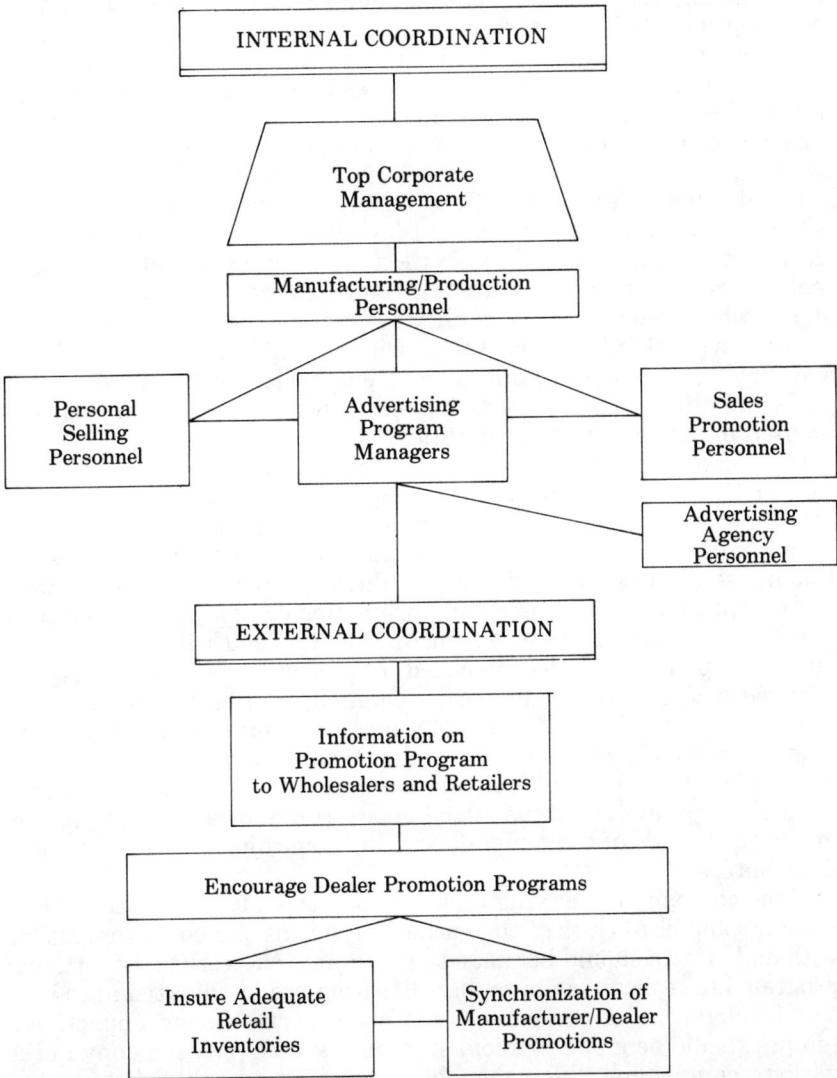

formed as to marketing and advertising plans and objectives in order to develop and maintain the proper appreciation for general values and contributions to these areas to company operations and profits. Adequate coordination, however, is more than a communication task. Coordination also involves explaining and interpreting the requirements which marketing, advertising, and sales plans may impose upon product modification and development, production schedules, and financial requirements.

Since advertising results depend so directly upon personal sales and sales promotion efforts, it is important that the personnel in these departments below management echelons be acquainted with advertising plans and an effort be made to build enthusiasm and support for the program. This support and enthusiasm may not come easily. Salespersons frequently do not think well and favorably of company advertising. This often may be attributed to a lack of understanding of advertising and of the advertising efforts. If sales personnel are to have a proper appreciation of advertising and make effective use of it in their sales work, they must be relatively well informed on advertising and advertising plans. They should be shown the advantages which advertising offers them and how it can be of direct benefit to them in their sales work. This is the type of approach which offers a real opportunity to build enthusiasm and support. In addition to being shown what kind of assistance they are going to be given, they should be told what kind of assistance will be expected of them. More specifically, the coordination should emphasize such phases as the goals and objectives of advertising and how advertising materials can be used in personal selling activities.

Coordination of Advertising with Advertising. A phase of integration of the promotion program frequently overlooked is that of the coordination of company advertising itself. Some companies will carry on a number of campaigns concurrently. The difficulties involved in this phase of integration increase in direct proportion to the number and complexity of advertising and promotion campaigns which a company is conducting. The problem reaches its zenith in the case of a large company with decentralized organization and a variety of branded products with advertising campaigns in both industrial and consumer goods fields. It is usually preferable for such a company to plan in terms of a company-wide advertising program rather than to execute a series of individual campaigns, some of which are directed toward the promotion of industrial goods, some toward the promotion of various brands of consumer goods, and some directed to dealers and distributors.

If the company is carrying on more than one advertising campaign, the aims and objectives of the various programs should be compatible with and efforts should be made to coordinate the various advertising programs to realize maximum benefits from brand advertising toward the development of company name or corporate image impact. Attempts should be made to avoid statements in advertising copy in the various campaigns which may be conflicting or contradictory and which might be confusing to customers or detrimental to another division of the company.

Coordination of these advertising efforts may be achieved through joint planning sessions, with the active participation of the company advertising director and the advertising managers of each of the various company divisions. It is desirable that agency representatives attend such meetings. In some companies, this problem has been of sufficient importance as to justify the use of a "coordinator" of advertising whose assigned responsibilities are to encourage and work toward the development of complementary advertising objectives and timing and the elimination of wasteful or undesirable competition in intra-company advertising.

This type of coordination obviously is not as important in the case of a company whose policies deliberately encourage competition among company brands and company divisions. Procter & Gamble brand policies illustrate a situation where greater emphasis is placed on competitive brand promotion and less on promotion of company name.

EXTERNAL COORDINATION

In this phase of the coordination function, the objectives are to reach and motivate those individuals connected with outside business firms which distribute the advertiser's product. The total impact of the manufacturer's brand promotion on consumers is the objective of the promotion program. This means tying together the manufacturer's promotion efforts with the advertising, personal selling, and other brand promotion of dealers and distributors.

The first step in external coordination is to inform wholesalers and retailers in adequate detail of company promotion plans, including advertising schedules and dates of insertion. This both encourages dealer interest and promotion support and gives an opportunity for those who use a planned promotion approach to correlate their release and insertion dates with those of the manufacturer. Dealers and distributors should be encouraged to give the manufacturer's brand a reasonable level of promotion support. This step is especially important because it provides necessary direct-action effort at the retail level. The final step is to attempt to tie together the timing of manufacturer and retailer advertising for special promotions which feature manufacturer brands or special promotion events initiated by the manufacturer such as special sales and seasonal price reductions.

If such a promotion suggested by the manufacturer is to be successful, retailers must be given advance information. Retail inventories must be adequate, and the chances of sales success will be enhanced if retailers can be encouraged to support this sale by placing advertising of their own and giving the product acceptable personal sales effort.

MECHANICS OF COORDINATION

Integration of the factors of sales promotion will not take place naturally and automatically. A *positive program* of coordination of promotion methods and departments must be developed if satisfactory results are to be realized.

Within the manufacturer's own company, there are likely to be two groups toward which coordination efforts should be directed. Those people actively engaged in sales and sales promotion activities make up one group, while key company executives and other influential company personnel comprise the second group. It is desirable that these executives both understand and appreciate the contributions made by advertising and sales activities to company sales and profits. Effective company management requires an integration of marketing plans, sales forecast, and promotional plans with financial requirements and production capacity and schedules.

It should be the joint responsibility of the advertising, sales, and sales promotion managers to keep other key personnel in the company adequately informed on sales and advertising plans. Meetings, discussions, and correspondence are the usual methods of accomplishing these objectives.

With members of sales and sales promotion departments, a fully integrated advertising and selling program is the goal. This means that during the planning stages the managers and directors of the departments involved must work together in establishing common goals and objectives and assigning specific tasks and functions for each of the various selling methods used. There should be a mutual understanding of the support which each sales division of the company can give. The advertising manager and the manager's staff must understand and appreciate the plans, contributions and problems of the personal sales staff. The sales force, in turn, must know the advertising plans and the contributions of advertising to company sales.

While an interchange of ideas and information is needed, it seems there is more change involved in advertising plans and campaigns than in personal selling and sales promotion. The task, then, of informing sales personnel on advertising is generally a greater one than that of keeping the advertising personnel informed on activities of sales personnel. It has been suggested that salespersons should know, at minimum, the following items about the advertising program:

(1) How advertising solves specific problems
(2) How salespersons can use advertising
(3) Place of advertising in sales program
(4) Proof of effectiveness
(5) What media are used
(6) Reasons for using these media
(7) Coverage of media
(8) How advertising is prepared
(9) Why current theme is used
(10) How advertising is tested
(11) Advance information on plans
(12) Supporting promotion
(13) How inquiries are handled
(14) What others say about the advertising
(15) How appropriation is determined
(16) Comparison with other years.[1]

Among many other suggestions, the following items indicate ways in which salespersons might be effectively informed about advertising:

(1) Sales meetings
(2) Portfolios
(3) Manuals

(4) Bulletins
(5) Company magazines
(6) Reprints
(7) Sales schools
(8) Media representatives
(9) Copies of letters
(10) Field trips
(11) Special promotion personnel
(12) Advertising exhibits.[2]

There are at least two advantages of using sales personnel as a source of ideas and suggestions regarding advertising plans. One value lies in the constructive nature of the suggestions made, particularly when they pertain to a campaign currently in preparation. Knowing marketing conditions in their territories, salespersons can often give helpful advice on localizing the selling effort. Another value lies in soliciting ideas from salespersons; it has the additional value of breaking down their resistance or indifference to advertising generally, and of arousing their enthusiasm in a particular campaign. In the final analysis, the number of and combination of methods used by a company to get sales understanding support of advertising should be influenced by needs and requirements of the situation.

With such a variety of effort, there may be insufficient attention given to such possible interrelationships as timing, complementary advertising objectives, and copy themes. Studies of such a diverse advertising program have revealed the use of copy statements which are opposing and contradictory and which oppose rather than support, and confuse rather than help customers.

Manufacturers can attempt to reach dealers and distributors through personal representatives, advertising, and both national and regional conventions and meetings. The personal representatives used may be regular company sales personnel, missionary salespersons, or sales promotion personnel; they may also be from the advertising agency. Such personal efforts may be very valuable in communicating information to wholesalers and distributors about the advertising program and in developing interest toward it. Visual aid materials such as portfolios, slides, and films have been found helpful. As a rule, the most effective approach to building interest and cooperation with distributors is to show how it will be to their advantage to tie in their advertising and promotion efforts with those of the manufacturer.

Advertising is also an effective method, for non-personal methods are generally more important as a means of communicating promotion plans to the trade than of persuading these middle-level organizations to schedule local tie-in advertising and use point-of-purchase materials. Personal contact has generally proved more effective in securing action. These efforts may be buttressed by portfolios of advertising, slide films, and complete descriptions of advertising plans including media, scheduling data, dates and frequency of insertion, size of space or time to be used, and estimates of market coverage.

Dealer meetings and conventions often create enthusiasm for product and promotion plans. There is a certain mass motivation and stimulation to be gained when dealers and distributors are all brought together, exposed to effective speakers, and shown new product models and promotion plans. Such efforts frequently result in an expansion in dealer promotion efforts and a closer coordination with manufacturer promotion. A retailer's interest in supporting and promoting a branded product other than the retailer's own is generally based upon the profitability and value of that brand to the retailer, although personal factors sometimes enter the picture also. Volume and profit margins have the most direct influence upon brand profitability, thus allowing higher than average margins is one device for gaining additional retail support.

POINT OF PURCHASE MATERIAL

It is difficult to overestimate the sales influence of point-of-purchase displays. The manufacturer who gets the sales message across to customers at the final moment before purchase has a decided advantage over competitors. There is, consequently, keen competition for this scarce space.

The approaches and appeals used in preparing this material should be selected with a view toward support of and coordination with national advertising themes. The possibility of retailers making effective use of manufacturer point-of-purchase display material should not be left to chance. A well-organized plan should be developed and followed in order to achieve maximum utilization at the retail level.

There seems to be considerable variation in successful plans. Some manufacturers (Hart, Schaffner, and Marx, for example) have found that utilization of manufacturer display and advertising material is increased if retailers are asked to pay a nominal sum for such material. This seems to attach a greater value to the material than if it were distributed free. Other companies, in the food industry for example, find that it is desirable to pay retailers and chains a small fee for the use of the space occupied by their displays. Competition for the use of this space and the value of the line to retailers seem to be important factors which vary from one situation to another.

RETAIL ADVERTISING

Persuading retailers to support a manufacturer's product through retail advertising goes a step beyond devoting space for its display in retail stores. Here the retailer is asked to invest what sometimes amounts to substantial sums in the promotion of a product which belongs to the manufacturer. The task is to show the retailer how sales and profit opportunities are linked with those of the manufacturer and that what benefits one will benefit the other.

If the manufacturer or the manufacturer's representatives can appeal to the self-interest of the retailer and at the same time offer help with local advertising problems, a great deal may be accomplished along this line. One method of encouraging retailers to increase their advertising for a manufacturer's brand is to make a mat service available to them. Such a mat service may offer as many as a hundred ads contained in a book or a catalogue from which the retailer may choose. If retailers have a wide selection of advertisements suited to their needs from which they may choose, a larger volume of retail advertising of manufacturer brands will generally result. One of the best methods of producing retail advertising which will be used by retailers is to examine what all types of retailers are doing in their advertising, and then provide retailers with advertising which will appeal to them. To be successful, retail advertising material offered by manufacturers must recognize the retailer. It must appeal to the special needs of the retailer and produce results. Advertising representatives of local media may be of help in regard to the manufacturer's efforts to stimulate greater use of advertising by the retailer.

VERTICAL COOPERATIVE ADVERTISING

The use of an advertising allowance to retailers (vertical cooperative advertising) is a further step which manufacturers may take in encouraging retail advertising support of the product. These allowances may take a variety of forms. The manufacturer, for example, may agree to pay 50 percent of the advertising for the brand which the retailer places. This means that the manufacturer is paying 50 percent of a local rate. In some cases, the manufacturer may agree to share some percentage of the cost (perhaps 50 percent) of the national rate even though the retailer pays for the advertising at the local rate. It is not uncommon in some industries, in the promotion of canned fruits and vegetables for example, for the retailer, perhaps a food chain, to bill the producer at the national rate for the full cost of space devoted to the manufacturer's brand while the retailer pays a local rate which may be less than half of the national rate.

The decision to use or not to use some type of an advertising allowance to retailers as part of the promotional program is an important one since the cost may be high and the quality of retail support may hinge on this decision. The problems and complexities involved make this a difficult decision for most manufacturers.

This type of cooperative advertising is supposed to help build manufacturer-retailer cooperation in brand promotion and to expand volume and quality of retail promotion of manufacturer brands. Manufacturers are not in complete agreement as to the values of granting retailers such an allowance. These differences in opinion may be attributed to different promotional problems and promotional mixes due to differences in product requirements, marketing, and competitive situations. Some of the differences, however, are to be explained only by inherent conflicts with the cooperation concept itself.

In the usual concept of cooperation there is an assumption of mutual interests and common objectives. This seems only to be partially true in the case of manufacturers and retailers. Their interests are, to some degree, mutual. Both are interested in sales and profits; in some cases these sales and profits come from the same merchandise. The principal interest of the manufacturer lies in maximizing sales and profits of the manufacturer's own brand. This calls for developing selective demand through the use of long-run, indirect-action advertising to build brand preference and insistence. The retailer is an essential element in this program, since it is the retailer who provides distribution and contact with the ultimate consumer market and promotion at point of purchase.

The retailer, while interested in sales and profits, is not as limited in brand interests as the manufacturer. The retailer's main objective is in the reputation of the store and store facilities and services and in the sale of the entire stock of merchandise. Retail sales come usually from a group of products and brands from many manufacturers; some of these are competitors. Retail advertising tends to be direct-action in order to build customer traffic and loyalty. After the customer is in the store, the main interest of the retailer is in making a sale and less in which particular brand is sold. Retailers have usually concentrated their promotional efforts on a single brand only when they have developed their own distributor or "private" brand or brands.

APPENDIX A

THE ADVERTISING ALLOWANCE

When dealing with a subject as controversial as the advertising allowance, it is necessary that management be intimately acquainted with the advantages and disadvantages involved before attempting to arrive at a workable decision. Because of the differences in the points of view between manufacturer and retailer, it may be desirable to consider these from the points of view of both business institutions.

Manufacturer: Possible Advantages

(1) The allowance helps the manufacturer get additional retail interest in and promotion of the brand and to synchronize manufacturer-retail advertising.

(2) It may increase the amount of retail advertising of manufacturer's brand if the manufacturer pays a sizable proportion of the bill.

(3) If the cooperative arrangement is based on the local rate, it is possible for the manufacturer to buy more space and time in local media than could be done at national rates. It must be determined, however, whether or not the objectives of the two types of advertising are similar.

(4) The allowance can be a selling device; it helps open new territories and

new distributors; it helps sell merchandise.

(5) The association of the brand with the prestige of the local store may be beneficial to the manufacturer's brand.

(6) Because of the knowledge of local conditions and local media, the retailer may be able to do a better job of advertising than the manufacturer.

(7) The allowance may enable the manufacturer to bring some influence to bear upon the promotional policies of the store.

Manufacturer: Possible Disadvantages

(1) The control of advertising expenditures is difficult when cooperative contracts are used. Budgetary allocation problems are encountered; retailers may spend the money in the wrong area; some retailers tend to overspend, some to under-spend; advertising may be done at the wrong times. Scheduling decisions are difficult to stop once started.

(2) The allowance to retailers may increase the total expenditures for advertising. There is a tendency for it to draw funds from manufacturer's own advertising program.

(3) The cooperative arrangement is subject to abuses. Since local rates are not readily available to the manufacturer, retailers may bill the manufacturer at rates above those actually paid. The manufacturer may be billed for ads which never ran; the manufacturer may be billed twice for the same ad. The retailer may take advantage of large numbers of issues run by some metropolitan newspapers. The retailer may include an intentional error in an advertisement, stop this ad after the first issue and order standing ad B to be run, then bill the manufacturer for both ads. Gains from this type of practice may act as a subsidy for promotion of retailer's own brands. From the manufacturers' point of view, these abuses may dissipate whatever savings may be obtained from the use of a local media rate.

(4) The retailer may place cooperative advertising in inferior media.

(5) Troublesome legal problems are involved. The Robinson-Patman Act indicates that all recipients of cooperative advertising funds be given an equal opportunity to share in the cooperative funds.

(6) The retailer may not use manufacturer-supplied mats. Actual ads used may be of poor quality; the manufacturer may be billed for excessive production costs.

(7) Allowances may create discontent or dissatisfaction between dealers if they believe that discrimination exists.

(8) Cooperative advertising may feature the retailer's point of view and interests; ads may not properly feature the manufacturer's brand. The retailer may be more inclined to use direct-action advertising than indirect-action, reputation-building advertising.

(9) The allowance tends to become an accepted custom after a period of use; it tends to lose its effectiveness in gaining special interest and promotion for the manufacturer's brand.

(10) Many retailers have come to consider cooperative funds as a source of revenue rather than a promotional device.

(11) The producer may, in some cases, actually subsidize advertising efforts of the retailer in the promotion of the distributor's brands. The extent of this depends upon the rate at which the retailer bills the manufacturer.

Retailer: Possible Advantages

(1) The retailer receives some aid and compensation from the manufacturer for efforts to promote a brand which is distributed by the retailer but is not owned and may not even be handled next week or next month.
(2) The allowance offers retailers a means of adding to their advertising funds.
(3) Some retailers may gain prestige by tying promotional effort to the manufacturer's brand.
(4) The total amount of advertising allowances may be sufficiently large to make an appreciable contribution to store profits or to the promotional budget of store brands. This is especially true if contracts are at the national rate.

Retailer: Possible Disadvantages

(1) The allowance may permit the manufacturer to interfere with retail promotion. This may hinder store promotional planning. Selection of merchandise may tend to be on the relative size of the advertising allowance rather than on the basis of merchandise qualities. Restrictions of cooperative contracts may emphasize the manufacturer's objectives and aims more than the retailer's interests. For example, some clothing manufacturers pay nothing on ads which show any product except their own. It may be more advantageous for the retailer to feature an ensemble rather than devote the entire ad to one item.
(2) The lure of an advertising allowance may deter the buyer from the most satisfactory performance of his or her function. The buyer may over-buy in order to qualify for a larger allowance. The buyer may not act in the true capacity as purchasing agent for the clientele. The buyer may purchase less desirable merchandise in order to get the allowance.
(3) The buyer may use the advertising allowance as a means of getting more advertising for a department than it should have in relation to the store as a whole. This tends to be more true of department store buyers than some other retailers.
(4) There may be a tendency for a manufacturer to try to recover the costs of the advertising allowance by increasing the price of the merchandise or by lessening the quality level of the merchandise.

QUESTIONS AND PROBLEMS

1. How would you evaluate the relative importance of advertising in the overall promotion program for a new product in the snack-food market as opposed to the importance of sales promotion methods such as point-of-purchase displays? How would your evaluation of the relative importance of sales promotion versus advertising change in conjunction with the introduction of a new product in the durable goods field such as stereo equipment for the home?

2. List some criteria which you believe would be important to keep in mind when a new advertising agency was being selected for an existing brand at your company?

3. What types of corporate organization in terms of the marketing function do you believe would be most compatible with a synchronized functioning of the advertising, personal selling, and sales promotion functions of the overall promotional program? Present two alternative organizational forms in chart format.

4. In this chapter it was indicated that the major internal factors governing the selection of promotion methods and their relative importance in the overall promotional program were: (1) type of product involved; (2) general company policies; and (3) the type of distribution channels used. Show how these three factors have an influence on promotion mix selection by giving three different examples.

5. What is the relative importance of sales promotion methods in relation to shopping goods versus convenience goods?

6. How might an argument be made to top management in a particular instance that more funding should be given to advertising and less to the personal selling activities of the firm? What type of evidence could be assembled in attempt to convince top management that such a fund transfer would be desirable? How would this argument be conducted in relation to the relations of the advertising department with the sales department?

7. What are the primary problems which are likely to arise from the manufacturer's point of view in the use of point-of-purchase displays?

8. Examine the Robinson-Patman Act with respect to cooperative allowances. What does it mean to make cooperative allowances available to retailers on an equal-opportunity basis?

ENDNOTES

1. Paul N. Nystrom (ed.), *Marketing Handbook* (New York: The Ronald Press, Inc., 1948), p. 391.
2. *Ibid.*

CASES IN PROMOTION MANAGEMENT

- Fox Lines, Inc. (B)
- Gold O'Roast Corporation (B)
- The Monsanto Chemical Company
- Homemaker Appliances
- Minneola Canning Company
- The B & B Manufacturing Company

CASES IN PROMOTION MANAGEMENT

Case 17-1—Fox Lines, Inc. (B)

Executives of Fox Lines, Inc., a subsidiary of the Fox Corporation, were engaged in a major review of company marketing strategy. The factors which were of prime concern to these executives in this analysis were: the relatively small share of total intercity travel business carried by buses and the highly seasonal pattern of Fox Lines travel business. Fox executives were of the opinion that economic conditions were such that it would be an opportune moment to increase their share capitalizing on the increasing fuel prices.

COMPANY BACKGROUND

Fox Lines is recognized as the largest intercity bus line in the United States. It has held this position for nearly 50 years. As of 1980, it served approximately 14,000 American communities. Fox Lines owns, directly or partly, various other companies performing terminal, supply, and other auxiliary services. The affiliated companies function as a unified national system through interline tariffs, connecting schedules, and joint advertising. The company operates under the supervision of the Interstate Commerce Commission and various state commissions.

The buses of Fox Lines are built for comfortable long distance travel. The current versions of the bus are noted for their wide picture windows and comfortable air suspension ride. Bus seats are adjustable and well upholstered; they have the usual ash trays, foot rests, etc. An important feature of passenger comfort of the buses is the availability of complete washroom facilities right on the bus. Fox Lines Food

Management operates restaurants and fast-food facilities in the bus terminals which posted an outstanding year in 1979. In 1975, the decision was made to convert a number of the restaurants to part of a large franchise. With an average of a half-million dollars invested in the conversion of each of 19 sites, every Fox Lines franchise has come to represent a major generator of earnings for the food service group. Each of the restaurants averages $1.2 million in sales annually.

Fox Lines tickets are sold at company owned terminals and commission agencies. Fox Lines owned terminals are usually located in the heart of the downtown districts, near hotels and shopping districts. They have the usual waiting room facilities, benches, ticket windows, newsstands, and baggage lockers. The commission agents also provide ticket service, waiting rooms and washrooms, and earn a commission on each ticket sold. Usually the principal business of these agents is a hotel-restaurant, drug store, or other retail establishment.

Although not expanding rapidly enough to satisfy Fox Lines officials, operating revenues have shown reasonable increases over the past years. (See Exhibit 17-1).

Exhibit 17-1   Fox Lines—Operating Revenues 1969-78

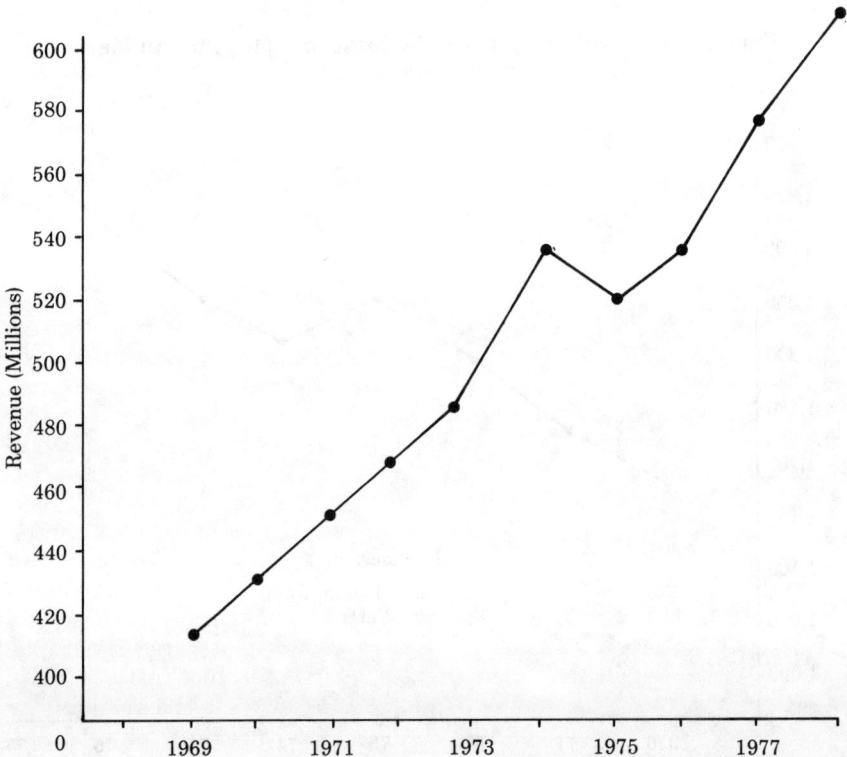

Total operating revenues for the company (which are equivalent of sales for a manufacturing company) were $414,496,559 in 1969. By 1978 these revenues had increased to $594,071,172. Net income in 1978 was $18,741,216.

Although the company is engaged in numerous activities including package express service, bus charters, a toll service, and post houses, the travel market comprises a large percentage of Fox Lines business. It was in this area that company officials directed their attention.

THE INTERCITY TRAVEL PICTURE

As background for their analysis, company officials reviewed the transportation travel picture nation-wide for the period 1969-78. Their sources of information included studies by the Interstate Commerce Commission, the National Association of Mutual Bus Operators, as well as Fox Lines' own operating data for the period.

Interstate Commerce Commission reports revealed that total intercity travel increased by 22.4% in the period 1970-77. Exhibit 17-2 shows this increase in total passenger miles of intercity travel during this period by passenger automobiles, railroads, airways, buses, and waterways with about 85 percent of this travel done in private automobiles.

Exhibit 17-2   Intercity Travel in Passenger Miles by All Means of Transportation

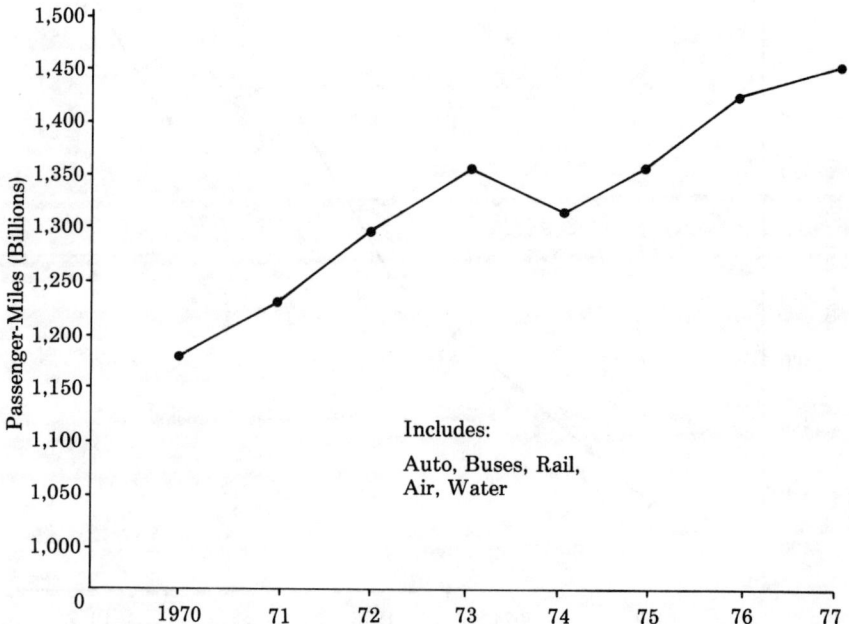

Exhibit 17-3   Intercity Travel in Passenger Miles
for Private Automobiles

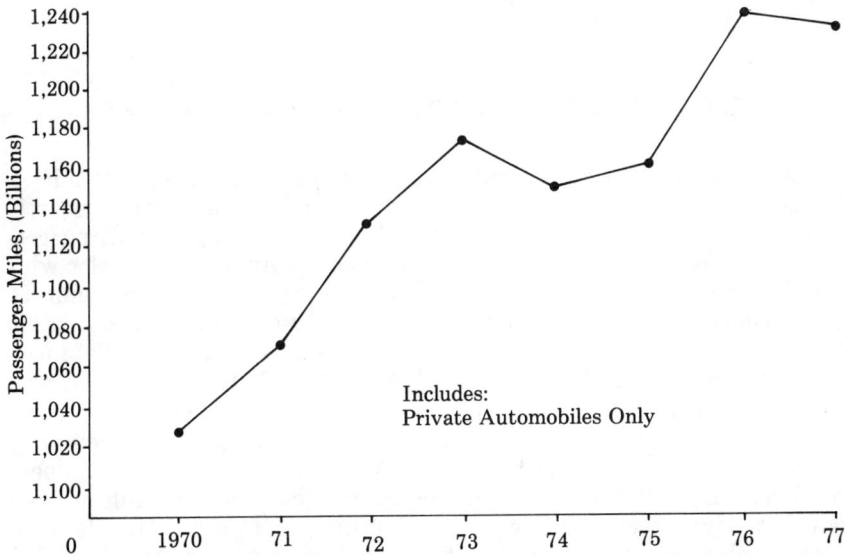

Includes:
Private Automobiles Only

Total consumer expenditure for intercity travel during this period also showed considerable increase.

A comparison of Exhibits 17-2 and 17-3 indicates that most of the rather sizable increase in total intercity travel miles was accounted for by private automobiles rather than public carriers. When passenger miles by public carriers alone are examined, the increase is shown to be a modest one of 35 percent—from 159 billion passenger miles in 1970 to 216 billion in 1977.

One of the peculiarities of the bus business, or any travel business for that matter, is the perishable nature of its service. Travel, like any other service or non-tangible product, has certain characteristic features which affect its marketing. It is highly perishable; it cannot be mass-produced and stored. A trip planned but not taken may be lost to the seller forever. Services are quite unlike durable products in this respect. Timeliness, good will, customer comfort and convenience, and the need for constant customer reminders are all important in the sale of travel service. These characteristics of the travel product were considered by Fox Lines officials as one of the special problems they faced in attempting to expand their business.

Company officials took a careful look at the competition which Fox Lines faced. Some at Fox Lines did not consider the numerous small bus companies scattered throughout the country as offering much real competition. The 4 percent share of the total travel market which all buses enjoyed was so small, and Fox Lines had such a large share of it, that they believed very little potential existed for the company if it were to direct its efforts toward obtaining for itself the volume possessed by other bus companies. The biggest portion of the intercity travel pie was retained by automobiles which accounted for 85 percent of this travel in 1977.

EXPANSION POTENTIAL FOR FOX LINES

Company executives were interested in appraising the opportunities for the expansion of their business by inducing travelers to switch from other modes of travel to the use of buses. It was generally agreed that the most logical prospect for a bus company was a traveler who was in the habit of using public rather than private transportation. It was believed that the airplane traveler did not represent the most likely bus prospect since most plane travel covered long distances and speed was generally an essential factor. The Amtrak, however, was considered as a logical source of additional volume. Some of the company's executives believed that the inflexibility of railroad scheduling made Amtrak a particularly vulnerable competitor. Rail travel does, however, have inherent advantages of comfort and sleeping service which are important on long trips. Fox Lines company officials were very much aware of this competitive disadvantage, and the additional comforts and conveniences built into the new equipment represented attempts to reduce this.

Another important area of possible exploitation lay in attempting to expand the entire travel market—that is, in getting all people to travel more. Increased consumer purchasing power and leisure time gave encouragement to this approach. The widespread construction of turnpikes, thruways, and other superhighways which reduced travel time substantially was further development favorable to this proposal.

Since the suggestion of promoting increased travel was based upon positive and constructive thinking, it was the subject of wide discussion. It was pointed out, however, that it is a difficult and expensive task to attempt to change the habits and patterns of behavior and leisure of an entire populace. Increases in leisure and consumer purchasing power did indicate the possible receptivity of the people to this type of campaign. New modes of behavior, however, were generally the result of deep-seated sociological forces which may be encouraged by advertising but are usually not engendered by it. One company official reminded the group that even if the campaign were successful in encouraging more travel, there was no certainty that Fox Lines would get more than its regular share of this new travel market.

By far the largest possible area for new business development appeared to be users of private automobiles which accounted for 85 percent of intercity travel. If only 5 percent of these people could be induced to use Fox Lines buses instead of their own cars, the company could double its volume of business. The private automobile offered many advantages which indicated that diverting travel to buses would not be a simple matter. The car traveler enjoyed the privilege of controlling his own movements, starting and stopping when he pleased, detouring if he so desired, and eating when and where he wanted to. This privacy is important since company studies showed that over 50 percent of these travelers had children with them. In addition, their travel costs were proportionately reduced since relatively little more gas and oil are consumed if one drives alone or takes four or five passengers along. Company officials recognized that these are desirable advantages which auto travelers would be reluctant to give up.

THE SEASONAL FACTOR

In deciding how to orient their marketing strategy, Fox Lines executives had to face one more important problem. This dealt with the seasonal factor of their business. Sales and net revenue peak during the summer months.

This non-use of equipment again brings up the perishable nature of travel service and emphasizes an acute problem—the unused, available seat. Every mile it travels empty, every minute that it sits in a garage, is lost forever. Seats cannot be stocked up for rush seasons, days, or hours. The Fox Lines company keenly felt this aspect of perishability which was compounded by the extremely seasonal nature of the travel market. During the summer months every available piece of physical equipment capable of transporting passengers was pulled out of the garage to help accommodate the peak loads. In spite of this, many would-be passengers had to be turned away because of the unavailability of more equipment. During the winter months when travel was at an ebb, the company had to garage some of its newest and best equipment because there was not enough traffic to require its use. If efforts to increase the volume of business during the peak travel season were successful, new investment in buses and equipment would be required. Although the company was financially capable of this, the only way it could recoup sufficient funds from this increased investment was by increasing off-season business. This has been a perennial problem for Fox Lines.

CONSUMER MARKET DATA

As a guide for the development of marketing strategy, *the company undertook an extensive survey based upon a nationwide probability sample.* The findings were considered significant. Some of the results of this research were:

1. During the year prior to the research, it was found that about 75 percent of all people over 18 years of age took a trip of 50 miles or more.
2. The preponderance of trips were taken for pleasure and vacation.

3. Buses were third in frequency of use for these trips.
4. The bus traveler was more likely to have a relatively low income.
5. In their choice of buses as a mode of inter-city travel, time was considered of secondary importance.
6. Buses had the lowest social status of any form of popular transportation.

QUESTIONS FOR DISCUSSION

1. Prepare a promotion plan for Fox Lines. Include in the plan: A brief statement of the alternatives available to Fox Lines as competitive targets and sources of new business, a recommendation on the market positioning and competitive strategy which Fox Lines should adopt from among these alternatives, reasons to substantiate your choice and an outline of a copy strategy to implement your recommended marketing strategy.

Case 17–2—Gold O'Roast Corporation (B)[1]

Gold O'Roast is one of the major regional coffee brands in the New York metropolitan area. While the company has been expanding its market outside of the Eastern market over the past 20 years, 35 percent of the company's present coffee sales is made in the New York metropolitan area. This figure implies that the Eastern market is the most important market for the Gold O'Roast coffee operation.

Consumer price promotions are one of the major marketing tools in the competitive coffee industry. Gold O'Roast is also using such price deals to promote its coffee, although the company's coffee has been known for its premium quality.

SALES PROMOTION FOR INSTANT COFFEE

Various promotional methods are used in the instant coffee market. Sampling, direct mail, coupons, point-of-purchase displays, and heavy advertising are often used for the introduction of new brands of coffee in order to promote trial and repeat purchases. Cents-off coupons and bonus-size jars (larger-size jars) are the most widely spread practices for both new and relatively established brands of instant coffee. Of course, a wide distribution is an important requirement for the use of coupons through advertisements to meet consumer demands.

Cents-off coupons are usually carried within newspaper ads or with containers. For example, in 1975, General Foods ran newspaper ads for Maxwell House Coffee offering a 20-cents-off coupon. The same company also ran newspaper ads for Sanka regular, instant and freeze-dried coffee with a 40-cents-off coupon. The amount of price reduction through coupons went as much as 50 cents in the mid 1970's.

Bonus-size jars offer consumers more coffee at no additional cost. For example, Nestle introduced 10-oz. jars, in addition to 8-oz. jars, for Taster's Choice regular and decaffeinated freeze-dried coffees. Nescafe, another Nestle's instant coffee, went from 10- to 12-oz. jars in the mid 1970's.

PROMOTION METHODS FOR GOLD O'ROAST INSTANT COFFEE

When Gold O'Roast introduced its special process instant coffee in 1972, the company offered a 2-oz. sample jar with a special retail price of 29 cents in end-aisle displays in grocery stores and supermarkets. The jar contained a 15-cents-off coupon, good toward purchase of a 4-oz. or 8-oz. jar. The advertising campaign for this instant coffee in the Eastern market, including New York, New Jersey, Pennsylvania, Massachusetts, Rhode Island, Connecticut, Delaware, Maryland, and Washington D.C., consisted of 4,000 spots of radio advertising and newspaper ads in black and yellow (yellow is the color of the container's cap). Initial newspaper ads for the instant coffee featured "Just this once! A little of heaven . . . only 29 cents." The second advertisement carried a coupon and it compared the company's product with Taster's Choice freeze-dried coffee and Maxwell House instant coffee with a headline, "Now . . . Which instant do you think tastes most like premium-priced ground roast coffee?"

REGULAR COFFEE MARKET ON THE EAST COAST

There are three major regional regular coffee brands, Gold O'Roast, Savarin, and Martinson's, in the New York metropolitan area, and Maxwell House is the largest national brand in this area. These brands' market shares in the past are shown in Exhibit 17-4.

Exhibit 17-4   Percentage Share of New York Regular Coffee Market: 1954-1960

	Gold O'Roast	Martinson's	Maxwell House	Savarin
1954	5.2	4.9	21.5	16.8
1955	7.8	6.0	24.9	20.2
1956	9.2	7.8	23.9	22.8
1957	9.9	7.2	23.3	22.8
1958	11.8	7.7	24.5	21.2
1959	12.5	7.9	26.4	20.0
1960	11.6	6.4	29.3	19.4

SOURCE: New York World Telegram and Sun Grocery Audit

In 1960, Gold O'Roast ranked third with an 11.6 percent of share behind Maxwell House and Savarin. The company's share was more than doubled, from 5.2 percent to 11.6 percent, during the years between 1954 and 1960 in the New York market.

In 1978, the price competition in the East coast market had an increased intensity with the expansion of two major coffee brands, Hills Bros.' High Yield and Procter & Gamble's Folger's, into this market. High Yield, as its name implies, was advertised as yielding as many cups as a single pound does from its 13-oz. can. Folger's Flaked coffee was also advertised as requiring four measures instead of the usual five measures for making regular ground coffee. These two brands were priced 18 to 20 percent less than those of regular coffee: High Yield was priced at $2.56 per 13-oz. can, and Folger's Flaked coffee was priced at $2.42 for the same size can, when the average regular coffee price was about $4 a pound. Hills Bros., which had an approximately 6.5 percent share in the national market, gained an almost 13 percent share in New York when it was introduced into this area. Some competitors in the New York area, however, estimated that Hills Bros.' share had soon declined to less than 1 percent in New York in spite of its heavy advertising program, with $11,000,000 expenditures, for its introduction.

Folger's, which entered into the New York market shortly after Hills Bros., started an aggressive promotion in March, 1978. Although Folger's gained the first position in the national regular coffee market with its total share increased from 21.4 percent to 26.5 percent in 1978, the East Coast market was one of its weakest regions in sales and distribution. Folger's set a goal to gain 15 percent of the New York market within 6 months from its introduction. In addition to the price cut, Folger's mailed coupons offering 45 cents off on a one-pound coffee to 70 percent of the 6 million households in the New York area. General Foods met Folger's promotions with competitive measures.

In the two-month period of March and April of 1978, it was estimated that a total of $24,700,000 was invested in coffee advertising in this market alone. The market shares in New York during the April-May period of 1978 are shown in Exhibit 17-5.

Exhibit 17-5   Percentage Share of New York Coffee Market: 1978

Maxwell House	24.0%
Savarin	16.0%
Gold O'Roast	13.0%
Martinson's	9.3%
Folger's	7.4%

SOURCE: *Advertising Age*, August 7, 1978

Although Folger's did not attain the goal of 15 percent in this time period, it gained 7.4 percent of the New York market. Maxwell House's share in this market was about 28 percent in the fall of 1977, and it decreased to 24 percent in the spring of 1978. It is believed that

Folger's will also introduce its instant coffee in the East in a few years.

Folger's entry into the New York market created keen price competitions between itself and Maxwell House coffee. However, the regional coffee roasters were not necessarily panicked at the Folger's entry. They rather believed in strong consumer loyalties to the brands that they have established over the years. In the middle of the Folger's expansion into the New York market, a Gold O'Roast executive mentioned with confidence that New York and New England have many discriminating coffee users who buy Gold O'Roast coffee for its quality.

QUESTIONS FOR DISCUSSION

1. Evaluate the Gold O'Roast's promotional strategies for its instant coffee described in this case. If you were the brand manager for this instant coffee, what combination of promotion methods would you recommend to use in the Eastern market for next year?

2. What kind of promotion methods do you recommend for the Gold O'Roast regular coffee for the second half of 1978, assuming that there are continuous price competitions between Folger's and Maxwell House?

3. Do you recommend different promotional strategies for the Gold O'Roast instant coffee and regular coffee in the Eastern market, or do you recommend any promotion methods that may be used for both its instant and regular coffees simultaneously?

ENDNOTE

1. For a more detailed background, see Case 12-1(A).

Case 17-3—The Monsanto Chemical Company

COMPANY BACKGROUND

The Monsanto Chemical Company manufactures and sells a widely diversified line of chemical products. In 1960, total sales were $890,114,000, the bulk of these sales coming from industrial goods. The company makes such products as sulphuric, nitric, and phosphoric acids, caustic soda, alum, calcium carbide, sulphur dioxide, chlorine; plastics; pharmaceuticals, such as aspirin, sulfas, antibiotics, penicillin, antihistamines; saccharin, flavors and condiments; insecticides, herbicides, and many petrochemicals. Manufacturing plants are located in over 20 cities, laboratories in over a dozen cities. The company operates either itself or through subsidiary and affiliated companies in over some 20 countries. The company conducts an extensive chemical research and development program. In 1956, over 1,200 people, including 774 scientists, were employed in Monsanto research laboratories.

DECISION TO ENTER CONSUMER GOODS MARKET

Prior to 1952, all products entering the consumer market were sold to other manufacturers who packaged and sold them under their own brands or who utilized raw materials purchased from Monsanto in production of consumer products. In early 1952, however, company management organized a new division of the company to produce and distribute products directly to the ultimate consumer market.

Krilium, a soil conditioner, was one of the first products developed by Monsanto research and marketed by this new division under the Monsanto brand. Other consumer products were added to the line. Folium, a fertilizer soluble in water, Bogey, an insecticide, D-Leet, a herbicide, and Rez, a wood sealer, and Red Wood Rez, a wood sealer and stain. It also added All which was a low-suds detergent for use in automatic washing machines. By 1955 when Monsanto introduced Dishwasher All for automatic dishwashers, the company had a total of 9 consumer products in the market. Sales to the ultimate consumers inevitably required the company to develop different promotion methods.

SALES PROMOTION FOR "ALL"

All has been the most successful consumer product in Monsanto. In 1947, Westinghouse Electric Corporation approached Monsanto, asking them to develop a controlled suds detergent for the new automatic clothes washer that Westinghouse was planning to manufacture. Neither Westinghouse nor Monsanto was interested in marketing All at that time. All was distributed by Detergent, Inc. which was established by a company of agricultural specialties. In 1953, however, Monsanto acquired Detergent, Inc. and started the marketing of All. At this time, there was a growing interest in synthetics. In 1952, as much as 46 percent of total detergent sales came from synthetic detergents, whereas only 16 percent was accounted for by the same category in 1948. A major advantage of synthetics over natural fats and oils was that the former worked even in hard water.

Various promotion methods were used to sell All by Monsanto. The company developed a tie-in program with manufacturers of automatic washers. In 1955, approximately 60 percent of automatic washers were sold carrying a package of All, and those manufacturers used All for the demonstration of their washers. Premium systems were used to establish a tie with appliance distributors and servicemen. When a serviceman repaired a washer, he demonstrated the machine with All and left the package with the housewife. A serviceman received 20 cents for this promotion from Monsanto. In addition to these tie-in promotions, the company's own home laundry consultants were sent to stores for demonstrations. Monsanto also introduced large-size packages: when most detergents were sold in 24-oz. packages, All was sold in a 10-lb. package, 50- and 100-lb. drums, and in a 25-lb. pail. Newspaper advertising and cooperative magazine advertising were also used to promote All.

PROBLEMS IN CONSUMER GOODS MARKET

All gained fourth market position, following Procter & Gamble's Tide and Cheer and Colgate Palmolive's Fabin, in a few years. Its annual sales were $30 to 40 million in the mid 1950's. All was so successful that it found that many imitation products were sold under the name of All. However, All met competition from other low-suds detergents sold by the other three large detergent manufacturers. Procter & Gamble's Dash, Colgate Palmolive's Ad, and Lever Brothers' Vim were already in test-marketing stages when All was increasing its sales.

In spite of its success, the sales of All created two major problems for Monsanto. First, the company was now in direct competition with its customers since it was also supplying raw materials to Procter & Gamble, Colgate, and Lever Brothers. Secondly, since the competitors started heavy promotions for Dash and Ad, Monsanto had to meet them with a continuous heavy promotion to keep All in the market. It was estimated that Monsanto had a $3 to $4.5 million promotional budget when Lever Brothers was spending $60 million for the promotion of its products. Also, other detergent manufacturers were trying to establish tie-in programs with manufacturers of washing machines as Monsanto did for promoting All. Procter & Gamble, for example, acquired 15 washing machines and paid $1.20 to distributors for promoting Tide when Monsanto was paying $1.00. Another problem was an increasing competition in the raw material field. Although Monsanto was producing 35 percent of the country's phosphate, three competitors, Victor Chemical Works, Westvaco, and Shea Chemical Corporation, were moving into the phosphorous field and they were producing an increased amount of the raw material.

Meanwhile, Lever Brothers approached Monsanto to negotiate its acquisition of the distribution right for All. Monsanto is now deciding whether to remain in the consumer market or to specialize in manufacturing All and leave All's distribution to Lever Brothers.

QUESTIONS FOR DISCUSSION

1. What action should Monsanto take for All? What is your solution for Monsanto in the consumer market? In your recommendation, discuss whether Monsanto should stay in the consumer market or not.

Case 17-4—Homemaker Appliances[1]

Homemaker Appliances is a medium-sized manufacturer of appliances in a field which is dominated by such giant names as General Electric, Westinghouse, and General Motors. The company enjoys a market share of approximately 6 percent of the total home appliance market.

The year 1979 had been a relatively poor one for the appliance industry, and the management of the Homemaker Appliance company was concerned with their sales situation. The economic recession which began during this period reflected itself in a strongly diminished rate of consumer purchases of such items as refrigerators, washing machines, ranges, etc. This situation led to a major re-examination of marketing and advertising policies.

BACKGROUND OF APPLIANCE MARKET

In many of the major appliance categories a high degree of market saturation exists. For example, fully 98 percent of wired homes own a refrigerator. Similarly, 93.1 percent of homes possess an electric washer. Radios are owned by 99 percent of homes and television by 97.5 percent. Accordingly, in many appliance categories a substantial portion of sales represent replacement units, with the balance accounted for by new household formations or purchases by existing households which did not previously possess the appliance.

In 1978, of total refrigerator sales 73 percent represented replacements. On the other hand, with dryers, which possess a lower degree of market saturation, only 24 percent of sales in 1978 represented replacements. Generally, as the saturation level of ownership for a particular appliance rises, selling becomes more and more a replacement business. Thus, with the major appliances, which represent the bulk of the industry, the selling problem is not a generic one, as it is, for example, with room air conditioners, but rather one of brand preference.

DISTRIBUTION CHANNELS

The conventional distribution channels for major appliances are manufacturer to distributor to retailer to consumer, and manufacturer to chain store to consumer.

Of the types of retail outlets, appliance stores account for some 50 to 60 percent of sales, followed by department stores with an estimated 15 percent of total. Mail order houses and chains such as Sears and Ward are relatively important in the sale of appliances; most of these are their own brands. They are particularly active in the sale of washers and dryers with market shares in these products of 16 and ten percent respectively. Discount stores and furniture stores account for the balance of the purchases in these lines.

Distribution for Homemaker products is achieved through thirty-two independent distributors throughout the country who devote their efforts exclusively to the sale of the company's full line of appliance products. The distributors, in turn, sell these products to retail dealers. Some 5,000 dealers, representing about 7 percent of all retail outlets that sell appliance products, carry the Homemaker line. Homemaker distribution suffers from the fact that a substantial portion of these dealers represent relatively small dealers that have negligible sales volume. Moreover, almost all of the dealers handle Homemaker in addition to a number of other appliance brands, frequently those of leading companies. Among the more important dealers where good volume potential existed, Homemaker is carried as a third or even fourth brand and is handicapped by a corresponding lack of promotion support and aggressive merchandising at the retail level. Company management considered the weak nature of its dealer organization one of its major marketing problems and one of the barriers to significant sales increases.

CONSUMER PURCHASE PATTERNS

In their appraisal of marketing and advertising policies, company management gave some attention to a study of consumer purchasing habits of appliances. It was generally agreed that the decision to purchase a major appliance consists of a considerable number of sub-decisions that take place at various stages in the purchase cycle. These would include the original idea of purchasing a major appliance, the actual decision to make the purchase, decisions concerning brand, and the retail outlet in which the refrigerator, for example, is to be purchased.

In each of these decision areas different individuals play roles of varying degrees of importance. Generally, a fair measure of consistency applies as between the relative importance of the husband and wife in making these various decisions. Considering the total of all decisions leading to the final purchase from the initial idea to buy to the completion of the purchase, Homemaker research findings indicated that about 52 percent of the decisions were made by the husband and wife jointly, 30 percent by the wife alone, and about 18 percent by the husband alone. With respect to the brand-selection decisions, the data seem basically similar. It appears that about 52 percent of the brand-selection decisions are made by the husband and wife jointly, about 34 percent are made by the wife alone, and some 14 percent are made by the husband alone. Thus, it is apparent that, while both husband and wife play important roles in the formulation of decisions leading to the purchase of an appliance, the wife has somewhat of an edge and is at least a participant in the decision over 80 percent of the time. When the decision is a joint one, it may be assumed that the preponderant role and major influence in the process is the wife.

The major element influencing the selection of the store from which a major appliance is purchased seems to be the reliability of the store. This answer was given by almost 45 percent of respondents in a magazine survey. (See Exhibit 17-6).

Exhibit 17-6   Factors Influencing Selection of Store in the Purchase of TV, Washers and Refrigerators

Factors	Refrigerator, Percent of Total	TV, Percent of Total	Washers, Percent of Total
They are reliable and stand behind their merchandise	45.3	39.6	46.8
Their prices are low	30.5	26.1	25.8
They're the authorized dealer for the brand I decided to get	14.6	15.2	24.8
We have credit there	11.8	18.0	13.5
They carry only good merchandise	10.0	9.9	10.4
They really want to satisfy their customers	11.5	10.0	9.5
They carry many different brands so you can really compare them	11.0	12.4	8.5
The store is near where I live or work	9.3	9.0	8.4
I have a friend or relative there	7.1	9.2	8.3
They know me and always want to treat me well	12.7	10.3	4.2

NOTE: The totals exceed 100 percent because of multiple answers.

As figures in Exhibit 17-6 indicate, price is the second factor in importance, being mentioned by 26 percent of respondents. Other reasons are concerned with various facets of the dealer's activities. Although some respondents may have been hesitant to mention their concern with price, by far the preponderance of reasons given were related to the type of store run by the dealer rather than with the prices that he charges. This tends to support the contention of some industry representatives that merchandising, selling, and service can be used satisfactorily to overcome price competition. While this may be true to some extent, the plight of the standard appliance retailer has been a difficult one since the advent of discount selling. In a survey in 1979 among dealers, retailers listed price cutting, or price instability, and discount-house competition as their most important problems.

HOMEMAKER ADVERTISING

In 1980 Homemaker spent approximately $10.5 million for consumer advertising. Of this total, however, fully $2.78 million was budgeted for cooperative advertising. By far the major part of the coop budget was used by the dealers for newspaper advertising. Of the $7.72 million which remained for national advertising, approximately $6.18 million was used for the purchase of network television programs and the balance went into magazines.

Dealer promotion is an important part of the total promotion program in the appliance industry. The increased competition in the retail sale of appliances has caused many dealers to increase their use of advertising and promotion. The survey of dealers indicated that during 1978 and 1979 an expenditure of 4.8 percent of sales was devoted to advertising and promotion as compared to 3.5 percent during prior years. Successful retail promotions have been based on many varying themes, from the traditional birthday sales and seasonal sales periods, to such far-ranging promotions as giving away ten pounds of potatoes, displaying "two-headed" cars, etc.

Cooperative advertising also plays an important role in the marketing structure of the appliance industry. It is estimated by MART magazine that at least 60 percent of the nation's appliance dealers participate in cooperative advertising programs of some type. For the manufacturer, cooperative advertising serves a variety of purposes. It is a means of securing retail distribution, of encouraging retailers to stock adequate inventories and of giving the manufacturer's product advertising and promotional support.

Dealers who receive a large amount of coop funds justify the use of these funds by promoting the line aggressively, by stocking a representative amount of merchandise, and by acting generally as a leader in promoting the manufacturer's products and, to some extent, generating business with non-advertising dealers who handle the same brands.

Dealer advertising usually places strong emphasis on price or on individual promotion themes. They are often almost devoid of the type of advertising copy which builds brand preference. Dealers believe that this approach is necessary because of the availability of the particular brand in competitive outlets and the resulting need of the dealer to emphasize his own sales problems and not those of the brand which he believes should be presold by the manufacturer in manufacturer-national advertising. The typical dealer advertisement, in which the manufacturer shares the cost, frequently includes a variety of brands and items, although this practice is frowned upon by the manufacturers.

Cooperative advertising arrangements exist primarily between the distributor and the dealer. Although the manufacturer supplies the funds, he generally does not enter into the specific arrangements at the dealer level. While distributors often do some advertising on their own, most of the advertising is done with funds supplied by the manufacturer. Some of this advertising takes the form of dealer listings and is generally paid for by the manufacturer through special funds in addition to those included in the normal cooperative advertising. In general, the appliance industry is so notoriously lenient in administering cooperative advertising that, in many cases, the programs are almost "give-away" plans.

Under these arrangements, the manufacturer simply deducts a given percentage from each distributor's invoice and leaves it up to the distributor to spend and allocate the money as he sees fit. Thus, there is an absolute minimum of control on the part of the manufacturer with respect to the administration of the coop plan by the distributor. Manufacturers justify this practice by stating that it is the full responsibility of the distributor to build the market for their goods in his area and that the manufacturer discharges his duty by allocating the means by which the distributor can perform the task established for him. As long as the distributor's sales are satisfactory, the manufacturer frequently does not interfere in his territory.

An evaluation of the coop advertising plan was given a prominent place in the reappraisal of the advertising program. Since this was an involved problem, management representatives were divided in their opinions, and at the conclusion of the second meeting to decide the issue, no solution was in sight.

QUESTIONS FOR DISCUSSION

1. What specific role do you believe cooperative advertising should play at Homemaker Appliances?
2. Does the distribution system used by Homemaker have implications for a certain type of advertising program? What type specifically?
3. How does "reliability of the store," as involved in purchasing decisions, relate to the promotion programs developed by Homemaker?

ENDNOTE

1. Company name is disguised.

Case 17-5—The Minneola Canning Company (The Use of an Advertising Allowance)

The executives of the Minneola Canning Company are in the process of re-evaluating the company advertising program. This company, which is a producer of pickles, relishes, jams, and jellies, is experiencing a severe financial crisis brought on by an attempt to introduce a new product which did not succeed in gaining satisfactory consumer acceptance. There is such a serious shortage of working capital that management is exploring every possibility for cutting expenditures and the consumer advertising program appears to be an attractive possibility.

COMPANY DISTRIBUTION

The Minneola Company, located in Camden, New Jersey, has never attempted to expand distribution west of the Mississippi River. The company which sells part of its products under the Minneola brand has two distinct markets: restaurants, hotels, and soda fountains, which it reaches through various food wholesalers and wholesale confectioners; and the consumer grocery market, reached through wholesale grocers to independent food retailers and supermarkets, and by direct selling to chain and voluntary chain organizations. Some direct sales by company salesmen are also made to large supermarkets. Company sales, which range between $15,000,000 and $20,000,000 annually, are made principally through company salesmen, although food brokers are used in some sales territories.

BRAND POLICIES

About one fourth of company sales are made to hotels, restaurants, and soda fountains. Although these products are sold originally under the company brand, they do not reach the public as Minneola products. Company sales executives believe that these are industrial-goods products in which purchases are made on the basis of quality and price and that brands are not important in determining choice of supplier.

About 30 to 40 percent of the output of the company is sold to distributors for sale under their brands. These brands are owned by large grocery wholesalers, chains, and voluntary chain organizations. The owners of the distributor brands typically price their brands lower to consumers than the Minneola brand although these products of both brands are identical in quality. Sales to distributor-branders yield a lower gross margin than sales of the Minneola brand, but company management considers this volume important as a means of increasing output and contributing to a more efficient utilization of plant capacity. Some of these brands are showing very rapid increases in sales volume. For example, the sales of Shop & Save brand sweet pickles have more than doubled during the past year.

Sales of the Minneola brand make up the remainder of company volume. These sales represent the highest gross margin for the company and, because of sales stability and the profit possibilities, the expansion of sales of the Minneola brand is one of the principal objectives of company management.

COMPANY ADVERTISING AND SALES PROMOTION

In order to achieve this objective there has been a steady increase for several years in the advertising appropriation for Minneola brand products. Last year this amounted to $250,000. This advertising, combined with a high quality product and a sound marketing program, has resulted in a steady and gratifying increase in consumer sales of the Minneola brand. Most of the advertising budget has gone into newspapers, radio, car cards, and outdoor posters.

In addition to appropriating funds for promotion of the Minneola brand, the company has also followed a policy of offering an allowance to distributor-branders to be spent as they see fit to advertise their private brands. Minneola management believes this allowance is worthwhile in that it encourages distributors to advertise their brands. They believe the rapid increase in sales of distributor brands may be directly attributed to the combination of this advertising of relatively high quality products sold at a lower price than Minneola and other producer or national brands.

They also believe that they are getting a better buy for their money with this advertising than for the Minneola brand advertising. The advertising allowance to distributors results in a type of cooperative arrangement in which the distributors share in the cost of the advertising which is purchased at local—or lower—rates than Minneola brand advertising. Thus, the company saves two ways.

After a review of the above information the company treasurer proposed that the consumer advertising program for Minneola brands be suspended but that advertising allowances to distributors for cooperative advertising be continued. This approach, he emphasized, would save Minneola over $200,000 each year.

QUESTIONS FOR DISCUSSION

1. What should be the relative role of consumer advertising for Minneola brands and the advertising allowance program?
2. Is the $200,000 savings suggested by the company treasurer through the reduction of consumer advertising a realistic figure? Why or why not?
3. Should cooperative advertising play a role in the promotion program at Minneola? Should it play a *significant* role?

Case 17-6—The B & B Manufacturing Company
A Proposal to Advertise Stillson Wrenches
to Householders

The B & B Manufacturing Company produced a line of steamfitters' and plumbers' tools. These products were noted throughout the industry for their high quality and long life under hard usage and were, correspondingly, a relatively high-priced line.

The company distributed these industrial tools on a nation-wide basis through eight sales branches which sold to supply firms reaching industrial users and to hardware wholesalers.

In the summer of 1981 the sales of the B & B Company decreased sharply as a result of a nation-wide slump in the construction industry. This caused company management to look for new markets and methods of distribution. A five-man management committee was appointed to study the problem and work toward a solution. At one of the meetings of this committee a Mr. Jones, who seemed to have given the problem much more thought than other members of the committee, proposed that the company pick one product out of the company line and conduct a sales promotion campaign directed toward the ultimate consumer-homeowner market. He suggested that a medium-sized Stillson wrench suitable for use in the home be advertised in appropriate consumer media as an essential item for the homeowner, utilizing the general slogan: "Every home needs a Stillson wrench."

Stillson wrenches were not a large dollar volume item for B & B, as total sales for this type of tool through the entire United States averaged about two and a half million dollars a year. This was a long-life, relatively infrequently purchased tool. It was a profitable product, however, since it carried a mark-up of 50% based on selling price.

Mr. Jones presented a rather well-filled out marketing plan, emphasizing the large number of prospective purchasers and suggested an advertising appropriation of $250,000 for the first year to reach this market. About 90% of this would be spent in consumer magazines in which generic demand buying motives would be stressed by showing the different ways in which the Stillson wrench could be used in the home. The brand advantages of B & B dependability and superior quality would also be developed in the copy.

Other members of the committee found this proposal very interesting because the home market was an entirely new market area for the B & B Co. The prospect of a B & B wrench in every home was very attractive and, if successful, could very well take up much of the slack caused by the decline in sales in the industrial market.

One member of the group was somewhat skeptical, however, and raised several questions. He was concerned, first of all, with the size of the proposed advertising budget. He pointed out that the company had never spent so much money on advertising. He was also concerned about competition. He said that he had noticed Stillson wrenches on sale in hardware stores, in discount houses, and in such chain stores as Sears. These wrenches sold for about half the price of a B & B Stillson.

Mr. Jones dealt with these objections very quickly. The B & B Company had never spent as much money on advertising as he proposed but neither had they ever attempted to reach such a broad and rich market as the ultimate consumer market represented. The competitive product problem was not of great concern to him. He pointed out that these were cheaper wrenches in every sense of the word; they did not approach the quality and durability of a B & B Stillson. He said that if a plumber or a steamfitter, accustomed to the quality of a B & B tool, slipped a piece of pipe over the handle of one of these cheap wrenches for additional leverage, they would readily bend or break. The B & B Stillson could take that kind of treatment because of the higher quality metal used in its manufacture. The discussion continued.

QUESTIONS FOR DISCUSSION

1. Is it feasible for B & B to conduct an effective consumer advertising program? If so, how would you select the particular product to serve as the object of this campaign? What criteria would be used to select the particular product?
2. What role might promotion methods other than consumer advertising play in the marketing program at B & B?
3. Are other forms of promotion than consumer advertising more or less appropriate for the situation in which B & B finds itself?

PART 5:
CONSIDERING THE
REGULATORY
ENVIRONMENT

- Advertising Regulation and Advertising Decision Making
- Cases in Regulation and Advertising Decision Making

ADVERTISING REGULATION AND ADVERTISING DECISION MAKING

- Federal Regulation of Advertising
- Deceptive Advertising
- Remedies
- Advertising Substantiation
- Self-Regulation

Decision Making Organization of This Text

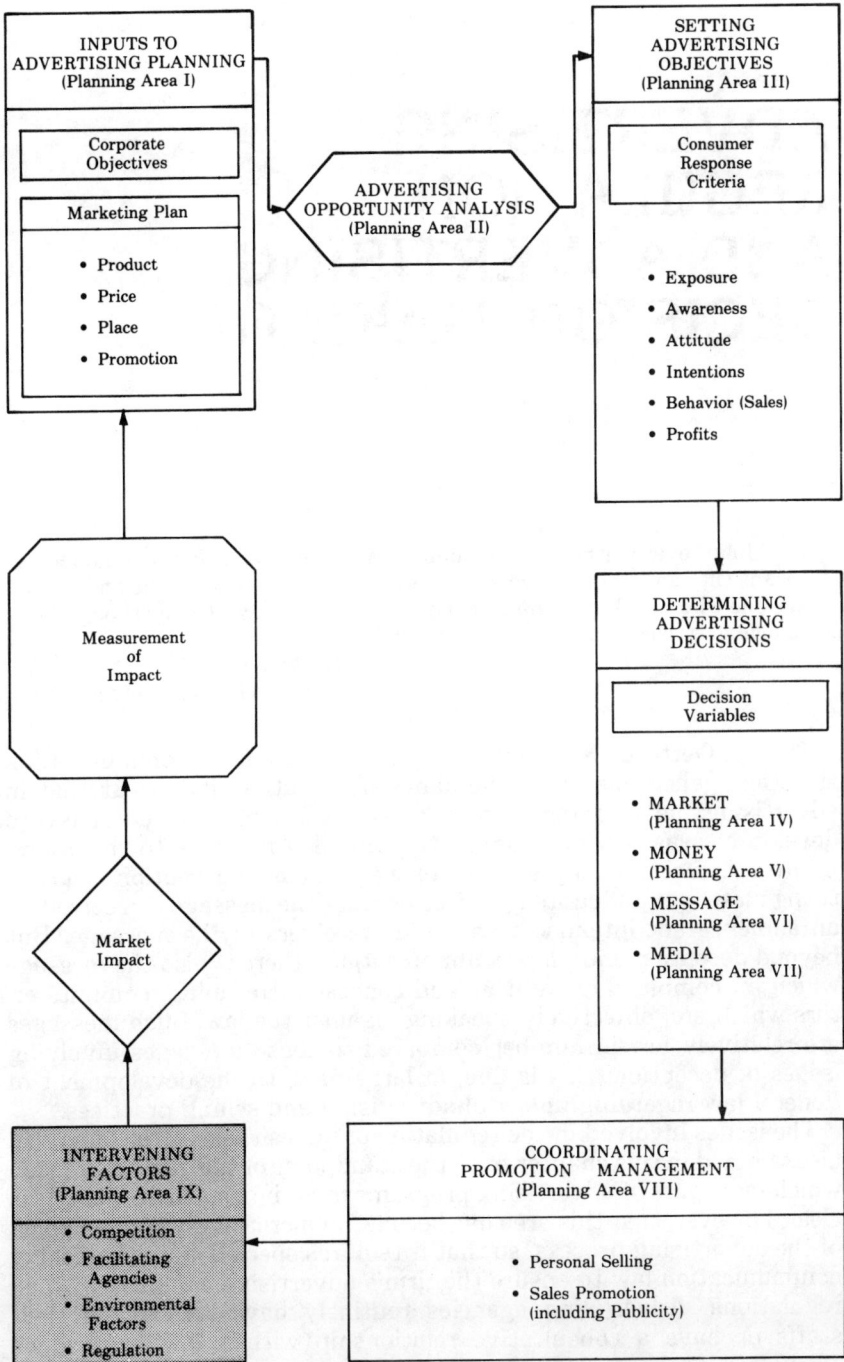

ADVERTISING REGULATION AND ADVERTISING DECISION MAKING

"About every other thing nobody is of the same opinion nobody means the same thing by what they say as the other one means and only the one who is talking thinks he means what he is saying even though he knows very well that that is not what he is saying."
—Gertrude Stein
Everybody's Autobiography

Though Gertrude Stein was referring to two-person communication situations when she made the above observation, it is clear that in advertising, as in interpersonal communication, it is not easy to develop messages which convey the intended message to the appropriate audience. And a great part of the problem of deception in advertising messages undoubtedly arises because the message is received by an audience not intended to serve as receivers of the message. But beyond deception and "mis-communication" there is also the message which, in combined denotative and conotative meaning, commits errors which are, objectively speaking, against the law. Such messages are relatively few in number compared to those messages involving issues of deception; this is due, in large part, to the development of Federal law regarding unlawful advertising and selling practices.

The issues involved in the regulation of undesirable advertising will be examined in this chapter from the standpoint of the general areas in which managers of advertising programs must be knowledgeable. It is clear, however, that this area has become an increasingly complex part of the advertising process, so that it requires specialists in the field of communication law to ensure the firm's advertising complies with all regulations. Advertising agencies routinely have lawyers on their staffs or have a consultative relationship with a law firm which specializes in communication issues in the law. The advertising manager is not expected to be a legal scholar or practitioner. Yet the manager should understand the underlying issues involved so that effective communication with the specialists in this area can take place. The manager should be generally aware of the major Federal legislation impacting on advertising, the nature of deceptive advertising viewpoints, the remedies available to the Government when an advertising program or advertisement is found to be in violation, and the general role of self-regulation in the industry.

FEDERAL REGULATION OF ADVERTISING

The Federal regulation of advertising has developed largely in response to a number of criticisms of advertising dating back to the founding of the United States.[1] Such criticisms can be summarized under two categories: (1) Social criticisms of advertising; and (2) Economic criticisms of advertising. The general issues under each of these headings are summarized below:

I. Social Criticisms of Advertising

Advertising Encourages Materialism and False Values
Advertising Encourages Business Control of the Media
Advertising is Misleading and Deceptive
Advertising Insults Consumers' Intelligence
Advertising is Too Pervasive
Advertising Makes People Buy Things They Do Not Need

II. Economic Criticisms of Advertising

Advertising is Anticompetitive
Advertising is Wasteful
Advertising Promotes Market Concentration, Monopoly
   Prices, and Exorbitant Profits.

A great deal of legislation developed since the 1960's has been due directly to the Consumerism movement. Modern Consumerism started around that time with the issuance by then-President John F. Kennedy of the Consumer Magna Carta which emphasized the rights of all consumers in the United States to have the right to safety, the right to be informed, the right to choose, and the right to be heard. But modern consumerism could be traced fairly directly back to the woman's rights movements at the turn of the century; such organizations were not only concerned with women's rights to vote in elections, but they were also concerned with the role of women in the workplace, especially in terms of compensation issues. Such activities corresponded to the passage of acts such as the 1906 Food and Drug Act and the Federal Trade Commission Act of 1914. Later, during the New Deal era, such consumerist organizations as Consumers Union were founded in response to such muckraking books as *The Jungle*, Vance Packard's famous book on advertising called *The Hidden Persuaders*, and many more books of the same variety. During this time, the Wheeler-Lea Amendment of 1938 to the Food, Drug and Cosmetic Act was passed which gave the Federal Government considerable control over advertising activities. But the most aggressive consumerism came in the 1960's during and after the Kennedy administration; by 1969 there were over 400 consumer protection bills before the Congress. Recent history has shown some decline in Federal interest in advertising regulation, however. The Congress has not passed the Consumer Protection Agency-enabling legislation and has shown considerable interest in curbing the power of the Federal Trade Commission. It is clear, however, that the basis of Federal regulation, that is, the Consumerism movement, is here to stay. Advertising managers must learn to deal with a consumer who is becoming increasingly sophisticated in knowledge, communication powers, and buying habits.

Figure 18–1 summarizes the most important Federal legislation impinging upon advertising which the advertising manager should become generally familiar with as a constraint on the day-to-day activities of the firm's promotion program. State and local legislation are largely subsidiary and of secondary importance to Federal legislation.

DECEPTIVE ADVERTISING

One of the most serious issues facing advertising management today and in the coming years concerns the issues inherent in deceptive advertising. The difficult issues which come into play in this area can be seen in the slogan used several years ago by the Jos. Schlitz Brewing Company. The slogan was, "When you're out of Schlitz, you're out of beer." Clearly, if truth or falsity were the test of harmful advertising, this statement could be objectively proven to be false if the consumer has another brand of beer in the refrigerator but no Schlitz beer. But as is the case with so much advertising, this slogan involves the application of a value judgment and, as such, the truth or falsity standard does not apply.[2] Clearly, it is a matter of taste as to whether a person will accept a brand other than Schlitz for consumption when Schlitz is not available.

The issue which must be confronted is whether or not the above statement and others involving value judgments, which undoubtedly make up the large volume of messages in advertising, is deceptive. Deception can be said to occur in advertising under two conditions: (1) if consumers' perceptions of a situation as a result of exposure to advertising differs from the reality of the situation; and (2) this differing perception process affects consumers' buying behavior. From a legal point of view, deception was defined in the Wheeler-Lea Amendment of 1938:

> ... "false advertisement" means an advertisement other than labeling, which is misleading in a material respect; and in determining whether any advertisement is misleading, there shall be taken into account (among other things) not only representations made or suggested by

statement, word, design, device, sound or any combination thereof but also the extent to which the advertisement fails to reveal facts material in the light of such representations or material with a respect to consequences which may result from the use of the commodity to which the advertisement relates under conditions prescribed in said advertisement, or under such conditions as are customary or usual.[3]

This definition of deception has since been modified by the FTC in its rulings. The FTC's Trade Regulation Rulings are derived from hearings and cover entire industries' unlawful trade practices. The FTC rulings can be appealed in the court system, which is the ultimate source in the definition of deceptive advertising.

Specific issues in deception include the following: (1) The persons deceived; (2) overall impressions generated by an ad; (3) the ambiguous statement; (4) the sin of omission; (5) materiality of the damage; and (6) puffery.[4] Each of these areas is briefly discussed below.

DEFINITION OF DECEIVED PERSONS

Two issues which must be confronted in the deceptive advertising area are the number of people who must be deceived in order for deception to occur in conjunction with a particular advertisement and the nature of the people to be protected.

In 1937, the Supreme Court of the United States indicated that the FTC was supposed to protect the "trusting as well as the suspicious."[5] In the *Gelb* v. FTC case, the low intelligence level of people which the court expected to be protected reached a low.[6] In this case, the FTC had prohibited the company from using a claim that a hair-color product would color the hair "permanently." The claim was that the word "permanent" could imply to some people that new hair would also grow with the color on it. One woman indicated that although she would not be so naive, some people might think this is so; based upon her testimony, the court found the word to be used in a misleading way.

In another case in 1963, the Kirchner case, the court became less liberal in its definition of the persons to be deceived.[7] It was decided that most people would not think that "thin and invisible" actually meant a swimming device was invisible underneath a swimming suit; in addition, the court determined in this case that the target audience to whom the message in the advertisement was aimed should be taken into account when deciding who is deceived. For example, if the intended advertising target market is children between 12 and 15 years of age, then deception should be defined with respect to this group of people.

Still, and despite the 1963 Kirchner case, there is a marked tendency for deception to be defined based upon a relatively small number of people being deceived and with respect to audience segments relatively low in intelligence levels.

Figure 18-1   Major Federal Legislation Relating to Advertising Management

Year	Legislation	Major Advertising-Related Provisions	Advertising Management Concerns
1890	Sherman Act (as amended)	Prohibits: 1. Contracts, combinations, conspiracies in restraint of trade (Section 1). 2. Monopolizing; attempting to monopolize, combinations or conspiracies to monopolize (Section 2).	The courts can regulate monopolistic advertising and refer to the Sherman Act if that advertising acts as a potential barrier to competition, as was done in the ordered divestiture of P&B and Clorox.
1914	Clayton Act (as amended)	Prohibits: 1. Brokerage *per se*, non-proportional advertising and sales allowances, and price discriminations, except where cost justified or where in good faith to meet equally low price of competitor, where effect is substantially to lessen competition or to tend to create monopoly (Section 2), as amended by the Robinson-Patman Act of 1936.	Advertising managers must caution against offering advertising allowances to competitors in a discriminating way that may have some effect on competition.
1914	Federal Trade Commission Act (as amended)	Prohibits: 1. Unfair methods of competition (Section 5). 2. Unfair or deceptive practices in commerce (Section 5, as amended by the Wheeler-Lea Act of 1938).	Recent concepts of deception and unfairness, particularly among special audiences (children, aged, minorities, etc.) present serious limitations on advertising managers even when the truth is told completely and claims can be substantiated.
1936	Robinson-Patman Act	Prohibits: 1. Advertising or sales allowances not made on "proportionately equal terms" to all purchasers.	Same as Clayton Act with respect to discriminatory advertising and promotional allowances.

Year	Act		
1938	Wheeler-Lea Act	Prohibits: 1. "Unfair methods of competition in commerce" (original prohibition in FTC Act) but also prohibits "unfair or deceptive practices in commerce."	Same as FTC Act of 1914 except this Amendment gave the FTC real, very broad powers with respect to potential harm or deception as a result of unfair advertising practices.
1938	Federal Food, Drug and Cometic Act (Amended Pure Food Act)	Added cosmetics and therapeutic devices to the FDA's responsibility. The Act requires specific and informative labeling of foods, drugs, and cosmetics. Broadened the definition of misbranding to include a "false and misleading" label. The FDA was subsequently removed from the Department of Agriculture and is now a part of the Department of Health and Human Services.	
1939	Wool Products Labeling Act	Requires full disclosure of the percentages of new wool, reprocessed wool, and other fibers or fillers used. Such information must be shown on the labels of products containing wool, except carpets, rugs, and some other textile items.	All of these labeling acts have the potential of spreading to advertising. Since they deal with adequately informing the consumer about product ingredients, they could ultimately have impact on advertising campaigns, in the light of the FTC's outlook on affirmative disclosure.
1951	Fur Products Labeling Act	Requires labels that fully disclose the name of the animal and from what part the fur derives, whether the fur is new or used, and whether the fur is bleached or dyed.	
1953	Flammable Fabrics Act	Prohibits the shipment in interstate commerce of wearing apparel and fabrics so highly flammable as to be dangerous when worn.	

Figure 18-1 Major Federal Legislation Relating to Advertising Management (Continued)

Year	Legislation	Major Advertising-Related Provisions	Advertising Management Concerns
1958	Textile Fiber Products Identification Act	Protects consumers against misbranding and false advertising of the fiber content of textile fiber products not covered by the Wool or Fur Products Labeling Acts.	
1958	Automobile Information Disclosure Act	Requires auto manufacturers to affix to the auto the suggested retail price, detailing the price of all extra equipment and transportation charges on all new passenger vehicles.	
1960	Federal Hazardous Substances Labeling Act	Requires warning labels on hazardous household chemicals.	
1962	Kefauver-Harris Drug Amendments (amended Food and Drug Act)	Requires manufacturers to produce drugs in accordance with accepted standards of safety and purity, to provide substantial evidence of their effectiveness and to accurately label them.	
1966	Fair Labeling and Packaging Act	Requires packages to be honestly and informatively labeled and attempts to reduce package size proliferation.	
1966	Cigarette Labeling Act	Requires cigarette manufacturers to label cigarettes: "Caution: Cigarette Smoking may be hazardous to your health."	

Thus, for example, the FTC could in the future require advertisers to make harm and safety disclosures in their advertisements, for example, in cigarette advertising the health warning label may become mandatory; or in the case of harmful toys, the advertisers might need to warn parents.

1967	Wholesome Meat Act	Provides the Secretary of Agriculture specific authority to require inspection and authorizes the Secretary to require denaturing and identification of meat not suitable for human consumption.
1968	Consumer Credit Protection Act	Requires all persons extending credit to another to make full disclosure in writing of all finance charges prior to consummation of the transaction.
1969	Child Protection and Toy Safety Act	Allows FDA to ban products that are so dangerous that adequate safety warnings cannot be given.
1970	Public Health Smoking Act	Bans cigarette advertising on radio and television and revised the caution on cigarette packages to read: "Warning: The Surgeon General has determined that cigarette smoking is hazardous to your health." An amendment in 1973 extended the ban on broadcast advertising to "little cigars."
1970	Poison Prevention	Requires safety packaging for products that may be injurious to children.
1970	Federal Deposit Insurance Act Amendment	Prohibits the issuance of unsolicited credit cards, limits a consumer's liability to $50, regulates credit bureaus, and provides consumers with access to their credit files.

Figure 18-1 Major Federal Legislation Relating to Advertising Management (Continued)

Year	Legislation	Major Advertising-Related Provisions	Advertising Management Concerns
1972	Drug Listing Act	Provides FDA with access to wide information on drug manufacturers.	
1972	Consumer Product Safety Act	Created the machinery for government-enforced quality control and is designed: (1) to protect the public against unreasonable risk of injury from consumer products; (2) to assist consumers in evaluating the safety of consumer products; and (3) to develop uniform safety standards for consumer products and to promote research and investigation into the causes and prevention of product-related injuries and deaths.	
1975	Consumer Product Warranty and Federal Trade Commission Improvements Act	Establishes minimum disclosure standards for written consumer product warranties and defines federal content standards for those warranties. In addition, the Act extends the consumer protection authority of the Federal Trade Commission when deceptive consumer warranties and other unfair acts and practices are found to exist.	

| 1975 | Fair Billing Credit Act | Permits the consumer to withhold payment from the issuer of a credit card when seeking restitution from a merchant for defective merchandise. The Act also provides greater legal protection against credit practices and billing errors by establishing a procedure with which all merchants must comply or else face legal redress. It also prohibits agreements barring discounts to cash-paying customers. |

SOURCE: Adapted from Robert F. Gwinner, *et al., Marketing: An Environmental Perspective* (St. Paul: West Publishing Company, 1977), pp. 348-349 and 366-367, as reprinted in R.L. Anderson and T.E. Barry, *Advertising Management: Text and Cases* (Columbus, Ohio: Charles E. Merrill, 1979), pp. 494-498.

OVERALL IMPRESSIONS OF ADS

When deception is to be ascertained, it is clear that such deception shall be determined based upon the *general impression* created by the ad as a whole. An ad may be literally true, yet deceiving.

For example, in a 1950 decision, the courts ruled that P. Lorillard Company was guilty of deceptive advertising in its campaign against a *Readers' Digest* article which had included a list of cigarette brands with their tar and nicotine content and indicated that all cigarettes were harmful since the differences between them were minor. P. Lorillard ran advertisements which claimed that their brand had the lowest tar and nicotine as indicated by the *Readers' Digest* article; the difference between the Lorillard brand and all others was insignificant.[8] Though Lorillard's claim was literally true, their brand did have the lowest tar and nicotine of all brands in the *Readers' Digest* article, the advertisement led to an incorrect conclusion about the safety of its cigarette relative to other companies' brands.

THE AMBIGUOUS STATEMENT

If an advertisement can be interpreted in any of several ways, and one of these ways could be interpreted as deceptive, the advertisement would be judged to be deceptive. For example, an advertisement by Sterling Drug company indicated that some research was "government supported." The courts decided that this statement could be *interpreted* as "government approved" and was, therefore, deceptive in nature.[9]

In a related matter, if a product has characteristics such that a term must be applied to describe the product even though this term is not completely accurate, this will be allowed. For example, a drink might be described as an orange drink even though it is artificially made to look and taste like oranges. Since this is really the only way to describe the product so that consumers can have some perception of what the product is like generally, this non-literal use of the term will be allowed.[10] However, the FDA also has strict regulations governing the application of label names to products; orange drink rather than orange juice, for example, has a very specific meaning and must be complied with.

THE SIN OF OMISSION

The defense lawyer in a murder trial is not required to divulge all negative material about the client in the courtroom proceedings; this is so since the prosecutor will undoubtedly correct any obvious omissions in this regard. But in advertising, since it is not clear the competition will always provide the "other side" of the story, there are many instances where the FTC and courts have ruled that an advertisement

was deceptive because it did *not* mention some important characteristic of the product, service or idea.

For example, Geritol was required to indicate that its product would
not effectively treat the "tired feeling" which its ads claimed it would
cure.[11] Baldness cures have also been required to directly indicate that
baldness is usually of a hereditary nature and, therefore, untreatable.

MATERIAL FALSEHOODS

The final major consideration in the deception area concerns the
magnitude of the damage inflicted upon consumers by the deceptive
advertisement. For an advertisement to be ascertained as deceptive, it
must contain what is called a "material untruth." A material untruth
is one which, essentially, can have an effect on the consumer's purchasing decision. It must be highly likely that the advertisement would
cause injury to the public. This injury must not necessarily mean that
the consumer suffers actual injury but rather that the consumer is induced to take action which might not have been taken had it not been
for the advertisement, for example, purchase of the product.[12]

The Colgate-Palmolive case involved the use of Rapid Shave cream
to shave sandpaper in a demonstration advertisement. The FTC held
that the ad was deceptive since the sandpaper had to be soaked for
some time before it could be shaved. The FTC claimed this information
was material since consumers were likely to rely upon it when making
purchase decisions. However, the courts disagreed that such a "mock-
up" would affect consumer purchasing decisions. As a result, the FTC
modified its ruling saying that only mock-ups which were intended to
demonstrate visually a quality of the product which was material to
the sale of the product would be prohibited.[13]

PUFFERY

It has been a well-established rule that "puffing" is an acceptable
thing to do in advertising. Puffery has two different forms: (1) It can be
a subjective statement of opinion about a product using terms such as
"best" or "greatest;" (2) It can be an exaggerated claim which is so
outrageous as to be obviously untrue. An example of the first type of
puffing might be the statement "You Can't Get Better than First,"
which was a slogan for a local bank called First National Bank. An example of the second type of puffery can be found in the Pillsbury
Dough Boy; obviously, even though this character is made to talk, it is
not a "real" character.

Preston has the view that over the years the puffery "defense" made
by companies has been upheld by the courts when, in fact, the issue
went beyond puffery and was really deception.[14] There are signs that
the courts are becoming less receptive, however, to the use by companies of the puffery defense. For example, the 1970 case involving the
Standard Oil Company of California in which this company made the

claim in its advertising that Chevron's F-310 additive was "the most long-awaited gasoline development in history" was held to be false.

REMEDIES

The primary formal procedure which has been established by the Federal Trade Commission Act for enforcing its rulings against deceptive practices is the cease and desist order. In some instances involving food, drugs, and cosmetics, the commission has the power to obtain injunctions to stop the use of advertising immediately; however, in most cases the FTC relies upon the power inherent in the cease and desist order. The cease and desist order has been described as a command to "go and sin no more." The suggestion is that it has little practical effect. Sometimes the delays inherent in the cease and desist procedure are lengthy. For example, it took the FTC 16 years to have the Carter Products Company remove the word "liver" from their advertising of "Carter's Little Liver Pills."[15] The FTC has, however, gone beyond the remedy of cease and desist orders; in the 1970's, it developed a remedy called "corrective" advertising.

CORRECTIVE ADVERTISING

The development by the FTC of the concept of corrective advertising stemmed from the famous incident involving advertising for Campbell Soups. It was learned that Campbell advertising included glass marbles in the bowl so that the vegetables would remain on the top of the bowl and be visible, thus giving the impression that the soup was plump with vegetables. The FTC obtained a consent order stopping this process. A consent order is obtained when, within ten days of receiving a complaint, the company agrees to comply with the order and waives rights to the normal administrative procedures and appeals. About 75 percent of the cases brought before the FTC are settled by consent orders. A group of law students organized under the acronym of SOUP (Students Opposing Unfair Practices) filed a petition requesting permission to intervene and proposing that Campbell be required to include affirmative disclosure in all its future advertising for soups. The FTC decided that although Campbell's case did not warrant such corrective advertising, the idea did have merit and could be applied by the FTC in future cases. In the Campbell Soup case, the FTC also accepted SOUP's plea for outside parties to intervene on behalf of the public in deceptive advertising cases. The Chevron F-310 case, mentioned earlier, was actually the first to which the FTC applied corrective advertising remedies, although the first company actually required to conduct corrective advertising was Continental Baking Company. One of its corrective advertisements read as follows:

> I'd like to clear up any misunderstandings you may have had about Profile bread from its advertising or even its name. Does Profile have

fewer calories than other breads? No, Profile has about the same per ounce as other breads. To be exact, Profile has 7 fewer calories per slice. That's because it's sliced thinner. But eating Profile will not cause you to lose weight. A reduction of 7 calories is insignificant. . . .[16]

The concept of corrective advertising has been examined in recent years by several authors. For example, Sawyer suggested that benefits from corrective advertising can decay rapidly.[17] Kuehl and Dyer support this notion and their work showed that the claim-belief form of deception was not significantly affected by corrective advertising messages.[18] However, a significant study by Hunt dealing with the Chevron F-310 case mentioned previously showed that corrective messages reduced favorable attitudes and that various intensities of corrective advertising could produce degrees of favorableness reduction.[19]

It should be noted that the recent case of Listerine has set precedent in the corrective advertising area. The FTC required Warner-Lambert, the makers of Listerine mouthwash, to spend $10,000,000 to correct false impressions given the public regarding the ability of its Listerine product to kill germs and cure colds and sore throats.[20]

ADVERTISING SUBSTANTIATION

In 1971 the Federal Trade Commission adopted a documentation program which shifted the burden of proof in deceptive advertising cases by requiring an advertiser to submit proof to the FTC that advertising claims were truthful. In other words, advertisers would be required to *substantiate* their claims. The new program included the right of the FTC to make advertisers conduct tests to support claims made in their advertising if such evidence was not already in existence. In addition, the new program allowed the FTC to make all such information, except that which would reveal trade secrets and the like, available to the public at large. During this program entire industries were selected, one at a time, in which the major companies were systematically requested to provide such evidence. The first industries affected were the automobile, air conditioner, and electric shaver industries. These were closely followed by the television, shampoo and aspirin product categories.

It should be noted that such a program can have benefits as well as detriments to the advertiser. For example, the FTC tested color television sets to determine which manufacturers were "puffing" and which were not. The Sony company used the results of the testing in its print advertising since the government-conducted tests showed that Sony Trinitron color out-performed all other color televisions. On the other hand, advertising substantiation has had a dampening effect on the amount of research the advertiser will do and the ultimate value of such research to the advertiser. Since it is known that any research can be seized by the FTC and used against an advertiser in a court of law, (copy research results would be a good example), advertisers routinely destroy all research results within a given period of time. This means that historical information on the performance of a brand becomes lost to the advertiser; this may have an effect on the managerial efficiency of the advertising decision making process. In addition, some say that the rule, since it makes advertisers very leery about making any claims which cannot be objectively proven, has resulted in "no-advertising" advertising; that is, much advertising now is advertising which says essentially nothing of substance since such substance would need to be demonstrated to the FTC. Due, in part, to this type of dilemma from such programs, the advertising substantiation program of the Federal Trade Commission has been dramatically reduced in scope through pressure from the United States Congress in the very recent past.

SELF-REGULATION

The notion that self-regulation can be an effective force in the regulation of market forces has always been a compelling idea. This has become particularly true in light of the problems which developed, as outlined above, with the Federal Trade Commission's program of advertising substantiation. In 1971, acknowledging the need for better self-regulation than existed at that time, representatives of the American Association of Advertising Agencies, American Advertising Federation, Association of National Advertisers, and Council of Better Business Bureaus met to establish a National Advertising Review Council. The council then formulated by-laws and operating procedures for a National Advertising Review Board (NARB). The board consists of 30 advertiser members, 10 advertising agency members, and 10 public members. To expedite and begin the process of review and evaluation, complaints are directed to the National Advertising Division (NAD), a division established within the Council of Better Business Bureaus. In addition to review and evaluation of complaints, the NAD has responsibility for monitoring of print and broadcast advertising.

The overall procedure involving the NARB and NAD is as follows and as shown in Figure 18-2. The NAD first requests substantiation of claims from an advertiser accused in a complaint. Following its investigations, the NAD may dismiss the complaint or find it justified. If the advertiser disagrees with the NAD decision, this decision may be appealed to the NARB, where a five-member panel of board members may be appointed to review the case. If the panel members find against the advertiser and the advertiser refuses to change or stop the advertising, the case is then referred to the appropriate government agency, perhaps the FTC.

In his study of the first five years of operation of the NARB, Zanot found that in 1976, 36 percent of the cases were substantiated, 35 percent led to modification or discontinuation, 28 percent were closed administratively, and only 1 percent reached the NARB panel level. In the same year, he found that 52 percent of the complaints were in-

Figure 18-2 The Mechanisms of the
National Advertising Review Board (NARB):
Advertising Self-regulatory Procedures Step by Step

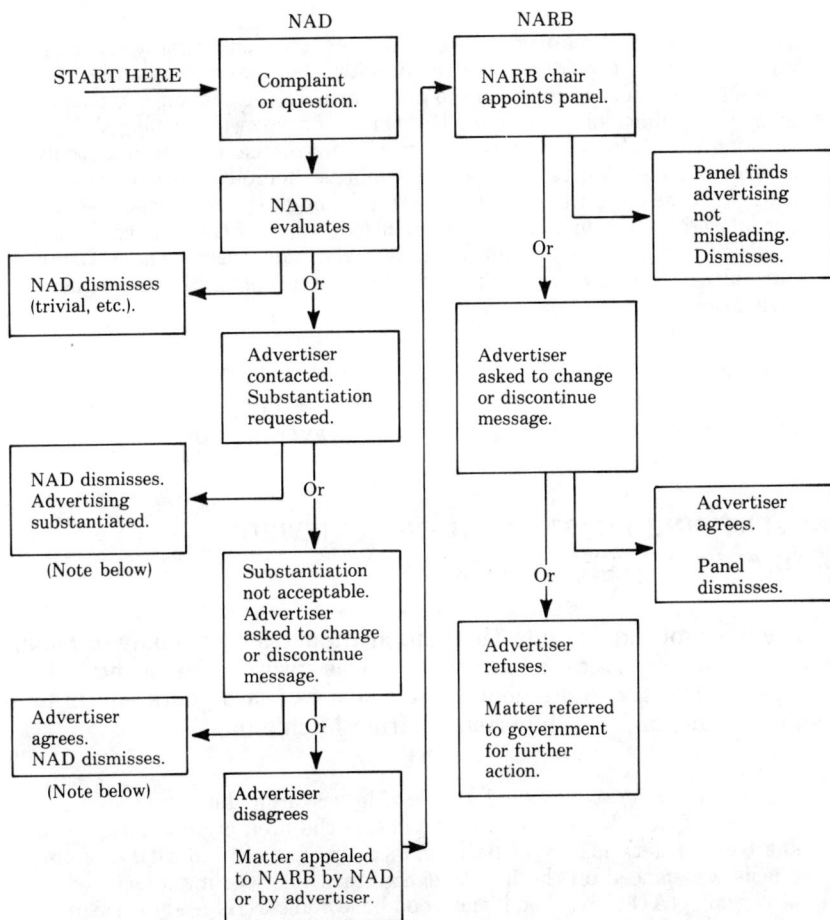

NAD   NARB

START HERE → **Complaint or question.**

NARB chair appoints panel.

NAD evaluates

Or

Panel finds advertising not misleading. Dismisses.

NAD dismisses (trivial, etc.). ← Or

Advertiser contacted. Substantiation requested.

Advertiser asked to change or discontinue message.

NAD dismisses. Advertising substantiated. ← Or

(Note below)

Advertiser agrees. Panel dismisses.

Substantiation not acceptable. Advertiser asked to change or discontinue message.

Or

Advertiser agrees. NAD dismisses. ← Or

(Note below)

Advertiser refuses. Matter referred to government for further action.

Advertiser disagrees. Matter appealed to NARB by NAD or by advertiser.

Note: If the original complaint originated outside the system, the outside complainant at this point can appeal to the chairman of NARB for a panel adjudication. Granting of such appeal is at the chairman's discretion.

SOURCE: *The National Advertising Review Board 1971-1976* (New York: NARB, 1977).

itiated by NAD monitoring, 26 percent by competitors, and only 10 percent by consumers or consumer groups.[21] Zanot drew the following conclusions about self-regulation upon the termination of his study of the NARB process.

Apparently, self-regulation has been a response and a reply to forces impinging upon the trade from the outside. Self-regulation can be considered a reaction by the trade to downturns in the economy, criticism from the public, or especially, the threat of government legislation. Although the altruistic motive of protecting consumers undoubtedly enters to some degree, the primary motive behind self-regulation is thought to be enlightened self-interest. Although this analysis does not permit tight cause-and-effect statements, it appears that the trade has used self-regulation to not only eradicate false and deceptive advertising but also to dampen public criticism and forestall government legislation.[22]

It is instructive to examine two examples of the NARB in operation as illustrated by the British Industries Company situation and the Sterling Drug Company's problem with Bayer aspirin.[23]

ADVERTISING SUBSTANTIATION REVIEWED AND FOUND ACCEPTABLE

The basis of inquiry into the British Industries Company (a manufacturer of phonograph turntables) was print advertising which claimed, "The turntable nobody had heard of two years ago is now Number One, and it's imported . . . from Michigan."

The advertiser was asked to provide research data to prove the "Number One" designation and to define the area of superiority, i.e., share-of-market, quality of performance, and also to indicate why emphasis was placed on the fact that the turntable was manufactured in Michigan. NAD also asked if the wood base and cartridge shown as part of each turntable in the advertisement was included in the prices for each model.

The advertiser submitted data to show that BIC's two top-selling models had a greater percent of total unit sales than the best-selling models of major competitors. The reference to Michigan was stressed with humorous intent since most turntables are of foreign import. Representative dealer ads from different U.S. regions were also presented to indicate that in many cases cartridges and wood bases were included in the approximate costs listed in the advertisement for each model.

The advertiser further stated that the information provided was no longer germane since the subject advertisement had been discontinued and there are no intentions to use it in the future.

While the advertising had been discontinued, NAD felt that the claims had been supported.[24]

ADVERTISING MODIFIED OR DISCONTINUED

The basis of inquiry with regard to the Sterling Drug Company's Bayer aspirin brand was television and print ads which stated: "A government-sponsored study showed 99 times out of a hundred, people got no stomach upset with Bayer ... so get genuine Bayer Aspirin. Proven effective. Gentle to the stomach." The commercials also stated "As to how they work, substitutes can't equal Bayer. You sacrifice an important therapeutic action with an aspirin substitute."

> As to the "gentle to the stomach" claim, NAD felt that the government-sponsored study referred to in the advertising only considered the subjective symptom of upset stomach. It did not consider overall product gentleness or objective symptoms which can be present in many cases where aspirin is taken. Therefore, NAD felt it inappropriate to say Bayer Aspirin is "gentle to the stomach."
>
> The therapeutic action referred to in the advertising is the relief of inflammation. NAD knows that Bayer Aspirin has an anti-inflammatory property while acetaminophen, i.e., "Aspirin substitute," does not. While the advertiser has submitted evidence that aspirin has an anti-inflammatory effect at label recommended dosages, NAD is concerned that describing this effect as an "important therapeutic action" may overstate the case.
>
> The advertiser, while not in accord with NAD's opinion, has not made the claims in question for some time and has no plans to use them in the future. NAD has no objection to the claims in the advertiser's current television commercial, the text of which is as follows:
>
> Woman: I switched to Bayer. I thought I had a sensitive tummy and I heard aspirin might upset it. So I began taking aspirin substitutes. Then I read that inflammation often accompanies pain and aspirin substitutes have nothing to relieve inflammation. Also a major hospital study showed 99 times out of 100, Bayer aspirin doesn't upset the stomach. So I switched to Bayer.
>
> Voice-over: The kind of relief you can't get from an aspirin substitute.[25]

Throughout the 1970's, the emergence of the NARB and the toughening of media acceptance standards (for example, the television networks' and the National Association of Broadcasters' codes) have generally led to a self-regulatory climate far more serious than any of the past. And, given the presence of the Federal regulatory structure discussed earlier in this chapter, albeit in the context of a somewhat weakened FTC, it is likely that it will remain so into the 1980's.

A contrast of the NARB examples above with some of those litigated cases referred to earlier in this chapter clearly shows that the desirable path for advertising management involves self-regulation involving tough standards so that government is not required to be involved in advertising management decision making processes. Just as clearly, the most desirable course for advertising management is to pursue a managerial course whereby there is no reason to involve either the self-regulatory processes of the NARB or the Federal regulatory processes of the FTC. Not only is truthful and non-deceptive advertising healthy for the individual manager's company, but it is also healthy for the advertising industry and society as a whole.[26]

QUESTIONS AND PROBLEMS

1. Should advertising to children be banned? Would this ban only include television advertising? Why or why not?
2. Examine the Canadian Broadcasting code for children. What elements would you add or subtract to such a code? Should a similar code be developed for other groups in the society? Which groups?
3. Should certain kinds of appeals be restricted in advertising? For example, should the use of sex in advertising be banned? How would this ban work if it were to be implemented?
4. How does the NARB compare with other self-regulation forms in other sectors of the society, for example, with the American Medical Associations' Code of Ethics and other self-regulation in the medical sector?
5. Do you agree or disagree with the trimming by Congress of the power of the Federal Trade Commission? What does this mean in terms of the Consumer Movement in the United States?
6. What proportion of problem advertising do you believe is untruthful and what proportion is deceptive? What is the difference between truth and nondeception?
7. Examine any recent issue of your local newspaper. Count all advertisements which are display ads (i.e., do not count theatre bills or want ads) and categorize them as informative or persuasive in nature. Are any of these untruthful or deceptive?
8. Would you be in favor of the government taking action in the cereal industry? What action? In what regard would advertising be involved? What is the basic problem in this industry as you see it?

ENDNOTES

1. See, for example, S. Watson Dunn and Arnold M. Barban, *Advertising: Its Role in Modern Marketing* (New York: The Dryden Press, 1978), Chapters 4 and 5, for a detailed discussion of the criticisms of advertising in the United States.
2. See the discussion of this matter by E. John Kottman, "Truth and the Image of Advertising," *Journal of Marketing* (October 1969).
3. 52 Stat. 114 (1938), 15 U.S.C., 55(a) (1958).
4. This categorization of deceptive advertising issues has been suggested by D.A. Aaker and J.G. Myers, *Advertising Management* (New York: Prentice-Hall, Inc., 1975), pp. 570-575.
5. FTC v. *Standard Educ. Society,* 302 US 112, 116 (1937).
6. *Gelb* v. FTC, 144 F 2d 580 (2d Cir. 1944).
7. Trade Reg. Rep. 16664 (FTC, Nov. 7, 1963).
8. *P. Lorillard Co.* v. FTC, 186 F. 2d 52 (4th Cir. 1950).
9. FTC v. *Sterling Drug, Inc.,* 215 F Supp. 327, 330 (S.D. N.Y.) aff'd. 317 F. 2d 699 (2d Cir. 1963).
10. FTC v. *Morrissey,* 47 F 2d 101, 103 (7th Cir. 1931).

11. *J.B. Williams Co.*, 3 Trade Reg. Rep. 17, 339 (FTC Dkt. No. 8547, 1965), appeal docketed, no. 16, 969 (6th Cir. Dec. 3, 1965).
12. Ira M. Millstein, "The Federal Trade Commission and False Advertising," *Columbia Law Review* (March 1964), p. 438.
13. *Colgate-Palmolive Co.* v. FTC, 310 F. 2d 89 (1st Cir. 1962).
14. Ivan L. Preston, *The Great American Blow-Up* (Madison: The University of Wisconsin Press, 1975).
15. *Carter Products, Inc.* v. FTC, 186 F 2d 821 (7th Cir. 1951).
16. "Mea Culpa, Sort of," *Newsweek* (September 27, 1971), p. 89.
17. Alan G. Sawyer, "The Need to Measure Attitudes and Beliefs Over Time: The Case of Deceptive and Corrective Advertising," *Proceedings,* American Marketing Association (August 1976), pp. 380-385.
18. Philip G. Kuehl and Robert F. Dyer, "Brand Belief Measures in Deceptive Corrective Advertising: An Experimental Assessment," *Proceedings,* American Marketing Association (August 1976), pp. 373-379.
19. H. Keith Hunt, "Effects of Corrective Advertising," *Journal of Advertising Research* (October 1973), pp. 15-22.
20. George Hartman, "Courts Affirm, Spell Out Rules for Corrective Ads," *Marketing News* (October 21, 1977).
21. Eric J. Zanot, *The National Advertising Review Board: Premises and Performances,* unpublished doctoral dissertation, College of Communications, University of Illinois at Urbana-Champaign, 1977, p. 202.
22. *Ibid.*, p. 326.
23. *News From NAD* (New York: National Advertising Division, CBBB), April 18, 1977.
24. *Ibid.*
25 *Ibid.*
26. For a discussion of issues involved in the perception of advertising as an institution see C.H. Sandage and John D. Leckenby, "Student Attitudes Toward Advertising: Institution vs. Instrument," *Journal of Advertising* (Vol. 9, no. 2, 1980), pp. 29-32, and Kim B. Rotzoll, James E. Haefner, and C.H. Sandage, *Advertising in Contemporary Society: Perspectives Toward Understanding* (Columbus: Grid Publishing Company, 1976).

CASES IN REGULATION AND ADVERTISING DECISION MAKING

- The Borden Company
- The American Thermos Products Company
- The Parkinson Company
- Wonderland Toys, Inc.

CASES IN REGULATION AND ADVERTISING DECISION MAKING

Case 19-1—The Borden Company
(Advertising and Value)

The Borden Milk Company, since 1938, has packed evaporated milk under the private labels of distributors in addition to the milk which they sold under the Borden brand.

PRODUCT QUALITIES

The company has always packed the same grade and quality of milk under both types of labels. Thus, the distributor brand milk which Borden sells is chemically identical to Borden brand. It is processed and packed in the same plants and in the same way, the only difference being that distributor brand labels belonging to the customer are put on the cans instead of Borden brand labels.

PRICE POLICY

As a matter of policy Borden has always sold its distributor label evaporated milk at lower prices than its Borden brand evaporated milk. The price for the distributor label milk varies from plant to plant and from month to month at each plant, but it is always substantially lower than the Borden brand price which is uniform throughout the country.

DUAL BRAND DISTRIBUTION

The distributors who purchased the product for sale under their own labels all continued to buy and stock the Borden brand along with their own private brand. In spite of the price differential the Borden brand was generally a big seller in most of these outlets. Although the distributor brands carried a larger gross margin, the owners of these brands did not always get a larger net profit than they realized from the Borden brand sales.

FEDERAL TRADE COMMISSION, CEASE AND DESIST ORDER

The Federal Trade Commission reviewed the pricing policy of the Borden Company and considered the policy to be a violation of the Robinson-Patman Act and on January 30, 1963, issued a cease and desist order of this pricing practice. The Federal Register of February 19, 1963 carried the following reference to the FTC action:

> Order requiring the producer of Borden brand evaporated milk since 1892, and which since about 1938 has packed the same grade and quality of evaporated milk under the private labels of the purchasers as well as under its own Borden brand, to cease discriminating in price between its customers buying the milk under the Borden label and those buying the product under private label.
>
> The order to cease and desist, including further order requiring report of compliance therewith, is as follows:
>
> It is ordered, That respondent The Borden Company, a corporation, its officers, representatives, agents and employees, directly or through any corporate or other device, in, or in connection with, the sale of food products in commerce, as "commerce" is defined in the amended Clayton Act, do forthwith cease and desist from discriminating in the price of such products of like grade and quality by selling to any purchaser at a price higher than the price charged any other purchaser who, in fact, competes with the purchaser paying the higher price or with a customer of the purchaser paying the higher price.
>
> It is further ordered, That respondent The Borden Company, a corporation, shall, within sixty (60) days after service upon it of this order, file with the Commission a report, in writing, setting forth in detail the manner and form in which it has complied with the order to cease and desist set forth herein.

THE BORDEN DEFENSE

The Borden Company did not dispute FTC claims that the products sold under different labels at different prices were physically and chemically of like grade and quality. They did, however, contend that the grade and quality of products may vary either because of differences in "intrinsic superior quality" or because of "intense public demand" for one product as compared with another.

The record in the market clearly establishes that Borden brand evaporated milk does command a higher price than distributor brand milk at all levels of distribution. Customers at the retail level are willing to pay more for it than for distributor brands because of the Borden name.

QUESTIONS FOR DISCUSSION

1. Evaluate the claims and counter-claims made in the Borden Company case.
2. Do you agree or disagree with the order set forth by the Federal Trade Commission with respect to Borden? Why or why not?

Case 19-2—The American Thermos Products Company[1] (Problems Involved in Protecting a Trademark)[2]

COMPANY BACKGROUND

About the turn of the century the Thermos-Gesellschaft MBH, a German concern, was producing and marketing a vacuum bottle as a commercial product for general use both in Germany and the United States. This bottle was an adaptation of a vacuum flask developed about 1893 by Sir James Dewar for laboratory use.

In 1907 The American Thermos Bottle Company was formed and took over the U.S. business of Thermos-Gesellschaft, and the name "Thermos" was registered with the U.S. Patent office. Sales of this bottle expanded rapidly and was a very profitable product for American Thermos.

EARLY PROMOTION EFFORTS OF AMERICAN THERMOS

Vacuum ware was being produced and marketed at this time by several other companies in addition to American Thermos. When the company started operations such generic terms as "vacuum-jacketed bottle" were in use in the industry. From the beginning of their operations, however, the Thermos Company avoided the use of these generic terms. All of their advertising was directed at popularizing the name

"Thermos Bottle," and in this they were very successful. The following are examples taken from American Thermos Company's 1910 catalogue showing an encouragement for the generic use of Thermos as a synonym for "vacuum insulated."

" 'Thermos' is a household word."

"Today we are housed in the twelve-story fireproof Thermos Building located in the heart of Manhattan."

"That Thermos is a household word and that the Thermos Product is known, used, and appreciated throughout the civilized world;

"That Thermos is sold and recommended by every good store everywhere;

"That Thermos has become indispensable in the nursery and in the sick room and for other household purposes;

"That Thermos has become alike indispensable to the sportsman, workman, yachtsman, automobilist, aeronaut, explorer, student—in a word, everybody needs Thermos;

"Please bear in mind: Thermos is a GLASS PRODUCT, but will last a lifetime if handled with care—as a glass product."

During this early period, the Thermos Company was aware of what it later described as *"careless" use by the public of the trademark in a generic sense. At the time, however, this was considered to be advantageous, free advertising*. The Thermos Company estimated that in 1917 this was equivalent to three to four million dollars worth of advertising.

This is the line which the company pursued vigorously until 1923 when it brought a trademark infringement action against the W. T. Grant Company. Although American Thermos won this case, it was decided on a technicality. The judge who decided the case suggested that "Thermos" might have become a descriptive term, i.e., generic, and, hence, invalid as a trademark. A defense based on this position was dismissed, however, because it had not been raised in time by W. T. Grant.

EFFORTS TO PROTECT THERMOS AS A BRAND NAME

Following the W. T. Grant Company experience Thermos Company management recognized and became concerned with the possibility of losing the exclusive right to the use of "Thermos" as a brand name. The company changed its advertising approach and utilized the generic names, "vacuum bottle" and "vacuum jug," by displaying them prominently in advertising and in their catalogues. This was the first time that these generic names had been used by American Thermos, although the company had been in existence well over fifteen years.

In spite of the adoption of this new policy, the company was not always consistent in this practice. Occasionally they reverted to the use of thermos as a generic term in the hope, obviously, of gaining additional "free" advertising through the popularization of the Thermos name. Other efforts made to protect it were generally inconsistent and ineffective. The company began to protest the use of thermos in a generic sense in dictionaries and other publications. No affirmative action was taken, however, to seek out these generic uses specifically. American Thermos protested only those cases which happened to come to its attention. Furthermore, if a publication or a writer, after receiving a protest letter, failed to comply, the company usually did not pursue the matter further. The number of protests registered by American Thermos during the period from 1923 to the early 1950's was small in comparison with the number of generic uses of "Thermos."

In a letter from A. H. Payson, vice president of the American Thermos Bottle Company, dated January 8, 1952, to F. S. Slyder, a field representative, Payson wrote:

> "We have had numerous instances of having protested the misuse of 'Thermos,' however, a short time later another violation pops up. The only real answer, of course, is a suit, the winning of a judgment and the broadcasting of the result to all of our customers.
> Action has been contemplated; however, management here as well as our attorneys *are very loath to go to law to enforce our trademark rights. There is a very real danger that some . . . might decide, particularly, if he himself has been in the habit of using 'Thermos' as a generic term,* to declare it that. Damage of an adverse decision would be irreparable as you know. I question very much if the decision were left up to you that you would decide to go to law."

The period from 1954 to 1962 was one in which American Thermos put on a determined campaign to protect the word "Thermos" as a trademark. The name of the corporation was changed to The American Thermos Products Company, and all items such as tents, camp stoves, lanterns, and bottle openers manufactured by the firm were labeled "Thermos" brand. The policing activity against improper uses of the term was intensified. In 1957 the company sent 178 letters of protest, 270 in 1958, 1109 in 1959, 950 in 1960, and 1171 in 1961. These numbers indicate the extent of the use of thermos as a generic term. In 1959 the company's clipping service was extended to include editorial and literary references to "Thermos." Prior to that year the clipping service had been limited to appearances of "thermos" in advertising. Protesting letters were sent to writers and editors who misused the trademark by spelling it without an initial capital.

Aladdin Industries, Incorporated was one company which had been very openly infringing on the Thermos trademark for several years. Aladdin made a variety of products among which was a line of vacuum ware. In 1958 Thermos Products Company charged Aladdin with selling vacuum bottles under the name "thermos" bottles. Aladdin acknowledged that it had been doing so, but they claimed they were doing this because the word had become a generic term. Claims and counter-claims were exhanged between The Thermos Company and Aladdin until 1962 when Thermos Company management decided they could no longer permit Aladdin to continue this flagrant infringement and that they had no alternative but to take legal action. They did this in a suit filed in 1962.

The Thermos Company lost the case. The court ruled that the name had become so well known that it had finally become generic, and American Thermos Products Company was no longer its exclusive owner. The judge ruled that the recent, almost frantic, efforts of the owners to protect the name had come too late. He was also of the opinion that the company itself had contributed greatly to the loss of exclusive ownership. From the beginning the advertising objective had been to popularize the term "Thermos Bottle." The company's 1910 catalogue stated that "Thermos is a household word." In the trial the court pointed out that, intentionally or not, this was "an encouragement for generic use of a synonym for 'vacuum insulated.' " The judge said further, "The plaintiff's extraordinary efforts, commencing in the middle of the 1950's and carried on into the time of the trial, came too late to keep the word 'thermos' from falling into the public domain: rather it was an effort to pull it back from the public domain—something it could not and did not accomplish."

QUESTIONS FOR DISCUSSION

1. How would you have modified, changed, or expanded the efforts employed to protect the "Thermos" brand name?
2. What role could advertising play in the protection of such a brand name?
3. Do you agree or disagree with the judge's decision in this case? Why or why not?

ENDNOTES

1. The collaboration of Professor Emeritus F.M. Jones on this case is duly noted.
2. A trademark is a brand name of a product. This is a word, name, symbol, or device used to identify a manufacturer's or distributor's goods and distinguish them from others. It must be in use in interstate commerce before it can be registered at the Patent Office. The certificate of registration remains in force for 20 years (providing an affidavit of continued use is properly filed) and may be renewed without limit for additional 20-year periods.

Case 19-3—The Parkinson Company

USE OF ADVERTISING ALLOWANCES TO REPLACE CONSUMER ADVERTISING

The Parkinson Company, a manufacturer of pickles and relishes, faced the necessity in early 1982 of curtailing its program of consumer brand advertising because of a serious shortage of working capital. As a means of retaining retail distribution and of stimulating aggressive selling on the part of retailers to compensate for the discontinuance of its own advertising, the company considered adopting the policy of granting advertising allowances to customers.

The Parkinson Company had two distinct markets: the soda fountain market, which it reached through wholesale druggists, wholesale confectioners, and wholesale tobacco firms; and the grocery market, reached through wholesale grocers and by direct sales to chain store organizations. The total annual sales of the company amounted to several million dollars.

Almost 50% of the output of the company was sold under distributor (private) brands, most of which were owned by chain store groups. The portion sold to the soda fountain market, although sold under the Parkinson brand, did not reach the public as the company's brand. Company sales executives believed that soda fountains and lunchrooms purchased on a price and quality basis with little reference to brands.

In 1975, the Parkinson Company had set up an annual advertising budget of $100,000 for consumer brand advertising; most of this advertising had been placed in newspapers, car cards, and outdoor posters. The company officials had been highly satisfied with the effectiveness of this brand advertising and would have continued to advertise had not an unsuccessful attempt to market a sandwich spread in 1978 brought on a severe financial crisis.

One of the voluntary chains which had done business with Parkinson for several years, the Shop and Save Stores, began to develop rapidly. In 1976 this group of stores purchased one-fifth of the Parkinson Company output. A large portion of the purchases made by the Shop and Save Stores was sold under the Shop and Save brand.

At the beginning of 1981 the Shop and Save stores placed an unusually large order for Shop and Save Sweet Pickles, with the understanding that the Parkinson Company would give, in addition to its usual 2½% rebate, a cash advertising allowance of 15 cents a case. The advertising allowance was to be spent entirely at the discretion of Shop and Save retailers.

During 1981 sales of Shop and Save Sweet Pickles had more than tripled under the stimulus provided by the increased advertising. The experiment was regarded by the Parkinson Company as so successful that the executives considered making a standard offer of an advertising allowance, both to firms selling Parkinson products under the Parkinson brand and to firms using their own brands.

QUESTIONS FOR DISCUSSION

1. Would you advise the Parkinson Company to continue offering such advertising allowances? Why or why not?

Case 19–4—Wonderland Toys, Inc.[1]

Wonderland Toys is one of the ten largest toy companies in the United States. The company has been known for its innovative product development in the toy industry. Recently, the company developed a product line, Space Travelers,[2] which is a series of toys modeled after the popular TV program of the same name. The whole product line consists of a plastic spaceship, five 8-inch-tall dolls which resemble the captain and the four crew members in the TV show, and several accessories such as a radar and a telescope.

Wonderland's promotional policy is to heavily advertise its products to children through television which is a primary medium to the young audience. The heavy advertising has been supported by the company philosophy that "children are the best salesmen": Even though children are not able to purchase expensive toys by themselves, they have the most powerful influence on the parents' purchase decisions for toys. Like many other toy companies, Wonderland Toys allocates a larger amount of its total advertising budget to the Christmas sales season than in other seasons. Since Wonderland was one of the first companies that introduced the "sci-fi" (science-fiction) or space toys, they launched an extensive advertising campaign for the Space Travelers series on television before Christmas in order to capture a larger share of the market before the competitors might introduce similar products.

INFLUENCE OF TELEVISION ON CHILDREN'S TOY DEVELOPMENT

Hundreds of companies are competing by introducing new items in the toy industry. In the 1977 Toy Fair, more than 7,000 new items were introduced by 700 companies. Many of such new items do not stay in the market very long: a market research firm estimates that nearly three-quarters of all new toys never succeed. And, many of the top-selling toys disappear in a short time when a fad has passed. The "sci-fi" toys, which were initially inspired by the movie, Star Wars, as well as many other TV-inspired toys, may be fad items since new, attractive characters are introduced in TV shows one after another. In addition to the characters of popular children's programs such as Mr. Rogers or Sesame Street, those of adult-oriented programs, such as Six Million Dollar Man or Charlie's Angels, are featured in children's dolls and games today. A recent trend in toy marketing is that several items are sold together under the same character with one basic media campaign in order to extend the lifespan of the same series.

ADVERTISING PRACTICES IN THE TOY INDUSTRY

The total toy industry sales exceeded the plateau of $1 billion in 1962, passed $2 billion in 1969, and the industry sales in 1976 were estimated to be approximately $3.8 billion. A large amount of advertising expenditures is spent on television. In 1976, as much as 94.8% of the measured advertising expenditures went to television.[3] In the same year, over half of the 47 million network TV advertising dollars were invested in the Saturday morning children's shows. Also, $35 million out of the total of $47 million were spent in the fourth quarter of the year, the best season to advertise for Christmas.

Television is, indeed, the predominant medium in children's advertising. The 1975 Nielsen study indicates that children aged 2 to 5 years watch television, on the average, 3 hours and 47 minutes a day and children aged 6 to 11 years watch television 3 hours and 41 minutes a day. Based on these viewing hours, it is estimated that children are exposed to approximately 20,000 TV commercials per year on the average.[4]

Although television is considered to be a most effective medium to reach children, some toy companies have been reaching parents, especially mothers, through magazines taking different approaches. For example, Dunbee-Combex-Marx, Ltd. ran a special promotion in women's magazines on the safety of its products for preschoolers. While children tend to respond to particular items such as Barbie Dolls, parent-oriented advertising appears to aim at building long-range brand or company loyalties.

A new trend in toy advertising is an increased use of different times other than Saturday mornings. Exhibit 19–1 shows the allocation of advertising expenditures by day part.

Exhibit 19-1   Allocation of Network TV Advertising Expenditures for Toys (in thousands)

Commercial Time	1975	1976	% change
Children's shows	$21,684.8	$26,407.5	+ 21.7%
Mon-Fri Daytime	4,468.0	7,709.8	+ 72.6
Primetime	3,878.8	5,317.6	+ 37.1
Evening Entertainment Specials	1,180.4	2,780.2	+135.5
Sports events	491.2	2,540.0	+417.1
PM Variety	190.7	674.5	+253.7
News	106.1	428.9	+304.2
Mon-Fri Early AM	335.4	140.2	− 58.2
Other	530.5	901.1	+ 70.0
Total	$32,865.9	$46,900.6	+ 42.7%

SOURCE: Broadcast Advertising Reports. Adapted from *Marketing and Media Decisions*, November 1977, p. 146.

As it is shown in Exhibit 19–1, sports events and evening entertainment specials gained as much investment as Saturday morning shows in 1976. It may be noted that some regulations such as the NAB code apply to children's programming time.

LEGAL ENVIRONMENT OF TOY ADVERTISING

Toy advertising involves two major regulatory issues, i.e., product safety and the fairness of advertising to children. The former is embodied in the Toy Safety Standards of 1969. The latter is incorporated into several self-regulations as well as it is guided by the Federal Trade Commission. The 1970's saw an especially increased concern by the public and in government about children's advertising.

REGULATIONS BY THE FEDERAL TRADE COMMISSION

The FTC is responsible for the *content* of commercial messages, whereas the Federal Communications Commission (FCC) has jurisdiction over the *amount* and *scheduling* of advertising. Below are some of the examples of the FTC cases of toy advertising.

In the early 1960's, the FTC charged Levis Marx and Company, Remco Industries, and Ideal Toy Corporation saying that they "exploited a consumer group unqualified by age or experience to appreciate the possibility that representations may be exaggerated." The former two companies, Marx and Remco, accepted consent orders which forbid them to make such exaggerated implications in advertising. On the other hand, Ideal Toy Corporation, which was charged for its deceptive commercials that implied that its robot and doll products can move automatically, denied the FTC charges. However, this company voluntarily withdrew the disputed commercials.

SELF-REGULATIONS

The major self-regulations on toy advertising are listed chronologically below.

1961 *Toy Advertising Guidelines* issued by the National Association of Broadcasters' (NAB) TV Code Review Board.

These are general guidelines dealing with the following issues:

1. Commercial dramatizations that unfairly glamorize a toy and make it seem to be more than it is.
2. Over-simplification such as "only" and "just" applied to the price of a toy exceeding a few dollars.
3. Implications that possession of the toy is a status symbol.

1975 *Children's Advertising Guidelines* issued by the Children's Advertising Review Unit of the National Advertising Division (NAD) of the Council of Better Business Bureaus. This review unit was established within the NAD in 1974.

The purpose of the Guidelines is "to ensure that advertising directed to children is truthful, accurate, and fair to children's perceptions." The guidelines are applicable to "children's programs" and to those "programs in which audience patterns typically contain more than 50 percent children."

1975 *Children's Television Advertising Guidelines* issued by the National Association of Broadcasters' (NAB) Television Code. The NAB Code prohibits certain products such as drugs from being advertised directly to children, lists certain presentational techniques which may and may not be used in commercials, and sets time limits for advertising during children's programming. The guidelines are applicable to weekend mornings and other programs oriented specifically to children.

The Children's Television Advertising Guidelines by the NAB has a special section which deals with all television toy advertising and other advertising designed primarily for children which emphasizes a product's play value. The following six provisions are included in this section.

1. Advertising shall present the toy on its actual merit as a play thing. It shall neither exaggerate nor distort play value.
2. Audio and visual production techniques shall not misrepresent the appearance and performance of toys. Any view of a toy or any demonstration of its performance shall be limited to that which a child is reasonably capable of reproducing.
3. When a toy is presented in the context of a play environment, the setting and situation shall be that which a child is reasonably capable of reproducing.
4. The use of stock film footage, real-life counterparts of toys, fantasy, and animation are acceptable if: (a) they are confined to the first one-third of the commercial, (b) no child or toy appears within them and, (c) the commercial as a whole conforms to the Children's Television Advertising Guidelines.

   Any other use of stock film footage, real-life counterparts, fantasy, and animation and any overglamorization (e.g., large displays, dazzling visual effects) is not permitted.
5. The original purchase must be clearly disclosed in the body copy of the commercial. There shall not be any implication that optional extras, additional units or items that are not available with the toy, accompany the toy's original purchase.

   In the closing 5 seconds of the commercial the original purchase must be disclosed by video with audio disclosure where necessary for children.
6. Advertising shall not employ costumes and props which are not available with the toy as sold or are not reasonably accessible to the child without additional cost.

CONSUMER GROUPS

In 1971, a consumer group, Action for Children's Television (ACT), submitted a petition to the FTC asking for prohibition of toy advertising in children's programs. ACT and other consumer groups such as the Council on Children, Media and Merchandising (CCMM) have been pursuing reform in children's programming and advertising through various methods, including testimony at government hearings, publications, conferences, filing petitions with the regulatory commissions and courts, and research sponsorship.

ADVERTISING CAMPAIGN BY WONDERLAND TOYS

Wonderland Toys started the advertising campaign for its Space Travelers series in mid October of 1978. More than $3 million was spent for network and spot TV advertising to reach 70 percent of the children between 6 and 11 years old in the national market. A 30-second commercial described a scene within the spaceship which was often seen in the TV program. In this commercial five dolls, including the captain and the crew members, are standing and announcers' voices are used to describe a conversation between the captain and the crew. The commercial ends when one of the dolls looks into a radar and five flying spaceships are shown. A super appears on the screen which indicates that each item of this series can be purchased separately.

Shortly after Christmas, the company received a letter from a consumer, a mother of a 4-year-old boy. That boy's uncle purchased a whole set of Space Travelers for him as a Christmas present. The letter had two complaints about the products from the boy.

1. The dolls do not speak at all as shown in the commercial.
2. Nothing can be seen from the radar. Instead, a static picture of the space is attached to the radar.

This mother claimed that the company's commercial was misleading since it resembled the TV program so closely that her child believed that the toys would perform the same things as those shown in the program. The letter was reviewed carefully by the Wonderland people. One group of people argued that their commercial had no misleading implications for the following reasons.

1. It was made clear that dolls cannot speak by showing each doll's face in a close-up shot when an announcer's voice was over the screen: In these close-ups dolls' mouths were not open.
2. There is a clear transition of scenes from the close-up of a radar to the long shot of five spaceships. Those spaceships were simply shown as an environment, and it was not implied that they were seen from the radar.

This group of people also argued that they should not worry about this issue since the complaints came from a 4-year-old boy who was outside of their target audience. However, another group of people proposed that the commercial should be revised promptly since the company is responsible for any misunderstanding of its commercials by any member of the audience. And, they suggested that the revised commercial should be subjected to a more careful copytest with children, including those under 5 years old.

QUESTIONS FOR DISCUSSION

1. What actions should Wonderland Toys take with regard to its present commercial?
2. Provide reasons for your recommendation including your evaluation of the present commercial from regulatory perspectives.

ENDNOTES

1. Fictitious company name
2. Fictitious brand name
3. Based on the estimate of the Leading National Advertisers. Expenditures for newspaper and spot radio are not included.
4. The estimation method of the averge number of commercials is described in the *Research on the Effects of Television Advertising on Children,* Principal Investigator R. Adler, Report Prepared for National Science Foundation, 1977.

INDEX

Epic coffee, 427
Essentials of Media Planning: A Marketing Viewpoint, 204n, 479
Estimation, 257
Expansibility, 57, 58
Exposure estimation,
distributions, 508-511, 519
importance of, 506-508
measures derived from, 511-514
message/media response values, 514-516
Exposure estimation models,
ad hoc, 516-519, 535
ad hoc/stochastic combination, 522
simulation, 522, 523
stochastic, 519-522
Exxon Company, 436, 437
Faison, Edmund W. J., 174, 175n
Falstaff Brewing Company, 314
Family Circle magazine, 495, 523
Family Health, 495
Federal Communications Commission (FCC), 645
Federal Trade Commission, 616, 617, 624, 626, 627, 628, 632, 637, 638, 645, 646
Federal Trade Commission Act, 618, 626
Federal Register, 637
"Fee System," 33
Festinger, Leon, 164, 170
Finance, relation to business, 5
Folger's coffee, 424, 425, 426, 596, 597
Foote, Cone & Belding, 285, 475, 521
Ford Motor Company, 32, 337
Fortune magazine, 545
Frank, R. E., 199n, 202, 205n
Freeze-Dried Sanka, 301-303
Friskies cat food, 123, 125
Gallup & Robinson, 374, 375, 377
General Electric Company, 600
General Foods, Inc., 144, 299, 301, 424, 425, 426, 594, 596
General Motors Corporation, 32, 600
Generic demand, 66
Gerhold, Paul E. J., 463
Geritol, 625
Gilchrist, Warren, 284
Glade Glass Ovenware Company, 446, 447
Glow toothpaste, 382, 387, 388, 389, 390
Glower Corporation, 483
"Glue Seal Method," 173, 469
Gompertz functions, 284
Good Housekeeping magazine, 456, 461, 495, 542, 543
Goods,
definitions of, 74
types of, 570, 571
Gordon Textile Company, 119-121
W. T. Grant Company, 638
P. Green, 23n
Greene, J. D., 522, 523
Grey Advertising, 367, 369

Greyser, Stephen A., 223
Gross Rating Points (GRP's), 473, 494, 500, 513, 517, 518, 522
Gulfcrest, 441
Gulf Oil Company, 436-446
Gulftane, 438, 440, 441

Hafer, W. Keith, 357
Haley, Russell I., 386
Halibut Association of North America, 419
Hallmark Card Company, 459
"Hall of Fame" series, 38
Hart, Schaffner, and Marx Company, 580
Harvard Business Review, 180n
Haskins, Jack B., 162
Hathaway Shirts, 330, 337, 340, 360
Headon, R. S., 522
Heeler, R. M., 169
Heller, Harry E., 398
G. Heilman Brewing Company, 313
Hendry Corporation, 240
Hep Cat cat food, 125, 553, 554
Heuristic models, 487
The Hidden Persuaders, 615
Hierarchy of effects concept, 161-170, 185, 402
and copy research, 370-381
criteria, intermediate, 170-181, 185, 248, 249, 347, 352, 353, 469, 470, 499, 514
factors influencing, 166
perspectives on, 162
shortcomings of, 162
types of, 166
"High Assay" search procedure, 492, 493
Hills Bros. coffee, 425, 596
Hodock, Calvin, 399
Hofmans, P., 518, 519, 521, 523, 524, 530, 531
Holbert, Neil, 381
Holiday Inns, Inc., 436
Horowitz Brothers and Kramer, 544, 547
House, James S., 76n
Hovland, Carl, quoted 366, 403
Hunt, H. Keith, 627
Hyett, G. P., 516, 519

Ideal Toy Corporation, 645
Implementation for advertising models, 11
Individual difference measures, 183
Industrial Revolution, relation to marketing, 4
Information Processing, steps in, 162
Institutions, principal, in national advertising setting, 28
Integrative approach, 169
Interactive Market Systems, Inc. (IMS), 519, 521
Intermediate criteria,
affective, 176-179, 185, 347, 352, 353, 470, 499, 514